OAKLAND COMMUNITY COLLEGE

3 2355 00040877 3
ML 417 .H8 P6 1983
Horowitz : OCOR

Oakland Community College
Campus Library

DI032047

ML 417. H8 P6 1983   /

Plaskin, Glenn.
Horowitz : a biography of
   Vladimir Horowitz /
1st ed.

FEB 0 5 1990

L 8 1

Oakland Community College
Orchard Ridge Campus Library
27055 Orchard Lake Road
Farmington Hills, MI 48018

Horowitz

A BIOGRAPHY OF
VLADIMIR
HOROWITZ

BY GLENN PLASKIN

Macdonald & Co
London & Sydney

OR 10/86

First published in Great Britain in 1983 by
Macdonald & Co (Publishers) Ltd
London & Sydney

Copyright © 1983 by Glenn Plaskin
Published 1983 by William Morrow & Co Inc., New York

Grateful acknowledgement is made for permission to reprint the following:

Portions of Chapters Fourteen and Nineteen were adapted from the author's article 'The Secret Career of Horowitz', published in the *New York Times Sunday Magazine*, 11 May, 1980.

Excerpts from *Musical Chairs* by Schuyler Chapin. Reprinted by permission of G. P. Putnam's Sons from *Musical Chairs* by Schuyler Chapin. Copyright © 1977 by Schuyler Chapin. Also reprinted by permission of Schuyler Chapin and The Lantz Office Incorporated. Copyright © 1977 by Schuyler Chapin.

From *My Many Years* by Arthur Rubinstein. Copyright © 1980 by Arthur Rubinstein. Reprinted by permission of Alfred A. Knopf, Inc.

Excerpts from *Cellist* by Gregor Piatigorsky. Copyright © 1965 by Gregor Piatigorsky. Some material appeared in *The Atlantic Monthly* copyright © 1962 by The Atlantic Monthly Company. Reprinted by permission of Doubleday & Company, Inc.

Excerpts from John Pfeiffer's 'Manhattan Holiday', *High Fidelity*, October 1957. Reprinted by permission of *High Fidelity*, all rights reserved.

Back jacket photograph by courtesy of Marilyn Meyer.

ISBN 0 356 09179 1

Published in Great Britain by
Macdonald & Co (Publishers) Ltd
Maxwell House
74 Worship Street
London EC2A 2EN

Printed and bound in Great Britain by
Hazell Watson & Viney Ltd
Aylesbury, Bucks

With love and gratitude
to my grandmother,
Essie Feinberg,
and to
my mother and father

PREFACE

When Vladimir Horowitz walks onto the stage, he always appears in a black cutaway jacket, gray striped pants, vest, and silk bow tie—a "uniform" (as he calls it) reminiscent of the elaborate frock coat and cravat worn by performers in the nineteenth century. By his own admission, Horowitz feels closer to that age than to the present. He disdains the modern school of musicians who play with computer-like perfection and pedantic loyalty to the printed score. He terms himself the last pianist to play "in the grand manner," to search for the "spiritual values" behind the notes while daring to imprint his own personality on them, seducing and then "wrapping" his audience with the sort of near-infernal energy once ascribed to Niccolò Paganini and Franz Liszt.

Even before Horowitz touches the piano he feels, he has said, "an electricity" that becomes transformed at the keyboard into "the demon," through a ferocious piling up of sonorities and a perhaps unmatched command of dynamic and coloristic contrasts. In his heyday, Horowitz could hold an audience silent and spellbound, generating excitement that drove listeners to near-hysterical ovations. Having pushed virtuosity and romantic freedom of expression to its limits, Horowitz not only established himself as a modern Liszt but succeeded in creating an aura of mystery equaled by no other performing musician of his day.

Despite Horowitz's preeminence in the history of the twentieth-century piano performance, he has never before been the subject of a biography. His musicianship has been analyzed to some extent in separate chapters of books such as Harold Schonberg's *The Great Pianists,* Kurt Blaukopf's *Les Grands Virtuoses,* Joachim Kaiser's *Great Pianists of Our Time,* Ronald Gelatt's *Music Makers,* and most recently, in Harvey Sachs's *Virtuosos;* and entertaining vignettes of him have appeared in Abram Chasins's *Speaking of Pianists,* Samuel Chotzinoff's *A Little Nightmusic,* Schuyler Chapin's *Musical Chairs,* Elyse Mach's *Great Pianists Speak for Themselves,* and in a few autobiographies written by colleagues of Horowitz such as Arthur Rubinstein's *My Many Years* and Gregor Piatigorsky's *Cellist.* However, I find it astonishing that until now many of the essential facts of biography have been ignored: an accurate itinerary of Horowitz's activities; a detailed description of his personal character and relationships to his family and friends; a systematic discussion of his repertory, his musical style, and the impact of his playing on younger pianists. The absence of a biography was perhaps most surprising considering that Horowitz abandoned the stage during three separate periods of his career, totaling twenty-two years. Details of these retirements were unavailable to the press—in fact, having gone out of his way to cultivate a reputation as an enigmatic recluse, Horowitz once beamed with pride when a critic dubbed him the Greta Garbo of the piano. As one of his managers explained: "He had the best sense of self-promotion I'd ever come across in any artist. He was very careful not to be overexposed. The whole image he projected was that you never knew whether his hands would fall off or not." Yet to those interested in understanding the man and his art, none of Horowitz's well-rehearsed anecdotes or carefully tailored autobiographical sketches seemed adequately to reveal the pianist or his "demon." By 1978, the year marking the fiftieth anniversary of his American debut, a comprehensive study of Horowitz seemed long overdue.

Because I wanted to incorporate Horowitz's personal recollections into any book I might produce, I tracked down thirty-five previously unpublished, unedited tape-recorded interviews granted by Horowitz to trusted friends and handpicked journalists. Many of these were recorded at important junctures in Horowitz's career: an extended conversation with his close friend Abram Chasins at the time of his dramatic return to the stage in 1965; hours of talk taped by the Canadian Broadcasting Corporation when he was again rejuvenating his career in 1976; an interview with New York Philharmonic program editor Phillip Ramey just before his historic Golden Jubilee performances in 1978; and numerous others referred to in the source notes.

Comfortably ensconced in his own living room, Horowitz seems relaxed and spontaneous in these wide-ranging discussions—chuckling over favorite anecdotes, detailing his personal routine, reminiscing about his friendships with such luminaries as Arturo Toscanini and Sergei Rachmaninoff, often going to the piano to demonstrate favorite Scarlatti or Clementi sonatas or enthusing about a new work in his repertory. Those recorded interviews—in addition to unedited tapes of press conferences and radio interviews—have been immensely valuable to me, not only for their content, but because they are imbued with Horowitz's special humor and piquant sense of irony.

Notwithstanding Horowitz's high spirits during such sessions, it is clear that he is never unaware of the microphone, and the tapes are remarkable for their relentless repetition of stock information that rarely extends beyond a guarded recollection of an event or emotion. While Horowitz superficially discusses his childhood and training in Russia, the effect of the Russian Revolution on his family, and some of his views on music and musicians, he hardly broaches other, critical, subjects. There is little mention, for instance, of the prolonged illness in the 1930's that forced his first retirement, his ambivalent attitudes as father and husband, or the physical ailments that drastically affected his ability to perform in public. However, everything that Horowitz is apparently willing to say publicly about his life is said in those recorded interviews. Having had access to them, I was able, I hope, to shade this book with his presence.

The aforementioned conversations have served as a basis for the reconstruction of some events in Horowitz's life, but they are by no means the primary—or, it should be said, the most reliable—source of information. With the help of my research and editorial assistant, Paul Genega, I assembled thousands of printed interviews and concert and record reviews from American, European, and Russian newspapers and periodicals published between 1921 and 1982. Moreover, concert programs, photographs, recording and managerial contracts and letters were collected from library archives, private collections, Steinway & Sons, RCA Victor, Columbia Masterworks, the New York Philharmonic, and many other sources. I have also, of course, been able to study carefully Horowitz's commercial and "pirate" recordings, his transcriptions, and videotapes of his playing (including a previously unknown slow-motion film of him performing Chopin etudes on the stage of the Paris Opéra, in 1928).

The final and most illuminating step of my research consisted of interviews with approximately 650 friends and associates privileged to have known the private Horowitz. These included childhood friends and fellow students at the Kiev Conservatory, colleagues who witnessed his first triumphs in Europe in the 1920's, intimates who supported him through periods of nervous collapse and physical illness, pianists who associated with him, and people who took care of his day-to-day needs while he was on concert tour. Some of these sources were especially valuable and call for separate mention: extended interviews with both Arthur Rubinstein and the late Alexander Steinert, the last of whom kindly read from the diary he kept in Paris in the late 1920's and 1930's; conversations with Rudolf Serkin and Nathan Milstein; an extensive discussion of Horowitz's fam-

ily history and childhood with his first cousin and only relative in the
United States, Natasha Saitzoff; lengthy interviews with all six of
Horowitz's former students: Gary Graffman, Byron Janis, Ivan Davis,
Ronald Turini, Coleman Blumfield, and Alexander Fiorillo; numerous
talks with Lowell Benedict, Horowitz's traveling companion during the
1940's, who generously loaned me his diary and correspondence from the
period; and invaluable interviews with a number of individuals closely
associated with Horowitz who have requested anonymity. In addition, I
conducted interviews with music critics, concert managers, record producers and engineers, and executives of Steinway & Sons, RCA Victor,
and Columbia Masterworks.

All verbal statements and other forms of secondhand testimony have
been verified to the greatest degree possible, and throughout the book
any speculative remarks of mine are clearly identified. By cross-checking
the previously mentioned interviews against written documentation and
against Horowitz's own recollections, important themes came into focus:
Horowitz's troubled associations with RCA Victor and Columbia Masterworks; his fluctuating allegiances to impresario Arthur Judson and to
his other managers; his intense rivalry with Arthur Rubinstein; his adoration of Sergei Rachmaninoff; the volatile dynamics of the Toscanini-
Horowitz family; Horowitz's complicated relationship with his wife and
daughter; and, perhaps most striking, the contrasts between the flamboyant public Horowitz and his private persona, anguished and torn by conflict and insecurities. The portrait that finally emerged will, I hope, fulfill
my original goal of providing a credible outline of Horowitz's life and an
accurate record of the development of his career.

At the time of this writing, Horowitz continues to perform with the
physical enthusiasm of a younger man, determined to conquer new repertory and win larger audiences. As he approaches his eightieth year, he
remains vital in spirit, eager, as he says, to "make new challenges" for
himself.

His life story is as rich-veined and provocative as his playing. In this
first biography, my intention has been to capture some of this drama and
to foster as thorough an understanding as possible of one of the great
musical figures of our time.

—GLENN PLASKIN
July 1982
New York City

ACKNOWLEDGMENTS

First and foremost, I am indebted to Paul Genega, my research and editorial assistant, who, for a period of three years, faced the formidable challenge of helping to compile a comprehensive Horowitz bibliography. Moreover, with his sympathetic perception of the subject and eye for detail, he helped define, in style and content, the parameters of this biography. His patience and enthusiasm fueled and refueled my enthusiasm and his contributions were, altogether, indispensable.

I am deeply grateful to Robert McAlear who worked for two years to research and compile the first complete Horowitz discography—a prodigious task that he approached with boundless energy.

I want to thank Ellis J. Freedman who, from the inception of the project, provided not only good counsel but steadfast encouragement and keen insight into the subject.

I also wish to express my gratitude to Phillip Ramey, New York Philharmonic program editor, for his valuable editorial advice.

I am much obliged to Erica Kaplan Kellermann who typed the manuscript twice and offered many helpful suggestions.

Most personally, I will always be indebted to my friend Harvey Schwartz. His daring imagination and deep-felt friendship gave me the fortitude to begin a new career.

Warmest thanks go also to the following institutions and individuals:

Owen Laster of the William Morris Agency; James Landis, Deborah Karl, Don Patterson, Ann Barret, Lela Rolontz, and Joan Amico at William Morrow and Company; John Hawkins and Gail Hochman of the Paul Reynolds Agency; Ken Larose of the National Film Archives, Ottawa, Ontario; Kenneth W. Duckett of the University of Oregon Special Collections Library;

ACKNOWLEDGMENTS

Digby Peers of the Canadian Broadcasting Corporation; Victor Hertz of the Columbia University Translating Agency; Howard Klein of the Rockefeller Foundation; John Steinway of Steinway & Sons Pianos; Joseph Klugar of the New York Philharmonic Orchestra; Mary Drugan, Gregor Benko, Francis Crociata, Caine Alder, James O'Connell, Jim and Carol Goodfriend, Dora Romadimov, Harvey Sachs, Elyse Mach, Schuyler Chapin, Claire Brooke, Myroslava Basladynsky, Ann Katcher, Lydia Heineman, Julius Bloom, Steven King, Freda Rosen, Phillip Berg, Steven Heliotes, Martin Lobenthal, Doug Smith, Scott Parris, Peter G. Davis, Seymour Rauch, Dana Perelman, Jason Kaatz, Nicolas Slonimsky, Wilfred von Wyck, Leonard Altman, David Dubal, Evans Mirageas, Winthrop Sargeant, Helen Epstein, Fred Calland, John Ardoin, Marilyn Holzer, Edward Greenfield, John Gruen, David Lowe, Mary Rousculp, Norman Pellegrini, Michel Glotz, Victor Ledin, Arthur McKenzie, Michael Maxwell, Marlys and Bill Ray, Buddy Dikman, Sheldon Shkolnik, Herbert Barrett; the Lincoln Center Library of the Performing Arts. Finally, I am indebted to the hundreds of concert managers, music critics and individuals at concert halls, libraries, and music societies from around the world who generously forwarded reviews, programs, and interviews and to the many friends and associates of Horowitz who generously shared their recollections.

CONTENTS

CONTENTS

PART ONE
1904 ~ 1925

CHAPTER ONE

MUSIC LANE

*"I wasn't a wunderkind, never. I had very intelligent
parents—a very cultured papa and mama—and although I
could perform, my father said no: 'Till he reaches maturity, I
will not let him play.' "*[1]

In 1911, Czar Nicholas II presented Josef Hofmann with the keys to
the Russian Railroad, enabling the great pianist to travel the breadth of
the empire as a guest of the ruler. This rare accolade symbolized Hofmann's immense popularity with the Russian people, a phenomenon
demonstrated most dramatically during his 1912 tour, which began in St.
Petersburg. After each of five scheduled concerts in that city, patient
crowds lined up outside La Salle Noblesse in sub-zero weather, willing to
stand all night for a chance to buy tickets for the next evening's performance. Capitulating to public demand, Hofmann augmented his five appearances first to ten and finally to a marathon of twenty-one consecutive
recitals, later advertised as "The Most Remarkable Concerts Ever
Given."[2] Hofmann's stamina and mastery of the piano repertory were
legendary, and by the time he was finished, he had played 255 compositions before combined audiences of 67,000 persons. Each program was
different with no single work repeated. The thirty-six-year-old artist then
set out on his tour, traveling to Moscow, Kharkov, Odessa, and Tiflis. In
early December 1912, Hofmann arrived in Kiev to present two recitals at
the conservatory. The director of the school, Vladimir Puchalsky, greeted
Hofmann at the train station and escorted him to the school. Surrounded
by aspiring virtuosos and newspaper reporters, Hofmann inspected the
magnificent Blütner grand piano in the concert hall and then returned to
his hotel to rest for the evening's performance.

The recital had been sold out for weeks, and Sophie Gorovitz,* an avid

---

* The closest transliteration of Vladimir Horowitz's name from Russian to English is Vladimir Samoliovich Gorovitz. (His middle name, in the traditional Russian manner, is derived
from his father's name, Samuel, later westernized as Simeon.) However, as did many Russian

concertgoer and alumna of the conservatory, had been unable to obtain tickets for this musical event of the season. Her youngest son, Vladimir, however, was undeterred, stubbornly insisting that he would find a way to attend at least one of the concerts. That evening, the chubby-cheeked eight-year-old stood at the conservatory's entrance, watching for the approach of any tall man. Eventually such a person appeared and the sly boy followed closely behind, suddenly dashing between the man's long legs just as the ticket was presented at the gate. Evading the pursuit of ushers, Vladimir rushed into the auditorium and hid in a dark corner, curled up on the keyboard side. For the next two hours he sat wide-eyed through his first recital, spellbound by Hofmann's amazing fingers and by the velvety sound that the master coaxed from the piano in the program of Bach, Beethoven, Chopin, and Moszkowski.

Grasping what he could, Vladimir returned home, and inspired by Hofmann's example, resumed piano practice with renewed enthusiasm. His parents, Sophie and Simeon, were delighted by the industry of their son but maintained a cautious perspective about his talent, remembering that Hofmann had already astounded audiences at age six and by age ten had had an international concert career. That particular prodigy had been exploited mercilessly until the Society for the Prevention of Cruelty to Children drew attention to his case, provoking Hofmann's father to retire his son from the stage until age eighteen. In the interim, Hofmann had studied in Berlin with the legendary Anton Rubinstein, who proclaimed him "a boy as the world of music had never before produced."[3]

Vladimir Gorovitz was quite a different case, for he had barely touched the piano at age six and was certainly not considered a *wunderkind*. In fact, during the boy's first two years of lessons, his parents viewed him merely as somewhat above average. They nonetheless remained absorbed by and supportive of their son's efforts, careful to allow the boy's interest to grow, encumbered neither by their ambition nor by a torturous practice routine. In his first years of lessons, Vladimir had demonstrated sensitivity to whatever he played, willingness to study, and ability to learn music quickly. Beyond what appeared to be a natural propensity toward the keyboard, however, there was no evidence that anything extraordinary would develop, not the slightest hint that their son would one day

immigrants of the 1920's, Horowitz chose to westernize his name; he did this at the time of his 1926 Berlin debut by changing Gorovitz to Horowitz.

be hailed as the king of piano virtuosos, the most charismatic performer since Franz Liszt.

Although there were no virtuosos in the family, nearly every Gorovitz played an instrument. Vladimir's mother, Sophie, was not a professional musician, but she had diligently studied the piano at Kiev's Royal Music School and was more than technically proficient. One by one, she gave her four children their first piano lessons. Vladimir, known by the Russian diminutive Volodya, was not the only energetic young music student in the family, for there was his older sister Regina, called Genya, who early on demonstrated a formidable talent for the piano. Also musically inclined, if less talented, were Volodya's older brothers, Jacob and George, who played the piano and violin respectively. Their father, Simeon, helped his children with their music whenever possible, but unlike his wife, he had only the rudimentary music training then typical of an upper-middle-class upbringing. Volodya's paternal grandmother, on the other hand, had been an excellent pianist who supposedly had been encouraged by none other than Anton Rubinstein. Her hopes for a concert career were never fulfilled, and it was Simeon's brother, Alexander, who became the first professional musician in the family. Alexander had studied both composition and piano with Alexander Scriabin at the Moscow Conservatory and had established himself as a successful teacher, pianist, and critic in the city of Kharkov. By the time of Vladimir's birth, Alexander was the director of the music school in Kharkov. Over the next years, he demonstrated a proprietary concern for the training of his most talented nephew.

The Gorovitz residence was located on a street named Musikalnyi Pereulok—Music Lane—in a lush, hilly area of the city, just a few blocks from the Royal Music School (later renamed the Kiev Conservatory). It was a large, sunny apartment, dominated by a music room with grand piano and well-stocked shelves of sheet music. As Sophie explained fundamentals of musical notation to her only daughter, Genya, three-year-old Volodya would wander about listening intently to his mother's voice, often imitating her keyboard technique by tapping on the windowpanes. Not knowing his own strength, he once became so excited with his imaginary manipulations that he pushed his hands through the windowpane and shattered the glass, lacerating his hands. But the world of the music room was usually one of peace and security. There Volodya could sit for hours, transfixed by his mother's playing. She was a great beauty with chestnut-brown hair, luminescent skin, and expressive brown eyes that she had passed on to all her children. He later remembered her as a sensitive, kind, gentle woman, and those hours in the music room remained his earliest and happiest memories.

When the music making ended and it was time to attend to other tasks, mother and son proceeded hand in hand past a long hallway table laden with black bread, pastries, and a great bubbling samovar of hot tea. Entering the kitchen, they greeted Sophie's aged mother, Yefrosina, whose greatest delight lay in supervising a servant girl in the pickling of cucumbers, melons, and apples or in the making of *zakuski*, hors d'oeuvres of pickled herring, pastries, or meat to be nibbled before dinner. Yefrosina was a plump, affectionate woman whose major passions were endless games of solitaire and equally endless doting on her four grandchildren. She loved to tell the story of the marriage of her daughter. It seemed that all her friends and relatives had complimented her on the gorgeous bride and groom, saying: "My God! This couple, with the way they look, what kind of children will they have?"[4] Yefrosina would later muse that, after all, Sophie and Simeon had produced something much better than mere beauty: the extraordinary talent of their son Volodya. The boy was watched over by French and English governesses and pampered by his aunt Evelyn, Simeon's unmarried sister. She lived with the family on Music Lane and was the first member of the Gorovitz household to insist that her nephew was a genius.

Simeon was proud that his family enjoyed a prosperous life. Living in the capital of the Ukraine, to say nothing of the imposing apartment building at the corner of Music Lane and Groriesnaya, was an exceptional accomplishment for a Jewish family. In Russia, Jews had traditionally been restricted by czarist statutes to live and work in what was known as a pale of settlements and had been allowed into the major cities only on market days. It was in one of those settlements, the dirty, industrial town of Berdichev, sixty miles southwest of Kiev, that all of Simeon Gorovitz's children had been born. The young father, however, had no intention of remaining in Berdichev. Settlement laws had been liberalized during Alexander II's reign, and by 1897 the Jewish population of Kiev numbered 32,000; by 1910, over 50,000. Despite occasional deportations and the constant threat of pogroms (which decimated the Jewish sections of the city in 1881 and again in 1905), families such as the Gorovitzes were eager for the expanded opportunities which life in Kiev offered

Shortly after the birth of his youngest son, Vladimir, on October 1, 1904,[5] Simeon joined the mass of emigrants and moved his family there.

Kiev was the queen of Russian cities. Situated on the banks of the Dnieper River, the verdant capital of the Ukraine was lush with meadows and forests and was ringed by fifteen miles of formal parks and gardens. In the springtime, the city was luxuriously scented with lilac, chestnut, dogwood, and acacia. From the forested heights of Kiev, known as the Perchersk, a view swept east for miles across the fertile plains, and south where the river wound its way toward the Black Sea. The Dnieper provided welcome opportunity for swimming and boating during the hot, humid summers. It was the lifeline of the city: The rich soil and waterway had made Kiev the agricultural and industrial nucleus of the Ukraine as well as its cultural center—with a large university, fine orchestra, opera and ballet company, and the esteemed Conservatory of Music. The autonomy and prosperity of the Ukrainian people and Kiev's close proximity to Eastern Europe made the city a home for Jewish families, like the Gorovitzes, fortunate enough to escape the pale. Kiev was a treasury of medieval art and architecture; ruins of the eleventh-century Golden Gate of the original walled city still stood on the right bank; the cathedral of St. Sophia, modeled on Constantinople's Hagia Sophia, was filled with exquisite icons, mosaics, and frescoes. Up and down the bluffs and hills, the onion domes of splendid churches and monasteries punctuated a cityscape of sandstone buildings and a countryside of sparkling cottages, all meticulously whitewashed twice a year. From Kiev's busy main boulevard, the famous Kreschatik, or Crossroads, the city glistened, itself a kind of icon.

Simeon Gorovitz was a member of the emerging class of bourgeois Jews who had benefited from the expansion of private business and the improvement of education. Trained as an electrical engineer both in Russia and at the University of Liège in Belgium, he was a tall, elegant man fluent in both French and German. He took his place in Kiev's business community by entering into a partnership with his two brothers-in-law, Alexander and Michael Bodick. Their firm—Gorovitz & Bodick— represented the Westinghouse Corporation as well as German electrical firms in Kiev. The business prospered by selling everything from household light bulbs to motors and transformers for powering the region's steel and sugar mills.

Simeon's economic success allowed his family to live a leisured upper-middle-class life. Sophie, leaving housework to servants, often went for long walks on the Kreschatik, shopping and mingling with the city's established *grandes dames.* Simeon energetically filled his library with an extensive international collection, books he encouraged his family to explore, some of which he had supposedly translated from Russian into German and French for foreign publishers. His aspirations were high, not only for himself but also for his children. Often, however, his ambitions gave way to social pretensions. Proud of his mother's alleged Polish gentile background, Simeon could be snobbish and moody—aloof and haughty one moment, convivial and generous the next. His exaggerated elegance served him as protection from the general vulnerability of Jews in Russia. Police surveillance, deportations, and pogroms were vivid memories, and like many successful Jewish merchants, Simeon knew that residing in a well-to-do section of Kiev was no guarantee of safety. He therefore had good reasons for de-emphasizing his family's Jewishness (indeed, religious observances did not figure in the Gorovitz homelife) and for aligning himself with the wealthy of the city's gentile leadership.

In 1905, Simeon's worst fears came true when the tranquillity of his home was broken by the sound of gunfire. A pogrom, inspired by the reactionary "Union of the Russian People," was bent on liquidating the Jewish merchants of Kiev. This assault, however, was only a small part of the so-called "First Revolution" which enveloped Russia that year, heralding a series of devastating national strikes that ultimately forced the czar to promise full civil rights to all citizens. Although Volodya was too young to remember the 1905 pogrom or the general turmoil of the period, he was often told of these things, including the story of how he was nearly killed when the windows of the family apartment were shattered by bullets. The events of 1905 stood as a frightening reminder of the precarious position of all Jews in Russia.

After 1905, the firm of Gorovitz & Bodick expanded and throve, and political worries aside, Simeon made every effort to see that music was prominent in his home. When Volodya was ready to begin lessons at age six, he demonstrated a retentive memory and a sensitive ear and was neither elated nor bored with the piano. After a few years of lessons, Sophie was amazed at the enthusiasm and ease with which her son took to the keyboard. His small hands seemed to have a natural predisposition for the piano, one that allowed him to play his beginning scales and arpeggios easily and efficiently. But his greatest gift was his innate and intense musicality—his capacity for becoming completely absorbed in the emotions engendered by music and his inclination to identify so closely with those emotions that even when he was not at the piano, they seemed to envelop him. One of Vladimir's cousins, Natasha (Bodick) Saitzoff, remembered him "sitting at the piano with his feet barely touching the pedals, explaining to us as he played: 'Now you see, the sun is shining and the birds are singing and everything is fine.' At this moment his playing was soft and tender. Then he would become very agitated and scream: 'Boom, boom, boom, boom!! Now a storm, and it is going to rain.' His huge brown eyes reflected the passion of his playing."[6]

A photograph taken at age eight shows a sturdy little boy with prominent ears, an imperious nose, and a rather coy, self-possessed expression. Volodya, the baby of the family, was shamelessly spoiled by everyone around him. When he was napping, the entire household had to wear special slippers so as not to disturb him. Although he was introverted, distant, aloof, and occasionally volatile, Volodya's moods were tolerated at home, and no one dared reprimand him for his capricious, sometimes unpleasantly aggressive behavior. Dressed in a black sailor suit with white stripes, he would solemnly present little piano improvisations to his captive family-audience or to a steady stream of guests that included aunts, uncles, and cousins.

By the time Volodya was nine years old, his inquisitive nature had led him to the family's tall, mahogany music cabinet, where he rummaged through a tantalizing assortment of sheet music. Skipping over works of Chopin and Liszt, whose notation looked impossibly complicated, he eventually settled on two composers, his "two loves" as he later put it: Edvard Grieg and Sergei Rachmaninoff. Grieg's *Lyric Pieces* appealed instantly, and they were well within his grasp. Sophie discovered that the simple structures of these character-pieces were perfectly suited to her son's abilities and she encouraged him to sing the folksong-inspired music as he played the melodies. After bounding through the *Sailor's Song* or the *Norwegian Peasant March,* he would put aside Grieg and turn eagerly to Rachmaninoff's pieces from Op. 3 or Op. 10, and a few of the preludes from Op. 23, which were equally alluring, if usually too technically demanding. But more important to Sophie than seeing her son master any one work was her insistence that he read through many different kinds of music and become exposed to the melodies, chords, harmonies, and diverse styles that he would later explore in depth at the conservatory. With his mother's constant encouragement, the boy eventually did come to admire a wide range of repertory, not only compositions for piano but also operas, orchestral and chamber music, songs, and ballet scores. Records were not then easily obtainable, and Volodya was obliged to familiarize himself with different music by playing it himself; sifting steadily through sheet music that interested him, he slowly developed into an extraordinary sight reader. Sophie spent hours introducing him to four-handed reductions of Haydn and Mozart symphonies, and she also encouraged him to listen to her impromptu performances of the Russian composers then in vogue—Arensky, Liadov, Glazunov, Glière, and Grechaninov. Many of these mother-son sessions ended with a spirited performance of Rachmaninoff's *Six Piano Duets*.

Volodya easily memorized many of his favorite pieces and continued to indulge in minirecitals for anyone in the family who would listen, performances partly inspired by music he heard outside his home. Many nights, after dinner, there were recitals in culturally rich Kiev, and Sophie took all four of her children as often as possible. Even when her oldest sons were not interested, she insisted on dragging the entire family to symphony and chamber-music concerts and to her favorite French, Italian, and Russian operas,—works she had heard performed in Europe before the birth of her children. After such events, she was especially adamant that Volodya practice slowly and carefully, but as the boy was impatient to devour new repertory before he had even half-mastered the old, it was a losing battle. Technical facility seemed to come easily, but as he once said of his early development: "I cannot tell you how I learned technique any more than I can tell you how I learned languages. I only know that, in the music, I found out what the fingers had to do and I did it. Music was the only source."[7]

By 1912, Volodya was tackling difficult piano reductions of operas, even attempting Wagner's *Der Ring des Nibelungen,* humming his favorite melodies without looking at the music. The boy's memory was not photographic but was facile enough to astound Sophie and Simeon when, for instance, he played, by heart, a passage from Rimsky-Korsakov's *Snow Maiden* and then, without missing a beat, switched to a favorite aria from *Lohengrin*. It was not long before the Gorovitzes decided that their precocious son merited formal conservatory training. So it was that, in September 1912, they paid a 125-ruble tuition fee and enrolled Volodya at the Kiev Conservatory.

CHAPTER TWO

APPRENTICESHIP

"There was a devil in me and an angel too. I could be both.
And all my life I was like that."[1]

$\mathscr{S}$ophie wanted the perfect mentor for her son, and she initially considered enrolling him in Vladimir Puchalsky's class. Puchalsky, the conservatory's director, had been her teacher years earlier and was widely regarded as the finest piano teacher in the Ukraine. In 1876, following an apprenticeship at the St. Petersburg Conservatory under the legendary Austrian piano pedagogue, Theodor Leschetizky, Puchalsky joined the Kiev music faculty. By the time Volodya Gorovitz entered the conservatory, Puchalsky was sixty-five years old, hard of hearing, gruff and inflexible in his teaching methods. Sophie became convinced that he was the wrong teacher for her son and decided to enroll Volodya in the piano class of Professor Marian Dombrovski, second in seniority at the conservatory, who had a reputation for being gifted and personable. When Sophie's old teacher heard he had been bypassed, he went into a rage: "You were my pupil!" Puchalsky screamed, "and here you have a talented son and you dare enroll him in another professor's class!"[2] Embarrassed, Sophie begged his forgiveness and reluctantly reregistered her son in Puchalsky's class.

It was then Dombrovski's turn to feel slighted, and henceforth he refused to listen to young Gorovitz perform. Volodya was considered one of the most promising pianists in the school and Puchalsky always scheduled him to perform toward the end of student recitals. When Volodya walked onto the stage, Dombrovski would leave the hall, storming past a puzzled group of students and their parents. The temperamental teacher was nonetheless curious to hear the boy and often paused outside the door to listen, to the amusement of spying students. Years later, during the 1920's when Horowitz was conquering European audiences, Dombrovski finally swallowed his pride and attended one of Horowitz's concerts in Warsaw, going backstage afterward to pay homage to this rising star who had so nearly been his student.

At the Kiev Conservatory Volodya easily settled into the routine. Unlike public gymnasiums, the conservatory was not restricted by sex or religion, and no drab uniform was required. Students attending the conservatory were considered an elite. Usually from upper-middle-class backgrounds, they socialized freely and divided their time equally between music studies and academic subjects. Every morning after breakfast, at 9 A.M., Volodya and his sister, Regina, walked together from their home on Music Lane the few blocks to the conservatory. This was an imposing, elegant structure, sand-colored, with oval arches on the bottom two floors and classical columns at the top. Dominating a small park in front of the school was an imposing statue of Mikhail Glinka, the "Father of Russian Music," which seemed to urge his musical progeny to greatness.

The first floor of the building held the large private studios of major teachers like Puchalsky and Dombrovski. Marble staircases led to the upper floors, where classes in harmony, music history, aesthetics, and theory were offered in the mornings. At noon, Volodya and Genya passed through the cloakroom to the noisy cafeteria where they ate a lunch of bread-and-butter sandwiches, sausage, French pastries, and tea. After lunch on Tuesdays and Fridays, Puchalsky's small and select piano class met in his spacious studio. The group consisted of the two Gorovitz children, Alexander Eydelman, Ariel Rubstein, and a few others.

Tuesday was "technique day." Lessons were given to each of the students individually while their classmates observed. Lasting from thirty minutes to an hour, these sessions with Puchalsky were a nightmare for Volodya. Much later, he would reminisce: "That old man's screaming never stopped. His teaching ability did not equal his virtuosity and he was not able to implant a love of the instrument in me so I undertook my daily compulsory exercises unwillingly."[3]

Each student marched grimly into class, armed with carefully prepared scales, arpeggios, and the despised exercises of Carl Czerny and Muzio Clementi. Rubstein remembered one of Volodya's lessons distinctly: "That day his scales were absolutely magnificent—clean, fast, perfectly articulated—yet Puchalsky yelled at him as much as at anyone else for an incorrect fingering or for some other minor infraction."[4] Because of Puchalsky's scathing reprimands and the constant peer pressure, piano lessons were nerve-wracking experiences. Volodya was always tense, did not enjoy playing in front of even a small group, and deeply resented the regimented study Puchalsky demanded. Already introverted, he seemed to retreat further into himself. "He was a strange fellow—quite shy," remembered one classmate. "In his personal appearance and playing he was meticulous. He used to spend much time outside Puchalsky's door before the class, fixing his hair. He had very flat hair and finding the part was always difficult for him. He stood in front of a mirror endlessly, scrutinizing his appearance and patting his hair into place."[5]

After being browbeaten by their cantankerous, dogmatic teacher, many of Puchalsky's students became inured to criticism and less frightened of performing at student recitals. In fact, their playing improved despite the stolid routine. Puchalsky's methodology was derived from the principles of his teacher, Leschetizky, who had counted among his former pupils giants such as Ignace Jan Paderewski and Artur Schnabel. Like Leschetizky, Puchalsky stressed the Romantic repertory, concentrating on Beethoven, Schumann, Chopin, Liszt, and the Russians, assigning little Brahms. The "Leschetizky System" emphasized the importance of relentless technical drill with an arched hand position, flexibility in the wrist, and total relaxation of the forearm and shoulder muscles. Some of Puchalsky's students became so bored with repetitious exercises that they placed a newspaper on the music rack and practiced their scales while reading books or daydreaming.

Wisely, Puchalsky paid special attention to the anatomical differences among his students. He explained that pianists with thick, fleshy fingers, such as Anton Rubinstein, usually produced a suave, velvety tone, while those with long thin fingers, such as Liszt, produced a lyrical but rather metallic sound. Within the context of this generalization, Volodya seemed to fall into the second category, and his lessons were guided by that fact. Puchalsky recommended that he sink into the cushions of the fingertips rather than play on the tips. Regardless of the anatomy of the hand, however, Puchalsky's main goal throughout Volodya's apprenticeship years was the production of a beautiful, singing tone—a *cantabile* melody produced with the weight of the arm, a melody that stood out in bold relief against the bass, and one that approximated qualities of the human voice. Once mastered, Puchalsky explained, such a tone was not percussive when *forte* yet it could penetrate to the last row of a concert hall when *pianissimo*. This reflected the very essence of the traditional Russian approach to the piano.

Friday was "repertoire day" at the conservatory, the day when students performed standard works of Bach, Mozart, Beethoven, Chopin, and Liszt. Also on the agenda was music by composers seldom heard today— Sgambati, Strobel, Moscheles, Graf, and Medtner. Of contemporary composers, Rachmaninoff and Scriabin were most popular. Puchalsky was also inordinately fond of Glinka's *Capriccio sur des Thèmes Russes,* and many of his students were made to learn it. Along with such conventional repertory as the Chopin *Berceuse* or the *Italian* Concerto of Bach, Puchalsky also assigned many works of Hummel and Moszkowski. Although he perfunctorily insisted that his pupils learn preludes and fugues from Bach's *Well-Tempered Clavier,* he knew that most of them disliked this music and he could not have been surprised that the results were seldom impressive. Other more indulgent professors capitulated to their students' insistence that it was difficult, if not impossible, to memorize the "dreadful fugues," and they were permitted to play with the sheet music. But the stubborn Puchalsky would not modify his demands, and he continued to assign Bach, bellowing admonitions when a performance fell below his expectations. Volodya, like his classmates, detested learning works of Bach and continued to concentrate on his two favorite composers, Grieg and Rachmaninoff. Years later, when questioned about his early attraction to unabashedly Romantic music, he said: "I was a long time in reaching a composer like Beethoven. One must develop in one's own way, without apologies and certainly without the attempt at taking an artificial position and claiming to admire what one does not."[6] No matter what the repertory, Puchalsky tolerated no letup from practice, even during summer vacations.

In 1914, after two years of study with his stern taskmaster, Volodya had progressed impressively in spite of his resentment toward Puchalsky. Alexander Gorovitz was so taken with his nephew's abilities that he asked his friend and mentor, Alexander Scriabin, to listen to Volodya's playing on his next visit to Kiev. A special bond had existed between the two men since the time Alexander Gorovitz was a student at the St. Petersburg Conservatory. When the young Alexander was given the silver medal instead of the gold, Scriabin had resigned from the faculty in protest, believing the top award had been denied Alexander because of an anti-Semitic jury.

The meeting between Volodya and Scriabin was arranged in 1914, only a year before the composer's death. This encounter, though brief, left an indelible impression on the pianist. As he later remembered it:

Scriabin came to our house only a few hours before his piano recital in Kiev, where he was going to play his Eighth and Ninth Piano sonatas. He was like a crazy man, sitting in his chair, very nervous, and he probably hated me; you know, Momma and Poppa came in with the prodigy and he must have been thinking: "My God! How can I get rid of him?" And so he sat very quietly and I played a few small pieces—ten minutes' worth of music. A nocturne and waltz of Chopin, a little piece by Ernst von Dohnányi, a melody of Paderewski, something of Borodin. When I finished, my father asked Scriabin what he thought of me and how he should handle my education. Scriabin answered, "Your boy will probably be a very good pianist. I don't know how far he will go, but he has tremendous talent. Make sure, however, that he gets a good general education, that he is exposed to all kinds of music, that he reads a lot, that he sees paintings, that he knows the classics of literature. He should not only play scales, but to be an artist, he must know many things." So my father and mother followed his advice and gave me a good education.[7]

Within the czarist quota system that limited Jewish enrollment, Sophie and Simeon registered Volodya at the local gymnasium, and he attended this concurrently with the conservatory. Although the boy went through the motions of receiving a general education, he had little genuine interest in his academic studies and his grades often reflected that fact. In his early teens, he developed some appreciation for the theater, and he read the Russian masters—Tolstoy, Dostoyevski, Pushkin, Gogol—along with Dickens, Proust, and Hugo. But he much preferred listening to recordings of opera or avoiding music entirely by hiking with his brothers through the forests surrounding Kiev or swimming either in the Dnieper River or at Sviatosino, a spa outside the city where the entire Gorovitz family often vacationed in the summertime.

Although Sophie was sometimes distressed by Volodya's neglect of academic work, Simeon was far more indulgent. Simeon concentrated on his son's musical talent, but he never considered exploiting him and vowed that Volodya would not perform in public until he had completed his formal schooling and was mature enough for such appearances. Not that Simeon was reluctant to establish connections in the music world that might later promote the development of his son's career: "You know, my father was not a timid man, not at all," remembered Horowitz. "Through a friend, he begged Rachmaninoff to hear me play when I was twelve years old. And Rachmaninoff, who *was* a timid man, was afraid to say no to such a request. So the composer agreed to an appointment with me and my mother at a hotel in Kiev; but when we arrived for my audition at 4 P.M., the concierge told us that Rachmaninoff had left Kiev by train at 3 P.M.! Many years later in America, when I finally met Rachmaninoff, I asked him why he ran away from me and he laughed. He said it was because he hated child prodigies, that he worried that if I was no good he would have to lie to my mother and tell her I was good, which he would not do."[8]

However, despite Volodya's pianistic precociousness, he was not considered a child prodigy and caught the attention of no important Russian musician during his early conservatory years. By 1914, even his musical studies had deteriorated. Puchalsky—old, emaciated, and tired—seemed to be in constant ill humor and screamed at his young protégé during violent flares of temper. Fortunately for Vladimir, Puchalsky would soon lose his position as director of the school. Rising nationalist feelings in Russia, amplified by approaching war, were working against this Pole who had filled many faculty positions with fellow countrymen. In 1914, Sergei Rachmaninoff held the post of inspector general of Russian conservatories, and it was he who finally recommended that Puchalsky be replaced by an eminent composer or musicologist of Russian extraction. Rachmaninoff's eventual choice was Reinhold Glière, a prolific composer who was a true successor of the Russian nationalist school. The energetic forty-year-old was a native of Kiev and had been a composition professor at the Kiev Conservatory before his appointment as director in 1914. He would hold this post until 1920, the year of Volodya's graduation.

Upon Glière's arrival at the school in September 1915, Volodya and Genya Gorovitz looked forward to being assigned a different piano teacher. Genya's choice was Sergei Tarnowsky, a dashing new faculty member who had graduated from the St. Petersburg Conservatory in 1907 with both the gold medal and Rubinstein prize. A brilliant pianist, Tarnowsky had studied with the famed Anna Essipova, the second of Leschetizky's three wives and the most sought-after piano teacher in St. Petersburg. Under Essipova, Tarnowsky had mastered a lush, singing tone and a breathtaking *legato*. Although his performances were technically dazzling and also graceful, his playing lacked a certain passion, and many of his former students later remembered him as a musician of limited abilities. Tarnowsky also had an awkward stage presence, aggravated by his fear of performing, and this had prevented him from gaining a firm reputation during three seasons of European recitals. He was therefore grateful when Glière offered him a teaching position in Kiev, and he accepted the post with enthusiasm. Tarnowsky, young and inexperienced as a teacher, hardly ranked as one of the conservatory's top piano professors, yet his arrival attracted considerable attention. Hordes of young pianists waited to audition for his class. Puchalsky was enraged by the prospect of losing his prize students, especially the Gorovitz children, and the demoted director forced his successor to negotiate a compromise: Volodya and Genya would have lessons with *both* teachers. While Tarnowsky supervised their week-to-week progress, Puchalsky assessed their overall development by hearing them play every few weeks. This equitable arrangement lasted for nine months, after which responsibility for the piano lessons reverted entirely to Tarnowsky.

The young teacher was captivated by the brilliant, intensely musical playing of his new student, Volodya, and was surprised to learn that he had not been considered especially prodigious as a child. "If Horowitz was not a child prodigy," Tarnowsky later remarked, "then there never had been such a thing."[9] Tarnowsky found that his pupil's exceptional ear and flawless memory enabled him to assimilate new repertory with ease, that he sight-read effortlessly and his improvisational talent even extended into operatic scores—Rimsky-Korsakov's *The Golden Cockerel,* Mussorgsky's *Boris Godunov,* Tchaikovsky's *Queen of Spades* and Puccini's *La Bohème.* German opera was not generally favored by Russian audiences, but Volodya loved piano reductions of Wagner and within a few years had memorized large portions of *Tannhäuser, Lohengrin* and *Das Rheingold.* Tarnowsky was impressed by his student's passion for operatic literature and, one day, nearly fell off his chair when Volodya re-created portions of Strauss's *Salome* by ear, after hearing it performed only once.

Tarnowsky became the most decisive influence in the formation of Volodya's pianism. Guiding him from age twelve to age sixteen, perhaps the most important years of a pianist's development, Tarnowsky particularly strove to expand Volodya's sensitivity to variations in color and dynamics. In doing so, he demanded more attention to the gradations of the pedal, aiming, like Puchalsky, for an expressive singing tone. Volodya's temperament suited Tarnowsky's approach, but the boy's enthusiasm for experimenting with different sound effects was not always matched by diligent practice. Unlike the young Liszt or Paderewski, who worked intensely in their early years, Volodya practiced no more than four hours a day and usually less than that, only applying himself rigorously if he had to learn something new. He practiced much less than his sister, Genya, and although he sometimes spent most of the day at the piano, he often ignored his assignments, playing, instead, music that appealed to him, especially operas and orchestral scores.

Tarnowsky knew that the key to redirecting Volodya's attention to diligent piano practice was the assignment of interesting and technically challenging repertory that would broaden the boy's mastery of differing styles. He craftily delineated an alluring new program of works, which were unknown to Volodya and therefore instantly appealing. Volodya was delighted, for instance, by Tarnowsky's very first assignments—*Ten Woodland Sketches* by the American Edward MacDowell and the more familiar *Kinderscenen* of Schumann. Volodya especially liked *Träumerei,* the seventh piece of the Schumann set, which many years later became one of his encore trademarks. A few weeks after assigning the Schumann, Tarnowsky introduced the *Giga con Variazioni* of Joachim Raff and the *Six Etudes de Virtuosité* of Camille Saint-Saëns, both difficult studies that preoccupied Volodya for much of the semester. Also, like many piano teachers at the conservatory, Tarnowsky emphasized the Chopin etudes. While the *Black Key* and *Revolutionary* etudes presented few problems for Volodya, the *Winter Wind* Etude seemed an insurmountable challenge. Even many years later, the pianist admitted that too much tension in his arm and wrist drained his endurance, so that midway through the piece he felt as if his right arm might fall off.

Tarnowsky believed strongly that technical problems should be tackled from within the music itself rather than through the pedantic exercises of Clementi or Czerny. Although Volodya had mastered the scales, arpeggios, and other exercises required of every conservatory student, by his own admission he nonetheless had "terrible difficulty with technique." Years later, he echoed his teacher's philosophy: "I wanted to solve my problems through the music I played, not by calisthenic exercises. I never approached the piano in a mechanical way. I would look at the music and say to myself: 'Well, that should be very fast, so I have to work. That voice has to be emphasized, so I will try and it *will* come out.' "[10] Tar-

nowsky introduced his student to the most efficient way of playing octaves quickly and accurately—with the eye anticipating the hand, each
octave was played with all motion concentrated in the wrist, while the
forearm remained nearly motionless, the shoulder relaxed. Volodya
quickly grasped the importance of allowing only enough rebound so that
the key came up before the next repetition.

Despite Tarnowsky's willingness to appease Volodya, repertory selection proved to be the one serious problem in the boy's work with Tarnowsky. Sophie Gorovitz was convinced that Bach, Beethoven, and
Brahms, along with the stultifying exercises she had practiced as a girl,
were the key to piano study. When she heard her son practicing works
such as the Moszkowski etudes, reductions of Wagner operas, or newly
published works of Russian composers, she began to doubt Tarnowsky's
discipline. Volodya was not unaware of the irritation he was causing at
home: "Ha, ha! I was a little devil. I never worked when I was young. My
mother would scream at me: 'You don't practice!' And I never did practice the Etudes of Chopin, [or] Bach, Mozart, or Schubert. I went to
sleep with *Götterdämmerung* under my pillow. So my mother was going
out of her mind because I brought to Tarnowsky the music I liked, not
the music I was supposed to play. Finally she went to my professor and
said: 'What are you doing? Instead of Bach, he's playing Rachmaninoff!' "[11]

Tarnowsky, being more open-minded than many of the other professors at the conservatory, went out of his way to encourage Volodya's
bubbling enthusiasm. As he grew closer to the Gorovitz family and
observed the overbearing behavior of the boy's parents, Tarnowsky concluded that both were excessively involved in their son's studies. Eventually, he offered Sophie some stern advice: "Don't force him to play
anything because it *has* to be played. Allow him to play what he feels an
affinity for and what he likes. When he grows up he will come to the
classics by himself."[12]

Although still skeptical, Sophie capitulated and allowed her son to buy
whatever scores interested him on her carte blanche account at the local
music store. Rather than force any particular repertory on his student,
Tarnowsky wanted, above all, to rein in Volodya's vain fascination with
his rapidly developing virtuosity. Thus, he worked at emphasizing the
meaning and stylistic demands of music. At the piano recitals which the
boy attended, salon pieces by composers like Moszkowski were much in

fashion, and Volodya was instinctively drawn to music with surface glitter. Tarnowsky chastised him for superficiality and urged him to take the refined playing of Josef Hofmann as a model.

Although Tarnowsky did everything possible to make Volodya's lessons interesting and to provide nonthreatening discipline, there were nonetheless conservatory requirements that even Volodya could not escape, including semiannual recitals in which the best students were made to play. These last anguished the boy. For weeks before one of them, he would be extremely nervous and irritable, sometimes hurling dishes or breaking whatever came to hand. His family refused to reprimand Volodya for these tantrums, a reflection of his long-standing position as "family pet." Instead, Sophie routinely hid all valuables before recital dates, while Genya stood passively by as her brother pushed his piano from one spot to another in the music-room. Genya, three years older and more extroverted and self-confident, appreciated her own talent for the piano but realized that she could never expect to receive the attention lavished on her baby brother. Her contemporaries note that she seemed to accept this and, being good-natured, even to enjoy her brother's glory.

On the day of a recital, Volodya, overwrought, would spend hours at home in front of the hallway mirror, combing and recombing his stubborn cowlicks. But by the time he sat down at one of the conservatory's two superb Blütner pianos, he exuded self-confidence and filled the hall with his passionate playing. Sophie and Simeon displayed strangely divergent demeanors at these concerts. Simeon, handsomely groomed with a small pointed beard, was extremely proud of his son's talent and sat nervously attentive in a first-row seat. Sophie, elegantly dressed, hair formally braided in the back, scrutinized her son's performance and appearance with a lorgnette from the back of the hall. She was more reserved and considerably more discerning than her husband. At one recital, both parents were especially proud when Volodya performed Anton Arensky's popular Concerto in F Minor with Genya accompanying on the second piano; at another, he played Tchaikovsky's *Dumka* and Moszkowski's *Étincelles* (*Sparks*)—the latter a staccato study perfectly suited to the boy's taste and temperament. But whether he performed Rachmaninoff etudes and preludes or Chopin waltzes and mazurkas, Volodya was always successful, to Dombrovski's consternation, and at the end of a program Sophie and Simeon would receive envious congratulations from the other parents.

Volodya's skittishness also plagued him in Tarnowsky's piano class. Although this was a small group, consisting only of Volodya, Genya, their friend Anatole Kitain, and three others, Volodya clearly resented the presence of those he felt were his inferiors. Tarnowsky understood the situation and, when Kitain joined the class, he urged him "to pick on Horowitz because he thinks he is the best."[13]

Volodya was often unsympathetic to the playing of his classmates. Once, one of the young girls in the group performed the *Dumka*. When Tarnowsky asked for constructive criticism Volodya replied: "She played it well, but I can do better."[14] Tarnowsky, angered, showed the upstart to the door, snapping that since he was already such a great pianist, there was obviously little he could learn from either his teacher or fellow students. On another occasion, Volodya attended a special master class for one hundred students, for which he was to play Beethoven's *Emperor* Concerto. As he tended to underpractice works that bored him, he arrived completely unprepared. The exposition of the first movement was a disaster, and he was again shown the door. This time he stormed home, vowing never to return to school. Sophie, rather than pressing her son to apologize, instead begged Tarnowsky to make some gesture of forgiveness to Volodya. But Tarnowsky was not inclined to so indulge the spoiled boy. Inevitably, there were frequent periods of estrangement between pupil and teacher. After one student recital, Volodya sulked for months because he had been upbraided for what Tarnowsky considered his cavalier approach to Chopin's G Minor Ballade. Until word came that he was forgiven, Volodya stayed home, enervated and despondent, neglecting the piano and his other studies. Generally, during crises, Sophie served as intermediary and peacemaker.

Such adolescent episodes dramatized important ingredients in the young artist's personality—his moodiness and sensitivity to criticism, his high opinion of himself and self-righteousness. Volodya was not only often estranged from his piano teacher but was detached from his family and friends as well. "He knew everybody," one acquaintance of the time remembered, "but nobody really was his friend. It's difficult to know if he wanted it that way. He was quite strange and did not mix easily with people. There seemed to be an insecurity, an alert pessimism that made him shield himself from some sadness he felt. His loneliness was dissipated by playing the piano; it was his way of establishing himself. So, if anyone criticized his playing, his entire identity was in jeopardy."[15]

One very real threat to Volodya's peace of mind was the unpredictable behavior of his brother George. A handsome boy who resembled his younger brother, George played the violin haphazardly and was, in general, overshadowed by the precocious Volodya and Genya. Volodya was embarrassed by George's erratic behavior, so much so that he seldom invited his fellow students home. "George was not the kind of boy anyone wanted to associate with," recalled one classmate at the conservatory. "He had many problems and, like his brother Volodya, had few friends. Of those children, only Regina was friendly and mixed with everybody."[16] Later on, George's mental condition deteriorated, but during those school years, the Gorovitz household still was loving and supportive to him. Besides, whatever consternation George's problems caused were certainly offset by Volodya's burgeoning talent. When Sophie walked on the streets of Kiev, the mothers of other piano students would often rush up to her and exclaim, "Your son is a genius!"

CHAPTER THREE

REVOLUTION

*"The {Russian} Revolution was no box of chocolates. What it
was, was the incentive to get out. Every two months we had a
new government and finally in twenty-four hours we lost
everything and didn't even understand what happened. I am a
product of the Revolution. I'm a product of general privation,
not personal privation."*[1]

By the fall of 1919, Volodya had been studying with Tarnowsky for
five years. Increasingly resentful of attempts to curb his virtuosity, Volodya desperately wanted to change teachers. His parents, however, saw
no diplomatic way of altering the situation, especially since Tarnowsky
had ingratiated himself with the family and had become a regular dinner
guest. Moreover, they saw that their son's progress had been extraordinary under Tarnowsky's tutelage. Although Volodya was bored by academic studies at the gymnasium and had begun to avoid theory and
history classes, which he sometimes failed, his industry at the piano had
increased notably. He had recently discovered the Rachmaninoff Third
Concerto and was engrossed in memorizing that difficult score, a work
which represented the very pinnacle of Russian Romanticism. Tarnowsky sculpted every phrase with his student, laying the groundwork
for an interpretation that would someday astound audiences.

The Rachmaninoff Concerto proved to be the last music that Volodya
would study with Tarnowsky, for his dissatisfaction with his teacher
coincided with bizarre circumstances in November 1919 that precipitated
a change in his studies. Tarnowsky, on a short vacation, received word
that his father had died and immediately left for the Crimea. But he
never got farther than Rostov-on-Don, where he contracted the typhus
that was then ravaging many areas of the Ukraine. Rumors reached Kiev
that Tarnowsky had died, and after a few weeks, Director Glière began to
look for a new instructor for the Gorovitz children and the remainder of
Tarnowsky's class.

The First World War and the 1917 Revolution had left Kiev relatively unscathed, and until 1920, it was a mecca for intellectuals and artists seeking to escape the fighting and famine in other Russian cities. Although huge stretches of the Ukraine had been occupied by German soldiers since 1915, Kiev enjoyed adequate food supplies. Notwithstanding governmental instability and successive invasions by German, White Russian, Bolshevik, and independent Ukrainian Socialist forces, between 1918 and 1920 Kiev did not suffer the violence and famine that plagued Moscow and St. Petersburg. Among the refugees who arrived from the latter city was Felix Blumenfeld, a composer, conductor, and pianist who became Volodya's third and last piano teacher.

In his mid-fifties, Blumenfeld was renowned in the capital cities of Europe and considered a far greater musician than Tarnowsky by the conservatory professors in Kiev. He had studied composition with Rimsky-Korsakov and aligned himself with the respected "Kuchka," or "Five" (Cui, Balakirev, Borodin, Mussorgsky, Rimsky-Korsakov), who energetically fostered the spirit of Russian nationalism in their compositions. Blumenfeld premiered many works by these composers, and his own Symphony in C Major, Op. 39, subtitled *To the Beloved Dead,* reflected their influence. As a pianist, his memory was extraordinary and he had accompanied the celebrated bass Feodor Chaliapin in all the song cycles of Schumann and Schubert without the music. Continuing to perform, Blumenfeld had joined the faculty at the St. Petersburg Conservatory, while simultaneously assuming the positions of principal conductor at the Maryinsky Theater and guest conductor at the Imperial Opera. His musical associations extended beyond Russia's border, not only because of his own recitals but also because he had served as guest conductor of Russian repertory in Paris during the "Russian Season" of 1908.

Blumenfeld's knowledge of opera and his respected position in the Russian music world excited young Vladimir Gorovitz. Even more alluring was his new teacher's piano style, which had developed under the tutelage of Anton Rubinstein, revered father of all Russian piano virtuosos. As a student, Blumenfeld had been given the highest grades by Rubinstein at the St. Petersburg Conservatory, founded by Rubinstein himself. Blumenfeld's playing mirrored much of Rubinstein's brilliant, sensuous lyricism, and the virility of his style had been highly praised in his early years. Vladimir saw the opportunity finally to learn firsthand about this heroic style (dogmatized by Puchalsky and suppressed by Tarnowsky), the grand Russian pianistic tradition that had captivated him since childhood.

One day in April 1920, Vladimir was understandably shocked when his former teacher Tarnowsky walked through the conservatory doors. After five months in the Crimea, Tarnowsky had completely recovered from typhus and had returned to find that everyone believed him dead and all his students transferred to Blumenfeld. Glière now assigned new students to Tarnowsky, but Tarnowsky resented losing his favorites, especially Vladimir and Genya Gorovitz. Volodya, however, was determined to remain with Blumenfeld, who had quickly become his favorite teacher—his idol, in fact—and Blumenfeld would subsequently be credited for much of his early development as a pianist. Many years later Tarnowsky was still bitter about this. "Blumenfeld," he maintained, "was primarily a conductor and composer. He seems to have been a good musician but not that interested in the piano, certainly not in teaching piano. He never reached the heights in either conducting, composing, or playing the piano, and he gave Volodya largely a carte blanche in his studies. Volodya always had had a strong tendency toward brilliance and the freedom he was given under Blumenfeld allowed the purely virtuoso side of the young pianist to take a dominant position."[2]

In fact, many musicians familiar with Vladimir's background attributed much of his unique style to Tarnowsky. "Volodya was a stinker," said classmate Rubstein. "He later gave credit to Blumenfeld because nobody knew who Blumenfeld was in America and there was no chance of professional entanglements since Blumenfeld remained in Russia until his death. But Tarnowsky came to live first in Chicago and later in Los Angeles, and he might have benefited from Horowitz's reputation. Much to Tarnowsky's chagrin, however, Horowitz did not want to be bothered with him."[3] In the United States, Tarnowsky sometimes went backstage after a Horowitz recital. Still thinking of himself as *the* teacher, he lectured his former student, even after the name Horowitz was a legend. Horowitz did not appreciate his former professor's advice, and once snapped to a friend, "I don't need Tarnowsky anymore!"[4] Horowitz did at one point, however, give a cursory recognition to his former mentor. In a 1930 press release, he stated: "From the time I was twelve years old until I was sixteen, Sergei Tarnowsky was my teacher. I shall always be grateful for all that I learned musically and technically from Professor Tarnowsky."[5]

In his student years, however, it was Blumenfeld who provided a link to the great Russian composers and to Anton Rubinstein, and Vladimir revered him, willing to do almost anything to please. "Blumenfeld was sitting for hours, days, weeks, close to Anton Rubinstein, listening to him play," he said. "They often played four-handed music together and so I consider Rubinstein my grandfather a little bit since much of what I learned about the piano from Blumenfeld actually came from Rubinstein."[6] Had Horowitz carried his musical genealogy back a bit further, Franz Liszt, whose influence on Rubinstein had been enormous, would have had to be cited by him as his "great-grandfather."

The Kiev Conservatory was nearly turned upside down by Blumenfeld's appearance there in 1919. He was an opinionated and critical teacher who wasted little time on social niceties, yet, despite his frequent gruffness, his chamber-music and piano master classes were always jammed with curious and eager students. Unlike Puchalsky or Dombrovski, who sometimes had as many as fifty pianists in their charge, Blumenfeld accepted very few private pupils, only those he considered technically advanced and extraordinarily talented. Sharing Blumenfeld's private piano class with Volodya and Genya were Vera Resnikoff, Anatole Kitain, Simon Barere, and Alexander Dubiansky, and Blumenfeld considered Dubiansky, not Volodya, his most talented student. But Dubiansky, an impetuous youth, became embroiled in an ill-fated romance and committed suicide in his twenty-first year.

When the heat and hot water malfunctioned at the conservatory or class routine was interrupted by German troops or Ukrainian nationalist forces, lessons were switched to Blumenfeld's living room. Volodya had never liked either the atmosphere at school or having to participate in master classes, so he welcomed private lessons in his professor's home. Blumenfeld was an unusual pedagogue in that he was no longer able to demonstrate effectively at the keyboard for his students by the time he joined the faculty at the Kiev Conservatory. The effects of syphilis had left his entire right side partially paralyzed.

A handsome man of medium height with a thick handlebar moustache, this prodigious womanizer, gambler, and drinker now walked with a cane and often found himself embarrassed by an uncontrollable slurring of his speech. Although he attempted to play passages with his left hand, he was quite clumsy at this, even in the few compositions for only one hand which he had composed as demonstration pieces. But Blumenfeld's disability had its advantages for Volodya, who was forced to find his own technical solutions to problematic passages without the aid of his teacher. In any case, Blumenfeld's experience as a composer and conductor brought an unusually broad outlook to Volodya's study, as well as a de-emphasis on technique. Although Blumenfeld perfunctorily suggested that Volodya and the others might benefit from studying Brahms's *Fifty-one Exercises,* he was not a pedagogical nitpicker, and fortunately his students were advanced enough not to require detailed supervision. "I don't care if you play with your nose," he would declare, "so long as you get the right feeling."[7] He was similarly permissive about practicing, merely recommending four hours a day as a minimum. If his pupils were sincerely interested in making something of themselves, he explained, it was up to them to practice more.

At lessons, Blumenfeld occasionally pushed Volodya impatiently aside and, with his crippled, flat-fingered technique, played a passage, bringing out strange inner voices the young man had never heard before. Although Volodya was at first incredulous, he was strongly influenced by the flat-fingered approach, and began experimenting with outstretched fingers and a lower wrist. This was the antithesis of the Leschetizky approach, taught by Puchalsky and Tarnowsky, which stressed a level wrist and curved fingers. But Blumenfeld encouraged Volodya to continue such unorthodox experimentation, and the boy soon mastered a semi-staccato finger technique which allowed for tremendous brilliance and clarity. Every note was detached. In slow motion, the outstretched finger approached a key, nearly flat. Appearing to scratch the key's surface, the finger then quickly snapped back toward the palm, simultaneously depressing the key while preparing for the next one. This sequence required enormous strength when repeated in rapid runs. "In my rapid passage-work, I played this half-staccato technique much of the time—*portamento*—so that every tone was very clear. I later found this to be effective, even necessary, in a large hall. If I played such passages *legato,* the effect would be blurred."[8]

Lessons with Blumenfeld were flexible, with no time restrictions, so that teacher and student had ample opportunity to investigate many scores, not only piano music but also the orchestral and vocal literature. Volodya was still headstrong about what he would play, and Blumenfeld bewailed the fact that his student was far more sophisticated in technique than in knowledge of the standard repertory. Feeling that performing conventional showpieces and transcriptions of operas like *Otello* and *La Bohème* was not sufficient preparation for a concert career, Blumenfeld turned Volodya's attention to those operas of Wagner with which he was not yet familiar and to a wide range of symphonic music. In this respect, Blumenfeld's influence was crucial. Remembered Horowitz: "He and I played duets together all the time—reductions of symphonies of Haydn, Mozart, Bruckner, Mahler, Brahms, and Tchaikovsky. He guided me as a conductor guides an orchestra. The idea of imagining different instruments at the piano was often dwelt on by Anton Rubinstein and by my teacher too. 'How would a violin, cello, or oboe play that?' he would ask me. 'Do not try to imitate the instruments, but think of their colors.' Whatever the effect he sought, I myself had to find out the way to make it. Our talk was of music, not the piano."[9]

Among the works Volodya studied with Blumenfeld were the First Concerto of Tchaikovsky, the Second Concerto of Rachmaninoff and both concertos of Liszt. Less important to his subsequent career but equally interesting to young Horowitz were concertos of Arensky, Saint-Saëns, and Glazunov. Most of his time, however, was spent learning solo works of Chopin and Liszt and pieces by the Polish composer Karol Szymanowski, at the time one of Volodya's favorite composers. Blumenfeld especially liked Volodya's clean, straightforward approach to Chopin, which used rubato properly and did not overromanticize. "As a young man, I was always criticized because I was unorthodox, particularly in Chopin. Why? Because I thought the late-Victorian tradition of Chopin playing was an exaggeration—just like the furniture and literature of the period—that Chopin himself must have played his music completely differently than his disciples."[10]

In all repertory, Blumenfeld discouraged his student from exploiting the piano's intrinsic percussive quality and insisted on a vocal approach. Like Puchalsky and Tarnowsky, he stressed the Russian School's expressive treatment of technique, demanding "singing" scales rather than the typical metronomic monotony that often emanated from student practice rooms. He was, then, understandably pleased by Volodya's avid interest in listening to and transcribing vocal music. Volodya and his favorite cousin, Natasha, sometimes barricaded themselves in her bedroom for hours, huddled around her phonograph listening to the most famous Italian *bel canto* singers of the time: Luisa Tetrazini, Enrico Caruso, Tita Ruffo, Mattia Battistini. Whenever possible, the two would also purchase tickets to performances of their favorite operas: Verdi's *Rigoletto,* Rossini's *Barber of Seville,* Gounod's *Faust,* Puccini's *La Bohème.* "I wanted to sing at the piano," Horowitz later recalled, "and I listened to those *bel canto* singers from morning to night. This was a major influence on everything."[11]

During the last two years of study at the conservatory Volodya's lessons with Blumenfeld were supplemented by frequent coaching sessions at the Gorovitz home, informal evenings attended by Professors Puchalsky, Tarnowsky and Blumenfeld and the esteemed pianist Heinrich Neuhaus, Blumenfeld's nephew and the first cousin of Szymanowski. The handsome, thirty-year-old Neuhaus was an articulate teacher, self-effacing and witty, given to wearing extravagant bow ties which looked like exotic butterflies. Volodya took an instant liking to the man and later insisted that, next to Blumenfeld, Neuhaus was the most important influence on his early development. In 1919, Neuhaus introduced Volodya to the Polish violinist Paul Kochanski, a new teacher at the Kiev Conservatory who became a frequent chamber-music partner with Volodya and Genya. Although both Kochanski and Neuhaus were amazed by Volodya's pianism and impressed and entertained by his opera transcriptions, they were taken aback when he lightly dismissed those composers he did not favor. "Volodya told me with great emphasis," recalled Neuhaus, "how much he loved Mozart and Schumann and how alien Beethoven was to him. Beethoven did not move him in the slightest. [Beethoven, he said,] was no Mozart and certainly no Schumann, but something halfway between the two."[12] However, Neuhaus indulged Volodya and agreed to appear with him in two-piano recitals at the conservatory. He also encouraged him in his early efforts as a composer.

During his middle teens Volodya had become intrigued with the idea of being a composer-pianist, in the tradition of Liszt and Rachmaninoff. He had accumulated a modest portfolio of original works, which began with his opera transcriptions and extended to ballades and sonatas for piano, songs, and sonatas for violin and for cello. He began to divide his time at the piano equally between practicing standard repertory for Blumenfeld and improvising, sketching out, and then writing down a new repertory of his own. In 1919 his ambitions as a composer were bolstered when a well-known soprano visited the conservatory and included some of his songs on her program, songs he had set to verses by Anna Achmatova and Alexander Blok and some of his own poems. But despite his interest and talent for composition, Volodya did not apply himself in harmony and counterpoint classes. Later he admitted that his negligence in academic discipline was a liability in his development. Influenced by the works of Grieg and Rachmaninoff, his early, derivative efforts never pleased him, and in later years he did not perform his chamber music or songs in public. He was, however, fond of two piano works he had composed when seventeen years old: a Waltz in F Minor and a *Danse Excentrique* modeled on the *Golliwogg's Cake-Walk* from Debussy's *Children's Corner* Suite. Volodya especially liked the *Danse Excentrique,* and he both recorded and occasionally performed it during the early years of his professional career.

With Blumenfeld's blessings, Vladimir continued to entertain the notion of being both pianist and composer until 1920, the year of his graduation from the conservatory. By this time material circumstances made continued study impossible. "As a composer I missed the boat,"[13] he said; and despite the extraordinary success of his later concert career, he steadfastly maintained that he had always planned to be a composer and had only abandoned the idea when the effects of the Revolution forced him to concertize.

During the tumultuous years after the 1917 collapse of the czarist regime, the Ukraine had seen seemingly endless and chaotic changes of government that slowly weakened and then nearly destroyed its rich agricultural and industrial productivity. In January 1918, the Ukraine declared itself an independent republic, and the next month Kiev was occupied by Bolshevik troops. In March, in order to extricate itself from the First World War, Russia was forced to sign the devastating treaty of Brest-Litovsk which yielded the Ukraine to Germany, but by the following November, the government in Kiev had changed hands again when Germany surrendered to the Allies. At this point, civil war erupted between the contending "White Russian" armies and the Bolsheviks. The White forces at first scored impressive victories, but their achievement proved ephemeral, for the war that Poland instigated against Russia in the spring of 1920 allowed the Bolsheviks to appeal to national patriotism in order to oppose foreign invasion. Although Polish troops did occupy Kiev for a short time in May 1920, a counteroffensive by the Red Army quickly drove them out, and, simultaneously, the Bolshevik forces squelched the last opposition from the Whites. The civil war ended with the Bolsheviks in firm control of the Ukrainian capital.

In the winter of 1919, at the height of the civil war, Volodya was nearly killed when a bomb landed ten feet away from him as he walked home from school. At the conservatory, conditions had deteriorated so badly that the institution was barely able to function. Group activities were suspended. Parents withdrew their children in order to save money, and faculty salaries remained unpaid. The decline of industry and the disorganization of transport now led to the decimation of the Ukrainian economy. Manufactured goods and articles for daily use, staples such as sugar, molasses, and flour, were nearly impossible to buy, and the catastrophe increased with severe drought in 1920 and 1921. Loss of life was estimated at five million.

When the Bolsheviks took control in Kiev, Simeon's electrical business had been appropriated by the government, and the family was forced to move from its comfortable apartment into a small house on the Bolshaya Zhitomizkaya, in a poorer part of the city. There, cramped into three tiny apartments, were the Gorovitzes, Sophie's brother Alexander and his family, and Simeon's two sisters, Pauline and Evelyn. For Simeon's youngest son, the trauma of those days was excruciating, inspiring a lifelong vow never to return to Russia: "In twenty-four hours my family lost everything. With my own eyes I saw them throw our piano through the window, into the street! The Communist motto was 'Steal what was stolen,' so they stole everything! All the clothes in the closets were taken. Books, my music, furniture, everything. Hundreds of people were killed and the streets were filled with bullets and blood. I could have been killed too. After nine o'clock at night, we were not allowed to walk in the streets. Sometimes I would be coming home with my friends and we would be interrogated."[14]

His business and home destroyed and his money gone, Simeon found that the need for food had become the all-consuming preoccupation. Provisions were requisitioned and distributed by a system of ration cards, but since the average ration per day was only half a pound of bread, everyone remained hungry. Farmers, distrusting the Bolsheviks' ability to supply manufactured goods or to pay for produce in stable currency, refused to work the land. In desperation, Blumenfeld wrote to Rachmaninoff in America, pleading for flour, rice, and condensed milk, and Simeon Gorovitz was forced to stand in line for hours with his family's ration cards to exchange for grain and sugar the few belongings he had left. Diamonds were frequently traded for a loaf of bread, and soon huge signs appeared in the streets ordering all citizens to deliver their money, silver, and jewelry to the party headquarters, by coincidence housed on Music Lane in the same building where the Gorovitzes had lived.

Simeon and Sophie had originally intended Volodya to continue his training at least until the age of twenty, but it was now decided that the sixteen-year-old should graduate from the conservatory immediately, despite his insistence that he wasn't ready. For his diploma, three performances were required: a concerto played with the student orchestra, a chamber-music concert, and a solo recital. Each stage of the ordeal threw the shy youngster ("sad-eyed and long-faced,"[15] according to one classmate) into paroxysms of terror, but there was no choice except to go through with the requirements, for they had been decreed by Anton Rubinstein himself and were mandatory.

On the first program, Volodya was soloist in the Rachmaninoff Third Concerto, and Blumenfeld was so pleased with the performance that he decided to write Rachmaninoff himself, in America: "From August 1918, up to last spring, I had as an advanced student an extremely talented youth of seventeen, Vladimir Gorovitz—a passionate admirer of your music and of Medtner's. He graduated, by the way, with your Third Concerto at the conservatory and later at his own recital he also played your B-flat Minor Sonata very well. As you can see, you are very much loved here."[16] Blumenfeld's mention of Volodya to Rachmaninoff presaged a close friendship between the two to be forged later in Europe and the United States. When Sophie found out that Blumenfeld had mentioned her son in a letter to the composer, she told the teacher about the time that Simeon had tried to persuade Rachmaninoff to hear Volodya play, and Rachmaninoff had failed to keep their appointment. Blumenfeld assured Volodya that at some point he would certainly meet Rachmaninoff.

After passing the chamber-music requisite, which included performances in the Schumann Quintet and the *Winterreise* of Schubert, Volodya presented his full-length recital program. In addition to the fiendishly difficult Rachmaninoff sonata, Vladimir also chose the Bach-Busoni Toccata, Adagio, and Fugue in C Major, the Beethoven Sonata, Op. 110, and the Chopin Fantasy in F Minor. He closed the concert with Liszt's tour-de-force, the *Don Juan Fantasy*. At the last note, pandemonium erupted in the hall. Normally, the one hundred or so invited guests, professors, students, and parents sat as dour judges during student exams, but on this occasion the entire audience leaped to its feet and applauded. Vladimir himself was flabbergasted. "This had never happened before in the history of the conservatory, [and] everyone made me know that I was above the typical pianist. I didn't know it. I was always very modest with myself."[17] Members of the jury congratulated Sophie, who was, as always, sitting in the back, and told her they had not heard such playing since Josef Hofmann's last performance in Kiev.

Even before the graduation concerts, Blumenfeld had tried to convince Simeon and Sophie that their son was ready for a public career, but both of them were adamant that Volodya should not play professionally until fully mature. Now, however, Blumenfeld and other musicians and friends pressed harder and finally gained tentative approval from Simeon and Uncle Alexander. Eventually Sophie too relented, and on May 30, 1920, Volodya presented his first concert outside the conservatory, a trial debut in Kiev for an audience of two hundred which was quickly followed by another appearance with the same program. As a tribute to his teacher, Volodya played six of Blumenfeld's Preludes, Op. 17, and then selections from Rachmaninoff's *Etudes-Tableaux,* Op. 39, the Bach-Busoni *Chaconne,* and Chopin works, including the G Minor Ballade, a nocturne, several mazurkas, and two etudes. As Volodya completed the Chopin group with the *Military Polonaise,* the sounds of guns and bombs could be heard in the streets, the last strife marking the Bolshevik subjugation of Kiev.

Onstage, the young pianist's appearance was striking, for he resembled, to a remarkable degree, Delacroix's famous portrait of Chopin: pale skin, brown almond-shaped eyes, and chestnut-colored hair worn long in the Russian style, falling in a lock to one side of a high forehead, face dominated by a prominent nose the family insisted he had inherited from Uncle Alexander. Fellow students remember that the resemblance to Chopin was apparently not accidental, that the "Chopin look" was deliberately cultivated.

Unfortunately, the debut in Kiev of Vladimir Gorovitz went largely unnoticed. For the next year and a half he returned to the role of student, practicing and taking lessons without any further public performances. In 1921, Simeon attempted but failed to find full-time employment, and as the family's economic condition worsened, it became obvious that Vladimir was going to have to help support his family by pursuing a concert career. "My father lost everything and I had to help him; my parents gave to me and now, I thought, I must give something back to them."[18] But this was no easy task, especially for an introverted, thoroughly spoiled eighteen-year-old who knew nothing but the routine of the conservatory and had hated even the pressure of student recitals. He dreamed one moment of being a composer like his idol, Rachmaninoff, and the next of having a glamorous concert career. But the grim reality of life in Kiev in 1921 acted as a strong antidote to romantic notions. Much later he declared: "I am a product of the Revolution, a product of privation. Coming out of this kind of life gives a young person a certain amount of dynamism. It was important to do something and to be somebody. I could not continue to study. I said to myself, all right, now I start to play the piano and maybe I can be a success. I began."[19]

CHAPTER FOUR

"ELECTRIC-LIGHTNING PIANIST"

"God was very generous to me and gave me facility so I didn't have to work too much and I had right away success. I didn't expect it. I didn't want it even. I still wanted to be a composer."[1]

When Horowitz began his professional concert career, he was "an un-finished product,"[2] according to Vera Resnikoff, one of his classmates in Blumenfeld's piano class. "Had the Revolution not brought hardship on his family and forced him into concertizing, we would have heard a different Horowitz in later years. Recognition came swiftly in Russia because of the public's appreciation of acrobatic ability over musicianship. Capitalizing on this, Horowitz soon found himself playing very brilliant programs to catch the audience's favor as well as their admission price." Vladimir was compelled to earn money for his family and his no-nonsense motto became "success above all." In his determination to establish himself as a pianist, he was buttressed not only by Sophie and Simeon but also by his indefatigable uncle Alexander, who was willing to court and exploit anyone who might be of help to the family. It was Alexander, an ambitious and astute businessman, who masterminded Vladimir's formal concert debut at the Kharkov public library in the fall of 1921.

Vladimir and his uncle arrived from Kiev by horse-and-carriage, both simply dressed in black trousers and open-necked white shirts, the pre-scribed concert attire in the first years of post-Revolutionary Russia. Once inside the library, however, they were dismayed to discover the one-thousand-seat hall about four-fifths empty. Moreover, the ticket seller informed them that most of the audience appeared to be deadheads who had accepted free passes in order to spend a few hours in a warm room. Undaunted, Volodya marched onto the stage and his playing managed to

rouse the audience to an ovation that encouraged Alexander to arrange
another recital that he advertised as a repeat performance by popular demand. This time there was a larger audience, one that had paid for its
tickets, and news began to spread by word of mouth about the sensational Gorovitz boy. Money from the second concert was used to book
the library for a third appearance and this time the hall was completely
sold out. Even after Alexander had paid for the auditorium and for advertising, there was money left to buy the necessities the Gorovitzes
badly needed: flour, sugar, fish, and meat.

Vladimir's career was then quite literally at the service of his family,
and he derived enormous satisfaction from providing for them while
proving himself as an artist. The approval of the public quickly became
intoxicating and his tentativeness about performing was replaced by an
eagerness for still more appearances. As an intelligent and sensitive young
man who had been overwhelmed by the destructive force of the Revolution, Vladimir came to understand his playing as an expression of the
startling social drama that had enveloped his country: "I felt the atmosphere in Russia. I felt the pessimism of the Russian people because of
deprivation, both intellectual and physical, like a feudal society. I identified with them and tried to put it all into my playing."[3]

By June 1922, Vladimir had given over a dozen recitals which
Alexander had arranged in Moscow, Tiflis, Odessa, Kiev, and Kharkov.
Now moderately successful, he became impatient for better coverage in
the press and more money. Alexander advised him to be patient. "You
play a concert, you go into the second and you keep playing," he told his
nephew. "Your reputation will develop and grow slowly."[4]

One stimulating benefit of travel and increased public attention was
that Vladimir was able to broaden his circle of acquaintances. In different
cities he met other musicians, both of his own age and older. The new
friend he liked most was a young violinist from Odessa, Nathan Milstein. Milstein had first studied with Professor Peter Stoliarsky at the
Odessa Music School and then in St. Petersburg, where he had been a
pupil of Leopold Auer, at that time Russia's most esteemed violin
teacher. In the winter of 1921, Milstein visited Kiev to give four recitals
at the conservatory, with Tarnowsky as accompanist. "The local musicians in Kharkov had told me that Horowitz played wonderfully," remembered Milstein. "Tarnowsky must have told Volodya and Genya
about me because they both attended my recitals and came backstage. I
remember he was so handsome—thin and elegant, like a greyhound."[5]

Vladimir and Genya invited Milstein to come to their home for tea. After an hour with Sophie, Simeon, Aunt Evelyn, and Professors Tarnowsky and Neuhaus, Milstein, Vladimir, and Genya became restless. "We grew tired of the talk of our elders," recalled Milstein. "Anybody over thirty was old to us then! And Regina said: 'Come to my room. I have a piano there.' "[6] After Genya had played a few works of Chopin and Schumann, Vladimir sat down at the piano. "He looked unusually revolutionary," said Milstein. "Beautiful, like a Pre-Raphaelite [portrait]."[7] Rather than the usual Liszt or Rachmaninoff, Vladimir regaled Milstein with his own arrangements of symphonies and operas. "Can you imagine how surprised Milstein was?"[8] Horowitz asked later. Indeed, the violinist was shocked and delighted by the unbridled enthusiasm for Puccini and Wagner. "He knew *Götterdämmerung* by heart!" exclaimed Milstein. "A seventeen-year-old pianist has to be burning up—and he was. My God, he broke the string when he played! Time flew."[9] Professor Neuhaus remained happily in the living room, a distance away from what he termed "the banging and thumping," and he later reflected that "Horowitz used to bang so mercilessly that it was almost impossible to listen to him in a room."[10] But that day Milstein was intrigued by the fire of Vladimir's technique and his versatility with opera, chamber music, and solo repertory. Sophie finally interrupted the young musicians to announce dinner, but immediately after eating Milstein and Vladimir returned to Genya's room. "Volodya and I played sonatas and concertos of Prokofiev, Grieg, Szymanowski, Glazunov and Beethoven. It became so late that I was asked to spend the night. We slept four in the same room—Papa, Volodya, his brother [George], and me. The next morning when I woke up I was asked to stay on."[11]

According to Horowitz, Milstein "came to tea and stayed in our house for three years because of me."[12] It was not long before the violinist was being treated like a son by Sophie and Simeon, and Milstein and Horowitz became inseparable. They ate lunch and dinner together, attended concerts, played chamber music, and finally teamed up to give concerts—all the while discussing how to leave Russia and make reputations in Europe. Said Milstein, "Horowitz and I were called 'children of the Soviet Revolution' and were made honored Soviet artists, although of course we were really children of a different stock. Whenever there was a Communist meeting from then on, we were asked to play. We were an elite. There was no competition—it was like playing tennis by yourself."[13]

The duo became a trio when Vladimir and Nathan were joined on-stage by Genya. A typical program featured Nathan accompanied by Genya in the first half followed by Vladimir's appearance, as the star, after intermission. In 1921, the three also appeared in public with a slightly younger but brilliant cellist from Tiflis, Raya Garbousova. "We played the trios of Franck and Beethoven together," she recalled. "Milstein and Horowitz were phenomenal talents, overwhelming in their musical, virtuoso playing of the Romantic literature. After performances, instead of money, we received chocolate. And we regretted the chocolate very much because we would rather have had bread and salami!"[14] So common was payment in sweets to young performers that many rising musicians jokingly referred to themselves as "chocolate babies."[15] Food was scarce, however, and few could be overly selective about what they would or would not eat. The popular trio were often invited to dinner at private homes after their performances in Kiev, Tiflis, and Odessa, but, oddly, their hosts inevitably seemed to serve something called "rabbit ragout." Since it tasted good no one really minded the monotony. In fact, it wasn't until they noticed the lack of stray dogs and cats on the city streets that they realized just how many they might have consumed.

In 1922, Alexander's role as concert manager for his nephew was largely usurped by the state-run concert bureau, which had been established by the Soviet regime to bring art to the proletariat. Anatole Lunacharsky, Lenin's commissar of public education, nationalized and coordinated the activities of theater and concert managements, conservatories, ballet companies, and symphony orchestras, and in the Ukraine all recitals and orchestral appearances were now booked by Paul Kogan, who was ordered to form "mobile artistic brigades" to introduce music into factories, collective farms, and workers' clubhouses. Vladimir, Genya, Milstein, and Garbousova were now placed directly under Kogan's jurisdiction, instructed to crisscross the Ukraine, presenting concerts for anyone who would listen—peasants, farmers, factory workers, soldiers, sailors. The Soviet concert bureau may have had lofty ideals about educating the masses, but for Horowitz, Milstein, and the others the imposed program was a horror. Delayed trains and uncomfortable hotels made traveling arduous, and playing conditions were unspeakable: improvised stages, decrepit pianos, and unheated halls which sometimes necessitated the performers' wearing overcoats and gloves. Moreover, the audiences were frequently uninterested and rowdy, forced to attend because of mandatory political lectures that followed each performance. They often arrived late, talking, smoking, eating nuts, and throwing the shells onto the stage, and among musicians this mass circuit became contemptuously known as *Khaltura* or "patchwork." But Vladimir's physical resiliency and conspicuous success with audiences allowed him to accept unpleasant conditions with relative equanimity, and his manager, Kogan, recalled that both Horowitz and Milstein were welcomed by the new musical establishment for being "kind-hearted and warm without pretension."[16]

Kogan observed the striking contrast between "the boys," as he affectionately called them. "Horowitz was tall, fair, quiet, serious, [and] kept to himself, while Milstein was dark-haired, short, broad-shouldered, very masculine, and a bundle of temperament, not given over to pessimism and very extroverted." When visiting Kiev, Kogan stayed in the Gorovitz home, where he noted the pianist's favored status over other family members: "He considered this superior position in the family to be proper; his behavior evoked in them both a feeling of pride and a certain degree of inevitable envy."[17] Although sometimes appalled by Volodya's egocentricity and imperiousness toward his family, Kogan held him in high regard as an artist. The young pianist's curiosity, willingness to take risks, self-discipline, and total concentration on and devotion to his instrument astounded the manager. "He was completely in love with music, as faithful to his piano as a medieval knight to his lady."[18]

Kogan booked Vladimir primarily for solo recitals and concerto dates, but sometimes also asked him to accompany singers. On one occasion, he played for Zoya Lodaya in Schubert's *Winterreise* and amazed everyone by performing the entire song-cycle by heart. The daily Kiev newspaper, which seldom reviewed concerts, praised the ensemble work as "near perfection."[19] Nonetheless, Vladimir lacked a firmly established reputation, and he was viewed by at least one diva with disdain. Even before hearing him play, one soprano flared at Kogan: "What, you couldn't get me a better accompanist?"[20] Indignantly, Kogan retorted that Vladimir had already accompanied the well-known tenor Leonid Sobinov and *he* had not complained. When at last the bickering pair were persuaded to begin rehearsing, the singer's reservations quickly melted away.

The highlight of Vladimir's short Russian career as a chamber musician came in 1922, when he gave a series of recitals with the famed soprano Nina Koshetz of the Moscow Winter Theater. Kogan, who had arranged the tour, noted with astonishment that, despite Koshetz's reputation, it was Horowitz who was the center of attention everywhere the pair performed. "In the *Romances* of Rachmaninoff, Horowitz inspired the entire evening," he said. "In vocal recitals, the singer is usually the center of everything. But this time it was different. Horowitz was incomparable. His accompaniment was not simply an addition to the singing—it seemed that he was the dominant force and the singer was in the background. Yet he maintained perfect balance with Koshetz and never exploited the piano part at her expense."[21]

In his solo recitals as well, Vladimir was beginning to achieve critical success, and he settled into a repertory of proven crowd pleasers. In addition to the Liszt B Minor Sonata and Rachmaninoff Second Sonata, he concentrated on such works as the *Danse Macabre,* arranged by Liszt from the Saint-Saëns symphonic poem, Liszt's *Fantasia on Two Motives from Mozart's* "Marriage of Figaro," Francis Poulenc's *Pastourelle, Presto,* and *Toccata,* Rimsky-Korsakov's *Flight of the Bumble-Bee,* and Tchaikovsky's *Dumka.* Most of his recitals were in small halls, and aside from flashy encores, Vladimir often selected single-composer programs of an intimate nature—Chopin, Schumann, or Bach-Busoni. "I could play a program of all Medtner compositions and make a sold-out house in Russia," he remembered. "But later, in the West, that was impossible. In Russia I could; it was a different time."[22]

Following his initial concert in each city, Vladimir was hailed as "a miracle" or some similar superlative, and Kogan, delighted with the audience response, began to book concerts for nearly every other night of the week. Pianist and musicologist David Rabinovich recalled the first time he heard Horowitz in 1922: "News about him began to appear more often and I was intrigued to hear this pupil of Blumenfeld. The success which accompanied his tours pleasantly exceeded that which was usual at the debuts of most young virtuosos. His interpretation of the *Don Juan Fantasy* was astounding. The victorious power and composure of his playing seemed inconceivable for a man his age. The quality of his technique was sensational: it incorporated an unheard of dexterity, a brilliance of tone, an indomitable spirit, a flaming temperament, an all-conquering drive and certain other traits in his 'piano musculature' that were second nature to him. As with the majority of geniuses, Horowitz seemed to appear suddenly and take his place immediately among great artists."[23]

Upon hearing Horowitz for the first time in Leningrad in 1923, no less a figure than Artur Schnabel pronounced himself "very impressed." Horowitz, he remembered, "wanted a lesson with me, but I decided he was not in need of any. I also asked him whether he was composing and he said, very shyly, 'Yes.' He had an enormous success, was rather spoiled, and tired—he was really the hero at that time. I thought it was absolutely necessary for him physically and mentally to leave Russia."[24]

Although Volodya seemed to enjoy his place in the limelight, he was sometimes plagued by terrible fears and insecurities during these early years. "His complexion became even paler than usual before each solo re-cital," recalled Kogan. "He couldn't look at anyone or talk to anyone and he walked back and forth in his room with heavy, despondent steps." But not long after, onstage, a miraculous transformation would occur. "I often asked myself," said Kogan, "whether I really knew this poetic youth in the long jacket who sat at the piano so simply, carefully dusting the keyboard with his white handkerchief before beginning to play. As he performed, the hall seemed so quiet it seemed one could almost hear his heart beating." According to Voltaire, one must have a tiny devil in the heart in order to be a successful performing artist, and Kogan re-marked, "Hearing Horowitz, I could experience the activity of this demon, something that Liszt and Paganini must have had."[25] That par-ticular demon, however, was, partly at least, consciously fabricated by Vladimir in order to generate enthusiasm for his concerts. "When I was young, I wanted to 'épater la bourgeoisie.' I had a tremendous facility. God was very generous to me and gave me technique so I didn't have to work too hard. I could make people throw their hats off. This was my goal. . . . I wanted them to acknowledge me and be a success right away. So I took the easy way."[26]

He was not, however, lackadaisical in preparation of repertory, and it was during these lean years of the post-Revolutionary period that he practiced most industriously. "I was extremely cold and I was extremely hungry and there was nothing else for me to do but sit at the piano from morning to night,"[27] he said. Vladimir's large repertory made it possible for him to present an unusual series of concerts in Leningrad which dra-matically illustrated his versatility as an artist and the reason for his popu-lar appeal. Competitive and ambitious, he planned a string of recitals that, he said, would even exceed Josef Hofmann's record of twenty-one different programs during one season. Although the documentary evidence of those Leningrad performances remains buried in the Soviet archives, Horowitz later reported that during the winter of 1922–23, he played twenty-three concerts of eleven different programs containing more than one hundred different works and never performed the same composition twice. "That is written in the Golden Book in Leningrad," he recalled proudly, adding, "They loved me there."[28]

Vladimir was, in fact, so extraordinarily popular in Leningrad that he was honored with an "official" fan club, a group of eight adoring females known as "the Green Girls" because of their emblematic green cardigans. "Why precisely green?" laughed one, Lydia Zhukova, in an interview sixty years later. "I don't remember. Once we had chosen Horowitz as our pianist, we decided that we needed some sign of adoration to distinguish us as his fan club. The Russian poet Vladimir Mayakovsky [1894–1930] had a fan club which wore only yellow sweaters, and we decided on the color green as our trademark. We were in love with music and a little crazy. We were also poor. We couldn't buy jackets so we sewed them ourselves from our grandmothers' old clothes, each of us wearing a different shade of green. At every one of his recitals we had to dress in green so that everyone in attendance would know who we were—and they did."[29]

Those eight girls were from families that had lost everything during the Revolution, and they did not even pay the admission price for Volodya's concerts. Some of them cleaned the concert hall for the privilege of hearing him play, while the craftier ones stole ticket stubs from people who either left the concert during intermission or dropped their tickets on the floor. "We took the tickets like thieves," recalled Zhukova, "and attended as many concerts as we could on these stolen stubs. Throughout the years that we listened to Horowitz play, we never spent one penny for a ticket. I always found a seat in the last row, which gave me a feeling of spiritual separation from the figure on stage. When he was playing, I was unaware of the luxurious chandeliers of the Philharmonic Hall, the red velvet, the seats filled with people; I only heard the silver, musical sounds recalling another world, quite different from the one created by the Revolution."[30]

According to Zhukova, the Green Girls were especially enraptured by Vladimir's renditions of their favorite works by Liszt (the Second and Sixth Hungarian Rhapsodies, *Mephisto Waltz,* and *Feux Follets* from the set of *Transcendental Etudes*) and by many of the all-Chopin recitals featuring the B-flat Minor Sonata, the ballades, the scherzos, and some of the etudes, waltzes and mazurkas. In the midst of the austerity then prevailing in Leningrad, how strange it must have been to see a gaggle of eighteen-year-old girls rushing through the streets in their green uniforms, before and after Horowitz concerts, chanting over and over again a simple jingle:

Volodya Gorovitz
Makes girls have fits.

All of them are wild
About his piano style!

Later, when the Green Girls heard reports that their idol was planning to leave Russia to make his fortune in Europe and America, they panicked. Previously, they had worshiped the pianist from afar, never even attempting to meet him, but now they were determined to have some souvenir. After one of Vladimir's final Leningrad concerts, they cornered the terrified young man backstage. Armed with scissors, they grabbed a tail of his formal coat and started snipping. "We grabbed the black tail rapaciously and Horowitz became so angry, he hit us with his hands— with those beautiful long fingers—his face flushed with hate and desperation. Although it seemed that he was willing to fight to the death for 'his tail,' we struggled with him and finally got as much of his coat as we wanted."[31] The girls then cut the seized material into eight thin strips and fashioned them into black roses to be worn on their green cardigans in subsequent seasons as symbols of mourning for their beloved.

During that Leningrad season, Horowitz was labeled the "electric-lightning pianist."[32] Sometimes his audiences became so excited that they actually rose silently from their seats *before* a piece ended to stand staring in amazement at the slight figure on stage. Said one observer of the period, "The essence of the music spoke so directly to their hearts, they were so hungry for release from ugliness and poverty, that the audience became frenzied and could not sit passively."[33] Vladimir's classmate Rubstein recalled that "after many of his Leningrad concerts, people who didn't even know one another were seen smiling and talking together, full of emotion."[34] Once, he was actually carried back to his hotel by a crowd of fans. ("It was very uncomfortable," he remembered.)[35] At a time when many people did not even have enough to eat, the pianist was able to draw three thousand people into the Great Hall of the Philharmonic, enthusiasts who somehow managed to scrape up an admission price ranging from 10 kopecks to 1.5 rubles. If the crowds were shabbily dressed or behaved poorly, they seemed nonetheless sincerely moved by what they heard.

Vladimir gained confidence from such enthusiasm and was also encouraged by the critical hyperbole he received after each of his concerts in major cities. Music coverage during this period was sparse, usually amounting to nothing more than a tiny news article, but Soviet newspapers often made an exception when reporting a Horowitz recital. After one of his all-Liszt concerts in Leningrad, an enthusiastic critic noted: "His finger dexterity was incredible . . . the rapid scales seemed weightless and surrounded by air, each note gleamed and sparkled like tiny diamonds permeated by the sun. A musical magician! His interpretations of the Chopin mazurkas left a lasting impression that had nothing to do with bravura. They were a treasure: delicate with an astounding variety of timbre; so much fantasy and simple good taste."[36]

Despite the positive reviews, Vladimir's artistic progress was not keeping pace with his virtuosity. When he played the Liszt First Concerto with the Leningrad State Philharmonic under composer Alexander Glazunov in 1923, his former teacher Blumenfeld attended the concert and was disappointed with the performance. "Very bad, too fast, too superficial,"[37] Blumenfeld told Anatole Kitain. Of course, to some extent Vladimir was playing down to his audience by emphasizing his command of fiery repertory, but then, he realized that his listeners were mostly poor and uneducated and that only pyrotechnics would arouse them. "He made mistakes," remembered Kogan, "miscalculated balances—but the mistakes were made out of enthusiasm, temperament which could be easily forgiven."[38]

In October 1924, Vladimir played the Rachmaninoff Third and the Liszt First concertos with Valeria Berdiayev, one of the few women conductors assigned to the State Philharmonic. Following these performances, he gave two recitals with Milstein, whose success as a concert performer had not yet matched that of his friend. On December 12, both Milstein and Horowitz performed with the State Symphony, conducted by Glazunov, who was at this time also the director of the Leningrad Conservatory. Glazunov conducted his own Violin Concerto with Milstein as soloist and then Vladimir repeated the Liszt and Rachmaninoff concertos. The concert had been arranged to raise badly needed funds for the conservatory, and much to Glazunov's satisfaction, the profits from it were substantial.

By 1924, the twenty-year-old Vladimir had been heard in the Rachmaninoff Third in every major Russian city, so that it had become one of his trademarks. Perhaps his most unusual performance of the Concerto occurred in the fall of that year, in Moscow with the Persimfans (*Pervei Simf*onicheskii *Ans*ambl, or "First Symphonic Ensemble"). This orchestra, a fascinating example of the Soviet collectivist spirit, functioned from 1922 to 1932 entirely without a conductor. Under the guiding spirit of Lev Zetilin, former concertmaster of the USSR State Symphony Orchestra, the Persimfans gained worldwide recognition for its conductorless performances, and many internationally famous artists such as Darius Milhaud and Sergei Prokofiev welcomed the opportunity of playing with the ensemble. An appearance with Persimfans was considered prestigious for any young artist and Simeon Gorovitz had traveled to Moscow to secure an engagement for his son. At his first rehearsal, Vladimir was flabbergasted to find that members of this orchestra grouped themselves in a large circle so that they could see one another easily, which meant, for some of them, turning their backs to the audience. Tempo changes were agreed upon in committee meetings and an elaborate system of cues (glances, raised eyebrows, jerks of the head or shoulders) was devised to keep the ensemble together. More dismaying to the soloist was that the rehearsal period for his Rachmaninoff concerto would stretch over a two-month period, with no fewer than nine sessions. Because of the difficulty of coordinating nuances of rubato with the Persimfans orchestra, Vladimir felt that he played "less well than usual,"[39] but when the performance finally took place, he was proud of it, one of his more unusual accomplishments.

In Russia during the decade of the conductorless orchestra, there was a resumption of Western contacts, with many foreign artists invited to play there for the first time since the Revolution. Vladimir heard many European composers conduct their own works during this liberalized period, among them Darius Milhaud, Paul Hindemith, Franz Schreker, and Alfredo Casella, and he had the opportunity to hear operas by Verdi, Bizet, Wagner, Gounod, Rossini, and Saint-Saëns. Most important, he now was able to compare and contrast his playing with the performances of older, internationally renowned pianists: Alfred Cortot, Artur Schnabel, Edwin Fischer, Wilhelm Backhaus, Eduard Erdmann, and Egon Petri. Although intensely curious to hear these men, the highly competitive Horowitz later maintained that then "there were only a few very good pianists," and that they did not influence him interpretatively but only in repertory. "I heard the Schubert sonatas for the first time played by Artur Schnabel," he recalled, "and that was good. But Petri, for instance, was a good technician, but he was dry and academic."[40]

The Russian musical world's seemingly boundless enthusiasm for Vladimir made Kogan's job easy. It was no longer necessary for him to advertise the pianist's concerts; just the mention of his name was enough to sell out a hall. But celebrity status produced a change in the young man, and this was duly noted by Kogan, who had now been organizing his tours for five years. Horowitz, he said, "was generally plain and easygoing with people, but he sometimes, for no apparent reason, would become boringly serious, playing the celebrity. He would wave his monocle with his long, ring-covered hand, blink as if nearsighted, then raise the monocle to his half-closed eye, even though his vision was perfectly normal."[41] Kogan himself didn't find anything interesting or original in this aspect of Vladimir. Despite such affectations, he found him to be an ordinary person full of common sense about everyday matters, a man whose thriftiness bordered on stinginess. Vladimir was squirreling away his money with the hope of someday leaving Russia; at night he slept with black-market dollars under his pillow and during the day he carried them in his shoes. He was learning to be frugal despite his passion for well-tailored suits, fashionable silk ties and elegant dinners.

Vladimir's new public status meant that he could play the artistic eccentric without reproach. In the capital cities of early post-Revolutionary Russia, staid provincialism had given way to permissiveness, reflecting Lenin's initial determination to forge a society tolerant of diverse social behavior. In sex-related matters, the Bolshevik government made sweeping reforms that ushered in a new atmosphere of sexual freedom—in the words of a recent study, "absolute non-interference of the state and society into sexual matters, so long as nobody is injured, and no one's interests are encroached upon."[42] Moves to extend sexual freedom were then considered an integral part of the social revolution, and the large cities became a haven for groups of sophisticated musicians and artists who enjoyed the Bohemian atmosphere. Responding to the freedom of the times, Vladimir would occasionally make something of a spectacle of himself by walking the streets of Moscow in an enormous fur coat, apparently wearing makeup. It was rumored that he spent time with a group of effete poets and artists who, it was claimed, took drugs and frequented sailor bars in Odessa.

The impish and affected aspects of Vladimir's personality were, however, always balanced by an absolute sobriety concerning his career. He firmly believed that the success he had achieved in Russia by 1924 had prepared him to face the more critical audiences of Europe, and the influx of Western musicians had whetted his appetite for such exposure. On one visit to Leningrad, Schnabel had not only advised him to leave Russia as quickly as possible but had suggested a concert tour of Germany and France. "We were all famous in Russia," Horowitz said years later, "but when we finally came to Berlin nobody knew who we were."[43]

The question of how to escape Russia and establish a career in Europe had vexed Vladimir until 1923, when he met a professional manager who was to have an enormous influence over the development of his career. Alexander Merovitch, "Sasha" as he was called, first heard Vladimir in Leningrad during the 1923–24 season. Merovitch had just returned from a trip to Western Europe and the United States, where he had begun to establish his credentials as an impresario, and he was now on the lookout for young Russian talent to introduce to Western audiences. Merovitch became intrigued by Vladimir's reputation in Leningrad, but, upon hearing him play the Liszt First Concerto, was not very favorably impressed. He reversed this opinion only after hearing the Rachmaninoff Third, when he concluded that the young man might have potential for a major international career and invited him to his hotel for a preliminary discussion. Vladimir arrived for the early afternoon meeting in audacious black patent-leather pumps, set off by bright powder-blue socks, his hair quite long, "cut in a geniuslike fashion,"[44] his face frightfully pale, almost translucent. He later admitted he was trying very hard to make an impression, and that he did. Merovitch, of course, was more impressed by Vladimir's devotion to the piano than by his dandified costumes. After hearing him play a few more times, he decided the young man had everything: "a mastery of the keyboard, musicianship, and an inborn stage personality."[45]

Merovitch was a native of St. Petersburg who had studied economics and political science before opening his own small concert bureau, Kamerat, in 1912. He had been drafted into the army during the First World War, and after the Revolution was employed in the music division of the Ministry of Education, where he worked from 1918 to 1921. In 1923, at the time of Lenin's "New Economic Policies," Merovitch had begun work on a grand scheme to take Russian opera and ballet to America. For two years he slaved at the elaborate project, attempting to persuade no less than Feodor Chaliapin and Anna Pavlova to become involved as heads of the respective companies. Ultimately, it all fell through, and by 1924 Merovitch was looking both for a way out of the Soviet Union and one or two artists to sustain his career as an independent concert impresario.

Merovitch became convinced that Horowitz and Milstein were his tickets to fame and fortune. He courted them assiduously and began negotiations with Simeon Gorovitz, who traveled from Kiev to Leningrad to negotiate on behalf of the two. Merovitch promised Simeon that he would arrange European debuts for each and requested in return 20 percent of all their earnings for the first three years and, thereafter, 15 percent of all sums realized on their careers for the rest of their lives. Neither artist liked the idea of being bound to anyone "for life,"[46] but Merovitch was insistent. As the arrangement seemed an expedient way to escape Russia, a verbal contract was concluded in April 1925. According to Milstein, Merovitch's initiative was supported by the Soviet government: "Trotsky asked us to go abroad to study, and to play, to show the outside world that they were not just materialists but were producing talented young boys."[47]

In May 1925, Merovitch arranged a nine-recital farewell tour of Russia for Vladimir: three each in Kiev, Leningrad, and Moscow. The first program was a mixture of Bach-Busoni, Rachmaninoff preludes and etudes, the Chopin B-flat Minor Sonata, a Medtner sonata and three Moszkowski etudes; the second was all-Chopin; the last was all-Liszt. But Vladimir dreamed of nothing but Europe and the West, looking forward to fine concert halls and pianos and to turning his back on the perpetual disorganization of the USSR. Having saved the equivalent of five thousand American dollars, he was prepared to finance his initial concerts in important cities where reputations were made: Berlin, Paris, London, and perhaps New York. Merovitch began to communicate with European managers—arranging halls and performance dates, and forwarding programs judiciously structured to display both Vladimir and Milstein as firebrand virtuosos. Although Vladimir felt confident psychologically about presenting himself to a wider audience, leaving his homeland would still be painful. There were people who had become an integral part of his life, such as Kogan, the state-appointed bureaucrat who had become a close friend. "We were," says Kogan, "practically inseparable in concerts, at rehearsals, in hotel rooms, on the trains. They were difficult years with 'the boys' [Horowitz and Milstein], but wonderful." In one of Vladimir's final letters to Kogan, he wrote: "I would like it if you would never leave me and always be near."[48] But the two would never see each other again.

For Volodya, the most difficult part of venturing abroad was taking leave of his family. After Simeon had lost his electrical business, he was assigned a mundane bureaucratic job in a government department. His technical training and linguistic expertise were ignored. He complained bitterly that he had been "turned into a machine"[49] and tried to find salvation in his son's success, pondering every detail of the Merovitch deal. Sophie, however, felt she knew best how Vladimir's career should proceed. The two argued constantly. The Gorovitz family had become troubled and embittered, even plagued with tragedy. Vladimir's elder brother, Jacob, who had shown promise as a pianist in earlier years, had been drafted and was killed during the Revolution.[50] George, living in Leningrad during Vladimir's concert years there, was a lost soul—emotionally unstable, highly nervous, a compulsive gambler. Sophie had begged a close friend of the family, the conductor Nicolai Malko,[51] to watch over George when he visited the capital, but George's behavior became increasingly erratic, and finally the family was forced to commit him to a sanatorium. When in Leningrad, Vladimir visited his brother daily until George's condition had so deteriorated that the doctors barred all visitors, even family. Nevertheless Vladimir arrived at the hospital doors every day, hoping for good news, and perhaps the chance to see George. One day, according to several accounts, an attendant became irritated with his persistence and snapped that he shouldn't bother coming back because George had hanged himself a week before.[52]

With Jacob and George dead, Simeon was grief-stricken and became overbearing and neurotically overprotective of his youngest son. Withdrawn and brooding, he would sometimes burst into wild, incoherent chatter about Vladimir's concert plans. Sophie attempted to maintain calm at home, but she was overwrought and emotionally fragile. Milstein, who continued to live in the Gorovitz house when not on tour, remembered that, except for Genya, the entire family seemed unbalanced and unstable. "Even with Horowitz," Milstein mused, "one must understand that his art is born out of his own neurotic-hysterical nature."[53]

Although twenty-three-year-old Genya was apparently the sturdiest member of the family, she too led an anguished personal life, sacrificing much for her parents and remaining brother. When Genya was wed in her early twenties, she continued to give chamber-music concerts with Vladimir and Milstein. Her marriage, however, was unsuccessful, and she was soon left alone with the responsibility of raising a young daughter.[54] Like her brother and Milstein, she desperately wanted to leave Russia and embark on her own European career, but she knew this was all but impossible. She too had a vested interest in Vladimir's success, and hoped he would send her money to join him once he was established abroad. But Regina's dream of a European career never would be realized, and once Vladimir left Russia they would not see each other again.

Apart from one visit with Simeon in Europe in the 1930's, the break Vladimir made with his family in 1925 proved to be a permanent one. In interviews over the years, the pianist declined to discuss details of his family's life in Russia, and close friends felt he had attempted to erase from his memory much of his early life. "Never mention my family, never!"[55] Vladimir once cried to Anatole Kitain. When success and public curiosity finally made it necessary to discuss his background, he sometimes invented an idealized family. He claimed that his brother Jacob was fourteen years older than he and that they had never known each other. George was alternately pictured as "playing in the violin section of the Moscow Symphony" or "teaching the violin at the Taganrog Conservatory,"[56] and never once did Vladimir mention this brother's tragic death. In Europe, as Vladimir began to move in aristocratic circles, he was always concerned with presenting a "respectable" public image. So it was that the concept of the "musical" family was encouraged, and the realities played down. Russia, he felt, had scarred him. "I have no desire to return. I don't like the Russian approach to music, to art, to anything. I lost all my family there. I never want to go back and I never will."[57]

In the fall of 1925, however, Vladimir had focused on what might lie ahead, not on what was to be left behind. His career took precedence over everything else, and there was never any question of his remaining in Russia. Unfortunately, a desire to leave was no guarantee of exit. Securing a visa was especially difficult since he was then of the age for military service. Simeon's solution was to lie about his son's age and claim that Vladimir wanted to study with Schnabel in Germany. The authorities accepted this story and granted a six-month visa, but they held firm on the rule that no one could leave the country with more than $500 (U.S.) in Russian currency. Merovitch advised his young protégé to stuff money into his shoes as he had always done, and hope for the best.

Many years later, Vladimir vividly remembered the evening of his escape. "At the border, I was nervous and white. I thought they would stop me with the money hidden in my shoes. When a soldier at the border examined my passport, I began to tremble. He looked at me for one long moment. At this point, my heart—I don't know where it was. The soldier looked into my eyes and said: 'Do not forget your motherland.' It was very touching."[58]

PART TWO
1926 ~ 1939

CHAPTER FIVE

"TORNADO FROM THE STEPPES"[1]

"My Russian success meant nothing at all in Europe. Germany was the citadel of music and until the time of Hitler everyone was there. I knew I could make such a wild sound—with such speed and noise—that the public would go completely crazy. And I wanted to do it, but unconsciously, in order to have success so that I would not have to return to my country."[2]

In no European city was the audacious vitality of the 1920's reflected more vividly than in Berlin, and to a wide-eyed young Russian like Vladimir Horowitz, Berlin was as convulsive culturally as his own country was politically. Vladimir arrived in Berlin in 1925, just when the Weimar Republic's renaissance was at its zenith. "All the eminent artistic forces were shining forth once more . . . imparting a many-hued brilliance before the night of barbarism closed in,"[3] wrote Peter Gay about Berlin in his book *Weimar Culture.* There, luminaries such as Albert Einstein, Thomas Mann, Bertolt Brecht, Wassily Kandinsky, Max Reinhardt and Arnold Schoenberg were redefining the twentieth century in the arts and sciences. Berlin was, in fact, the center of the German cultural upheaval, a magnet for every aspiring composer, writer, actor, and performing musician. It was a city that "gobbled up talents and human energies with unexampled appetite," remembered the playwright Carl Zuckmayer. "One spoke of Berlin as one speaks of a highly desirable woman whose coldness and coquettishness are widely known. She was called arrogant, snobbish, parvenu, uncultivated, common, but she was the center of everyone's fantasies."[4] Ten or fifteen years earlier, Paris had been the undisputed queen of Europe, the *mise en scène* of any young pianist's aspirations for a debut. But Berlin, with its sensitive restlessness and unerring instinct for quality, had emerged after the First World War as Paris's rival, and by 1926 the city had become an irresistible challenge to the intrepid.

Sophisticated, cosmopolitan Berliners supported nearly 120 newspapers, while 40 theaters, some 200 chamber groups and more than 600 choruses gave performances in 20 concert halls and innumerable churches. Vladimir found himself surrounded by hundreds of ambitious, energetic pianists, most of whom had neither the talent nor the money necessary for a major career. Notwithstanding Vladimir's phenomenal success with the unsophisticated audiences of Leningrad and Moscow, he now had to prove himself all over again. But the young man's strategy of dazzling the public with virtuosity was no insurance for popular success in Berlin; indeed, his musical philosophy and personal style were in direct opposition to the staid and accepted main-line German school of piano playing. The German ideal was, as one writer put it, "strength rather than charm, solidity rather than sensuousness, intellect rather than instinct, sobriety rather than brilliance,"[5] with scrupulous attention always paid to the score. The epitome of this school was the Austrian-born pianist, pedagogue, and composer Artur Schnabel. In both his concerts and his influential class at the Hochschule für Musik, the analytically minded Schnabel concentrated largely on the German repertory, from Bach and Mozart to Beethoven, Schubert, and Brahms. Vladimir's obsession with the grand manner was exactly opposite, and he would always regard with scorn the anti-Romantic, antivirtuoso philosophy of the Germans. Considering Vladimir's predilection for Romanticism and his Lisztian demeanor, it seems rather ironic that Merovitch chose Berlin as the first battleground of the pianist's campaign for world conquest.

Berlin aroused powerful emotions in everyone—"delighted most, terrified some, but left no one indifferent"[6]—and Vladimir was no exception. Arnold Schoenberg's master class at the Prussian Academy of Arts was attracting young composers intrigued by atonality and by Schoenberg's own recently developed twelve-tone method. Schoenberg and his two principal disciples, Alban Berg and Anton von Webern, symbolized a postwar music faction that was in rebellion against traditional laws of form, tonality, and rhythm. But Schoenberg's discipline was only a small part of the heterogeneous new-music scene, which also saw widespread interest in folk music, jazz idioms, and neoclassic forms. The conservative young Vladimir was shocked: "I wrote home to my mother that this was the *Götterdämmerung* of Germany. Everything was going to pieces here."[7] In an interview two years later in Chicago he made his own musical tastes absolutely clear:

"What music do I like? The Romantic school—Schubert, Brahms, Liszt, Chopin, and the operas of Wagner. And of the composers today—the French music of Debussy and Ravel. The modern Germans—No!"[8]

Vladimir attended the opera as often as possible, and after only a few weeks in Berlin, he realized how confining Russia had been, with its paucity of first-class troupes. The Berlin State Opera, alternately under the baton of Wilhelm Furtwängler and Erich Kleiber, was considered among the best in Europe. There, Richard Strauss, perhaps the most powerful force in German music since the turn of the century, was a frequent guest conductor of his own works. The varied repertory reflected Berlin's open-mindedness to contemporary music: among the sixty-six different operas presented during Vladimir's first Berlin season, for instance, was Alban Berg's *Wozzeck* in its world premiere. Moreover, the Berlin Municipal Opera under Bruno Walter and the Kroll Opera under Otto Klemperer were flourishing, and over the next few years these two companies introduced such diverse works as Igor Stravinsky's *Oedipus Rex,* Paul Hindemith's *Cardillac,* Kurt Weill's *The Threepenny Opera,* and Schoenberg's *Die Glückliche Hand.*

But most of all, Vladimir was obsessed with hearing other pianists. Josef Hofmann, Sergei Rachmaninoff and Ignace Jan Paderewski (all of whom Horowitz would meet a few years later, after his American debut) were established as the three giants of the keyboard. Aside from this trio, competition between performers was keen, rivalries fierce. Of contemporary pianists, the Pole Moriz Rosenthal was perhaps the most similar to Vladimir in taste, style, and temperament. Nicknamed "the little giant of the piano"[9] because of his short stature and phenomenal strength, Rosenthal was a stupendous technician who stormed with the instrument. His violent impetuosity, speed, power, and endurance rendered his performances of Liszt's E-flat Major Concerto legendary, and this fittingly enough, since in 1926 he was considered by many to be the greatest living Liszt pupil. Observers of the period have noted that until the career of Vladimir Horowitz took off, no pianist was known to match Rosenthal technically.

Another Polish-born artist whom Vladimir came to admire was Ignaz Friedman, among the most brilliant of Leschetizky's students and a renowned interpreter of Chopin. "I remember Friedman's performance of the F Major Etude [Op. 10, No. 7] as matchless," said Horowitz, "and I was also impressed by a recording of the E-flat Major Nocturne [Op. 55,

No. 2]."[10] The latter was an interpretation thought by some critics to be the most perfect ever recorded. In Chopin, Friedman's playing could be anarchic, however, musical freedom sometimes crossing the line to eccentricity. His performances were riddled with dynamic extremes, jagged accents, and sporadic rhythms that unsettled traditionalists. As in the case of every pianist Vladimir heard at that time, there were too many unattractive episodes in Friedman's playing to consider him a model.

Although Vladimir did admire, with reservations, Rosenthal, Friedman, Schnabel, and Wanda Landowska ("magnificent embellishments" was his term for them[11]), he generally disliked the other pianists whom he heard during his first three months in Berlin. Attending concerts as often as three times a day in order to hear popular Germans such as Wilhelm Kempff, Edwin Fischer, Wilhelm Backhaus, Carl Friedberg, Egon Petri, he found their performances insufferable: "I hated them all! I would go to a concert and one artist would play only five Haydn sonatas for the program and another only Mozart sonatas. I was terribly disappointed in what I heard. I had imagined much more warmth and sensuality, much more life in the playing. I heard and liked all the repertoire, but when it was played in Berlin it was too pedantic, square, boring."[12]

Feeling that German performers had never equaled German composers, Vladimir had genuine admiration for only two fixtures of the Berlin piano world: Artur Schnabel and Walter Gieseking, the edge going to Gieseking in those early years. Of mixed German and French background, Gieseking was generally considered the finest interpreter of Debussy and Ravel. His great musical intellect and versatility encompassed not only a vast range of French music but all of the Beethoven sonatas as well. He had first performed the entire Beethoven sonata-cycle at age fifteen and sometimes boasted that "the most difficult part was memorizing them—and that wasn't very difficult."[13] Known to master a score one day and perform it the next, Gieseking had a keen mind that was complemented by a technique that needed little practice to maintain. He devoured huge chunks of the German repertory, and then works of Prokofiev and Rachmaninoff, still finding time to make his own transcriptions of Johann Strauss songs. His exquisite pedaling was the envy of every pianist in Berlin, and no one equaled the triple-*pianissimos* of his Debussy. Vladimir was understandably flabbergasted by the then thirty-one-year-old Gieseking and found little to criticize in his playing. "The first time I heard Gieseking in Berlin, he performed the twenty-four preludes of Chopin and as many by Debussy," he remembered. "As an artist, not as a person, he left a deep impression on me. To me he was a sphinx, an enigma—because he did some very strange things; he had a beautiful *pianissimo* but applied it to all kinds of music whether it suited the score or not. But he was a very beautiful musician."[14]

Schnabel, known in Berlin as "the man who invented Beethoven,"[15] was even more intimidating. He was Vladimir's opposite in many ways, even in appearance. A stout, masculine, cigar-smoking Prussian with a large head and stubby fingers, Schnabel was anything but elegant, anything but Romantic. Although Vladimir would frequently play for Schnabel, he avoided the temptation of studying with him. As he put it: "Most young artists tried to imitate Schnabel in all the Beethoven concertos and they all played like little typewriters and sounded the same. Just the notes, just what was written, without a free approach to the phrasing."[16] Vladimir had no interest whatsoever in imitating Schnabel even though he admired much in his playing: "The first time I heard both Brahms piano concertos was in Berlin; Schnabel played the B-flat Concerto with the Berlin Philharmonic conducted by Furtwängler. I was so enraptured that I learned the work in one summer. But I didn't play any music like Schnabel; he was a very intellectual pianist. I heard him play five Chopin etudes and the B-flat Minor Sonata in Berlin and he played them beautifully. The last movement of the Chopin Sonata was technically superb. But then he told me that the Chopin pieces were superficial, only virtuoso, not important."[17] The first half of Schnabel's programs usually consisted of two Beethoven sonatas, the second half of smaller works, sometimes more romantic and virtuoso. "Schnabel could be a very witty, funny man," Vladimir remembered years later. "He once asked me, 'You know the difference between me and my colleagues? When I build a program, the second half is as boring as the first!' And it was true. He would sometimes play a Schubert sonata in the second half of the program, which is very difficult for the public to take. I didn't want to do that."[18]

Always eager to assert his individuality, Horowitz would claim in later years that he had not been significantly influenced by any of the pianists giving concerts in the German capital, and he clung steadfastly to the idea of his unique gifts, seeing himself as above the competition. "I am an individualist as every artist should be. I heard and knew all the pianists and they influenced me negatively. I criticized them. They had no effect on me. I kept my personality like a piece of steel, and no one ever shook it."[19]

At this time Volodya was almost completely controlled by Merovitch, who considered himself expert at "adjusting a musical personality to the stage"[20] while playing the role of father-confessor, manager-adviser, and constant companion. Merovitch believed, contrary to the approach prevalent in the late 1920's of de-emphasizing virtuosity, that mechanical ability was the most important asset of an interpretive artist, and he was determined to exploit the virtuoso side of Vladimir in order to make a "Friedmanesque" splash that would bulldoze the public into enthusiasm for yet another pianist. Or violinist: In December 1924, Nathan Milstein joined Vladimir and Merovitch in Berlin, and Merovitch admonished his charges not to be intimidated by the academic approach of the Germans. He reminded them that *virtuoso* was a much abused word which, in its original Latin, meant the possession of virtue of unsurpassed quality. Craftsmanship and absolute command of the instrument were primary in Merovitch's thinking, and he encouraged his "boys" to continue refining their technique and to choose repertory that would make the best use of it. The manager frequently lectured them on the necessity of choosing a balanced program that took into account physical endurance, sequence of works, and above all, the public's relation to repertory. "The artist has to 'take' the public before the big intermission,"[21] he told Vladimir as he encouraged him to play works easily digested by the average concert-goer—most often virtuoso pieces of Chopin and Liszt.

The nucleus of Vladimir's debut programs was the Romantic works which had so impressed his Russian audiences. The Liszt B Minor Sonata, which demonstrated by its vivid contrast of moods and severe technical demands every pianistic weapon in the pianist's arsenal, served as centerpiece. Three Busoni transcriptions also figured in nearly all the first European concerts: the Bach Toccata and Fugue in D Minor or Toccata in C Major, one of which began every program; and the Liszt *Fantasia on Two Motives from* "The Marriage of Figaro," which Merovitch insisted should end every program.

Aside from the Liszt Sonata, the only other large-scale landmark of the nineteenth-century literature scheduled frequently was the Schumann Fantasia in C Major. The remainder of Vladimir's early recitals consisted largely of miniatures such as Rachmaninoff preludes, Chopin etudes, mazurkas, polonaises, nocturnes and the *Barcarolle;* there were also selected Schumann *Novelettes* and pieces from *Kinderscenen,* and an occasional Scarlatti sonata or the Scarlatti *Capriccio.* Alternate ending pieces were Liszt's *Spanish Rhapsody* or *Don Juan Fantasy,* or the Saint-Saëns–Liszt *Danse Macabre.* Vladimir's favorite encores were the Schubert-Liszt *Liebesbotschaft,* Tchaikovsky's *Dumka,* Debussy's *Serenade for the Doll* from *Children's Corner* Suite, and a miscellaneous Brahms or Chopin waltz. For orchestral appearances, there were four concertos: the Tchaikovsky First, the Rachmaninoff Third and the two Liszts.

Merovitch was determined to mold Vladimir's career and stage personality in other ways than repertory, for he viewed his managerial role as having both "production" and "distribution" aspects. "Production" activities concentrated on "molding the young artist to become mature,"[22] juggling programs to suit different audiences, and monitoring the ability to "project" in cavernous concert halls—all of which presumed a knowledge of the psychology of the artist and the expectations of audiences in different countries. No detail was too small to fret about. For instance, before a month had passed in Berlin, Merovitch was dismayed that Vladimir's long hairstyle was causing scenes in the streets, where German boys chased the pianist, pointing and making jokes about "the mad Russian." After long conferences and with much hesitation on Vladimir's part, the long, wavy locks were snipped.

Merovitch's "distribution" technique was founded on the assumption that constructing the career of an artist was equivalent to masterminding a military invasion. First it was essential to pinpoint "strategic" cities to be conquered as quickly as possible. Cities of "retreat" were simultaneously mapped out in the event that the "frontal attacks" were unsuccessful and a "surrounding technique" was necessary. In his journal Merovitch noted that "you either take the capital of the country and the smaller provincial cities fall into your lap automatically, or you take the provincial cities first and the capital surrenders itself."[23]

During this planning period in Berlin, Vladimir and Merovitch moved into a modest boardinghouse near Beethoven Hall in order to save funds for their critical debuts in Germany and France. After three months of saturating themselves in the music world of Berlin, Vladimir concentrated solely on practice during the Christmas and New Year holidays of 1926, while Merovitch continued "distribution" maneuvers. In negotiations with music editors, critics, and concert administrators, Merovitch used any tactic that came into his head to arouse sympathy and enthusiasm for Vladimir, his intriguing "firebrand from Russia." Stocky, round-faced, and resolute, he would march into offices waving the pianist's Russian reviews in the air. But he could also be suavely elegant, obsequious, and even fawning.

A few weeks before the debut, Vladimir had to make a decision about what instrument he would use for the concert. Suddenly, he was approached by representatives of a number of piano companies, who hoped he would endorse their product, anticipating a repeat of the Russian successes, which Merovitch reported. Many of these firms were new to him. "I didn't know what piano to play and nobody told me," he recalled. "Some said 'Go to Weber,' and others something else. So I visited Blütner, Bechstein, Bösendorfer and Steinway."[24] Paul Schmidt, vice president of European operations for Steinway in Hamburg and a cousin of the Steinway family, proved persuasive in demonstrating the unique qualities of the Steinway concert grand—the clarity and brilliance of its treble and the sonorous, virile bass that put to shame the Blütners Vladimir had used in Russia. Schmidt emphasized the Steinway's ability to project more effectively in a large concert hall than either the Bechstein or Bösendorfer, pianos that many believed better suited to chamber music or solo performances of Haydn, Mozart, and early Beethoven than to the Romantic repertory. For Vladimir, the Steinway was the most satisfactory—"and I decided 'that's my piano' and never played any other piano, anywhere, at any time again."[25]

In Berlin, Vladimir also decided that his stage name would be "Vladimir Horowitz," and he made certain that the printers used this spelling on his debut programs. Even before he left Russia, his father had advised him to use the name Horowitz because he had noticed that German electrical companies had always addressed their correspondence to him in that way, no matter how many times he clearly wrote "Gorovitz" in his replies. Simeon reasoned that his son might as well conform in this regard, especially since he himself had already used the surname in his German translations of Russian books.

His piano and name resolved, Horowitz set his Berlin debut for January 2, 1926, in Beethoven Hall. The night before the recital, anticipation and nervous tension kept both the pianist and his manager wide awake, Merovitch worrying that Horowitz might have success with the public but not with the critics, and vice versa. Berlin was not easily aroused by unknowns, and it seemed to Merovitch that there were already too many pianists performing in the German capital. Also to be contended with were professional jealousy and a notoriously anti-Semitic public and press quite capable of vilifying a performer of Russian-Jewish background. The enormous expectations that had been fueled by Merovitch's machinations were nothing compared to the fear that failure here would mean returning to the despised homeland.

The recital proved disappointing, a letdown in light of the buildup although not disastrous. The hall was half empty and the audience consisted mostly of Russian émigrés, a group of Jewish musicians, and friends of friends who had been urged to attend by the indefatigable Merovitch. It was not, however, a large enough group to allow the concert to break even on expenses. None of the music critics came, which turned out to be a blessing because Horowitz's playing was as disappointing as the size of the audience. "I was very nervous," he remembered, "and I just didn't play well."[26] Merovitch, trying to save face, optimistically proclaimed the concert "good but not outstanding."[27] He decided to consult a doctor about Horowitz's nerves, and also increased his efforts to make Horowitz less self-conscious and rigid at the repeat performance scheduled two days later.

The night before, Horowitz was given an injection that the physician guaranteed would allow him to relax and sleep soundly. The second recital was at least encouraging, with a larger, more enthusiastic audience, although it was hardly the "historic event" that Merovitch, with characteristic hyperbole, dubbed it.

Nor was this recital without its practical difficulties. Just before intermission, the powerful Horowitz broke a string. As this had happened many times in Russia, Merovitch always made certain that a piano tuner was standing in the wings. Luckily, Horowitz had, as his manager put it, "taken the public before the big intermission," because the interval turned out longer than anticipated. It seemed that the tuner had left early for a drink, and so Merovitch had rushed out of Beethoven Hall in a panic, eventually spying him in a nearby beer garden.

After the concert, the first person backstage was Artur Schnabel. Recalled Horowitz: "I had played the [Liszt] *Marriage of Figaro* Fantasia and he said to me, 'Oh, very good!' And I said, 'Maestro, you never play pieces like these?' He answered, 'My God! I have only so much time to learn Bach and I don't even have time for all that he has written. I have no time for this kind of music.' I sort of looked at him and said, 'Maestro, you know, I do the opposite. First I play this music and I will have time for Bach later in my lifetime.' "[28]

Horowitz was, of course, disappointed that the hall had not been full, but at least the critic from the prestigious Berlin journal *Allgemeine Musikzeitung* had attended. So it was that he received his first review in the Western press, one which, although not an unqualified rave, provided a base upon which to build: "After the first bars of the Bach-Busoni Toccata in C Major you could feel it immediately—Vladimir Horowitz is one of the chosen, an artist with a piano-sound completely his own. With virtuosic ease, this youngster plays the Liszt *Don Juan Fantasy* and Rachmaninoff preludes with precision and elasticity and the most finely differentiated colors. No, he has not yet heard 'the silent sound for those that listen secretly' in the Schumann C Major Fantasy. Here his conceptual powers failed. But it is no wonder that a sense of romantic poetry and equanimity could not have evolved on the bloody soil of Soviet Russia. His obvious musical intelligence and intensity of feeling would appear to guarantee this very young man's road to success."[29]

As a result of this review, Horowitz received an immediate invitation to play the Tchaikovsky Concerto with the Berlin Symphony under the direction of Oskar Fried, which he did on January 8, 1926. The subsequent reviews, which resembled those Horowitz was accustomed to in Russia, delighted Merovitch. Wrote one critic: "The octave passages were thrown off with eminent bravura and the tender, lyrical passages—usually neglected by such tour-de-force players—were played with consummate charm."[30] Four days after this appearance, Horowitz gave his final Berlin recital, and it was successful enough to recover the expenses of all three. This time Beethoven Hall was nearly sold out, although once again almost exclusively to the city's large and culturally active Jewish population. Berlin was not yet conquered.

After the disappointment of Horowitz's debut, Merovitch decided on a completely different concert itinerary for Milstein, booking him in smaller cities so that he could more gradually acclimate himself to the new environment and build an audience. Neither Horowitz nor Milstein was adequately prepared for the musical tastes they found in Germany, and both of them quickly had to fashion amenable programs. "There was *tremendous* chauvinism in Germany," remembered Horowitz. "You had to play German music, and I felt this from the audiences. I tried playing

Russian music, which nobody played, but they didn't like it. So I had to change. I played the compositions of Nicolai Medtner, for instance, a whole evening of Medtner in Russia. But two pieces were too much for them in Germany and in France they were not interested at all! So I broadened in one way and shrank in another. But the Tchaikovsky Concerto I continued to play, so much that I got sick of it."[31]

An article in the *Deutsche Zeitung* of January 28, 1926, gave Horowitz and Merovitch particular reason to pause. Wrote their critic: "We hear dozens of pianists but only strong musical personalities can hope to make their way—once in a while a great technician. If I had heard Liszt play only once, I am sure the impression would have been incomparable. But today? Within the span of eight days I heard Mieczyslaw Horszowski and Vladimir Horowitz. I already confuse them, cannot tell them apart. And since then I have heard six more pianists. Had I not made notes during the concert I could hardly report on them. I have asked my colleagues and they feel the same way. A strong personality remains in one's memory. If he or she doesn't have one, it is his or her fault, not mine."[32]

What may have been merely the hasty criticism of an overworked critic nonetheless demonstrated Berlin's intolerance toward new performers, especially Jewish ones. Negative commentary of this sort was fortunately balanced by more objective and sympathetic accounts of Horowitz's effort to please German audiences, but the consensus of German critics was that Horowitz seemed to be in his element only when playing the virtuoso repertory, especially Liszt.

Horowitz had been hypersensitive to criticism ever since his classes with Puchalsky and Tarnowsky. As articles began now to appear in the press, Merovitch advised him as to the "proper attitude" to maintain. Remembered Horowitz: "In the beginning of my career I read the reviews, but only from a materialistic point of view. My manager told me it was very important to have good reviews because then I will be engaged. But the critics never influenced me musically, not from the first day I arrived in Berlin."[33]

While coaxing and soothing Horowitz and chastising Milstein for not taking his German debut seriously enough, Merovitch decided to find other young musicians who were not yet contracted to a professional manager. Although his two Russians were breaking even on their concert appearances and promotion expenses, they were not making a profit, either for him or themselves. All three men were dipping into their dwindling savings to pay for hotels, food, and transportation. Merovitch reasoned that perhaps promoting another, as he put it, "world-class talent" might alleviate his precarious financial position and, quite accidentally, he discovered Gregor Piatigorsky, a brilliant young cellist who had emigrated from Russia in 1921. Piatigorsky, the third and last performer Merovitch managed during this period, was to play an important role in Horowitz's personal and professional life for many years to come.

Merovitch first heard Piatigorsky—"Grisha" he was nicknamed—at a concert of the Berlin Philharmonic in which Schnabel performed the Brahms B-flat Major Concerto. At the tender age of twenty-one, Piatigorsky was already first cellist of the orchestra. He played the cello solo in the slow movement of the Brahms with such beauty that Merovitch hurried backstage after the concert to introduce himself and to suggest that Piatigorsky consider embarking on a solo career.

Exactly the same age as Horowitz, Piatigorsky had not enjoyed such a protected childhood and leisurely conservatory training. He was born in Ekaterinoslav, a small city in the southwestern Ukraine, into a small family whose life was complicated by a father forever "searching for a career" as a musician, theologian, philosopher, sportsman, and biologist. When Grisha was only eight years old, Piatigorsky *père* had abandoned the family to pursue violin studies with Leopold Auer in St. Petersburg. His son found a job at a local nightclub, where he played gypsy music on his inexpensive little cello to help support his mother and sisters. Tall for his age, Grisha was let go when his employer discovered how young he was. He then went on to play in the local movie-house orchestra.

In 1912, the family was reunited with the elder Piatigorsky when they moved to Moscow, and that was the point at which Grisha began formal cello lessons. Only two years later, when he was eleven, he had a bitter argument with his father and was told to leave the house and never return. Over the next few years Grisha was often evicted from boardinghouses because of overdue rent and had no place to sleep. But he was enterprising, and by the time of the 1917 Revolution was first cellist of the Bolshoi Theatre.

In 1920 Piatigorsky had been "drafted" into the state-run concert bureau. Disgusted with the performing conditions and poverty of Russia, he finally begged for permission to study in Germany and France, and when his request was denied he escaped across the Polish border, all six feet, four inches of him marching stalwartly through the water with, as he remembered, "My cello above my head."[34] Within three years he had secured the most important orchestral chair in Germany by sheer will, talent, and determination. Understandably, he was at first reluctant to jeopardize his safe and lucrative position in the Berlin Philharmonic to pursue a solo career, and Merovitch's offer came as something of a shock.

"Merovitch," wrote Piatigorsky in his memoirs, "was a man in his thirties, meticulously dressed and with the overall appearance of a Russian old-guard squire. By way of introduction, he unhurriedly went about with his autobiographical sketch. He had been a student of music, political scientist, economist, and cultural organizer, and he revealed at length his philosophy on the function of art."[35] Merovitch's aesthetics, however, impressed Piatigorsky far less than his success in securing engagements for Horowitz and Milstein.

Piatigorsky remembered Merovitch's backstage speech as being delivered in a pompous, melodramatic tone: "I took upon myself," declared the manager, "the responsibility of guiding the careers of two great exponents of their instruments, and I wish you to be the third. I can offer you my energy, experience, and my very life." Startled, Piatigorsky replied, "Why, it's very nice of you, really, but—" at which point Merovitch, grinning, interrupted, "I know, I must explain. Horowitz and Milstein entrusted their careers to me unconditionally as their personal representative first in Russia. Believing in each other, we arrived abroad with their genius and my managerial capabilities as our only contract and promise. My obligation is to protect their unique gifts from the pitfalls of their profession and to help reveal their art to the world." Merovitch then took a deep breath, stood up, and began slowly to pace about. "The whole world," he exclaimed, "will share my fanatical belief in them. And it won't be long [for] they are great artists and wonderful people and, as yourself, they are in their twenties. I know our lives will be bound together."[36]

Piatigorsky, by nature perspicacious and pragmatic, was intrigued by Merovitch's enticing, if farfetched, plan for making him world-famous. The following day, with Merovitch exerting pressure for a decision, he was introduced to Horowitz. The pianist was nervous about his next series of concerts, scheduled in the "retreat" city of Hamburg, and he bit his nails while listening to Merovitch's lengthy introduction. "Horowitz," recalled Piatigorsky, "was frail and poetic looking, and resembled the young Chopin, a gravure of whom hung in my room." Finally, Horowitz spoke: "I have never been to Germany. At home they frightened us with the German profundity." And then, with a touch of sarcasm: "We called them deep-sea divers!" Horowitz also talked of Milstein, whom he missed, and enviously described "Nathanchik's" recent successes in Spain: "I bet that son-of-a-gun already speaks Spanish!" Eventually, he moved toward the piano and asked apologetically, "May I, Grisha?" Piatigorsky's reaction to Horowitz's playing was typical of many who heard him at that time: "It's a curious phenomenon with some performers that even before they touch their instrument one instantly expects a miracle to be revealed. Horowitz was such an artist. He tried the piano hesitatingly at first, but hours later I still listened to his playing of unequaled force and poetry."[37]

Over the next few days, Horowitz visited Piatigorsky's apartment every afternoon to discuss music and performing. They agreed, ultimately, that words and theories were inadequate in solving specific difficulties, that experience was the only dependable education. Then Horowitz was off to Hamburg, even as Milstein returned to Berlin, excited and happy after his first Spanish tour.

"Two seconds" after they met, Grisha and Nathanchik were fast friends. Piatigorsky was struck by Milstein's "lively eyes, shiny black hair and strong medium-sized frame which suggested youth that would stay with him forever." Unlike Horowitz, who preferred staying close to Merovitch, Milstein was independent and willing to tour by himself. "It didn't take me long to realize that Milstein stood squarely on the ground and was equal to any situation he might encounter," recalled Piatigorsky.[38]

As a fellow string player, Piatigorsky was extremely respectful of his talented colleague. "[Milstein's] violin belonged to his body no less than his eyes and his legs. There are violinists who could have been flutists and cellists, and pianists who could as easily have been musicologists or conductors, but Nathan could only be what he was, a marvelous violinist."[39] During the hours they spent together in Grisha's apartment, Milstein would run through the violin repertory, playing bits of this and that and demonstrating clever solutions to every technical problem.

While Milstein and Piatigorsky enjoyed one another's company in Berlin, Horowitz faced audiences in Hamburg, where two recitals had been scheduled in the ballroom of the Atlantic Hotel. It was the turning point of his German career. Because no significant impression of the pianist had been relayed to Hamburg from Berlin enthusiasts, at the first recital the hall was only half full—"a good artistic success but, as usual, no money,"[40] reported Horowitz. Merovitch's verve in planning consecutive Hamburg recitals was noted in the city's press: "Alexander Merovitch had the courage to announce two evenings of piano music and Vladimir Horowitz did not disappoint the expectations of his audience his first time in Hamburg. His emphasis tends to be on virtuosity. The Chopin *Barcarolle,* for instance, is a piece more suitable emotionally and artistically to a more mature pianist and Horowitz's tended to be a surface performance. But the etudes and mazurkas were played with casual brilliance and elegance of design. The Octave Etude [Op. 25, No. 10] was astonishing. Finally, the beginning of greater intellectual substance was demonstrated by his dramatically pointed rendition of Liszt's B Minor Sonata."[41] Another critic finished by applauding Horowitz's dynamic control, "Slavic *rubato,"* and letter-perfect rendering of the *Marriage of Figaro* Fantasia.

The day after the first Hamburg concert, Horowitz and Merovitch spent a quiet day strolling in the city's famous zoo. When it began to snow, they headed back to their hotel, tired and chilled. Entering, they found the local impresario waiting in the lobby. When he saw them, he began a torrent of German which Horowitz did not understand, urging them to hurry with wild gestures. Merovitch's face began to glow with excitement as he listened. It seemed that the manager had been searching for them since the morning because a woman pianist scheduled to perform a concerto with the Hamburg Philharmonic that evening had fainted during the dress rehearsal and was unable to play. Horowitz was being asked to substitute. "It's the chance of your life!" cried Merovitch. "What do you say?" Horowitz, exhausted, cold, and unnerved by the unexpected offer, hesitated. After all, he had not eaten or shaved that day, much less practiced. "What time is the concert?" he asked nervously. The impresario said that the concert was about to begin and he must be at the hall within forty-five minutes to perform immediately after intermission. "All right. Tchaikovsky Concerto!" he snapped. "Has the orchestra got the score and the parts? Get me a glass of milk."[42] As he shaved and dressed, he reviewed the score in his mind, all too aware that he had not practiced a note of it since his appearance two weeks earlier with the Berlin Symphony.

Horowitz and Merovitch arrived at the concert hall out of breath, just as the conductor, Eugen Pabst, was finishing the Beethoven Sixth Symphony that concluded the first half of the program. Pabst was not sure there would even *be* a second half, nor did he know what music he would have to conduct. But the orchestra's librarian had been told to fetch the parts for the Tchaikovsky Concerto, and when Pabst came to the greenroom at intermission he was informed that one Vladimir Horowitz was to be the evening's soloist. Never having heard the name, Pabst nodded impatiently, and without greeting, gave Horowitz a cold stare, opened his score, and started giving instructions in their common language, French. "Look you," he said, "I conduct like this. Now, this is my opening tempo. Here, I take it this way. There we will have a little *ritardando . . ."* *"Oui, monsieur—oui, monsieur,"* Horowitz replied accommodatingly, bowing from the waist. Before walking out onstage, Pabst's final patronizing words were: "Just watch my stick, you, and nothing too terrible can happen."[43]

After the Concerto's short orchestral introduction, Horowitz's first crashing chords sent Pabst spinning around, staring in amazement at the slim, pale young man at the keyboard. A few more measures and Pabst abandoned the podium altogether, approaching the piano to stand conducting absentmindedly, incredulously watching Horowitz's hands. Until the end of the first cadenza, Pabst's face was reportedly a study in disbelief, as his hands beat time mechanically, following Horowitz's tempi. The flood of sound continued and by the end of the work orchestra and conductor were euphoric and overwhelmed, the audience was beside itself, and the piano "lay on the platform like a slain dragon"[44] while a perspiring Horowitz stood nearby with a modest smile on his face. The entire house had risen two measures before the end with a thunderous roar of applause. Bravos resounded, programs waved. Pabst rushed over to Horowitz, grabbed him by the shoulders, and hugged him repeatedly. One critic declared that "not since Hamburg discovered Caruso has there been anything like it."[45]

"That was my big break," said Horowitz years later. "Who knows? If not for that concert maybe my career would never have amounted to much. If one plays well it is not always enough. But in Hamburg they loved me right away!"[46] The second recital, originally booked into the same small hotel ballroom, was now rescheduled at a hall seating three thousand people, and within two hours of the announcement all tickets were sold. Merovitch was ecstatic about what seemed a miraculous turnabout, coming as it did only a month after the unmemorable Berlin debut, and he later pronouced the second recital "another tremendous triumph for Horowitz. His performance caused a sensation and the foundation in Germany was laid down perfectly."[47] With the Hamburg success behind him, Horowitz signed a lucrative contract for ten concerts in Germany during the next season, his appearances to be sponsored by the two most prestigious German management firms, Wolff & Sachs in Berlin and J. H. Bohme in Hamburg. Merovitch carefully arranged a trust agreement between the two companies to avoid possible conflict between them regarding future engagements.

From the moment Merovitch arrived in Berlin, he had been involved in negotiations with the Welte-Mignon recording company. Established in 1904 by Edwin Welte, this was the first manufacturer of player pianos equipped with reproducing mechanisms. Welte's magnificent instruments were delivered with a complete selection of piano rolls made by such distinguished artists as Rachmaninoff and Paderewski. The pianos were remarkably accurate at reproducing articulation, dynamics, and tempi, and the rolls competed well with the still-primitive disc recordings. Merovitch's agreement with Welte coincided with the company's heyday in the 1920's, when nearly half a million player pianos were manufactured every two years. Anxious to take advantage of this focal point of home music-making, he signed a contract with Welte in the winter of 1926. Although never corroborated by Horowitz, the supposed site of his first recordings was "a castle on the Rhine,"[48] and one of the rolls included Horowitz's own *Danse Excentrique,* marking his debut as a composer. In later years Horowitz would speak disparagingly of the piano rolls he had made, arguing that the inferior quality of reproduction gave an inaccurate impression of his interpretations. Nevertheless, making such commercial recordings only a few months after arriving in Europe was an important coup.

Horowitz's early piano-roll recordings turned out to be valuable documents, since some of the works he played were never subsequently transferred or rerecorded on the discs he later made for RCA and HMV records. In fact, some of the repertory on those piano rolls disappeared not only from Horowitz's recordings but from his concert programs as well, including such staples of his early European years as the Bach-Busoni Toccata and Fugue in D Minor and the Liszt-Busoni *Fantasia on Two Motives from* "The Marriage of Figaro." Also recorded for Welte were two Rachmaninoff preludes (Op. 32, Nos. 5 and 12) and the Chopin Mazurka in C-sharp Minor (Op. 30, No. 4).

Milstein realized that Horowitz had a genius for Chopin's mazurkas and encouraged him to schedule them frequently. "Horowitz's first reviews in Germany were not especially good," he said. "But then I suggested he play a Chopin mazurka—the one in C-sharp Minor—and it caused a sensation. I take credit. A reviewer by the name of Weissman wrote something under a headline like: CHOPIN-HOROWITZ: WITH HOROWITZ OUR PIANISTIC CULTURE IS AGAIN AWAKENED."[49]

Milstein was also indirectly responsible for another Horowitz trademark, his transcription of the *Carmen* Variations, based on the gypsy song (*Chanson Bohémienne*) and dance from the second act of the Bizet opera. Horowitz had first considered making his own set of variations on Bizet's music after performing Pablo Sarasate's violin and piano arrangement of themes from *Carmen* with Milstein many times during their Russian tours. He had become so bored with the simple *habañera* piano accompaniment that he decided to produce variations of his own, influenced by Moritz Moszkowski's piano transcription of the same material. The result was a glittering blend of Bizet, Moszkowski, Sarasate, and Horowitz—but with a virtuoso stamp and an élan that was his alone. During the protracted evolution of his own *Carmen,* Horowitz would record three different versions, spaced twenty years apart—1928, 1948, 1968. Each was slightly different but they all manipulated the chosen themes with uncanny ease, great attention being paid to the orchestral and vocal qualities of the piano.

In 1926, however, making transcriptions and Welte recordings were activities peripheral to Horowitz's goal of establishing himself firmly on the European concert scene. Even before his first Berlin recitals, Merovitch had cannily paved the way for his eventual Paris debut, arranging two dates there through the venerable Zerbason Concert Agency that were to be followed by further appearances designed to complement the debut and spread Horowitz's fame in France as quickly as possible. The first Paris recital was scheduled at the Salle Gaveau, an intimate hall often used by young performers who could not expect a large audience. If this concert was successful—and, after the triumph in Hamburg, Merovitch was positive it would be—a second would follow immediately in the much larger Salle Pleyel.

Before leaving for Paris with Horowitz, Merovitch received good news: Piatigorsky had decided to accept his offer of a solo career. The cellist had noted that Merovitch was, as he put it, "able to turn the vagueness and insecurity of a solo concert career into an exciting and daring venture."[50] Merovitch cautioned him that there would be no headquarters, no salary, no guarantee, no concentration on any one city or country. Piatigorsky, like Horowitz and Milstein, would have to be available for concert engagements anywhere and must fulfill tours in the manner prescribed. "The long meetings with 'Sasha' [Merovitch] revealed the drastic change I was to expect in my professional life," said Piatigorsky. "I had to acquire my almost-forgotten uprootedness all over again and to make the wide world my home."[51] As a result, Merovitch now left Berlin with Horowitz, the first of his "Three Musketeers,"[52] secure in the conviction that he had acquired the three most promising virtuosos of the day.

CHAPTER SIX

RUE KLÉBER

"All my early successes followed a similar pattern. Prestige galore, but only enough money to pay off some of my debts, to cover the expenses of halls, hotels, transportation and food."[1]

*H*orowitz arrived in Paris in early March 1926 and quickly became aware that that city's cultural life was intimately connected to the private world of the salon. It was in salons that he eventually met some of the pillars of the Parisian music world (Olivier Messiaen, Bohuslav Martinů, Louis Durey, Darius Milhaud, Maurice Ravel) and had the opportunity to listen to the works of contemporary composers like Erik Satie, Arthur Honegger, Francis Poulenc (and other members of that famous fraternity known as "Les Six"), Paul Hindemith, Igor Stravinsky, and Sergei Prokofiev. Merovitch understood the importance of securing the assistance of a well-connected Parisian hostess, and to this end, he cultivated Madame Jeanne Dubost, an intelligent and charming woman whose passion for art and music equaled her delight in fashionable entertaining. Merovitch had first met Madame Dubost at one of the many parties he attended on his first trip to Paris in 1923, when he was trying to establish himself as an impresario. Since returning he had courted her assiduously and, it turned out, successfully, for she agreed to present Horowitz in her salon the week before his public debut, and to invite forty or fifty of her most musically astute friends.

Horowitz was nearly fluent in French, and he was immediately at home in the Parisian social world. The young Russian seemed to conquer everyone with his playing and with his self-effacing charm. "[At Madame Dubost's] I played some pieces of Chopin and Liszt and finished with Ravel's *Oiseaux tristes* from *Miroirs* and his *Jeux d'eau*," Horowitz recalled. "At the end of the recital, a little man came up to me and said, 'Bravo! you play very well. But *we* play more impressionistically here; *you* play like Liszt.' Then he gazed up at the ceiling and said, 'But I think you're right. How do you do? I'm Ravel.' "[2]

The enthusiasm of Madame Dubost's guests was contagious: the two recitals Merovitch announced at the Salle Gaveau were almost immediately sold out, and three more dates were announced in quick succession—the first two at the Salle Pleyel (for a predominantly Russian audience) and the last at the Opéra. Horowitz's success in Paris surpassed the initial impression he had made on Berlin. One important French seal of approval quickly came from Henry Prunières, the distinguished musicologist and critic who had founded *La Revue Musicale* in 1920. Prunières was among Horowitz's most enthusiastic supporters: "Sometimes an artist appears who seems to be a genius incarnate, a Liszt, a Rubinstein, a Paderewski, a Kreisler, a Pablo Casals, a Cortot. . . . Vladimir Horowitz belongs to this category of Artist Kings."[3] One year later, Prunières wrote that "in this matter all the French critics have found themselves agreed. I cherish nonetheless the honour of having been one of the very first to point out the importance of this great artist as soon as he arrived on French soil."[4]

Horowitz's reputation was made in the press in less than three months. After such success, it is hardly surprising that Horowitz and Merovitch decided to make Paris their base. Almost immediately, they had begun searching for a flat, a hotel being beyond their resources. Finally, they found a small but attractive apartment on the Rue Kléber with a living room and two small bedrooms. In the fourth and smallest room lived the owner of the building, a generous, elderly Frenchwoman who was fascinated by her new musical tenants. Thanks to Horowitz's concerts in Berlin and Hamburg, Merovitch had sufficient funds to pay the first month's rent in advance, but the cost of the Paris recitals depleted their resources. Merovitch pleaded with the landlady for more time for the second month's rent, and soon a regular pattern was established. On the last day of each month, Merovitch and the landlady battled, yet this always ended with the old woman commiserating with his efforts to make a career for "this young genius."[5] She not only relented on collecting the rent, but sometimes gave Merovitch money to continue his good work.

Despite Horowitz's popularity in Paris, Merovitch knew they could hope for nothing better than to break even financially, so he worried constantly about keeping pace with rent and living expenses. He was therefore particularly excited by the interest shown by a Count San-Martino after one of Horowitz's performances at Madame Dubost's salon. The count, director of Rome's Augusteo concert society, gave every sign that he might consider becoming Horowitz's patron and promised to arrange at least one recital in Rome. Merovitch lavished attention on Count San-Martino and finally persuaded him to come to tea one afternoon at Rue Kléber, to hear Horowitz play a second time. Begging some francs from his sympathetic landlady, Merovitch bought petits fours and other gourmet treats which he hoped would make a good impression on their aristocratic guest. Then, the apartment cleaned and the table arranged, Merovitch, Horowitz, and their landlady sat down to await the arrival of the count who, as it turned out, came accompanied by Madame Dubost. After some amiable conversation, Merovitch signaled that Horowitz was to play and invited the count to sit down in the only armchair in the living room, an antique. As he settled into it, the seat fell through. Mortified, Merovitch apologized profusely, convinced that his hopes for a patron had gone the way of the chair. After much confusion, the count finally was ready to listen, but from the other side of the room. After over an hour of music Count San-Martino, clearly impressed by what he had heard, the unfortunate chair incident forgotten, promised Merovitch to arrange concerts for Horowitz in Rome late that spring.

The count proved true to his word. Merovitch waited impatiently for a few weeks and finally received a letter from Rome explaining that two concerts had been set which would pay Horowitz 2,000 lire each. Horowitz was ebullient, but Merovitch looked more troubled than ever, for he had determined that they didn't even have enough money to get to Rome. After days spent unsuccessfully trying to scrape together cash for train tickets and accommodations, Merovitch one morning told his tale of woe to a barber who was shaving him. When the recitation was finished, the man, nearly in tears, pulled out his wallet and counted out 1,000 francs.

Immediately after his recital at the Opéra, Horowitz found himself hustled onto a late-night train to Rome. The audience reaction that evening had been as wild as Horowitz's playing, and vanloads of gendarmes had been summoned to control an overly enthusiastic crowd that refused to leave the opera house and had begun breaking up everything not nailed down. Now, as Horowitz munched wearily on a cheese sandwich in his third-class coach, he began "meditating wryly on the exuberance of [the] ovation and the concert that had taken his last sou."[6] Even with the praise of Ravel and the most important music critic in France under his belt, the glamour of his position somehow eluded him.

The hard fact was that the pianist and his manager would be beleaguered by money problems until Horowitz's 1928 New York debut. Merovitch, an inventive and persistent fund raiser, was often compelled to rely on the generosity of others. One favorite patron was Madame Panowsky, a Russian émigré who had escaped the Revolution with diamonds inserted in her molars. "Madame P.," as she was affectionately called, adored the impresario and his three "boys," and every time they were desperate for money she would simply go to the dentist to have a gem removed.[7]

Merovitch was anxious to ensure Horowitz's comfort even at his own inconvenience. The third-class compartment to Rome could hardly be termed luxurious, and Metrovitch, determined that the pianist should be rested for the concert, stood most of the time so that Horowitz could try to sleep on their two seats. Upon arriving, they were invited to lunch by Count San-Martino, who had graciously prepared a sightseeing schedule for them, alas one which they couldn't possibly undertake for lack of funds. The concert proved to be a critical success and a financial disaster. As the two weeks in Rome turned out to be far more expensive than Merovitch had anticipated, the fees barely covered hotel expenses, much less the return to Paris. For two sleepless nights, Merovitch plotted. Then he went to the count and told him that Horowitz, who normally never went out alone in any city, had nonetheless decided to go for a solo walk and had somehow lost all of the money. Whether gullible or simply gracious, the count advanced Merovitch enough to return to France.

Back in Paris, Merovitch pursued another impresario, a person of far greater international importance than Count San-Martino. Arthur Judson, the most prominent concert manager in America, handled both the Philadelphia Orchestra (1915–1935) and New York Philharmonic (1915–1954) and was director of his own firm, Concert Management Arthur Judson, which, over the years, launched the American careers of such artists as John Barbirolli, Josef Szigeti, Jascha Heifetz, Robert Casadesus, Rudolf Serkin, Eugene Ormandy, Alfred Cortot, Wanda Landowska, and Béla Bartók. As manager of the two of the most important orchestras in the United States, Judson was in the enviable position of being both the buyer and seller of talent, for he hired conductors and soloists on his own extensive management roster to appear with his orchestras, thus nearly monopolizing the American music market. Judson's astuteness as a businessman made him the ultimate "salesman of fine music,"[8] as he liked to call himself, and his political power was matched by his knowledge of music (he had studied to be a concert violinist) and his identity with the artist. Moreover, he was a pioneer in radio broadcasting, one of the first to understand the potential of that medium in the arts, and a founder of the Columbia Broadcasting System. If so inclined, the forty-five-year-old music magnate was capable of establishing a reputation for a young artist in six months.

Merovitch was minor league professionally compared to Judson. Even in physical appearance, the Russian seemed dwarfed by the aristocratic-looking American, for the six-foot-one-inch Judson was "a huge man, with a massive head, a rectangular, ruddy face, and great hands that had the strength of a lumberjack and the sensitivity of a violinist."[9] Merovitch persistently followed this imperious impresario around Paris, until Judson finally agreed to hear Horowitz in recital at the Opéra. Judson had read with interest Henry Prunières's cables to New York describing Horowitz's successes, but had actually come to Paris to sign the Spanish pianist José Iturbi for an American debut. As it turned out, Iturbi did not become connected with Judson at that time, but Judson returned to New York with more than he bargained for: exclusive contracts to manage Piatigorsky, Milstein, and Horowitz, with Merovitch retaining his position as their "personal representative."

By the end of Horowitz's first season in Europe, Merovitch had booked sixty-nine concerts for the following 1926–27 season, in Germany, France, Italy, Belgium, Hungary, Austria, Holland, Spain, and England. The emphasis was on playing with as many leading European orchestras as possible in preparation for a crucial appearance with the New York Philharmonic early in January 1928. Meanwhile Merovitch, initiating contacts for other tours, began corresponding with concert managers in South America, Indonesia, India, Japan, South Africa, and Australia.* Clearly, he was hell-bent on global conquest.

Over the next year and a half Horowitz's tours were replete with enervating, if extremely successful, debuts, and adventurous mishaps that ranged from the amusing to the mildly disastrous. One of the stranger emergencies occurred during his second visit to Italy during the 1926–27 season. In contrast to the mere two concerts he had given there the previ-

---

* Horowitz never played in any of these countries; Merovitch did schedule and then cancel two consecutive summer tours to South America which became impractical because Horowitz was exhausted and needed to rest for his fall concerts.

ous spring, this time an extensive tour was arranged, with concerts booked in Rome, Milan, and Naples. On October 3, after an afternoon recital in Naples, Horowitz and Merovitch immediately boarded a train for Rome, with the pianist still dressed in his concert garb—a simple black suit, by that time rather rumpled and stained. The next day, as soon as they arrived at their hotel, the telephone rang, and Count San-Martino announced breathlessly that the King and Queen of Italy had invited Horowitz for tea and to perform for them at the Quirinal that afternoon. When Horowitz heard the news, he grumbled that he was tired and had no interest in playing for anyone anywhere, but Merovitch explained that, in Italy, an invitation from royalty was a virtual command. Furthermore, he would have to go to the palace alone since neither the count nor Merovitch had been invited. Reluctantly, Horowitz agreed.

There were only three hours to prepare, and Merovitch realized that Horowitz's crumpled suit would not do for such an occasion. After many telephone calls, he finally found a valet who was willing to clean the suit on short notice. But fifteen minutes before the royal carriage was to arrive, the suit had not been returned and both men began to panic. Just five minutes before the deadline, the valet walked through the door with a box, but when Merovitch tore it open a horrendous odor filled the room. It seemed that, in an effort to do a thorough job, the overindustrious valet had used an entire bottle of kerosene on the suit. Thinking fast, Merovitch sprinkled it with every last ounce of cologne in the room.

During the time Horowitz was at the palace, Merovitch waited anxiously in his bedroom. The pianist, returning later that evening, reported, with a touch of sarcasm, that everything had gone perfectly well. After playing for the royal family, he had been invited into the dining room for tea. A butler held out a large silver tray to Horowitz, then began to serve him a pastry. "I remember the royal butler bent over me, sniffed, and nearly passed out," said Horowitz. Whether Queen Elena noticed this aroma, I shall never know." But the butler's expression was quite enough, for it conveyed both dismay and scorn for a guest who would dare come to the palace so doused with perfume. "At any rate," finished Horowitz, "the queen passed it off like a good sport, but I was never so embarrassed in my life."[10]

Queen Elena presented Horowitz with an affectionately inscribed photograph which would be useful in Horowitz's subsequent European trips. Traveling with temporary visas, Horowitz had continually found himself being detained at borders, but now such crossings became easier. He would carefully place the queen's picture on the top of his suitcase so that custom officers would see it immediately. After one look at the autograph, they tended to close the bag quickly and allow Horowitz to enter their countries without further scrutiny.

Because they had violated their agreement with the Soviet authorities to return within six months, Horowitz and Milstein now relied on the League of Nations' Nansen passport issued to refugees. They did consider returning to Russia about two years after they left, but were persuaded by a Soviet representative to remain in Paris, presumably to demonstrate to the West the superiority of Soviet artists. "By 1929 when they wanted us to go back," remembered Milstein, "we had tasted too many of the pleasures of Western life to want to return. In any case, the regime under Stalin had become much more despotic, and the new Ambassador said we would have to do military service. That decided us finally not to go."[11]

With Horowitz and Milstein no longer Soviet citizens, Merovitch was forever trying to explain to border police that they were harmless souls, and that they would leave the country immediately following their concerts. Often he was asked to sign papers to that effect. Holders of Nansen passports were considered a risk because there was no country to which they could be deported. Yet there was a certain cachet about a Nansen. "I respected my mile-long document with innumerable visas, stamps, stipulations, and warnings," wrote Piatigorsky. "In fact, I was quite fond of my Nansen, an emblem of honesty and truth. To travel with a Nansen, one had to be endowed with patience and tolerance, and no little sense of humor. To be a fugitive in the morning and the government's guest of honor at night after the concert made the procedure amusing."[12]

Nonetheless, the Nansen passports caused Merovitch many headaches and he finally decided to do something about the problem. He arranged for Horowitz, Milstein, and Piatigorsky to make contributions to the charities of Haiti, with the result that the three became honorary citizens of that distant Caribbean nation. Subsequently, they had no problems with their visas, although disgruntled border police remained puzzled by the discrepancy between their Haitian citizenship and their light-colored skins and Russian accents.

Horowitz's recital debut in Budapest in 1926 was a traumatic experience, reminiscent of the fiasco with the Italian royal family. On the day of the concert, his trunk had not arrived, and it was only one hour before the performance that Merovitch located a tailor willing to accommodate him. The only dress suit in his shop was large enough for a three-hundred-pound man, but the tailor and his family managed to cut it down to the pianist's size in less than an hour. Horowitz seated himself to play at 8:40, only ten minutes late, and was cited the next day by one critic as "an elegantly tailored young man."[13] Back in his own concert attire a few weeks later, Horowitz was dismayed by yet another clothing problem during his first Spanish tour in December: "I was playing a recital in Pamplona. When I arose after my first group I discovered that the chair rose with me. My cutaway had caught in it. There was tremendous applause and laughter. When I realized what had happened, I sat down, released my cutaway and then rose again, but, to my disappointment, the applause had already stopped."[14]

Such mishaps seemed to occur regularly during the early years, when Horowitz often performed on makeshift stages and unreliable pianos. He depended entirely on Merovitch to smooth over every detail related to traveling and concert performance, and the manager had to leave Milstein and Piatigorsky more or less on their own as he lavished attention on his favorite: "Merovitch was solely interested in Horowitz, whom he considered his greatest possession," recalled a close friend.[15] In agreement, Anatole Kitain noted that "the careers of Milstein and Piatigorsky developed more slowly—in part because Merovitch was constantly tending to Horowitz, aware of his vulnerability and naïveté."[16] Yet within a year of arriving in Europe, Horowitz had become independent enough to spend time away from his manager.

Occasionally he gave mildly indiscreet interviews to the press. For instance, he was fond of telling of an incident that happened in Dortmund. During rehearsals of the Brahms B-flat Major Concerto, the concertmaster took Horowitz aside and told him what he really needed was a night out in a fancy bordello. They went to such an establishment and, said Horowitz, giggling, "the madam showed us seven naked girls, but I thought I had better be good, with a concert the next day. So while the concertmaster took a girl, I sat down at the upright piano and practiced. Once, I looked up to find myself surrounded by these naked girls, [and] the next day at the concert, when I went out onstage, there in the first box of the hall was the madam and seven girls!"[17]

Actually, Horowitz was titillated by the permissiveness he found in

Europe, and nowhere more so than in Berlin. Compared to the austerity of Russia, Berlin's pubs, cabarets, musical theaters, and revues were like a glittering carnival of decadence. In the book *Weimar Culture,* Peter Gay described in vivid detail the fermenting whirl:

> *The Germans brought to perversion their vehemence and love of sys-*
> *tem. Made-up boys with artificial waistlines promenaded along the*
> *Kurfürstendamm—and not professionals alone; every high school*
> *student wanted to make some money, and in darkened bars one*
> *could see high public officials and high financiers courting drunken*
> *sailors without shame. Even the Rome of Suetonius had not known*
> *orgies like the Berlin transvestite balls, where hundreds of men in*
> *women's clothes and women in men's clothes danced under the benev-*
> *olent eyes of the police. Amid the general collapse of values, a kind of*
> *insanity took hold of precisely those middle-class circles which had*
> *hitherto been unshakable in their order. Young ladies proudly*
> *boasted that they were perverted; to be suspected of virginity at six-*
> *teen would have been considered a disgrace in every school in Ber-*
> *lin.*[18]

In such an atmosphere (which Horowitz saw as only "a little bit deca-dent"[19]), Merovitch spent much time trying to keep his young charges in line, lecturing them paternally. He demanded that they live in a disci-plined way during their concert tours and that they appreciate the special demands of concert work, a profession which he saw as completely differ-ent from any other since the artist must be at his best between the hours of 8:30 and 11:00 P.M. Nonetheless, Horowitz more and more frequently took to slipping away to sample the night life of Berlin and Paris. He also decided to hire his own valet, a blond German, square-shouldered and handsome, who was to be his traveling companion and, it was gen-erally thought, lover, for the next six years.

Engaging the German valet may have been a kind of declaration of in-dependence from Merovitch, at least so far as Horowitz's private life was concerned, but he remained dependent on the older man in all profes-sional matters. Merovitch effectively advertised Horowitz as the most brilliant pianist since Liszt and encouraged him to "take the audience" with all of the pianistic tricks of the trade. Milstein later would view

Merovitch's effect as harmful: "Merovitch had a bad influence on him. He exploited the virtuoso side of his personality to the exception of everything else. Horowitz could have been a greater pianist and he knows it. But in these early years he would not play . . . things like Mozart and Beethoven—perhaps for fear that he would be criticized, perhaps because he thought audiences would not accept him in that repertory."[20]

Although immensely popular with audiences, Horowitz was subject to telling criticism from those who perceived his limitations. Wrote the critic of the *Hamburger Fremdenblatt* in 1926, "As with most primarily technically oriented talents whose significance is more surface than content-oriented, this image of Horowitz has not changed very much. Virtuosity, even if it is not his end, remains the most prominent aspect of his personality and he seems only in his element when playing the works of Franz Liszt, which is unfortunate. Someone who can play the Liszt B Minor Sonata with such demonical greatness and the Schubert *Liebesbotschaft* with such soulfulness and poetry, should not let himself be carried away by virtuosity and occasionally even render interpretations that are egotistical. Yet Horowitz played the *Spanish Rhapsody* with great verve, an enormously difficult if somewhat empty showpiece, and the elasticity in performance is something you will hardly hear better."[21]

During his second and third seasons of European performances, Horowitz became aware of strict divisions in musical taste from country to country, and he learned to adjust his programs accordingly. It seemed to him that the French were as chauvinistic in their preferences as were the Germans. "In Paris," he recalled, "I had to play French music."[22] So he added works of Ravel and Debussy as well as a few pieces of Poulenc and Dukas to his repertory. Debussy's *Serenade to the Doll* often figured as an encore, as did separate movements of major Ravel works: *Scarbo* from *Gaspard de la Nuit* and *Oiseaux tristes* from *Miroirs*. While his interpretations of Ravel's *Sonatine* and *Jeux d'eau* were enthusiastically received in Paris, "in Vienna the audience just laughed at [such music], even though today it would be like playing a Mozart sonata."[23] As no country seemed to appreciate the all-Medtner programs he had given in Leningrad, Horowitz, always the good businessman, discarded them.

Nowhere was Horowitz so well liked as in Paris, and his reappearance there during his second European season was an extraordinary success. The mainstays of Horowitz's programs were the Liszt B Minor Sonata, the Mendelssohn *Variations Sérieuses,* the Schumann Symphonic Etudes and generous samplings of Chopin—mazurkas, waltzes, etudes, the ballades, and the B Minor Scherzo. When he played the Liszt-Paganini Etude No. 2 in E-flat Major, the enthralled audiences would not applaud when he finished but, rather, laugh with amazement and stamp the floor for another encore. Horowitz would oblige, often with Liszt's *La Campanella* or the Saint-Saëns–Liszt *Danse Macabre*. From Henry Prunières's writings at this time, one would think that the pianist had been established in the French capital far longer than a mere twelve months, for Horowitz was termed "the king of the concert stage"[24] and named the successor of Anton Rubinstein and Ferruccio Busoni.

His stage demeanor was unmannered, always modest. His immobile posture at the piano, wrote, a Breslau critic, seemed to make the more astonishing "a nearly insurpassable technique—the most difficult problems are solved with astonishing clarity and ease."[25] In Germany, however, aside from Hamburg and the small cities, the press was especially critical of Horowitz—far more dogmatic about the niceties of performance than in France and Holland and less easily won over by Horowitz's pyrotechnics. But then, according to one chronicler of the period, German critics were noted for being "cruel, pitiless, aggressive and filled with bloody irony."[26] As an example: Horowitz had had great success with the Tchaikovsky Concerto in Paris and also in Hamburg, but in general, German critics were far more interested in hearing Bach, Beethoven, and Brahms. When he played the Tchaikovsky Concerto in Berlin, they referred to "the dreadful themes which are tolerable only on some 'blue coast' in a gambling hall or in some other 'elegant establishment.' "[27] Praise of his achievement with the Tchaikovsky was given only grudgingly: "He played it without missing a single note and with machine-like precision. Whether he is a great interpreter cannot be decided by a performance so unmistakably shallow, so exclusively devoted to grand effects."[28]

When Horowitz attempted to accommodate German audiences by programming Classical works, he was patronized for straitjacketed, immature if "correct," performances that "lacked the color and interpretative depth"[29] he brought to the Romantic repertory. Once, for instance, after he had performed Mozart's Sonata in E-flat Major, K. 282, the *Berliner Tageblatt* complimented him for the clarity and energy of the bass figurations and the tender simplicity of the melodic playing, but continued: "It was shown once again how difficult Mozart is to play. The artist approached the Sonata with sincere simplicity, but he did not do it complete justice."[30] Beethoven, except for the Variations in C Minor, was studiously avoided by Horowitz, causing one critic to muse: "We assume that Horowitz has enough insight to know that he can master Beethoven technically but that he could probably not yet succeed in making his spirit come alive. Confirmation of this fact was in his performance of the Bach-Busoni Organ Prelude and Fugue in D Minor. The dynamics and colors were all beautiful, but pure Bach it was not. Too lyrical, too romantic, not sufficiently sober."[31]

Horowitz would not have argued the fact that he was most comfortable playing extremely difficult works like the Liszt Sonata or miniatures like Scarlatti sonatas, Chopin mazurkas, Ravel pieces, and such relatively unknown delicacies as the Schubert-Liszt *Liebesbotschaft,* the Scarlatti-Tausig *Capriccio* and the Schubert-Tausig *Marche Militaire.* In these last, which had no technical obstacles to be overcome, Horowitz experimented with an improvisatorial approach that always irked die-hard critics in Germany. Through his variety of touch and a pedal technique* described as "a miracle in itself,"[32] Horowitz exhibited a tonal palette that awed critics and audiences alike, even when they considered it unorthodox. "If I succeeded with all the colors, then I knew it was a success," Horowitz declared. "It's like a painting. Here you plan a little rose, here a little blue, and some parts you don't know what the colors will be."[34] He could, of course, afford to take all the liberties he wanted in those of his own compositions that he performed: the Waltz in F Minor, the *Danse Excentrique,* and his *Carmen* arrangement. Likewise, in Russian works (the Rachmaninoff preludes, the Tchaikovsky *Dumka*) few questioned Horowitz's obvious affinity and command.

Because Horowitz was still trying to prove himself, his playing was often extreme. He was frequently compared unfavorably to more established colleagues like Friedman, Rachmaninoff, Hofmann, and Rubinstein. But despite that, and despite his strong competitive streak, Horowitz could be quite open with other musicians. This was particularly evident in his first meeting with Rudolf Serkin, arranged through Francesco Mendelssohn, the son of a German millionaire who had become a close friend of Horowitz's in Berlin. On a short holiday with

* "The pedal is everything," Horowitz would say. "It is our lungs and we breathe through the pedal. You can blend two harmonies which are completely dissonant for one millionth of a second and create possibilities for endless varieties of color."[33]

Horowitz in Basel, Switzerland, Mendelssohn had told Serkin he would bring Horowitz to see him, along with other friends. Serkin remembered, "Mendelssohn said that, out of politeness, I should ask Mr. Horowitz if he would play the piano. Horowitz was very shy and quiet. At that time, I was preparing many Schubert sonatas, and Horowitz was very interested because he did not yet know some of them. He asked me questions and I played a few things. Then the young, slim, delicate-looking man sat down at the piano and played the Chopin G Minor Ballade. I nearly fell off my chair, it was so amazing. The 'white heat' of his playing, the fire and passion were incredible, and my hair stood on end. I never in all my life heard a performance like that and I will never forget it."[35] From that day, Serkin and Horowitz became friends and saw each other frequently in Germany and Switzerland, and later in America.

But there was little time for such socializing during Horowitz's busy concert season. After completing a tour of Spain, southern France, Holland, and Italy in the winter of 1927, he prepared for his London debut. Unfortunately, this required the second phase of Merovitch's original attack plan, quick retreat, for the two recitals at the Aeolian and Albert halls were "unqualified disasters,"[36] according to the manager. Those concerts, said Horowitz, "brought nobody and nothing."[37] Merovitch partially blamed the English impresario Harold Holt, who had booked Horowitz into the vast Albert Hall, which seated over ten thousand people, and the acoustics of which left something to be desired. Conversely, Aeolian Hall was too small to suit Horowitz's grand manner. "It was difficult to play in a small hall. All my technique, touch, and acoustical feelings are geared for a large, full house,"[38] he said. Although the critics admitted he was "an exceptionally gifted pianist" (London *Times*), Horowitz was nonetheless taken through the wringer. "Execrable," was the way the London *Times* described his Chopin Etude in F Major (Op. 25, No. 3), while the C Minor (Op. 25, No. 12) was "horribly noisy." *The Times* concluded: "Horowitz confirmed his claim to an exceptional virtuosity in everything he did but the hard brilliance of his tone became very tiring to the ear."[39]

The fact was that the sensitivity of Horowitz's playing was not readily apparent in the concert halls Holt had chosen, and as a result, he was pigeonholed as being a virtuoso and little more. A planned third recital was canceled by Merovitch. Horowitz, spoiled by his ecstatic reviews on the Continent, raged that he would never return to England, quoting

Napoleon's alleged remark that the British had the souls of shopkeepers. In 1930 in London, the tide would turn after he played the Rachmaninoff Third Concerto at Queen's Hall with the London Symphony under Willem Mengelberg, but meanwhile Merovitch felt he had to get Horowitz out of England so that the recent debacle might be forgotten. All things considered, the two must have been relieved to return to Paris.

By early summer, Horowitz was exhausted, for he had given sixty-nine concerts that season throughout Western Europe. As the next season was packed with an extraordinary eighty-eight recitals and orchestral appearances that would include his American debut, the pianist clearly needed a vacation. However, despite all of his activity during the 1926–27 season, funds were low, seriously depleted by travel and hotel expenses. The always resourceful Merovitch soon began scheming to raise enough cash to enable them to relax during the summer. In Paris, upon meeting a kindly and wealthy man who sold pearls, he began to describe their plight, and how badly his young genius needed a rest. When the long-winded speech was finished, the pearl magnate asked the amount of money that was required, and not long after, Merovitch was back at Rue Kléber with 10,000 francs in his pocket, announcing that they would spend the summer in the south of France. Horowitz, always a potential clotheshorse, had never had the means to spoil himself properly. Now Merovitch bought him suits and concert attire and watched him fuss with the tailor and indulge his passion for pink and red shirts. A few months later, after a summer spent cycling, swimming, and planning programs, Horowitz and Merovitch returned from the Riviera to Paris.

Before Horowitz's American debut with the New York Philharmonic in January 1928, Merovitch had scheduled for him orchestral appearances under the batons of such luminaries as Bernardino Molinari, Bruno Walter, Wilhelm Furtwängler, Otto Klemperer and Pierre Monteux. The manager was convinced that this was a good way of gaining recognition for Arthur Judson's publicity machine and would also be a means of increasing their cash reserves. Nonetheless, although Horowitz's orchestral concerts were extremely popular with the public, they often had only limited critical success. Tired of the Tchaikovsky, Horowitz reverted to the Liszt E-flat Major Concerto or the Rachmaninoff Third. To his dismay, the Rachmaninoff seemed to be as disliked in Germany as the Tchaikovsky; so after programming it there a few times, "I played it in Italy at La Scala, [and] in Paris, where they didn't like Rachmaninoff too much. Perhaps the piece was too modern for them; I mean 'modern' as a concerto conception, not as music. When Rachmaninoff premiered it the virtuosi were playing concertos by Anton Rubinstein, Tchaikovsky, Chopin, Liszt. Maybe they thought the Rachmaninoff was too long and diffuse, too complicated, too thick-textured. The piano part is somewhat overwritten."[40]

Horowitz also began programming the Brahms B-flat Major Concerto in 1927. During a performance in October with the Hamburg Philharmonic, Karl Muck conducting, "the limits of Horowitz's talent became visible,"[41] reported one Hamburg paper—this after noting that Horowitz had usurped Edwin Fisher as Hamburg's favorite pianist. The critic of the *Hamburger Nachrichten* asserted that the performance was "irreproachable in all technical aspects" but that Horowitz "played the piece with more attention to the virtuosic than to the musical aspects."[42] Surprisingly, even when Horowitz played the Liszt A Major Concerto, where virtuosity is a foremost requirement, he was criticized for the fact that his technique was "more dominant than poetical ideas." Still, his fans did not seem to care.

His first all-Chopin recital in Berlin, on November 26, 1927, was a huge success, with a mass of automobiles crowded around Beethoven Hall two hours before. But: "Neither the emotion nor the wonderful lyricism of Chopin's works bloom in his hands, and the poetry is still missing," wrote one critic, continuing, "The B-flat Minor Sonata seemed more a bravura piece than a mystically fraught poem. We are sure he will mature."[43] Horowitz admitted that he had "played like a wild man,"[44] and he would later pay an enormous price for the acrobatic display of these early years. As early as 1927 a Berlin critic took note of the necessity of his slowing his pace: "We would wish the artist a time of quiet and contemplation to familiarize himself not only with a score but also with its spirit. Horowitz's uneven impression is not due to lack of skill but to his not yet fully mature emotional development."[45] One German newspaper, in one of the more disturbing critiques of Horowitz, stated: "Fear of unreserved expression of true feeling is an illness and Vladimir Horowitz seems to be subject to it."[46] The issues of emotion in his playing, and of balancing the spiritual and technical, were openly addressed by critics, such reviews being perfunctorily filed away by Merovitch in the back of his press-book. For Horowitz, this was a time dominated by ambition and virtuosity. Introspection was yet to come.

CHAPTER SEVEN

THE AMERICAN DEBUT

"I was just a wild Russian. I played louder, faster and more notes than Tchaikovsky wrote, and there are plenty of notes in {his} concerto. But my greatest musical triumph in New York was not playing the Tchaikovsky but in meeting Rachmaninoff, who was a god for me at that time. From that moment, Rachmaninoff and I were friends, until he closed his eyes."[1]

"Until I heard Horowitz, I did not realize the possibilities of the piano."—SERGEI RACHMANINOFF[2]

oth Horowitz and Merovitch were superstitious men, and they considered it a good omen that the ship that they boarded on December 24, 1927, to take them to the United States was named the S.S. *Hamburg*. Hamburg, after all, had been the first European city to enthusiastically receive the then-unknown Russian, the first successful stop on the arduous path to the all-important American debut. But Horowitz was fearful about the trip, for European friends had bid him bon voyage with the lugubrious warning that there was no place for him in the United States. The reigning favorites there were Paderewski, Rachmaninoff, and Hofmann, and close behind them Josef Lhévinne and Walter Gieseking, so why should the American public bother about yet another pianist? Horowitz would certainly not receive the kind of ovations he was accustomed to in Paris, they said.

After twelve leisurely days at sea, Horowitz and Merovitch docked in New York City on January 6, 1928, anxious and apprehensive, especially in light of the advance publicity. For Judson's public-relations department was billing Horowitz as "a superhuman combination of Rubinstein, Rosenthal, Paderewski, Busoni, Rachmaninoff, and Hofmann,"[3] and he felt keenly the weight of impossible expectations. And as if it weren't enough to have to live up to his nickname "Tornado from the Steppes," Horowitz would also have to share his debut spotlight with Sir Thomas Beecham, a conductor already well established in his native England, who, like him, was appearing in America for the first time. During the crossing, Merovitch had tried to reassure Horowitz, patiently answering endless questions about the accomplishments of Rachmaninoff and Hofmann, but nothing he said seemed to make a dent in Horowitz's self-doubt. Indeed, Merovitch seemed only to increase the young man's terror when he declared, "Nobody ever has or ever will play as well as you."[4]

Disembarking, the two were greeted by Dorle Jarmel, a Judson representative sent to make certain they got comfortably settled into a two-bedroom suite at the Majestic Hotel on Manhattan's Central Park West. But at the dock Horowitz was in a state of nerves. Meeting Miss Jarmel, he began to worry aloud about the safety of his baggage. His suitcases, he explained, were new, just purchased in Paris, and he had pasted colorful labels of different designs and colors on every square inch of them. "Do you think the labels will wash off?" he asked anxiously.[5] After passing through customs, he insisted that Merovitch blindfold him during the drive uptown, so that he would not be overwhelmed by the sight of New York's busy traffic and tall buildings. "The first two or three days I was like a somnambulist, not seeing anything," he later recalled. "But after that, it was all right. [Then,] I am seeing and hearing everything."[6]

It became clear that Horowitz's almost childlike needs were both unpredictable and insistent. Still, it was not Judson's policy to attend personally to his artists. Rather, he would perform the minimal courtesies, in this case arranging comfortable accommodations, briefing Merovitch on the upcoming twelve-and-a-half-week tour, and seeing to it that Steinway & Sons was aware of Horowitz and accorded him the necessary attention.

At Steinway, Horowitz found a friend—artist representative Alexander ("Sasha") Greiner, keeper of the concert grands and court diplomat of the company's New York offices. Greiner, another Russian-born émigré, worked for Steinway for thirty-three years, from 1925 to 1958. His fluency in languages, musical training, and easygoing temperament made him a great asset to Steinway's international network. Horowitz and

Greiner became close immediately and would maintain a friendship for the next thirty years, Horowitz relying on him not only for excellent instruments but also for advice on every aspect of his life and career. Meanwhile, in 1928, neither Merovitch nor Horowitz spoke English well, so they could not have been other than delighted to have a fellow Russian to help them through the strange maze that was New York.

Almost at once, Horowitz told Greiner that he wished, above all else, to meet Sergei Rachmaninoff: "The musical god of my youth,"[7] he explained excitedly. He had never met his idol in Europe and would not hear him play until 1931, but he knew by heart practically every piano work Rachmaninoff had composed and felt that his own pianistic technique and early compositions were rooted in the style and spirit of that master. Only forty-eight hours after arriving in New York, Horowitz's dream was fulfilled, thanks to Sasha Greiner. Arranging the meeting had been easy, for Rachmaninoff had phoned his friend Greiner on Horowitz's first day in New York. He had heard from Fritz Kreisler that Horowitz had played his Third Concerto in Paris and was scheduled to perform it in early February with Walter Damrosch and the New York Symphony. "I hear Mr. Gorovitz plays my Concerto very well," said Rachmaninoff. "I would like to accompany him."[8] So it was that on January 8 the two Russians met at Steinway on Fifty-seventh Street, in the famous basement where the concert grands were stored. Horowitz was asked to arrive at five minutes to four o'clock. "Nervous? I thought I would *die*! To think that this great man should accompany *me* in his own Third Concerto, a young pianist. This was the most unforgettable impression of my life! This was my real debut!"[9]

Typically, the taciturn Rachmaninoff said little after they had gone through the Concerto (the composer, of course, playing the piano reduction of the orchestra part and Horowitz the soloist's part). He merely called attention to a few passages and made occasional suggestions about dynamics and small cuts in the score. But, in fact, Rachmaninoff had been highly impressed with what he heard, and he later told friends that he had listened open-mouthed as Horowitz "pounced with the fury and voraciousness of a tiger." "He swallowed it whole," Rachmaninoff told Abram Chasins. "He had the courage, the intensity, the daring."[10] Over the next twenty-five years, Horowitz had even more success with the Third Concerto than did Rachmaninoff himself. In fact, the work became a Horowitz trademark. "Rachmaninoff gave this Concerto to me," said Horowitz. "He would always say, 'Gorovitz, he plays that better than me.' He told me he composed it 'for elephants,' so maybe I was one!"[11]

After meeting with Rachmaninoff, Horowitz felt as if he were sleep-walking. With only four days remaining before his Tchaikovsky Concerto at Carnegie Hall, he had no time to acclimatize himself to New York or to test American audiences with solo recitals. On January 11, he was introduced to Sir Thomas Beecham at the Majestic Hotel, just before a run-through of the Concerto. Actually, Beecham was no one's ideal choice as conductor for Horowitz's American debut, for Merovitch, Judson, and Greiner all worried that the Englishman's independent and flamboyant platform manner would detract from the soloist. Beecham, no master of baton technique ("In full conductorial flight his arms suggested the flapping pinion of a giant bird,"[12] one critic had written), was nonetheless a formidable presence, and he exercised complete authority on the podium. His impatience with soloists was legendary. Once, during the finale of a Beethoven concerto, Alfred Cortot's memory had failed him, as it frequently did, and Beecham's quoted reaction was typical of his urbane and searing wit: "We started with the Beethoven," he recalled, "and I kept up with Cortot through the Grieg, Schumann, Bach, and Tchaikovsky, and then he hit on one I didn't know, so I stopped dead."[13]

Even in England, the arrogant Beecham's reputation was not terribly sound. Heir to an immense pharmaceutical fortune ("Beecham's Little Liver Pills"), he had the means to buy his own symphony orchestra, with which he practiced conducting. When he had initially made his debut, the notices were lackluster. In fact, aside from his inflexibility and authoritarianism on the podium, Beecham's notoriety had been built primarily on patriotic service during the First World War, when he had refused to play German music, and had organized a series of promenade concerts at Albert Hall to help the war effort. For this, he gained a celebrity status which led to his being knighted in 1916 by King George V.

During the initial meeting with Horowitz, Beecham, proud of his memory, informed the pianist that he would be conducting without the score. From this Horowitz surmised that Sir Thomas not only wanted the spotlight during the orchestral part of the program, but also during the Concerto. Horowitz's competitive spirit immediately came to the fore: "My Englishman, my Lord," he remembers thinking to himself, "I am from Kiev and I will make the octaves so fast in the treble you won't believe it!"[14] The two musicians' ideas of tempi and shading were as divergent as possible, the conductor intent on somber stateliness, the soloist determined to play with dazzling speed. Even after two full rehearsals for the Thursday evening and Friday afternoon concerts, no compromise was reached. "If it isn't successful," Horowitz decided, "I'll just go back and play in Europe."[15]

On the night of January 12, Horowitz hurried up the back steps of Carnegie Hall, looking worried. Merovitch, trailing behind, noted that his anxiety appeared worse than ever before, but this time it was well founded. "Everyone is here!" exclaimed Horowitz. For one, Rachmaninoff could be seen in the audience, and there also sat many other luminaries of the music world: Josef Lhévinne, Benno Moiseiwitsch, Mischa Levitzki, Moriz Rosenthal, Mrs. Josef Hofmann—"a convention of Eastern European Jews, with an honorary membership for Rachmaninoff,"[16] as Merovitch sardonically put it. Also present were representatives of Steinway & Sons, recording executives from RCA Victor, Arthur Judson and every other manager in New York, and the principal critics from all the dailies. Carnegie Hall was filled to capacity, with standing room only.

Backstage, Horowitz pulled off his hat and coat, took a photograph of Liszt from his pocket, glanced at it prayerfully, and then began pacing back and forth, rubbing his hands to keep them warm. Finally, it was time. With Beecham striding behind, he walked onto the stage of Carnegie Hall, bowed perfunctorily, and sat down to adjust the piano bench.

From the very opening of the Concerto, the performance was a tug-of-war between orchestra and piano. Beecham began the orchestral introduction at a slower pace than he had promised, and Horowitz, at his entrance, seemed determined to quicken the tempo. But Beecham paid no attention, and when the strings declaimed the famous theme over the piano's clangorous chords, they did so at the opening tempo, "with what could be called, politely, a sturdy British independence."[17] As Horowitz continued the improvisatory-sounding passagework that leads to the restatement of the opening theme, he again established a faster pace, and once again Beecham refused to yield to his wishes. Horowitz played with disbelief, for no conductor in Russia or Europe had ever done this to him. Conducting without a score and with his usual aplomb, Beecham made a grand spectacle, striding about the podium "as though equipped with seven league boots."[18] Horowitz watched him incredulously. As if the theatrics were not disconcerting enough, he soon realized that Beecham's memory of the Concerto was faulty, for the conductor kept missing orchestral entries as well as piano cues.

"It was as if two performers had memorized, exactly and inflexibly, two different conceptions,"[19] wrote the *New York Times*'s Olin Downes. With the audience murmuring its surprise and the critics' pens flying, Horowitz started the slow movement, and the battle over tempo resumed. During the waltzlike allegro section, Sir Thomas miscued the brass and timpani in a loud chord, but thanks to timpanist Saul Goodman's familiarity with the score, disaster was averted. Horowitz looked startled, grinned, and kept playing, and even Sir Thomas smiled and shook his head. But by the third movement the soloist's patience was at an end: "I knew my career was at stake, and at the moment we were no longer together at all. I thought, you go your way and I'll go mine. Maybe in the restaurant after the concert we'll meet again, but not during the performance."[20] Horowitz's final cascade of octaves brought the piano part to a finish almost a full measure before the orchestra. Horowitz's *cheval de bataille* had literally become a runaway horse. Beecham was in a rage, while the audience was in a frenzy—stomping, clapping, hollering, as Horowitz beamed with delight. However, at the repeat performance the next day, Beecham put the young pianist in his place by cutting off the applause after only two curtain calls, and then delivering a witty little speech in defense of himself and the orchestra as Horowitz hung around like a fifth wheel. But, once again, the crowd obviously belonged to the soloist.

Horowitz's volcanic tone, his electric stage presence, his muscular, nervous energy seemed all out of proportion to his slight physique. He may have created a furor with his audiences but the critics, as usual, were divided about his performance. The *New York Times* assessed his playing as "ragged, superficial and frequently inartistic,"[21] and *The Nation* called it "a wild crazed flight without rhythm or reason, ending in a terrific clash of octaves that brought down the house and saved the performers, but not the Concerto."[22] Yet, there were those who were won over. "A volcano of the piano" was the reaction of W. J. Henderson of the *Evening Sun,*[23] while Pitts Sanborn of the *New York Telegram* termed Horowitz "a breathtaking talent," although he added a reservation: "Rarely if ever have I heard a piano so unashamedly banged as was his in the grandiose prelude of the Concerto."[24]

Even the harshest critics, such as one who felt that Horowitz's performance was "an exhibition of piano playing in its most degraded state,"[25] did not fail to see Beecham's role in the fiasco, especially since it was customary for a conductor to follow his soloist regardless. Beecham was taken to task, in particular for his careless effort to memorize the Concerto, since the botched attempt was "not only superfluous but directly injurious." Some blamed the pianist's "unseemly burst of speed" on too great a desire to impress the American audience, while others maintained that Beecham's lethargic tempi had resulted from jealousy in having to share his own New York debut with the Russian upstart. In any case, most agreed that the result had been a performance more like a circus than a serious concert.

While every critic agreed on the subject of the pianist's virtuosity, not one of them appeared convinced that he was a complete musician. "Certain tempi created curiosity to hear Horowitz in recital," mused Olin Downes condescendingly in *The Times,* "to find out in what degree he is a musician and in what degree merely a virtuoso with more than his share of technique, strength, and tricks of the trade."[26] In addition to inappropriate tempi and imperfect balances, Horowitz was also roundly taken to task for an unnecessarily strident and prominent tone. This would be a constant theme in written criticism over the next few decades. "His gift is technique and also it is his curse," said *The Nation* in a particularly astute analysis. "Based on a loud, clear tone obtained from the forearm, it [the tone] has extraordinary brilliance and clarity, like a pianola. Unfortunately . . . this method of production is anathema to overtones, legato, and tonal variety. It reduces every emotion to black and white, and every intention to technique. Undoubtedly there is a great musical talent buried beneath this virtuosity, but one fears that Mr. Horowitz has been following a blind trail."[27]

"Blood is blood," remarked another critic with a kind of exaggerated hyperbole that seemed an endemic reaction to Horowitz. "The call of the wild is heard whether it is a savage beating of a drum or a young Russian made with excitement, physical speed, and power, pounding on a keyboard."[28] Clearly Horowitz had suddenly become notorious. Merovitch was ecstatic.

Indeed, for Horowitz's manager, the debut was an unmitigated success. It mattered not that some critics considered Horowitz's playing "degraded." He had made headlines, and, as one newspaper declared, "it has been years since a pianist created such a furor with an audience."[29]

In retrospect, Horowitz admitted that his American debut was a bit "wild" and that at the concert he had "speeded up and slowed down when it was not necessary." But he was never to abandon Merovitch's notion of theatrical concertizing. "That was to *épater la bourgeoisie,*"[30] Horowitz later said defensively. Certainly, he had shaken up the normally staid Carnegie Hall audience, and no real harm could be said to have been done, since he would have subsequent opportunity to display his musical sensibility in solo recitals and orchestral appearances. He was pleased and optimistic, and he even managed to establish a friendship, albeit a cool one, with Sir Thomas Beecham. Five years later they would again play together, and it was on that occasion, in London, when Beecham said wryly, "Mr. Horowitz, this time I have the score with me!"[31]

For Horowitz, the most personally meaningful outcome of his American debut was that it led to a second meeting with Rachmaninoff. The day after the concert, he was surprised and pleased to receive a short note from the composer offering warm praise but also an admonition not to play quite so quickly next time, especially in the cadenza. "Come and have dinner with me and we will talk it over," Rachmaninoff suggested. Declared Horowitz, "Even if he had said I played miserably, I would still have been happy."[32]

The meeting, arranged again by Greiner, took place one evening in Rachmaninoff's apartment, and it turned out to be a getting-acquainted session, with little music. "Rachmaninoff told me, 'You may be the loudest and the fastest but I must tell you, it was not musical and it was not necessary.' So I explained to him why I did it and he laughed."[33] In the midst of discussing Horowitz's upcoming performance of the Rachmaninoff Third Concerto in New York, the composer warned him not to expect easy success with that work: "He told me that the only success *he* had with his own Concerto was when he played it with Mahler in 1909. Musicians loved it but not the audience or critics. 'They thought,' he said, 'it was too complicated.' "[34] At the end of their evening, Rachmaninoff played for Horowitz a group of Medtner's *Fairy Tales,* and it seemed to Horowitz that he and the composer had always known each other. Nonetheless, the rapport that developed between the two over the next years had elements of mentor and pupil. Rachmaninoff was twenty-five years older than Horowitz and looked upon him rather as a school-boy—talented, but very young. "Twenty years later we were equals," recalled Horowitz, "but not at that time. He was like a father to me from the first day we met."[35]

Unfortunately, during that first American season Horowitz had little time to savor the new friendship. His itinerary consisted of thirty-six concerts spread over twelve and a half weeks, sixteen of them with prestigious orchestras and conductors, such as the Philadelphia Orchestra with Leopold Stokowski, the Boston Symphony with Serge Koussevitzky, and the Chicago Symphony with Frederick Stock. After triumphant performances of the Rachmaninoff Third Concerto in Philadelphia, Cincinnati, Chicago, and St. Louis, Horowitz returned to New York to play it with Walter Damrosch and the New York Symphony. Although Damrosch was irritated because Horowitz would not perform the Concerto the way Rachmaninoff himself did, the composer attended and was delighted. So were the critics. With this appearance, Horowitz redeemed himself with them and dimmed the memory of his chaotic Tchaikovsky Concerto. "He proved he can play with a delicate touch, exquisite color, fastidious phrasing and a beautiful sense of proportion and tonal control,"[36] declared Olin Downes, who awaited Horowitz's first solo recital at Carnegie Hall on February 20. "It is one thing to play with an orchestra, and quite another thing to impress the discriminating audience which usually attends a piano recital, when seated alone with a bare ebony instrument on the stage."[37]

When Horowitz duly made his United States recital debut, critical reaction was mixed. *Musical America* summed up much of the negative commentary a week afterward: "Mr. Horowitz is too uncomfortably brilliant, too nervously attractive for our personal taste. His fingers allow him no repose. They are still in the puppy stage. They want to run around a lot and do interesting things; that is, things interesting to their owner. And if one is often annoyed with the ceaseless antics of canine limbs, he is in deadly earnest about it all. He means, we think, to be intensely absorbed within the walls of musicianship and to be communicative of that intensity. In this he succeeds in some degree for he is at times positively austere; he can never be accused of sentimentality.... The spirit was strong but the flesh and bone of Mr. Horowitz's two manual extremities was stronger."[38]

Most critics agreed that the Chopin selections of three etudes (G-flat Major, Op. 10, No. 5; C-sharp Minor, Op. 25, No. 7; F Major, Op. 10, No. 8), the Polonaise in A-flat Major, and two mazurkas in C-sharp Minor were "sadly lacking"[39] in grace and opulent tone. "With the exception of the mazurkas," wrote Downes, "the Chopin failed in a measure to impress the audience."[40] The rhythmic elasticity that Horowitz had mastered in the mazurkas worked to his disadvantage in the etudes, which he played with a freewheeling rubato that tended to weaken the formal structure of those works. Even the most sympathetic reviewers were essentially negative here, pointing out that the young man simply did not yet have the emotional maturity necessary for such music. Pitts Sanborn, who became Horowitz's nemesis, railed in the *Evening Telegram* against the pianist's "incredible liberties" and a "sinister dexterity that was positively Schoenbergian."[41]

Other selections, however, received different and more favorable responses. Horowitz opened his recital, as he had so many European programs, with the Bach-Busoni Toccata in C Major, but as often happened when he became nervous, his playing was hard-surfaced and didactic, with a glassy tone produced by the nonlegato finger stroke he had learned from his teacher Blumenfeld. His Scarlatti sonatas, on the other hand, were a considerable contrast to the Bach-Busoni, completely convincing, and played, said one critic, with "fluency, sparkle and charm."[42] The Scarlatti-Tausig *Capriccio* and an unfamiliar Scarlatti Sonata in C Major came as a delightful surprise, the impressive pedaling establishing Horowitz as a master colorist in such miniatures.

It was, above all, Horowitz's performance of the Liszt B Minor Sonata that separated the critics. Downes, clearly won over by the young Russian, called it "a noble and powerful conception, a reading that towered above everything else . . . stamping Horowitz with most if not all of the qualities of a great interpreter."[43] Sanborn, perhaps more discerning, felt differently, writing that the Sonata "oscillated between ineffectual moonings and orgies of high-speed massacre, achieving a general obliteration of rhythm and destruction of design."[44] While Downes did question Horowitz's tendency to overdramatize the work while exploiting the piano's sonorous capabilities, he felt that Horowitz's art would "mellow and ripen."

Merovitch was delighted to read in one paper that Horowitz's prodigiously powerful hands had "terrorized the piano into some amazing sonorities,"[45] for, from his point of view, his charge had once again triumphed. Although Horowitz was now generally viewed as a highly effective rather than a poetic pianist, Merovitch believed that what ultimately mattered was that audiences should stand and applaud enthusiastically. The final words of *Musical America*'s appraisal proved a point

Merovitch had always made: "You may think his tone is stimulatingly clean or you may think it just brittle and colorless. Whether or not you agree with him, you have to pay attention when he plays. In other words, Mr. Horowitz is one of those not-too-common events—a distinctive personality."[46]

Another important indication of success occurred on February 21, the day after Horowitz's Carnegie Hall recital, when recording company executives, mindful of the pianist's newfound popularity, rushed in to capitalize on the sensation he was creating. By early March, Merovitch had negotiated contracts with both the Duo Art paper-roll company in New York and RCA Victor in Camden, New Jersey. Benefitting from an advanced electronic process devised by Victor for 78-rpm shellac phonograph records, Horowitz faced the microphones for the first time on March 28, recording in three takes his own *Carmen* Variations. He had included this as an encore at his New York recital, and the thunderous applause had convinced Merovitch, Horowitz, and RCA Victor that such paraphrases were what audiences craved and would come to expect from him. Although serious piano recitals did not usually contain works of that nature, Horowitz reasoned he might thus give new life to the nineteenth-century tradition of improvisation, which seemed only fitting since he was constantly being touted as the "second Liszt."

Over a five-day period, Horowitz also recorded one of his favorite Chopin mazurkas, Op. 30, No. 4 in C-sharp Minor, the Scarlatti-Tausig *Capriccio,* and Debussy's *Serenade to the Doll,* brief works suitable for release on 78's and with instant appeal for the public. It turned out that Horowitz's *Carmen* Variations proved such a crowd pleaser that Duo Art asked him to record it again, along with the Tchaikovsky *Dumka,* the Schubert-Liszt *Liebesbotschaft,* and his own Valse in F Minor. During the next year, Horowitz found himself recording for three firms simultaneously: his two new American contractors plus the German piano-roll company, Welte-Mignon. Indeed, by the fall of 1928, three different versions of *Carmen* were available, but such duplication ended in 1929, when Horowitz began to record exclusively for Victor and its London affiliate HMV. This was a consequence of the decline in popularity of the player piano and the subsequent reduced production of piano rolls. Phonograph records, if still in their infancy, were clearly the wave of the future.

Horowitz now directed his attention to the grueling schedule of his first whirlwind American tour, which began in Baltimore on February 3.

He soon found that the same pattern that had emerged in Europe also appeared in the United States: just as Hamburg had embraced him rapturously while Berlin at first received him ambivalently, so in America Horowitz found more enthusiasm outside New York City. In Chicago, Boston, and Philadelphia, "Horowitz cities" from the very start, pressures were less fierce, and Horowitz seemed to play better and receive more positive notices. A case in point was his first Boston appearance on March 16 in a performance of the Rachmaninoff Third Concerto with Serge Koussevitzky and the Boston Symphony Orchestra. At Symphony Hall, the polite Friday afternoon audience became nearly delirious at the sound of the Rachmaninoff, behaving like a bleachers crowd at Fenway Park—cheering, yelling, pounding their seats. Wrote Philip Hale in the *Herald American,* "There was a sense of enthusiasm such as has not been aroused by any performance of a pianist in Symphony Hall since its opening."[47] Said the *Boston Globe:* "He makes stories told of Liszt and Anton Rubinstein rousing audiences to frenzied excitement credible. He has something of the almost demonical force ascribed to Paganini. [Horowitz is] the most successful concert artist with the American public since the debuts of Heifetz and Galli-Curci."[48]

Horowitz reveled in the hyperbole and wrote to friends in Europe to tell them they had been wrong about America. In less than three months, he had proved that there was indeed room for him on the American concert scene. Merovitch boasted that Horowitz, who was now receiving his first fan mail, rivaled most tenors in the way he charmed and fascinated his audiences. Humbly, Horowitz tried to return the compliments he received in Boston: "The Boston Orchestra is wonderful," he said. "With the Philadelphia Orchestra and New York Philharmonic, these are the three greatest in the world"[49]—a vast improvement, he felt, over some of the slipshod ensembles he had been forced to play with just two years earlier, when he was unknown.

The press found Horowitz personally irresistible, for his courteous and bashful yet humorous manner was a startling contrast to the volcanic image he presented on stage. "No fortress-browed giant, no fierce and haughty eagle, disdaining a crawling world from a pinnacle of genius," proclaimed the *Boston Globe.* "Instead he is a charming, wistful child, wondering naively what makes the world go round."[50] Horowitz's appearance was striking—the thick, dark brown hair, slicked down and parted in the middle emphasizing the large, expressive eyes, and the smooth, clear complexion that had always been a source of pride to him. A wistfulness was apparent when he discussed his childhood and training in Russia, but he became exuberant when asked about his impressions of America, a country which he already clearly loved. "You are so unexpectedly enthusiastic," he responded. "European audiences are more conservative. It is very hard for a newcomer to get started, but here you are like the Russians—you seem to like youth and a new face. In France and Germany they are so loyal to their old favorites that it usually takes twenty-five years for an artist to become well-known."[51]

America's innocent fervor was close to Horowitz's own, and the pianist delighted in the questions he was often asked about the foibles of virtuosos. "Do you soak your hands in hot water for an hour before a concert as Paderewski is supposed to?" asked one reporter.

"No," Horowitz laughingly replied. "I warm mine with the music."

"How long would it take to commit another work like the Rachmaninoff Third Concerto to memory?"

"A month would do—you must remember that I have to learn the orchestral score as well as my own."

"Do you practice during the summers?"

"I try to practice two hours a day, if I am a good boy, but sometimes I skip"[52]—then he would giggle and look at Merovitch.

Either Merovitch or Horowitz's newly hired secretary stood next to the pianist during such interviews, offering moral support and, more important, serving as a translator. Horowitz's English was poor, and he often answered in Russian, French, or German in order to be quoted accurately. When it came to his Russian background, he quickly glossed over sensitive questions. Once, for instance, asked why his father had not visited him in Europe or America, Horowitz replied, "Our difficulty in getting him out arises from the fact that he is a well-known engineer and therefore valuable to the Soviet government at this time."[53] Never did he mention his family's continuing hardships or the fact that he would not be allowed to return home. Rather, he tried to present a positive picture of his motherland. Merovitch would then call attention to Horowitz's Russian training as a composer, describing his abilities in exaggerated terms: "a prolific composer of many sonatas, quartets, ballades, etudes, waltzes, and songs."[54] Pressed on this point, Horowitz modestly insisted he was not yet ready to publish his own compositions.

Despite Horowitz's retiring and sometimes coy demeanor with the press, he was impressed by his own success and was not above name-dropping, especially those of the aristocratic or socially prominent. The King and Queen of Belgium and the royal family of Italy, for instance, were his "close acquaintances"; the Prince of Monaco and Duke of Connaught were his "dearest friends." Material manifestations of his recent success also began to appear. After an adolescence of poverty, he was fascinated by cars ("I have just buy, what you say, automobile"[55]) and colorful clothes, and he took to wearing the best Bond Street fashions "with originality of detail bordering on the bizarre."[56] His taste in clothes often charmed and amused the public, especially the red and pink shirts he was fond of. Horowitz seemed an overgrown boy who liked to "dress up," even when there was no occasion for it. The American public soon adored him.

CHAPTER EIGHT

STEINERT, RUBINSTEIN, AND CORTOT

"In the late 1920's, Horowitz wrote beautiful letters to me and I always thought a terrific lot of him. Later, he never wanted to be bothered with old friends like me and so I just let it go."—ALEXANDER STEINERT[1]

"Steinert had a lovely house with two pianos and every night Horowitz and I went there and played four-hands. He was very conceited, only interested in making a big impression. He behaved as if Mozart, Beethoven, Schumann and Schubert had only lived to provide 'showy' music for his encores."—ARTHUR RUBINSTEIN[2]

"I could see in about thirty-six seconds the exact range of Horowitz's intelligence and was not interested, indeed contemptuous, of someone who made a game of using his own physical resources cleverly."—ALFRED CORTOT[3]

In only two and a half months in the United States, Horowitz had created a sensation that surpassed even Merovitch's wilder dreams. Manager and protégé left New York for Paris on April 7 with Judson's guarantee of forty-five American appearances during the coming fall season. Horowitz now had nearly a full month to rest before his final concert, at the Paris Opéra on June 5—the finale of a phenomenally successful season. In the City of Light Horowitz could do no wrong; there critics and audiences practically howled with delight. Horowitz was "an Arabian thoroughbred of the highest quality possessing everything,"[4] wrote one newspaper. His technique became a lively subject for discussion among conservatory students: the economy of motion, the low sitting position, the outstretched, nearly flat fingers and elevated wrists. Horowitz consented to make a film on the stage of the Opéra, a valuable document of this early period. Michel Hirvy, in collaboration with Louta Nouneberg, shot the silent film at both normal speed and in slow motion, with close-ups of Horowitz's hands in the *Octave* Etude of Chopin, and that performance was included in a film series also made of such pianists as Alfred Cortot and Wilhelm Backhaus.

Horowitz had given more performances and more interviews during the 1927–28 season than ever before in his career, and he felt exhausted. For the next few months he planned only to relax, dividing the summer between swimming at Antibes in southern France, mountain climbing and playing tennis in Switzerland's Engadine, and motoring in the new American car he had brought back on the ship from New York.

The automobile was a prized symbol of recent financial solvency. Merovitch had bought a modest apartment in Paris to serve as headquarters for Horowitz and his other artists, but Horowitz could now afford his own room at the Majestic Hotel. Life had been made easier by the impressive box-office receipts from his first American season.

However, the pace had taken its toll. Horowitz found he needed time by himself, to be away from all pressures, and in a letter to Sasha Greiner from Vichy written at the end of that summer, he described his condition: "Please do not be angry with me for my chronic silence. Believe me, this letter is the third or fourth one I wrote during the past five months. I was much fatigued by the past year, and I underwent a terrible reaction which is disappearing gradually, only in the course of time."[5] Although the exact nature of this "terrible reaction" is unclear, Horowitz was known to be chronically susceptible to colds and bronchitis, and his nerves were easily frazzled. That summer, he began a habit to be continued during many subsequent summers in Europe—"taking the cure" at the various luxurious health spas and sanatoriums that dotted the French, German, and Swiss countryside.

Horowitz still felt most comfortable in Europe during the 1930's, and spent most of his free time in France and Switzerland. During the hectic years of traveling back and forth across the Atlantic, his European friends—most of them in Paris—sustained him and gave him opportunity to relax. One important new friend made during the summer of 1928 was Alexander Steinert, an American composer and conductor who had settled in Paris after studying at Harvard and winning the 1927 Prix de Rome. "Alex" was a rambunctious, amiable, talkative character who was eager to become a part of the Parisian music world. Easily recognizable because of his glasses and thick blond hair, the inquisitive, social young man became a fixed figure at recitals and operas. Horowitz and Steinert first met that July at the Versailles chateau of the Italian composer Prince Rofredo Bassiano. "Wherever Horowitz went, people fell at his feet because of his sensational success in Paris, Berlin, and New York,"[6] recalled Steinert, and he himself was immediately captivated by Horowitz's boyish humor.

Soon after, Steinert accompanied Horowitz, Francesco Mendelssohn, and other friends on a short trip to Belgium, where Horowitz hoped to have a reunion with his sister, Regina; however, it turned out that she had not been allowed to leave Russia for fear she would stay in the West. Steinert soothed Horowitz, and upon returning to Paris the pianist was a frequent guest at his home at 69 Rue Raymond. Thanks to the wealth of Steinert's father, a New England piano manufacturer, he and his wife, Sylvia Curtis, lived quite lavishly, and their studio was a lively music center. Two magnificent concert grands graced it, and an army of performers and composers passed through, practicing, playing chamber music, discussing new compositions, and exploring Steinert's impressive collection of scores. "Vladimir was at my home all the time," recalled Steinert. "He had a strange elegance—beautiful manners, immaculately turned out, and quite self-contained. Yet he always displayed the lovely sense of humor that first struck me at Bassiano's lunch. He did not know the works of Scriabin very well at that time, and was always trying out new pieces of Poulenc, Rachmaninoff, and Prokofiev. He was also insane about Wagner, and we used to play things like *Die Walküre* and other portions of the *Nibelungen* cycle. He idolized Liszt, always placed his picture on my piano, and once even brought Liszt's granddaughter—Blandine Ollivier—to our house. She was delighted to have found the modern-day Liszt of Paris!"[7]

Among Horowitz's new admirers in Steinert's salon was composer Sergei Prokofiev, who had settled in Paris in 1920 when he became associated with Diaghilev and the Ballets Russes. Horowitz vividly remembered their first meeting in Paris in 1927: "I was just a kid at the time and he brought five or six pieces of music to my room and said, 'I want to dedicate two pieces, you choose.' So I said, 'I want that etude and that scherzo.' . . . Prokofiev went to all my recitals in Paris and wanted me to play his Third Concerto. He said, 'Don't play the second one, it's too many notes and I don't like it myself.' " As it turned out, Horowitz never played any of the Prokofiev concertos in public, although he did enjoy the Third and proclaimed it "a good concerto."[8]

Beyond the glass doors of Steinert's music room, Prokofiev was often to be found on the terrace playing bridge, Germaine Tailleferre led discussions on the avant-garde works of "Les Six," and Milstein and Piatigorsky (who had not yet made their New York debuts) discussed the American jazz bands then producing a sensation in the European capitals. Baron Robert de Rothschild and his beautiful wife, Nellie, Prince Pierre of Monaco, and other aristocratic figures mingled with the musicians during evenings of music and conversation. Although there were other musical parties to attend in Paris—for instance, the salons of the Princess de Polignac (Princess "Winny"), the Viscountess de Noailles, and Jeanne Dubost; the Rothschild home; and the apartment of the Samuel Dushkins, where Horowitz first met George and Ira Gershwin— the Steinert house was dearest to Horowitz.

Not that he restricted himself exclusively to the glittering world of the salons. There was also a large if rather unglamorous Russian expatriate community in Paris, and Horowitz often visited his fellow countrymen. One story, recalled by Steinert, illustrates well Horowitz's compassion for and interest in his fellow refugees. "There was a little diamond merchant who had known the Horowitz family in Russia, a short Jewish fellow named Mr. Gourian who lived in a tiny attic up in Montmartre. At this time Horowitz was a top drawing card in France and a terrific success already in America, yet he always befriended this dull little man. Gourian was very grateful and decided to have Horowitz for 'high tea'—and went to a lot of work for the visit. We went to his grubby little apartment and the table was beautifully laid out. Horowitz invited all of his new friends. There was an old upright piano and brass candlesticks and to my horror Gourian asked Volodya, 'Won't you play something for me?' The piano was entirely out of tune, many of the keys were missing ivories—but Horowitz, who was in love with Wagner, played his own transcription of the *Valkyries' Ride* and poured himself into the performance—just as if he were playing a Steinway at a recital. He loved the guy, and it was the most touching thing you can imagine."[9]

Pianists were the stars of Steinert's salon—not only Horowitz but also José Iturbi, Jacques Février and Arthur Rubinstein, the last a frequent guest who became an important new friend of Horowitz. Many years later, after the deaths of Rachmaninoff, Paderewski, and Hofmann, Horowitz and Rubinstein would be generally considered the two foremost exponents of the Romantic tradition, fixed in the public's mind as approximate contemporaries. There was, however, a seventeen-year age difference between them—a crucial fact in understanding an intense rivalry that developed both professionally and personally.

The Polish-born Rubinstein had made his American debut in 1906, when Horowitz was only two years old, and although he had not been particularly successful in New York, he was immensely popular in France, Poland, Italy, Spain, and South America long before Horowitz arrived in Berlin. Rubinstein's fiery temperament and poetic lyricism made him as much at home in the works of Chopin as in those of Spanish composers, all of which he imbued with "a sheer healthy masculinity and athleticism . . . expressed in a gorgeous tone, with bigness, sanity, directness and emotional clarity."[10] Rubinstein's active repertory, aside from the Spanish music that Horowitz never touched, included many of the Beethoven sonatas to Op. 81A, most of the Romantic concerto repertory and several Mozart concertos, chamber music from Beethoven to Fauré, and a large chunk of Brahms's solo works. Rubinstein's remarkable memory made possible an encyclopedic grasp of differing music that was far more comprehensive than Horowitz's.

Beyond repertory, the two men were opposites in nearly every way. Rubinstein, short and bulky with a nose as striking as Horowitz's, considered himself a *grand seigneur par excellence*. Fearing nothing, extroverted, well-read and sophisticated, he constantly indulged a gargantuan appetite for, as he put it, "good food, good cigars, great wines, and women."[11] During the 1920's and 1930's, Rubinstein coasted on his temperament and physical vitality at the keyboard, dropping many notes. This caused him to be less than popular with German, English, and American audiences, who felt that their admission price entitled them to all the notes. Rubinstein admitted he was lazy and was not interested in practicing, but, he declared, "To hell with the German pianists and their exact fingers."[12]

In Paris, Rubinstein's premier position with the public was unchallenged until Horowitz's arrival. Rubinstein, widely known as one of the greatest living Chopinists, had also championed the works of contemporary composers like Villa-Lobos, Dukas, Stravinsky, Prokofiev, Ravel, and

Debussy. He was welcome in the grandest salons, where his suave and aristocratic manner proved an asset. Yet, Rubinstein later admitted that "the great ado and excitement about Horowitz gave me a little pang of jealousy even before I met or heard him. My staunchest friends and supporters, my most loyal admirers, were talking of nothing else but young Horowitz. I couldn't believe that a serious pianist would play *Carmen* at a concert, but I was very impressed by my friends' enthusiasm and promised myself to hear him as soon as I could."[13]

Before going to Horowitz's May 29, 1931, recital at the Théâtre des Champs-Élysées, Rubinstein had the opportunity to listen to a few of Horowitz's recordings and he did so with an astonished, unhappy expression on his face. The playing, he thought, was fantastic, and friends assured him it was even better in live performance. "No pianist should ever attend another's recital," Rubinstein has written, perhaps remembering the first time he heard Horowitz. "If a rival plays badly it's irritating. If he plays well, it's annoying."[14]

Hearing the young Russian turned out to be more than just an annoying experience for Rubinstein. "I shall never forget the E-flat Major and E Major Paganini-Liszt Etudes," he said. "There was much more than sheer brilliance and technique; there was an easy elegance—the magical something which defies description. He also played two major works by Chopin—the *Polonaise Fantasie* and *Barcarolle,* both masterly performances even if they went against my conception of Chopin. The greatest success of the evening was his encore, his own arrangement of the dance from the second act of *Carmen.* He brought the three repetitions to a shattering climax which made me jump up. We were all flabbergasted by him. When he played his final encore, in a high state of excitement I rushed with the others to see him backstage. While he was dressing, his admirers, among them most of my friends, were shouting enthusiastic comments at each other and I was the loudest. Horowitz came out of his dressing room, sweating and pale, and received the great homage with regal indifference. When I came up to him, he said, 'Ach, I played a wrong note in the *Polonaise Fantasie.*' I would gladly have given ten years of my life to be able to claim only one wrong note after a concert. On the way out, one lovely and very musical lady, a great friend of mine, said to me, '*Artur, pour la* Barcarolle, *il n'y a que vous.*' ('Artur, the *Barcarolle* will always be yours.') The words went into me like a dagger."[15]

Horowitz's technical brilliance and fastidiousness in playing every note of a score prompted Rubinstein to reevaluate his own development. The then-forty-three-year-old artist was caught in the changing tides of Romantic pianism. In the past, he had been forgiven wrong or missed notes because of the emotional impact of his playing; but such license had given way to a concern for perfection, and now audiences were quick to criticize the slightest inaccuracies. It began to look as if pianists who were too old or too stubborn to change would be pushed aside.

Rubinstein well remembered his own trauma. "It caused me to feel a deep artistic depression. Deep within myself, I felt I was the better musician. Frankly, I think Horowitz was always most interested in the actual success of the gallery, in the applause and in being called the number-one technician.[16] My conception of the music was more mature, but at the same time, I was conscious of my terrible defects—of my negligence for detail, my treatment of some concepts as a pleasant pastime, all due to that devilish facility for grasping and learning the pieces and then playing them lightheartedly in public; with all the conviction of my own musical superiority, I had to concede that Horowitz was the better pianist.[17] My self-esteem was at its lowest. The pianistic exuberance and the technical ease of Vladimir made me feel deeply ashamed of my persistent negligence and laziness in bringing to life all the possibilities of my natural musical gifts. I knew that I had it in me to give a better account of the many works which I played in concerts with so much love, and yet with so much tolerance for my own lack of respect and care. It came to a point where I seriously considered giving up my ambition of a great pianistic career to become a piano teacher, giving concerts here and there, especially in places like Spain and South America where my public accepted me unconditionally, just as I was. I knew that I was born a true musician but instead of developing my talent I was living on the capital of it."[18] Rubinstein determined to become a better pianist. After a period of concentrated study during the 1930's, he made "a grand re-entry" into New York in November 1937 and eventually conquered the musical worlds of both the United States and England, earning in them those critical plaudits that had for so long eluded him.

Rubinstein was to remain inspired by Horowitz's example, but in their personal relations he was often distressed and hurt by Horowitz's superior attitude. At Steinert's, the two pianists had quickly become friendly, addressing each other by their Russian diminutives. Often they entertained guests with impromptu performances of two-piano arrangements of Wagner's operas, Rimsky-Korsakov's *Capriccio Espagnol,* Chabrier's *España,* Debussy's *Fêtes* from *Nocturnes.* Sometimes the next morning Horowitz visited Rubinstein, and Rubinstein greeted his colleague with a friendly hug. But the older pianist would become irritated when Horowitz seated himself at the piano and began playing bits and pieces of Haydn sonatas or Moszkowski etudes, in search of the perfect encore for his next recital. "I need a piece which is really brilliant," Horowitz said, and Rubinstein was appalled by what he regarded as Horowitz's "immense conceit." "For him," declared Rubinstein, "Mozart, Beethoven, Schumann, Schubert were only vehicles for Mr. Horowitz—the material with which he could make a big impression on audiences. Every pianist should get down on his knees before touching the piano and give thanks for these giant geniuses who give us life, happiness, talent, and enthusiasm!"[19]

Rubinstein was also exasperated by what he regarded as the younger man's careless attitude toward their friendship. On the surface all was amicable, yet Rubinstein detected "a subtle difference" between them. "Horowitz's friendship for me was that of a king for his subject. In short, he did not consider me his equal."[20] Rubinstein frequently received a phone call from Horowitz in the morning—"What are you doing today?" "I took the hint," recalled Rubinstein. "Horowitz showed his friendship by accepting, without difficulty, my hospitality."[21] Horowitz would wangle an invitation for lunch at Fouquet's, then disappear for the afternoon and reappear at Rubinstein's home at dinnertime. The evening might end with Rubinstein taking Horowitz to a few nightclubs. According to Rubinstein, such favors were rarely returned, and Rubinstein found himself in the unpleasant position of being both professionally overshadowed and personally patronized by Horowitz. He remembered that both Horowitz and Jascha Heifetz "treated me as an inferior in our profession from the heights of their American dollar superiority," but insisted nonetheless that he "never envied either of them their great success" and took it for a fact that "Heifetz was the greatest violinist of the time, who never touched my heart with his playing, and Horowitz, the greatest pianist, but not a great musician. On such premises, our trio got along together quite well."[22]

For Horowitz, another important relationship on both a personal and professional level developed during this period with France's premier pianist, Alfred Cortot. Born in Switzerland of French parents, Cortot was a musician with indefatigable energy and little patience for the flamboyant indulgences of virtuosos. In fact, Cortot, then fifty, had little interest in technique for its own sake, or in the cutthroat competition among fellow pianists. As well as concertizing and recording, Cortot had founded his own school, the École Normale de Musique, and also an internationally renowned trio, with Jacques Thibaud as the violinist and Pablo Casals as the cellist. Cortot's considerable range of activities limited his piano practice, and his recitals often suffered from missed notes and memory slips. Yet his intellectual force and clarity of expression remained uncompromised, and when he was pianistically in shape, he was an astounding technician. Cortot's playing blended in perfect proportion the elegance and emotional force of the Romantic school with the sobriety and logic characteristic of pianists like Schnabel and Friedberg. It is no wonder that Horowitz was eager to forge a friendship with this highly cultivated musician. In fact, Horowitz would always gravitate toward such powerful, complete artists: Rachmaninoff was one example, Cortot another, and later there would be Arturo Toscanini.

Horowitz must have been surprised by Cortot's appearance when they first met, for it contrasted sharply with his reputation as a no-nonsense, dominant personality. Elegantly dressed to the point of foppishness, Cortot was a small, moonfaced man with a puckered mouth, a rather girlish stance, and enormous hands—at least for a man who stood only five feet tall. His intimates, however, knew that the effete surface belied a virile determination to control every situation. Impressive displays of temper often punctuated his teaching at the Paris Conservatory, yet five minutes after such an outburst the large brown eyes were once again benign.

Although Horowitz could not rightfully be called a Cortot student, the French master did give him occasional lessons and assignments. These began in 1928 and continued sporadically for the next few years. Cortot was instantly struck by the clarity and projection of Horowitz's tone but showed disdain for the idea of making a career on temperament and technical brilliance. *"Horowitz a un grand génie,"* he would tell his students, *"pour la mise au point."*[23] ("Horowitz has great genius for getting things ready for performance.") But Cortot made no secret of his reservations about Horowitz's intellect, and was never convinced that as a performer he desired to be a re-creator in service of the composer.

From the very start of the association, there was friction. A Cortot pupil, Thomas Manshardt, remembered that Cortot believed Horowitz "came to study in order to discover how he, Cortot, managed the double notes in the *Étude en Forme d'une Valse* by Saint-Saëns, which Horowitz considered a miracle of velocity and light brilliancy as played by Cortot. Cortot thought this an inadequate reason for studying. Years later he gleefully declared, 'I never told him how it was done!' "[24]

The results of one of the first assignments Cortot gave Horowitz during the summer of 1928 showed that Horowitz was not to be easily weaned from his obsession with virtuosity. The first part of the *travail de vacances* consisted of transcribing selected Beethoven quartets for four hands. It was the sort of chore normally given a composer, but Cortot had wide views on piano study and regarded the exercise as essential in preparing for the second part of the assignment—a systematic survey of all thirty-two Beethoven sonatas. Cortot was impressed by Horowitz's gift composition, and his transcription of the Beethoven quartets delighted him, for Horowitz had displayed unusual sensitivity to changes of timbre and an instinctive understanding of orchestration and voice-leading. However, the results of the second half of the assignment were far less satisfactory. After studying all of the Beethoven sonatas, Horowitz proudly declared, "I can do everything but this trill"[25]—pointing to a passage in Op. 106. Cortot was disgusted. Clearly Horowitz viewed Beethoven's sonatas as nothing more than a technical challenge.

Perhaps the most significant influence Cortot exerted had to do with the repertory Horowitz chose for the 1928–29 season. With Beethoven in his fingers, he decided to program the romantic, technically challenging *Appassionata* Sonata. In Germany, his interpretation inevitably received negative reviews, causing Horowitz to doubt whether he had really learned anything at all from Cortot. Later, he twice scheduled and twice deleted the *Appassionata* from Carnegie Hall programs, replacing it with two of his war-horses, the Chopin B-flat Minor Sonata and G Minor Ballade.

Oddly, the passion that Horowitz brought to the music of Liszt and Rachmaninoff was absent from his self-conscious performance of the *Appassionata*. In Hamburg, a local critic wrote: "The conception presented was the work of the intellect, more forced than mastered, more harsh than usual, unnatural in effect."[26] Another Hamburg paper nearly apologized for criticizing the *Appassionata*, because Horowitz was so loved in the city: "As a virtuoso pianist he is of the first rank, but as far as depth of feeling is concerned he is still among the struggling."[27]

One exception to the generally bad press that greeted Horowitz's Beethoven and Brahms at that time in Germany was a much-improved performance of the Brahms B-flat Major Concerto, with the Berlin Philharmonic, Wilhelm Furtwängler conducting, given just before leaving for the United States in early October. (Horowitz's rethinking of this work would later mute many of his harshest critics in America, and the Brahms Concerto was by far his most successful repertory choice of the 1928–29 season.) The Berlin engagement had not been easily arranged, for Horowitz had appeared with Furtwängler two years earlier in a performance of the Liszt A Major Concerto and at that time the conductor had decided he was, according to one account, "definitely not his type."[28] After much pleading from Merovitch, Furtwängler finally agreed to try Horowitz a second time, so long as he played Brahms and not Liszt or Tchaikovsky. This would be their last appearance together, thanks to the ill feeling sparked by Furtwängler's remark to Horowitz at the first rehearsal: "Unlike America, we don't play like such virtuosos here"— which Horowitz took as a sneer at his quick success in the United States. "Right away I felt some animosity and belligerence from him,"[29] he remembered.

Horowitz was also offended by Furtwängler's choice of program. The first half consisted of the mammoth Bruckner Eighth Symphony— "without cuts!" Horowitz observed incredulously. He was convinced that putting the Bruckner before the Brahms was a deliberate attempt to undermine his performance. As he had feared, by the second movement of the Brahms the restless audience had begun to leave the hall. Eventually there was hardly anyone left, except for some stragglers in the back, standing at a sandwich buffet. Enraged and humiliated, Horowitz vowed never again to play under this "ignorant" man's baton.

CHAPTER NINE

"GREATEST PIANIST ALIVE OR DEAD"[1]

*"When I came to America I am very happy. I am young man,
absolutely twenty-five. I make the success and the lots of money.
I buy large Studebaker and hire chauffeur. Then, sad, come
crash. I lose lots of money, maybe seventy percent. But in few
years I make moneys again and I buy Rolls-Royce. Imagine!"[2]*

orowitz arrived in New York on October 10, 1928, fresh for his second American tour. His novelty value there had diminished, and now it was time for consolidation—sustaining his popularity while perhaps winning the respect of his more severe critics. Unfortunately, as in Hamburg, former enthusiastic admirers in the press had by now become more objective. So it was that Horowitz's Carnegie Hall recital, on November 2, unleashed a much more negative commentary than he expected. Every New York critic, even his devotees, agreed that, as one put it, "the thunderous applause lavished by a large audience whenever Mr. Horowitz pounded his loudest"[3] could not mask the uneven quality of his playing. "Altogether, the discrepancy between the potentialities of the pianist and the artistic results achieved was, in a sense, the feature of the occasion," wrote Pitts Sanborn in the *New York Telegram.* "His appearances here have given rise to some misgivings regarding the true significance of his deeper musical gifts, and last night the doubters had further justification for their fears."[4]

Part of the problem was Horowitz's repertory, which meant that Merovitch's supposed talent in program planning was being exposed as inept. The miscalculations, however, were prompted by Horowitz's strong, if somewhat premature, desire to play Brahms, Beethoven, and Schumann. "Viewed from any standpoint, it was an odd program," Sanborn concluded. "Horowitz had decided to open ... with the last Schumann *Novelette* from the set of eight pieces which the composer himself had described as 'longish tales of adventure.' "[5] Horowitz's performance of this seemed "cold and analytical," thought Olin Downes, cast in a virtuoso mold "with a scale of dynamics not always drawn to Schumann's scale but rather [to] what we might consider necessary to make music effective in Carnegie Hall."[6] When Horowitz identified with a composition (like the Liszt B Minor Sonata or Rachmaninoff Third Concerto) such things were executed with a careless, breathtaking abandon, but in a work he did not completely understand or immerse himself in, the opposite could be true.

Naturally, any mention of careless execution was anathema to Horowitz. He must also have tired of reading about his metallic tone. At this particular recital, his performance of the Brahms Rhapsody, where "the clamor at the end was positively grotesque," was denounced by the *New York Times*. Horowitz "ranted" at climaxes "with singular outbursts of pounding and sudden spasms of speed for speed's sweet sake."[7] Complained the *New York American:* "The typical inner suffused warmth of Brahms wasn't in evidence. That Mr. Horowitz can be delicate in touch and deft in shading he proved again and again, but though a master of the technique of finesse, its use in expression and structure apparently meant very little to him."[8]

The Carnegie Hall recital, even in Merovitch's mind, was an unmitigated disaster, and Horowitz must have been glad to escape New York on November 3 to begin two months of touring. Judson had arranged forty-two concerts over the next eighty-one days, with appearances not only in major cities like Chicago, Philadelphia, and Boston but also in small towns like Winnetka, Illinois; Sioux City, Iowa; Utica, New York; and Hamilton, Ontario. These less-prestigious appearances, however, were not part of a "retreat" strategy by Merovitch; they constituted an important part of Judson's huge network of so-called Community Concerts that were formally organized during the 1929–1930 concert season. These concerts enabled Judson to put serious music into hundreds of American cities that could not afford a local manager. Eventually, the series included nearly a thousand small cities and towns from coast to coast, and any artist under Judson's management was compelled to fulfill a prescribed number of these less-desirable engagements if he expected to be signed for appearances with the New York Philharmonic or the Philadelphia Orchestra.

Arthur Judson's business was growing rapidly, and in October 1928, Columbia absorbed the Wolfsohn Musical Bureau, the oldest concert management company in the United States. Two years later, Judson merged with four of his key competitors—Hansel and Jones, the Metropolitan Musical Bureau, Evans and Salter, and the American Opera Company—to form Columbia Concerts Corporation. The Columbia Broadcasting System then bought a half-interest in Columbia Concerts and Judson became president of the new organization, making him the most powerful man on the American classical-music scene. No concert-management firm could compare with Judson's, with its specialized departments for sales, transportation, field representatives, recital programming, auditioning, publicity, and community concerts. Even the offices were plushly appointed, a far cry from the stark, formal settings of European management firms. Yet there was something impersonal about the Judson headquarters. Merovitch came to dislike spending time there, preferring instead the more interesting role of traveling with his artists. When Horowitz first began giving concerts under Judson's management in 1928, Merovitch had been hired directly by the firm and put on the payroll as personal representative of Horowitz, Milstein, and Piatigorsky. Thought of as a prima donna by many at Columbia, the temperamental Slav clashed often with the imperious Judson. "Merovitch was a sentimental Russian full of emotional extremes, with many ups and downs,"[9] remembered Kurt Weinhold, past president of Columbia Artists. Merovitch was strongly opinionated and subject to fits of rage when crossed, and Judson soon put him out of the New York office and took him off the Columbia payroll. Once again, Merovitch was to be paid directly out of Horowitz's earnings, and this would eventually cause enormous problems when the double financial burden on Horowitz of paying two commissions—to Columbia and to Merovitch—became intolerable.

Merovitch's anger with the Judson office was initially provoked by the Community Concerts. Horowitz himself was not opposed to playing in small towns; in fact, he rather enjoyed doing so, since in those places he did not keenly feel pressures from the press. Merovitch, however, believed that such concerts were "the ruination of both the artists and the musical culture that [the management] ostensibly claim to nurture."[10] As he saw it, Horowitz didn't need those engagements; besides, the fees were lower and Merovitch didn't see why Horowitz should tire himself unnecessarily. But neither Horowitz nor Merovitch had a chance against the powerful Columbia organization, which had laid out a schedule that consistently gave the pianist little time to relax or practice before facing yet another audience. Dressing for a concert on a train became the rule, as Judson's booking department all but ignored the fact that human beings need rest.

Horowitz not only had little say in negotiating his contracts, he did not even see the documents. Merovitch signed both his own name and Horowitz's, even though he hadn't the legal authority to do so. The seeds of an immense distrust and dislike of managers and a reluctance to sign contracts in advance were sown in Horowitz during those early years of exploitation by Judson. Nonetheless, at that time Horowitz seemed oblivious to such pragmatic matters as contracts. He rarely protested the engagements booked all out of proportion to his physical strength, so strongly did he want to prove himself to audiences and critics, and, of course, to make money.

Horowitz was fast becoming a celebrity, and fan mail came pouring into the Columbia offices. The public wanted to know everything about him. When asked in Chicago what interests he had other than music, Horowitz, in typically rehearsed fashion, responded, "Sports." Then he laughed, admitting that he really had little interest in the subject but that it seemed a good answer for a young man to make. "No, I will tell you," he said. "I read now a great deal because in these few years I am going to play everywhere, all over the world."[11] Horowitz had a vague notion of touring until his fortieth birthday and then retiring with what he hoped would be a fortune. "I will soon be twenty-five. You must not say I look thirty-five; that is not a compliment. And all my time—it is only from one train to a hotel to a concert hall, and to a hotel again, and on to a train. I play nearly every day, and on the train I read."[12] If Horowitz sometimes felt exhausted from his rigorous schedule, he nevertheless continued to look as fresh and boyish as ever. He was even slightly irked by his youthful appearance, thinking he would seem more distinguished if he looked more mature. Once, on his way to have photographs taken, a friend suggested he postpone the session because there were dark circles under his eyes. "Good!" he exclaimed. "Then I will look older!"[13]

Horowitz's preoccupation with his age and appearance was fostered by the reactions of interviewers, who tended to stress the contrast between his impressive stage personality and his sometimes childlike demeanor offstage. At a press conference before his December 3, 1928, Carnegie

Hall recital, the second of the season, the reporters gathered at Steinway Hall couldn't help but note the dissimilarity between the public and private Horowitz. "Vladimir Horowitz the virtuoso and Vladimir Horowitz the man are two totally different personalities," stated the *Musical Courier*. "The impression we had carried of him since having heard him last year with orchestra, was one of the dominating, overpowering creature, fearless in the face of all difficulties, with a tense fire raging within him which would carry him on to unlimited success. Imagine the conflicting emotion we experienced upon finding Mr. Horowitz a gracious, retiring, unpretentious young man."[14]

As always, Horowitz faced the journalists with a nonchalant air, on that particular occasion surrounded by a large group consisting of Merovitch, Steinway representatives (including Sasha Greiner) and members of the Steinway family, Calvin Franklin from the Judson office, and RCA Victor agents. Speaking Russian, French, and some German, all spiced with comical dashes of bad English, Horowitz quite enjoyed himself, discussing music and his desire to be a composer. Asked which he liked better, composing or performing, he replied, gesturing urbanely with one hand, "Feetee-feetee."[15] ("Fifty-fifty.") He told of his recent fascination with the tone poems and operas of Richard Strauss, many of which he had heard conducted by the composer himself in Berlin. Toward the end of the previous summer, while studying with Cortot, Horowitz had even begun a piano transcription of Strauss's *Salome,* which he felt he could finish "before not so very long." He also remarked, in his offhanded way, "I think that Strauss is the greatest living composer, despite the fact that recently his works have not been as great as his earlier ones." Mildly interesting to Horowitz was American jazz, which he considered "something totally different and apart from other music, an excellent source of amusement."

Horowitz liked to characterize himself as an experienced and versatile musician. Asked if there were a "secret" to his playing, he answered, "Perhaps my approach is a little different than most other pianists, because I was interested in all music—composition and chamber music especially—long before I specialized in piano. I tried to understand and study music in general."[16]

Late in December 1929, the second American tour ended, and on January 2 and 4 Horowitz went to the Victor studios in New Jersey to record the Liszt *Valse Oubliée* No. 1, the Schubert-Liszt *Liebesbotschaft,* and the Paganini-Liszt E-flat Major Etude. But the performances did not satisfy him, and he rejected all of them, putting off further recording activity for a year. By the time he returned to Paris in mid-January, he was overwrought, and his doctors suggested that a rest was in order. Since Milstein was busy with concerts, and Francesco Mendelssohn was recovering from an illness, Horowitz asked Steinert to travel with him to a sanatorium in Dresden. Steinert agreed and left Horowitz at the spa on February 4, continuing on to Rome. Horowitz felt completely exhausted and was suffering from an influenza which his physicians feared might develop into bronchial pneumonia. After a few weeks' rest, he felt recovered enough to play a recital on February 23 in Vienna, a city largely avoided during the first four seasons in Europe. "It is only now that I have been accepted in Vienna, the city said to be the most difficult for a pianist to conquer,"[17] Horowitz told the Austrian press.

Later that spring, Merovitch decided it was time for Piatigorsky's Paris debut, and he proposed to use Horowitz, already a celebrity there, to assist the cellist. The Piatigorsky-Horowitz program consisted of Brahms and Beethoven cello sonatas, an unaccompanied cello suite by Bach and a piano sonata by Mozart—an uncharacteristic choice for Horowitz, but one which he agreed to in keeping with the Classical dimensions of the concert. Years later, Piatigorsky recalled that Horowitz's considerable abilities as a chamber musician were overshadowed by his reputation as a soloist: "Though of the highest artistic level in chamber music, he was a different Horowitz from what his clamoring audience expected. After the delicate Mozart piano sonata, there were demands for an encore. 'What shall I do? What shall I do? It is a chamber music concert,' said Horowitz between bows. 'Hell, give them what they want,' I said, clapping him on his shoulder."[18] That is exactly what Horowitz did—his scintillating performances of Chopin, Liszt, and Dohnányi made the Classical repertory seem like forgettable preliminaries.

One prominent member of the Piatigorsky-Horowitz audience, Arthur Rubinstein, concluded that Piatigorsky was "certainly the best cellist I had heard since Casals."[19] Rubinstein and Piatigorsky became fast friends and the cellist would later join with him and Jascha Heifetz to form an ensemble that came to have the nickname, "The Million Dollar Trio," to Rubinstein's intense disgust. However, the Horowitz-Milstein-Piatigorsky trio never gave many recitals or produced even one recording. In those early years, all three artists were far more interested in establishing themselves as star solo attractions than in playing for the considerably smaller audiences devoted to chamber music.

A few weeks before the Piatigorsky concert, Horowitz had traveled to Berlin for his first appearance with the Concertgebouw Orchestra, under the direction of its principal conductor Willem Mengelberg. An engagement with the famous Dutch orchestra, which was regularly guest-conducted by such luminaries as Pierre Monteux, Richard Strauss, Erich Kleiber, Adrian Boult and Igor Stravinsky, was considered highly prestigious, equal to playing with the Berlin Philharmonic. Horowitz had long been hoping for such an opportunity. Following the May 3 performance of the Rachmaninoff Third Concerto, Horowitz's engagement with the Concertgebouw was to become an annual event. His appearances usually occurred during the orchestra's series in Paris at the beginning of May, and were followed by extremely successful solo recitals at the Paris Opéra, which capped off his season with sellouts. "Horowitz came back to us in better form than ever," enthused *Lyrica Paris,* in June 1929, calling his interpretations of Brahms and Liszt "some of the most interesting we have heard this season."[20] It was about this time that Horowitz first played the Brahms F Minor Sonata, a work that was in his active repertory only a short time. "Poesie, ardour, stormy passion still appeared acted rather than experienced,"[21] wrote one critic in Vienna. It was not long before Horowitz began to concentrate on newly learned miniatures such as a group of Szymanowski mazurkas from Op. 50, the Liszt E Major Polonaise, and a Hummel rondeau and gavotte. He also worked on the Balakirev's *Islamey* Fantasy.

Following his Opéra recital, Horowitz had remained in Paris at the Majestic Hotel to spend time with Milstein, Piatigorsky, and the host of friends he had made over the past few years in the Proustian salons of Princess Winny and the Viscountess de Noailles. After months of concerts only, there was now conversation and amusement. While Horowitz relaxed with Piatigorsky one afternoon at the hotel, Francis Poulenc suddenly appeared. Poulenc was given to rushing in unexpectedly, crying "Allo, allo, allo!"[22] and then trotting to the piano to play one of his short, witty pieces—after which he would back out the door throwing kisses.

Later that summer, Merovitch left Horowitz to spend a few hours with Piatigorsky in Berlin—all the time he had to spare as he accompanied Horowitz across the continent, making practical arrangements, guarding his somewhat frail health, and bolstering his easily damaged spirits. There was good news to report. First, Merovitch had completed arrangements with Judson for both Piatigorsky and Milstein to make their American debuts during the 1929–1930 season. As in Paris, the two string players would be billed as "friends of Vladimir Horowitz" to try to capitalize on the pianist's success. "The demand for you three is fantastic," Merovitch told Piatigorsky excitedly. "Some dumbbells say we're lucky—as if you had no talent and your concerts were not planned and worked on with blood and sweat."[23]

All four would sail that fall on the *Mauretania,* the first of many trips to New York together. Their personalities were strikingly dissimilar, and they behaved differently aboard ship. Milstein, suspicious and fearful of all modes of transportation, could often be found on deck, day and night, standing watch and supervising the ship's passage—"ready to save his life should the opportunity arise,"[24] joked Piatigorsky. Nonetheless, Milstein, pragmatic and wryly humorous, gave the trio stability. He seldom became emotionally involved in an issue and was always straightforward. Horowitz spent much of his time secluded in his stateroom reading and resting, saving energy for dinnertime conversation. Piatigorsky was moody and temperamental like Horowitz, but he often joined Milstein for a game of bridge and was a frequent escort to eligible women passengers. In the middle of a social occasion, however, he might suddenly bolt for his cabin to practice, even if it meant leaving a beautiful lady in the lurch.

Horowitz's 1929–30 American tour was the longest and busiest to date: no less than seventy-seven concerts scheduled over a six-month period. According to the Judson office, Horowitz had been "a novelty" his first season and "a sensation" his second. For his third, he was billed as "a lion"[25] of the keyboard, and his concerts sold out everywhere despite the economic collapse of 1929. In fact, Horowitz's fee and number of engagements were initially unaffected by the Depression, and in 1929 he was receiving $1,000 per solo recital, double what he had gotten the previous year; in 1930, his fee jumped to $1,500. This made Horowitz the fifth-highest-paid pianist in the world, exceeded only by Rachmaninoff, Paderewski, Hofmann (who received as much as $2,500 per concert), and Ruth Slenczynska. (Fifty years later Horowitz's fees would dwarf theirs, even considering inflation; he would be the highest-paid classical performer ever.)

Horowitz's fee structure had been carefully determined both by Merovitch and by Columbia Concerts general booking manager, Calvin Franklin. Franklin later reasoned that it was worth losing some engagements during hard times to preserve the scale for the future, so from 1930 to 1935 Horowitz's fee remained at $1,500 per concert. When Community Concerts, which had been the foundation of Horowitz's extensive tours, began curtailing their series, Franklin and Merovitch refused to lower his fee. After 1931, Horowitz—who had always been proud of his full concert calendar—would complain to friends that his engagements had dwindled down to a mere handful, and that he was not even able to meet expenses.

The expenses he referred to were, however, no longer merely a matter of bed and board, as during the first seasons in Paris and Berlin. As soon as his budget allowed, Horowitz had acquired extremely elegant tastes. He seemed determined to indulge himself, perhaps in compensation for the years in Russia when he had had nothing. Already he owned a large Studebaker, complete with chauffeur, and though he would later estimate that he lost 70 percent of his wealth during the early years of the Depression, he nonetheless additionally became the proud owner of a Rolls-Royce. Automobiles were an obsession. "A great car," he would say, "is a thing of beauty. It is for life; it is forever!"[26]

Horowitz insisted upon a chauffeur, and once, in London when he advertised for one, the response from unemployed drivers nearly caused a scandal. "The hotel lobby looked like military headquarters," reported the London *Times*, "with hundreds of uniformed men standing in line. Literally an army of unemployed chauffeurs!"[27] Horowitz's favorite publicity shots had him posed on the running board of his Rolls, dressed to the nines in the Paris fashion of Knize (a clothes designer "who charges plenty,"[28] Horowitz told *Esquire*). Merovitch attempted, with absolutely no success, to instill a sense of prudence in his young protégé. Often exasperated with what he regarded as Horowitz's silliness and naïveté on his buying sprees, he told one friend, "If a book of matches cost 100 dollars, Horowitz would pay it."[29]

Now Horowitz had little time for pampering himself, and he had to work harder than ever for his small pleasures. The third United States tour included three Carnegie Hall recitals and his first visit to the West Coast. Eventually the strain of endless train connections and anonymous hotel rooms began to show in dark circles under Horowitz's eyes. Although he preferred Russian food if it was available, he would wolf down almost anything trying to satisfy his nervous hunger. Staring out a train window, biting his nails in anticipation of the next concert, reading little and talking less, Horowitz would while away the tedium of long trips by playing game after game of poker with Merovitch or his secretary. "I live in the Pullman," Horowitz told reporters. "When I invite a friend to dine, I have to say, 'please come to the diner.' "[30]

While Horowitz headed west to Denver from Chicago with Merovitch on the Union Pacific's *Los Angeles Limited,* Milstein and Piatigorsky remained in the East to make their debuts. Both were well received, although they did not create the sensations Merovitch hoped for. Unlike Horowitz, who consciously used his keyboard mechanics to wow an audience, Piatigorsky had a platform manner that was measured and a technique that was described by one critic as "a vehicle for his musical thought and completely fused with it."[31] Milstein had many of the same attributes, and was likewise complimented for his serious musicianship. Still, Merovitch was disappointed by the tame commentary, and he came to realize that the furor Horowitz had created in New York was unique, not to be repeated.

Meanwhile, Horowitz was enjoying his first view of the majestic Rockies, and ten minutes after checking into Denver's Brown Palace Hotel, without even discussing concert details with the local manager, he rushed off with Merovitch to Lookout Mountain. "These mountains, I love them!" Horowitz exclaimed to Denver reporters. "I would like it here for six months. I know it affects some people in the ears and nose, but it makes me feel grand."[32] He then announced his intention of buying a chalet in the Swiss Alps, near Montreux, and hinted that he wanted to retire within two years to devote his time to composition. Questioned about his upcoming concerts in Los Angeles and San Francisco, Horowitz beamed at the thought of at last visiting Hollywood, for movies had become one of his favorite diversions. He often bought a ticket and walked into a theater without checking what film was playing. (In his later years, films would become an effective escape mechanism for Horowitz at times when stage fright and fatigue got the better of him; canceling that day's concert, he would sometimes telephone Milstein and ask him to accompany him to an afternoon movie.)

Western newspaper reporters were curious to see Horowitz in the flesh, after two years of reading stories about him by their colleagues back

East. As always, Horowitz was eager for publicity. A minor sensation was caused by the three concert-grand pianos traveling with him along with a piano tuner. "One very large for appearances with orchestra," Horowitz would carefully explain. "Another somewhat smaller for solo appearances in large auditoriums, and the third still smaller for concert halls."[33]

In the West, Horowitz was often aghast at the lack of sophistication of his audiences. He had long since accustomed himself to changing his repertory according to nationalistic preferences—in Berlin, Vienna, or Paris—but he was not prepared for a telegram from a small-town manager in Lincoln, Nebraska, requesting him to delete from his program so standard a selection as the Chopin G Minor Ballade. "That piece," said Horowitz, "was too much over the heads of the audience. They asked me to substitute something lighter!"[34] Audiences everywhere, however, were astonished by Horowitz's super-brilliant reading of the Rachmaninoff Third Concerto. He programmed the work with Koussevitzky in Boston, Stock in Chicago, Reiner in Cincinnati, Damrosch in New York, Monteux in Philadelphia, and Molinari in St. Louis, all during the 1929–30 season. It seemed almost as if the Concerto had been written for him, though he was only five years old when Rachmaninoff himself had first played it. In fact, the essence of all that was right about Horowitz's pianism was to be found in his rendition of the Rachmaninoff Third. As Eugene Stinson noted in the *Chicago Daily News,* "In all my musical experience there is nothing even remotely comparable to his performance of this concerto as evidence of the emotional effect to be derived solely through the acoustical, the physical agency of sound."[35]

In Chicago, the seventy-year-old Ignace Jan Paderewski was in the audience. "I must admit," he said, "that I liked him very much. I liked both his playing and his general bearing. He was self-disciplined, and, above all, he has rhythm and tone. I only heard him play the D Minor Concerto by Rachmaninoff, but it was very fine indeed. Without any doubt he is the most convincing among the younger pianists."[36]

RCA Victor's English subsidiary, HMV, wasted no time in capturing Horowitz's performance of the Rachmaninoff. This, his concerto debut on discs, was recorded with Albert Coates and the London Symphony Orchestra on December 29 and 30 at London's Kingsway Hall. The Concerto filled nine sides of a five-record set, with Rachmaninoff's Prelude in G Minor, Op. 23, No. 5, on the tenth (a curiously pallid, sloppy rendering). Despite some faulty balances between orchestra and piano, and a memory lapse in the solo during the first statement of the third movement's second theme, this was one of the outstanding recorded performances of Horowitz's career, a masterly reading that was received with great enthusiasm. "In this work, at least, Horowitz is the greatest pianist of the present,"[37] wrote one American critic; and *The Gramophone* in England cited Horowitz's bravery in playing a score that had not been all that well known or especially popular with the public until he had begun programming it. After the appearance of this album and after a London recital at Queen's Hall a year and a half later, in April 1932, Horowitz found himself firmly established in London. Until 1936 he would make all of his recordings there, at Kingsway Hall.

But for seventeen months after the Rachmaninoff recording, Horowitz had no further sessions before the microphone. Instead, he concentrated on his busy itinerary. The 1930–31 American season began with his being detained (as in the past) on Ellis Island because of passport red tape. This time the immigration officials were embarrassed when Horowitz explained he was on his way to Washington, D.C., to play at the White House for President and Mrs. Hoover. The recital, arranged by Henry Junge of Steinway & Sons, was scheduled for January 8, 1931. Horowitz's English was still "pretty groggy,"[38] as he put it, and the thought of playing for the President and conversing with the distinguished guests afterward worried him. On the train to Washington, Junge coached Horowitz, assuring him that the receiving line would present no problem if he said, "I am delighted"—and nothing more. When the concert ended, and President Hoover—who much preferred light popular tunes to what he had just heard—had sighed with relief, Horowitz was positioned on the receiving line with Junge stationed directly behind him. There, with great solemn poise, he stood in the East Room and, as each of the seventy-five diplomats in attendance greeted him, declared amiably, "I am delightful, I am delightful!"[39] Perhaps everyone agreed, for nobody corrected the malapropism.

Before departing for Paris on the S.S. *Bremen* in early April, Horowitz and Merovitch met with reporters, and the manager gloated over the overbooked European concert itineraries not only of Horowitz but also of Milstein and Piatigorsky. The violinist, he said, was to give spring concerts in Vienna, Bucharest, and Budapest, and the cellist was to tour Italy. Horowitz, prior to a five-month tour of America the following fall, would play in Berlin, Hamburg, Cologne, Vienna, Budapest, Prague;

then would come his first solo recital in England since 1927, three appearances with Mengelberg and the Concertgebouw Orchestra in Amsterdam, and a tour of South America. Merovitch also proudly announced that his "boys" would appear together for the first time in a chamber-music concert the following March at Carnegie Hall.

In fact, Merovitch intended to make chamber events a regular part of the itineraries of Horowitz, Milstein, and Piatigorsky. "We will hold our own subscription series in all centers of the world," he grandly told his charges. "The life of a virtuoso should be as permanent and as fruitful as that of Philharmonic societies, which outlive wars and depressions and build traditions in their perpetual service to music. We will present the best of music in all forms, and we will invite other virtuosos of our own choice, who later, in turn, will be our successors!"[40] It was usually Milstein who became impatient during one of these diatribes. "Meanwhile, let's have lunch," he would suggest dryly.

For the trio's summer vacation of 1931, Merovitch had chosen Crans Sur Sierre, a small Swiss resort with tiny houses and hotels spread over a lovely valley surrounded, recalled Piatigorsky, "by gentle mountains on all sides."[41] All three looked forward to a marvelous working holiday, with side trips to the Engadine where Horowitz, especially, enjoyed mountain climbing. Piatigorsky and Milstein settled in a local hotel, but spent most of their time at a house Horowitz and Merovitch had rented together. Occasionally, Horowitz would abandon his colleagues to holiday in the south of France with his secretary, and with Steinert and other friends. Early that summer, in Paris, he had met an American composer, Sam Barlow, who had offered him use of his chateau above Nice and Monte Carlo. The pianist adored the sun and water, and stayed at the Château d'Èze for two weeks. "Horowitz and his friend were just acting like lunatics and having fun," recalled Steinert who took home movies of the interlude. "In those days, Horowitz was not a recluse and he enjoyed being with people—even begged to be with them."[42]

For Merovitch, it was one of the best summers ever. "I live at Volodya's place as a 'guest' and I feel blissful," he wrote Sasha Greiner from Switzerland, "because for these six years of my wanderings at hotels, I became homesick and it is wonderful here. We take care of the household and have a remarkable lady-cook. I have even taught her to cook genuine Russian *pirozhki* [puff pastries]."[43] However, only a few weeks into the summer Merovitch began lecturing on the need to prepare for the next season. In all matters, he tended to assume an authoritarian role, but this was especially so in the matter of repertory. He advised all three of his protégés to avoid "ungrateful works," stressing the need to perform "effective" short pieces to assure good box-office receipts. "Fast ones that had to sound still faster, and all kinds of transcriptions for encores" was Piatigorsky's summary.[44] Secretly, the three musicians grumbled about Merovitch's ideas, but in the end they all abided by his decisions, with Horowitz the one most easily led. "When Mr. Franz Liszt performed in public he put himself down, and that's what I did too," Horowitz was quoted as saying years later. "But the audience identified with my transcriptions and that's what I played. That's the only reason I did it. I made lots of money and I'm very glad!"[45] Milstein didn't much care one way or the other about the issue of giving the public what it wanted. Only Piatigorsky seems to have been bothered by the notion of capitalizing on his technique, for he was not yet accustomed to his, as he put it, "fairly new role as a virtuoso." Milstein and Horowitz were puzzled by his reservations about concentrating on showpieces. However, as Piatigorsky saw it: "Professionally I had lived many lives, while since childhood their field and destination had been solely that of the virtuoso. Without the experience of playing in orchestras, operas, operettas, chamber music, teaching, playing in restaurants, movies, and weddings, they could not be expected to understand my concern about embarking upon a strictly soloistic career. In this I was the youngest."[46]

Nonetheless, for encores the cellist acquired "a fine collection of 'bugs' "—*Bee* by Schubert, *Mosquitoes* by Fairchild, *Bumble-Bee* by Rimsky-Korsakov, *Butterfly* by Fauré, and lots of tarantellas. All three musicians, in fact, learned versions of Rimsky's *Flight of the Bumble-Bee* and all three played them a year later in Vienna, spaced only a few weeks apart. "I was rather perplexed in comparing three kinds of bumble-bees," a Vienna critic admitted. "Milstein's fiddle bee was more like a mosquito; Piatigorsky's cello bee had a more threatening droning quality, while Horowitz's was the elegant, playful kind, reminding those who know the story of the Tsar Saltan that the bumble-bee is really a prince in disguise."[47]

Horowitz's catalog of flashy encores was already well stocked, so during the summer of 1931 he spent most of his time working on more serious repertory: Brahms's *Paganini* Variations, Prokofiev's Third Sonata, Stravinsky's *Petrushka* Suite, a prelude and fugue from Bach's *Well-*

Tempered Clavier, and several of Szymanowski's mazurkas. Horowitz's industry was partly inspired by Arthur Judson's decision to offer him a minisubscription group of three recitals in the winter of 1932, which he was billing as "The Season's Most Significant Piano Series." The first program was to be devoted to "the three B's" (Bach, Beethoven, Brahms), the second to Slavic works (Rachmaninoff, Prokofiev, Szymanowski, Stravinsky, Chopin), and the last to Liszt. Judson's publicity department intended to generate great excitement with the series, even designing an opulent red program with a picture of Horowitz's hands on the cover. The advance billing and hyperbole, of course, meant increased pressure on the pianist.

Piatigorsky remembered that that summer "Horowitz worked tenaciously, with meticulous care to every note, every phrase, until all was fitted together."[48] Unlike Milstein, who enjoyed breaking up the day with visits to the practice studios of his colleagues, Horowitz worked in solitude, remaining the most isolated member of the trio. "Nathan was always in full view, Volodya had to be found," said Piatigorsky. "I liked to watch one and search for the other. Volodya was complex and elusive, and this searching had to depend on the light in which he wanted to be seen or to see himself. He did not make it easy."[49] The vivacious Milstein, on the other hand, gave the impression of not practicing at all, always eager to greet visitors and willing to drop an entire day's work when Steinert or pianist Alexander Brailowsky visited Crans Sur Sierre. It was Milstein who made Horowitz laugh, and Milstein who calmed Piatigorsky with pungent sarcasm when the cellist lurched into anxiety attacks or fiery speeches: "Come on, Grisha," he would tease, "some more passion!"[50] It was also Milstein who had the least patience with Merovitch's lectures on repertory and self-discipline. When the manager pontificated at length about "the downfall of human morality and the labyrinth of the Russian soul," Milstein defused him by offering congratulations "on his light touch and brevity."[51]

Of the three, Milstein was the most relaxed. Remembered Piatigorsky: "His friends, his surroundings, his violin, his exquisite cashmere sweaters, all existed to augment his pleasure."[52] Horowitz was always the nervous one, the worrier biting his nails, who sometimes separated from the group, and although Milstein and Horowitz had known each other far longer than they had Piatigorsky, it was the violinist and the cellist who spent the most time together. Horowitz was sometimes estranged even from his closest friends and colleagues, but if he needed support or encouragement, Milstein, Piatigorsky, and Merovitch could be relied upon.

Despite the striking differences in temperament among Merovitch's three virtuosos, they had committed themselves to joining together musically, and during the summer of 1931 they prepared for their first trio concert in Carnegie Hall the following March. Piatigorsky, who had had extensive experience as a chamber musician, often became the leader at rehearsals. Their program comprised the Brahms Trio in C Major, Op. 87, the Beethoven Trio in B-flat Major, Op. 97 (*Archduke*), and the Rachmaninoff *Trio Élégiaque,* Op. 9, the last a favorite as all three men worshiped their fellow Russian. Rehearsals sometimes concluded with Horowitz showing his friends manuscripts of his own compositions from his student days—"music for the piano, a sonata for violin, an unfinished piece for cello . . . all had the mark of a true gift for composing,"[53] remembered Piatigorsky.

As far as they were concerned, the fruitful summer ended too soon. After celebrating Horowitz's twenty-seventh birthday in Vienna on October 1, Milstein and Piatigorsky went their separate ways, beginning tours of Germany, Holland, England, and South America, not to see Horowitz again until their March chamber-music concert. As it happened, this long-awaited debut of the Horowitz-Milstein-Piatigorsky trio was something of a disappointment. The Rachmaninoff *Trio Élégiaque* turned out to be the most successful performance of the evening, certainly the best played, while the Beethoven and Brahms unfortunately tended to call attention to the group's inexperience as an ensemble. Merovitch insisted to the *Musical Courier* that they had "the same musical understanding and are able to play together in complete sympathy,"[54] that they had played together often for their own amusement and thus were not novices. However, Olin Downes of the *New York Times* found it necessary to observe that "the whole can be less than the sum of its parts."[55] Although individual playing was crisp and clean, ensemble was sometimes ragged, and shading was close to nonexistent, especially in the Brahms which, said Downes, "was whirled along on a wind of spectacular bravura and immense fortes that distended its outlines and ignored the content. . . ." More given to solo passages, ensemble-wise the Beethoven was an improvement, but the group lacked a really cohesive sound. There seemed to be no common denominator except for brilliant technique, so that the playing was "presented with the utmost finesse of detail and a profile always clean and vitally etched, if untouched by those impalpable veils of emotion which attend a performance less immaculately and more poetically conceived."[56] It was finally dawning on Merovitch that the contrasting temperaments of his protégés simply did not lend themselves to ensemble playing—although this should not have surprised the manager, since he had been grooming all three to be virtuosos, an attitude at odds with chamber-playing philosophy.

Despite the less-than-favorable notices, Horowitz, Milstein, and Piatigorsky continued to play chamber music, if only for their own pleasure, during their stay in New York. There were two particularly memorable occasions. One evening at Jascha Heifetz's palatial Park Avenue penthouse, they played without pause until the early hours. Toward morning, recalled Piatigorsky, they stopped to fortify themselves with "delicious little Russian chicken cutlets, of which the thin and poetic Horowitz consumed fifty-six!"[57] Always unpredictable, Horowitz turned up a few nights later at Rachmaninoff's apartment accompanied by his two comrades, ready to play their entire program. Shy at the prospect of performing for the master, Horowitz begged Rachmaninoff to play the piano part. "Nathan declared that there were no critics present and no risk whatsoever involved," reported Piatigorsky. Rachmaninoff laughed, but firmly declined, so Horowitz finally capitulated. At the end of the *Trio Élégiaque*, Rachmaninoff's wife and daughters exclaimed together, "What pretty music! Who wrote it?" "I," said Rachmaninoff, rather guiltily. "Sergei Vassileivitch," Milstein cried, "why don't you write anything for the violin?" "Why should I, when there is the cello?" Rachmaninoff replied, to Piatigorsky's delight.[58]

Before returning to Europe in late March, Horowitz played one recital in Havana, Cuba, and prepared himself for the highlight of his spring season: his recital reentry into London, arranged by Merovitch with England's foremost concert manager, Harold Holt. Thanks to Horowitz's recording of the Rachmaninoff Concerto, his popularity in England was on the rise and Holt had sought exclusive rights to manage Horowitz in the United Kingdom. Merovitch, mindful of protecting his status as Horowitz's personal manager, wanted to restrict Holt's management to a period of two years, but the impresario replied that "two years would be the period during which I may have to sacrifice in order to establish Horowitz as a first-class attraction."[59] As Merovitch could not risk another lukewarm reception in England, he agreed, unwillingly, to Holt's terms.

Horowitz's Queen's Hall recital on April 10 displayed the same virtuoso fingerprints that had left the British press so unimpressed five years earlier. "Owing to a certain conservatism (some would say obtuseness) the English public did not [then] properly value his extraordinary qualities," wrote the London *Times*. "This time he went over with a bang."[60] Even his British nemesis, Sir Thomas Beecham, admitted that the pianist was irresistible when Horowitz played the Tchaikovsky Concerto with his Royal Philharmonic Society the following fall. Horowitz's octaves in the first movement were twice as fast as Beecham had ever heard them played, and he genially twitted him by saying, "Really, Mr. Horowitz, you can't play like that. It shows the orchestra up!"[61] Remembering the frenetic pace of Horowitz's 1928 performance of the same work in New York, Beecham was now struck by the incisiveness and refinement of Horowitz's playing. According to one critic, large sections of the outer movements were "performed in such a quiet, unpretentious manner that many listeners seemed disappointed and did not think they had gotten their money's worth." Overall, the press loved it, praising Horowitz's ability at turning the Concerto's "blatancy to majesty, its sentimentality to fine feeling."[62]

Great Britain and Ireland were was the most important part of the 1932 fall itinerary, with stops in Glasgow, Sheffield, Manchester, Birmingham, Liverpool, Belfast, Nottingham, and Leicester, dates coordinated around a rigorous series of recording sessions in London. Recording during the day and playing concerts practically every night was wearing, and Horowitz concluded that performing for the microphones "is certainly the most exhausting work there is." Never before had he made so many records, one after another. "I began with a sonata by Haydn [No. 52 in E-flat Major], after that the Liszt B Minor [Sonata], which alone required eight sides. After that I played many short works by Chopin, Schumann, Stravinsky, Poulenc and Rimsky-Korsakov. All together twenty-five records. That is quite enough."[63] Not only were these the most extensive sessions to date, but the eleven works actually released were among his most brilliant recordings. His Liszt Sonata, for instance, was considered then, as now, one of the most impressive ever registered on disc.

Aside from the Haydn sonata, that fall Horowitz had expanded his

Classical side by also programming the Beethoven Sonata in A Major, Op. 101. In his Beethoven playing, Horowitz was nearly always accused of compromising style and structure, of employing a scale of tonal colors "better adapted to Chopin than Beethoven."[64] He bristled over such commentary, for he believed that many of Beethoven's works were "not of sufficient listening value to recommend them for recitals in large auditoriums,"[65] and certainly not as effective as the Ravel, Debussy, Poulenc, and Saint-Saëns pieces that figured prominently in his 1932–33 recital programs.

His concerto repertory (the two Liszt concertos, the Rachmaninoff Third, the Tchaikovsky First and the Brahms Second) showed no sign of expanding. He might never have learned the Beethoven *Emperor* had he not received an invitation in the fall of 1932 from Arturo Toscanini. Just a week before the November 10 Tchaikovsky with Beecham in London, a telegram arrived from the famed Italian conductor inviting Horowitz to play the *Emperor* Concerto that April with the New York Philharmonic at the final concert of Toscanini's 1933 Beethoven cycle. This, coming from Toscanini, was in the nature of a command. But, as Horowitz admitted to a friend, he had never even heard the *Emperor,* so he borrowed a record. "It may sound unbelievable," Horowitz told an interviewer that fall, "but this will be the first time I have ever played the Beethoven in public. Not that I perform exclusively Russian music, but people ask for that everywhere."[66]

Ten days before the April 23 concert with Toscanini, Horowitz tried out the *Emperor* in Chicago. His Rachmaninoff Third with the Chicago Symphony a few days earlier had been a triumph, but—in the press at least—the *Emperor* was a disaster. The performance "was neither Horowitz nor Beethoven as we are accustomed to thinking of them,"[67] reported the *Daily News.* Instead, it was "a painstaking, indeed a mincing performance. Finicky throughout, hard, brittle technically, the great flowing melodic lines broken out of all recognizability, the spirit eluded entirely and the whole a drawing-room exercise in youthful finger exercises." Ordinarily meticulously economical in his physical movements, Horowitz "bounced and bowed extravagantly over the keyboard, tremulously tugging at his chair, fingering his collar, his tie betimes, wiping from his face copious perspiration of which there was nearly a deluge. It was all rather amazing, but obviously the young modern feels out-of-key with the classics."[68]

Horowitz left Chicago highly agitated, nervously anticipating his first meeting with the universally feared Toscanini. His New York performance would be remarkably improved, yet he would rarely perform the *Emperor* Concerto again in the United States after the spring of 1933. But through it he met a man who was to have an immense influence on both his development as an artist and his personal life.

CHAPTER TEN

THE TOSCANINIS

"Toscanini was like a priest in music . . . like a flame. He could conduct any orchestra but there were problems working with him. We talked music for hours and hours. Oh, the man was stubborn and would not change. Toscanini had his conception and I followed it when I played with him. Even if it was against my wishes."[1]

"To be the daughter of Toscanini, I didn't have any merit because I could have been born to anybody. But to be the wife of Horowitz, in that I take a little bit of pride."—WANDA TOSCANINI HOROWITZ[2]

*A*fter the February 1933 appearances in Chicago and Philadelphia, Horowitz had returned to New York to attend a lavish party at the Hotel Astor, in the heart of Times Square. Arturo Toscanini, a resident of the hotel when in town, was at the party, so Horowitz had the opportunity of observing the celebrated conductor at close range weeks before their appearance together. Toscanini was perhaps the most important and powerful musician in the world, notorious for his fiery and formidable personality, and Horowitz's first reaction to the charismatic presence was a puzzling one: rather than exhibit his usual ebullient party pose, he retreated into a corner to sit alone, silent and glum. Later, he would tell friends that he was "merely awed at being at last in the presence of the Maestro whom I had worshipped from afar for so long,"[3] but in retrospect his behavior on that occasion seems portentous. In the years to come, there would be many such withdrawn, introspective reactions to the cobalt-eyed Italian.

Horowitz had first heard Toscanini conduct at the Salzburg Festival and at La Scala, and he realized then that the conductor's Apollonian temperament and fanatic fidelity to the score were diametrically opposed to his own outlook. Understandably, the upcoming rehearsals weighed heavily on Horowitz, especially since Toscanini had the reputation of a relentless tyrant who demanded absolute perfection and was given to violent fits of temper when musicians failed him in this respect. As with Beecham, his impatience with soloists was legendary—he dominated them and displayed his wrath and disgust if even small mistakes were made. And he did not tolerate virtuoso display, but demanded an equable balance between soloist and orchestra. "Toscanini didn't want to take any stars, and he didn't like them,"[4] said Horowitz.

Horowitz's constant need to prove himself, and his fascination with the rich and famous, explain, in part, his willingness to submit himself to such a trial by fire. Also, his great love for opera may have turned mere respect into exaggerated worship. Toscanini, after all, had served as artistic director at La Scala and as principal conductor of the Metropolitan Opera, and he had conducted the world premieres of Leoncavallo's *I Pagliacci* and Puccini's *La Bohème* and the Italian premieres of Wagner's *Götterdämmerung* and *Siegfried*. Above all, Toscanini was the complete musician, an unchallenged genius who conducted by memory a huge portion of the Romantic and Classical repertory.

A few days after Horowitz's March 29 Carnegie Hall recital, his second that season, he received a message from Bruno Zirato, the New York Philharmonic's assistant manager, requesting that he come to Toscanini's suite at the Astor to review the piano part of the *Emperor*. Horowitz was terrified, especially because his recent performances of the work had been so badly reviewed. Friends had warned that the Maestro would not tolerate his being one minute late, so Horowitz walked up and down Broadway in front of the hotel for half an hour to make sure he would be on time. Other snippets of advice went reeling through his mind: "If he starts to shout, don't be frightened; if he insults you, don't respond."[5] At last, it was time. When he arrived at Toscanini's door, his hands were almost paralyzed, shaking horribly, and when Zirato thumped him encouragingly on the back all Horowitz could do was to croak, *"Nyet, nyet.* Can't play a note."[6] Ushered in, he managed to introduce himself to the great man. For a few minutes the two spoke of Horowitz's teacher Felix Blumenfeld, whom Toscanini had met years before in Paris when Blumenfeld conducted an opera with Feodor Chaliapin. Toscanini told Horowitz that Blumenfeld was an excellent musician and that he was lucky to have studied with him. So far, Toscanini was not being the gruff, tempestuous ogre Horowitz had expected. The Maestro pointed to the piano, Horowitz sat down and played without interruption and the audience was over. "That's very good," was all that Toscanini said. "Now I must ask you to leave because I have a lot of work to do. I'll see you at the first orchestral rehearsal."[7]

At the rehearsals, Horowitz recalled, "there was no battle," and Toscanini even asked Horowitz to play freely. "I expected tension, stormy scenes, shouting. I was afraid he would laugh at me. But we got on famously."[8] On the night of the concert, Horowitz sat backstage. For company, he had Toscanini's dog, Picciu, who was always growling and trying to bite. Horowitz wasn't scheduled to play until after intermission and Toscanini never left Picciu home alone, so the pianist was assigned the task of watching the animal during the entire first half of the concert, dodging his teeth and trying to still his barking.

Under Toscanini, the *Emperor* turned out far more polished and relaxed than in Chicago. Toscanini had lavished great care in rehearsals to achieve, according to the *New York Times,* "complete harmony of intent and accompaniment between orchestra and soloist,"[9] though it seemed that the beauty of the orchestral part detracted from the piano. Nevertheless, in the prayer-like theme of the *Adagio,* where Toscanini carefully worked his magic and held his soloist in strict rein, Horowitz's playing was described by the *Times* as "a thing of beauty, its loveliness increasing as it progressed."[10] Although many critics still criticized the virtuoso reading as too "impetuous," Toscanini was satisfied, exclaiming, "I like to play with this boy!"[11] Although it was clearly the Maestro's evening, Horowitz had proved, the *Times* concluded, that "he, too, could stride with Beethoven and Toscanini."[12]

It was at a supper party following the concert that Horowitz was reintroduced to Toscanini's youngest daughter. Wanda, then twenty-six, was traveling with her father during the American spring season and was at that time living with him at the Astor. She and Horowitz had met briefly a few years earlier at another New York party, but it had been one of those occasions when Horowitz was basking in his own celebrity, clusters of fans and friends surrounding him as he alternately played violin sonatas with Milstein and Ping-Pong with his chauffeur. Now, however, Horowitz's attention was riveted upon Toscanini and his daughter.

Two years earlier Wanda had heard one of Horowitz's recitals in Milan and since then had avidly followed his career, for she was infatuated with his playing and appearance. "He was the best,"[13] she declared. Until the performance of the *Emperor,* Wanda had not mentioned his name, fearful, she said, "that I'd have to take the responsibility"[14] for whatever the outcome of the performance. At the post-concert party, Wanda fell under Horowitz's spell, while he was captivated by her father. He hovered about Toscanini, playing Chopin mazurkas on the host's piano and pointing out striking harmonies and modulations, eager to please and interest him. Toscanini, impressed, listened intently, as if he had never heard the music before, smiling indulgently.

Near the end of the evening, when Toscanini had become engaged elsewhere in conversation, Horowitz drifted into a corner with Wanda, and the two began to speak animatedly in French. (As Horowitz knew no Italian and Wanda no Russian, French was their language from this initial meeting.) The next day, Horowitz sent Wanda a photograph that said only, "To you." Thus began an eight-month courtship that would ultimately unite the world's most brilliant young pianist with the daughter of the world's most famous conductor, a marriage destined to have dramatic and unexpected effects on Horowitz's professional and personal life.

To properly understand the various changes in Horowitz's playing over the years and the emotional problems that drastically affected his career, it is essential to view him within the context of the Toscanini family. After leaving Russia and his own family, Horowitz had been almost completely dependent, both practically and emotionally, on his manager, Merovitch, his secretary-valet, and a few friends such as Milstein, Piatigorsky, and Steinert. Although often vivacious, Horowitz was by nature a solitary, isolated man with few close attachments. In 1933, the Maestro, Wanda, and the entire Toscanini clan began to fill an enormous emotional vacuum, initiating a permanent shift away from the Merovitch circle.

Not that the Toscaninis were an easy family to fit into. The conductor's wife, Carla, and her four children had shaped their lives around the intimidating brilliance and puzzling contradictions of their "Papa," who ruled them with absolute authority. Toscanini loved the idea of having a family, yet he threatened its stability with frequent philanderings; he was fond of his children but sometimes treated them like orchestra members; he wanted them to be successful, but imposed the impossible standards of his own genius upon them, effectively circumscribing their independence and self-esteem. "As a child, I feared him not for what he said but for his silence," Wanda once said. "Of course there were explosions at home, but not very often. When angry, he didn't talk to us. He was very silent and I think silence for a child is very scary. You didn't know what he was thinking. So as a child, I always felt guilty. We were a very strange family, the Toscanini family, we never talked. We took example from my father; he never praised us. He always told us when we were wrong; never when we were right."[15]

Before 1908, when Toscanini was appointed principal conductor of the Metropolitan Opera, he had been able to spend time at home in Milan with his sons, Walter and Giorgio, and his daughter Wally. Convinced of the importance of a solid homelife, he sometimes took care of the babies himself, spending many hours reading from pediatric and child-care books. But after his La Scala appointment, he was occasionally absent from the house for as much as eighteen hours a day working on a new opera production, not only conducting it but taking a hand in stage direction, lighting, and costume design. Although categorically opposed to divorce as he was to anything that might imperil the family structure, Toscanini nonetheless spent much of his spare time having affairs, often with his own sopranos. ("He could not forgive himself but neither could he control himself in the sexual-amorous aspect of his life," wrote one biographer. "He ate and drank extremely sparingly, slept little, worked like a beast of burden, shunned high society, and demanded the utmost of himself at all times; but he could not resist women and they could not resist him."[16]) Carla Toscanini was therefore left with the task of raising the children and of relaying messages to them from Papa. "There was a law which had to be observed by everyone in our house," remembered Wally. "Papa told Mama what he wanted of us and she passed it on. We always obeyed."[17] Added Wanda, "We knew what we could do and what we couldn't do."[18] Especially after 1908, nearly all of Toscanini's life was absorbed by artistic activity and he no longer had much time to attend to his family.

Eighteen months before Wanda was born, four-and-a-half-year-old Giorgio contracted diphtheria and died in Buenos Aires, where Toscanini happened to be conducting. Toscanini was grief-stricken and regarded his child's death as a kind of divine retribution, punishment for his infidelities. Carla, who had always adored her husband, who had traveled with him and made his life easier in every imaginable way, was beside herself with sorrow. She now determined to leave him. But somehow things were patched up and on December 7, 1907, the fourth and last Toscanini child was born in Milan. She was christened Wanda Giorgina, a name chosen by Toscanini himself.

Filled with peasant superstition, the Maestro took the choice of a new-born's name very seriously. For instance, he had championed the works of the Italian composer Alfredo Catalani, and the close friendship between Catalani and Toscanini continued until the composer's death from tuberculosis at age thirty-nine. Thus, Walter had been named after the hero of Catalani's opera *Loreley* and Wally after his last and most successful opera, *La Wally.* Since both Walter and Wally had been healthy infants, Toscanini had concluded that a name which began with *W*—a letter that does not exist in the Italian alphabet—would bring the new baby good luck. And even if it did not have a talismanic effect, the Polish name he chose for his fourth-born seemed rather exotic and alluring.

Wanda Toscanini was born only a year before her father began annual trips to New York, so she would never enjoy the same close attention from him that her siblings had received. Rather, Wanda spent the early years of her life with a nursemaid, Nena Rama, who, in the tradition of those who care for the children of absent parents, became a kind of second mother.

The Toscanini children both feared and adored their father from afar but felt more comfortable with their mother. Carla was strong, quiet, and domestic and dealt with the pressures of fame and scandal with dignity. "My mother was a wonderful woman," Wanda remembered. "Very musical, very critical of my father, and very practical. She always traveled with him—packing valises, trying to see that everything was there when it had to be there, signing for and collecting his fees. She loved people and did a lot of good for people. If somebody needed something, she was always ready to help. She had an instinct for music and understood. She would say to Papa: 'I may be stupid, but that singing will not go.' And she was always right."[19]

Largely under Carla's influence, Wanda was raised and schooled in Italy and graduated from the *liceo* at age eighteen. Fairly early on, she decided not to pursue an education or independent career and chose instead to travel with her father and learn music through his performances. "I was taught to listen," Wanda recalled. "My mother did the same."[20] In her early and middle teens, however, the girl had harbored a deep interest in a musical career, an idea quickly squelched by her father's exacting standards and intolerance for anything less than genius. Until age fifteen,

Wanda had studied the piano. Toscanini approved of her taking lessons, for she was the most musical member of the family, but he could not refrain from berating her for every wrong note. "A mistake was like a stab in his stomach,"[21] said Wanda, not mentioning the state of her own stomach at such moments. As she practiced, Toscanini would shout, and it got to the point that the young girl's hands shook every time she tried to play. "Ah! Impossible!"[22] she finally exclaimed, quitting the piano.

Wanda subsequently took up singing, having often been told that she had "a natural voice." Unknown to her father, she had vocal lessons and, a friend remembers, was eventually able to render a fine, professional performance of *"Ah, fors' è lui"* from *La Traviata*. She also sang in the Verdi *Requiem* with a choral society in Milan, but as she knew what her father's reaction would be, was careful to use an assumed name when appearing in public. When Toscanini finally became aware of the deception, he was furious, and screamed at her that there would be no second-rate performers in the Toscanini family. Demoralized, Wanda gave up music completely, for with her father there was no such thing as compromise.

All hopes for a career destroyed, Wanda traveled sporadically with Toscanini from 1927 to 1933. She modeled herself after her mother and became assistant caretaker "to Father." Eventually, they became close, and she would stay with him in the United States for two or three months at a time, depending on his conducting schedule. She found she could talk frankly and openly with him, and she became quite a good judge of his performances—the family's resident critic. "I was not blinded by his fame," she said, "and could always say when a concert was better than the other."[23] So Wanda received her real musical education at La Scala and in Carnegie Hall.

In 1933, when she met Horowitz for the second time, Wanda had defined for herself a mothering role she would play for her entire life: traveling companion, valet, and critic. Her years of apprenticeship with her father had prepared her in many ways for the life she would live with Horowitz. With both Toscanini and Horowitz, she assumed her duties with enthusiasm and dedication, a fiercely determined woman eager to protect the men she loved and to share in their successes. "To be the daughter of Toscanini, I didn't have any merit because I could have been born to anybody," she said. "But to be the wife of a Horowitz, in that I take a little bit of pride." Pride, surely, but also, in her own words, "quite a cross to bear,"[24] as she was to discover.

In April 1933, Horowitz sailed back to Europe with the Toscaninis soon after the performance of the *Emperor* Concerto, which had marked the end of the Maestro's New York season. In early May, he gave a recital in London at Queen's Hall. One of the most successful concerts of his entire career, it caused the usually biting critic of the *Manchester Guardian,* Neville Cardus, to declare him, in a headline, "THE GREATEST PIANIST, DEAD OR ALIVE." Horowitz's Brahms *Paganini* Variations overwhelmed Cardus: "His fingers might have had brains in them, so subtly pointed was every note. The witchcraft of this performance might easily have come to pass because of some private transaction with the devil. This was Brahms-plus!"[25] The hyperbole of Cardus's headline provoked a barrage of irate letters from fans of Wilhelm Backhaus, Egon Petri, Moriz Rosenthal, Alfred Cortot and Rachmaninoff, one literal-minded writer even demanding to know whether the critic had ever heard Liszt play. In later years, Cardus explained that the notorious headline had been meant ironically (he was a well-known devotee of Schnabel at the time), since Horowitz's publicity was forever billing him as the "greatest living pianist."

Along with Horowitz's other spring triumphs in Milan and Paris, the *Manchester Guardian* article had further piqued Wanda's interest in him. "I don't know, maybe that's why I married him, thanks to Mr. Cardus," she said years later. "I don't say I chose him for this reason but he was my favorite pianist and I found him very attractive. I fell in love with his pedaling—not on the bicycle, on the piano. And I was one of the few who agreed with Cardus."[26] Toscanini had cast a shadow over her, and if she could not be a musician she would assert herself in another way.

Horowitz ended his seventh European season on June 2, 1933, in Paris, with a recital at the Théâtre des Champs-Élysées. In need of rest, he began spending time with Wanda and her family, watching the Maestro conduct in Vienna, sightseeing with Wally in Rome, and gradually becoming more comfortable with the formidable Wanda. Violinist Yehudi Menuhin wryly recalled that "it was a time of infatuation—with Wanda Toscanini, whom he was then courting, and with a two-door Rolls-Royce which he had lately bought."[27]

The courtship began in earnest that summer, and it was almost immediately clear what Wanda had on her mind. Her determination was etched on her face. She had inherited her father's cobalt eyes, his beetling brow, and some of his darker moods. Friends remember her as being a complete contrast to the well-behaved and ladylike Wally, for even as a child Wanda was bad-tempered and ready at any moment to make a scene. "I did not inherit my father's musical talent, but I did inherit his good health!"[28] she would declare. And this sturdy Italian woman, with her thick black hair and olive complexion, had her sights set square on Horowitz. Bored with her staid life in Milan, and having a passion for travel, Wanda may well have viewed marriage as a path to freedom, independence, and self-esteem.

Not that it was going to be easy to obtain her father's approval, even if Horowitz should propose marriage, for her sister Wally's difficulties were a vivid illustration of how Toscanini treated his children when angered. In 1924, Wally had fallen in love with Count Emanuele Castelbarco of the Piedemonte Rezzonico branch of a proud aristocratic family. But the count was already married with children, and for the next seven years the two had carried on a clandestine romance in face of the strong disapproval of Papa Toscanini. Finally, Castelbarco was able to obtain a divorce, and in 1931 he and Wally were married in Budapest. Toscanini categorically refused to speak to his new son-in-law, although he did eventually reconcile with Wally after she gave birth to a daughter. Finally, during the summer of 1933, when Toscanini was conducting in Vienna, Wanda put her foot down. She said, "It's time, Papa, that you stop this!"[29] and the count was then welcomed into the family. But Wanda always remembered Toscanini's violent reaction when he first discovered that Wally was involved with a married man. Glasses, dishes, and anything else he could put his hands on went flying; and for the first time in his life, Toscanini had struck one of his children.

Although Horowitz was spending that summer in Switzerland, at Sils Marin in the Engadine, Wanda managed to see him by having her mother and father invite him to northern Italy to visit their island home on Lago Maggiore. "The Isolino," as Toscanini named it, a pristine retreat just a rowboat's ride from the town of Pallanza, was covered with trees and flowers that rose to a hill crowned by a picturesque villa. Its tranquillity and utter privacy had immense appeal for the Maestro. Until the time Italian politics and the threat of war drove him to America, Toscanini spent each summer on the Isolino, and he would return to it after the end of the Second World War.

During Horowitz's stay, he and Wanda discussed marriage, but with trepidation, knowing that it all hinged on the approval of Toscanini. Although Horowitz was Jewish and Wanda Roman Catholic, religion is not known to have been a major factor in Toscanini's opposition that summer to the union. After all, the Maestro wasn't especially religious and the rest of his family was rather nominal in their practice of the faith. "I was brought up half religious, half not,"[30] said Wanda, who, anyway, had no intention of being dissuaded by mere convention. Toscanini's objections lay in other areas. Although he felt warmly toward Horowitz and greatly admired him as a pianist, he had warned his daughter how problematic living with such a high-strung musician would be. "You know very well that life with an artist is very difficult," Toscanini admonished. Growing more recalcitrant, he said enigmatically, *"Moglie e buoi dei paesi tuoi."*[31] ("Wife and cattle from your own village.") Family friends suggested that Toscanini was concerned about Horowitz's other friendships, worried that because of such friendships he would make neither a good husband nor a good son-in-law. Ultimately, however, he gave his blessing to the union.

Not that Horowitz himself was free of doubts. In an interview a few years earlier he had asserted that "marriage and a successful musical career are incompatible. To be a great artist, one must live alone."[32] He now worried about the obligations and responsibilities of family life and confided to friends: "Women are like unnecessary baggage. My fiancée doesn't know how to do anything—just to tell if I play good or bad."[33] Horowitz said he didn't know how he would cope with someone for twenty-four hours a day, and when the wife of a colleague said that she helped with her husband's correspondence, Horowitz decided that might not be a bad idea: Wanda could write letters for him. "In those days the pressure to get married was tremendous," recalled one close friend, "and Horowitz needed someone to take care of him, to replace the family he had lost. Wanda and the Toscaninis gave this sense of stability to a life which had been desperately chaotic and lonely. She gave him a home and the iron control he needed."[34] Horowitz was filled with the reservations any young man might have had, fearful of losing his freedom and not yet emotionally ready to commit himself to anything beyond his career.

But above all, Horowitz was enchanted by the idea of becoming Arturo Toscanini's son-in-law. At home, a picture of the Maestro was always prominently displayed on his piano, and he would proudly declare, "I am a pupil of Toscanini."[35] Horowitz at that time tended to parrot Toscanini's ideas about music and performance, insisting, for instance, that "performers should not insert too much. We should try to understand as much as possible the intentions of the composer and not invent anything of our own."[36] Yet a moment later he would be at the keyboard demonstrating quite the opposite, his own amazing technique and un-canny talent for producing colors—"like a painter," as he put it. He bragged to one conductor that he could create sixteen different colors in the Debussy *Serenade* and frolicked at the piano in immodest escapades of high velocity and near-orchestral dynamics. "Horowitz would be playing a very fast passage wonderfully," recalled a friend, "then he would stop now and again, saying, 'Oh, my goodness, what wonderful little fingers I have!' Then he would giggle and kiss his 'darling little fingers.' "[37] None-theless, Horowitz continued to issue a litany of Toscanini's ideas, ideas that were opposed to nearly everything he did at the piano.

Over and over, he recounted the same anecdotes about his perform-ance of the *Emperor* with the Maestro in New York. "Toscanini told me that he could not understand why the piece usually sounded so dull and he decided that it should be played much faster than usual. And oh! how we played this concerto!"[38] Obviously, Horowitz was proud of himself and his new status with Toscanini. European critics, however, liked his performance of the Beethoven Concerto no better than they did his read-ing of the sonatas. He played the *Emperor* that fall in Vienna, Brussels, Amsterdam, and Paris without the cachet of Toscanini, and his rendition was dismissed by one critic as "delightful to some" but "empty, cold and unemotional,"[39] still self-consciously restrained.

With Wanda still pressing heavily on his mind, in the fall of 1933 Horowitz faced yet another overloaded itinerary, including concerts in Hungary, Italy, Denmark, Sweden, Switzerland, Belgium, England, Hol-land, and Austria. One engagement he looked forward to was in Copen-hagen, where he was to play the Rachmaninoff Third with the State Radio Symphony under the direction of Nicolai Malko. Malko was a fel-low Russian who had conducted Horowitz's first concerto appearances in Kiev, Odessa, and Kharkov in the early 1920's. He and his wife had been frequent visitors at the Horowitz household in Kiev and they had looked after Horowitz's brother George before the boy was institutionalized. Horowitz enjoyed bantering with Malko's wife, Berthe, and he cherished the couple as an important connection with his past.

On October 3, the day of his first rehearsal in Copenhagen, Horowitz told the Malkos that he had finally decided to marry, and he showed them a photograph of his intended, keeping her name a secret. In his schoolboy way, he teased about how surprised they would be when they learned his fiancée's family background because her father was terribly famous. Two days later, he could contain his excitement no longer and announced to the Malkos that his bride-to-be was none other than the daughter of Arturo Toscanini. He told everyone he knew that he felt as if he were eighteen years old, that everything seemed new to him, and that it was the first time that he had felt anything at all for a woman.[40]

Many close friends of the period were surprised by Horowitz's decision, though delighted for him. They could not, however, help noticing his ambivalence and anguish as he tried to accustom himself to the prospect of marriage. For Horowitz had grown used to and content with his male friends. Once, he shyly asked intimates if they had heard rumors that "he fancied men." Then, in a devil-may-care but aloof manner, he exclaimed, "Well, let them talk!"—and pointed to his male secretary, who had traveled with him for the past six years.[41] The secretary empathized with Horowitz, for he was also engaged to be married. Traveling together, the two husbands-to-be would put pictures of their respective fiancées on their nightstands and shake their heads in self-mocking disbelief before turning in.

In jest, Horowitz would flirt with Berthe Malko, complimenting her on her clothes, chattering away criticizing other women they knew, all the while being, as she saw it, "charmingly egocentric." "Women are too feminine and I don't like them," he told her once, suddenly erupting into self-conscious giggles as if not believing what he had just said.[42] Among friends, Horowitz had acquired a reputation for having a roving eye, and even as he told the Malkos about his future wife, he couldn't help flirting with one of Malko's conducting students, who was part of the supper party that followed Horowitz's performance of the Rachmaninoff Concerto. As he talked to the student, he became animated and his eyes seemed to light up.*

* Horowitz's romantic interest in other men seems to have been common knowledge among friends and associates during this early period of his career. Serge Koussevitzky once confided to composer David Diamond that this dated back to Horowitz's performing days in Russia. (David Diamond interviewed by author, February 5, 1980) In a letter dated April 3, 1928, Josef Hofmann wrote his wife that Horowitz "has temperament, although he is not said to care for ladies. . . ." Nathan Milstein appears to have regarded Horowitz good-humoredly. Said one intimate: "Milstein and I met in Prague. He was not going to be able to see Horowitz on October 1, his birthday, and wanted to give Volodya a present, so he gave me some money and asked me to take Volodya out to a club when I saw him in Copenhagen. He knew Volodya would appreciate it." (Interview with author, January 23, 1980) Arthur Rubinstein remembered: "Horowitz adored his male friends and bachelor freedom and told me that he wouldn't know what to do with a woman. Everyone was astonished when he married Wanda Toscanini." (Interview with author, June 30, 1980)

Nevertheless, Horowitz sometimes spoke excitedly of his wedding plans. The news leaked out and was announced by the *Chicago Tribune* Press Service in Paris on October 6: "Wanda Toscanini hopes to become the wife of Vladimir Horowitz. The young man is awaiting the arrival of Toscanini, who is scheduled to arrive on October 12 in Paris for a series of concerts, in order to ask formally for Wanda's hand. Wanda is buying copiously from the world-famed Paris dressmakers."[43]

On October 8 the Toscanini family formally announced the engagement, and the Maestro privately suggested to Horowitz that he and Wanda travel together in England as a sort of trial run. This idea may have seemed logical to Horowitz because, in a state of confusion about his feelings toward Wanda and the marriage, he was still hesitant to take the plunge. "Maybe I shouldn't get married," he would say to friends. "But then again, Wanda knows I'm a little perverse, and she wants to try anyway. She has been in love with me for the past four years."[44] About his own affections, he would respond: "I? I am not in love. I can't love anyone. I love the piano."[45] A cynic might have wondered if his motivations were more involved with career than emotion, for he admitted the attraction of the Toscanini name. "Toscanini is like an icon to me and Wanda is part of the icon. Still, I like her as a woman," he admitted, "and when we kiss, I feel like a man."[46] Discussion of Horowitz's surprising marriage continued among his friends. To them, it was apparent that the transition from bachelorhood to married life was not going to be easy. For one thing, Toscanini "just didn't like the idea of Wanda marrying Horowitz," as one close friend put it. "He thought his daughter was going to walk into a hornet's nest and she did. But she married him because she really loved him. There is no question about it. And he loved her as much as he was able to."[47]

On November 2, Horowitz and Wanda arrived in London for his "Celebrity Tour" of England and Scotland, as arranged by Harold Holt. Young unmarried women then did not travel alone with a man, so Wanda's sister, Wally, agreed to chaperon the couple from London to Manchester, Glasgow, Liverpool, Edinburgh and Dundee. In London, Queen's Hall (later destroyed during the war) had wonderful acoustics, and Horowitz savored them at his two recitals there. The two major works of the evening—Liszt's *Dante* Sonata and Beethoven's Sonata in E-flat Major, Op. 81—were heralded as great athletic feats but criticized because of Horowitz's tone, which one writer found "frankly dull . . .

monotonous at anything above *mezzo-piano* and thin at its loudest."[48] However, riding on the crest of Neville Cardus's headline, Horowitz was generally touted everywhere he went. The tour was not only a professional success but, despite fears and misgivings, Horowitz and Wanda enjoyed their time together and decided to go ahead with the marriage. As Horowitz left England for concerts in Belgium, France, and Hungary, Wanda returned to Milan to prepare for the December 21 ceremony.

Many of Horowitz's friends believed he would cancel the marriage at the last moment. Some of his colleagues—perhaps jealous of Horowitz's coup in snaring Toscanini's daughter—tried to second-guess his motives. Pianist Vera Resnikoff, an old friend from Russia, remembered that "we Russians always thought he married Toscanini's daughter hoping he would learn to play Classical music. He had a tremendous capacity for the Russian composers and Liszt but when it came to the classics, his playing was a bore."[49] Resnikoff had concluded that Horowitz "was not the marrying kind" and remained skeptical. Other friends familiar with the situation predicted, according to Wanda, "that the marriage wouldn't last three weeks,"[50] but she was determined to prove them wrong. It was true that *she* had chosen *him,* but his passive role during the short courtship did not justify, in her own mind, the barrage of criticism she now received.

A sympathetic friend pointed out the practical advantages of the match, noting that "from the start, Wanda and her father understood that Horowitz was an exceptional creative genius, and all three respected one another. They knew an enormous amount about how the music business worked and each recognized the other as an asset in what was to become a marvelously effective family machine."[51] Horowitz would not have denied that he expected to learn much from Toscanini. Years later, in a rare reflective mood, he said, "Wanda made a man out of me—and her father made me a musician. He was uncompromising and I began to play more straight."[52]

Arthur Rubinstein viewed Horowitz's decision to marry as gratuitous and believed Horowitz was copying him, since he had married only three months earlier. Rubinstein's analysis reflected the intense competition between the two men: "Horowitz saw that getting married was good for me. I was able to concentrate on my work and was happy. But marrying Wanda Toscanini was so typical of him because he was after a career and adored making money and thought more of himself than of anything else. He had told me that if he was going to get married he was going to marry someone celebrated. That he should have married Wanda is self-evident, more so than if he had married the daughter of Barbirolli or Beecham."[53]

At the end of Horowitz's fall season in Europe, four days before Christmas 1933, the fateful day arrived in Milan. "It wasn't a conventional wedding. I don't like those affairs,"[54] said Wanda years later. Indeed, the simplicity of the ceremony also reflected her father's "instinctive aversion for celebrations, for official receptions."[55] The Maestro had no patience with social pretension, hated publicity, never gave interviews, and was scornful of everything that "was not spontaneous and sincere." Wanda's Paris designer, Lucien Lelong, dressed the bride in a black coat with a silver-fox collar. He kept urging her to wear a touch of pale blue, but she refused, insisting on the stark outfit she knew would please her father. Likewise, there was no ostentatious wedding ring, only an engagement band with two small diamonds that Horowitz had given her during the summer.

None of Horowitz's family attended. Standing beside the Maestro were Carla; Wally and her husband, Count Castelbarco; Wanda's brother, Walter; Milstein, Piatigorsky, and a few other close friends. The event turned out to be satisfyingly "spontaneous" because of Horowitz's poor Italian. Toscanini, who as a wedding present had given the young couple a gold plaque bearing a likeness of himself, had hired an interpreter to translate the civil ceremony for the groom. This man was a Milanese musician of some standing and he remained absolutely tongue-tied with awe and fear when it came time to perform his duties. The combination of Vladimir Horowitz and Arturo Toscanini was too much for him, and he could only stare helplessly as Horowitz listened, trying to follow the ritual so as to make the proper responses. The celebration afterward was also short and simple, and then there was little time for a proper honeymoon since Horowitz immediately had to begin preparations for another American tour. On December 28, 1933, exactly one week after the marriage, the couple departed on the Italian liner *Rex,* accompanied by Toscanini, Molinari, Milstein, Piatigorsky, and Yehudi Menuhin, certainly one of the most notable musical entourages ever to cross the Atlantic on the same ship. "What a honeymoon!" grumbled Horowitz.

Arriving in New York on January 5, the group was met by a sizable press contingent, and the newlyweds were naturally the center of attention. In a photograph, Wanda strikes a characteristic pose: solid, stony-eyed, her heavily painted lips resisting even the hint of a smile. In contrast, Horowitz flashes a wide grin, and looks debonair with one hand folded into his double-breasted suit, his hair slicked back. It is a portrait of an improbable match.

Settled into the Hotel Astor with the Toscaninis, the couple was soon bombarded with requests for interviews. In one of these, Horowitz spoke enthusiastically about his fall concerts in England and his upcoming appearance at Carnegie Hall on January 30. As always, he expressed his preference for the musical life of the United States. "London is now like New York was a few years ago, just too many concerts. Germany is out of it, of course. And Paris was never really musical. There has been a considerable reduction in the number of concerts in New York and I personally think this has its advantages."[56] At that moment, the papers reported, Horowitz suddenly launched into a monologue on the exchange rate and various traveling problems. The phone rang, and his wife, dressed in a long brown-velvet dressing gown, answered. Jascha Heifetz was calling with congratulations. The famous newlyweds—who were described as "radiantly happy"—seemed to the American public a fairy tale come true.

Two weeks later in Chicago, Horowitz's close friend, pianist Gitta Gradova, and her husband, Dr. Maurice Cottle, honored the Horowitzes with "one of the most interesting parties of the winter,"[57] according to the *Chicago Tribune*. Horowitz had first met Gitta in Paris at the time of his debut recitals, and had been instantly captivated by her command of the Russian repertory—especially the works of Scriabin—and her nononsense, riotous good humor. Gitta and Horowitz became lifelong friends who supported each other unconditionally through professional and personal crises. The Chicago-born pianist was like a sister not only to Horowitz, but also to Milstein and Piatigorsky, and she spent part of each summer with the trio, in Lucerne or at St. Moritz. Her fashionable home in Chicago became a salon for every important musician visiting the Windy City, especially her Russian idols and intimate friends, Sergei Prokofiev and Sergei Rachmaninoff—her most frequent houseguests aside from Horowitz and Milstein.

Wanda also found a sympathetic friend in Gitta Gradova, and the two women were amused by 1934 news reports in Chicago that described

Horowitz as "the upstart who married the Emperor's youngest daugh-ter."[58] Wanda was seen by the public as attractive but not beautiful or glamorous—"not remarkably social in the usual sense,"[59] as the Asso-ciated Press put it. Aside from her propensity for expensive clothes and jewelry, she was by now entirely taken up by her husband's career. In a crepe dress worn under a mink wrap and set off with a diamond brooch, Wanda would spend the last moments before a recital fussing over him, adjusting his tie, smoothing his coat, worrying about the adjustment of the piano bench, and then sitting on the edge of her chair in the audi-ence until he was safely onstage.

They traveled widely in America that season, including some of the western states, and at one point were able to take a few days off in Colo-rado Springs for a "second honeymoon." Musically the marriage seemed to agree with Horowitz, for some of his harshest critics were impressed by his growth that season. After his January 30 recital at Carnegie Hall, both Olin Downes and Pitts Sanborn applauded the pianist for his at-tempt to be "a musician first . . . and a technician only to serve the com-poser."[60] Sanborn, in particular, was surprised by the changes in his playing: "Anybody who supposed Vladimir Horowitz to be merely syn-onymous with strength and speed would hardly have believed his ears at Carnegie Hall last evening, [for] his prodigious technique was the ser-vant, not the master of his artistic aims."[61]

Two weeks later his performance of the Brahms Second Concerto with the New York Philharmonic under Hans Lange was coached by Tos-canini himself. During the rehearsals, the Maestro had "sat hunched down in a seat, his distinguished head bent forward, a frown on his brow," recalled Charles Cooke of *Esquire* magazine. "He arose and paced up and down, listening directly under Lange's podium [and] afterwards he and Horowitz left together, the venerable Italian talking earnestly, the famous young Russian listening with head deferentially inclined."[62] As Horowitz had hoped, the Maestro now took an interest in all of his major appearances. The pianist was completely under the conductor's spell, and since his playing seemed to have new depth, it almost seemed as if Horowitz had gained something of Toscanini's mastery by marrying his daughter.

CHAPTER ELEVEN

FIRST RETIREMENT: SECLUSION

*"From the time I left Russia, I never stopped for a second. I
had only three months in the summer when I didn't play and
sometimes I even played then. Routine, routine, routine, and I
was feeling that I was an assembly-line pianist, which I was not."*[1]

Nineteen thirty-four was a landmark year for Horowitz. In one
twelve-month period he became a father, saw his own father for the first
time since leaving Russia, moved from Paris to Milan, toured extensively
with Wanda, and—not least important—ended his professional relationship with Alexander Merovitch. Merovitch's name, which had hitherto
appeared on Horowitz's concert programs as "Personal Representative,"
now disappeared. The first public announcement of the change appeared
only much later, in a 1935 *Esquire* article: "Two years ago," the magazine
reported, "in the old, old custom of artists and their managers, the two
parted company."[2] Behind this polite statement of fact lay a complicated
and painful story.

The custom of artists routinely leaving their managers may have been
traditional, but Merovitch was not having it. In 1932, he had tried to negotiate a written contract assuring his job as Horowitz's personal manager "for life," as they had once verbally agreed back in Russia. Horowitz
had positively bristled at this idea and told Merovitch that as he didn't
expect to be performing for more than another fifteen years, being
"bound for life" was hardly necessary.

Actually, it had been Horowitz's father who had agreed to the for-life
concept. In 1925, when Horowitz was unknown and frightened of the
future, Merovitch had been indispensable. He had brought Horowitz out
of Russia and had taken good care of him when there was little money
and few prospects. With considerable savvy Merovitch had arranged

Horowitz's European debuts and orchestrated his highly effective publicity campaign. He then introduced Horowitz to the most important concert impresario in the United States, Arthur Judson, assuring a career there. He had tolerated Horowitz's shifting moods, fits of temperament, and the often embarrassing quirks of his personal life, while protecting him against his own naïveté in negotiations with other managers and with record companies. He had advised him on repertory and even acted as a personal valet in the days before Horowitz could afford one. Perhaps most important, he had seen to it that Horowitz's intense feelings of insecurity had not sabotaged his career before it had begun.

After Horowitz's marriage, Wanda assumed many of these tasks, and Merovitch suddenly seemed less essential. Merovitch had invested much emotional energy in Horowitz's career, even after this was unnecessary. As Horowitz's friend Gitta Gradova would observe years later, "Sasha was solely interested in Horowitz—that was his great possession."[3]

Once Merovitch had also developed the careers of Milstein and Piatigorsky, he had envisioned spending his entire life with the trio—traveling with them and establishing concert series throughout the world. But by 1933 both Milstein and Horowitz had lost patience. "He didn't take us under his wing," said the violinist. "In 1925, he didn't *have* any wings. He only talked big. We didn't know anything, we were naïve, so we followed his advice. At first, we did need someone who would be with us, and he adopted us and treated us like [he was] some kind of ministration nurse. If he thought of himself as our father, we didn't feel like his sons."[4]

By 1933, Horowitz required only a small fraction of Merovitch's immense energy, and it was not in his nature to be generous about paying for something he did not need. The fact that his career and finances had been furthered by an extraordinary marriage had effectively undermined Merovitch's position. As for Horowitz's personal life, the manager had become a troublesome mother hen, and in his professional life, Judson and the Columbia operation were handling everything satisfactorily. Now that the number of his American engagements was reduced because of the Depression, retaining Merovitch on the payroll and paying him a 20 percent commission was a costly and unnecessary drain.

Over the next several years Merovitch would continue to manage Piatigorsky (even when he had finished with Milstein) and to function as an occasional consultant to Horowitz, but in 1933 his role as Horowitz's personal representative came to an end. "Sasha's experience with Horowitz was something that he relived from the time they separated until he died,"[5] recalled Merovitch's sister-in-law, Maria Merovitch. Having suffered a substantial loss of income, Merovitch chose to open his own firm in New York, Musical Art Management, which he ran from 1933 to 1936. He continued to introduce young artists to the American public, but never with the same success he had enjoyed with his famous trio. Although Merovitch occasionally arranged single concerts for illustrious figures like Feodor Chaliapin and Igor Stravinsky, he remained obsessed with the past and would pester his "boys" and their wives for years to come. "He became a strange, psychopathic personality," recalled one contemporary whose husband was managed by Merovitch during this period. "He would get into fits of rage and start screaming, eyes inflamed, for no apparent reason, and it was absolutely impossible for anybody to work with him."[6]

Over the years, Merovitch's business ventures were consistently beset with financial difficulties and he suffered from fits of depression that resulted in two nervous breakdowns. His second wife, Rosamond, and the rest of his family bitterly blamed the insensitivity of Horowitz, Milstein, and Piatigorsky—most specifically Horowitz—for many of his problems and would never forgive Horowitz for what they viewed as his disloyalty. "Horowitz was indifferent to Sasha's problems, couldn't have cared less about other people," said Maria Merovitch. "He didn't give a damn. Milstein and Horowitz exploited him, not the other way around. They gave him nothing and Sasha was the one who paid and sacrificed everything during their first years in Europe."[7]

Other colleagues also found Horowitz difficult during the first years of his marriage, among them Arthur Rubinstein. Rubinstein had long ago become resigned to Horowitz's quirks, but two incidents in the spring and fall of 1934 strained their friendship. When Horowitz returned to Paris with Wanda on May 5, 1934, the Toscanini clan settled there for a month. Toscanini was to conduct on the twenty-fifth and twenty-seventh, while Horowitz was to play with the Paris Symphony Orchestra under Cortot on the ninth and then give a recital on the fifteenth. A few days after Horowitz's highly successful performances of the Beethoven *Emperor* Concerto and Liszt A Major Concerto, all the Toscaninis attended the Paris Opéra. Rubinstein was also there, and he remembered that at intermission "Horowitz came out to the same corridor where I was walking, escorted by the entire Toscanini family. He avoided me, I believe, because he did not care to introduce me to Toscanini. I didn't particularly care if he did introduce me, but politeness called for it and anybody else would have done so. But at the second intermission, my wife, Nela, and I went to get a glass of champagne at the bar and out of the box came Horowitz, this time alone. He eagerly came over to us and asked, 'Can I have a glass of champagne too?' In our language we call that chutzpah, tremendous chutzpah—generally discourteous behavior. That he was full of, and I became very angry about these little things."[8]

Not long after, Horowitz surprised the Rubinsteins by making a date with them for the day following his recital. Rubinstein recalled:

> We spent the entire day after his concert with Horowitz. Later that night, when we took him back to his hotel, as we were parting he said very amiably: "Will you lunch with me next Sunday?" My wife and I were flabbergasted! It was the first time I had heard him invite anybody anywhere. "Well, well, Volodya, this is quite an honor, but unfortunately on Saturday night I am playing the Tchaikovsky Concerto with Mengelberg in Amsterdam and there is always a supper afterwards, so I couldn't be back before Sunday afternoon."
>
> But Nela was on his side. "Arthur," she said, "we cannot refuse Volodya's first invitation. We can easily give up the supper and be here on Sunday morning." That's just what we did. Nela and I rushed to the train after the concert, arrived in Paris at seven in the morning, had a quick breakfast, and lay down to await the call from Horowitz. There was no call. At eleven, Nela impatiently telephoned the Prince of Wales Hotel. "Hello, Volodya, where are we lunching?" she asked. He replied, "Yi, yi, yi, yi? . . . I, ah, would like to go to the races today. Look, you can come if you like to my room. I can give you some sandwiches before I leave." So he had forgotten his invitation and offered us a snack in his room as a compromise. That really was something, something I will not take from anyone. We were dead tired from rushing back on the train and I felt like going over and slapping him. But instead, we dressed and drove to his hotel. In the lobby I wrote him a short note which I

remember well: "Dear Volodya, I hate to interfere with your wish to go to the races, so I invited my beautiful wife Nela for lunch in a good restaurant and she accepted." We lunched in the Bois, saw a movie, and returned late in the afternoon to Montmartre. I assured my wife that when we returned to the hotel there would be apologies from Volodya or flowers or something.

When we returned there was a call from my German manager, Dr. Paul Schiff, who said that he had had a telephone call from Horowitz saying that he had received a little letter from Rubinstein and that he did not like the tone of the message. I gasped and said: "Look here, tell Mr. Horowitz's manager that Mr. Horowitz should go to hell and that I won't see him again unless he apologizes in a letter." For many years to come, nearly twenty, we were not on speaking terms. I would meet his wife with whom I would exchange a few polite words, but we never mentioned Horowitz's name.[9]

So it was that, at about the same time, two of Horowitz's most important colleagues, Merovitch and Rubinstein, disappeared from his life. However, Horowitz was now a member of the Toscanini family. The summer of 1934 was split between Paris, Milan, and Lago Maggiore, with a visit to St. Moritz, where Volodya and Wanda vacationed with Gitta Gradova, Milstein, and Piatigorsky. Late in August, Horowitz went to Austria for the Salzburg Festival, where Toscanini was conducting an all-Wagner program. The principal events of his summer, however, were not musical, but personal. Wanda was then six months pregnant, due to deliver early in October, and Horowitz was already nervous about his impending role as a father. Also that summer, Simeon Horowitz had finally been granted permission by Soviet authorities to leave Russia to see his son. Over this, Horowitz was ecstatic.

Simeon was an unhappy man at the time he visited his son and daughter-in-law in the late fall of 1934. Formerly a successful and prominent engineer, he now held what he regarded as an inferior position with the State, and made a poor living. He told his son in detail the circumstances of his mother's death four years earlier of peritonitis after an unattended case of appendicitis. When Horowitz had first learned of her death, he had gone into a rage, convinced that she had not received proper care. Deeply despondent, for he had adored his mother, he blamed her death on the Soviet government. He would feel the loss for many years to come.

After Sophie's death, Simeon had moved to Moscow, and he subsequently derived his greatest satisfaction from following as best he could the meteoric career of his only remaining son. He was also enormously proud of his daughter, Regina, who had an active and distinguished career in Russia as a concert pianist and chamber musician. Simeon had spent years trying to obtain a visa for travel abroad, but it was not until his second marriage, to a much younger woman, that he received this, on condition that his new wife stay behind in Russia. The government evidently reasoned that an old man with a young wife at home would quickly return.[10]

That fall, Simeon accompanied his son on a tour of Italy, Belgium, France, and Switzerland, and Horowitz was delighted that his father was finally able to share in and witness his success. In Paris on November 18, Simeon was introduced to Alex Steinert after a recital at the Théâtre des Champs-Élysées. Steinert remembered: "My wife and I went backstage and there was this magnificent man, six feet tall, with the saddest face you've ever seen but with great nobility. 'Tell me, how is your life in Russia today?' I asked. 'How are things in the capital?' And he replied: 'Oh, we have a four-room apartment in Moscow.' And I said, 'Aren't you glad to come back to France?' And he looked at me and said, 'I don't want to like it here.' "[11]

Horowitz was soon able to give Simeon a very special gift, a granddaughter, born in Milan on October 2. The child was named Sonia, after Horowitz's mother Sophie. In many ways, this was one of the happier times of Horowitz's life. But nonetheless, there was an underlying sadness to the long anticipated reunion of father and son, due to the fact that it would all too soon be over. Simeon wanted to extend his stay in Europe indefinitely, but knew he could not and doubted that he would ever be permitted to leave the Soviet Union again. Horowitz was certain that he would never return, for he had relinquished his citizenship and feared punishment. He knew that if *he* went back, he would never again be seen in the West.

When Simeon finally returned to Russia, the worst happened: he was arrested and sent to a prison camp, where he died. Horowitz and family members in Russia presumed Simeon had been arrested because, as he spoke fluent German and French, it was thought he might be a spy; during the Stalin era, everyone was suspect. Regina was the last member of the family to see Simeon alive, at the camp. Already in a state of mental deterioration, he did not even recognize his daughter. He died alone—a broken, tormented man.[12]

Back in Paris, Horowitz was much occupied with his wife and child during the 1934–35 concert season. The pressures of marriage were already weighing heavily on him, and friends began to notice the first signs of a developing crisis. He seemed unusually nervous, distracted, and morose. In addition, his playing showed less attention to detail. At a rehearsal of the Tchaikovsky Concerto in Copenhagen, Horowitz kept stopping, repeating passages, and "making many mistakes," according to conductor Nicolai Malko, while playing with "a strangely harsh, metallic and strident" tone. "Maybe his new family has aged him?"[13] surmised Malko in his journal, only half in jest. The conductor was especially dissatisfied with the second movement during rehearsal ("not enough poetry"), but was relieved when the performance went reasonably well. "He played rather better than at the rehearsals, but not as good as in past years. He made many mistakes and muddled numerous passages with the damper pedal. Some passages were played too superficially and the sound was not always beautiful. The success with the audience was terrific, but I expected more."[14] Similarly, while rehearsing the Liszt A Major Concerto, Malko saw that "not everything is going well. Horowitz came to rehearsal late and we didn't have time to finish playing through the Concerto with him. Afterwards, Horowitz seemed very nervous and capricious. He explained that he was agitated because he was supposed to telephone his wife in Paris. Every time he had to call Wanda, it was very nerve-wracking for him and he was perspiring profusely."[15]

The following day, he did not even show up for rehearsal. When Malko telephoned the hotel, Horowitz said that he had completely forgotten about it and, besides, he had fifteen visitors in his room. The conductor chided him, and Horowitz insisted that he had to see the visitors and that the one rehearsal of the Liszt would be enough. "How can you talk like that?" Malko exclaimed angrily, concluding, "I thought the way he was behaving was terrible. It didn't help the music very much."[16] Not surprisingly, the performance was less than memorable. "Horowitz began the piece beautifully," wrote Malko, "but then it suddenly became uninteresting, more erratic. His success with the audience was once again great, but not everyone applauded and the press was negative."[17]

Horowitz's puzzling behavior and the uncharacteristic carelessness of his playing were, many friends believed, related to his new alliance with the Toscaninis. One intimate remembered that "although Horowitz had, admittedly, been conceited and self-possessed, he was egocentric in a delightful kind of way. He loved to be loved and could be very childish. Stingy, egotistical, but charming. He was used to getting all the attention. After his marriage, however, he found that he was now in the orbit of another great figure and this bothered him. He seemed prone to depression much more of the time. He had always been seen with a big grin on his face, but Wanda told him she did not like the ingenuous smile. She told him not to smile so much because he looked like all the other Russian émigrés who always smiled to ingratiate themselves. If Horowitz was one of the most brilliant pianists in the world, his education and knowledge were no match for Toscanini's, and this fact was implicit in Wanda's intolerance."[18]

The pressures of associating with Toscanini, of having a wife and child and an important career, weighed heavily on Horowitz. More and more often he told friends that he was afraid to play, unable to concentrate on music. He felt hemmed in by the Toscaninis, who were around most of the time monitoring his activities. Even when Wanda had to remain in Paris to care for their infant daughter, her brother-in-law, Count Castelbarco, traveled with Horowitz on his European tours instead of the German secretary whom Horowitz much preferred. The watchdog count was not even of much practical use, for when Horowitz wanted him before a concert he was usually off exploring the local museums. Horowitz complained bitterly that he was not getting the help he needed, but no one listened.

When Horowitz visited his new in-laws either in Milan or on the Isolino San Giovanni in the Lago Maggiore, he had to endure the ranting and raging of the Toscaninis. The Maestro and his younger daughter, lamented Horowitz, constantly criticized other people. Toscanini would pace the floor, foaming with fury when told that rival conductors were attempting to imitate him. "We screamed," recalled Wanda years later, "but, in the end, we were always right."[19] Indeed, at home as everywhere else, the Maestro was determined to have his own way in everything.

Much of the time, Horowitz was treated like a guest who had no right to an opinion. Piatigorsky sympathized with him, terming Toscanini "the damndest lump of macaroni to swallow,"[20] and Arthur Judson had nicknamed Toscanini, more simply, "son-of-a-bitch."[21] *En famille,* Horowitz was astonished both by the steely willfulness of his wife and the tyrannical insensitivity of her father. "It is very sad to have a person like that," he reflected years later about him. "It is not an easy person. He was a difficult character. Much more difficult than me."[22] Indeed, a friend who watched Horowitz's general unhappiness at the time later commented that "the autocratic brutality of Toscanini could have killed anyone, and Horowitz simply did not have the resources to combat such pressure."[23]

Eventually, the relentless bickering and backbiting became intolerable. One friend of the family later remarked, "It was not surprising that a nervous, high-strung man like Horowitz would have found it difficult to acclimate himself to the kind of cat-and-dog screaming typical in this family. I remember Wanda once standing at the top of the stairs in her negligee, screaming as if the house was on fire. It turned out that she and the other members of the family were discussing whether or not the chauffeur should come at ten or ten-thirty A.M. to take them somewhere."[24]

On the subject of the Maestro, Horowitz was of two minds. His respect for him as a musician remained unchanged and in later years he described his father-in-law thus: "He was like a priest in music. He was like a flame. He had true, natural rhythm, so seldom [found] even in good musicians. Most artists, they imitate rhythm. It comes not from the inside. But he was a genius, and he never stopped studying."[25] Likewise, Toscanini was proud of his son-in-law, telling anyone who would listen that Horowitz was possessed by demons. Said Horowitz, "When he spoke to others about me he would say that only Horowitz and Liszt could play like this. I used to tell him, 'Maestro, please, not in my presence.' "[26] Yet when alone together, the two squabbled over music, especially orchestral works, for hours at a time. Toscanini seemed to win every battle, which was psychologically debilitating for Horowitz. But, then, Piatigorsky once admitted that Toscanini was the only conductor who frightened him and made him feel like a pupil, and Horowitz realized that "he liked to play with me because I gave in. Toscanini had his conception and you followed it when you played with him. Sometimes I was not completely in accordance but I changed my interpretation. . . . I was an easy fellow."[27]

Horowitz gradually experienced a downward spiraling effect from his career and family life being too intimately connected. The Toscaninis did not provide respite from the pressures of concert life; they contributed to them. The free time Horowitz had enjoyed as a bachelor was now a thing of the past. After only one year of marriage, he seemed disillusioned with his wife, nervous about his daughter, and discouraged by life in the shadow of a father-in-law he feared.

As it turned out, the 1934–35 season, which consisted of seventy-five concerts, was to be Horowitz's last until 1939. After eight years of touring America and ten years in Europe, personal and professional pressures led to the first of Horowitz's "sabbaticals" from the concert stage, during which he would lose confidence in his abilities and become immobilized by illness.

Meanwhile, January 1935 began with an extensive tour of Britain and Ireland with stops in Glasgow, Sheffield, Manchester, Birmingham, Nottingham, Leicester, Dublin, Belfast, and of course, London. The six-week American season included his first performance anywhere of the Brahms D Minor Concerto, under Toscanini's baton, and one Carnegie Hall recital, billed as Horowitz's last scheduled appearance in America for two years. Wanda, in Milan preoccupied with Sonia, could no longer travel overseas, so Horowitz had opted to concentrate on Europe for a while, after the spring season in the United States.

With a backbreaking itinerary ahead of him, it seemed to Horowitz that dealing with his family and playing concerts were quite enough activity, and that there was simply no time for learning repertory. In fact, the only new works featured in his 1934–35 recitals were Liszt's *Mazeppa* (one of the *Twelve Transcendental Etudes*) and Schumann's *Humoresque*. The latter reflected Horowitz's growing interest in the works of Schumann—he had previously programmed the *Arabesque, Presto Passionato, Toccata,* and *Traumeswirren.*

Although Horowitz was not expanding his repertory, he seemed to be working harder than ever onstage. During his recitals he soaked at least two large handkerchiefs with perspiration, and between movements of the Schumann *Humoresque* he methodically dried each finger of each hand and at the finale wiped his face and neck thoroughly before launching into the next work. His playing was more feverish than ever, the *Mazeppa* chiseled with "a savage and transported passion,"[28] thought one critic. Because of his frenetic schedule and the considerable time he had to give to his family, neither his fingers nor his mind ever had enough chance to rest, and the nervous energy of his playing never quite turned to true emotion. Horowitz's tone, rather than being round and full like Hofmann's, was now even more than usually brittle and harsh. The London *Times* declared, "The *Mazeppa* exposed most clearly the one weakness in the pianist's technique, which is the inability to produce a really resonant *fortissimo*. Where it is required, he forces the tone and sometimes almost loses control of those extraordinarily deft fingers."[29]

Yet in that season's only Carnegie Hall recital on April 13, the heroic grandeur of the Chopin B-flat Minor Sonata seemed to herald a new maturity. Leonard Liebling of the *New York American,* who continued to refer mistakenly to Horowitz as "that Polish keyboard artist," perceived "a deeply serious communion" with the Chopin work in which "fingers are in service to the music rather than to personal exhibitionism."[30] Horowitz's continuing swing between the ironclad classical rule of Toscanini and his own more capricious virtuoso nature left one writer with the impression that the pianist was "always on the brink of escape from the brilliant virtuoso class and about to develop into an interpreter of deep insight and romantic feeling, but his programs usually contain numbers which call for all the resources of his extraordinary technique and then his audiences become demonstrative in the extreme."[31] Instinctively attracted to such demonstrations because of his vanity and his ever-present desire for more success and money, Horowitz could not quite bring himself to follow Toscanini's dictums.

Nonetheless, it was Horowitz's musicianship that was to the fore when he played the Brahms D Minor Concerto with Toscanini and the New York Philharmonic on March 14, 15, and 17. "The undercurrent during rehearsals was one of fear," recalled violinist Edwin Bachmann. "Not only did Horowitz follow the Maestro but his eyes were nailed on that stick."[32] The results were superb. "His playing has seldom had the splendor of tone, the firmness of grasp and outline, the awareness of the composer's requirements that were manifest last night,"[33] wrote Olin Downes. Toscanini conducted with his usual iron hand and it seemed to one commentator that "the soloist was practically in a straitjacket of rhythm and tempo most of the time."[34] Still, overall it was the Maestro who was given the most credit for the evening's success, Horowitz's measured playing being attributed by one writer to the "eagle eye of his pappy-in-law [who had] put a slight quietus on his hitherto tempestuous style."[35] At the end of the last movement, the audience thundered applause, and cheers came "from all over the house, that would have done credit to a football game."[36] Toscanini, despite a general impression that this was "a public family party," allowed Horowitz most of the bows. The one time he came out with his soloist, the Maestro only went so far as center-stage.

On April 19, 1935, Horowitz and Wanda returned to Europe on the S.S. *Berengaria,* en route to Milan to prepare for his performances of the Tchaikovsky Concerto and Brahms D Minor at La Scala in May. Horowitz subsequently repeated those works in Bologna and Paris, and then began his first reasonably relaxed summer with his wife and daughter. That summer was highlighted by a much-publicized cycling tour of northern Italy, during which Wanda and Horowitz, with Piatigorsky, used Milan as their home base and traveled leisurely through the Dolomites, with side trips to Venice and Salzburg. In *Musical America*'s October 25, 1935, issue there is a picture of the athletic trio at lunch at an outdoor café, their bicycles standing near the table. Horowitz seemed in fine health during the escapade, enthusing that "in one single day we cycled 162 kilometers." The summer ended on the Isolino with Horowitz, Wanda, Sonia, the Maestro, and Carla; Walter and his wife and their six-year-old son, Walfredo; Wally, the count, and their daughter, Emanuela. There was no hint of an impending crisis.

Indeed, when Horowitz began his new season in October 1935, he appeared well rested and in good spirits. As usual, he began with a tour of Scandinavia and he was the picture of exuberance at his first concert in Stockholm—"my October City," as he told the Swedish press: "This is my fourth time here."[37] His only worry was whether or not a suitable piano could be found for his recital, and he expressed a desire to expand his travels to China, Japan, and Mexico, and also said he would like to return to Russia. His present itinerary included a tour of Norway, Denmark, and Sweden, followed by appearances in Holland, Austria, France, Switzerland, and Hungary. Early on, however, on November 8, a concert in Rotterdam was canceled due to "illness of the artist."[38] Horowitz retired with Wanda to St. Moritz, where he spent the Christmas holidays. In January he was to tour Italy, but upon his arrival in Milan, one newspaper reported, he "had suddenly fallen ill. He will probably have to spend several weeks in complete rest."[39] In fact, the entire tour of Italy was canceled, and not long after, projected concerts in Egypt and Palestine.

Horowitz did, however, fulfill an important engagement on February 22, 1936, in Amsterdam, when he played the Brahms D Minor Concerto with the Concertgebouw Orchestra conducted by Bruno Walter, his all-around favorite conductor. In March, Horowitz summoned the energy to go to London, where in addition to a recording session on the sixth, he gave two solo recitals and made one orchestral appearance. The recording session was to be his last until 1940. At age thirty-three, Horowitz was more hypertense than ever, "suffering pitifully" before each appearance; if he was able to brood for twenty minutes backstage, he sometimes left without playing at all. Therefore, it was necessary for him to arrive just in time to hang up his hat and coat and then run onstage, without a moment to pause or reflect.

Exhausted and overworked, Horowitz went through the motions of playing when he was physically capable of doing so, but his performances clearly reflected his worsening psychological state. "I played certain works so often that I couldn't hear them anymore, even while my fingers were performing them,"[40] he later said. If there was no discernible depth of emotion, the surface grace, agility, and brilliance remained. But the fire of earlier years had been quenched. "Routine, routine, routine," Horowitz grumbled. "From the time I left Russia, I have never stopped for a second. I had only three months in the summer when I didn't play and sometimes I even played then. I am not an assembly-line pianist!"[41] The London press noted the change at once: "I do not think it is fanciful," wrote one critic, "to trace in his playing during the last four or five years a steady retreat from all depths. His fire, when it burns, feeds on his nerves and not on his heart: his brilliance is not the brilliance of an exuberant, but of a crippled emotional personality. Fingers, brain and nerves all contribute and make him a wonderful technician and a clever musician, sensitive to all external promptings of the music: but at the core his whole playing is dead."[42] Even pieces with which he had become identified were played now with a forced, exaggerated style. His Chopin mazurkas, for instance, were too obviously charming and his tone above *forte* was thin and hard. "Lyrical passages were played with an exaggerated tenderness, an over-stressing of the rubato which destroyed all rhythm and continuity."[43]

More concerts were canceled, including a projected April tour of Spain, his first there in five years. After a few scattered recitals in Rome, Paris, and The Hague, the season came to an end. Horowitz's last performance until 1938 was in Trieste on May 2, 1935. He spent the month of June in Paris with Wanda and Sonia, July in Switzerland, and August at the Salzburg Festival listening once again to Toscanini. Despite these months of rest, he still felt unable to resume the pace he had sustained for the past decade.

Nonetheless, his calendar was booked two years in advance. In the spring, he had announced a 1935–36 season that included twenty performances in England, plus tours of Scandinavia, France, Italy, Holland, and Belgium. Forty concerts were planned in the United States in early 1937 to be followed by a spring tour of Australia and New Zealand. As it turned out, none of these events took place.

In September 1936, Horowitz was suffering extreme abdominal discomfort, and suddenly decided to have his appendix removed. According to Nathan Milstein, Horowitz's abdominal pain was caused by spastic colitis, "but Horowitz insisted that his appendix was the cause." The trauma of the operation and its aftereffects caused a nearly complete collapse of body and mind. He had always been bothered by a nervous stomach and subject to cramps and chronic diarrhea. Since his mother's death after a delayed appendectomy, he had worried about the state of his own appendix. In 1935, during concerts in Chicago, he stayed with Gitta Gradova and consulted with her husband, Maurice Cottle, an eminent nose-and-throat specialist, about the possibility of having an appendectomy. Dr. Cottle, who for years had tended Horowitz's various minor ailments, took him to a number of the city's leading surgeons and their decision was unanimous. "There's nothing the matter with you or your appendix," they each declared. "You don't have to have it taken out. For heaven's sake, forget it!"[44] By 1936, though, Horowitz was plagued by pains both real and imagined, and had become convinced that his appendix was to blame. Recalled his first cousin, Natasha Saitzoff, "He was always afraid that something bad would happen. His outlook was tinged with a little pessimism always."[45] So it was that, perhaps thinking once again of his mother's death and fearful for his own life, Horowitz had the operation in Paris.

Whether or not it was necessary is not clear. A friend of later years observed that "both Horowitz and Milstein had consuming phobias about appendicitis; they couldn't wait to be operated on. There was nothing wrong with their appendixes, but they had their operations."[46] However, there is no question that the removal of Horowitz's appendix proved the catalyst for a great many unexpected complications. Because of the customary medical practice of the period, Horowitz's physicians insisted he stay in bed for ten full days after the operation. Consequently, he contracted phlebitis and became completely immobilized. For three months he lay despondent in the hospital with his foot propped on a pillow. "Horowitz was not a happy creature and did not take such things in his stride,"[47] said his cousin Natasha. Horowitz later told Gitta that when the doctors finally got him out of bed, he just passed out, and "from then on," she recalled, "it was a long, drawn-out, disheartening recuperation."[48] His London engagements for the fall and his American tour of 1937 had to be canceled indefinitely.

Horowitz's recovery from phlebitis was retarded by his psychological reaction to the deterioration of his health and the disruption of his career. The press made much of the "nervous breakdown," despite Wanda's protest that "it is absolutely untrue that his illness affected either his mind or his hands, as some rumors have it."[49] After his recovery in 1939, Horowitz insisted that his "intermission" was a necessary step "to regain not only health, but strength."[50] No other explanation was offered, and some newspapermen speculated on "nervous derangements so severe that it seems uncertain whether he would ever return to his brilliant career," while others explained Horowitz's withdrawal from the stage as essential to his artistic growth. The latter part of the problem was readily admitted by Horowitz. As Kurt Blaukopf asserted in his book *Les Grands Virtuoses,* "for the first time, Horowitz realized the limits of his artistic possibilities and . . . he tried, in taking two years of rest, to unravel this crisis. The true reason behind it lies in the excessive value he had given pure technique up until then. The mechanical precision of his playing had become so stupefying that no listener could any longer pay attention to the truly musical aspects of the work. Horowitz himself had finally become aware of this."[51]

Even Horowitz, who in later years admitted to close friends and associates that the "intermission" had indeed been a nervous breakdown, did not believe his collapse could be entirely explained in exclusively artistic terms. But he only hinted at other possible factors when he told his friend Abram Chasins, "I had a lot of things to think about. One cannot go through life playing octaves."[52] It seems incontestable that Horowitz had pushed himself beyond endurance and that his artistic maturity had failed to keep pace with the adulation of his admirers. But, said one close friend of the time, "I don't believe Horowitz's breakdown resulted from too much performing. It was an inner conflict related, at least in part, to his new family and the one he had left behind in Russia—a kind of delayed effect that finally burst. The trauma of getting sick, the nightmarish fate of his family in Russia, the unending scrutiny of his activities by Wanda, and the enormous chasms between his private feelings and family responsibilities would have been enough to exhaust anyone."[53]

Pressure exerted by the Toscanini family in conjunction with Horowitz's new role as a father must also not be underestimated. Horowitz had feared the nuisances of family life even in the fall of 1933, before he married. So long as his freedom had been protected by bachelor status and by Merovitch, Horowitz was in excellent control of himself. But when he entered the tumultuous, demanding world of the Maestro, any illusion of personal inviolability and security was shattered. One friend recalled: "Horowitz was emotionally still very childlike, but was now saddled with gargantuan adult responsibilities. He had learned that Toscanini could be an insensitive tyrant and was both influenced by him in his interpretations and afraid of him at home."[54] By 1936, Toscanini, much concerned with the deteriorating political situation in Italy and the plight of Jews in Germany, had become more distracted and difficult than ever and quite intolerant of those around him.

After leaving the hospital in Paris, Horowitz had gone to Wally's house in Venice to recuperate. In the late fall of 1936, leaving little Sonia in the care of her grandmother Carla and her aunt Wally, Horowitz left with Wanda for Switzerland. He spent most of the next two years in Bertenstein, in a rented house overlooking Lake Lucerne. Switzerland had always been his favorite summer retreat, full of happy memories: hilarious evenings with Gitta Gradova at the Palace Hotel near Rachmaninoff's home, delightful days spent swimming and bicycling with Milstein and Piatigorsky, and the many hours devoted to plotting out European tours with Merovitch. Switzerland's tranquil political environment, free of the turbulence then rocking Germany and Italy, seemed to Horowitz ideal for recovering and sorting out the tangled affairs of his life. And, of course, excellent medical care was available there. He took the cures, making short trips to Basel, Orne, Gstaad, and Engelberg, and even traveled to Paris once he felt stronger. Wanda, meanwhile, could easily go to the Toscanini home in Milan and visit her father in Paris and Salzburg.

Horowitz's recovery took far longer than anyone anticipated. A year after contracting phlebitis, his leg was still bothering him and the "cure" at Orne, which had helped him in the past, now had only mixed results. In a letter to Rachmaninoff, Wanda described the ups and downs of that difficult year: "Volodya promised he would give you his news, and I want to keep his promise. The beginning of the cure was not too brilliant. . . . Volodya had no luck with the Doctor, who at once gave him baths that were too protracted and a lot of medicines that were too strong, so that by the end of the first week he had to keep to his bed for three days. After this unhappy experience, we immediately quit the Doctor and are now in the care of another doctor (a Russian lady-Doctor!) who is conscientiously following the progress of the cure and Volodya is taking quite well to the baths, although the cure is very tiring. We'll remain at Bagnoles until July 10, and after a two or three day stop in Paris, Volodya will leave for Engelberg and I will stay with my sister in Venice."[55]

Rachmaninoff was immensely fond of both Horowitzes and went out of his way to be friendly during this distressing period of Horowitz's life. The disparity in their ages, along with their busy concert schedules, had kept both men apart much of the time during the first years of their friendship, but Horowitz's physical collapse now prompted a new intimacy. Horowitz admired Rachmaninoff more than any musician alive, and his relationship with his idol now helped immeasurably in restoring his self-confidence and stimulating a desire to once again perform in public. Shortly before his marriage, Horowitz had declared that Toscanini was his "icon," but in reality it was Rachmaninoff who was his greatest inspiration—not only then, but throughout his life. And during the summer of 1937 it was Rachmaninoff who encouraged Horowitz to think seriously about returning to his career.

When Rachmaninoff first met Horowitz in 1928, he had been amazed by the young man's brilliant pianism and pleased that he was championing his music, especially the Third Concerto. Yet during the early years of their friendship, Rachmaninoff remained rather aloof, somewhat "nose in the air,"[56] according to a mutual friend. There seem to have been reasons for this. Before Horowitz married, Rachmaninoff had frowned at rumors of Horowitz's personal life that had reached him. In addition, Horowitz's materialism and lust for success irked the composer, and Rachmaninoff made no secret of the fact that he much preferred the playing of Josef Hofmann and Benno Moiseiwitsch.

In 1936 Rachmaninoff wrote to a friend in the Soviet Union that "the best pianist, probably, after all, is still Hofmann, but only under one condition—when he is 'in the mood.' If not, then you could not recognize the old Hofmann. Lately Horowitz has acquired a big name. He has colossal octaves! After his marriage to Toscanini's daughter, many hoped that his playing would gain a little musicality.... So far this has not happened. Everyone is consoling himself that he has not been married a very long time."[57] Hofmann was the only pianist whose photograph hung in Rachmaninoff's living room, and despite Hofmann's slow disintegration from alcoholism, Rachmaninoff still considered him to be "sky-high above Horowitz."[58]

Horowitz enjoyed spending a good part of every summer at the Palace Hotel on Lake Lucerne, just a ten-minute drive from Rachmaninoff's Villa Senar (an acronym derived from the first two letters of the composer's and his wife Natalia's first names, plus the R from Rachmaninoff). Built in 1931, Rachmaninoff's house was a modern, white brick-and-glass structure set on a cliff overlooking Lake Lucerne, his permanent and beloved home until 1939, when he left Switzerland for the United States. Rachmaninoff liked to know that friends and colleagues were nearby, but not so close that they would invade his privacy. In Lucerne, Horowitz reveled in his close proximity to Rachmaninoff and was flattered when the older man would consult him on a work-in-progress. For instance, in 1934, when composing his *Rhapsody on a Theme of Paganini,* Rachmaninoff telephoned him nearly every day: "I have a new variation to play for you," he would announce. The composer's caustic humor about his own works endlessly amused Horowitz. "I have composed this one for my manager," he joked about the eighteenth variation. "Well, maybe this will save the piece."[59]

The young pianist spent as much time with Rachmaninoff as possible. He was a frequent dinner guest and, like Rachmaninoff, much enjoyed dining with the family in the leisurely Russian manner. Certainly an important element of their friendship was their common heritage. Rachmaninoff loved everything Russian and had remained faithful to the language, customs, and holidays of his grievously missed homeland. His frequent depressions—in fact, the melancholy for which he was legendary—were largely the result of an acute homesickness, which only increased as the years passed. Some of his friends regarded Rachmaninoff as the saddest man they had ever known, and a few thought that they had never seen him smile. "He was a very gloomy man," recalled Horowitz, "and was not easy to approach."[60] Indeed, Rachmaninoff presented a formidable demeanor: his monklike tonsure, the manner in which his thick Slavic lips curled downward at the edges, the deep creases of his brow and face. Igor Stravinsky was given to describing his colleague as "a six-and-a-half-foot-tall scowl," and Rachmaninoff's eyes gave the uncomfortable impression that whatever light had once glowed there had long ago been replaced by world-weariness.

The dour Rachmaninoff seemed an unlikely personality to help anyone in the throes of physical and psychological collapse. But he and Horowitz shared more than national heritage and musical temperaments. Rachmaninoff empathized with Horowitz's plight because nearly forty years earlier he had experienced a similar breakdown. Extremely shy and self-critical, Rachmaninoff had been prone to depression even as a young man. In 1897, after listening to the badly executed premiere performance of his First Symphony and experiencing the lashes of the critics, Rachmaninoff suffered a nervous collapse. Eventually seeking help, in 1900 he had gone to a celebrated Moscow neurologist and hypnotist, Dr. Nicolai Dahl, who spent many hours telling him, over and over, "You will compose again. You will write with great facility."[61] Soon Rachmaninoff regained confidence in himself to such a degree that he produced his Second Piano Concerto which, in gratitude, he dedicated to Dahl.

So Rachmaninoff understood quite well Horowitz's anguish and feelings of inadequacy, and was willing to help in whatever way he could, even writing to Dr. Dahl to inquire about possible treatments for "a sick person"[62] suffering from neurological-psychosomatic disorders. Sedentary, Horowitz had become overweight and his health remained precarious. It was said that he was convinced that if he played in public again his fingers would become like glass, and break. Rachmaninoff listened to his fears with compassion, all the while softly assuring him that they were imaginary, and Horowitz paid attention as he would not have with anyone else. In later years, after Rachmaninoff's death, Horowitz would sometimes say with great emotion, "The man was like a father to me!"[63]

During his illness, Horowitz was also aided by the friendly ministrations of pianist Rudolf Serkin and Serkin's father-in-law, violinist Adolf Busch. In April 1937, Horowitz had begun to practice sporadically and he took a short trip to Basel to visit Serkin and Busch. Recalled Serkin, "I saw Horowitz almost every day, and he was exhausted at this time.

Still, we played a lot of two-piano music—Reger and Rachmaninoff. He was a fantastic sight reader. During one of his visits, I caught him practicing the fugue of Beethoven's *Hammerklavier* Sonata. It was incredibly beautiful. Horowitz was phenomenal, but he didn't think that much of himself."[64]

After returning to Bertenstein, Horowitz continued practicing and also playing four-hand music with Rachmaninoff—anything from Haydn symphonies to Godowsky transcriptions. The composer encouraged these sessions, which he hoped would distract Horowitz's mind from his physical condition, and he asked Wanda to keep him informed about all aspects of medical treatments. At that time, Rachmaninoff was suffering from what was then thought to be sclerosis but was later diagnosed as cancer, which caused muscular and skeletal ailments and difficulty in walking. But not even arthritis in his hands had deterred him from planning a full 1937–38 concert season, and his example was an important factor in Horowitz's decision to return to the stage the following year.

As part of Horowitz's treatment, Rachmaninoff recommended long walks, declaring that if one didn't walk, one's fingers "would not run."[65] He also encouraged him to reexamine the Russians, insisting repeatedly, "Tchaikovsky is the greatest Russian composer. He has enough melodies for hundreds of composers."[66] Horowitz would become animated during lively discussions with Rachmaninoff about music. "Rachmaninoff and I had a tremendous affinity of conception,"[67] Horowitz said. Sometimes they talked about Rachmaninoff's Third Concerto, and the composer would pencil in phrasings and possible cuts in Horowitz's score.

Horowitz also adored gossip about other pianists. Once, Rachmaninoff delighted him by recalling the time, in 1935, when he was listening on the radio to someone playing the Chopin Etudes with a multitude of wrong notes. "It happened to be Cortot, who soon began to rubato-ize. Rachmaninoff laughed: 'Cortot is *so* musical. The more difficult the etude, the more sentimental he gets. Isn't that so, Gorovitz?' he would say."[68]

Rachmaninoff also gave Horowitz much practical advice about concertizing. "Look to see if the gallery is full. That is the real public. When the boxes are full, they go because they have to do it—Society!"[69] He advised Horowitz to play some concerts in the afternoon, when his energy level was at its peak, a practice he would exclusively subscribe to in the later years of his career. Rachmaninoff also encouraged Horowitz to search for unhackneyed repertory for his concerts. His reserve gone, in all of his advice, Rachmaninoff revealed himself a true friend. "He was the most emotional pianist I ever knew," Horowitz remembered. "He told me, 'I'm always crying; I'm too sentimental.' You can hear it in his music and he played like that."[70]

Rachmaninoff's effect on Horowitz was enormous, and he eventually persuaded him to try playing in public again. He suggested that Horowitz return to France and initially perform in small towns where he was unknown. He would then quickly see that there was nothing the matter with either his hands or his endurance, and could gradually reacclimatize himself to the concert platform without pressure from critics. "There are three kinds of critics," Rachmaninoff told Horowitz, in an effort to defuse the pianist's fear of them. "The first kind cheat and sleep very well; the second kind cheat but sleep badly; and the third kind are honest and good and you never read them because they are not printed!" Years later, Horowitz mused: "Very cynical, but this is a little true."[71]

On October 1, 1937, Horowitz's thirty-fourth birthday, he gave a private concert at his sister-in-law Wally's home in Venice. Both she and Wanda urged him to heed Rachmaninoff, and he agreed to play again the following season. For one thing, he realized that his long absence was hurting his career. There were repeated rumors of "insanity, suicide, or death," even though he was now spending time in Paris and Milan with Wanda and Sonia. In July 1938, while listening to a radio broadcast from his house in Lucerne, Horowitz was startled to hear a news report that was printed in the Paris *Figaro* not long after: "We wish to announce the passing of Vladimir Horowitz, one of the most famous pianists who ever lived. He was born in Kiev, Russia, and his interpretations of Chopin and Liszt are in the memory of all who heard him. Horowitz suffered for two years from an incurable malady. The deceased was the son-in-law of Toscanini."[72]

This was followed the next day by an obituary in one of the largest Swiss newspapers. Wanda had been delegated the task of disclaiming rumors, and it was she who telephoned the newspapers and corrected the incredible error. Noting Horowitz had had an unusually long convalescence after his appendectomy, she stated that "he is now fully recovered and all rumors that he will be unable to resume his career are ridiculous."[73] Thus a few days after Horowitz's obituary appeared, European newspapers were compelled to print retractions: "Contrary to published news, the famous pianist Vladimir Horowitz is far from having been affected by an incurable malady," wrote one. "He has wonderfully recovered from an operation of appendicitis and is now preparing to renew his concert activities in October."[74]

Horowitz's return to the stage occurred in Zurich on September 26, 1938, at a charity concert for refugee children which he shared with the Busch String Quartet. Although Horowitz's portion of the program was to consist only of the Schumann Fantasy, at the last moment he substituted a group of Chopin pieces that he had performed frequently—the *Polonaise Fantasie, Barcarolle,* and several etudes. With Rachmaninoff in the audience, Horowitz felt ill at ease. He seems to have played well, however, and was welcomed back with favorable notices, which applauded his "virtuoso elegance and noble musicality."[75] Not long after, Horowitz scheduled concerts for 1938–39. "In contrast to earlier," he told local managers, "I now want to take a few days off between concerts. It's necessary. It's not the playing of the fingers, but rather the things your heart gives to the music which demands so much. For that reason I want to put this limitation on myself."[76]

Taking Rachmaninoff's advice, Horowitz decided to begin his tour in smaller cities such as Monte Carlo, Marseilles, St.-Étienne, and Lyons in December 1938 and January 1939, saving his two major solo recitals in Paris for February and March. Almost immediately, the practical problems involved with touring asserted themselves. In France the quality of pianos was in general quite poor and the cost of shipping good instruments to the lesser cities was high. Horowitz wanted to have two or three decent Steinway concert grands shipped from Paris to the provinces and to have his favorite concert grand in London sent to Paris for his solo recitals, but the cost was prohibitive. After the three-year hiatus, with no income and high medical bills, Horowitz was feeling a severe financial strain, as was reflected in his letters to Alexander Greiner at Steinway in New York. He asked for help, explaining that it was impossible for him to assume the full cost of shipping pianos, especially in view of the low fees he was offered in cities outside Paris. "I am not writing to intimidate you," Horowitz said, "but to ask for help (which is also connected with financial difficulties); I am writing also because of the concern with artistic *higher* principles."[77]

The rather aggressive tone resulted from Horowitz's realization that Steinway did not "have a real interest on the Continent in the countries where I want to or can play." Because he was Jewish, Germany was out of the question, and because he was Toscanini's son-in-law, it was danger-ous to appear in Italy. His engagements that season were therefore cen-tered in France, Switzerland, Holland, Belgium, and Scandinavia. He knew that a pool of excellent instruments was available in Switzerland and Holland, but he pointed out to Greiner that "in all of France exist only two or three Steinway concert grands, and these instruments are al-ready twelve years old and in very bad condition so I cannot really con-sider them as Steinways." Horowitz proposed that Steinway split the cost of shipping the pianos with him, as they had always done in America. He reminded Greiner that "from the first days I played in France only the Steinway, when all your great drawing artists were playing other firms. In those times all the French firms like Gaveau [and] Pleyel were offering money to me if I played their instruments. I refused it and I must say that in those days that money would have been very welcomed from me!! And now, my dear friend, what have I to do? After having played for twelve years in France the Steinway, and after an intermission of three years, you will force me, if you refuse, to see under my eyes during the playing a different name of firm "[78] The threat was understood, Greiner conveyed Horowitz's message to the Steinway family, and the request was approved.

During Horowitz's first round of concerts in late 1939, he discovered that he was more out of shape than he had imagined. "To my great cha-grin I did not have a chance to listen to you this evening," he wrote to Rachmaninoff at one point. "When I returned to Gstaad and resumed my piano work I realized that my musical affairs were in a very deplorable state. Therefore, I cannot miss even one day of work."[79]

To others, however, Horowitz presented a new self-confidence and en-thusiasm. "I seem to have completely recovered," he wrote Greiner, "and little by little I start to give concerts. I enjoy giving public performances and it seems to me (and up until now I have never been mistaken) that my musical outlook has undergone a great change."[80] In press interviews, Horowitz asserted that during his "retirement" he had made new discov-eries about music and about himself. "I will say," he told one reporter, "that in the many months when I didn't play I learned a great deal about music, perhaps more than I could have learned if I had been forced to practice every available minute, then jump on a train and give a concert. I could get outside, mentally speaking, of my music. I could contemplate it from a new point of orientation and I could see things about the forest, which, so to speak, I had not been able to perceive on account of the leaves. I had played certain works so often that I couldn't hear them anymore. During the break, I had nothing to do except rest and concentrate on music, music itself. I was able to bring myself into direct contact with it without any of the ulterior considerations which are inevitable when one knows that, within a few days, or a few weeks, he is going to play it before an audience. I think I grew as an artist. I needed to regain not only health but strength. It is impossible for anyone to play well without it. I do not mean that in order to hammer a piano loud enough it is necessary to be a giant. There are even brawny persons who only have a small tone and small people who draw a big sonority from the instrument. But it must be *your* tone, born of your special strength, physique, temperament, and unless there is the reserve of health back of it, you cannot carry your intention to your audience."[81]

Indeed, the first thing audiences and critics noticed about the new Horowitz was a change in his physical appearance. Wrote an observer: "Good healthy flesh has filled out his meager frame, although he is still far from being overweight; his face has lost the drawn and tired look which I remember so vividly from previous meetings with him, and he has obviously discovered how to be a reasonably happy human being while continuing to meet the demands imposed upon him by his gifts. Genius sometimes consumes its possessor, unless he has the physical and spiritual strength to keep it in balance. During his long retirement, Horowitz has found that strength."[82]

Despite his renewed physical vitality and his assertion that he was "spiritually replenished," many perceived no significant change in his playing except that his clean-edged virtuosity and concentration onstage were not unmarred by fatigue or boredom. "It is impossible to say that his playing was coming more from within, or was more charged with spirituality," wrote one astute critic. "During those years of reflection, he did not arrive at a more intimate approach to the spirit of the great composers. His interpretation of Beethoven was still as cold, and his way of playing Chopin [had] lost nothing of its dazzling and frivolous elegance."[83]

Some thought Horowitz's playing had grown worse. The Amsterdam newspaper *De Telegraaf,* for instance, remarked that "the introductory Scarlatti sonatas usually would have sounded elegant, with typical dryness of pedal and with a sharp and business-like finesse, but now they sound cruel. Every accent got a sharp, raw rap, so hard that the string grinds, so merciless that it seemed as if metal was being pounded against metal—an iron hammer with all its strength upon a naked, iron anvil. The objectivity seems to have taken on something possessed. Scarlatti's flourishing joy now contains something demonic. In other repertoire, no change was forthcoming. One felt like a pain, sometimes even as an irritation, the hardness in each piece that undercut the romanticism and emotion of works like the *Sonetto del Petrarca* of Liszt—which was not understood. One piece that symbolized the change was a mazurka of Chopin which was played with a distressing tone, bitter nostalgia, hardly the magnificent sonority remembered, but now tortured."[84]

After Horowitz's first few appearances, he became more relaxed, and even if his playing did not always reflect a deepened spirituality, his technical achievements—the amazing speed, the kaleidoscopic range of colors—remained undimmed. "His use of the pedal," wrote a Rotterdam critic, "is perhaps the biggest secret because it is practically unnoticeable in fast passages—he can isolate timbres (which usually flow together when played by every other pianist) and at the same time he can achieve a *legato* that makes each melodic line absolutely fluid."[85] It was the sensuousness of Horowitz's playing that was new and that accounted for its "sheer witchery" according to the London *Times,* which concluded that "the intellect with him plays a secondary role."[86] Horowitz's return was an enormous success with his audiences. He was still, as the *Times* put it, "a magical presence."

For his four most important engagements of the season—two recitals in London and two in Paris—Horowitz chose a program of Scarlatti sonatas, Debussy etudes, Chopin (the *Barcarolle,* etudes, mazurkas, A-flat Major Impromptu), Brahms (*Paganini* Variations), and Liszt (*Sonetto del Petrarca,* No. 104, *Au bord d'une source, Paganini* Etude in E-flat Major). New repertory included a Fauré nocturne, the Beethoven Sonata in E-flat Major, Op. 31, No. 3, and the Schumann Fantasy. If Horowitz's claim to a new maturity was to be taken seriously, the test was the Schumann, a demanding landmark of the nineteenth-century piano literature. That he had meticulously studied the work was obvious at his Queen's Hall recital on February 29, where "not only his finger work but every aspect of the pianist's technique, every phrase and gradation of tone" was found to be "controlled and employed to contribute to his thoroughly thought-out conception of the work."[87]

When he subsequently played the Schumann at his Paris recital, the

New York Times sent its music correspondent, Herbert E. Peyser, to judge whether Horowitz's playing had actually changed, in anticipation of an American tour the next season. Peyser reported that the Schumann Fantasy "was a singularly uneven performance with moments of eloquence and beauty offset by others curiously exaggerated and willful. Considering he had just returned to the stage after a long absence, the old qualities may return. The Christmas-tree glitter and fascinating shimmer are still evident though not as consistently as before."[88]

If Horowitz's success with critics was mixed, his popularity with audiences was as notable as ever. After all the surmises that he would never play again, concertgoers in Paris and London now clamored for tickets. With many critics saluting him as "a changed and greater artist," the recitals quickly sold out. Half an hour prior to the concert at the Salle Pleyel, "the junction of Faubourg St. Honoré and Avenue Hoche looked like a tolerable imitation of an opening night at the Metropolitan,"[89] wrote Peyser. Horowitz ended each recital with his *Carmen* Fantasy, and his fans behaved with characteristic abandon. "Whatever new elements critics may have detected," said *Le Figaro,* "the general public appeared to see in the popular artist just about what it has always seen. And for thousands this will undoubtedly be welcome news."[90]

Horowitz was in excellent spirits. He spoke admiringly of "his young, charming wife"[91] and expressed interest in the raising of his four-year-old daughter, Sonia. He promised he would make other transcriptions to equal *Carmen* and looked forward to recording the Brahms Second Concerto with the BBC Orchestra under Toscanini, if the Maestro's schedule permitted. During this time Horowitz kept Greiner posted, writing excitedly on one occasion: "I already played a recital at The Hague and the success was enormous! All the critics and public are saying that my playing and my musical conception has attained a new height of achievement. I will say that I feel a great change in all myself and I see that all the time I was kept away from the platform was not lost but went to the profit of my art."[92]

His confidence restored, Horowitz thought of increasing the number of his engagements. With concert fees low and only a handful of appearances expedient in Europe because of political tensions, Horowitz badly wanted to tour the United States during the 1939–40 season. He signed a contract with Judson to present twenty concerts for the period of January to April, and requested from Greiner "a great choice of good instruments," especially "the piano with the signature of Rachmaninoff which I played during my last season in America."[93] Although Wanda wanted Sonia to grow up in France and loved spending time with her family in Milan, it was increasingly evident that the Toscaninis would be in danger if they remained in Europe.

From the time of Benito Mussolini's ascent to power in 1922, Toscanini had repeatedly defied the Italian dictator, refusing to display Mussolini's photograph at La Scala or to perform the Fascist party hymn, the "Giovinezza," at the opera. "If I were capable of killing a man, I would kill Mussolini,"[94] the Maestro raged to a friend. Using his position as Italy's premier musician, Toscanini took every opportunity to embarrass the *Duce* and his government, most dramatically in May 1931, at the Teatro Comunale in Bologna. On that occasion, Toscanini was instructed to begin the program with the "Giovinezza," and, as always, refused. That evening, when he and Carla arrived at the theater, they were, in Toscanini's own words, "attacked, injured and repeatedly hit in the face by an unspeakable gang."[95] Mussolini despised Toscanini and after this incident had the conductor's Via Durini home in Milan placed under constant surveillance and his telephone tapped. Moreover, in 1931 and again in 1938, Toscanini's passport was taken away and only returned after an uproar in the world press. In the government-controlled Italian newspapers, there was little to be found about the Maestro unless there was occasion to insult him, and when Toscanini attacked Mussolini's anti-Semitic policy, he was viciously denounced as "The Honorary Jew."[96] In August 1939, in Lucerne, Toscanini came to the conclusion that it was unwise for him or his family to return to Italy.

Horowitz also spent the summer of 1939, his last in Europe, in Lucerne, relaxing with his family. He was preparing for an August 29 performance of the Brahms Second Concerto with Toscanini at the Lucerne Festival, which had been organized the previous year as an alternative to the Salzburg Festival, in which many musicians were either unable or unwilling to play. A Swiss Festival Orchestra was formed with members of the Busch Quartet as string-section leaders and five of Switzerland's other leading quartets in the ranks. The festival had expanded in its second year, and a distinguished group of artist-refugees gathered together in neutral Switzerland for it. Rachmaninoff, Pablo Casals, Bruno Walter, Adrian Boult, Rudolf Serkin, Willem Mengelberg, Emanuel Feuermann and Bronislaw Huberman joined Toscanini and Horowitz in what turned out to be a musical farewell to Europe. The mood was grim; a sense of impending catastrophe was in the air.

For Horowitz's appearance, the Mozart A Major Concerto, K. 488, had originally been chosen. But ticket prices at Lucerne's Kunsthaus were scaled extraordinarily high in an effort to raise money to aid political refugees, and both Toscanini and Horowitz agreed that "you raise more money with Romantic music than with Classical."[97] Horowitz therefore decided to play the Brahms B-flat Major Concerto, and sure enough, the hall was filled to capacity. The performance was a success. "His playing had passion, strength and in the *Andante* poetic serenity of a very exalted order," wrote one American critic who was present. "The impression left was profound and the pianist was wildly acclaimed."[98]

Three days after the concert, on September 1, 1939, Germany invaded Poland. Rachmaninoff had already left Europe on August 23, and Toscanini and his family sailed for the United States in early September. Until World War II ended, the Maestro would not conduct again in Europe, while Horowitz would not return until eleven years later. Ever since the pianist had left Russia, he had had no real roots and no genuine citizenship. Over the next thirteen years, America became his adopted land, the setting for perhaps the most productive periods of his professional life.

PART THREE
1940 ~ 1952

CHAPTER TWELVE

TOURING ON
THE SUPER CHIEF

*"What I saw in the front row was sometimes terrible and
spoiled the whole concert. There was once a woman who shook
her head at everything I did. An old woman. Everything I did,
she disapproved. She came backstage afterwards and I saw she
had a nervous tic. And in Milwaukee, there was a
three-hundred-pound man sitting back in his seat with his legs
stretched out, picking his nose. I was to begin with Beethoven
and was in a rage. So I sat down on the bench, put my legs
apart, and stared straight at him. Nobody understood what
was going on. He became red. I wasn't embarrassed."*[1]

In the autumn of 1939, Horowitz, Wanda, and five-year-old Sonia
moved into an unfurnished rented house in Fieldston, New York, ten
minutes from Villa Pauline, the Toscanini residence in Riverdale. After
living in Lucerne and Paris for four years, Horowitz may have found
Fieldston a bit dull, yet he seemed to prefer it to the frenetic pace of
Manhattan. "New York? No! I hate that crazy place. I like the country
best."[2] As Horowitz planned his December programs, Wanda and her
mother indulged their passion for shopping while settling into their new
homes. Returning to America with the Horowitzes under that September's immigration quota, the exiled Maestro and his wife had decided to
move from their usual New York headquarters in the Hotel Astor to the
more peaceful environment of a five-acre estate just north of the city.
Toscanini wanted his family close to him, and while Wally had decided
to remain in Italy, the rest of the Toscanini clan was now in the United
States. Wanda's brother, Walter, had settled with his wife and son, Walfredo, in Camden, New Jersey, and was working, thanks to "Papa," for
RCA Victor Records. If Horowitz had any qualms about living in such
close proximity to his in-laws after the relative seclusion of Switzerland,

he would find that it was only a temporary situation. A year later, the Fieldston house was abandoned as Horowitz once again took to the road.

In the meantime, the Horowitzes spent most of their time at Villa Pauline, an imposing house with a dark wood-paneled central hall, enormous parlor, library, and a glass-enclosed sun-room and external balcony. From Toscanini's second-floor study, he could survey the entire estate, down to the Hudson River and across to the New Jersey Palisades. At seventy-three, the Maestro, as vigorous as ever, was absorbed in his plans for the NBC Orchestra and his new membership in the Mazzini Society, comprised of Italian expatriates who planned to establish a democratic Italian republic upon the fall of Mussolini.

Still, he always had time for Sonia, who had inherited her father's naughty humor and her grandfather's independent will. Toscanini adored his granddaughter and insisted on supervising every aspect of her upbringing. The dark-haired little girl bore a resemblance to his side of the family: She had inherited Wanda's olive complexion and the Maestro's penetrating eyes. Her serious, intense expression was also strikingly similar to her grandfather's, and "Nono," as he was called, reveled in Sonia's irreverent behavior. Often, when Horowitz came to Villa Pauline to practice, Sonia danced merrily to her father's playing, yet would resolutely decline to do so when Toscanini was at the keyboard because, she once said, "he plays so badly."[3] For weeks afterward, Toscanini delightedly told colleagues that his granddaughter had pronounced him "not such a hot pianist."[4]

To carry on the Toscanini musical tradition, Sonia began piano lessons that fall. A member of the NBC Orchestra had recommended a student from the Juilliard School to be her teacher, and when the young man arrived at Villa Pauline, the door was answered by Horowitz, who took the wide-eyed pianist into the living room to introduce him to his new pupil. Also present was Toscanini, comfortably positioned in an easy chair. The boy was quite terrified by the idea of "teaching" before the two musical giants. "You're not going to stay here now, are you?" he pleaded. Horowitz responded, "Yes. I'm the father and he's the grandfather. We stay!"[5]

Sonia was also a regular visitor to Studio 8-H in the RCA Building, where the NBC Orchestra performed. There, she observed her grandfather's temper in full force. As Toscanini rehearsed a Beethoven work for his third season with the orchestra, Sonia sat transfixed in the empty studio. Suddenly, the orchestra made a mistake and Toscanini directed a tirade of abuse at the musicians. Sonia listened to the outburst and inquired calmly and audibly, "Why don't those musicians talk back to Nono? If they don't agree with him, why don't they just walk out? I would."[6] On another occasion, a few years later, Horowitz and Toscanini were rehearsing the Tchaikovsky Concerto and Sonia's account of the performance became a stock family joke. "Papa just sat there and didn't do anything a lot of the time," the high-spirited girl observed. "But Grandpa stood up and worked hard all the time!"[7]

During that fall of 1939, both musicians were working especially hard. After a five-year absence from the concert platform in the United States and only a modest roster of European appearances in 1938 and 1939, Horowitz was nervous about the upcoming season. He did not, however, have any intention of resuming the backbreaking schedule he had abandoned in 1935. "Before thirty no man knows how to live," Horowitz told the press, adding that his appearances would be limited to those he felt he could undertake "with a genuine sense of joy and fulfillment. Two or three concerts a week is enough playing."[8]

To satisfy public curiosity after his absence, Arthur Judson did everything possible to spruce up Horowitz's image in press releases, and to project him as a vastly matured artist: "Horowitz is still in his thirties, a simple, natural person, without affectation, who has traveled a long way from the very young man who loved loud ties, luxurious bathrobes and elaborate automobiles."[9] Horowitz was now portrayed as an art collector and a family man, a connoisseur of literature (Racine, Molière, Tolstoy)—and to round out the image, as a devotee of detective stories, especially while traveling on trains. His press book continued: "He collects old boxes, a small but rare group of gold, lapis and enamel boxes. . . . The prize of the collection [consists of] boxes once owned by Empresses Catherine and Elizabeth of Russia; others are precious examples from the Napoleonic and Louis XVI periods. They are all lit by a lamp which has nothing but sentimental value for Horowitz. Its shade is composed of color photographs of a small, dark, curly-haired girl, sitting on the floor with her legs straight out before her . . . Sonia Toscanini Horowitz."[10]

Describing his musical tastes, Horowitz asserted in interviews that little music beyond Debussy or Ravel interested him or seemed worth playing. Bemoaning the fact that contemporary composers were employing the piano "as an instrument of percussion, to be beaten or whacked in order to make rhythm," Horowitz declared his new programs would reflect his Romantic ideal "because I feel that romantic things are badly needed. I'd like to give people something that they don't find in their daily lives nowadays. Our time, our kind of life, does not inspire romantic music. I do not say that is unfortunate, however, because it is very possible that it will inspire other kinds of music, equally good."[11] Horowitz also maintained that he was on the lookout for "the great American composer," and conjectured that such a man would probably come "from the folk culture of the country." He often said, "The Skyscraper, now there's a great American theme. Someone should write a musical piece about that."[12] (In fact, John Alden Carpenter had composed *Skyscraper Suite* ten years earlier.)

Horowitz's abbreviated itinerary for 1940 reflected his desire not to overwork. Still in the process of reacclimatizing himself to giving concerts, he planned three recitals in California for December, even before the "official" opening of his tour at the Mosque Theater in Newark, New Jersey, on January 17. Only after appearances in Cleveland, Toronto, and Philadelphia would Horowitz face a New York audience at his Carnegie Hall recital on January 31.

Horowitz now claimed to be more concerned with poetry than pyrotechnics, but his programs over the next several years were not markedly different from those of the past. They still demonstrated a slavish determination to play repertory that would be the most effective for large halls. Continuing to avoid Bach, Mozart, and Haydn, Horowitz rationalized that "the smaller pieces of the 18th century would not either fill a hall from the standpoint of effect, or prove sufficiently attractive to the audiences."[13] Likewise, with the exception of the E-flat Major Sonata, Op. 31, No. 3, Horowitz avoided Beethoven, stating that Beethoven's sonatas "have drawn me very much, though I would seldom try to play them in public, since the musical thought, partly on account of Beethoven's bad piano writing, remains inaccessible to the majority of listeners."[14] To many critics, playing Scarlatti and Mendelssohn but ignoring Haydn, Mozart, and Beethoven was untenable—"in all ways ridiculous," huffed B. H. Haggin in *The Nation*.[15]

The January 31 Carnegie Hall recital was sold out a full month in advance, and the audience that evening greeted Horowitz enthusiastically. After taking his place at the piano, Horowitz then had to rise for an extra bow before beginning the program of Mendelssohn, Schumann, Chopin,

Debussy, and Bizet-Horowitz (the *Carmen* Variations, which he had re-vised in 1937). Olin Downes, in the *New York Times,* failed to detect any dramatic change in Horowitz's playing, emphasizing in his review the coruscating technical resources which made the Chopin etudes and *Carmen* the highlights of the evening. Downes was reserved about the understated dynamics and excessive rubato evident in the Schu-mann Fantasy, though most other critics detected in his interpreta-tion hints of more profound musicality and emotional sensitivity than before. Francis Perkins of the *Herald Tribune,* for instance, noted the "matured interpretative powers ... and exceptional ability to convey his hearers into a desired imaginative atmosphere. His technique was convincingly revealed as the instrument of a fully integrated expressive artistry."[16]

The second high point of the season was Horowitz's February 15 per-formance of the Rachmaninoff Third Concerto, with the New York Philharmonic under John Barbirolli. The critics were unanimously laud-atory. "Even five years ago when the pianist last appeared here with or-chestra, he was miles from the goal now attained," stated Downes. "Mr. Horowitz brings to [Rachmaninoff's] works a maturity of understand-ing, a depth of human feeling and a glory of highly sensitized tone that give his playing entirely different and exceedingly greater values."[17] An-other critic wrote that "even the composer's own superb interpretation of the same work earlier in the season with the Philadelphia Orchestra was not its peer in fiery intensity and irresistible sweep."[18] The evening was a special triumph for Horowitz since Rachmaninoff himself was an appre-ciative member of the audience.

Another performance with Barbirolli followed on March 30, with Horowitz playing the Tchaikovsky Concerto in commemoration of the composer's centenary. Horowitz then retreated to his home in Fieldston to make final preparations for his second Carnegie Hall recital on April 12, which featured the Chopin *Funeral March* Sonata, the Beethoven So-nata, Op. 31, No. 3, and an assortment of Chopin, Liszt, and Ravel. Once again, the evening's fireworks were provided by the *Carmen* Fantasy and also, in Horowitz's own adaptation, the Paganini-Liszt Etude in E Major. Despite a rainstorm, the house was packed.

Only the Beethoven was poorly received, "leaving even his warmest admirers at loose ends," according to the *Times.* "Nowhere did Mr. Horowitz display any keen understanding of its essential character of style or content."[19] But in Liszt's *Sonetto del Petrarca,* No. 104, *Au bord d'une source,* and the treacherously difficult *Feux Follets,* Horowitz played, said Olin Downes, "with breathtaking virtuosity [and] complete conviction to a degree not quite attained in the rest of the evening's contributions."[20]

The final major event of the 1939–40 season was a long-awaited performance of the Brahms Second Concerto with Toscanini and the NBC Symphony Orchestra. The benefit program, for the Greater New York Fund, took place at Carnegie Hall on May 6 and was broadcast live over the NBC radio network. RCA made a live recording of the event, which marked Horowitz's first recording session since 1936, his first in Carnegie Hall, and his first commercial recording of the music of Brahms. However, this was never issued, and three days later the Maestro, Horowitz, and the NBC Orchestra returned to Carnegie Hall to rerecord the work without an audience. It was this second version that became available. Since there is little difference between the two performances, it is likely that the first version was put aside for technical reasons related to the difficulty of recording in four-and-a-half-minute segments during the 78-rpm era. Pauses between segments and slight changes in the score were loathsome to Toscanini but essential to the engineers.

The concert performance was hailed as "magical" by Olin Downes in the *New York Times:* "Nothing Mr. Horowitz has done here has indicated more impressively his growth as interpreter as well as virtuoso of his instrument. What Horowitz achieved with the keyboard part . . . was something to make giddy the heads of those it most stirred and gratified."[21] Just as in their performance of the Brahms First Concerto five years earlier, Toscanini planned this reading, said Downes, with one purpose only—"the revelation of Brahms, and this with a cohesion, balance and precision of the interweaving parts of the piano and the orchestra past praise."[22]

"When I played the Brahms [Second] Concerto with Bruno Walter it was completely different," Horowitz said later. "Toscanini had his own conception and I followed it, even if it was sometimes against my own wishes. Toscanini was more Schumannesque, more romantic than Walter—more precise, more dynamic, stronger."[23] At the rehearsals, there had been little discussion between Toscanini and Horowitz, for the interpretation had already been carefully planned in Riverdale. "There was no dialogue," recalled orchestral violinist Edwin Bachmann. "The undercurrent was one of fear—Horowitz's fear of Toscanini."[24] Prominent among the few words that issued from Toscanini's mouth were *canta* (sing) and *vida* (life), and the results, with Toscanini holding sway over both his orchestra and son-in-law like a martinet, were memorable—a performance "of breath, masculinity and withal a heroic spirit which would have satisfied the composer," according to Olin Downes.[25]

The Brahms disc, released in 1941, was a tremendous commercial and critical success, displacing previous versions by Rubinstein and Schnabel. It was heralded as one of the most lifelike recordings ever made, with none of the dead qualities associated with the acoustics of Studio 8-H, where the NBC Orchestra usually recorded. For sheer visceral excitement, the mesh between Toscanini and Horowitz, in which neither artist overshadowed the other, seemed unbeatable. In addition, their crisp, clean, slightly nervous approach, with faster-than-usual tempi, allowed the Concerto's architectural lines to emerge clearly and with grandeur, even if some critics took issue with Toscanini's rigidity and Horowitz's unyielding tone. Naturally, the marketing executives at RCA Victor understood the immense draw of having both Horowitz and Toscanini together and immediately planned a second record, to be made the following spring, of the Tchaikovsky Concerto.

The Brahms performance in May 1940 was one of Horowitz's last appearances that season. A few weeks afterward, he accidentally caught his left hand in a door at the Fieldston house. Three physicians examined him, and concluded that he was suffering from "a traumatic tenosynovitis of the flexor digitorum sublimis and profundis muscle at the metacarpophalangeal joint"—or, as the *New York Tribune* translated: "Mr. Horowitz has an injured finger."[26] It was consequently necessary to cancel upcoming concerts at the Ravinia and Robin Hood Dell Festivals. Later that summer, hoping to fulfill a promised appearance at the Hollywood Bowl, Horowitz traveled as far as Colorado, but on August 10 canceled due to the continued inflammation of his hand. He retreated to Chicago to consult with Dr. Cottle, who continued to minister to his numerous physical ailments over the next fifteen years. Cottle advised Horowitz to cancel his autumn and early winter engagements and to resume playing only in the middle of January 1941. Almost at once, rumors began circulating about Horowitz's having suffered another nervous breakdown, periodically forcing him to assure the public that his hand was "constantly improving." Likewise, Judson's press releases stated that "the owner of one of the most valuable pairs of hands in the world can't be blamed for making doubly sure that they're at their maximum strength before he starts out."[27]

Meanwhile, Horowitz much enjoyed his relaxing stay in Chicago, for few friends meant as much to him as did Gitta and her husband. Gradually, he resumed practicing, as Wanda shuttled back and forth between Chicago and New York trying to tend to both husband and daughter. During Horowitz's return season in America, Wanda had traveled with Horowitz whenever possible. But he needed more attention than she could provide. Moreover, he sometimes seemed uncomfortable having her along on tour.

With thirty-two concerts booked for the winter and spring of 1941, it became apparent that Horowitz would need a steady companion. The idea of working with Merovitch was again broached, for the manager had spent some time with Horowitz during the short 1940 season, but their relationship, though cordial, remained strained. After the break, Merovitch had slowly worked himself into the role of advisory consultant, acting as a liaison between Horowitz, RCA Victor, and Columbia Management. Although this lasted until 1949, his status as "personal representative" was never restored. He was paid piecemeal for his work—$200 to $500 at a time—and not on a percentage basis. One of Merovitch's continuing responsibilities involved the planning of future foreign tours. During most of the 1940's, for instance, he attempted to arrange a South American tour with the impresario Ernesto de Quesada. After nine years of voluminous correspondence, it seemed as if Horowitz might finally make such a tour in the summer of 1948, but as had happened so many times in the past, he called it off at the last moment. In fact, the only trip he ever made south of the American border was to Havana, on December 7, 1949.

Merovitch was repeatedly embarrassed by having to cancel concerts, and although he never complained directly to Horowitz and tiptoed about in fear that his position might be further undermined, he did express irritation and frustration to others. "I am only an old, loyal friend of Horowitz and his advisor, when he needs, or better say, when he asks my advice," Merovitch wrote to Quesada on one occasion. "I do not control him."[28] After the cancellation of the South American tour, Merovitch, who suffered one of his two nervous collapses during this period, said sadly, "Once more I have lost for nothing so much time, energy and nerves."[29]

The emotionally volatile Merovitch was not the ideal person to fulfill the role of tour companion for Horowitz, so on November 28, 1940, a mysteriously worded advertisement appeared in the domestic-help-wanted section of the New York Times: "Traveling companion, secretary wanted for concert musician, one of the world's greatest artists. Please send résumé and photo."[30] Lowell Benedict, a twenty-one-year-old student who had been forced to leave college and return home to New York City to find work, answered the ad and remembered that "getting the job was the weirdest, most unbelievable circumstance in the world. It was the tail-end of the Depression. I got myself a chauffeur's license and took to reading the domestic-help section of the Times. Three weeks after I read about the 'famous musician,' I received a response from Wanda, who used an alias—'W. Martini, secretary to V. Horowitz'—an elusive reply, inviting me to the Hotel Park Crescent for an interview with her alone. At this, she told me that the position was a very responsible one and, though I wasn't terribly musical myself and was only vaguely aware of Horowitz's name, it seemed a terrific adventure for a young man." Wanda liked Benedict and introduced him to Horowitz, and with little more discussion the young man was hired "for the princely sum of twenty dollars a week."[31]

On January 8, Horowitz and Benedict left New York for the first recital of the season, in Chicago. During the extensive tour that followed, the two spent much of their time in trains and hotel rooms. "I thought the life of a traveling virtuoso must be the most glamorous in the world," said Benedict. "It was the Golden Age of trains, and their compartments, drawing rooms and bedrooms were extremely comfortable and beautiful. Before you hit your city on lengthy trips, the crack trains had a passenger agent who would come aboard to see if Mr. Horowitz was happy." Benedict quickly discovered that, often, Horowitz was not happy, that he was passive and inactive a good deal of the time. Wanda had instructed Benedict to keep her fully informed about her husband's health and state of mind. "He was," remembered Benedict, "extremely tense about concert touring, and performing was traumatic for him and required a great deal of effort. It was enough for him just to withstand traveling and playing. He did absolutely nothing else during those five months of the tour." Although Judson's publicity portrayed the pianist as an exuberant, active man who swam, collected art, read, and researched composers' manuscripts, Benedict soon learned the truth about

Horowitz: He did not play cards, go to the theater, read books, study music, or even practice. In earlier years, Horowitz had traveled with a dummy, or silent, keyboard, to keep his fingers in shape, but now he had abandoned that. Aside from rehearsal before a recital, Horowitz simply did not practice at all. "In fact, I packed his bags, and he didn't even travel with his music," said Benedict. "During the summer he prepared one program, and once it was tucked away in his mind, I can't recall his ever having any lapses of memory. He played the same things wherever he went and once the program was established he made no changes."

Horowitz explained to Benedict the difficulties in choosing a program that would appeal to audiences in Kansas City and Dallas as well as to the more sophisticated concertgoers of Chicago and New York. "He knew that many people in each audience were there only to show off their mink coats, but to his dismay, Horowitz found that many concertgoers in the lesser cities did not even recognize his name. Nevertheless, he would always throw in something a little avant-garde for that small portion of the really musical public. Structuring a recital was like architecture to him, and a very painful process. He was tremendously conscious of what his audience wanted, and he tried to present a program with something in it for everyone."

Horowitz liked to have long hours of conversation with Benedict and it was not long before the young man was his closest confidant. "We did an awful lot of talking," Benedict remembered, "and I discovered that one of the big reasons he chose me was because I was *not* a musician, and in fact knew very little about music. He didn't want a musician with him and preferred having somebody sort of neutral. He liked educating me during those long train rides. I knew that he studied during the summer because he would come up with details about the composers, their times, and the history of each composition. He knew all the letters that described their lives and work."

As Horowitz told Benedict of his past American tours, his dislike of Arthur Judson and the entire Columbia Management operation became apparent. He blamed Judson for the grueling schedule into which he had been forced ever since he first came to the United States. "Horowitz said they had been killing him with a concert almost every day, that sometimes he had even had to dress for them on the train. He swore he would never go through that kind of ordeal again." One concession Horowitz eventually had won from Judson was the guarantee that he would arrive in a given city the day before a concert and not have to leave until noon the following day. This was necessary because he had difficulty sleeping on trains and wanted a decent rest in a hotel before moving on to the next stop. ("Although he had been given sleeping pills, he took them very sparingly, because he didn't want to be fuzzy on the day of a concert," remembered Benedict. "He had fantastic self-discipline and was very aware of his body, like an athlete. To play well, he knew he had to be in peak physical condition.") But nonetheless, Horowitz remained resentful of Judson's high-handed manner and rattled off to Benedict a long list of complaints.

He hated performing in Columbia's Community Concerts series. Those engagements brought in too little money and tired him for his important appearances in the larger cities. Horowitz wanted to play fewer concerts and to receive higher fees for them, preferably with a reduction of Columbia's standard 20 percent commission. He had already won some concessions and now was not obligated to play everywhere his management wished, but he was still irritated by the manner in which he was treated by Columbia personnel. "There was absolute hysteria when he discussed Judson," said Benedict. "He felt that the people of Columbia were purely businessmen, venal capitalists with no regard for an artist of his stature. He recited the names of other artists, not only pianists, who had literally been played to death by Columbia."

Although Horowitz doubtless had justification for his negative feelings about Judson, his dislike had become an obsession, and he was convinced that Judson was coldly taking advantage of him. According to Benedict, Horowitz's paranoia on the subject was at least partly related to his attitude toward money. "When it came to his finances," he recalled, "Horowitz could be extremely penurious and was always delighted, for instance, when I was able to get him some shirts at a discount. He had a morbid fear of the stock market crashing again, so he never put his money into stocks. First, he spent it on expanding his snuff-box collection and later on French Impressionist paintings and the jewelry which Wanda often wore."

Horowitz had left Merovitch in charge of negotiating the details of his contract with Columbia for the 1941–42 season, but by January 27 he felt compelled to write Judson to express his "extreme surprise and considerable disappointment" that Columbia had chosen to disregard all of his proposals for the tour. Horowitz's threatening letter ends with the admonition to Judson that "you leave me no other choice but the painful alternative of abruptly terminating all of our plans and arrangements for the season 1941–42, and thereby ending, forever afterward, a business relationship which had endured, to our mutual pleasure and benefit, for nearly thirteen years."[32] Among the points of contention was Horowitz's desire for a guarantee of at least four Pacific Coast appearances and a guarantee that no press criticisms of his concerts would appear in his advertising material (he had been livid whenever this happened). He also insisted that the special 40 percent commission that Columbia wanted on Horowitz's Chicago engagements be eliminated. "I pay no commission to Columbia for Chicago recitals," Horowitz stated in a telegram to Merovitch.[33] Eventually, Merovitch's diplomacy yielded results, for Judson capitulated on all the demands.

As Horowitz and Benedict traveled around the country, their lives settled into a predictable pattern. After checking into a hotel and unpacking, an appointment was made through the local Steinway dealer for a piano tuner for one or the other of the three pianos shipped ahead by the company. When Horowitz arrived at the concert hall, the piano was already onstage and he then worked with the tuner on voicing it. He was extremely demanding about the placement of the instrument. Recalled Benedict: "It was usually put almost directly under the proscenium arch, but he would move it around to find the best acoustic."[34] After the rehearsal, Horowitz sometimes met with the local manager, whom he often found crude and unmusical. In Kansas City, for instance, the manager had Horowitz's piano positioned on a nightclub-like runway that jutted out from the stage, all so the audience could get a better look at his hands. Horowitz issued an ultimatum: "I'm not going to play unless you take that thing away!"[35]—and after an ugly scene with raised voices, the offending platform was removed.

By the evening of a concert, Horowitz was nervous. "He told me he had suffered from colitis in past years," said Benedict, "but although he carried a great many medications in his suitcase, he had no trouble with the affliction at this time. I would be with him backstage just before the concert to see that everything was in order. He was always extremely tense and perspiring. I tried in every way I knew to relax and comfort him but he was like a man about to jump into the rapids. He would grit his teeth as he went onto the stage." After the performance, Horowitz met with his fans in the greenroom. However, he did this only reluctantly, for he detested that part of the evening, much preferring to return immediately to the hotel, order dinner in his room, and seclude himself. He had never enjoyed autograph sessions, and sometimes Benedict took program books from admirers, had Horowitz autograph them on the train, and then mailed them back from the next tour city.

The day after a concert, Benedict always asked Horowitz what percentage of the audience he felt had understood the music. One of the pianist's amusements was rating his audiences in different cities, and Benedict had agreed to keep a log of percentages. After his recital in Ann Arbor on January 15, 1941, Horowitz gave a poor grade to students at the University of Michigan—only 40 percent, while Toledo scored 60 percent and the students at Oberlin College an impressive 80 percent. Two performances of the Tchaikovsky Concerto with the Detroit Symphony under George Szell rated a 70 and 80 percent, and so on: Chicago, 75; Denver, 60; Portland, 70; Seattle, 75; Spokane, 70; San Francisco, 50. Although Horowitz was quite pleased with his playing in San Francisco, its Opera House had not been entirely sold out (at his West Coast recitals the previous year attendance had been even worse). Clearly, after the five-year hiatus, Horowitz needed to rebuild his audiences in many parts of the country.

His February 18 Los Angeles recital was received with great enthusiasm, and there he rated the audience an unprecedented 85 percent. Thereafter he became bored with his ratings game and discontinued it during less glamorous engagements in Pasadena, Dallas, Houston, and Kansas City. Kansas City was one of Horowitz's least favorite stops, with a hall only half filled and a local manager pointedly blaming this on his long absence. The critics there were also less generous than in other cities, calling attention to, in the words of the *Kansas City Times,* Horowitz's "frail and nervous demeanor on stage, often crouched on the piano-bench, his body stooped above the keyboard."[36] Exaggerated pauses and lagging tempi were blamed on the pianist's nervous fatigue, and the *Times* unkindly concluded that "the marks of his illness are still upon him."

The major events of the spring of 1941 were a Carnegie Hall recital on March 19 and an April 19 appearance with Toscanini and the NBC Symphony. This would be Horowitz's first performance of the Tchaikovsky Concerto with the Maestro, observing the fiftieth anniversary of the composer's 1891 visit to the United States for the opening of Carnegie

Hall. For March 19, Horowitz programmed the Liszt Sonata, the Beethoven Thirty-two Variations, the Schumann *Arabesque,* a Chopin group,
and a new offering, *Six Short Etudes,* Op. 19, by the contemporary composer Valery Jelobinsky. (These last, "pleasant trifles"[37] according to one
notice, were apathetically received, and Horowitz never repeated them
after that season.) The pianist's tonal coloring, variegated dynamic palette, and digital wizardry were evident in everything he did, and in preparation for the Liszt and the Chopin A-flat Major Polonaise, Bill Hupfer,
the chief Steinway tuner, voiced his piano to provide a brilliant treble—
"too brilliant for comfort," said one critic, concluding that the resulting
tone, though glittering, lacked "the depth and heroism which prevented
him from attaining truly stirring climaxes."[38]

Horowitz had had to steel himself for this Carnegie Hall recital, and
New York critics noted the same tension that others had commented on
during the tour. He was, in fact, so anxious that he begged Toscanini not
to attend. The Maestro had promised to remain in Riverdale that evening, but after the performance Horowitz found him in the greenroom
thumping away on the piano with a big grin on his face.

At rehearsals of the Tchaikovsky Concerto that followed not long
after, Toscanini's well-known iron will was evident. Although Horowitz
believed that many aspects of the Maestro's interpretation were faultless,
he disagreed with a few of his tempi, and according to Benedict, he was
able "to gently persuade the old man to give in on some points."[39]
Rumors circulated that Horowitz's demanding father-in-law had exhausted him during those rigorous rehearsals—so much so that by the
end of the season Horowitz had "to seek the sheltering walls of a nerve
clinic,"[40] according to Joachim Kaiser in his book *Great Pianists of Our
Time.* Although Horowitz did admit to Benedict that there had been "a
slight bit of electricity" between himself and the Maestro, there were no
outward displays of anger or disagreement at the rehearsals nor even any
dialogue, for in large part Horowitz capitulated to Toscanini. But although Toscanini viewed the Concerto symphonically and worked to
make the orchestral part as interesting as the solo, it was Horowitz who
carried the evening, according to the *New York Times,* with a "truly stupendous exhibition of pianism, as emotionally expansive as it was amazing in its tonal hues and subtlety of nuance."[41]

The performance, broadcast live but not recorded, was repeated on
May 6 and 14 for the Victor microphones. After listening to the master

disc of the second session, Horowitz pointed out, at the beginning of the scherzo, one omitted note which was almost impossible to detect, and insisted that the error be repaired by mixing in the same note from the first session. Doing so was a matter of considerable difficulty in those days before the advent of tape and splicing, but it was eventually accomplished to Horowitz's satisfaction. But after forty thousand sets of the Concerto were released, Horowitz discovered that the wrong master had been used when the record was made, and to make matters worse, one portion of the music was not in tune with the rest. Although even record reviewers overlooked this, Toscanini and Horowitz were furious.

The error was enough to set off the characteristic Toscanini "feeling of outrage and resentment,"[42] according to Charles O'Connell, RCA's classical-music director. Also, the Horowitz-Toscanini Tchaikovsky was unfavorably compared by critics to the Rubinstein version recorded with Barbirolli in 1933, and even O'Connell admitted that "apart from certain details of recording technique, Rubinstein's was far more poetic and musical. He invests the superficial brilliance of the Concerto with his own imaginative concept, giving it warmth and virility infinitely more satisfying than the meretricious glitter, inflexible rhythms, and unnatural pace of the Horowitz-Toscanini recording."[43] Rubinstein, also a Victor artist, was outraged that RCA had released another version of the Tchaikovsky to compete with his own and had advertised it "as the greatest recording ever made." He declared: "When I bought a copy, I was amazed that not only were conductor and soloist not in accord, but the record was technically defective. My opinion was shared by everybody I met, and I was glad to hear that they also stated their great preference for my own record with Barbirolli."[44]

Even Toscanini was not happy with the record, and he summoned Horowitz to the Riverdale House. With the phonograph's volume turned up high, the Maestro lectured him at length about what was wrong in the performance. Said one close friend: "Toscanini was a man of opinions, and Horowitz was meek with him to the point of nonexistence. Wanda told me her husband just sat there."[45] Wanda, in fact, agreed with her father, and went so far as to warn Rachmaninoff in a letter that "if by any chance the occasion should arise, *do not listen to* the record of the Tchaikovsky Concerto by my father and husband. I don't like it at all. It's a streamlined train, coast-to-coast interpretation. Quick, and no stops! However, it appears to be good business."[46]

At the end of April, Horowitz suffered an attack of tonsillitis and had to cancel recitals in Michigan and Canada, going instead to Chicago for medical care supervised by Dr. Cottle. After a week in bed he was sufficiently recovered to return to New York. There, he ended his season, appearing with the Philharmonic under Barbirolli in the Rachmaninoff Third Concerto, broadcast live on WABC from Carnegie Hall. This was the summer for which Merovitch had arranged a twenty-concert South American tour, but the tonsillitis had so alarmed Horowitz that he decided to cancel this, opting for a rented house in Beverly Hills.

In California, Horowitz made a concentrated effort to relax. The season had been rigorous and he was still unaccustomed to hotels and trains. He slept until about eleven in the morning, had his breakfast in bed with the newspaper, and then read through his fan mail, directing either Wanda or Benedict to answer it. After his morning meal of tea, Holland rusks with honey, and perhaps an egg, he went to the piano for an hour or two, dressed in his pajamas all afternoon, and read through new repertory until five o'clock tea. Even on vacation the piano remained his focus. Insisting that driving would harm his hands, Horowitz hired a car and chauffeur to take him to and from the RCA Victor studios in Hollywood, where he began to record selections for 1943 release: the Tchaikovsky *Dumka* and his own transcription of the Saint-Saëns–Liszt *Danse Macabre*. After an early evening nap, dinner was served at eight, and then Horowitz sometimes listened to the radio—local news and politics—or entertained guests at the keyboard, not retiring until two or three in the morning. Wanda did not enjoy cooking, so servants prepared either Russian dishes, French specialties, or simple American cuisine. Corn on the cob (the national dish of the Ukraine, Horowitz explained to guests) was served nearly every night.

Even during the summertime, when Horowitz had time for seven-year-old Sonia, she was relatively peripheral to him. "She was a very charming but very subdued child," recalled Benedict. "Sonia was just learning her English and still used French when speaking to Wanda and Volodya. She had been displaced many times—France, Italy, Riverdale, New York City, California—and had already had many homes and tutors. She was quiet and there appeared to be a sadness in that little girl. Horowitz was not an adoring father, and had sort of an offhand attitude toward her. He never mentioned her while on tour."[47]

Beyond the demands of his career, Horowitz had little energy to spare for anything including his family. He was plagued by emotional problems that caused him to become the isolated and withdrawn personality Benedict had to contend with during tours. In December 1940, Horowitz had begun psychoanalysis with an eminent psychiatrist, Dr. Lawrence Kubie, a strict Freudian who was among other things attempting to exorcise any possible homosexual element in Horowitz. Kubie believed that homosexuality was an aberration that could be "cured." Horowitz, controlled by his wife and psychiatrist and bound in by the repressive social climate of that time, found little comfort. Kubie's unenlightened treatment only made him feel increasingly depressed. Benedict remembered that "during his analysis, Horowitz would just stay with me, completely secluded from everyone, completely passive. His doctor was trying to change him, and Horowitz's response was to cut himself off from the world entirely, from his own feelings as well. Much of the time, he was unhappy and depressed—a very bitter man. His was a stoic self-denial under extremely trying conditions and it wasn't as if he had any friends or activities to relieve the pressure." Dr. Kubie's treatment seemed, in fact, to be counterproductive, amplifying Horowitz's anguish. "We did a lot of jawboning on our train trips," said Benedict, "and he told me that his breakdown in Europe was hardly voluntary. It became clear that his attempt to deny his own personality, to mitigate it or extirpate it, had been a prime factor in that breakdown."[18]

On those few occasions when Wanda joined Horowitz and Benedict on tour (most often in Chicago, where she could visit with the Cottles), Horowitz's behavior vacillated between gregarious and depressed. According to Benedict, "sometimes he was totally uninhibited, and at other times he was very withdrawn and would remain seated in a corner of the hotel room, brooding." Conductor Lehman Engel, who visited the couple in Chicago at their hotel after one of Horowitz's triumphant performances of the Rachmaninoff Third Concerto in 1943, recalled that "Wanda and Volodya were not having a glamorous time in Chicago, and there was no apparent closeness between them. Wanda was motherly in a cool sort of way but seemed bored and wanted to have some fun, so we played gin rummy in the hotel room after the concert. No one was paying any attention to Horowitz and Wanda didn't seem to care. He seemed to be passive and childlike in her presence. Yet on another occasion he asked me to take him to some bars, and there he was completely animated, overeager—anything but timid."[19]

At the time, Wanda would not discuss her husband's problems, even with Benedict, but she was nonetheless extremely supportive of his efforts to overcome them. She had before her her own mother's stoic acceptance of Toscanini's philandering, and as an Italian woman, said Benedict, she felt that "you did not divorce, you stayed with whatever situation you were in, no matter what." Benedict voiced an opinion echoed by many of Horowitz's close friends: "I don't think he could have survived without her. She didn't only put up with his personality. When he would get hysterical over Columbia Concerts, or a bad piano, or a bad concert hall, or a bad review, he took it out on her. He screamed and refused to go out on tour, and she would gently pacify him, usually successfully. She tried to make his life as comfortable as possible, seeing that he got good medical attention. She was a consummately good caretaker."[50]

CHAPTER THIRTEEN

THE WAR YEARS

"In 1942, I experienced one of the greatest moments of my life—obtaining my final American citizenship papers. After being a 'man without a country' for so many years, this ceremony . . . made a great impression on my mind. Just before the close of World War II, I transcribed 'The Stars and Stripes Forever' and was proud to present to my fellow Americans what seemed to me to be the most fitting display of my great love for a great country and a great victory."[1]

he Horowitzes remained in Hollywood until the end of October 1941, with November recitals scheduled in Pasadena, Salt Lake City, and Los Angeles. In December, they returned to New York for a month, settling at Villa Pauline. Toscanini sometimes treated his son-in-law with respect and affection, although when music was discussed the air between them usually became heated. There was considerable difference of opinion on the subject of Rachmaninoff. Toscanini was adamant that Rachmaninoff was "not a good composer"[2] and refused to conduct his works. Horowitz believed Toscanini would not play his idol's music because he was jealous of his own close friendship with Rachmaninoff. According to Horowitz, after Rachmaninoff's death in 1943, Toscanini regretted his negative attitude, but still stubbornly refused to conduct the music.

Toscanini was also critical of Liszt and, once again, Horowitz leaped to the defense, arguing that Liszt was the real father of the piano and had invented the piano recital. Toscanini could not abide Liszt's "pose" of retiring from the stage, believing it to be fundamentally insincere. Horowitz countered that Liszt had produced "fantastic pupils," and that "if it was a pose, it was a good one!"[3]

Afternoons at Villa Pauline would sometimes end with Horowitz at the piano practicing Rachmaninoff. Horowitz's cousin, Natasha Saitzoff, remembered once touching Toscanini's arm and asking, "If Rachmaninoff is not a good composer, isn't he at least the greatest pianist today?" The Maestro, glancing toward Horowitz, replied vehemently, "He? Never in the world! It's Volodya who is the greatest because what he can do is superhuman!"[4]

On one subject Horowitz and Toscanini were in complete agreement: critics. Toscanini would say sarcastically that critics were only happy if a performance was not too fast, not too slow, not too loud, not too soft— just boring. From this, he concluded that the only solution to the problem was to be honest to one's own deepest impulses and aspirations. Horowitz quite agreed, but critics remained one of his horrors. Even when he received favorable reviews, he sometimes angrily told Benedict that the critics never knew what they were writing about. This was at least partly true, especially in smaller cities where city-desk editors sometimes assigned news reporters to cover a concert when the regular critic was unavailable.

Horowitz grappled with the problem of ill-informed criticism for a long time and eventually decided to educate the critics himself by providing detailed program notes for every recital. He persuaded Olin Downes, chief music editor of the *New York Times*. and Herbert Peyser, the *Times*'s Paris music correspondent, to write "analytical notes"—"a clever move," said Benedict, "which he insisted upon with Columbia Concerts. When Judson refused to pick up the entire tab for this service, Horowitz paid Downes out of his own pocket."[5] The plan seemed effective, for Horowitz noted that critics who "didn't know anything" would often quote copiously from the notes.

Wanda, who had seen both her husband and father suffer at the hands of critics, enjoyed taking revenge on them whenever possible. Her favorite anecdote concerned a performance of Verdi's opera *Falstaff,* conducted by Toscanini in New York, during which she observed the acerbic composer-critic Virgil Thomson, no admirer of either her father or her husband, snoozing. At the end of the evening, she marched over to him and announced, "I am Wanda Toscanini Horowitz. I saw you sleep from the first note to the last note." Then, swatting him with a program book, she concluded, "I hope you enjoyed the performance!"[6] When she told Toscanini, he cheered *"Brava! Brava!"* For good measure Wanda then telephoned a newspaper columnist about the incident, and the call was followed, whether coincidentally or not, by the best review Thomson ever gave Toscanini.

During the stay in Riverdale, Horowitz began practicing a major new work for his January 31 Carnegie Hall program, the Sixth Sonata, Op. 82, of Sergei Prokofiev, which the composer had sent to him the previous year. Horowitz was more nervous than ever about this concert, because he had agreed to allow the last portion of it to be broadcast on the radio as a personal birthday greeting to President Franklin D. Roosevelt, in observance of the "March of Dimes" campaign. He had also agreed to allow members of the audience to sit onstage for the first time. His only condition was that such seats be reserved for army or navy personnel, one of the many patriotic gestures he made during the war.

On January 12, 1942, Horowitz took out citizenship papers, and later that year he became an American citizen. This, he said, was "one of the greatest moments of my life; that I had been accepted as a free citizen in the country I loved made a great impression on my mind." As had Rachmaninoff and Hofmann, Horowitz now began each program with his own arrangement of "The Star-Spangled Banner," members of the armed forces forming a khaki-and-blue background in Carnegie Hall at the January 31 recital. Of Horowitz's rendition of the national anthem, one critic commented: "It may not have been everybody's 'Star-Spangled Banner' any more than his Bach and Brahms were everybody's Bach and Brahms, but the opening octaves brought the audience to its feet with a jerk. . . . The finale sounded more like a brass band augmented with pipe organ than any piano has a right to [but] the skyrocket drama set the house afire."[7] Later, to celebrate the end of World War II, Horowitz transcribed another tune, *The Stars and Stripes Forever,* as his glittering and very personal expression of patriotism.

Horowitz now focused more and more on his troubled relationship with Arthur Judson and the Columbia Management office. Merovitch had helped negotiate Horowitz's contract for the 1941–42 season, signed in February 1942. Horowitz had sought, once again unsuccessfully, to have the Columbia commission reduced from the standard 20 percent, but the contract did promise him thirty appearances at $2,750 per recital, or a minimum guarantee of $2,000 per recital plus 60 percent of the gross over $3,000. Horowitz had declined to play more than four college dates or four community and civic concerts in smaller cities; in addition, he refused to perform on the Pacific Coast that season. Particularly irritating to him was Columbia's longtime practice of taking 40 percent of the box-office returns in both Chicago and New York.

Judson had long regarded Horowitz's general nervousness and inclination to cancel recitals suddenly as a liability to his business.[8] It was known that when Horowitz received his usually overbooked itinerary from the Judson office each September, he glanced over the list and said to friends, "Ummm, now which ones shall I cancel?"[9] He knew in advance he would make cancellations, sometimes because two dates were too close together, sometimes because he disliked a certain town. During the 1930's, when Horowitz's nerves were often getting the better of him, Judson sometimes had to visit him backstage at Carnegie Hall to coax him into playing. "You have to," he would say; "I can't," Horowitz would retort. Once, the clever Judson had taken Horowitz's arm and walked him around the backstage area, maneuvering him so skillfully that the pianist was surprised to find himself suddenly standing onstage in front of three thousand people. Judson, concealed two feet away in the wings, had hissed, "Go over to the piano and play!"[10] and Horowitz had obeyed.

Although Judson was willing to extend himself with Horowitz from time to time, he would not compromise on a reduction in his commission. He feared that if he capitulated to Horowitz others would demand the same concession. Judson pointed out that for every recital Horowitz played, José Iturbi played twenty, and that if Horowitz wanted quality management he was going to have to pay for it. To smooth things over, Judson amiably invited Horowitz to "come anytime" to his office. Horowitz, who absolutely refused to set foot in the Columbia headquarters, retorted sarcastically, "Come anytime to my house."[11] Neither man would budge, for Judson made it a principle to conduct business only from his office, while Horowitz was seeking a signal that he was indispensable. Finally on March 7, 1942, Horowitz fired off a note to Judson: "Please be advised that I shall no longer be your artist because I am completely dissatisfied with the services of Columbia Concerts Corporation."[12]

Even after this letter of resignation, Calvin Franklin made a last attempt to persuade Horowitz to remain with Columbia at least until the spring of 1944 and fulfill the engagements already booked for that season. In a letter to Merovitch, Franklin suggested that "a friendly arrangement can be made without going into the details of a lengthy contract."[13]

Horowitz would not remain with Judson beyond the spring of 1943.

He replaced Columbia with Annie Friedberg, an ambitious and energetic woman who had established her own small management firm in New York in 1912. Miss Friedberg had introduced the British pianist Myra Hess to American audiences, and among her other clients were conductor Adrian Boult, the Budapest String Quartet, and pianists Carl Friedberg and Gyorgy Sandor. Although her operation could not compare to Columbia's in scale, she did provide the customized service Horowitz wanted. Miss Friedberg and Horowitz were in agreement on the pianist's fee structure, and in addition, he was allowed complete freedom to play whenever and wherever he chose. There would be no community concerts, no backwater cities with poor halls and unresponsive audiences. He had total control.

During his last full season with Judson, Horowitz agonized over whether or not to return to Russia for a concert tour. Because of the rapprochement with the Soviets during the war, overtures had been made about his playing again in his native land. Although tempted by the offer, if only because it would allow him to see his sister, Regina, again, Horowitz was afraid that if he set foot in the Soviet Union the government would find a way of keeping him there. Eventually, he decided not to go. He did, however, write to the first secretary of the Soviet embassy in Washington, to ask for assistance in procuring an orchestral score of the Prokofiev Second Piano Concerto, stating that he wished to play the work "not only from a musical point of view but also as an outstanding contribution to a deeper cultural relationship between two great allies."[14] Although Horowitz had plans to program the Prokofiev concerto with Serge Koussevitzky, the performance never took place, and Horowitz remained skeptical about Soviet intentions. "When the war is over," he predicted to friends, "this marriage will end in divorce."[15]

Profits from Horowitz's second New York recital at Carnegie Hall on March 6 were donated to the American Red Cross War Fund and to the Russian War Relief. The day after the concert one of the most devastating reviews ever written about the pianist appeared in the *New York Herald Tribune*. There, his old foe, Virgil Thomson, described him as a "master of distortion and exaggeration." Wrote Thomson: "If one had never heard before the works Mr. Horowitz played last night ... or known others by the same authors, one might easily have been convinced that Sebastian Bach was a musician of the Leopold Stokowski type, that Brahms was a sort of flippant Gershwin who had worked in a high-class night club and that Chopin was a gypsy violinist." Thomson concluded by stating that Horowitz "is out to wow the public, and wow it he does. He makes a false accent or phrasing anywhere he thinks it will attract attention."[16] Years later, Horowitz sloughed off that appraisal ("Virgil Thomson called me a master of distortion. I took that as a compliment. After all, so was El Greco. So was Michelangelo."[17]), but in 1942 it is likely that he and Wanda fumed over it. At any rate, a few days after the recital, Horowitz caught a severe cold and asked Columbia to cancel his remaining East Coast engagements. After a solo recital in Chicago on April 13 and further appearances in Milwaukee and Pittsburgh, as in previous summers he headed for California for a rest.

The most enjoyable aspect of that summer was Horowitz's continuing friendship with Rachmaninoff. The sixty-nine-year-old composer's health had by then deteriorated, and his doctors suggested he give up his Long Island home in favor of the warm climate of California. Rachmaninoff and his wife, Natalie, had rented an estate in Beverly Hills called the Tower Road House, which had a large garden, a swimming pool and a music room large enough to accommodate two concert-grand pianos. Their house was frequently filled with guests, many of them expatriate Russian friends delighted to have the Rachmaninoffs in California. Over dinner, Rachmaninoff would profess deep guilt about living so lavishly while war was ravaging his motherland. "Every time the conversation turned to the East European front and the sufferings being endured by his beloved native country, one could easily observe how strongly he suffered himself," wrote one biographer. "The mere thought of the millions of Russians meeting their deaths, and the barbarous destruction of priceless ancient Russian monuments, made him shudder."[18]

During this summer, Rachmaninoff's last, there were lighter moments that Horowitz and Rachmaninoff savored. Often, as in Switzerland, they played duets, warming up with the first book of Bach's *Well-Tempered Clavier* (each taking one hand), and continuing with Rachmaninoff's two suites for two pianos (Opp. 5 and 17). Another work they practiced together was Rachmaninoff's final composition, the *Symphonic Dances*, Op. 45, written in 1940 for Eugene Ormandy and the Philadelphia Orchestra. That same year Rachmaninoff had adapted this score for two pianos and now he wanted to play it publicly with Horowitz, but he died before he was able to. That summer the two men did invite about fifty guests to the Tower Road estate on two occasions for private duo-piano performances. The first program, on June 15, containing Mozart's Sonata, K. 447, for two pianos and Rachmaninoff's Second Suite, was so enthusiastically received that the next program was arranged for August, with a repeat of the Mozart and the first hearing of the two-piano transcription of Rachmaninoff's *Symphonic Dances*. According to one person present at these occasions, the impression made by Rachmaninoff and Horowitz playing together was one of "power and joy . . . experienced by the two players, each fully aware of the other's greatness. After the last note, no one spoke—time seemed to have stopped."[19]

The would-be duo never appeared in public together, but both Horowitz and Rachmaninoff performed separately that summer at the Hollywood Bowl—Rachmaninoff on July 17 and 18 in an all-Russian recital, Horowitz on August 7 and 8 in Rachmaninoff's Third Concerto under William Steinberg. In the past, Horowitz had declined to play outdoors because of inferior acoustics, but he made an exception with the Hollywood Bowl because, as he later explained, "I sounded good there."[20] Rachmaninoff attended the event, seating himself in the last row so that no one would notice him. When Horowitz finished his Concerto, the composer, as always modest and almost pathologically shy, paid Horowitz a supreme compliment by walking onto the stage, taking his hand, and declaring, "This is the way I have always dreamed that my Concerto should be played, but I never expected to hear it that way on earth."[21] The audience of 23,000 stood in homage to both men, and Horowitz would later call this "the greatest moment of my life."[22]

To celebrate Rachmaninoff's seventieth birthday in 1943, Horowitz wanted to play the composer's Second Sonata, composed in 1913 and condensed in 1931 when the composer decided it was too long and diffuse. Horowitz felt there were beautiful things in the first version that the composer had excised, and with some trepidation he approached Rachmaninoff about the possibility of combining the best of both editions. To his surprise, Rachmaninoff agreed. "Gorovitz," he said, "you are a good musician. Put it together and bring it to me and we see how it is."[23] He did just that, Rachmaninoff gave his approval, and Horowitz gave the first performances of this third version of the Sonata in his January and February 1943 concerts in Buffalo, Washington, Atlanta, and Chicago. Though the work itself did not much impress the critics, Horowitz's performance was commended as "music in the grand manner."[24]

As Horowitz played his last recitals under Judson's management, Rachmaninoff began his final concert tour. His first date was on February 3, 1943, at State College, Pennsylvania, but by the twenty-second he had become so ill in New Orleans that he decided to return to Los Angeles to see a Russian doctor. There he was diagnosed as having melanoma, a rapidly spreading cancer which had already attacked his liver, lungs, muscles, and bones. Rachmaninoff's doctors gave him less than a month to live, and the composer's closest friends, including Horowitz, hurried to California to see him a last time. A few days before Rachmaninoff's death, Horowitz paid his final visit to the man who had meant so much to him both personally and professionally. At the deathbed, he spoke tenderly, and Rachmaninoff's last words to him were, "Good-bye, good-bye, I will not see you again."[25] He died early in the morning of March 28, just a few days before his seventieth birthday.

Horowitz was so shaken that he canceled his concerts for one month. The following year, he accepted the presidency of the Rachmaninoff Memorial Fund, an organization established by the composer's widow to promote exceptional talent in those areas in which Rachmaninoff had excelled—piano, composition, and conducting. The first undertaking of the fund was a piano competition to ensure the winner a season's tour with leading American orchestras and a series of concerts in the Soviet Union. Horowitz took his role as president seriously and organized a board of directors which included Serge Koussevitzky, Mrs. Frederick Steinway, Mrs. Olin Downes, and Wanda Horowitz. The Rachmaninoff Memorial Fund, however, had to be discontinued six years later for lack of sufficient public support.

Horowitz was far more successful in raising funds for the war effort, and his most important contribution came from the legendary Tchaikovsky War Bond Concert given at Carnegie Hall on Easter Sunday, April 25, 1943, with Toscanini conducting the NBC Symphony Orchestra—the one appearance Horowitz did not cancel during the month after Rachmaninoff's death. The benefit concert was planned as the climax of the U.S. Treasury's April war-bond drive, and the price of admission was the purchase of a bond in any denomination ranging from $25 to $50,000. It proved to be the greatest fund-raising event in musical history: first-tier boxes went for $50,000, second-tier for $25,000, orchestra seats for $5,000 and $3,000, and standing room for $25. (In the entire house, only nine free seats were put aside, for music critics.) Although the

Treasury Department estimated that approximately $6 million would be raised, the total box-office take turned out to be $10,190,045.

The Tchaikovsky Concerto was broadcast live, nationwide, from five to six in the afternoon, and at its conclusion the applause and cheers would have continued much longer had not Toscanini raised his baton for a performance of his arrangement of "The Star-Spangled Banner." The War Bond Concert was the first Horowitz-Toscanini performance recorded live and approved for release on records. If anything, this collaboration was even more exciting than the 1941 studio version, but the disc was not made available by RCA until August 1959, when advanced technology and the long-playing format allowed for a suitable presentation. The Tchaikovsky was a triumph for both Horowitz and Toscanini, and Virgil Thomson concluded his favorable *New York Herald Tribune* review with the hope that "their loyal public will get one-half as much democracy for its money as it did music."[26]

Early in the week following the war-bond concert, Wanda and Horowitz left New York for the Great Lakes Naval Training Station in Illinois for his first concert at a military post. This was originally scheduled for March 30 but had been postponed until April 29 because of Rachmaninoff's death. Although Horowitz was eager to help his newly adopted country, he had declined past invitations to play at military bases, fearing poor acoustics and unsure of how to choose repertory for fighting men. However, the new Ross Auditorium at the Great Lakes station was well-suited for concerts. The recital had been organized by the composer and conductor Lehman Engel, who, after being drafted into the Navy, had already organized impressive entertainments for the armed forces, among them Milstein, Piatigorsky, Kreisler, Menuhin, Paul Robeson, and Lily Pons. Even in that company, Horowitz's appearance was billed as "the greatest event of our series."[27]

It wasn't every day that Horowitz shared a program with a brass band, a male chorus, and warm-up music like "Slaughter on Tenth Avenue," "Embraceable You," and *Porgy and Bess*—or a stage with a master of ceremonies, Lieutenant Commander E. E. Peabody, Engel's superior. Introducing Horowitz, Peabody waxed effusive: "Now, folks, it comes time for me to enjoy the highest privilege in all my career as master of ceremonies. I will next present to you the world's greatest artist, the world's greatest pianist, Vladimir Horowitz!"[28] There was a moment of hushed expectancy among the audience of two thousand uniformed men, and then thunderous applause as Horowitz, sleek and smiling, marched to the piano. He had designed a program which he hoped would have appeal: the Schubert-Tausig *Marche Militaire,* the Saint-Saëns–Liszt–Horowitz *Danse Macabre, Carmen* Fantasy, the Chopin C-sharp Minor Waltz, two Scarlatti sonatas. The audience was as enthusiastic as any in Horowitz's career, exploding in shrill whistles and whooping cheers after each selection. At the end, Horowitz returned numerous times for encores, among them Brahms's Waltz in A-flat Major, Liadov's *Musical Snuff-box* and more Chopin, all of which, according to one critic, "really got the boys." Finally, Horowitz coyly waved a white handkerchief of surrender to the crowd and left the stage to wild applause.

The next night, after playing a recital in Chicago at Orchestra Hall, he began to feel ill. He had caught a cold at the naval center and it developed into a throat infection and fever a few days later. He went ahead with a recital in Milwaukee and returned to Chicago for a week of bed rest, having canceled a concerto appearance with Eugene Ormandy at the University of Michigan in Ann Arbor. At the time, Horowitz was preparing new repertory—the Prokofiev Seventh Sonata and the Liszt Hungarian Rhapsody No. 6, and he asked Lehman Engel, whose musical opinion he held in high regard, to come to Chicago for coaching sessions. "Everything he did became a superhuman feat," recalled Engel, "but I found myself saying over and over again, 'It's too fast for the music.' He played one passage [in the first movement of the Prokofiev] with five-note chords jumping back and forth. He was playing this passage faster than you can imagine, looking away from the piano and grinning, not making one mistake. 'Good?' he asked me. 'No,' I replied. 'My God! It's too fast.' He looked surprised."[29]

Horowitz reveled in the technical challenges of Prokofiev's music and was honored that the composer had asked him to give the American premieres of all three of his so-called War Sonatas, written between 1939 and 1944. The Sixth Sonata was heard for the first time in the United States on January 30, 1942, at Carnegie Hall, the Seventh on March 14, 1944, and the Eighth on April 23, 1945. When Horowitz received the score of the Seventh Sonata from Russia one day in the early spring of 1943, he was in Chicago. He stayed up all night, and by dawn the entire work was memorized. He had previously programmed not only Prokofiev's Sixth Sonata but also two early pieces, the *Toccata,* Op. 11, and the selections from *Visions fugitives,* Op. 22. The Seventh Sonata, however, became his favorite Prokofiev work, and early that summer he played it exuberantly for Toscanini. The Maestro, sitting next to Horowitz's first cousin, Natasha Saitzoff, touched her arm and said, "It's not a great work. He makes it great."[30] But the pianist begged to differ with Toscanini, and he later told one interviewer that "Prokofiev would not have been able to achieve this consummation in his music had it not been for the effect of the war and the spirit of the Russian people."

Before the official Carnegie debut, Horowitz played the Seventh Sonata in New York on January 13 at a private concert at the Soviet Consulate before a distinguished invited audience of musicians and critics. A year later, he would also premiere the Eighth Sonata at the Consulate, and he was immensely proud of his connection not only to Prokofiev but also to the Russian people. "The quintessence of all musicians were present, two hundred people,"[31] Horowitz declared. Indeed, the audience was a musical who's who: Arturo Toscanini, Leopold Stokowski, Serge Koussevitzky, Bruno Walter, the young Leonard Bernstein, Samuel Barber, Aaron Copland, Virgil Thomson, Edgard Varèse, Artur Rodzinski, Nathan Milstein, Josef Lhévinne, Ania Dorfmann, Carl Friedberg. Prokofiev, of course, could not attend, but when Horowitz recorded the Seventh Sonata a year and a half later, he posted the first copy to him in Moscow, and Prokofiev in turn sent back an autographed copy of the score, inscribed "to the miraculous pianist, from the composer."[32]

At the public premiere of the Seventh Sonata at Carnegie Hall on March 14, Horowitz effortlessly rattled off the biting sonorities of the first movement and brought the toccata-like finale to a stunning climax. As an encore, the audience demanded a repeat of the last movement, and Horowitz's playing proved no less vigorous the second time. "Mr. Horowitz obviously loves this music, and plays every note of it with the spontaneity of an enthusiast and with the finish of a master performer,"[33] said the *New York Herald Tribune.* Critics compared the Prokofiev Seventh to works of Hindemith and Bartók, but although Horowitz's playing seemed beyond criticism, the Sonata itself received mixed reviews. "Mr. Horowitz did everything humanly possible for the new work, but neither in substance nor in style can it measure up to the composer's best,"[34] was one critic's reaction. Eventually, the Prokofiev would gain a firm place in the repertory and be widely accepted as a masterwork, but in 1944 it was severely criticized for "paucity of melody" and the "saccharine quality" of its romantic *Andante*. The following year, when Horowitz introduced the less aggressive, more lyrical Eighth Sonata of Prokofiev, it was as well received as Horowitz's playing.

After Rachmaninoff's death Horowitz seemed more conscious of his Russian roots, and his 1943 and 1944 programs featured not only works of Prokofiev and Rachmaninoff (the Second Sonata and four of the preludes) but also the Sonata in G Minor, Op. 22, of Rachmaninoff's close friend, Nicolai Medtner. Horowitz had long since abandoned attempting to convince audiences and critics of the worth of Medtner, and his experience with this Sonata, one of that composer's strongest and most appealing works, only emphasized the past: Medtner was unsalable outside of Russia. "Not a phrase of it quickens the pulse, or causes one to crave for further acquaintance with the composer's other creations,"[35] declared the *Chicago Tribune*. "Medtner at least owes a debt of gratitude to two of his countrymen—Rachmaninoff and Horowitz—for the propaganda which they have made to advance his reputation." The dense, neoromantic work was denounced as being cliché-ridden; further, "not even Mr. Horowitz's adroitness could bring it to life."[36] Horowitz soon dropped the G Minor Sonata from his active repertory, but he retained his affection for Medtner, and in the future often mentioned him in interviews and sometimes played through his sonatas, concertos, and chamber music at home.

Horowitz then began to favor Alexander Scriabin—"a composer who has been neglected and who has something to say of emotional importance," as he told one interviewer in 1948. "I would like to play some of his late music, like the Tenth Sonata, but I doubt if the public is ready for it yet."[37] A few years after the end of the war, Horowitz did program Scriabin—the *Vers la Flamme*, Op. 72, *Poème*, Op. 32, No. 1, and various etudes—and with great success.

Horowitz also examined music of Soviet composers like Dmitri Shostakovich, Aram Khachaturian and Dmitri Kabalevsky. He liked the idiomatic writing of Kabalevsky and gave the American premieres at Carnegie Hall of both the Sonata No. 2 in E-flat Major, Op. 45 (on February 3, 1947) and the Sonata No. 3 in F Major, Op. 46 (on February 2, 1948). Years later, Horowitz marveled that he had so easily learned and memorized the complex and dramatic Kabalevsky Second Sonata, which had proved an effective display vehicle for his digital facility, explosive dynamic range, and acute rhythmic sense.

Horowitz had long ago declared that he was on the lookout for "the great American composer." "I would like to find a good large piano work by an American composer," he told an interviewer. "They do not write much or very well for the piano. They only want to write big orchestral pieces."[38] Copland's often percussive piano works were not even remotely appealing, and although at one point Horowitz contemplated performing some pieces of George Antheil, only the music of Samuel Barber really interested him. Horowitz and Barber had been friendly via Toscanini since the 1930's, and in 1945 Horowitz had premiered Barber's first piano work, the small-scaled *Excursions*, Op. 20. Far more ambitious was Barber's Piano Sonata, Op. 26, composed in 1949 and premiered by Horowitz in Havana on December 9, 1949. This important work, commissioned by the League of Composers to celebrate its twenty-fifth anniversary, became so identified with Horowitz that many concertgoers have since assumed that Barber wrote it specifically for him. "But he didn't," Horowitz explained. "I saw [the first] three movements and told him the Sonata would sound better if he made a very flashy last movement, but with content. So he did that fugue, which is the best thing in the Sonata, and I suggested other changes too."[39]

Before introducing the Barber Sonata to New York, at Carnegie Hall on January 23, 1950, Horowitz tried it out in Cleveland, Washington, and at a private musicale at G. Schirmer's music store in Manhattan before an invited audience of close friends. He proved an indefatigable promoter of the work, talking enthusiastically about it everywhere he went. "The music is like Barber [himself]," he would state. "Aristocratic and full of taste. It is also very American and that is why I am proud to present it. Barber has put warmth and a heart into the work that the ultramodern compositions, with their mechanical pyrotechnics, lack. I don't, for instance, play Bartók because I don't like his percussive use of the piano. But Barber is very brilliant and very different."[40] Horowitz's high opinion of the Barber Sonata was echoed by most of the critics who were at the Carnegie Hall performance that January, and the work quickly entered the modern repertory. Horowitz was its principal champion. "Many pianists will now attempt its performance," wrote Olin Downes. "Few can expect to approach the authority and imagination, the power and the delicacy, on occasion, also the incredible virtuosity, which went into its performance [by Horowitz]."[41]

Horowitz's renewed attention to lesser-known Russian pieces and his newfound interest in American music were initially a response to the patriotic fervor of the war years, for the pianist had been an enthusiastic and generous fund raiser for the Russian War Relief, as well as for the American Red Cross and the U.S. Defense Bond Campaign. During the summer of 1944, his enthusiasm for his adopted country led to what was perhaps his most flamboyant pianistic accomplishment of those years: a transcription of John Philip Sousa's march, *The Stars and Stripes Forever*. While vacationing in Jackson, New Hampshire, he began work on the Sousa, which he considered "one of the greatest marches ever written," but one unfortunately hackneyed by bands all over the world. "My main goal in the transcription," he said, "was to restore the music to its purest and most correct form . . . and to be faithful to the original score. I didn't want to miss any of the outstanding coloring Sousa obtained from the use of solo instruments such as the piccolo."[42] By using the thumb of each hand to carry the main theme, Horowitz was able to add enough embellishment to the march to make it a staggering feat of virtuosity, and the transcription became a favorite of concert and radio audiences. It was first recorded at Hunter College on May 6, 1945, possibly so Horowitz would be able to sit back and listen to what he had wrought. Three days later, at the request of Mayor Fiorello LaGuardia, he played *The Stars and Stripes Forever* in Central Park before an estimated one hundred thousand people celebrating the end of the war on "I-am-an-American Day." During the later 1940's, *The Stars and Stripes Forever* became one of Horowitz's signature-pieces, requested so often by audiences that he almost began to wish he had never made the transcription. But, with it, he seemed to celebrate his recent American citizenship. "I think I am more American than anybody," he had declared in Chicago early in 1945. "I visit a thousand American towns, all states, small towns, big towns, everywhere—and I love them all. From now on, you can forget about my Russian birth and European career, if you will. Just call me, 'Vladimir Horowitz, the American pianist.' "[43]

The combination of the war and Toscanini's political ardor had clearly made Horowitz something of a patriot. This attitude was evident in the late 1940's when Horowitz joined Rubinstein and other pianists in protesting the presence of Walter Gieseking on the American concert stages. Because Gieseking had remained in Germany during the war and had supposedly supported the Hitler regime, Horowitz announced that he would not appear on any concert series during the 1948–49 concert season that engaged Gieseking. Akin to this was the opposition that blocked Wilhelm Furtwängler—the German maestro who had frequently performed for high Nazi leaders, including Hitler—from being appointed the principal conductor of the Chicago Symphony Orchestra in 1949. Once again, prominent musicians, including Milstein, Piatigorsky, Rubinstein, and Heifetz, declared that they would decline engagements with the Chicago Symphony if Furtwängler became its conductor. "If the Nazis had won, I am sure I would not have been invited to play in Berlin," Horowitz told the press on the subject of Gieseking and Furtwängler. "I have sympathy and understanding for little men who had to play before the Nazis in order to eat, but that was not the case with these two men. They made a choice."[44]

CHAPTER FOURTEEN

PROFESSOR HOROWITZ

"I have no method. I can often tell from a student's playing just who his teacher has been, and that is bad. Art should go by excellence, not imitation. I ask [a student] for a little more of this or a little less of that, perhaps for more emotion—but their own kind, not mine."[1]

During the summer of 1944, Horowitz decided to venture for the first time into teaching. His interest had been sparked the previous February in Pittsburgh. After playing a Saturday night recital, bad weather had prevented him from leaving the city the following day and he had passed the afternoon by attending a concert of the Pittsburgh Symphony. The featured soloist was a sixteen-year-old pianist named Byron Janis, who was making his debut in that city playing the Rachmaninoff Second Concerto under the baton of Lorin Maazel, himself only fifteen years old.

Born in McKeesport, Pennsylvania, and educated in Pittsburgh, Byron Yanks (later changed to the more attractive Janis in the interests of career) had come to the attention of the renowned Russian pianist Josef Lhévinne and his wife, Rosina, when he gave his first piano recital at age eight. After studying for two years with the Lhévinnes in New York, Janis had continued lessons with Lhévinne's assistant, Adele Marcus, who took the ten-year-old under her wing for the next six and a half years. By the time of the Pittsburgh performance, Janis had, according to Marcus, blossomed into "a great American talent with a great interpretative gift: a rich imagination, a tremendous warmth, and a spontaneous response to romantic music."[2] Horowitz's accidental presence at Janis's Pittsburgh concert led to an important four-year association between the two.

"Not long before this performance," remembered Janis, "I heard Horowitz's recording of the Brahms Second Concerto, and I felt this was one of the greatest performances I had ever heard. My God, I thought to myself, if I could just meet that man one day and talk with him! So it was very strange when he came backstage in Pittsburgh. He told me I reminded him of himself at my age, that I had a certain kind of nervous energy, some kind of electrical thing. I could hardly speak. Then he said, 'When you return to New York, will you call me? I want very much to talk to you. I would like to work with you!'[3]

Back in New York, Horowitz telephoned his friend Samuel Chotzinoff, musical director at NBC, and enthusiastically described the brilliance and the lyrical intensity of Janis's performance. "But that's the boy I was telling you about!" exclaimed Chotzinoff. "Toscanini already knows his playing."[4] Janis had, in fact, played the Beethoven Fourth Concerto for Toscanini and later performed it in a radio broadcast with the NBC Symphony under Frank Black. Chotzinoff went on to explain that he had been monitoring the boy's education since his twelfth birthday, first at the Chatham Square Music School in New York and then at the Juilliard School, where Janis studied composition and harmony with Roger Sessions while having piano lessons with Adele Marcus. In his role of musical godfather, Chotzinoff thought it a splendid idea that Janis begin to study with Horowitz. Over the next several months, Janis played privately for Horowitz and the transition away from Marcus was begun, albeit painfully. Janis, who had been quite satisfied with Marcus's teaching, was perplexed by the need for a drastic change. Even Chotzinoff admitted that it was likely that Horowitz would not really teach the boy but would probably "just push him out of the way and play."[5]

"Changing teachers was a political thing," declared Marcus. "Chotzinoff believed that the great name of Horowitz would establish Byron, and the lure of that name was too strong for me to stop the change, so I told Byron to go. He was sixteen, a very young sixteen, and I remember him lying on the floor, crying and kicking his feet, screaming, 'If my playing is that good, why do I have to change?' He did not entirely understand how important the connection to Horowitz could be for his career, and I told him, 'If Mr. Horowitz called me right now and asked me to come play for him, I would. And I'm your teacher.' That gave him an entirely different slant. Although I wasn't angry, I was naturally sad to lose him and sat down and wrote Horowitz a beautiful letter, telling him I thought it was wonderful that he was taking an interest in Byron. I had built up Byron's technique from the time he couldn't even play an octave, and now Horowitz had called me and said, 'Don't you think his octaves is faster than my octaves?' Horowitz recognized all of that and later gave me full credit. When Byron made his New York debut four years later, Horowitz came out of the box at intermission, and I said, 'Congratulations.' He answered, 'Only to you. You built the whole menu and I put the cherry on top of the ice cream!' Still, there were many things that Horowitz showed Byron about projection. Byron was working with a man who knew the piano better than anybody else."[6]

Total commitment and unswerving loyalty were expected from the start of Janis's lessons. "Horowitz did not want me playing for anybody else during this period because he felt other people's comments would confuse me. The Rachmaninoff Competition, then a major opportunity, was available, and I could have entered. Horowitz said that I would probably win it but people would think he was up to something, since he was the President of the Jury, as if it were rigged, so he said, 'Don't.' "[7] For Janis, though, competitions were unnecessary. Already, concert managers and recording executives were eagerly awaiting the start of his professional career, and Horowitz promised Janis he would make all necessary arrangements when it was time.

The interest in Janis even before his New York debut was partly due to the fact that he was known as Horowitz's only student. Actually, in 1944, Horowitz had accepted an eighteen-year-old girl from Milwaukee named Marilyn Meyer as a student, but nothing came of the relationship and it ended eighteen months later. Horowitz had been unhappy with Miss Meyer's interpretation of the Rachmaninoff Third Concerto, because he thought she did not have the necessary brilliance for it, and had continually canceled her lessons, until finally Merovitch interceded and told the girl that Horowitz did not want to teach her. In later years, Horowitz would never mention that she had briefly been his student.

So, in the fall of 1944 when Janis's lessons began, Horowitz had no real teaching experience. He would later admit that it was difficult to teach, and that he employed what Janis described as a trial-and-error approach. "There was a lot of experimenting going on—Horowitz deciding what to do and what not to do. Many of his ideas were sound, some not. After a long struggle, I discarded things that weren't me." For instance, Janis ignored Horowitz's recommended physical posture at the keyboard, which he found unsuited to the technique he had learned under Marcus. "Horowitz played with a very low wrist, a fair amount of tension in the arms; he sat extremely low on the bench, and held his fingers extended, nearly flat. Sitting that low suited his torso and he tried to show me how to play that way, but it didn't work for me."[8]

The occasional demonstrations given seated at the piano were the exception, for Janis discovered that Horowitz's standard teaching position was to lie stretched on his living-room couch, nattily dressed in bow tie and sport jacket, shoes highly polished, handkerchief jauntily peeping out of his breast pocket. His manner at lessons was a flamboyant potpourri of conducting, singing phrases, speaking in Russian-tinged English and French, and regaling Janis with humorous anecdotes of his own career. Unlike more conventional teachers, Horowitz usually listened without score, never touched a pencil to the music or used a metronome. With Janis, he was extremely generous with his time and an average lesson lasted two hours, Horowitz leaving his couch approximately twenty minutes of each hour to demonstrate at the piano.

Although Janis was accustomed to practicing four to six hours daily, Horowitz insisted that a shorter period of intense, concentrated work was more valuable than prolonged, tedious hours of routine. He himself, he said, practiced only two hours a day. When Janis became adamant about practicing more than two hours, Horowitz advised him to avoid the kind of mechanical repetition that could detract from the spontaneity of a performance. "A piece can be practiced a hundred times," he said, "and then, when it is taken to the stage, can sound simply like practicing the hundred and first time."[9]

Instead of scales and arpeggios, Horowitz demonstrated for Janis technical exercises that he had created for the purpose of developing strong, independent fingers. One such exercise involved playing a diminished-seventh chord, all five notes depressed simultaneously, emphasizing only one finger at a time while the other four played more softly. The exercise was then expanded to include different kinds of chords while making subtle changes in volume, quality of attack, and color—with or without pedal. Special attention was paid to the fifth finger of each hand—the melody and bass fingers—which Horowitz believed had to be especially well-trained. To bolster the endurance of the weak part of the hand (that is, the fourth and fifth fingers), Horowitz assigned Janis a stretching exercise that Rachmaninoff had shown him. Both thumbs were placed on middle C; then, with a gentle rotating motion of the hands, the fifth fingers played the distance of a tenth above and below middle C; and after that the fourth fingers stretched the distance of an octave, the third fingers a sixth and the second fingers a third. This exercise not only stretched the hand but also made it flexible and accurate over wide spaces. Gradually, the tempo was increased, with more frequent changes in key so that the fingers became accustomed to anticipating spacings with greater accuracy and strength. Horowitz explained that the bridge of the hand was not to be allowed to collapse under any circumstance. Another exercise involved holding up the third finger to create tension in the bridge of the hand, and then playing two notes at a time with the fourth and fifth fingers and second and first on the notes E-G and C-E, with rotating motion chromatically up the scale. As Janis played, Horowitz would lean the entire weight of his body on the bridge of Janis's hand to test its strength.

Horowitz also encouraged Janis to create his own exercises, and supplemented all repertory assignments with groups of Chopin etudes. In the course of demonstrating, Horowitz was careful to emphasize the distinction between "technique" and "mechanics." "Mechanics is the ability to play slow, fast, even chords, arpeggios, scales, octaves, trills—carpenter's tools toward an end but not the end itself," he said. Technique, on the other hand, was "the ability to project your own musical ideas through your instrument. It includes everything which makes possible the translation of musical thought into audible performance—control of pedal dynamics, coloration, and most important, the ability to project emotion. Technique means *savoir-faire,* knowing how to do. It is not part of musicianship, but its result. Mechanics and technique must be balanced; if mechanical ability exceeds musical thought, it sticks out and suggests a meaningless performance."[10]

Horowitz had himself, of course, often been criticized for just such an imbalance. He would therefore constantly make the point to Janis, stressing that "most important is the balancing of brain and heart with the means—the fingers. In a good artist there must be a coordination between these three elements. If any one element is lacking, the circle is not complete. The brain is the police. When the brain becomes the sole inspiration, music becomes sterile and static. But good brains are important, and young musicians nowadays have them in abundance, though too often the music sidetracks the heart and goes directly from the brain to the fingers."[11]

Although Horowitz clung to his theoretical belief that performances must be balanced thus, he admitted to Janis that one "must often do things simply for the sake of arresting the audience's attention—a sudden pianissimo, an unexpected accent. Students think you must always play a piece in the same way. But you cannot—you must exaggerate."[12] Years later, Janis declared that "the danger with too much mastery and craftsmanship of the piano is that it is sometimes difficult keeping this fantastic arsenal under control. The nervous energy should not be put into the music except where it is needed. It is like a person with too much money. Horowitz overspent sometimes. It was very difficult for him to maintain the balance he himself recommended. He was not the most intellectual pianist, and one of his main interests in a score was to find the effects that would show off what he could do at the piano."[13]

After working with Janis for a year, Horowitz scheduled a trial recital for the boy at the Ninety-second Street YMHA in New York, for he was anxious to gauge the success of his lessons by hearing his pupil in public performance. "For that concert," said Janis, "Horowitz gave me my first pair of tails, which had been his own when he was a young man, and I wore them for many years after."[14] Horowitz promised that he would give Janis a fee for the concert, as he strongly believed that when things were paid for they tended to be taken seriously. Correspondingly, Janis had paid Horowitz $100 per lesson. Although obviously Horowitz did not need the money, he did not want the privilege of studying with him taken for granted. Merovitch, who handled the business details, received a letter from Wanda in the summer of 1944 that reflected Horowitz's attitude: "Volodya's idea is to give back the money of the lessons for the expenses of a Carnegie Hall recital or two, according to the amount, naturally. By knowing it, the boy will have more 'pep' to work for that goal. If Volodya will not be satisfied with his work at the end of the year, he will give the amount of money to a charity."[15]

But Horowitz, in fact, was more than satisfied with Janis's progress and after the "Y" recital, he became concerned with showing Janis how to play in a larger hall. "An artist must in many ways be like a speaker. He must develop skill in projection," Horowitz would say. "He must exaggerate. Some people are so puritanical they are afraid to do anything when they play. Then nothing happens. It is easier to control an excess of something, rather than not to have enough."[16] It was on the subject of projection and the variation of tonal inflection that Horowitz proved most helpful. Knowing the difficulties inherent in cavernous concert halls, he stressed the importance of regulating the pedal according to different acoustics and showed Janis how to focus and project a singing tone. In contrast to playing in a living room, Horowitz said, in a large hall "you have to gauge everything differently—the levels of sound, the levels of emotion. *Underline them!* You are playing for twenty-five hundred to three thousand people. Young pianists forget this. They bang out the pyrotechnic parts but they do not project the singing ones."[17]

"Singing," after all, was what the Russian school of piano playing was all about, and Horowitz emphasized it constantly. He encouraged Janis to listen to great singers and to become familiar with operatic literature so that he could pedal and articulate inflections in Chopin just as a singer might phrase an aria of Bellini or Verdi.

Not surprisingly, the assigned repertory gravitated toward Horowitz's favorite Romantics—Chopin, Schumann, Liszt, and Rachmaninoff. While studying with Adele Marcus, Janis had been brought up on a very different diet of Bach, Haydn, Mozart, and Beethoven. Horowitz, he recalled, "wanted to add larger things to my repertoire—the Rachmaninoff Third Concerto, for instance—and he made me think more in oils and less in pastels, which I think young people are afraid to do. They are frightened of thinking in a bigger way and of projecting something. At lessons he would tell me: 'Say something of your own! Make a statement!' And if I had none to make, he'd become irritated and end the lesson, telling me to go home and think about it and return the next week."[18]

During Janis's four-year period of study, Horowitz was busily crisscrossing the nation on concert tours. Lessons continued uninterrupted, for it had been decided that the boy would accompany Horowitz on the road. "We really worked," remembered Janis. "Although he had other students in later years, I was the one he spent the most time with. I was almost like a substitute son and was around the house every day when he was in New York. Indeed, the problem with me was that I wasn't just working with Horowitz, I was part of the family. I would be there in the evenings for dinner, take lessons at the Toscanini residence in Riverdale, vacation with the Horowitzes during the summer, and sometimes stay overnight with him on weekends. Every evening he would play a hundred things for me; it was an extraordinary experience to hear all this, but when you are as young as I was and as sensitive, hearing him play that much got into my ear and the influence was unavoidable."[19]

At lessons, Horowitz tried to discipline himself not to overdemonstrate, believing "talented people must be guided rather than taught." Nevertheless, his effect on Janis was enormous. As Marcus had observed, Janis was "a very young sixteen," and he could hardly avoid the temptation of imitating Horowitz. In later years, Janis mused that "the most important thing is not the strength of the teacher but of the student. Studying with a great artist is like being dominated by a strong parent. It takes a very strong person to work with a personality like Horowitz and not be smothered or swallowed up by his way of thinking. I had an innate fear of falling into this trap, but I did, for quite a while, play a lot like him. I knew how he thought musically and how he breathed, and I could imitate him exactly. He would say, 'Don't be a second Horowitz, be a first Janis!' But it was impossible."[20]

Horowitz's influence did not at first inhibit the development of Janis's professional career. In 1946, at eighteen, Janis received an RCA recording contract and a year later was signed on by the famous impresario Sol Hurok. Early in 1946, Horowitz had helped to arrange concerts for Janis in the United States, both with lesser symphony orchestras and in recital series in Baltimore, Pittsburgh, Kansas City, and Dallas. Horowitz and Chotzinoff were convinced that Janis needed to have at least fifty concerts under his belt in smaller cities before making his official New York debut. Said Horowitz: "For a New York debut, because of nervousness, a young artist is usually twenty-five percent below par, and I wanted Janis to have a chance to prepare himself. A New York appearance should be the end of an artist's early career, not the beginning. A career has the healthiest chance for success when it doesn't start at the top. Before a young artist takes the important step of a New York debut, he should have six or seven programs at his fingertips, all routined through frequent performance."[21]

As Janis performed more frequently, Horowitz reminded him that a concert is not an examination and that spontaneity is most important. He warned against playing when he felt ill on the day of a concert and couldn't meet his own standards, explaining he never hesitated to cancel an appearance. "Horowitz also had a lot of business acumen, and advised me on my contract with management," said Janis. "Hurok was unable to produce as many concerts before my New York debut as Horowitz and Chotzinoff felt appropriate, so they replaced him with Arthur Judson."[22] Horowitz also thought it would be helpful for Janis to play before foreign audiences and helped arrange for a tour of South America in the summer of 1948. The excellent reviews and enormous ovations that Janis received there amply demonstrated to Horowitz the boy's potential as a major box-office draw. Wherever Janis played he created a strong impression, especially with the Rachmaninoff Second and Third concertos. At last, Horowitz was satisfied that his pupil was ready for New York.

On October 30, 1948, Janis made his Carnegie Hall debut before a packed house, and it was an unqualified success. "Not for a long time," wrote Olin Downes, "had this writer heard such a talent allied with the musicianship, the feeling, the intelligence, and artistic balance shown by the twenty-year-old Byron Janis. It was the concert of a young man whose singular gifts are matched by his seriousness and feeling and sincerity and the penetrating thought and aesthetic balance which go with his interpretation."[23]

At that point, Horowitz decided that it was time for Janis to make his own way. Naturally, Columbia Management wanted to use Horowitz's name on Janis's publicity, but Horowitz insisted that doing so could only hurt Janis in the end, as it would detract from his individuality. "Managers want to do that because you are my only pupil and it is good for sales,"[24] he told Janis. Horowitz's worries over possible professional damage seem minor when contrasted with the psychological difficulties Janis was then experiencing, problems that over the next two years interfered with the development of his career. Many of these were closely related to his work with Horowitz. "Lessons were not merely lessons," said Janis. "The difficulty was that I became emotionally involved with him—it was almost impossible not to, since Horowitz's personal makeup demanded this. Horowitz had such an enormous ego that he never let one forget for a moment that it was a great privilege to study with him. He could be rather childish and ruthless at times, even jealous of my successes."[25] On one occasion, Janis proudly brought Horowitz one of his first RCA recordings, of two Beethoven sonatas. Horowitz looked over the album carelessly, then refused it, scowling: "I don't like Beethoven. I don't want to hear that."[26]

Horowitz had many times overstepped the bounds of piano teacher and professional adviser to become a kind of father-confessor and intimate friend, quick to punish Janis for any real or imaginary offense. The emotional and professional dependency Horowitz had fostered in the boy made him overly vulnerable, frightened of Horowitz's opinion, and he struggled unsuccessfully against his teacher's dominating ego. In his twentieth year, Janis withdrew from concerts for two seasons. When the twenty-two-year-old reappeared, at Carnegie Hall on November 28, 1950, he came onstage with the aid of a cane and limped to the piano. "I had torn a ligament," said Janis, "but I admit that I also had many psychological problems related to those years with Horowitz. The weight of his personality was too much for me and I had a breakdown."[27] According to a Columbia manager, Janis's physical condition was "entirely affected and imagined. It was a sad thing. Janis was very fragile emotionally and his condition very much affected the development of his career."[28] Adele Marcus, among others, lamented that "studying with Horowitz ultimately hurt poor Byron. It was too early and the study should have been moderated. The situation simply got out of control."[29]

Gradually, Janis's self-doubt faded and, during the 1950's, he established himself as one of the most brilliant pianists of his generation, noted for his interpretations of Chopin and of Russian music. His RCA recording of the Rachmaninoff Third Concerto, released in 1958, was warmly received by the critics who favorably compared it to Horowitz's own interpretation, and his recording of the Prokofiev Third Concerto was considered outstanding. Moreover, Janis was the first American pianist to tour Russia, and his 1960 concerts there received, according to the *New York Times,* "an overwhelming reception" in which "men and women wept."[30]

Considering Horowitz's competitiveness, it is not surprising that his reaction to Janis's successes was less than generous. When Janis made headlines in 1967 and again in 1973 in connection with his discovery of Chopin waltz manuscripts, he brought the manuscripts to Horowitz. "Take them to Rubinstein!"[31] Horowitz growled. An incredulous Janis bitterly told an interviewer: "Horowitz didn't give a damn about those manuscripts, didn't care what was in them, and couldn't have been more rude."[32]

Without minimizing what he had gained from Horowitz pianistically, Janis ultimately came to regard his four years of study as "overall, a decided negative rather than a positive influence."[33] Janis would remain guarded and nervous over this traumatic period of his life, alternately appreciative and disdainful of his former teacher.

CHAPTER FIFTEEN

PIANO
ACROBATICS

*"An artist who is constantly before the public becomes an
extrovert without even knowing it; he is always giving out
instead of taking in. In the 1940's, my repertoire started to
change rapidly toward modern music and transcriptions.
Anything fast. My pianism became shrill, more brutal, and I
couldn't play certain kinds of music. I don't say it was bad, or
good, but that's what happened."*[1]

Until 1940, Horowitz's recording activity had been relatively modest.
There were twenty-one recording sessions between March 1928 and
March 1936, with thirty-five different works released at an average rate of
four per year (except in 1932, when eleven different works were recorded
and released). Aside from the 1930 Rachmaninoff Third Concerto and
the 1932 Liszt B Minor Sonata, nearly everything was short encore pieces
easily marketable by RCA and HMV and suitable for the limited playing
time of the 78-rpm disc.

After a four-year lapse from 1936 to 1940 due to Horowitz's illness,
there was a dramatic increase in his recording output: ninety-four different, generally more substantial, works recorded between May 1940 and
February 1953 in sixty-three sessions, yielding an average of twenty-one
works released a year. By 1953, Horowitz interpretations of more than
one hundred works were available on disc as compared to a meager
thirty-five up until 1940. RCA's growing classical-record market, the improvement of technology, and the incentive of more lucrative contracts
were important factors in Horowitz's willingness to spend more time in
the studio. He had been upset by the disparity between the actual sound
of his piano and the distortion he heard on records. It seemed impossible
throughout the 1930's to fully capture the breadth of Horowitz's dynamic range or the subtle variety of his tone color. Although the 1930

Rachmaninoff Third Concerto came to be regarded as one of the finest recorded performances of his early career, Horowitz had been unhappy with its sound and would later regret its release. He had hated the tedious, unnatural process of recording the work in four-minute segments and then listening to it on nine separate record sides. Although he could easily have recorded either the Tchaikovsky Concerto or the Liszt E-flat Major or A Major concertos during the 1930's, he had not done so. He did not, in fact, make another concerto recording until ten years after the Rachmaninoff—the famous 1940 collaborations with Toscanini on the Brahms Second and the two versions of the Tchaikovsky, studio (1941) and live (1943).

In the 1930's, Horowitz's busy schedule of eighty to one hundred concerts a year, divided between America and Europe, had rendered any concentration on recording next to impossible. However, living permanently in the United States after 1940 and paring down engagements to forty a year, Horowitz was able, at his convenience, to walk into studio facilities set up by RCA at various New York locations. This was especially so after the war. From 1941 to 1945, recording activity had come to a virtual standstill for two reasons: first, because the shellac used in making records was considered an essential military commodity by the War Production Board, which cut nonmilitary use of the substance by 70 percent; second, because the musicians' union imposed a ban on recordings in the hope of being able to collect royalties from radio broadcast of discs. Consequently, aside from performances with Toscanini, Horowitz had studio sessions only four times during that period, all of them occurring in Hollywood during the summer of 1942 at Republic Studios. Two discs were the result: the Saint-Saëns–Liszt–Horowitz *Danse Macabre* and the Tchaikovsky *Dumka*.

With the end of rationing, Horowitz resumed recording. In search of the best possible acoustics in New York, he alternated between Hunter College, Town Hall, and Carnegie Hall, with scattered sessions at RCA's East Twenty-fourth Street studio. He also recorded occasionally in Hollywood and also in London during his brief 1951 English tour. All recordings, then, made between 1944 and 1953 were produced under studio conditions, with the exception of the two Carnegie Hall recitals (March 5 and April 23, 1951) and two other Carnegie Hall appearances in 1953—one a recital (February 25, 1953), the other (the Tchaikovsky Concerto with George Szell, January 12, 1953) celebrating the twenty-fifth anniversary of Horowitz's American debut.

Merovitch proved indispensable in negotiating Horowitz's contracts with RCA, especially in 1946 and 1948. In return for relaying details of repertory choices and recording sessions, managing correspondence with RCA, forwarding master discs to Horowitz for approval, and overseeing liner notes and record-jacket design, Merovitch received payments in $250 and $500 amounts. He specified in the contracts that all recordings made for release would require Horowitz's written approval, that the number of records released would not be less than those made by any other RCA pianist, that the publicity for each record would be at least equal to that of any other RCA artist, that no pianist would receive prior mention except alphabetically in any RCA advertisement, nor any name appear in larger type. Further, the *Träumerei* from Schumann's *Kinder-scenen,* which Horowitz had played so frequently as an encore that the public now recognized it as one of his signature-pieces, would be reserved only for him; no other RCA pianist might record or have released an interpretation of that work except for use in a motion picture, an option Horowitz had ruled out for himself. The 1946 contract guaranteed Horowitz $1,250 per record side, up to and including twenty sides a year, bringing the total guarantee against royalties to $25,000 a year, or $75,000 for the three-year contract RCA favored. In return, Horowitz was required to produce no less than sixty 78-rpm record sides over the three years. He did not, however, like the idea of being tied down that long, and eventually agreement was reached on a two-year contract, with the additional understanding that for every concerto performed and approved for release he would be paid an additional $5,000 against royalties. Above and beyond his guarantees, Horowitz was also to have a 12.5 percent royalty on solo recordings and a 7.5 percent royalty on concertos, except for those with Toscanini, for which he would receive only 5 percent.

After Horowitz's contract was settled, RCA's principal concern was to coordinate his recorded repertory with the works he played most frequently in recital. Merovitch received an itemized list of over sixty pieces separated into three lists of ascending priorities. Number one on the most important list, "A," was the Beethoven *Moonlight* Sonata, which RCA had stipulated Horowitz must perform during the first year of his contract, and which he had, in 1946. Number two on that list was the Beethoven *Waldstein* Sonata which he recorded in 1944. He was not satisfied, however, and no recording of the *Waldstein* was released until 1956. In addition to Beethoven, List A included a wide variety of Chopin, the

Rachmaninoff Third Concerto, a generous selection of Liszt, and three of Horowitz's popular transcriptions: *The Stars and Stripes Forever, Carmen,* and the Mendelssohn-Liszt-Horowitz *Wedding March.* The order of recording and the placement of works in different albums was left to Horowitz; RCA executives asked only that they be informed of his intentions well in advance so that the selected compositions could be reserved exclusively for him for the period of his contract.

RCA's priorities were, of course, wholly determined by the preferences of Horowitz's audiences. Aside from the predictable appeal of the Liszt Hungarian Rhapsodies and the transcriptions, his public demanded a generous selection of Russian or Slavic works, including Prokofiev's Seventh Sonata, Kabalevsky's Third Sonata, Mussorgsky's *Pictures at an Exhibition,* Scriabin's *Vers la Flamme,* Moszkowski's *Étincelles,* and Tchaikovsky's *Dumka.* For his orchestral dates, Horowitz considered extending himself beyond the seven concertos in his active repertory (Brahms Nos. 1 and 2, Beethoven No. 5, Tchaikovsky No. 1, Liszt Nos. 1 and 2, Rachmaninoff No. 3) and put a number of other works on his own priority list, reflecting a somewhat ambivalent desire for a better-balanced musical diet. Among these works were the Grieg Concerto, the Tchaikovsky *Concert Fantasy,* the Prokofiev Third Concerto, and a group of Mozart concertos, none of them ever recorded or performed publicly by Horowitz. Years later, he said with some exasperation: "Audiences always wanted me to make a big noise in the concertos of Tchaikovsky and Rachmaninoff, to hear everything I could do in one half hour. But I could play softly, too! I could play four or five Mozart concertos and Chopin's Second, but I played the Tchaikovsky. It was a visiting card so that people would come to my recitals."[2]

Nonetheless, during the 1940's and 1950's, giving audiences what they wanted was the governing principle of Horowitz's performing and recording careers. He chose to return to his old stamping grounds for three recordings of the early 1950's: the Rachmaninoff Third in 1951 and the Beethoven *Emperor* in 1952 (both recorded with Fritz Reiner and the RCA Victor Symphony Orchestra), and the Tchaikovsky First in 1953 (with George Szell and the New York Philharmonic—never released because of contractual difficulties).

Whether in concerto or solo repertory, Horowitz had no interest in testing the patience or attention of his audience by scheduling Classical repertory. "If you play Classic music in correct style on a big piano and in a big hall, it will bore most of the audience," he stated. "This is not the listener's shortcoming. It just demonstrates that Classic music was written for small pianos and small rooms."[3] To the chagrin of friends like Rudolf Serkin and Nathan Milstein, Horowitz went on to assert that "the last sonatas of Schubert and Beethoven are boring. I think that the fugue at the end of Beethoven's *Hammerklavier* Sonata, for instance, is much too long. But if I said that to Rudolf Serkin he'd kill me."[4]

Many of Horowitz's colleagues joined with music critics in viewing his flashy programs with disdain. He was continually chided in the newspapers for descending to the lowest common denominator of taste, for capitalizing on his acrobatic ability, and for distorting standard repertory. As far as Horowitz was concerned, the standard repertory was not sacrosanct: "You can improve on Beethoven and everybody," he once declared for an interview. "I remember Casals was always saying: 'Just play Beethoven like you play Chopin.' Always. It was just in the conservatory that they teach the strict divisions."[5] Horowitz's Classical repertory during the 1940's was sparse—three Mozart sonatas, seven early Beethoven sonatas, a few works of Haydn, the *Emperor* Concerto—and he admitted that by concentrating on his transcriptions "my pianism started to change—it became more shrill, more brutal, so brilliant that I couldn't play certain kinds of music."[6] One critic commented that applying Horowitz's prodigious gifts to a Beethoven sonata—for instance, the frequently performed Sonata, Op. 10, No. 3—"was akin to using a bulldozer to level an anthill."[7] Another suggested that while Horowitz's detached fingering suited the Mozart Sonata, K. 331, "nevertheless I have an uneasy feeling, like poking around a humming generator. It's supposed to be safe and the million volts are under control; but there are a few suspicious voltage surges and one never knows exactly what's going to happen."[8]

B. H. Haggin of *The Nation* wrote that "one of the instrumentalists I stopped going to hear was Horowitz, whose prodigious mastery of the piano was not enough to keep me from being bored beyond endurance by the musical limitations evident in the program."[9] Irving Kolodin of the *New York Sun* declared that "if there is any reason why a Horowitz should devote half his program to brief pieces of Prokofiev, plus various etudes of Rachmaninoff, Debussy and Scriabin as preludes to the fantastic intricacies of his [transcriptions], I cannot imagine what it might be."[10]

During this period a Horowitz transcription was usually placed at the end of one of his recitals. Audiences were likely to be restless during Scarlatti, Bach-Busoni, Schumann, or Mendelssohn, keenly anticipating the moment when, as one writer put it, "the characteristic sound and fury would be turned loose [and] Horowitz would stop being respectful of the classic and start being his unafraid self."[11] During the eleven years from 1941 to 1952, Horowitz kept pace with the public's obsession with acrobatics by unleashing a string of his own transcriptions and arrangements. Into these, he poured his imagination and skill as a composer and extended the mechanical resources of the piano beyond what even Liszt might have imagined. Although some critics viewed these transcriptions as a meretricious form of self-display, Horowitz argued that he was merely returning to a well-respected, even common, nineteenth-century tradition of adapting orchestral works and operas for the piano.

Audiences of the past were not only entertained but were also afforded the opportunity to hear music they might never before have encountered. Horowitz's transcriptions, however, were not intended to be educational, but were an attempt to outdo Liszt by refashioning some of that composer's own transcriptions into technical feats accessible only to a Horowitz. The unique results became his trademark, and were endemic to the artistic problems of his career. "It was during the 1940's that I began to shrink intellectually and artistically," he later admitted. "My pianism became too brilliant. I played anything too fast, even my own transcriptions."[12]

The first of these was *Carmen*, written in 1923, revised numerous times over the years, and recorded three times—in 1928, 1947, and 1968. (In addition, Horowitz cut two piano rolls of *Carmen*—one in Germany about the time of his 1926 debut, the other in the United States in 1928.) There were no further transcriptions until 1941, the year of the Saint-Saëns–Liszt *Danse Macabre*. During the next eleven years, however, there was a veritable spate: the Schubert-Tausig *Marche Militaire* in 1942; Sousa's *The Stars and Stripes Forever* in 1945; the Mendelssohn-Liszt *Wedding March* in 1946; the Mussorgsky *Pictures at an Exhibition*, the Mussorgsky song, *By the Water*, and the Liszt *Legende: St. François de Paule marchant sur les flots*, all in 1947; a new version of *Carmen* in 1948; the Liszt *Rakóczy March* (Hungarian Rhapsody No. 15) in 1949; and the Liszt Hungarian Rhapsody No. 2 in 1952. After 1953, which marked the beginning of a long period of introspection and change of taste in repertory, Horowitz abandoned most of these technical tours-de-force in disgust. Later, however, in the 1960's, he produced a few new arrange-ments—the Liszt Hungarian Rhapsody No. 19 (1962), and Liszt's *Scherzo and March* (1967), Hungarian Rhapsody No. 13 (1969)—but he never again programmed his most popular transcription, *The Stars and Stripes Forever,* for this had come to symbolize for him the considerable artistic compromises he made during the 1940's, all for "a quick success with the public."[13]

The *Danse Macabre* or one or another of the Hungarian Rhapsodies usually appeared on the printed program of his recitals in the 1940's, and at the end of an evening Horowitz seldom denied his audience *Carmen* or *The Stars and Stripes Forever.* His astute showmanship could be seen in the logical and concise construction of all his arrangements. Each was of rela-tively short duration: the Hungarian Rhapsodies between six and nine minutes, the *Danse Macabre* eight minutes and the remaining works three and a half to six minutes. Playing with extreme speed, impeccable clarity, enormous power, and seemingly limitless endurance, Horowitz produced in each transcription a flamboyant personal impression display-ing both his compositional control and his technical command of every-thing it was possible to do on the modern piano. He presented them with implacable rhythm, biting dynamics, and a brassy, plangent tone.

In his transcriptions, Horowitz managed to heighten the tension be-tween background and foreground by adding new countermelodies, making contrapuntal use of subordinate themes and rhythmic motives. He eliminated direct thematic reiteration while expanding and/or rewrit-ing entire cadenza and coda passages. He began each transcription with a relatively simple presentation of the theme and returned to each succeed-ing stanza with the melody more ostentatiously ornamented, the texture thicker, the dynamics more orchestral, and octave displacements em-ployed more daringly—repeatedly proving in performance that he was able to fit the theme into the same amount of time with additional notes piled on top.

One of Horowitz's more fanatical fans, the pianist Arthur McKenzie, was the only musician known to have succeeded in writing down with any accuracy all of Horowitz's transcriptions, and he therefore came to understand some of the secrets of composition and execution, secrets that had long baffled even the most astute aficionados. Horowitz, said McKenzie in an interview, was, during the heyday of his transcriptions, "probably the finest living composer for the piano—no one but Rachmaninoff had had such an idiomatic command of the instrument. Horowitz brilliantly took advantage of the piano's geography. For instance, in playing descending or ascending chromatic notes, he skipped a step here and there to make the execution easier, the sound brighter. He understood that the ear cannot hear those skipped notes, that the rhythmic impetus was far more important than playing every note. He also rewrote passages, interchanging the hands when playing chords, thirds, and octaves. He kept the transcriptions in his safe, believing that by not publishing them he was certain to go down in history as the greatest piano virtuoso of all time. For no one knew how he did what he did in them, nor could they be played without the music. He told me it was humanly impossible to write down what he had played. When I did it and showed him, he was astounded." Horowitz, concluded McKenzie, "was very streetwise on the stage: he spent much of his time playing *pppp* so that when he felt he might be losing his audience he could jab them with one of his *fffff*s. He could manipulate an audience better than any other pianist."[14]

In Horowitz's transformations of Liszt, Mendelssohn, and Sousa, octaves became booming chords, and scales, cascading strings of double-thirds and -sixths. With extraordinary digital independence, Horowitz navigated the entire keyboard, sometimes sustaining two or more melodies simultaneously and almost persuading his audience that three, not two, hands were at work. Describing his arrangement of the Liszt Rhapsody No. 2, Horowitz told critic Irving Kolodin: "No changes in harmony, all the original themes, but look what I do here," and proceeded to play one theme in the bass, another with the thumbs of both left and right hands, as the upper octaves resounded with a third theme in broken thirds. "Is fun, no?" he asked. "Is fun, yes!" responded a dumbfounded Kolodin.[15]

In the *Danse Macabre* and Hungarian Rhapsody No. 15, Horowitz produced waves of sound at climaxes, fearsome in their power, shifting in and out of focus according to the pedaling. From this orchestral volume of sound, Horowitz could change gears in an instant to trills, octaves, repeated notes, and *tremolos* in the treble register that seemed to transform the piano into a gigantic celesta. Recordings at that time could not capture the richness of color and the dynamic range of these arrangements, and in the codas of the recorded versions of the Hungarian Rhapsodies and *Danse Macabre,* the sequences of interlocked octaves and pounded chords give the impression that the dials of a machine have suddenly been turned too loud.

Although Horowitz's recordings were usually praised for their transparency, there remained a glassy percussiveness in his tone during *fortissimos* which resulted in a distortion of the sound. At moments, his 1940's and early 1950's recordings seem tinny and out of tune. Horowitz had reconciled himself to the limitations of recordings, concluding that the finest reproduction of a performance was still no more than a photographic likeness. "The best you can expect," he would say, "is black-and-white effects."[16] Certainly, no recording equipment available during the 1940's could come close to re-creating what he did in the concert hall.

Horowitz may have been determined that no other pianist play his transcriptions and discover how they were done, but he could hardly avoid scrutiny of his arrangement of Mussorgsky's *Pictures at an Exhibition.* Working from the original edition of the work and also Maurice Ravel's 1922 orchestration, Horowitz was not exclusively concerned with displaying his own virtuosity. Rather, he believed that Mussorgsky had not sufficiently understood the potential of the piano and that his clumsy keyboard writing could be improved with no detrimental effect to the composer's intention. "The piano has to sound idiomatic, and Mussorgsky was not a pianist," Horowitz reasoned. "So I decided that in order to make the piece more extroverted, [I would] double things; but I didn't change very much of the music, only the sound."[17]

Aside from octave doublings, Horowitz also redistributed passagework between the hands, transposed brief passages an octave below or above the original pitch, and inserted effective rhythmic patterns to replace Mussorgsky's uninteresting *tremolandos,* while keeping the harmonies the same. Only in one place did Horowitz seriously tamper with the music: In the final bars of "The Great Gate of Kiev," he augmented Mussorgsky's writing with a clanging-bell motif. One critic wrote about this change: "Horowitz's finale to this work is overpowering in sheer sonorous impact: that so much music can pour from one instrument or that two hands can manage so many notes seems scarcely credible."[18]

Although, according to Horowitz's most supportive critic, Olin Downes, the pianist's purpose was "to realize the intention of the composer and to refrain from gratuitous ornamentation or officious correction of any detail of Mussorgsky's text,"[19] the final result was another demonstration of Horowitz's technical genius. Irving Kolodin concluded that evident everywhere was "the old basic Horowitz wizardry: the sharp-stabbing accents, the ability to play prodigiously loud and preposterously soft, [and] when it was all through, one had the feeling that Horowitz had enlarged nobody's repertory but his own." Horowitz himself was quite pleased. Nearly three decades later, he declared, "Of that transcription I am proud. Changing the work took courage because a pianist is very much open to criticism in tampering with an established master. But I did a good job there and played it very well."[20]

The discreet, essentially modest approach Horowitz had employed with the Mussorgsky was tossed aside for his haunting version of *Danse Macabre* and his Liszt Hungarian Rhapsodies. Of these, Hungarian Rhapsody No. 15 was the most drastically altered, for Horowitz deleted Liszt's short introduction, moving almost immediately to the main theme, which he introduced with a sequence of martial-sounding octaves. Horowitz's double-*forte* passages are as brutally strident as trombones, and the trills and melodic flourishes have a clangorous ring that frequently borders on the shrill. He composed a completely new cadenza for this work. Interlocking octaves run up and down the keyboard in a thick-textured rattle, rendering the bass notes nearly indistinguishable at the triumphant end. The *New York Times* noted that Horowitz had incorporated the Liszt setting, along with some ideas from Berlioz's orchestral version, "plus an assortment of pyrotechnical bedevilments of his own invention that go far beyond anything ever imagined by either composer."[21]

Technical feats abound in Horowitz's recordings of the Hungarian Rhapsodies. The repeated octaves of Rhapsody No. 6 sound as effortless as the repeated single notes of the Second; the shimmering trilled *tremolo* in the Fifteenth is as brilliant as most pianists' single-note trills. As he brings the *friska* portions to a close, he creates a body of orchestral sound, an illusion only he had mastered. "The impulse behind the performer's maneuvers . . . remains remarkably, almost inhumanly tense," wrote critic Arthur Berger. "No other soloist comes near Mr. Horowitz in this respect; a listener is impelled to hang on with nervous, breathless attention. And since Mr. Horowitz is constantly at work ringing new changes on his colossal gamut of pianistic touches and the stupendous range of the degrees of loudness he can achieve, a listener may find himself constantly on a nervous edge, wondering what the pianist will do next, or whether the next effect will be as good as the last one."[22]

In his Liszt Hungarian Rhapsody No. 2, Horowitz bedazzled his audience with a contrapuntal combination of three of the work's principal motives along with a rapid and accurate octave passage near the close. "The music is unquestionably superior in its original form," said *Musical America.* "But no one who has heard the performance would ever quarrel with Mr. Horowitz for having his way with it."[23]

During the period 1940–1953, Horowitz seemed driven to inform the world that he was its greatest pianistic technician, and that even Liszt himself might have gasped at his accomplishments. Yet the artistic, physical, and emotional toll was enormous. Years later he stated with regret: "I'll never know how I could ever have allowed myself to stray so far from the destination that I had set for myself in my youth. I did not want to put on a pianistic show, or an act. I would rather have done anything in the world, or nothing at all, than continue to be a sort of glorified juggler. I never wanted to be a superman of the piano."[24]

CHAPTER SIXTEEN

A TARNISHED
JUBILEE

*"In one way we are happy, in another way we are unhappy.
Every human being is born like that. People think I have
everything ... oh ... he is the greatest in the world, he is
making money, he is traveling. But I have my own ..."*[1]

ince Russia, Horowitz had had no permanent home. Most of his
summers had been spent in California, early falls and holidays at the
Toscanini estate in Riverdale, much of the rest of the year in New York
at the Madison Hotel on Fifty-eighth Street, where Wanda looked after
Sonia while Horowitz toured. This rootless existence ended in 1944
when Horowitz purchased a townhouse in Manhattan from the playwright George S. Kaufman. Located on East Ninety-fourth Street just off
Fifth Avenue and near Central Park, the house was a spacious, white-
stoned, five-story structure. In the second-floor front parlor-library
Horowitz kept his impressive collection of musical scores and recordings,
and in the living room at the back of the same floor, a growing collection
of nineteenth- and twentieth-century paintings.

Initially, Horowitz had collected only snuffboxes, which he meticulously displayed in a large wooden chest lined with green silk. Then the
conductor Vladimir Golschmann, a sagacious collector of modern paintings, interested Horowitz in the idea of investing in art. As a result,
Horowitz started a collection of French Impressionist paintings, financ-
ing it by selling a set of czarist Russian glasses he had purchased some
years earlier. "Nobody told me what to buy," Horowitz later declared
proudly. "I studied books about history of painting and went to all the
museums and then bought what I liked in 1945—and didn't pay much
money."[2] Aided by major New York art dealers—Sam Saltz, Daniel Sai-
denburg, Justin Tannhauser—Horowitz collected quickly. He became, in
fact, a fanatical buyer, stating that "all I earn from one art I spend on

another. No stocks, no bonds."[3] His collection soon contained works of Degas, Modigliani, Matisse, Manet, Pissarro, Rouault, and Picasso, the prize being Picasso's *Acrobat en Repos,* purchased for a mere $18,000. This last, which Horowitz was fond of showing off to friends, seemed to convey something of his own character: Picasso's acrobat sits with knees crossed and arms folded, facial expression and entire figure conveying a youthful power and a sophisticated innocence.

Guests invited to Ninety-fourth Street usually arrived around ten P.M. for music making and card games that lasted until two or three in the morning. Horowitz was an indefatigable host. After greeting people on the ground floor, he brought them up to the living room, where there were two Steinway grand pianos, one the 1933 wedding gift from the manufacturer. On one piano were photographs of Horowitz's favorite musicians—Toscanini, Rachmaninoff, Paderewski, Milstein, Hofmann—all inscribed. Surrounding them were the paintings. Horowitz sometimes crawled about the living-room floor on hands and knees, switching on the lights he had had attached to each frame, pointing excitedly to the canvases, declaring with gusto, "This is my fortune! Now, you know, it is better to put money into paintings because that grows. It's growing all the time!"[4] After the tour, it was time for cards, which Horowitz left primarily to Wanda and the guests. Occasionally, he would go to the piano and play new repertory from his latest concert programs—delicacies like Variations on the Aria "La Ricordanza" by Czerny or the Clementi Sonata in B-flat Major, Op. 47, No. 2; then there might be Scarlatti sonatas, unfamiliar pieces by Clementi, or some of Horowitz's transcriptions. The music was punctuated by rest periods, during which Horowitz stretched out on the couch underneath the Picasso and regaled his guests with his infectious good humor, appropriately reflected by his festive and colorful vest-and-bow-tie attire.

Horowitz attended the parties of others only infrequently, but when he did and was in form he could be an entertaining, witty guest. He had always enjoyed playacting and was an amateur actor of some ability. One evening, friends remembered, he assumed the character of a befuddled but determined aspirant for a scholarship at a music school. Clad in a skintight checked suit, his neck wrapped in a long woolen muffler, his hair slicked down and parted in the middle, he looked, acted, and spoke like a member of the Moscow Art Theatre. "I play the piano," was the only line allotted to him, and he repeated it desperately in answer to any

Steinway & Sons

Twenty-three-year-old Vladimir Horowitz at the time of his Berlin
debut in January 1926. His manager insisted that Horowitz's hair
be cut short in the European style then popular.

Steinway & Sons

During the summer of 1928, following his first American tour, Horowitz poses with his first automobile, a Studebaker.

Steinway & Sons

Horowitz with his German chauffeur. (1928)

Sporting a monocle and dressed to the nines, Horowitz vacations with Paul Schmidt in Cannes during the summer of 1928, following his triumphant first tour of America.

Steinway & Sons

Having created a furor in New York in January 1928 with his performance of the Tchaikovsky Concerto, Horowitz became a celebrity overnight, frequently sketched and photographed by newspapers.

Steinway & Sons

Steinway & Sons

Courtesy of James Dick

Alexander Merovitch (left), Horowitz's manager from 1924 to 1934, on the balcony of his Paris apartment with Horowitz and Paul Schmidt. (1930)

United Press International Photo

The great German pianist Artur Schnabel, who had encouraged Horowitz to leave Russia when they first met there in 1923, photographed with Horowitz in Berlin in 1930.

Celebrated in Paris as the "king of the concert stage," an elegantly attired Horowitz embarks on the *Europa* for his fifth American tour in October 1931.

Steinway & Sons

Horowitz mountain-climbing
in the Swiss Engadine,
following his 1929–1930
concert season.

Steinway & Sons

Nathan Milstein, Horowitz, an unidentified woman, and
Alexander Merovitch on the beach at Antibes in the
summer of 1930.

Courtesy of Berthe Malko

At a picnic in Copenhagen in October 1933, Horowitz
announced to friends his engagement to Wanda Toscanini. From
left: Berthe Malko, Horowitz, conducting-student Hans
Schroeder, conductor Nicolai Malko. (Malko points to
Horowitz's secretary, a young German who had been the
pianist's near-constant companion for almost six years.)

Courtesy of Marilyn Meyer (Cosmo-Sileo Co.)

The Piatigorsky-
Horowitz-Milstein trio
preparing for their first
chamber-music
appearance at Carnegie
Hall on March 30, 1932.

United Press International Photo

Arturo Toscanini suggested to
Horowitz that he and Wanda
travel on tour together in
England as a trial run for their
marriage. Chaperoned by
Wanda's sister, Wally
(Countess Castelbarco), left,
they arrive in London in
November 1933.

Courtesy of Marilyn Meyer (Cosmo-Sileo Co.)

Alexander Merovitch and "his boys" arriving in New York
on the S.S. *Leviathan* for their 1932–1933 American season.

United Press International Photo

Portrait of an improbable match: in
January 1934, two weeks after
their marriage, Mr. and Mrs. Vladimir
Horowitz arrive in New York.

Steinway & Sons

Leaving Milan on the S.S. *Rex* on December 28,
1933, are the newly married Horowitz, Milstein,
Piatigorsky, Toscanini, and Bernardino Molinari.

Wide World Photos

The hands of Vladimir Horowitz. (May 1936)

On August 29, 1939, at the Lucerne Festival, Horowitz and Toscanini receive a standing ovation after their performance of the Brahms Second Concerto, the last time either would play in Europe until after the war. Three days later, Hitler invaded Poland.

Courtesy of Harvey Sachs

In Los Angeles, on December
9, 1939, Toscanini and Bruno
Walter congratulate Horowitz
backstage after his first
American recital in five years.

United Press International Photo

In June 1942, Horowitz visited the Walt Disney Studios in
Hollywood with the great Russian pianist Sergei
Rachmaninoff, his idol and father-figure. This is the only
known photograph of Horowitz and Rachmaninoff together.
After viewing the film, *Mickey's Opry House*, in which Mickey
Mouse plays Rachmaninoff's famous Prelude in C-Sharp
Minor, the composer remarked to Walt Disney (center): "I
have heard my inescapable piece done marvelously by some o
the best pianists, and murdered cruelly by amateurs, but
never was I more stirred than by the performance of the great
Maestro Mouse."

Wide World Photos

Horowitz and actor Paul Henreid congratulate each other in Los Angeles on December 14, 1945, after they both received their final citizenship papers. Horowitz remembered: "This was one of the greatest moments of my life."

Walt Disney Productions

Photograph by the *New York Times*

In the living room of their New York
townhouse, Wanda and Horowitz pose with
their fourteen-year-old daughter, Sonia, for a
1948 *New York Times Sunday Magazine* family
portrait. Above them is Picasso's *Acrobate au
Repos*. (1948)

Although RCA Victor publicity photos
portrayed a contented couple, the marriage of
Horowitz and Wanda Toscanini was, in
reality, an extremely volatile one. Horowitz
and Wanda were frequently estranged. (1948)

Steinway & Sons

Courtesy of Carl Erpf, Jr.

Horowitz in Central Park in 1950 with Carl
Erpf, his secretary-valet and traveling
companion, who lived with him at the Elysée
Hotel after Horowitz separated from Wanda
in 1949.

Back together, in September 1951, Horowitz
and Wanda leave New York for London and
Paris, his first European appearances since
1939.

United Press International Photo

Courtesy of Byron Janis

HOROWITZ'S STUDENTS

(Studied with Horowitz, 1944–1948)
Lorin Maazel (left), fifteen, and Byron Janis, sixteen, backstage afte the 1944 Pittsburgh performance of the Rachmaninoff Second Concerto which Horowitz attended by chance Janis became Horowitz's first student.

(1953–1955)
Gary Graffman in 1948, age twenty five years before he began to study with Horowitz.

Courtesy of Gary Graffma

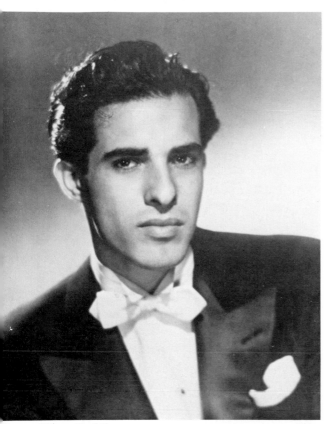

(1956–1958)
Coleman Blumfield in 1956. Two years later, Horowitz abruptly ended his lessons and forbade him to use his name in his publicity.

Courtesy of Coleman Blumfield

Courtesy of Alexander Fiorillo

(1960–1962)
Alexander Fiorillo. Horowitz promised him concerts and a recording contract but the pianist ended his lessons with ulcers and his career aborted by the draft.

Courtesy of Ronald Turini

(1957–1963)
Horowitz giving a pep talk in his
library to his favorite student,
Ronald Turini, before Turini's
1961 Carnegie Hall debut.

Courtesy of Ivan Dav

(1961–1962)
Ivan Davis. He began coaching with Horowitz after winning the 1961
Liszt Competition and was as much a confidant as a student.

question asked by the school's headmaster. By the end of the skit, his audience was exhausted from laughter. (Wanda also had her theatrical side. She bore a distinct resemblance to her famous father and friends remembered that at New Year's Eve parties at the Riverdale mansion, she was much given to donning Arturo Toscanini attire, down to the moustache, and tap-dancing on the Maestro's piano.)

Horowitz seldom went to concerts or visited nightclubs to amuse himself, but he did occasionally venture out to hear popular music. Since his first visit to the United States, he had become increasingly infatuated with jazz. A great fan of jazz pianist Art Tatum, Horowitz had improvised in the idiom for his own entertainment and that of his friends. On one occasion he was taken to a jazz club in New York to hear Joey Bushkin bang the ivories. That night Louis Armstrong was also visiting the club, so the trumpeter blew a New Orleans medley to greet him. Someone pointed out to the manager that Horowitz couldn't see Bushkin's fingers from where he was seated. "He won't learn a thing," was the sarcastic reply, and Horowitz shot back, "Don't worry. I see it here," pointing to his ear. "I won't try the fast, technical stuff," Bushkin declared, motioning to Horowitz, "because that man's got it covered hard!" Horowitz was obviously enjoying himself as he listened to Armstrong and Bushkin. "That Horowitz is a cat, a real gone cat!" someone shouted. "He digs the bit!"[5]

A friend who shared Horowitz's enthusiasm for jazz was pianist Oscar Levant, famous for his performances of Gershwin, a star of stage, screen, and radio and a professional wit. Levant shared Horowitz's passion for a good joke and was one of the few who could invariably make Horowitz laugh when he was feeling depressed. In return, Horowitz would resort to outlandish jokes and tricks to get a rise out of Levant. One of Horowitz's favorite parlor games was to play a short piece for Levant and Sonia, the tune with his right hand and the bass with his derrière.[6] He would also indulge in his own elaboration of the popular song "Tea for Two," replete with flourishes and brilliant double-thirds. In the late afternoon, the two pianists sometimes took long walks down Broadway, and invariably people would stop in recognition to ask for an autograph—from Levant. "Don't you resent that they never ask you?" Levant once asked Horowitz. Laughing heartily, Horowitz replied, "I'm glad, I'm so happy. Let them ask you. . . . Take his autograph; take his. He is the greatest pianist!"[7]

The two friends would commiserate with each other on the strains of touring and compare notes about audiences in different cities. "One spot that was not exactly inspiring to touring musicians was Des Moines, Iowa," recalled Levant in his autobiography, *The Unimportance of Being Oscar*. "One winter Vladimir Horowitz asked me where I would open my tour. I told him: 'Des Moines.' Horowitz rolled his eyes upward in sympathy. 'Dostoyevski!' he groaned commiseratingly."[8] Horowitz also told Levant one of his favorite stories about Rachmaninoff. Once, when Horowitz was scheduled to give a concert in Providence, Rhode Island, he asked Rachmaninoff if the acoustics were good there. The answer was: "If the check is good, the acoustics are good."[9]

Both Levant and Horowitz were notorious for canceling concerts and for sometimes refusing to play even after arriving in a tour city. "Horowitz gave me lessons in canceling concerts," said Levant. "I used to cancel as far ahead as two weeks when I was ill. 'Never do that,' Horowitz explained. 'Always cancel at the last minute.' The year my mother died I canceled all my concerts except one. For some reason I had to play Akron, Ohio. Among others, I'd canceled Cincinnati. The following spring, Horowitz suddenly canceled Cincinnati and the local manager called me to ask if I would replace him. I indignantly replied, 'But I already canceled Cincinnati!' "[10] When an advertising solicitor for *Musical America* tried to sell space to both pianists, Levant suggested they take an ad together reading "Vladimir Horowitz and Oscar Levant available for a limited number of cancellations."[11]

Actually, Horowitz's cancellations had become no joking matter. During the 1940's they steadily increased, and by the middle of the winter or early spring of each year, newspaper articles often would refer to his colds, attacks of influenza, bronchial infections, and bouts of tonsillitis. Horowitz was continually distressed by poor food and noisy accommodations, and usually at about midnight after a recital he telephoned Wanda to report on his performance and complain about his hotel. By the end of a season, Horowitz would be exhausted. With his wife and daughter he would retreat to a rented house in Hollywood for summers spent resting, swimming, bicycling, and seeing movie previews. During these vacations he carefully tended his health. In 1947, for instance, he was intent on losing fifteen pounds, and Wanda wrote to Merovitch: "Volodya has lost weight and looks like an Apollo. I wish I could say the same for myself. . . . We don't see many people and for the moment I don't miss them. I still prefer the climate to the people in California."[12]

In general, the only prolonged periods Horowitz had with Wanda and Sonia were during summers, and then the strains and pressures of touring were all too often replaced by family conflicts. Alex Steinert was host to the couple one summer in California before they rented a house of their own, and he remembered Horowitz as "tremendously temperamental, often throwing tantrums—and things on the floor. I wanted to get away from this and suggested that I leave them alone."[13] After a full season of concerts, Horowitz tended to be highly nervous, and according to Lowell Benedict, "he would get really hysterical about his management or a bad piano or a bad concert hall or review, and he took it out on Wanda. He yelled and screamed a good deal of the time, and she would gently try to pacify him and generally succeeded in doing so, trying to make his life as comfortable as possible."[14]

It seemed that anything could set Horowitz off. One summer guest said that "Horowitz and Wanda would fight like Spanish fishwives, really violent arguments that were quite unpleasant. It was unbelievable and so embarrassing that I couldn't take it and would go out for a walk. They fought over just about everything. Horowitz was having trouble with his stomach and with colitis, so if his food was not pulverized enough, that was cause for the beginning of an argument. Often, Horowitz was not feeling physically well and was very self-conscious about having to pass gas all the time. This made him extremely irritable. Still, he might sit down and play a whole volume of Scarlatti sonatas for the fun of it and could be marvelous company."[15]

One continuing subject of conflict with Wanda was Horowitz's friendships. After Lowell Benedict had amicably resigned from Horowitz's employ in 1942, he had been replaced by a young man, which aggravated the underlying tensions of the Horowitz marriage. Benedict was working in the public-relations department at MGM Studios in New York City when one day he received an urgent telephone call from Wanda begging him to come to Ninety-fourth Street as soon as possible. Not only had Benedict's successor not worked out, but there had been, he said, "an explosion." The assistant had been ejected from the house, and Horowitz, remembered Benedict, was "hysterical, impossible to deal with. Wanda had her bags packed and was ready to leave her husband, but first she wanted to make sure that somebody would be with him. And so my boss at MGM allowed me to take three weeks off and travel with him. Horowitz was very bitter and angry and did not want to finish the tour."[16]

Benedict managed to persuade Horowitz to play his last four recitals of the season but found keeping him ready and able to perform a formidable challenge. "Horowitz's feelings alternated wildly between hating his friend and missing him. During the tour, we were invited to, of all things, a wrestling match, and Horowitz, to my amazement, accepted. He sat there, watching two young thugs who couldn't have been more than twenty years old, and I thought to myself, Oh my God, what's going to happen now? At the last concert Horowitz refused to play; he simply didn't feel like performing. I got quite angry and told him to get the hell out on the stage, and he did. After we returned to New York, I didn't want to see him too soon again."[17]

Aside from such tensions, another source of unhappiness between Wanda and Horowitz was the matter of their daughter, Sonia. The charming little girl with the impertinent sense of humor had developed into a subdued and withdrawn child. Toscanini had always adored her and counted her among his favorite grandchildren, but Sonia had not been immune to the Maestro's violent flares of temper, nor to the cruel silent treatment that had distressed Wanda, also, while she was growing up. For instance, when Sonia had abandoned the piano for the violin, Toscanini had recruited Edwin Bachmann, first violinist of the NBC Orchestra, as her teacher. Bachmann remembered coming to the Riverdale house in 1947 and finding the thirteen-year-old Sonia upset, her eyes red from weeping. It turned out that two weeks before she had committed some minor infraction and Toscanini had been furious ever since. "Nono won't talk to me!" the girl wailed. Bachmann was astounded and decided that "Toscanini did not know the difference between a one-dollar bill and a fifty, for he was treating Sonia not as a child but as an equal."[18]

During her early teens, Sonia gave up both piano and violin and turned her attention to painting, poetry, and horses. Although Horowitz had never encouraged his daughter to practice an instrument ("If she must be urged," he said, "it's no use anyway."[19]), he did believe Sonia had a talent for painting, and proudly announced in a 1949 interview that she had just sold her first canvas. The purchaser was none other than Arturo Toscanini. Sonia had asked only $5 for it, but the Maestro explained that an artist must respect his craft and paid her $100.[20] The eighty-two-year-old Maestro carried the painting with him to Europe that year and hung it in his home in Milan, where he would insist that all visitors admire it.

Despite Toscanini's notorious fluctuations of mood, he appeared to give Sonia more sincere attention than did her own father, and the girl treated "Nono" with great respect and trust. But the affection and discipline Sonia needed could not be adequately provided by her grandparents or by the hovering governesses who took care of the girl during the week. Largely neglected by a self-absorbed father and a mother whose self-defined purpose was to minister to her genius husband, Sonia began to behave in an aggressive and unpredictable manner which was a considerable contrast to her former playful exuberance. This was characterized by extreme changes of mood and hostile behavior at school. Although still capable and energetic when she wanted to be, the girl now spent a great deal of time alone in her room, staring at the pictures of her idol, actress Ingrid Bergman, writing poetry, and sporadically painting. An only child abandoned by her parents for months at a time, Sonia became wild and impulsive, full of pranks, and as the years went by her attention-getting devices became more and more violent, dangerous to herself and to others. "Sonia was a kinetic girl, very spoiled, and allowed to do pretty much as she pleased,"[21] recalled a childhood friend who played with the girl at the Riverdale house. As evidenced by her actions—from smoking cigarettes and using four-letter words to setting curtains on fire and then trying to do the same to the dog—Sonia was highly antagonistic to her home environment. During the summers, both parents ignored the fourteen-year-old's cigarettes and swearing and apparently felt unable to control the situation. Horowitz's attitude ranged from indifference to feeling burdened by Sonia, while Wanda seemed to be more concerned with the child and to feel some guilt over her condition. In 1948, in desperation, she hired a psychologist, Anna Orentlich, to help look after Sonia, but the damage looked irreversible. It was, said Alex Steinert, "a classic case of the unhappiness of a child born to famous parents."[22] The one member of the family who seemed to be able to readily communicate with Sonia was her aunt Wally, with whom Sonia spent considerable time in Italy, in the process growing close to her first cousin, Emanuela. Sonia also relied on her grandparents, on Wanda's close friend, Olga Strumillo, and on Merovitch's wife, Rosamund.

In her late teens and early twenties, Sonia worsened considerably. Lashing back at the pressures of being Sonia Horowitz, she regularly embarrassed her family. In 1945 the eleven-year-old girl was registered in the George Junior Republic School, a home for delinquent adolescent girls in Courtland, New York, where, once, Horowitz came and played a mini-recital.[23] After she had run away from one corrective school in up-state New York, Wally offered to look after her for a while; then she entered another school and was soon dismissed for bizarre, violent behavior. Sonia resented being sent away and would always escape at the earliest opportunity. Schools were followed by reformatories, and reformatories were followed by sanatoriums. Gitta Gradova, who had constant access to the Horowitzes, recalled that Sonia "was extraordinarily gifted, writing poetry, and at age fourteen talking intelligently about *War and Peace*, studying deeply different religions, mastering a number of languages. But she was not going to execute or follow through with anything in the presence of her father on the one hand and her grandfather on the other. It was too much pressure, and it was not possible to follow in the footsteps of that kind of talent."[24] Horowitz's first cousin, Natasha Saitzoff, concluded from this that "there must be something strange" in the Toscaninis and the Horowitzes, "a dark quality with that kind of genius, which manifested itself in Sonia, in her extreme unhappiness."[25]

Compared with her parents, Sonia felt she was inferior and was certain that anything she might do would not be enough. When she was older, Sonia remarked bitterly that she had inherited only two things from her brilliant forebears: dandruff from her grandfather and a tendency toward spastic colitis from her father.[26] Horowitz did little to try to bolster the girl's self-esteem, essentially treating her as a burden to be tolerated. Steinert recalled spending one evening with Sonia at the Horowitzes and noting that she had grown into an attractive young woman of eighteen years. "At the party Sonia was, at first, rather belligerent, but I pushed her back into a chair and said, 'Now you sit down; you're not going to get away with that with me,' and suddenly this killing expression came into her eyes. But the minute I countered her, she sort of melted. She wanted to talk about growing up, about a possible career. She wanted to have people pay attention to her, but her mother and father were such stiff competition. Then, all at once, Horowitz's nose came over the stairway and he came down the stairs with his hands folded across his chest, as always, like Toscanini. I told him, 'You know, I've had the most wonderful talk with your daughter,' and he waved me off, and said '*Meshuga*,' 'crazy.' "[27]

Sonia, extraordinarily sensitive, was doubtless hurt by her father's apparently uncaring attitude. She grew progressively more estranged from both her parents, said Steinert. "Wanda tried to be nice to her but Sonia wouldn't have anything to do with her mother. It was perfectly awful. Sonia was jealous of Wanda."[28] Still, Wanda did make an attempt to be a mother to her daughter. Horowitz was quite another matter. "She was simply foreign to him," recalled one family intimate. "He didn't know what to do with her or how to deal with the situation, but intellectually they had a wonderful relationship at times. He respected her intelligence and was always in a kind of awe that she existed, that he had made her— he was very impressed by that."[29] In frequent and violent arguments, Wanda would blame Horowitz for Sonia's condition and the focus of hostility would spread to the other conflicts in the marriage and the various irritations involved with concert tours.

In the fall of 1949, the problems apparently irreconcilable, Horowitz moved out of the Ninety-fourth Street house and into the Élysée Hotel on East Fifty-fourth Street, subsequently transferring to the Hotel Volney on East Seventy-fourth Street. The separation lasted off and on until 1953. In a letter to Sasha Greiner in September 1949, Horowitz confirmed that he and Wanda had indeed decided "to separate. But *not* to divorce each other. This is why neither Wanda nor Sonia have spent this summer with me." Horowitz added: "Please do not spread this sensational news."[30]

Horowitz had been encouraged to experiment with this period of independence from his family by his psychoanalyst, Lawrence Kubie, who had developed a keen interest not only in the pianist's treatment but in his career. Even before Horowitz had made a definite decision to live separately from Wanda, Dr. Kubie realized that he was going to need someone to look after him full time. The analyst had therefore introduced Horowitz to his fifty-five-year-old brother-in-law, Carl Erpf, who became Horowitz's secretary-valet and traveling companion in late 1948. Erpf had been a successful lawyer in the securities market before alcoholism forced his retirement in 1944. Now, thanks to the ministrations of his brother-in-law, Erpf was back on his feet. Like Horowitz, Erpf was separated from his wife, Kubie's sister, and Kubie believed that the two men living together at the Élysée Hotel would be mutually therapeutic, as Horowitz needed someone to take care of him and Erpf needed something to do to keep his mind off his problems. There was also the hope that Erpf, who was something of a financial wizard, would assist Horowitz with his taxes and with the increasingly complicated negotiations over his RCA Victor contracts.

It turned out that Horowitz and Erpf immediately adored each other, and so Erpf was hired to take charge of Horowitz's domestic life and to travel with him during the 1948–49 season. He found Horowitz a demanding employer during this period, one determined to assert himself in new ways. Erpf's son, Carl junior, later explained: "It was my father's job to keep Horowitz under control as much as possible but he confided to me that he was nearly uncontrollable."[31] Horowitz frequently canceled concerts and recording sessions; he often woke Erpf for no good reason in the middle of the night. But the kindly rehabilitated alcoholic was infinitely patient, and stayed with Horowitz until his own death in 1951 at age fifty-eight.

During the first year with Horowitz, Erpf had realized that the job was too physically demanding for him alone, so in November 1949 another man entered the picture. He was Kenneth Leedom, an ambitious and aspiring actor in his twenties who was glad to give up the near-starvation wages of a job at the Columbia Presbyterian Hospital to work for the famous pianist. Leedom—tall, blond, and strikingly handsome—was hired to be a kind of touring stevedore. His duties consisted of loading and unloading Horowitz's suitcases, making every train trip with him, settling him into hotels, and acting as contact between his New York management and local managers. Although Erpf sometimes traveled with the pair, he spent increasing amounts of time back at their hotel in New York, tending to Horowitz's correspondence and preparing to make him comfortable upon his return.

Horowitz's entourage was now complete, and the pianist might have been described as leading a coddled life. He continued to see Dr. Kubie when in New York and would joke to the doctor's nephew, Carl Erpf, Jr., "your uncle is trying to take me back to the womb!"[32]

Merovitch, also, was occasionally about, still drifting in and out of Horowitz's business affairs, usually as a liaison with RCA Victor. The former manager was now reduced to expediting recording sessions, mailing test records to Horowitz for his approval, and suggesting new repertory.

Finally, in the background but ever present was Wanda, living alone with Sonia on Ninety-fourth Street but still occasionally traveling with her husband for a short segment of a tour. "Even when they weren't living together, Horowitz absolutely needed Wanda," remembered Leedom. "He wouldn't make a move without talking to her."[33] Nevertheless, Horowitz did not want to return to the house and spent summers with Leedom in rented houses on Fire Island and in East Hampton, cultivating a newfound hobby, fishing.

During those years, there was one other important figure in Horowitz's career, the Russian-born concert manager David Libidins, who was associated with Horowitz from 1951 to 1953. Annie Friedberg had handled Horowitz for eight seasons, but she was now elderly and could no longer provide the customized attention he wanted. He welcomed a change, and when she died in November 1952 he chose Libidins. On occasion, the Friedberg office had been driven to distraction by the complaints of local managers protesting Horowitz's cancellations, and patience with Horowitz's foibles was an essential prerequisite for his new manager. Libidins was known to be good-natured and relaxed, a businessman with a sense of humor. The two would be able to speak together in Russian, and Libidins was confident that he could deal with the highstrung Horowitz without too much trouble. When Erpf had first called Libidins in 1951 to inquire about the possibility of his taking on a new client, Libidins had responded, "No, I can't. Not for anybody. Nobody—not even if it were Vladimir Horowitz. Well, maybe for Horowitz."[34] To Libidins's amazement, the reply was, "But it *is* Horowitz."

Shortly thereafter, Horowitz and Libidins met and Horowitz found he liked the tall, broad-shouldered man with the loud, husky voice. Libidins's combination of candor and a no-nonsense approach to business was the perfect foil for the elusive Horowitz. As expected, Libidins was willing to manage him for even less than the usual 10 percent of the profits. Horowitz made three additional demands: "First, I don't want any plants onstage while I play. Second, no drapes or velvet or silk blackdrops onstage. And third, I don't want to be billed in any advertisement as 'King of Pianists.' Kings should be elected and not proclaimed. Besides, if you have to be advertised as a king, then you aren't one."[35]

Indeed, by 1951 such proclamations were unnecessary, for judging from his instantly sold-out houses and his fee structure, Horowitz was clearly the reigning monarch of the American concert stage. Gone were Hofmann, Rachmaninoff, and Paderewski, and although Rubinstein played many more recitals and concerto dates than Horowitz (one hundred a year to Horowitz's forty), Horowitz compensated by commanding the highest fee of any pianist. From $2,750 per recital in 1942, this had risen to as much as $8,500 for his 1953 Carnegie Hall recital—

from which was subtracted $1,250 for expenses, netting $7,250, an extraordinary profit for a classical artist at that time. Except in Chicago and New York, Horowitz did not produce concerts himself, and he therefore did not receive the entire gross minus expenses but rather a fixed fee—usually $4,000 per recital, although that could rise to $5,000 depending on the size of the house. Occasionally, when a manager doubtful of Horowitz's box-office appeal refused the $4,000 guarantee and opted instead to have him take a percentage of the gross, Horowitz was delighted, for then he could easily walk away with $5,600. Horowitz was a canny businessman who knew the size of every house, the scaling of tickets, and his travel expenses down to the penny. The only time he would reduce his fee to $3,500 or $3,700 was when, for instance, he wanted to play a concerto with a particular conductor, such as his 1949 appearance with the New Orleans Symphony under the direction of his Italian friend Massimo Freccia.

Horowitz had become increasingly selective about which concerto dates to accept, and between 1945 and 1953 his principal income was derived from solo recitals. Playing a concerto required extra rehearsals, accustoming himself to an ensemble, and the possible nuisance of a conflict with a conductor, whereas a solo recital allowed him complete free-dom. Also, he found playing the same few scores over and over boring, and he complained that in a twenty-five-minute concerto he could show the audience only a tiny portion of his ability. Finally, the money was considerably less rewarding than for a recital because for $4,000 Horowitz was obliged to appear at two or three subscription concerts during the same week. On the other hand, if he should give two solo recitals instead of the two repeat performances with orchestra, he could instead earn $12,000 in a given week. Considering Horowitz's near obsession with fees, it is hardly surprising that by 1953 the ratio between his solo recitals and his orchestral dates was four to one and his career had become immensely lucrative. During the 1952–53 season, he played only four orchestral concerts but thirty-four solo recitals, netting him approximately $171,800, which did not include his $40,000 guarantee from RCA Victor.

Nonetheless, Horowitz had chosen to limit his income by accepting no more than thirty-five engagements per year, by restricting the release of his RCA recordings to those which met his stringent standards, and by refusing to appear on television or on radio or in motion pictures. In 1949, for instance, he turned down a $100,000 offer to make a movie sound track. His principal reservation about the medium was that he didn't trust Hollywood moguls to make artistic use of his work. One day, while having his hair trimmed, he told his barber about the movie offer and the response was, "Just a sound track? And they won't see you playing? Don't take it!"—which settled Horowitz's mind on the subject.[36]

When he was invited to play a short, live television recital on the *Bell Telephone Hour* for a fee of $5,000, he likewise refused. "The studios make me nervous," he explained to his disappointed manager. "I worry that I may make a little extra pause or decide to play something a little slower, and they'll cut me off because the half hour is up. Not for me."[37] Horowitz reasoned that if he accepted radio, television or film offers, he might "enrich the government and myself," but "there's nothing like the personal contact of the concert hall."[38] He would declare firmly: "I want to be paid, but I will not be bought."[39]

The artistic standards of commercial broadcasting were simply not high enough for him, and despite constant pleas he would not give radio concerts. Not until 1951 did Horowitz's friend Abram Chasins (then music director of the New York radio station WQXR) persuade him to allow the second half of his April 24 Carnegie Hall recital to be broadcast. Libidins was pleased and asked Horowitz how much to charge for this. To his astonishment, the reply was: "Nothing! Well, I'm playing anyhow. It is Carnegie Hall, where I like to play. It is no extra trouble."[40] Aside from Horowitz's short birthday tribute to President Roosevelt in 1942, the 1951 recital was his first radio event, and he decided on another first by having RCA Victor record the concert live for future release. The radio program was a tremendous success, the station receiving the largest response ever for that sort of broadcast. "These are all raves," Chasins exclaimed to Horowitz a few days after the performance, holding up a huge stack of mail. "I was concerned, Abram," replied Horowitz, "because you once told me that people write in only when they're angry."[41]

Another important development in Horowitz's career that year was a fall tour of Europe. His appearances there would be his first since 1939 and his last until the spring of 1982. Although the trip was publicized as being for the duration of the 1951–52 season, in fact Horowitz traveled for only two months, playing three October concerts in London and two November recitals in Paris. By November 20, he was back in the United States.

The European tour was meant to be a triumphant return, and Libidins had arranged it with no little effort. Horowitz worried over the acoustics in London, for Queen's Hall, his favorite, had been destroyed during the war. He had put off playing in London until the new Royal Festival Hall had been finished.

So, after an absence of nearly thirteen years, Horowitz appeared once again in London on October 8, 1951, in a performance of the Rachmaninoff Third Concerto with the Royal Philharmonic Orchestra under Walter Susskind. His recordings on the HMV label were as popular as ever in Britain, and the hall was packed. Despite his long absence, Horowitz seemed to have the same hold on the English public as before the war. "Such is the magic of the name," wrote one critic, "that the hall was packed with people, cheerfully prepared to pay grossly inflated prices."[42] Of the Rachmaninoff performance, the London *Times* raved that while "memory of his individual quality may have become a little blurred . . . no one who heard him last night . . . on his return at long last is likely to forget for another dozen years. . . . Mr. Horowitz's handling of the top three octaves of the keyboard made one wonder whether it was, after all, a piano and not some new one-man orchestra that was being played."[43]

In his room at Claridge's Hotel, Horowitz prepared for the first of his two solo recitals on October 13. Apparently he and Wanda had patched things up for the tour, for she had accompanied him to London, her favorite European city. In a letter to Sasha Greiner dated October 9, Wanda told of Horowitz's enthusiastic reception, adding: "You can be happy about what they say about the piano. Volodya played his 347 [in the Rachmaninoff Concerto] after much debating and worrying that here in London they don't like the tone of the American Steinways. When I inquired when the public had ever heard an American instrument, [I was] told that it was thirty years ago when Hofmann played his own instrument brought from New York. Volodya has found a nice piano here . . . but still doesn't know which piano he will take to Paris. Here [i.e., the Royal Festival Hall] the acoustics are on the sound-proof side and quite deceiving."[44]

Two days before his first recital, Horowitz went to the HMV studios to record two Scarlatti sonatas and the Chopin Impromptu, Op. 29, and Nocturne, Op. 72, No. 1, all of which he had programmed for that concert. At Festival Hall he quite bowled over his English audience, although the critical reception was not as unqualifiedly positive as it had been after the Rachmaninoff Concerto. "A brittleness in Horowitz's playing became apparent," noted *The Musical Times.* "Underneath a brilliant shell of pianism there seemed to lurk something detached and calculating, something too far removed from the Byronic grandeurs, the luxuriating self-abandonments of Liszt's B Minor Sonata. In Liszt and in Chopin, Horowitz inserted plenty of *rubato,* but it was unspontaneous, sometimes mechanical—a distortion of melodies rather than an emotional intensification of them."[45]

Although Horowitz and Wanda enjoyed London, neither was entirely captivated by the English. Wrote Wanda to Greiner: "Volodya joins you wholeheartedly on your opinion of the English people!!! And I join you both [for] we had a lot of disappointments in meeting the people here and their principles. *We* came to the conclusion that the difference between the USA and England is that in the USA you can spot a crook right away—here they look distinguished and wear gloves, which makes it difficult to discover them."[46] On one occasion, Wanda bristled when an English society matron asserted, "In America, everyone must have an electric refrigerator. It's bad for the people." Retorted Wanda: "But it's good for the meat!"[47]

In Paris, Horowitz was received even more rapturously than in London. But although Libidins had wanted to extend the European tour, it was now cut short, with a scheduled recital in Brussels canceled. Horowitz returned home with words of praise for the United States. "America has no longer any need to feel inferior culturally to Europe," he told the press. "I was living in France ten years before coming here. When I went back I was very disillusioned. The country is wonderful, like a museum, but the people don't take a part in it. I don't blame them. They suffered much more than we in the war, but we should get rid of our inferiority complex that the whole world is over us. It is just the opposite."[48]

After the European tour, it was business as usual for Horowitz. He crisscrossed the country giving concerts, as tightly wound as ever. Still living in New York at the Hotel Volney, he traveled everywhere with Kenneth Leedom, who ministered to his nerves and made excuses for the cancellations caused by Horowitz's frequent ailments. Protesting that he couldn't go on, before a concert a perspiring Horowitz would hold on to Leedom's arm from dressing room to stage. But as he once put it, "I see the piano, I forget everything else."[49] Horowitz was now chronically fatigued, and the strain was reflected by his decreasing productivity at RCA Victor. From eleven recording sessions in 1950, the number dropped to seven in 1951, four in 1952, and three in 1953. He had become increasingly agitated, especially about concerto dates, and often just before a concert would tell the manager that he couldn't play that night. At a concert in New Orleans, Horowitz seemed fine until it came time to go onstage. Then, wrote a local newspaper reporter, "he went into his act. He became nervous and jittery. 'I feel like a mouse,' he told the manager. 'I feel like a mouse, and Rachmaninoff needs a lion.' "[50]

For Horowitz, the highlight of the early 1950's was the Silver Jubilee concerts he played to celebrate not only the twenty-fifth anniversary of his American debut but also the tenth anniversary of Rachmaninoff's death and the one hundredth anniversary of Steinway & Sons. Since 1945, Horowitz's appearances in New York with orchestra had been few and far between, reserved mostly for benefits or special occasions. His last concert with Toscanini and the NBC Symphony Orchestra, for instance, was on February 19, 1945, in the Brahms B-flat Major Concerto (perhaps their most successful collaboration), a benefit for the National Foundation for Infantile Paralysis. Then, on April 8, 1948, Horowitz had played the same work with Bruno Walter and the New York Philharmonic, in celebration of the twentieth anniversary of his American debut. Now, for his Silver Jubilee Concert of January 12, 1953, Horowitz chose Dimitri Mitropoulos to conduct the Tchaikovsky First Concerto in a benefit for the New York Philharmonic's Pension Fund. Mitropoulos, however, became ill and was forced to cancel all his winter engagements, so George Szell replaced him. In his review of the concert, Olin Downes reminisced about Horowitz's performance of the same music a quarter of a century earlier, noting "a comparison which astonished in ways not entirely expected. The ripening of the pianist's conception of the work was to be anticipated . . . [but] the power and sweep of it took the audience completely by storm. We do not remember any single concert in the twenty-five years . . . when an audience remained so long after the program, splitting its palms and remaining on its feet, cheering wildly. . . . What delighted us most . . . was the fact that Mr. Horowitz, whose intense and scrupulous self-discipline has always kept pace with or perhaps gone slightly ahead of his emotional currents, last night was in such a condition of tension and inspiration that he forgot niceties in favor of sheer magnificence and reckless and unlimited mastery. . . . The performance

[was] gigantic, unpolished, imprudent and overwhelming."[51] At the end of the concert Floyd G. Blair, president of the Philharmonic, presented Horowitz with a silver cigarette box engraved with his image at the piano and underneath, the notes of the opening theme of the Tchaikovsky Concerto.

To celebrate his anniversary, Horowitz had also scheduled two Carnegie Hall recitals for February 25 and March 23. The first featured two major works Horowitz had never before played in public—Scriabin's *Black Mass* Sonata (No. 9, Op. 68) and Schubert's posthumous Sonata in B-flat Major—along with Horowitz's latest and most scintillating transcription, the Liszt Hungarian Rhapsody No. 2. The second, but never-played, recital was to have included the Beethoven *Moonlight* Sonata and the Rachmaninoff Second Sonata.

Horowitz's decision to program the Schubert was surprising. Although he had always spoken of that particular work with reverent enthusiasm and had performed it privately for friends, he had never previously considered playing it in public. "It is too long, too introspective," he had said. "You cannot keep the attention of five thousand people through four long movements of Schubert. It would be a wasted effort."[52] But by the winter of 1953 he had changed his mind, although the Schubert Sonata still worried him. Before New York, he tried it out in Boston, San Francisco, and Los Angeles, experimenting with different tempi and gauging the different audiences' receptivity and attention span. After one of these concerts, Wanda came backstage and told him, "You played too slow. I thought it would never finish!"[53] Accepting her criticism, at the next recital Horowitz made a shortcut in the last movement and played the entire work slightly faster, shaving about five minutes from the performance time. He was encouraged by the glowing praise he received from critics in California. Said one: "He has met this new challenge and conquered it invincibly, and it was all in perfect Schubertian style, with no hint of the Russian feeling that has predominated in his playing."[54]

New York must have come as something of a shock. There, the *Herald Tribune* ranted that Schubert's intentions had been "corrupted and concealed."[55] The *Saturday Review* proclaimed that to play the piece Classically, Horowitz "would have to find a way of arising on a given morning, reducing all the gradations of his internal amplifying system, like the dials on a machine, for the impending occasion. Altogether this was an instance of temperamental miscasting."[56] Most New York critics were of the opinion that Horowitz's virtuosity and oversized sound had done in Schubert. Nearly three decades later, B. H. Haggin remembered the performance well and pronounced it "dreadful."[57]

Horowitz later admitted that programming the Schubert Sonata was a sign of his own impatience with his reputation as an acrobat. Although Howard Taubman wrote poetically in a 1953 *New York Times Sunday Magazine* article about Horowitz's transformation from "a fire-eating virtuoso into a self-critical, searching artist,"[58] the truth is that Horowitz was still addicted to giving audiences what they wanted. By the winter of 1953, he was mentally and physically overwrought to an unusual degree. He had put all his energy into the strenuous anniversary programs, and had little to give beyond that. In thirteen years of concert touring, he had changed very little in appearance. His body still had the leanness of an athlete and his nervous energy continued to propel him from one concert to the next. But he was now severely depressed and suffering acutely from colitis. More and more, he seemed frightened of playing for the public.

PART FOUR
1953 ~ 1964

CHAPTER SEVENTEEN

SECOND RETIREMENT: COLLAPSE

> *"Traveling shattered me and I wanted to rest. Four concerts a*
> *week and traveling on the train were just too much. I stopped*
> *like a car must stop or burn its motor out. I thought I would*
> *never play in public again."*[1]

Horowitz loathed trains, feared airplanes, and dreaded the inhospitable anonymity of hotels. Room-service food often nauseated him and aggravated his colitis, while dining in restaurants and attending post-concert parties provoked anxiety attacks which also upset his delicate stomach. The continual newspaper criticism and relentless curiosity of fans made him act more reclusively than ever, and he would often take shelter in his hotel room until the very hour of a concert. At unavoidable social gatherings, he was shy and impatient, unable to relax, distracted by the necessity of packing soon and moving on to the next tour city. Even more often than in the past, Horowitz found himself on display like an icon in dusty greenrooms, accepting homage from businessmen and society matrons who had no idea of what he considered the drab realities of his life.

Indeed, since 1940, his life had been mostly a dull routine of traveling and performing in uninteresting places. "All those towns!" Horowitz often wailed. Suffering from constant displacement and emotional disorientation, he isolated himself for protection, with no time allowed for recreation. Diffident and nervous, he did not enjoy his fame, for he was chronically enervated and edgy, always on his guard—anything, in fact, but the extroverted stage personality familiar to the public. Horowitz, lonely and increasingly uncommunicative, was alienated from both his wife and daughter and had little free time for friends. Bitterly, he lamented that he had no satisfying romantic relationship, and although

Kenneth Leedom, his secretary and constant companion, was solicitous and tried to make Horowitz as comfortable as possible, he could hardly begin to fill the enormous vacuum in his employer's life.

The 1953 Silver Jubilee season had been less celebration than endurance contest, and for the first time since 1936, it became apparent that Horowitz was losing the battle with his nerves. Cramps and diarrhea intruded during performances, making it difficult for him to concentrate. His incontinence made concerts a continuous horror, and sometimes immediately after finishing a selection he would rush backstage to the toilet. His physical ailments were also aggravated by insomnia, which further weakened and dissipated him. Well aware of the public's superman image of Vladimir Horowitz, he became demoralized by his inadequacies. "He was not insecure about his piano playing," Wanda would explain years later. "He was insecure about wanting to be able to be up to the expectations of the public. And the greater the name is, the greater the responsibility."[2]

Actually, Horowitz, driven for the most part by his own exacting standards, had grown contemptuous of his audiences as he was trying to please them. "They always listened to how fast I could play octaves, but they didn't listen to music anymore. It was boring. I played for two hours but they only remembered the last three minutes of the concert. I felt dissatisfied with . . . what I was doing and what I felt I had to do to fulfill my own identity as a musician."[3]

The conflict seemed insurmountable. From the very beginning of his career, Horowitz had created and nurtured expectations of fire-and-brimstone pianism, and he would not now disappoint his audiences, no matter what the cost to himself. As his personal anxiety increased, the drama and intensity of his playing (in, for instance, the Liszt Hungarian Rhapsody No. 2) became nearly unbearable. "One almost felt that there was a demon trying to get loose," wrote Harold Schonberg. "Surely that tensely controlled figure was wound up too tight."[4] Horowitz himself often referred to his temperament as "a little bit angel, little bit demon," and the latter, encouraged by external pressures, sometimes seemed to be literally eating him alive, devouring his nervous system and innards.

At a concert in February 1953, Horowitz knew that he was hanging on to his equilibrium by a mere thread of nervous energy and was terrified of slipping out of control on stage. He later confided to friends that playing then was like appearing in the Roman Colosseum with the public out for blood. "My God, people were sitting all over the stage, and I was going out to play an encore, Chopin's A-flat Polonaise. Big crescendo. I was exhausted and felt like my heart was going to burst. My stomach was tight and it felt like it was coming up into my mouth. The tension was unbelievable and I actually felt I might drop dead before I finished. When I played the last chord, there was the usual applause and stamping of feet and I heard a man say to his wife, 'My God, did you ever hear anything like that?' And she answered, 'That's nothing; wait until you hear what he does next. He's only beginning.' I played my heart out and she says, 'This is nothing, just wait. There's much more, much more, much more.' Well, there wasn't."[5]

A complete collapse was precipitated by a concert in Minneapolis on March 11, 1953. After the February 25 anniversary program at Carnegie Hall, Horowitz had traveled west with Leedom to begin a winter tour. Wanda joined Horowitz in Minneapolis, and shortly after their arrival on March 10, Horowitz ate something which made him violently ill. Libidins announced the cancellation of his concert that same evening, explaining that Horowitz had suffered "an attack of intestinal flu." Local managers and newspapers had long ago accustomed themselves to Horowitz's cancellations due to colds, tonsillitis, influenza, and digestive problems, so there was no reason to believe the latest Horowitz illness might be anything out of the ordinary; besides, Libidins had rescheduled the concert for April 15. But Wanda realized that Horowitz's condition now was more serious than before, so she refused the care of local doctors and hurried back to New York with Horowitz in a private airplane—the first time he ever flew. Two weeks later, Libidins was forced to cancel all scheduled appearances through the spring, and, in fact, for an indefinite period.

Most accounts of Horowitz's condition after arriving in New York make it seem unlikely that he was more than marginally aware of the plane ride. However, his own version of that traumatic time was different: "I went to the hospital. They checked everything and said I was all right. But the doctor told me, 'You have to take a sabbatical because your nerves are on the verge of collapse.' So I took."[6] Lowell Benedict, still a close friend, was one of the few people allowed into the house that winter, and he recalled Horowitz's condition as being horrifying and poignant: "When I went to visit him on Ninety-fourth Street, Wanda greeted me, telling me he was upstairs in his bedroom. 'He's just a mess,' she said, with a note of contempt in her voice. I went upstairs into the room and what I saw was a vegetable. He was totally incoherent, just blubbering away, speaking nonsense. A legion of doctors were going through the house—recommending absurd treatments such as an all-potato diet. He was of course still suffering from colitis, but nobody understood what was really wrong."[7]

Even thirty years after Horowitz's confinement, the details of his collapse are not fully known, and he has never explained the complex of factors which made him terminate his career at the height of his popularity. For it is unlikely that the strain of traveling, colitis, audience expectations, and press criticism alone could account for a retirement of twelve years. Fritz Steinway remembered that rumors and speculation began to circulate almost immediately, rumors that Horowitz had been institutionalized, that he was afraid of the piano, that he had gone mad. "Everyone wanted to know what happened to him," said Steinway. " 'He's got cancer. He's off his rocker'—et cetera, et cetera. He never was crazy and he's dumb like a fox. But emotionally, he had some sort of immense insecurity. Maybe age creeping up on him was a psychological blow—the realization that he didn't have the vim and vigor of a thirty-year-old anymore."[8] George Marek, director of RCA's classical division and a loyal Horowitz friend in the late 1940's and the 1950's, frequently accompanied him to New York's Columbia Presbyterian Hospital for treatment and tests. "The psychological reasons for his withdrawal and the sickness that followed are much too complicated to be adequately analyzed, even now," said Marek in 1979. "Frailties of health and growing older certainly played a part. The marriage had always been stormy and he had lived in hotels away from Wanda since 1949. There were also constant difficulties with Sonia."[9] Discussing Horowitz's breakdown, Arthur Rubinstein focused on domestic problems. "Wanda was a very hard woman—hard as stone. They really never had a happy marriage, and the weight of this fact certainly contributed to Horowitz's nervous collapse."[10] Another intimate, not sympathetic to either Wanda or her family, asserted that "after his marriage, Horowitz forfeited a chance for personal happiness. Toscanini and Wanda slowly broke his back, and he simply did not have the resources to combat such pressure."[11]

Many friends, however, have emphasized that Horowitz's life style was the real problem, that it finally incapacitated him to the point where he could not leave his house or play the piano. As he said: "The traveling shattered me and I wanted to rest. I told myself I need two, three years of quiet. I was completely exhausted. I was nervous. From 1953 to 1954 I did not play at all. To 1955, even. It was just physically impossible. Nothing . . . I told myself I need rest and reflection."[12]

So it was that in the early spring of 1953 Horowitz had finally moved back to Ninety-fourth Street. There, Leedom continued to tend to his reduced business affairs and dwindling correspondence over the next few years, although what he did for most of that period was simply to spend time with the pianist and hope for the day he would feel like playing again. During the first months of early spring and summer 1953, Horowitz was profoundly unhappy. "He wasn't in bed all the time and he did get up and dress," said Leedom, "but he was very uncomfortable because of his colitis and had trouble eating. He was depressed to begin with but the depression built on itself and that made him feel even worse."[13] By the middle of the summer, Horowitz was feeling better physically but still remained sequestered in the house, declining all social invitations. "In the twelve years I didn't play, I was in this room very happy," Horowitz declared in 1978 during a television interview filmed in his living room. "Not so happy," Wanda countered, continuing: "The doctor said he should stop for a while and then stopping became a bad habit. It was a difficult twelve years because, you see, from time to time, he would say 'I will never play again,' and I would say 'Fine, very fine,' and my heart was sinking to my feet."[14]

Said Horowitz: "Rumors began that I am in the crazy house. But there was nothing wrong with me. Americans like bad news. That sells the paper. 'What is wrong with you? We want to know.' I didn't care. Mae West told me that everyone wrote that she was a prostitute. . . . Everybody thought her life was terrible. She said that she would only worry when they stopped talking about her."[15]

For nearly two years, Horowitz rarely left his house, and for the first six months of that period, Wanda seldom left his side. As Horowitz's state of mind began to improve, she occasionally tried to persuade him to join her on an excursion outdoors. Once she complained to Henry Steinway that they had not been out of the house in months, and that *she* was going to have a nervous breakdown if there was no change. An opportunity had arisen for use of a cottage in New Hampshire with complete privacy, but Horowitz still refused to venture from the house, insisting he wasn't strong enough for a long automobile trip. Steinway suggested they rent an ambulance and Horowitz refused on the grounds that if someone saw him getting into it, the already terrible rumors about his condition would get even worse. Steinway then advised them, half jokingly, to furnish a piano truck with Horowitz's own bed and furniture—and that is exactly what they did do. In this manner, the Horowitzes traveled to New Hampshire incognito and in comfort.[16]

During the first stages of his recovery, Horowitz concentrated on regulating his physical system by changing his diet completely from haphazard eating patterns of the past. He now avoided foods high in fat and anything rich or spicy, and would drink nothing stronger than milk, eventually graduating to Postum. Unseasoned meat and baked potatoes were at the core of his new diet. His meals were separated by long naps, he slept a full twelve hours at night, and he continued to boycott the piano. Eventually a one-mile walk was added to the daily regimen.

Horowitz was not yet ready to resume socializing and his inner circle was a small one, consisting only of Wanda and Leedom, with occasional visits from Milstein and also from RCA producer John ("Jack") Pfeiffer, whose friendship became increasingly important. Pfeiffer was a knowledgeable musician, an innovator in recording technology, and a compassionate and understanding friend who handled his two prize artists, Horowitz and Heifetz, with expert care. Tall, dark-haired, well-dressed, with a comfortable smile, he seemed to calm Horowitz during the first years of withdrawal. Pfeiffer radiated confidence, and his silky bass voice and placid demeanor were inevitably reassuring, striking exactly the tone Horowitz needed as he faced the challenge of the piano again. Partly due to Pfeiffer's encouragement and support, Horowitz returned to a limited recording schedule during the years of public inactivity.

In his gentle but professional manner, Pfeiffer discussed with Horowitz the most pressing matter at hand during that fall of 1953—release of the recording of Horowitz's twenty-fifth anniversary recital the previous February (the recital was scheduled to be broadcast by the NBC radio network on January 2, 1954). Horowitz suddenly felt an urge to work, and he carefully listened to the master tape, pointing out places that would benefit from improved tone color and dynamic contrasts. As he became involved in the editing process, his enthusiasm and curiosity about music were suddenly reactivated, causing him to savor his present state of retirement: "I'm free! I don't have to go anywhere. I don't have any commitments."[17] Pfeiffer observed that "ideas which had lain dormant for years were rearing up to intrigue his interest."[18]

"In the past," said Horowitz, "I couldn't absorb anything new because I was constantly playing. I had one, two programs that I went around and played. You cannot have in your head too many pieces because you have to rehearse them all. But when I was alone, I absorbed a lot. I had the time. I could read and be interested in many things."[19] Now, in 1953, the focus of his interest was the eighteenth-century Italian composer and pianist Muzio Clementi, and for many years after Horowitz would bubble enthusiastically about the discovery. "I came to Clementi accidentally. Schirmer had only published two volumes of his piano music, about twenty sonatas, and not the best of them. My wife went to Italy for a visit and found a complete first edition of all sixty-four sonatas in twelve volumes. And I started to play them and read books about Clementi and learned that his influence on Beethoven's piano music was enormous."[20]

So after years of performing Beethoven's piano music only infrequently and with little enthusiasm or success, Horowitz, in a sense, came through Beethoven's back door by studying Clementi. He was fascinated to learn that Beethoven's scanty music library had contained a large number of Clementi's keyboard works, that bars written by Clementi foreshadowed passages in Beethoven's piano sonatas. Demonstrating a sequence of arpeggiated chords from Clementi's Sonata in F Minor, Op. 14, No. 3, Horowitz would exclaim to Pfeiffer, "Listen, Jack. Listen—this is Beethoven pure and simple!"[21] The romantic and dramatic aspects of Clementi's inventiveness, the progressive musical language woven into his Classical style, surprised and delighted Horowitz, and he quickly came to understand Clementi's pivotal role as one of the first composers to write well for the pianoforte and to master Classical sonata form in terms of that instrument. Clementi's career as a piano manufacturer, his pioneering expansion of piano technique in his *Gradus ad Parnassum,* his versatility as pianist, teacher, music publisher, and composer of concertos, symphonies, and operas—all of this astounded Horowitz. "I call Clementi the papa of the modern piano and of piano technique. Although he didn't have the genius of Mozart or Beethoven, he was as important as an innovator—in terms of finding the first idiomatic *hammerklavier* approach in his writing, in his development of sonata form. I think the last movement of the F-sharp Minor Sonata, composed in 1788 [Op. 26, No. 2], is one of the best movements written in the eighteenth century. The writing is very bold, even better than some early Mozart sonatas, yet you never hear anyone play them, nobody knows them. This is the greatest crime in music, that his compositions are not played, not assigned in conservatories."[22]

Horowitz's enthusiasm for Clementi did not immediately provoke plans for a recording, but discussion with Pfeiffer of Clementi's transformation of the piano from a percussive into a singing instrument often led to another favorite topic—opera singers and what he perceived as the lost art of *bel canto*.

Horowitz had sometimes accompanied singers in Russia, first at the Kiev Conservatory and later during his early concert tours in the Ukraine, but after 1925 his frenetic life as a soloist precluded that activity. Nor did he have the time he would have liked for browsing in record shops after favorite opera albums or for regular attendance at opera performances. During the early years of his retirement, Horowitz's interest in the *bel canto* singers who had thrilled him as a child revived. After reading about how much Chopin had loved to listen to and learn from great singers, Horowitz began to study the art of the Italian baritone Mattia Battistini (1856–1928), whose records were generally unfamiliar to a new generation of listeners, and whom Horowitz considered a "forgotten genius." He memorized details of Battistini's performances, fascinated by his plasticity of phrasing, breath control, tonal shading, and lyric expressiveness.

Beginning that October, Horowitz spent most evenings by his new phonograph, listening not only to Battistini but also to other *bel canto* masters, such as the Italian tenors Giuseppe Anselmi and Alessandro Bonci, and the Russian tenor Leonid Sobinov, whom Horowitz had once accompanied. By now, Horowitz was slightly better disposed to visitors, and he was pleased to discover a fellow *bel canto* aficionado in *New York Times* critic Howard Taubman. After reading a Taubman piece about Battistini, Horowitz invited his former program annotator to his home for an evening of records. He was eager to discuss *bel canto* style with Taubman, and to the critic, Horowitz seemed far more relaxed than he had the previous January when interviewed in conjunction with the twenty-fifth anniversary concert. Horowitz told Taubman that it did not bother him that Battistini had habitually taken what some might consider shocking liberties with an aria. "Even if we don't agree with such exaggerated freedom, there is much we can learn," he said. "It is better to control an abundance of spontaneous feeling than to hide that not enough is there."[23]

Horowitz's interest in Battistini became a near obsession and he proposed to Pfeiffer that the singer's best performances be rereleased by RCA in long-playing format. As his first professional activity since his retirement, Horowitz offered to supervise the project himself, making selections, writing descriptive notes, and approving the final product. But after many trial transfers to microgroove, it was clear, said Pfeiffer, that "too many compromises were necessary, since many of the best performances were too technically deficient for transfer . . . and some of the point of Horowitz's special objective was stolen away by the antique thinness of the sound."[24] In addition, other matters began to distract Horowitz, particularly his tentative decision to record several Clementi sonatas, which he continued to regard as undiscovered treasures.

After ten months of inertia, Horowitz had been prompted to consider making a new album, partly because the January release of his anniversary recital on disc was a resounding success—warmly received not only musically but also for its sound, which was for those days superb, despite applause, coughs, and rustling of programs. In addition, Horowitz wanted to make another record to quell speculation over his health and to prove that he was in good mental and physical condition. During the spring of 1954, he therefore began to weigh the commercial feasibility of an all-Clementi album and how well he would be able to bring it off. "You know, I can't play anymore,"[25] he insisted to pianist Gary Graffman. Yet he continued enthusiastically to run through Clementi's sonatas at home for any visitors, and became convinced that a record by himself would redress a historic wrong and establish a modern reputation for Clementi.

Horowitz's manner of making any decision was always a laborious process of studying, vacillating, collecting the opinions of others, asking friends to argue for or against a proposal, assessing financial, artistic, or personal gain, and then usually opting for the adventurous course of action. Finally, after months of this both before and during a summer spent in East Hampton, Long Island, Horowitz decided to proceed with a Clementi record. "It took courage to play again and I didn't know if I could do it. It was a surprise to the music world and a surprise to me too. I said to myself, 'OK. I will do it so the public will know I am not dead or something is wrong with me.' At least I would not have to be in the train—I would do the record and let the record travel."[26]

CHAPTER EIGHTEEN

PEACE AND QUIET

*"Nobody disturbed me. I still loved music and was having a
good time for myself. I loved talking with friends, playing
cards, talking philosophy, reading books, looking at my pictures,
reading music—not just piano music, but anything. I said to
myself, My God! I can earn big enough money with recordings,
why should I perform?"*[1]

To the few who associated with Horowitz during the first twenty
months of his retirement, it was clear that he had recovered quickly from
his physical exhaustion—which seemed to refute the frequently heard assertion that he had been incapacitated by fears and illness for the initial
years. Now he approached the Clementi project with characteristic zeal.
He would not, however, leave the cocoon of his home and insisted that
RCA make the recording in his living room. At that point almost any
demand by Horowitz would have been met because RCA was desperate
for a new album, worrying that Horowitz's continued absence from the
stage would jeopardize sales of his previous ones. Since the twenty-fifth
anniversary recital, RCA had put out two all-Chopin discs repackaged
from previous releases, but they did not want to dig any deeper into their
archive for older performances. So in October 1954, they willingly set up
equipment on the second floor of the Horowitz house, and the library
became a control room with recording machines crammed among massive Venetian furniture, an enormous desk, and Horowitz's second concert grand.

At 4 P.M. on a Saturday afternoon, Horowitz entered his living room-
cum-recording studio, now empty except for his piano and paintings.
Immaculately dressed in sport coat and bow tie, he seated himself on a
very low bench before the miked piano, ready to begin the session. As
Pfeiffer and the engineers adjusted dials in the study, Horowitz warmed
up. He had settled on three Clementi works: the Sonata in F Minor, Op.
13, No. 6, the Sonata in G Minor, Op. 34, No. 2, and the Sonata in F-
sharp Minor, Op. 25, No. 2, said to be Beethoven's favorite.

To Pfeiffer, the afternoon session seemed surreal. Horowitz began one passage of the F-sharp Minor Sonata, and "concentration arched his slim frame into the aspect of a mighty wizard from whose fingers notes sparked and ricocheted through the silent room. Finishing with a glittering cascade, he paused and quietly addressed his strangely unresponsive audience [of paintings]. 'I will repeat it.' A crisp voice [of an engineer] answered curtly, 'Right.' "[2] "Once again, the atmosphere was drenched with a torrent of music," recalled Pfeiffer. "But the Picasso dancer in pink tights didn't stir on his purple cushion; the benign gaze of the Rouault maiden didn't shift one degree; and the prim Modigliani lady stared unwaveringly from the opposite wall."[3]

During this first recording session, neither Horowitz nor RCA was convinced that a sound acceptable for commercial release had been achieved. Recalled Pfeiffer: "The type and placement of microphones to give suitable sound values were found rather quickly, and everything seemed tuned to the smooth functioning of creative art at work. Everything, that is, until a most unrefined and irritating rattle sliced through the monitor speaker with every note from the piano. . . . A frantic search of the living room finally uncovered a vibrating pair of glass prisms and an ornate candelabra which had a direct sound path to the microphone. From that point on, the search for Clementi began."[4]

Horowitz's habit while recording was to keep playing even if there were mistakes. With an irritable wave of his hand he would acknowledge an uneven phrase or wrong note and then circle back to the problem area by repeating four or five pages. He constantly asked questions: "Are these passages enough *forte?*" "Will it sound if I use soft pedal here?" Finally, said Pfeiffer, there emerged, "quietly and surely the performance, and in it the spirit of Clementi and the soul of Horowitz."[5]

Free of commitments, Horowitz subsequently concentrated his energies on every detail of the album, including its cover and annotations. Arthur Loesser, pianist and music critic for the *Cleveland Plain Dealer,* was chosen to write the liner notes. Horowitz had been impressed by the imagination and entertaining style of Loesser's book *Men, Women and Pianos* and had discovered that Loesser had programmed Clementi sonatas years earlier. After approving Loesser's commentary, Horowitz turned attention to the final pressing of the disc, during which, according to Pfeiffer, his exacting standards "threw the combined forces of the New York recording department and the Indianapolis pressing plant into production trauma."[6]

Reviewing the Clementi album, Irving Kolodin, who in the past had more often than not given Horowitz negative notices, conceded in the *Saturday Review* that "Horowitz has made his point, without question: namely that Clementi is a composer of individuality and idiomatic strength.... We will grant his premise that Clementi has not had it good for over a century, while adding Clementi *never* had it so good [as] in these incisive, fluid and wonderfully alive performances."[7]

Both Horowitz and RCA were excited by the universally positive response to the Clementi disc, and they immediately decided to do further recording. Once again Horowitz was interested in breaking new ground and exploring unusual repertory. He considered but then rejected an all-Medtner album, deciding instead to focus on the music of Alexander Scriabin. Horowitz had played Scriabin's Ninth Sonata, known as the *Black Mass,* as part of his anniversary program and had recorded two Scriabin etudes, but he had never strongly identified himself with that composer, although Wanda occasionally prodded him to learn more of a repertory that formed so important a part of his heritage. "It took me twenty-five, thirty years to persuade him to play it in public," she once said, "even though he knew all of it."[8] Horowitz had, of course, read through Scriabin's sonatas, preludes, and etudes, but not until the 1950's and 1960's did he emerge as a champion of the composer. Like his earlier interpretations of Rachmaninoff, his performances of Scriabin would come to be considered as being without peer. "I started very late with that composer," Horowitz said, "and started to feel that music and began playing it during my sabbatical. He is a mystic. Still, it's difficult for the general public even though it's Romantic. This is supersensuous, super-romantic, supermysterious. Everything is 'super'; it is all overboard. From the spiritual and emotional point of view, it is one of the most difficult chunks of music in the literature."[9]

The Artists and Repertoire department at RCA understood perfectly well that Horowitz had no present intention of recording more-commercially-viable selections of Liszt, Chopin, or Rachmaninoff and was extraordinarily solicitous of Horowitz's interest in the then little-known Scriabin. For his next album, Horowitz chose Scriabin's Sonata No. 3 in F-sharp Minor, Op. 23, and a group of sixteen of the eighty-five preludes, aiming for a representative sampling with a balance of contrast and mood. "I'm going crazy to decide," he told Pfeiffer. "Nobody knows how difficult it is to pick just a few pieces."[10] Horowitz was fascinated by the influence of Chopin in the early works of Scriabin and would demonstrate this for Pfeiffer by "transposing both composers' works to the same key and phrasing them together, punctuating the illustration with a running comment, a look of surprise, a shrug, or a nod of affirmation."[11] Eventually, Horowitz had picked fourteen of the sixteen preludes to be on the record from the early and middle opus numbers (Opp. 11, 13, 16, 27, 48, 51) where the Romantic influence of Chopin was most apparent, proceeding with caution for the last two into the late, near-atonal works (Opp. 59, 67).

Once again Horowitz declined to leave his house for the recording studio, and Pfeiffer was instructed to manage the unusual situation as best he could. "It was a perilous condition only from the engineering aspects, the [Scriabin] music differing enormously from the relatively restricted dynamic and tonal demands of Clementi," he remembered. "Here was a situation commensurate with planning the recording of an opera in a studio which had been validated only for a string quartet."[12] The sessions began in January 1955, with Pfeiffer and his engineers "as apprehensive as if we were trying to record a full symphony in a telephone booth."[13] To mitigate the small size of Horowitz's living room, the microphone was placed very close to the piano so that "standing waves would be minimized and reverberation would have little weight in the sound," said Pfeiffer. "There was a risk involved in this technique, however, for unless the microphone was placed in the ideal position, the piano would sound excessively percussive; furthermore, it imposed the need for extreme precision on the part of the performer."[14] Once the sound was regulated to Pfeiffer's satisfaction, the actual recording went quickly. Horowitz had prepared meticulously, and he managed to complete all sixteen preludes and the Sonata in only four sessions. As always, recalled Pfeiffer, Horowitz "reviewed, questioned, restated, altered, reinstated, and generally inspected for any slight flaw in content or procedure"[15] every aspect of the record's production.

The romantic intensity of Scriabin's music seemed to suit Horowitz's restless temperament, and critics once again applauded his adventurousness. RCA's new orthophonic process captured a clear, if somewhat hard, recorded sound. The elusive, flickering shadows of the preludes were the most successfully rendered, and even Horowitz later expressed reservations over the less substantial and less interesting Third Sonata, stating that the album was "a little disappointing because the work itself is a little weaker [than the preludes]."[16]

An amusing sidelight of the Scriabin release was its promotion campaign as planned by RCA's marketing department. For the "RCA Victor Showcase Series," many artists recorded short verbal introductions for their albums, most of which proved eminently forgettable. Monteux, Beecham, Rubinstein, and Reiner had consented to this promotion plot and Horowitz also agreed. His message was certainly the most original of all, though it never found its way onto the Showcase. "This is Vladimir Horowitz," he began. "If you, the buyer, if you will not get the records on time, so blame Mr. Alan Kayes. If the sound will not be perfect—there will be some blur and something not completely right—just blame Mr. Jack Pfeiffer and the engineers, too. If the composition appears to you fading and not so beautiful, first blame the composer. If the performance is lousy, blame Mr. Vladimir Horowitz. But please buy the record because we are all in great need of money!"[17] A few dubbings of this impish promo were sent to RCA Victor distributors and became collector's items.

But a recorded advertisement by Horowitz proved unnecessary, and the success of both the Clementi and Scriabin albums bolstered his self-confidence; Horowitz had proved both to his public and himself that his abilities were intact. Now he relaxed and began to spend more time with colleagues and friends like Milstein, Piatigorsky, Ania Dorfmann, Rudolf Serkin, Abram Chasins, and the ever-present Jack Pfeiffer. The first few years of retirement had been, at least before 1956, an unpleasant but necessary period of stabilization. "I had to impose new disciplines on myself," he said. "Becoming free as a bird after a lifetime of routine can make you feel awfully lost. At first, I just moped around. Then I had to work out new daily schedules for myself—so much time for study, for rest, for reflection, for exercise. In the first few years, besides walking, reading, and resting, I used to go to the pool at the Ninety-second Street YMHA to swim. But it took time, and the water was much too cold, so after a while I stopped. But I walked twenty-five to thirty blocks a day. I used to go to art galleries. Then I became more engrossed in musical matters. Soon my days had a new rhythm, a new serenity."[18]

Horowitz still associated going out of the house with his years of grueling travel. "Although a daily walk was part of the routine," recalled Pfeiffer, "he rarely went out socially, and a visit to his father-in-law in Riverdale, less than ten miles away, took on the proportions of a major journey."[19] Even walks on the Upper East Side of Manhattan could be traumatic. On one of his first ventures alone, he happened into Manhattan's Yorkville neighborhood, a German enclave, and looking about, grew panic-stricken when he realized that everything he read was in German.[20]

On occasion, opportunities arose to attend small dinner parties with Wanda, but he almost always declined, uneasy about answering questions concerning the reasons for his prolonged absence from the stage. When he did show up at a party, he could be a difficult guest, often sitting in a corner brooding. For Horowitz was still most relaxed and happy when in his own house, anchored by routine: one hour of practice every day and a walk, weather permitting, before an afternoon nap. Indeed the state of the weather began to take on mammoth importance in his daily routine, as it affected his moods and determined whether or not he would be able to exercise. Friends like Piatigorsky were amused by the seriousness with which Horowitz watched the skies; when they visited, Horowitz might excuse himself five or six times in order to listen to the weather report on the telephone. And if the temperature was just right, he would simply abandon his guests and disappear outdoors.[21]

One of the chief topics of discussion with intimates was the possibility of resuming concerts. Still adamantly rejecting the life of the performer, Horowitz appeared more contented than he had in years: "I love to talk to friends, look at my pictures, listen to recordings, study vocal and symphonic music I never previously had a chance to know. I don't know, but I don't think I will play again in public."[22]

Nearly a year passed before Horowitz agreed to make another album. To offset what the RCA marketing department now perceived as the ill-advised Clementi and Scriabin releases, the company reissued Horowitz's 1947 version of Mussorgsky's *Pictures at an Exhibition* only a month after the Scriabin and also repackaged the Schumann *Kinderscenen* and a group of Chopin mazurkas. In the late winter of 1956, RCA began to pressure Horowitz for an album that would appeal to a wider audience, and to their great relief he expressed an interest in "returning to the classics"— primarily Beethoven. Of course, RCA was eager to capitalize on his willingness to do two of Beethoven's best-loved sonatas, the *Moonlight,* which he had first recorded in 1946, and the *Waldstein,* which he had never recorded. However, the sessions for the Beethoven, occurring once again in Horowitz's living room, proved less satisfactory than either the Clementi or the Scriabin. At the first playback of the opening movement of the *Waldstein,* on May 10, 1956, Horowitz's only comment to Pfeiffer was: "The sound, it's a little bit lousy"[23]; and the producer spent the remainder of the day "revising the recording technique to eliminate the caustic sound of the piano."[24] The second and third movements were recorded the following day and the *Moonlight* Sonata was taped one month later. All during that summer in East Hampton, Horowitz brooded over the first movement of the *Moonlight,* worrying that he had played it too fast. In the middle of October, he was still vacillating over the tempo and finally decided to do the movement again, more slowly.

When Horowitz's recording was released, it was favorably compared to the Columbia Rudolf Serkin *Moonlight* Sonata, which must have pleased Horowitz since he revered Serkin's Beethoven. Horowitz's tempi were slower than Serkin's in every movement but "seemed to capture the poetry of the first movement and the vitality of the last with greater effect," said critic Robert C. Marsh. Overall, this was "a penetrating view of Beethoven in which the artist's own temperament and German tradition are combined in performances of stunning power."[25] One aspect of the album was criticized as being tasteless: In an attempt to make the release as "popular" as possible, RCA had slapped on the jacket a moonlit photograph in Liberace style, complete with candelabra—"unworthy of the pianist and the music," thought one critic.

Despite his close personal and professional relationship with Jack Pfeiffer and his trust in him, Horowitz was sometimes displeased with RCA's aggressive approach to repertory and marketing. Alan Kayes, manager of Red Seal's Artists and Repertoire department, had tried for nearly a year to persuade him to record the Rachmaninoff Second Concerto. Eugene Ormandy had been approached, even though the Philadelphia Orchestra recorded for Columbia, and Ormandy had teasingly responded that he would be glad to record with Horowitz if a hundred men could be squeezed into the Ninety-fourth Street living room. But Horowitz had never performed the Second Rachmaninoff, much preferred the Third, and did not at that time feel equal to the strain of an orchestral recording. Although Kayes "did everything to advance the realization of this project,"[26] Horowitz refused to consider the offer seriously, and seeds were being sown for an eventual rift between himself and RCA. An exasperated sales staff reasoned that if Horowitz was not going to perform in public, the least he might do was record some "popular" repertory that they could sell.

It was agreed that Horowitz's next release would consist entirely of Chopin, and for the first time since 1953, he wanted to leave the confines of his living room to record. Although Pfeiffer had achieved an agreeably rich sound for the Beethoven discs, Horowitz had grown impatient with the limited acoustics of his home. "Not satisfactory," he told Pfeiffer. "Something lacking still. Concert grand and small room. Let's go to Carnegie Hall."[27]

The Chopin sessions began in January 1957 in the auditorium of New York's Hunter College and continued through the late winter and spring at Carnegie Hall. After four years, Horowitz was excited at the prospect of playing in a concert hall again, and his renditions of the Second and Third scherzos, the *Barcarolle*, and four of the nocturnes testify that he was in magnificent form. He was also in an ebullient mood, so much so that he began to speak seriously of the possibility of playing again in public. He had become bored with the microphone and had begun to crave the excitement of a live audience. The previous November, David Libidins had announced that Horowitz might resume concertizing in the 1957–58 season. Early in 1957, Pfeiffer stated that "dates have been spread before him with complete freedom of choice. But the same delicate balance that allows him to retain or alter a tempo according to his feeling of the moment also gives him an instinctive sense of timing. When the right moment comes, and it will be sometime this fall, he will be performing those works he feels and understands."[28]

One indication Horowitz was ready to resume his career fully was that he began to rework his *Carmen* transcription. He had already performed *Carmen* twice for records, but now decided the piece could be improved. After at last putting down the original version on paper, he began to edit and recompose it with the idea of expanding the two earlier encore versions and making *Carmen* a real "concert composition" similar in length to a Chopin ballade. He even test recorded the new version at Carnegie Hall on May 14, 1957, and Pfeiffer became convinced this work would become "part of a program that will mark his concert reappearance." Further, said Pfeiffer, "by this one gesture he is indicating that devices which were once an end in themselves will now take their rightful place in the pattern of music. Virtuosity will be as prominent as ever, but it will serve a musical master. There will be differences born of four years of time but also four years of study, evaluation, and experimentation that must broaden and mature an artist at any stage of his career."[29]

Six weeks after Horowitz's final recording session at Carnegie Hall, he abandoned all plans for a return to the stage. The first several months of 1957 had been a traumatic time for the family. In mid-January Toscanini had died. Not long before, at the annual New Year's Eve party in River-dale, he had been together a last time with all his children and grand-children, for Wally, Emanuela, and Sonia had come from Europe for the occasion. The Maestro was lively and talkative, delighted by the news that Emanuela was soon to make him a great-grandfather. The next morning Toscanini suffered a cerebral thrombosis. During the afternoon he regained consciousness, and his favorite, Sonia, came to the sickroom, where he whispered in her ear, "*Cara, cara,* you've come in time, because your grandfather is dying."[30] Over the next several days, Toscanini's con-dition improved enough that he attempted to walk, but still, said Wally, "That iron will of his helped him to conquer the pain, but it was no longer he. For me, Papa died that New Year's morning."[31] Further strokes weakened him, and at 8:40 A.M. on January 16, less than three weeks short of his ninetieth birthday, he died in his sleep, surrounded by his family.

For three days Toscanini's body was viewed by thousands who filed past the open coffin at the Frank E. Campbell Funeral Home in New York, and on Saturday morning, January 19, at 10 A.M., a solemn requiem mass was offered in his memory at St. Patrick's Cathedral. Arriv-ing for this at the last moment, Horowitz behaved in a typically eccentric manner, announcing that the service could not begin until he had had tea and crackers.[32] To avoid a scene, Walter Toscanini hurried from the church and did his bidding.

Only five months later, there was another tragedy in the family. On June 30, twenty-two-year-old Sonia Horowitz was critically injured in a motor-scooter accident at San Remo on the Italian Riviera, suffering a skull fracture when she collided with a telephone pole. Since her father's retirement, Sonia had spent considerable time in Milan and Venice with her beloved aunt Wally and it was, in fact, Wally who saved her life. Wally was immediately called to the scene of the accident but when she arrived was told that there was no longer anything to be done, for Sonia was dead. The traffic police refused to touch Sonia, but Wally, seeing her lying senseless on the street, did not hesitate. She knocked one of the stubborn policemen to the ground, loaded her niece into a passing car, and arranged for a U.S. Army helicopter to fly Sonia to Milan for emer-gency brain surgery.[33] On a stretcher in the helicopter, Sonia was covered with ice packs and ministered to by nurses and military personnel.

Nearly a week after the accident, Sonia was still unconscious much of the time, and she would never completely recover. Her recuperation was to be long and painful, drawn out over the next two years. Wanda flew to Italy to be with her daughter, while Horowitz remained in New York, behaving as he always had during family crises: withdrawing deeper and deeper into himself. Not only were his plans for concertizing suspended indefinitely, but all musical activity, including recording, came to an abrupt halt. Horowitz never would speak of the effect of Sonia's near-fatal accident on his plans, and there was a virtual blackout on his activities during this period. He even stopped practicing regularly to retreat into his routine of rest, walks, reading, and occasional socializing. Sometimes he played canasta with friends, and he began to watch television a good deal—especially prizefights, a recent passion. When his colitis flared up, George Marek, then vice president and general manager of RCA, sometimes accompanied Horowitz to Columbia Presbyterian Hospital. "I remember driving in the car with Wanda and Volodya and he said to me: 'You are my only friend.' He was convinced that he had no real friends. Sometimes he was really sick with the colitis and sometimes it seemed like hypochondria. He felt lonely, depressed, and was in no condition to record or perform."[34]

For the next two years, Horowitz would not even consider recording. Marketing executives shook their heads in disappointment and compensated for his self-imposed silence by repackaging previously issued repertory with improved sonics. Portions of Horowitz's 1951 Carnegie Hall recitals were released in 1957, an all-Chopin album in 1958, and in 1959 the 1943 version of the Toscanini-Horowitz Tchaikovsky Concerto and yet another rerelease of the Mussorgsky *Pictures at an Exhibition.* It was the Tchaikovsky that attracted most attention. In 1943 both Horowitz and the Maestro had agreed that the famous war-bond broadcast was not sonically acceptable for commercial release. But by 1959 enterprising RCA engineers had located more than fifty different lacquers of the broadcast, and these had then been cut and spliced into a performance with astonishingly good sound. More than a few people believed the final result to be a great improvement over the 1941 studio version, a reading that had pleased neither conductor nor pianist. For the moment, RCA was placated by the excellent sale of the new Tchaikovsky record, but everyone impatiently awaited Horowitz's next move.

CHAPTER NINETEEN

THE NINETY-FOURTH STREET CONSERVATORY

*"I had pupils because I was bored. The only pianists I call my
ex-pupils are Byron Janis, Ronald Turini, and Gary
Graffman. If someone else claims, it's not true. I had some
others who played for me, but I stopped work with them because
they did not progress. They did not want to follow my advice,
or couldn't."*[1]

*H*orowitz's return to good physical health in 1954 had prompted not
only the Clementi recording but also a sudden renewed interest in teaching. Although making records seemed to him the most expedient way of
keeping in the public eye, it was far from satisfying. Horowitz was often
bored during the years he was not performing, and he regarded the few
students that he accepted as members of his musical family. Their function was both to stimulate and to entertain him.

He had not demonstrated any notable interest in involving himself
with another young pianist since 1948, when Byron Janis's lessons with
him had ended. That same year, however, he had heard of a gifted
twenty-year-old named Gary Graffman who was studying at the Curtis
Institute in Philadelphia with the distinguished Russian pedagogue Isabelle Vengerova. Vengerova had been grooming Graffman since age
seven and in 1946 had entered him in the preliminary regional auditions
of the Rachmaninoff Competition, which he won, although the top national award eluded him. Horowitz, then president of the competition,
had expected the first prize to go to Graffman, but as Horowitz recalled,
"there was another quite talented but more mechanical pianist [Seymour
Lipkin], not very much of an individual, and to me, that's what counts
in music, the personality and the individuality. But four judges voted for
Graffman and five for Lipkin. And so Mr. Lipkin won the prize."[2] Disappointed with the verdict of the jury, Horowitz continued to be interested
in Graffman.

The young man's career skyrocketed after he won the Leventritt Prize in 1949, for he subsequently appeared with George Szell and the Cleveland Orchestra and Leonard Bernstein and the New York Philharmonic. Graffman was still in his early twenties, however, and not yet ready to leave Vengerova, with whom he continued to study until her death in 1956. However, in 1953, Graffman had accepted Horowitz's invitation to begin regularly scheduled lessons with him too. Unlike Byron Janis, Graffman had had considerable success by the time Vengerova told him about Horowitz's offer to "help a young person," having already made an extensive tour of the United States and studied in Europe on a Fulbright Fellowship. Happily married, Graffman was considerably less fragile emotionally than Janis, and thus less vulnerable to Horowitz's quirks and moods. "I don't think anything fazed me at that time," Graffman remembered. "Although I was impressed by Horowitz's recordings, I was not intimidated by him and was not nervous at my first lesson. I admired Horowitz immensely. But as with all great artists, he had such a strong personality. And I had my ideas about certain things. I wasn't sure I wanted to be closely influenced by him, and I made all of this abundantly clear to Vengerova, who told me to shut up and go play for him."

Perhaps Horowitz's own collapse had made him sensitive to the at least partially negative effect he had had on Janis, for he approached coaching Graffman with great care and a sense of responsibility. "His method of teaching me, after the first or second visit, erased irrevocably all doubt in my mind about whether I wanted to be taught by him," said Graffman. "At no time did he ever even hint at imposing his ideas on mine. In fact, it was quite the opposite. After criticizing and making suggestions, he tried to find ways within my conception ... of playing a phrase more intensely or more lyrically, or both. He almost never went to the piano and said, 'Here's how to do it.' "[3]

Horowitz was a quiet, subdued teacher, in contrast to Vengerova who was given to screaming and throwing chairs. Although Vengerova idolized Horowitz, she was anxious to protect her protégé from picking up what she regarded as bad habits. Graffman recalled her shrieking and "waving her hands like claws in front of my face. 'Keep the fingers curved, curved, always cooooooorved, like this! Yes, yes, I know he gets a beautiful sound by hitting the keys with flat fingers, but *he* can do it, and you *can't*.' "[4] Yet Graffman realized that the important differences in his two mentors had nothing, really, to do with digital technique. "The real difference between them was that between someone who makes his living giving concerts in large auditoriums and someone who teaches most of the time in the studio and plays a good deal of chamber music. The sounds that Vengerova had in her mind were those of a large living room while Horowitz had Carnegie Hall in his mind. Horowitz told me that some things that may have sounded beautiful in his living room would have been lost in a large hall. He prepared me for pitfalls I might encounter rehearsing with orchestras, showed me how to practice problem passages—for instance, octaves in the Tchaikovsky Concerto—but he was most concerned with communicating across the footlights. Horowitz, always cognizant of his audience, wanted a big sound that would embrace and intoxicate his listeners."

Horowitz told Graffman that he was underpedaling and, to Vengerova's chagrin, encouraged him to strive for a "wetter sound." "This surprised me because there were passages in the Brahms *Intermezzi,* Opus One seventeen, or the Schubert *Wanderer Fantasy* where a tonic and dominant harmony would mesh together into the same pedal and sound terribly muddled in the living room, and yet, when heard this way in Carnegie Hall, such pedaling prevented the passage from sounding detached. There was a richness of color, a shimmer to the sound that worked perfectly."

Graffman's own predilections coincided with Horowitz's repertory preferences, so that the two spent much of their time working on Tchaikovsky, Chopin, Liszt, Prokofiev, Rachmaninoff, Schumann, Schubert, and Beethoven. Although Graffman occasionally brought in a contemporary work, like Benjamin Lees's *Sonata Breve,* they concentrated on the Romantics. Horowitz would constantly return to his old argument that the piano should be a "singing instrument," telling Graffman: "Imitating the string instruments and the voice are the only ways to make the piano—a percussive instrument—a singing instrument. That's why I do not recommend Bartók or Stravinsky, or Copland—because I am against using the piano this way. Maybe it's beautiful music, but I don't like to play it, but can still listen and enjoy it."[5] Horowitz shared with Graffman his Battistini recordings, lectured him at length about Bellini's influence on Chopin, and, said Graffman, "continually analyzed how a great singer would phrase any given passage. He spoke about breathing—the stretching and contraction of phrases—and there was a wonderful plasticity to each phrase he played, always with a great deal of freedom."

Graffman was pleased by Horowitz's consistently courtly demeanor during their two years of regular lessons. Horowitz was a night person and scheduled Graffman for eight or nine o'clock, immediately after dinner. Graffman remembered that "although he might have been considered something of a recluse at that time because he didn't go out much, he was always . . . extremely cheerful, enthusiastic, and full of enormous vitality." Horowitz also had a "bounding vigor and energy that left me breathless when, as sometimes happened, it was suddenly two o'clock in the morning and Mrs. Horowitz would come into the living room and shoo me out." Although Horowitz told Graffman about his stomach problems, the young pianist didn't pay much attention because he looked so healthy. "He always dressed elegantly for my lessons. The shoes would match this and the socks would match that, and he was handsomely decked-out in bow tie and sport jacket. He had rosy cheeks and told me he was sleeping ten to twelve hours a day." Horowitz's dress had become something of an obsession, particularly his concern with bow ties. "In 1953, he had hardly any bow ties,"[6] remembered Wanda. At some point, however, he began to collect them as a hobby, and within a few years he had close to six hundred, in every imaginable shade, which he kept in specially made drawers, the ties arranged by color. His sartorial splendor was augmented by a cigarette which he held in his hand but did not smoke; he would explain that he needed this prop because he was nervous.

The part of an evening Graffman most enjoyed would come after the formal lesson had ended. Then the discussion turned to music-business gossip, politics, museum exhibitions, recordings of other pianists—anything that happened to catch Horowitz's interest. Graffman, like the students who followed him, became an important connection for Horowitz with the outside world.

The real high point often came around midnight, when Horowitz would ask a question such as, "Do you, by chance, know the Sixth Sonata of Scriabin?" "No, not really," Graffman would eagerly respond. Then Horowitz would walk to the piano, saying apologetically, "It's a very great work. You should hear it. I would like to play it for you, but of course you understand that I cannot play the piano anymore." He then sat down at the keyboard. "If I could play, I would play it for you." His hands hovered over the keys and dropped back to his lap. "Since I cannot play the piano anymore this is not possible. However, I'll try to give you just an idea. But please forgive me, because, of course, you understand . . ." Then Horowitz would, as Graffman put it, "tear through the piece, often in a performance so brilliant and so perfect that it could have been recorded on the spot."[7]

Horowitz and Graffman spoke constantly on the telephone, and little by little the student-teacher relationship turned into a friendship. Between dates on his tours, Graffman would stop at Ninety-fourth Street for coaching sessions and for more midnight concerts, during which he heard Horowitz play through volumes of Clementi and Scarlatti sonatas, and also works of Scriabin and Medtner. Horowitz so enjoyed his association with Graffman that the young man never was asked to pay for lessons. "There was some talk about my either preparing better or being charged so that the lessons would not be taken for granted, but he never did charge and he gave me a hell of a lot of his time very graciously."

When Horowitz began working with Graffman, he also started to coach another young pianist, Arthur McKenzie. Horowitz had heard about him through the renowned vocal coach Frank LaForge, who told him that McKenzie had transcribed and performed two of Horowitz's transcriptions, Mendelssohn's *Wedding March* and Sousa's *The Stars and Stripes Forever*. Horowitz, who believed it impossible for any pianist to have duplicated his transcriptions, nonetheless contacted McKenzie to satisfy his curiosity. It turned out that McKenzie had indeed copied the works exactly, and Horowitz was so impressed with his ear that he agreed to work with him for a short period of time late in 1953. However, one day McKenzie's lessons came to an abrupt end. At Ninety-fourth Street Wanda appeared in place of Horowitz and curtly announced that Horowitz would not be able to see him anymore. Said McKenzie: "His colitis was bothering him and he broke off communications with everyone for a period."[8]

When Horowitz recovered, he had no interest in continuing with McKenzie, but he subsequently accepted four students: Coleman Blumfield from 1956 to 1958, Ronald Turini from 1957 to 1963, Alexander Fiorillo from 1960 to 1962, and Ivan Davis from 1961 to 1962. In the next decade Janis and Graffman became well-known performers, although neither pianist ever achieved anything near the superstar status of their mentor. Turini, Blumfield, Fiorillo, and Davis earned their livings performing, teaching, and playing chamber music.

Although Horowitz had accepted a total of seven students between

1944 and 1962, he publicly acknowledged only three: "Many young people say they have been pupils of Horowitz, but there were only three: Byron Janis, Ronald Turini, who I brought to the stage, and Gary Graffman. If someone else claims it, it's not true. I had some who played for me for four months. Once a week. I stopped work with them because they did not progress. They did not want to follow my advice—or couldn't. If I am here for a constructive purpose, I am here. I am not doing this for bucks. It was only to help, really."[9] The fact that Horowitz disavowed most of his students and blurred the facts regarding their periods of study says something about the erratic nature of his personality during this period of his life.

As with Graffman, Horowitz inherited both Turini and Blumfield from Vengerova, who had made it a principle that her finest pupils should go to him. The least-known of these Vengerova students, and the one never mentioned in any context by Horowitz, was Coleman Blumfield, a native of Chicago who had studied with Horowitz's own teacher, Sergei Tarnowsky, before beginning with Vengerova in 1952. During Blumfield's childhood years, Gitta Gradova had taken an interest in his training and it was she who introduced the boy to Horowitz in the late 1940's. Gradova remembered: "Coleman was about sixteen when I sent him to Horowitz for an audition. All he was interested in doing at that time was playing everything that Horowitz played, and badly. Horowitz said he was not ready and wouldn't take him, so we got him into Curtis in Philadelphia. He was a talented and ambitious boy, but was mishandled, and the fact that he wanted to play what Horowitz played nauseated me. This was somebody who thought he was going to emulate the one and only Horowitz, and it couldn't be done."[10] Seven years later, however, Blumfield had made excellent progress with Vengerova, and at Vengerova's funeral in 1956 her assistant, Olga Strumillo, a close friend of Wanda Horowitz, told Blumfield to call Horowitz for an appointment. It seemed that, before her death, Vengerova had arranged for the young man to study with him.

Like most pianists who have auditioned for Horowitz, Blumfield was petrified. Wide-eyed, he entered the Ninety-fourth Street townhouse and was dazzled by the Picasso over the couch and intimidated by the concert grand festooned with its autographed photos. In his own words, "I was completely awed by Mr. Horowitz's dedication to Art. At that moment I knew that I was in for a marvelous musical experience." Later, this naïve enthusiasm would turn to frustration and bitterness.

Horowitz accepted Blumfield only conditionally, stipulating a three-month trial period which was then extended to nearly two years, sometimes with as many as five or six lessons concentrated in a two-week period, followed by a month of separation as Blumfield prepared repertory. His new teacher stressed to Blumfield the importance of abandoning his "Horowitzian" style (then, as always, imitation offended Horowitz) that had so irked Gitta Gradova, of conceptualizing music in more than merely pyrotechnical terms, and of paying close attention to the actual meaning of a work. However, Horowitz was not pleased with his pupil's progress and granted lessons more and more sporadically, until the time came in 1958 when he finally told Blumfield bluntly: "I don't want to teach you anymore." Blumfield recalled, "I picked myself up, and—what do you do? You go out and try to make a living. I think Horowitz was irritated that I had auditioned for Columbia Artists without his permission." Blumfield was subsequently signed on by Columbia but was at the same time forbidden by Horowitz to use Horowitz's name in his publicity. "I think that just under two years' study should be considered a student," said Blumfield twenty-two years later, still smarting from the slap. After four seasons with Columbia, Blumfield went to Flint, Michigan, in a two-year artist-in-residence program and later toured American high schools in programs sponsored by the Ford Motor Company and the Office of Economic Development. But his growing interest in public-service projects could not compensate for his despair over his thwarted concert career. One Columbia manager explained, "We did as much for Coleman as we could and worked very hard, but his career did not develop. After four seasons, he left us by his own choice."[11] Blumfield's concerts continued to reflect the Horowitz repertory, and he never seemed quite able to shake off his negative experience with Horowitz. The two did not speak again.

Horowitz's experience with Ronald Turini proved far more satisfactory than the disappointing work with Blumfield. Turini, born in Montreal and trained at the Quebec Provincial Conservatory, had also studied with Vengerova, from 1954 until her death. He had then continued with Olga Strumillo, who took the young man under her wing and prepared him for his prize-winning performances in the 1958 Busoni and Geneva competitions. When Turini returned to the United States, Strumillo offered to introduce the twenty-five-year-old to Horowitz. "Shaking in my boots," recalled Turini, "I summoned the courage to audition and played the first movement of the Chopin E Minor Concerto and a movement from the Beethoven *Appassionata* Sonata." Turini was accepted enthusiastically by Horowitz, who nonetheless insisted on the usual three-month trial period.

Turini quickly became Horowitz's favorite pupil. Their relationship lasted from early 1958 through 1963, and Horowitz remained interested in Turini's career long after formal lessons ended. Like Graffman, Turini continued to perform during the period of study with Horowitz, and although Horowitz disapproved of contests, he helped groom Turini for the 1960 Queen Elisabeth of Belgium International Competition in Brussels, at which he won a gold medal. He also carefully coached Turini for his Carnegie Hall debut in 1961, and was later instrumental in helping to procure for him a Columbia Artists Management contract. Horowitz went on record as saying that Turini was "a very talented boy and I was very proud of him and I gave him lots of time. I was in complete disagreement with Vengerova and I changed everything even though . . . it was difficult. He had mechanics but I changed his sound— taught him the *savoir-faire* of real technique."[12] Turini's lessons sometimes went on for two or three hours rather than the customary one, for Horowitz was willing to devote a good deal of energy to him. "Teaching was more than just teaching for Horowitz," Turini remembered. "It was also a social occasion, because he saw so few people. I would call him the day before a lesson was scheduled, usually about once a month, although I sometimes had two or three in quick succession since I commuted down from Montreal. Sometimes he would say he was not feeling too well and I would call back in four or five days. There was no regularity to the lessons, and getting one depended on his mood. I would take it when I could get it, and it was worth every minute. You could never get that kind of teaching anywhere else."

Turini discovered that Horowitz employed an intuitive approach, focusing attention on musical style, mood, tone, color, and dynamics rather than mechanics. "Lessons were on a high level—not the kind where you put this finger here and that finger there. The teaching was coaching. I played an entire composition or entire movement, and then he would pick out the sections that needed improvement. He was a born demonstrator-teacher and his imagination was his greatest gift. His goal was having at his disposal as many approaches to one passage as he could imagine, and in performance he chose any one of them spontaneously. He would spring from the couch and sit down at the piano. 'Do something like this,' he'd say, and his playing was flabbergastingly beautiful, worth a thousand words. I knew immediately what he wanted, what he was driving at. Although he did demonstrate frequently, he also expected a lot of musical imagination from me and was not going to tell me exactly what to do."

The fact that Horowitz demonstrated frequently was fortunate, since Turini soon realized that his teacher was relatively inarticulate when it came to explaining technical matters. The inimitable Horowitz octaves, the orchestral sonority, the delicate pedaling, and the huge dynamic range all remained a mystery. "It was impossible to please him, for instance, with my pedaling of the Chopin B-flat Minor Sonata because he could never tell me exactly what he wanted. Also I was never able to find out how he played octaves so accurately and so quickly. I think a lot of it was natural technique, nothing he either learned or could necessarily explain in words, and he didn't even try." However, Turini did achieve an expanded dynamic range in his playing thanks to Horowitz's high-spirited demonstrations. "Usually I didn't have enough *pianissimo*, or enough *fortissimo*. I would feel his arm as he played and there was a tremendous amount of tension, but it was released immediately after he struck a note. When he played loudly, it came all the way from his back and was like an explosion. He used to stand behind me and feel my back when I played a loud chord and say: 'You don't have enough *forte* there.' Then he'd grab my shoulders and my back again and exclaim, 'Yeah, that's better! The strength and leverage come from the legs, stomach, and body weight, too.' "

Because Horowitz seemed to have a great deal of faith in Turini's abilities, he was intolerant of any letdown of standards. "He became irritated several times when I didn't play well because I had an off day or hadn't practiced enough, but it was nothing in comparison to the ranting and raving of Vengerova. In his own way, he was more encouraging and more demanding than Vengerova, and actually quite kind. He was a great gentleman to work with—a perfectionist. One could always do more, but he would always make his demands in a nice way."

After Turini won the second-prize gold medal in Belgium in 1960, he toured for the next few years in the United States, South America, and the Soviet Union. In 1963, his lessons with Horowitz finally ended. "He told me I should be on my own then and said, 'Try it by yourself for a while.' He also gave me some advice on critics: 'If you are going to have a career, you will have bad critics and lots of them, but you will have to be able to take it. It's part of the game, part of the business.' Sometimes, of course, Horowitz would mistake a bad critic for one who did not like his playing, but I appreciated the advice nonetheless."

Unfortunately, by the late 1960's Turini's career in America had come to a standstill. He moved permanently to Canada to teach and play chamber music, giving only occasional solo recitals. As late as 1976, Horowitz attempted to help him by procuring management with what was then his own firm, Harold Shaw Concerts. Turini played few dates in the United States and finally ended his relationship with American management to devote himself to full-time teaching. "He deserves a better place than he has," Horowitz declared. "But he is very shy and not a pusher."[13]

Horowitz would never feel as warmly toward any other of his pupils. Nevertheless, he did accept two pianists in the early 1960's—twenty-year-old Alexander Fiorillo and twenty-nine-year-old Ivan Davis. Fiorillo became perhaps the most bitter of Horowitz's former students. Born in Philadelphia and trained under Victor Babin at the Philadelphia Musical Academy, Fiorillo had already made his debut with the Philadelphia Orchestra and had appeared at New York's Town Hall as winner of the Leschetizky Piano Debut Prize before he met Horowitz. It was the Town Hall recital and the subsequent intervention of John Steinway that spurred him to study with Horowitz. Steinway asked Fiorillo about his future plans, which included a European tour and master classes in Italy and Austria, and suggested that he defer all decisions until he auditioned for an interested party. One week later, Fiorillo played his Town Hall program for Horowitz, after which Horowitz declared: "You are enormously gifted. If you are interested, I would like to teach you." Surprised, Fiorillo told him about his immediate plans, and Horowitz responded, "I want you to give up everything and start immediately." Like Blumfield, he was forbidden to enter competitions. "Horowitz also said not to tell anyone I was studying with him—that I should never reveal his concepts, his secret technical exercises, nor give out his telephone number or try to arrange auditions for friends. I enjoyed protecting him as much as he wanted to be protected and I respected his privacy."

While Fiorillo devoted himself to determined practice, Horowitz began to coach Ivan Davis, the seventh and last pupil he worked with during his nonperforming years. Davis, like Graffman, did not pay for lessons and was as much friend and colleague as pupil to Horowitz. He had won first prize in the 1957 Busoni and 1958 Casella competitions; in 1960 he also won the Franz Liszt Competition and received a surprise phone call from Horowitz the day after the announcement. With sixty concerts planned for his first cross-country tour and a CBS Records contract, Davis intrigued Horowitz because of his successes and the rumors of a Horowitzian technique. A meeting was arranged, and after dinner Horowitz asked Davis to play. "I understand you play the Sixth Rhapsody of Liszt," Horowitz said. "I hear you have good octaves."

Davis was shocked: "Oh my God, I thought to myself. It's like taking coals to Newcastle!" But after he played, the young man was touched by Horowitz's gentle response: "Well, Ivan, I'm not playing much myself anymore. You already have a personality, you're already a pianist, but sometimes I think you do things you don't hear yourself. I'd like to be big ears for you."

For the next year and a half, Davis dropped by Horowitz's home on the average of once a week at 9:45 P.M. "I was never a student per se, because I was already established, but he gave me suggestions about the repertoire I was playing in concerts, and we discussed my experience at Columbia Records since he himself was about to begin recording there. Also, I'm an opera buff, and we listened to Rimsky-Korsakov's *Sadko* and other Russian operas." Horowitz also played for Davis his collection of private recordings of many of his Carnegie Hall recitals in the late 1940's and 1950's and told him that he was both proud and ashamed of one recorded performance of the Liszt Hungarian Rhapsody No. 6. "It was the fastest damn thing you can imagine," recalled Davis. "Horowitz was just like a mischievous little kid—'Hee, hee, listen what I do here, very bad taste, but isn't it fun?' And it really was marvelous." Curious about the hands that had managed such a feat, Davis observed them carefully. "Although not king-size, Horowitz's hands were extraordinary looking. The fifth fingers were surrounded by the most incredible mass of white muscle."

In their evenings together, Davis much preferred Horowitz's demonstrations to any attempted explanations. He later stated that if there was a secret to Horowitz's brilliant technique, he never found it. "One time, when we were playing octaves," said Davis, "Horowitz said to me, 'You know, you've got a good wrist, most people don't. Want me to show you how I play my octaves?' And I thought, 'Here it is, the secret that all the world's been waiting for.' And Horowitz said, 'I practice slow, high from the wrist and in different rhythms.' Of course, everybody practices that way, so I didn't learn one thing!"

Horowitz enthusiastically told Davis of Turini's progress, and in fact, Turini was the only student ever mentioned. "At one lesson," recalled Davis, "I was playing something for both hands in unison, extremely fast, and was having trouble keeping my hands exactly together. Horowitz said, 'Oh, I have the same trouble. It's easier for me to play double thirds in one hand than to play them with two hands. Turini can't play the double notes as well, but he plays both hands together better than anyone I've ever heard." Horowitz's candor with Davis even led him to an assessment of his own strengths as a pianist. According to Davis, Horowitz once told him that he thought his playing had "the best of the masculine and feminine qualities. He said that some men are incapable of feminine warmth while a lot of feminine players did not have the aggressive masculine quality." Horowitz went on to assert that he had never heard a woman play as well as a man, no doubt the reason for his impatience with Marilyn Meyer years earlier. "I've also been told," Davis added, "that he has jokingly said there are three kinds of pianists: Jewish pianists, homosexual pianists, and bad pianists!"

As Horowitz ventured out of his house more often in the early 1960's, Davis became one of his favorite companions. "We once went to Carnegie Hall to hear Rudolf Serkin and his son Peter play the Mozart Double Concerto. When we went out in public he always told me that in case someone came over to us, I should introduce him as 'Mr. Howard.' I thought this was very funny because no one in the world would believe it—I don't know if he thought he was fooling anyone or not. After the Serkin concert, in the midst of backstage autograph seekers, Horowitz kept looking nervously at his watch and saying, 'We've got to go, we've got to go,' and I thought he was panic-stricken with all the people surrounding him. But that was not the problem. When we were in the car, he said, 'Got to get home because the Emmy Awards are on and I must see if *Naked City* wins!'"

Such camaraderie was not always part of Alexander Fiorillo's experience. "I went through a very regimented, sometimes demeaning routine regarding appointments," Fiorillo said. "From my home in Philadelphia, I had to call Horowitz on the Saturday before a lesson at nine P.M. sharp to confirm our appointment for Sunday at five P.M. When I called at nine P.M. on Saturday, he always picked up the phone on the first ring, but if I called at nine-fifteen he wouldn't talk to me and I would miss the lesson for that week. Even after the lesson was confirmed, I would drive from Philadelphia, and upon arriving at the Ninety-fourth Street house, very often I would be told by Horowitz's butler that Horowitz was not feeling well and that I should call him next week. It would never occur to him to pick up the phone to save me the trip to New York."

Although many lessons were canceled, Horowitz always, according to Fiorillo, received the standard $100 per lesson paid by his sponsor, the Martha Baird Rockefeller Foundation. "Even after I got in the house, I never knew what to expect," he complained. "For instance, one time I was scheduled to have a lesson on a very hot day during the summer and had driven all the way from Philadelphia with no air conditioning. It was a great relief to be in Horowitz's townhouse, which was entirely air-conditioned and very comfortable. I began practicing in the living room, and he walked in and said, 'It's humid today, huh?' I answered, 'Yes, it's very humid.' Horowitz said, 'It was hot driving here?' 'Yes,' I replied. Then: 'You know, I think it is too hot for a lesson today. You will call me next week. If you want to practice, stay. I will see you next week.' He left the room and I sat there amazed."

Despite such difficulties, Fiorillo discovered that Horowitz could be generous with his time. "When I began studying with him, I was not a superdooper rip-roaring technician, and Horowitz worked with me patiently, demonstrating exercises for stretching the hand, for making the fingers more independent. He assigned every one of the Chopin Etudes, Opus ten, which he played perfectly. His hand was very lean but deceptively strong. When he played octaves, for instance, his wrist was wonderfully resilient—almost as if there were a spring in it. After spending the first few months on exercises, we concentrated on the Romantic repertory." Focusing on Fiorillo's Town Hall program, Horowitz pointed out what he considered to be the young man's principal weakness, a lack of continuity and structure in his playing. "In the Chopin F Minor Fantasy, he told me that the key to the problem was understanding transitions. He discussed in great detail the preparation and adjustment to a new tempo and described the importance of a fermata, the dramatic purpose of a rest, and the psychological importance audiencewise of making a transition visually with a connecting gesture of the hand."

Byron Janis had welcomed the inconsistencies in Horowitz's criticism from week to week because they had the effect of forcing him to play more flexibly and spontaneously. Fiorillo, however, found this approach confusing and resisted studying certain repertory with Horowitz. Fiorillo was disconcerted, for instance, by Horowitz's ever-changing ideas about the Chopin G Minor Ballade. "I have never heard him play that piece the same way twice," he said. "I see this constant shifting of concept as a function of his enormous creativity. It must be very difficult for him to agree in his own mind about one way to do something. When I went for a lesson on this piece, he was never consistent in his criticism. He would ask me indignantly, 'What are you doing there?' and I would answer, 'Well, you asked me to do it that way last week'—and then he would snap, 'Well, I don't like that.'" Although Fiorillo admitted that Horowitz's comments about the Romantic repertory had been illuminating, he remembered that he tended to avoid playing Classical pieces for his mentor. "There were too many gimmicks in, for instance, his Beethoven. He overorchestrated the music; if there was a subordinate melody in the left hand that no one had ever brought out before, he would think of a reason to bring it out. I didn't hear all those colors, inner voices, and crescendos that Beethoven had not written and didn't want to superimpose them. As I mature in repertory, where I used to find Horowitz's playing terribly spontaneous, I now sometimes find it contrived. For him, nothing can be simple." Davis agreed that Horowitz's overdramatization was a problem in some music: "I must say that I never want to hear him play Schumann's *Scenes from Childhood* [*Kinderscenen*] again. So tortured! There is not a note of simplicity left in it. He wrings every note dry, and I don't think the piece can stand the weight of all that torture."

Although quick to criticize Horowitz years later, all his former students admit to having been overwhelmed during lessons by Horowitz's technical achievements. "His fingers could bring out anything, anywhere, at any time," said Fiorillo. "He was simply amazing in terms of color, endurance, and rhythmic vitality." Fiorillo had been curious about Horowitz's fabled transcriptions and had asked him if he would ever play them again. "I don't remember any of them," was the answer. "I don't play them anymore and don't want to be associated with them." Fiorillo then made his own arrangement of the Paganini-Liszt Sixth Etude, adding doublings, inner voices, and a dramatic coda—all in the Horowitz style. "When I played it for him he was furious. He said, 'Why are you doing that? You are trying to imitate my transcriptions? I don't want to hear it this way! Don't ever play it this way for me again!'"

But that was one of the few times Horowitz lost his temper with

Fiorillo, with whom he was oftentimes friendly and gregarious. During the summer of 1961, when Horowitz took a house in East Hampton, he rented a second house about two miles away for Fiorillo so that their lessons could continue uninterrupted. "He laid out seven hundred fifty dollars a month for my house, which came complete with gardener and Steinway piano. This was incredibly generous of him." By living in such close proximity to his teacher, Fiorillo was privy to many aspects of Horowitz's daily life. Horowitz told him that he spent his time following politics, current events, and for a while, baseball. "He was clever, like a child, but I would not say that he was an intellectual. I did not see him studying music much."

With some amazement, Fiorillo noted certain of Horowitz's foibles: his fear of the dark, his susceptibility to the weather, his fanatically strict daily regimen, his bizarrely restrictive diet. Still suffering from colitis, Horowitz ate only lamb patties for both lunch and dinner every day with RyKrisp crackers and milk or tea. That summer in East Hampton, he was still plagued by a host of illnesses, real and imaginary, and his bedroom looked rather like an apothecary's shop. "I never saw so much medication in my life," said Fiorillo. "Bottles everywhere. Black drapes and black shades drawn in the middle of a July afternoon. And there Horowitz would be, lying on his back with his eyes covered with plastic eyeshades, wearing earplugs. He was always complaining to me about his stomach problems, and I felt very sorry for him."

On the numerous days that Horowitz remained sequestered indoors, Fiorillo would drop by and encourage him to take a walk. He discovered that the weather dictated nearly everything Horowitz did. "One day, it was one hundred and five in the shade. Horowitz hesitated to take a walk but I insisted it would be good exercise. He then proceeded to don a tie and sport jacket, and I thought he must be out of his mind. I told him it was too hot for that outfit, so he took off the jacket. We took about three steps out of the house and he said, 'I am cold. How can you say it's so warm? It's very cold here. I am going back to get the jacket.' And it was true that he did not look warm; nor did he perspire."

Horowitz seemed to enjoy Fiorillo, not only as a student but as a companion and confidant. He sometimes spoke with him of the continuing problems with Sonia. When Horowitz received a letter from his daughter, he would show it to Fiorillo with irritation. "Some were very beautifully written," recalled Fiorillo. "Sonia would tell her father how proud she was to be his daughter, what a privilege it had always been, and how much she loved him. Then in the next letter she would declare that she hated him and everything he stood for and that he was a horrible parent. Yet I don't think these letters had much of an effect on him. He did not seem to care for her much. I don't think he cared much for anyone, really. He was terribly self-centered."

Horowitz did, however, seem to have at least a temporary attachment to Fiorillo during that summer, and it was his expression of affection that eventually precipitated a break. "Wanda would see me at the beach with women, and Horowitz appeared to be jealous and at the same time to take a vicarious thrill from my escapades. He wanted to know if I was sleeping with women and often questioned me about my habits. He said he was responsible for my behavior and that he did not want me to create any controversy." After returning to New York in the fall, Horowitz remained involved with his student: "I was quite athletic, and Horowitz enjoyed my demonstrations of strength, whether it was arm wrestling, handshakes, or breaking pencils. He was constantly testing me. One day late that fall, he said, 'You know, Alex, you once said you loved me. What did you mean by this?' I told him that I loved his playing and had always idolized him. Our relationship deteriorated from then."

Later that fall Horowitz explained to Fiorillo that he was going to be extremely busy making recordings for Columbia Masterworks soon, and that he contemplated returning to the stage and would thus not have any time to teach. He suggested Fiorillo work with Rudolf Serkin—"You could study Mozart, Schubert, Beethoven with him," he said. Fiorillo was shocked: "He was very polite and showed no animosity about our association ending, but I was angry and disappointed because I cared about it and I didn't think he ever really had. I also cared about him." Fiorillo worried about his future. "Although Horowitz had arranged for me to play for George Marek at RCA and had introduced me to some conductors, I had not played publicly or entered any competitions since I began lessons with him two years before. He had promised me, 'When you are ready, I will arrange everything'; but he arranged absolutely nothing. When I started lessons, I was making wonderful strides and there was no reason why I should have stopped performing. But I respected his wishes, because I thought this was a great man, a man whom I idolized, and I believed I should follow his advice and not question his authority. I put all my eggs in one basket and most of them cracked."

The twenty-three-year-old Fiorillo ended his lessons not only bitter but also ill. He began to have serious problems with his stomach and nerves and found he had lost confidence in himself. To make matters worse, he was drafted into the army, which all but aborted his career as a pianist. "When I got out of basic training, I visited Horowitz's home in uniform for cake and coffee. We discussed the possibility of my continuing lessons sporadically but Horowitz explained that his psychiatrist recommended that he discontinue teaching, that it was not good for him as he increased his recording activity."

Years later, Fiorillo remained angry and resentful. He eventually became a professor of music at Temple University and a member of a chamber group at that institution, but the damage to his career as a soloist left him with mixed feelings toward his former teacher. "On a scale of one to ten, I would give Horowitz a ten in terms of his ability to inspire," he said. "However, in terms of his responsibility and commitment as a teacher, less than five, due to his inconsistency and, at times, lack of interest. To yell out, '*Forte, piano, more crescendo!*' while lying on his couch—that, many people could do."

Of the seven students, only Graffman, Turini, and Davis seemed to have escaped any negative effects. Their careers were at least somewhat established before they began to work with Horowitz, and they were less dependent on him, therefore less vulnerable. Graffman, who had the most consistently successful performing career, was willing to discuss Horowitz as a person only guardedly. However, he made evident his disdain for Horowitz's erratic behavior. Only Davis, who had toured, recorded, and taught at the University of Miami, seemed relaxed when speaking of Horowitz.

In the context of teaching, Horowitz appeared blind to the sometimes devastating effects of his volatile temperament on the young. He was capable of kindness, but a kindness that could suddenly evaporate and be replaced by capricious insensitivity. He would arbitrarily postpone lessons and drop students without explanation; he undercut self-confidence by sometimes showing no enthusiasm for or interest in the concerts and recordings of his protégés. He would even deny that some of them had ever studied with him, assuring that their connection with him could do nothing to help their careers. It was Byron Janis who offered an explanation for Horowitz's evasiveness in this area: "He's happy to acknowledge his teaching when he has a successful student."

For those half-dozen students who spent years working with Horowitz, there remained a legacy of misunderstood motives and tangled emotions. It is clear that neither Horowitz—to judge from his aloof silence—nor most of his former students—as evidenced by their often resentful criticism—have managed to come to terms with the full impact of their shared experiences. Horowitz continued to show lively interest in younger pianists throughout the 1960's, inviting many artists—including Vladimir Ashkenazy, Alexis Weissenberg, André Watts, John Browning, Murray Perahia—for evenings of music making and talk. Contact with young people remained important to him, as is illustrated by a poignant anecdote told by Ivan Davis. "He called me one day and said, 'Ivan, I'm tired of staying in. I want to go out. Take me someplace.' I mentioned several restaurants, and he declared, 'I want to see young people. I want to go and look.' We settled on O. Henry's in Greenwich Village, and sat at a table on the sidewalk drinking Poland Water. A group of young piano students came over. They recognized me because they knew my Liszt record and they asked for my autograph. But they didn't recognize Horowitz. I thought, 'You fools, here is the most famous pianist in the world and you don't know it.' And Horowitz exclaimed, 'They don't know who I am!' I calmed him down by saying it was only because he had not played in such a long time. But I always felt this episode was one factor in his returning to the stage. It may have made him aware that there was an entire generation of young pianists who had never heard him play."

CHAPTER TWENTY

"GOOD-BYE, MR. RCA"

*"RCA told me if I didn't perform, people would forget me
and my records wouldn't sell. They said, 'At least play some
popular music for us, some Gershwin, more Wedding Marches,
and that will sell.' I said, 'Fine. If that's what you want
from me, I'm going.'"*[1]

*S*onia's accident in 1957 had brought on a hiatus in recording for
Horowitz, a two-year period of restlessness and depression. Then in May
1959, he was persuaded by Jack Pfeiffer and Wanda to return to the stage
of Carnegie Hall to make his first stereo recording, which proved to be
his last disc for RCA until many years later. Continuing the concept of
one-composer albums, Horowitz had decided on an all-Beethoven program that consisted of two sonatas not previously recorded by him: the
Appassionata and the D Major, Op. 10, No. 3. Released also in monaural,
the disc was generally well received. "The cruelest thing one can do to
any Beethoven sonata recording is to play it against the Schnabel version," wrote Robert C. Marsh in *High Fidelity,* "and if you do this to the
Horowitz, you will, I think, discover two things. First, that Schnabel gets
somewhat more from this music than Horowitz does; second, that the
Horowitz recording, which of course is incomparably superior technically, can withstand this comparison better than most."[2] Yet especially in
the D Major Sonata, Horowitz's forced tone at climaxes and the immediacy of the "under-the-piano-lid" engineering resulted in a hard, somewhat brittle sound—"quite ugly," according to one critic, who went on
to note that "in the slow movement, for instance, he allows it to get the
better of his sense of Classical proportion, and although the performance
is gripping, there are moments which border on hysteria."[3] The combination of playing in an empty Carnegie Hall and the strident tone of the
piano made Horowitz himself deeply unhappy with the result. "Playing
in Carnegie Hall gave me a depression a little," he recalled. "I said, no, I
don't want to play anymore—the recording doesn't capture the tone and

I still don't want to perform for an audience. I felt frustrated and did not record for three years."[4]

Of course, Horowitz's sudden decision to stop recording yet again infuriated RCA executives, especially as their advertising department had already announced that the Beethoven album inaugurated a new series of Horowitz releases. George Marek made every effort to get him to change his mind, but the pianist remained adamant. He was not interested in recording, and further, he had lost interest in the entire piano repertory. Still, Marek would not give up. "I encouraged Horowitz to record all four of the Rachmaninoff concertos, or possibly just the Second, which he played beautifully in private. I also suggested he record all five Beethoven concertos. But nothing happened. He remained withdrawn, sitting at home, not going out, just listening to the radio."[5]

Marek was irritated not only with Horowitz's inactivity but also by his concept of recording and his financial demands. "Horowitz was the most particular recording artist I had ever seen, and I had seen them all. He rerecorded constantly and often rejected a master the day after he approved it. Every day was different for him, and his responsiveness depended entirely on his physical and emotional condition. His behavior was erratic and unpredictable. Yet he was still under contract, being paid a yearly salary—for nothing."[6]

From Horowitz's vantage point, however, the merchandising department at RCA was vulgar, anachronistic, and even insulting. The company insisted that he record more "popular" music, such as George Gershwin's *Rhapsody in Blue* or the Concerto in F Major. "We quarreled because there were wrong people at RCA at that time," Horowitz later stated. "I just said to myself, if they don't want me, that's all right."[7] Alan Kayes, RCA's manager of Artists and Repertoire from 1951 to 1962, tried to act as an intermediary between Horowitz and the marketing department, and he admitted that there were internal problems at RCA, infighting between A & R and marketing, and that many of Horowitz's complaints were justified. "The merchandising people were trying to call the shots and A and R was being asked to persuade artists to play repertoire about which they had serious misgivings. In Horowitz's case, his records were not selling, and the marketing division did not want to keep him on the label unless he would tour again to bolster sales, or would at least record salable repertory."[8] At one point, marketing made a serious effort to persuade Horowitz to do an album of marches, including his popular transcription of *The Stars and Stripes Forever*. This notion was absolutely abhorrent to Horowitz, for he had, he felt, long ago shed his image as an acrobat.

But repertory was only part of the story, according to Kayes. "The merchandising people had never had much effect on Horowitz and he had always recorded anything he pleased—Clementi, Scriabin: hardly big money makers. Therefore, when Horowitz made his decision to leave RCA, he and Wanda developed their own rationale for the decision. The bottom line was money, more money than we were prepared to offer, the kind of money that he thought he really deserved. Horowitz prided himself on the fact that he was a skillful businessman. He always had uppermost in his mind the material aspects of a relationship, and that's why he could extract something a bit more than someone else from a contractual relationship—whether it was a reduced commission from a manager, a record company, or local presenter. The guarantee he wanted was entirely out of line, considering the kind of repertoire he wanted to play. Clementi and Scriabin, Medtner and Scarlatti didn't sell records, and we had absolutely no hope that he would ever play in public again."[9]

Near the end of 1961, Horowitz's RCA contract was up for renewal but negotiations were stalled, with both sides unable to agree on the financial arrangements. An all-Liszt album, "Homage to Liszt," released in conjunction with the composer's 150th anniversary, gave the illusion that Horowitz was still at work, but the material was merely a repackaging. Wanda, who had frequently acted as her husband's spokesman in negotiations, became incensed over the lack of adequate advertising and promotion of Horowitz's previous album, and the talks with RCA remained at a deadlock. "RCA was, admittedly, not going after the renewal of his contract enthusiastically," recalled Marek. Nor were company representatives pleased with the way Wanda railed on and on about RCA's paltry advertising budget—which had, after all, been reduced in proportion to Horowitz's declining sales. "It's true," said Marek, "that promoters and stores were not buying Horowitz's records, and we were continuing to lose money on our investment, which was over twenty-five thousand dollars per year."[10] With an enraged Wanda determined to terminate the relationship with RCA, the matter became exaggerated out of all proportion. Finally, in a last-ditch effort to keep Horowitz with the company, RCA President David Sarnoff became involved, sending Vice President Charles Odorizzi as his personal emissary. All efforts failed.

As soon as rumors circulated that Horowitz might leave RCA, other companies began courting him. Schuyler Chapin, in 1961 the director of Artists and Repertoire at Columbia Masterworks, telephoned immediately after Gary Graffman told him Horowitz was seriously considering jettisoning RCA. "Through the Steinways I had known Horowitz for many years," recalled Chapin, "but not intimately and never in a business sense. Nonetheless I telephoned his house and when his wife answered I came right to the point. Was it true Horowitz was leaving RCA and if so could we meet to discuss the possibility of his coming to Columbia? I spoke all this breathlessly and without pause. . . . Wanda said the news was true, and if Goddard Lieberson and I were interested enough to talk they would be interested enough to listen."[11]

Although Chapin faced the discussions with trepidation, he had complete faith in Goddard Lieberson, president of Columbia Records, a talented and persuasive man described by Chapin as "bright, funny, quick, outrageous, vain, enormously egocentric."[12] Since 1939, Lieberson had been a guiding force at Columbia and had given impetus to the recording careers of many musicians, from Bruno Walter, Igor Stravinsky, and Leonard Bernstein to Miles Davis, Barbra Streisand, and Andy Williams. Lieberson had himself been trained in composition at the Eastman School of Music, and his erudition and wit had the desired effect on Horowitz. During their first evening together, the two men sat swapping stories, leaving the hard bargaining to Wanda. According to Chapin, she "had her RCA facts and figures marshaled with the excellence and efficiency of a bank auditor. Nothing seemed to get past those wide, sharp eyes of hers and her Toscanini antecedents seemed to be very much in command. She recited tales of broken promises and professional carelessness, and every once in a while Horowitz would nod agreement or lean over in a conspiratorial manner as if to indicate his wife was a force to be reckoned with."[13]

During that evening Chapin and Lieberson not only sympathized with Horowitz's indignation at his shabby treatment by RCA but also caught his attention by presenting a point of view not previously considered. Both men explained that a new youth market was opening up for serious music and that Columbia was fast becoming the leader of the classical music market. After eight years away from the concert platform, Horowitz worried that his recordings were not enough to sustain a hold on the public. "He asked whether I thought that any young people had ever heard of him," said Chapin. "I could sense that this was a very important point and might indeed be a key to a more active professional life. I assured him that there was a market out there made up of people who had heard him and also those who knew him only as a myth. The longer he stayed away the more the myth was fed, and while I did not say so that night, I felt that it was possible for too much myth and too long an absence to finally remove him altogether from the public mind."[14]

The creation of a new youth market with the attendant possibility of winning new fans was an important consideration in Horowitz's eventual decision to sign with Columbia. He was not, however, easily persuaded, and Chapin's gentle persistence and almost parental reassurances continued during the fall months of 1961.

Ten years earlier, Chapin had worked as Jascha Heifetz's valet-companion for concerts, so he was accustomed to temperamental artists. He knew how to assuage Horowitz's fears, and his patience and charm were great assets for Columbia. Serious consideration, however, was being given by the Horowitzes to an offer from EMI-Angel Records, a London-based firm which had special sentimental appeal for Horowitz, since he had made his very first recordings for it. Still, in the early 1960's Columbia was clearly becoming the strongest bet in the classical-record business, and all things seemed to point to that company as the choice. In forsaking RCA's distinguished entourage of Rubinstein, De Pachman, Paderewski, and Rachmaninoff, Horowitz was joining an equally illustrious group at Columbia: Hofmann, Godowsky, Grainger, and Petri. It was, he said, Columbia's "human approach to artistic demands"[15] that finally won him over. Chapin recalled that "there came the night we'd been waiting for. The Horowitzes agreed to come to Columbia, and I was moved when he turned to me and said, very simply: 'Will you take care of me?' I said a quiet and heartfelt yes."[16]

In his three-year contract, which committed him to six releases at a rate of two per year, Horowitz was assured not only that he could record whatever repertory he wished, but that he would have the full support of the CBS public-relations department, which vowed to market and advertise his records aggressively. The contract also stipulated a generous raise in salary over what he had received at RCA—the figure reportedly approaching $50,000—but, in contrast to RCA, Columbia agreed to pay that fee only on a per-record basis rather than as an annual salary. The steep increase and per-record guarantee had a tremendous effect on

Horowitz's attitude, as even RCA's George Marek was forced to admit. "Signing with Columbia and being paid by the album, in fact, forced him to work," said Marek. "Horowitz wanted to show RCA that he could play, sell, and be successful and popular again. The psychological effect on him of changing companies was a tremendous boost and injected new life into his career and his desire to work."[17] Lieberson had promised Horowitz: "You will see, everything will start like a new life for you," and Horowitz had finally exclaimed, "Why not? Good-bye, Mr. RCA. I go with Columbia!"[18]

"Horowitz is nothing if not a consummate showman,"[19] declared Schuyler Chapin, and even before his first CBS recording sessions in April 1962, Horowitz had begun generating publicity for his fall release by calling a press conference the month before to announce his move to Columbia. The theatrics of the occasion were not lost on the *New York Times,* which reported that "if motion pictures have their Greta Garbo, music has its Vladimir Horowitz. . . . Last Tuesday the pianist made news by switching his allegiances. . . . It was a bit as if Garbo, who made nothing but Metro-Goldwyn-Mayer films, should turn up in a Paramount picture. Or if Yogi Berra should go to the Cleveland Indians."[20] Horowitz also conducted interviews from his home and during them enjoyed teasing the press about a possible return to the stage. "That is my little secret," he would say impishly, adding: "I am ready to go into Carnegie Hall and give a recital right now, but you cannot give just one recital. Immediately my friends in other cities would say, 'You have to come and play for us here.' I could not satisfy just a few friends and I do not think I can stand the ordeal of touring." Horowitz emphasized that everything depended on his upcoming date with CBS: "I want to see how I feel about my recording sessions next month. If I feel strong enough, then maybe."[21]

Columbia Records' first formidable task was to find a Jack Pfeiffer, someone not only to produce Horowitz's records but also to serve as an adviser and confidant. Tom Frost, a professionally trained violinist who had studied composition at Yale with Paul Hindemith, had been hired by CBS as a producer in 1959 and had worked successfully with Bruno Walter, Leonard Bernstein, Eugene Ormandy, George Szell, and Isaac Stern. When Frost heard that Horowitz had joined the CBS roster, he walked into Chapin's office one day and said that he would like to work with Horowitz.

Frost's patient demeanor and professional training as a musician were essential ingredients in dealing with Horowitz. Recalled Chapin: "We began a series of tests with Frost, who I felt was the right producer for him. He was a serious and experienced record man and musician and would understand the nature of the artist with whom he would now be involved."[22] The test tapings were made at Columbia's Thirtieth Street studio, a converted church which Horowitz found "not bad—very high ceilings, nice to play in."[23] Frost took an immediate liking to Horowitz, whom he later described as "a warm, gentle man with a wistful sense of humor."[24] At the session, Frost was amazed by the change in his playing, from the first time he had heard him in the 1940's to now, after eight years of retirement. "There was a mellowness, a warmth and introspective quality never before present. The hard, steely, percussive fever was gone. Although the demonic quality was still intact, there was a greater variety of tone color, and he was generally less nervous. We experimented with microphones and achieved a sound that was not overly immediate or brilliant, but warm and round. Although that studio was not as sonically rich as a concert hall, it was considered—as recording studios go—better than average, if a little dry. We could have moved to Carnegie Hall but Horowitz seemed content."[25] The test takes indicated that Frost and Horowitz might work very well together.

Horowitz had decided to break precedent with the one-composer albums he had made for RCA. Wanting to entice the so-called youth market, and increasingly pondering a return to the stage, he structured his first Columbia album as he would an actual recital. "I believe records should be like recitals," he told Raymond Ericson of the *New York Times*. "If a pianist plays nothing but Beethoven sonatas on a recital, then it is all right for him to play Beethoven sonatas on his records. But who plays only Chopin nocturnes on a program? Who wants to listen to all the nocturnes or waltzes in a row? I'm against the complete-recorded-edition approach. Boring."[26]

When Horowitz finally presented Columbia with the repertory for the first album in the early spring of 1962, Chapin was delighted: "One look and I knew that he had chosen cannily, with an eye on the largest public. There was something for everyone who knew his work—Rachmaninoff, Chopin, Schumann, and Liszt—a perfect recital program for the home and maybe, just maybe, for the concert hall."[27] Horowitz had regarded the B-flat Minor Sonata of Chopin as "a good friend" throughout his career and had been dissatisfied with his 1950 RCA recording—"a little slow, a little stagnant, especially in the first movement and the funeral march."[28] For the second side of the new record, Horowitz toyed with the idea of recording another large work—either the Schumann Fantasy in C Major or the Liszt B Minor Sonata—but he ultimately opted for a group of shorter pieces—two *Études Tableaux* of Rachmaninoff (Op. 39, No. 5; Op. 33, No. 2), the Schumann *Arabesque,* and a transcription of the Liszt Hungarian Rhapsody No. 19, his first entirely new such arrangement since the 1953 Hungarian Rhapsody No. 2.

Horowitz agreed with Frost's assessment of the change in his playing and pointed out that even in the Liszt transcription "there is more relaxation."[29] His chief purpose now was not merely to display his technique. "The ideas in the Rhapsody are sketchy sometimes and that's why I decided to fill it out—but in Liszt's vein, not in mine. In the *lassan* I did some doubling and expanding, but not so much. But in the *friska* I changed the form because he repeats the same thing too much. I made the ending more brilliant too—a musical brilliancy. It is rather bravura, for the sake of the musical spirit of the piece. And very Hungarian, too."[30]

Horowitz was just as meticulous in planning the advertising campaign for the new album as he had been selecting the repertory, insisting, remembered Chapin, on "a long-range promotion campaign designed for his world-wide fans of middle age and for the youngsters." Although the Columbia staff thought Horowitz's artistry would sell itself, he himself was, said Chapin, "very conscious of his image and place in history, and he wanted to reach a wider range of the public. And so the recording, packaging, and merchandising of the first album was given as much attention and planning as anything I had ever seen." Wanda, of course, was intimately involved with every detail of the merchandising plan. According to Chapin, "No detail escaped her, from the album cover and jacket notes to the smallest program ad in the remotest concert hall. Wanda had exquisite taste and on every point she gently but firmly challenged me. I rapidly learned that if she had chosen to do so she could have out-merchandised R. H. Macy himself."[31] Horowitz followed their discussions keenly but rarely added anything to his wife's comments. It was decided that an elaborate eight-page booklet would be enclosed with this premier album and that it would contain two long essays—one by Tom Frost and one by Horowitz's old admirer from the 1930's, the

English critic Neville Cardus. There would also be a short introductory statement by Goddard Lieberson and a series of photographs tracing Horowitz's career from the early Russian days to the present.

One thing remained: the actual recording. Chapin had taken special pains to arrange the session for 4:00 P.M., an unusual time for studio engineers, but the hour at which Horowitz liked to work. However, on the afternoon of the first session, March 31, Chapin received disturbing news. "About 1:00 P.M. on that day my phone rang and a message was delivered to me that he had cancelled his first session. I was jolted, for this was the behavior I had heard about for years. The phone rang a second time; now he wanted to speak directly to me. I picked up the instrument, my heart beating and spirits lowering, to hear a choked and stuffed-up voice apologizing for the cancellation and explaining that he had been fighting a spring cold that had gotten the better of him. He said that above everything else he did not want me to have the impression he was cancelling for temperamental reasons. He was ready and eager to work, but could not until he was better." For the next four days, Chapin was forced to endure the nods and winks and I-told-you-so expressions of his colleagues: "One or two patted me on the back, sighed and rolled their eyes to heaven."[32]

The session was rescheduled for five days later. On April 5, a limousine arrived at the Ninety-fourth Street house in mid-afternoon to pick up Horowitz, Frost having been instructed to bring him to the studio at least an hour before the actual recording time. Chapin was pleased with the chemistry between Frost and Horowitz. He relied on Frost to manage the afternoon, assisted by Fred Plaut, the senior recording engineer, and also Bill Hupfer, Steinway's chief tuner—"without whom Horowitz would not play a note," recalled Chapin. But it seemed that the only person who was relaxed that day was Horowitz, who approached his task with steely professionalism. It took only four more afternoon sessions to complete the album, each lasting between one and a half and two hours. Unlike many pianists, Horowitz did not indulge in excessive takes, replace mistakes with tiny splices, or repeat a ten- or twelve-bar phrase over and over again. Instead, he sat down and played an entire piece through, or a large section, always attempting to approach the recording process spontaneously. Between takes, he rested on a cot, sometimes smoking a cigarette and discussing the music with Frost.

During the session, the major complaint of the recording personnel was that Horowitz refused to listen to playbacks in the studio. It seemed that during his years with RCA Horowitz had become accustomed to doing this at home after dinner, and he intended to continue the luxury at Columbia, much to the irritation of Frost and Plaut. "I knew Horowitz would be a difficult customer," said Plaut. "Although he would come into the control room at the beginning of a session to hear how he sounded, thereafter we had to practically force him to listen to a playback. I would have preferred it if he had done retakes immediately because we had to match the sound of the previous master, and this was difficult due to changes in the temperature and humidity."[33]

Nonetheless, everyone at Columbia was instructed to be completely solicitous of Horowitz. Promptly at nine o'clock the evening of a session, Frost was expected to arrive at the house with that day's work. "Horowitz's recording equipment at home was little better than average," he said, "but he wanted to play the acetates on his machine as opposed to listening in the booth because, as he put it, he wanted to hear how it would sound to the average listener with average equipment." After listening, Horowitz might decide to discard everything and start all over again, or to accept only twenty bars, or, on occasion, approve the entire take. "Working that way, although it was much more time-consuming, did allow for more objectivity in assessing each day's work," recalled Frost. "Horowitz was a legend and could work however he chose. Because he could come in and record whatever whenever, his performances were spontaneous. This was most important."[34] Chapin stayed out of the studio but was well aware that Horowitz "wanted to retain the feeling of spontaneity, of a live performance that had accidentally been captured on tape. Above everything else, he wanted to avoid the plastic perfection of a studio creation. He wanted the best of both worlds and taxed the production and engineering staffs to the utmost to obtain what was right."[35]

The final session took place on May 14, 1962, and the meticulously produced and carefully merchandised album was released on September 24. The same changes in Horowitz's playing that Frost had observed were duly noted by the press. Poetry and refinement were seen to have finally taken precedence over digital dexterity. "The biggest measure of the 'new' Horowitz," said High Fidelity, "can be found in the lyrical passages, which have a basic simplicity now, and a relaxed flow which contrasts strongly with the former febrile neuroticism."[36] Sonically, Frost had left no stone unturned, and Horowitz's performances were backed up by a natural-sounding piano tone, rich and mellow. Unlike Pfeiffer, he had, said *High Fidelity,* avoided "gimmicked microphoning that made Horowitz's piano [in past years] sound like a cross between a harpsichord and vibraphone."

The new Horowitz record became the most popular classical disc of 1962 and received a Grammy Award for the best classical performance. "The album created a sensation," said Chapin. "Within days it had climbed to the top of the record charts and re-orders were pouring into the factories. Within three weeks the company had earned back its guarantee payment and both artist and firm were in a profit position. A nice way to start an artistic and business relationship!"[37]

Horowitz and Wanda were satisfied. As Wanda later sniffed at a press conference, "RCA said his records were not selling, but Columbia could sell one hundred and twenty thousand records in the first week!"[38] Horowitz joined in, incredulously: "This was my most successful record!"[39]

CHAPTER TWENTY-ONE

RENAISSANCE

"People went to a Horowitz recital expecting excitement—and I knew it. The effect showed in my playing. It was often tense and hysterical. I no longer have this pressure and my playing reflects it—whether for good or bad is for you to decide."[1]

*T*he positive response to his first Columbia album gave Horowitz the psychological boost he had long been waiting for. He enjoyed being perceived as a remade pianist, "an instrumentalist in full command of his resources, a musician at the summit of his perception and intelligence and a technician of unsurpassed power,"[2] as one critic put it. Such reinforcement and confirmation of his abilities encouraged him to make what were perhaps the finest recordings of his career during his period with Columbia in the 1960's and early 1970's.

Chapin immediately began to plan a second record. He hoped to entice Horowitz into the Rachmaninoff Third Concerto, and suggested either Ormandy and the Philadelphia Orchestra or Bernstein and the New York Philharmonic. Horowitz, however, played cat and mouse, so that Chapin finally realized his "chances of persuading him were almost zero."[3] In Columbia's effort to display versatility, Tom Frost even suggested that Horowitz consider making a four-hand album with Rudolf Serkin, arranging sessions that never occurred. "In our talks about other musicians," said Frost, "Serkin and Rachmaninoff were the only pianists that Horowitz did not speak badly of, and Ormandy the only conductor. Still, no record with Serkin or Ormandy."[4] Chapin recalled that Horowitz "would wax enthusiastic and we'd even begin to talk about halls and schedules. Once I almost went to the telephone to call Ormandy to make a tentative date but always, at the last second, Horowitz would pull back, smiling, eyes twinkling, and say that he had to think about it some more."[5] Andrew Kazdin became Tom Frost's assistant in 1964, and he remembered that "one evening Frost and I were over at Horowitz's house and he was again considering playing the Rachmaninoff with Ormandy. He said he would want a tryout first but did not wish to be embarrassed by everyone knowing he needed one. So he had the idea of playing with Ormandy and the Philadelphia Orchestra with a paper bag on his head. No one would ever know who he was, he reasoned—and he was absolutely serious."[6]

Originally, Horowitz had thought that his next five recordings would each be devoted to the works of one composer—Beethoven, Chopin, Liszt, Schumann, and Rachmaninoff—but the mixed-recital concept had been so successful as to change his mind. His next two records thus featured pieces by Schumann, Scarlatti, Schubert, Scriabin, Beethoven, Debussy, and Chopin. The Columbia sales department, like its RCA counterpart, were not very happy at the thought of Scarlatti sonatas and Scriabin etudes, but Chapin maintained that Horowitz could record the C major scale and it would sell. The second album, entitled "The Sound of Horowitz," was made in four sessions in November and December 1962 and released in April 1963. Once again, public and critical response was overwhelming, and both Columbia and Horowitz tallied up impressive profits.

Chapin was anxious that Horowitz's momentum continue and so began with increasing frequency to broach the subject of a return to the stage. "One night, after some superb cognac, I told Horowitz that I was without a doubt the best concert valet in the business, that I had started my career doing just that for Jascha Heifetz and though perhaps a little rusty I would be happy to do this for him if he ever should decide to try the concert platform again. He said, 'I will remember that.' "[7]

Horowitz had become expert at fielding questions from the press about performing again. "I'll tell you three days in advance," he joked to one interviewer, "then you'll be able to come." "I don't want to promise and to tell people and then disappoint them," he said to another. "But I do plan to do it. Before I die I'll do it. I want to play before an audience again for my own satisfaction, to show I can do it."[8] Nonetheless, he would not go so far as to commit himself. Even a petition signed by thirteen hundred musicians, actors, and writers demanding his return, provoked a sour response. "Everyone seems to think of his own pleasure and not of mine," he declared. "Can't they see that I am a retired pianist—or perhaps—just a tired pianist?"[9] Horowitz even received an invitation from Mrs. John F. Kennedy to play at a recital at the White House, but he declined that too.

With his third CBS record, Horowitz continued the practice of recording "a balanced program—like Streisand does it,"[10] as he put it—in order to appeal to the widest audience. With the exception of the Chopin Scherzo No. 1, which he had done with RCA in the early 1950's, this entire album was comprised of works he had never before recorded. Moving through the program of Beethoven, Chopin, and Debussy, Horowitz shifted stylistic gears with apparent ease. At the urging of CBS, he had agreed to include two popular works: the Beethoven *Pathétique* Sonata and the Chopin *Revolutionary* Etude. He was especially enthusiastic about the Beethoven ("to me, it is a fresh thing"[11]), and the final result, according to one critic, was "resolute but simple. . . . Indeed, the sonata discovered here is precisely 'pathetic,' not tragic, and I have never heard a more discerning statement of the peculiarly moving innocences of Beethoven's transitional period."[12] For the first time in his career Horowitz chose to record Debussy preludes (three selections from Book II), and many believed them the highlight of this particular album. *Hi-Fi/Stereo Review* stated, "In sheer beauty of sound as well as in ability to evoke an atmosphere, strike a mood, project an image without actually defining its perimeters, Horowitz has asserted an affinity with this com poser hardly suspected in the past."[13]

It took six months, from June to November 1963, to record the latest album, primarily because Horowitz was constantly juggling repertory (the Clementi Sonata in A Major, Op. 36, No. 1; the Mozart Adagio in B Minor, K. 540; the Beethoven Thirty-two Variations) and was unhappy with all takes of the Chopin, Debussy, and Beethoven he made in June, July, September, and October. It wasn't until the last two sessions in November that the material for the record was completed in a frenzy of work. However, Horowitz won his second Grammy for this release and was quite delighted with the state of his affairs at Columbia. RCA Victor, smarting from the loss of Horowitz and his subsequent triumph elsewhere, did not waste any time capitalizing on the new surge of interest in him. In 1963, RCA released an elaborately produced two-album set of previously recorded works entitled "The Horowitz Collection," complete with a booklet of photographs, color reproductions of Horowitz's paintings, and an introductory essay written by the pianist's friend Samuel Chotzinoff. Angel followed suit by rereleasing the Liszt Sonata and *Funérailles* along with pieces by Schumann, and this prompted Columbia to try again to persuade Horowitz to make a new version of the Sonata.

But by the fall of 1964 he was absorbed by the idea of an all-Scarlatti album to complement his 1955 all-Clementi record.

As mentioned earlier, Horowitz was now hesitant to put the works of only one composer in an album, but he believed that Domenico Scarlatti, like Clementi, had been so unfairly neglected that he was an exception to that rule. Thus, despite muffled grumblings from the CBS marketing department, he decided to go ahead with a Scarlatti album. Like Scarlatti, Horowitz was a master of the miniature, and he loved the challenge of scouring all the composer's 550 sonatas for a group of 12 that would both demonstrate Scarlatti's versatility and sustain the listener's attention.

Horowitz, of course, knew that Scarlatti had written his sonatas for the harpsichord. He now faced the problem of playing this music on the piano with stylistic integrity but without being confined by the limitations of the eighteenth-century instrument. "I didn't want to imitate the period," he said in an interview. "I wanted to play like it would sound today on the big piano and maybe Scarlatti would be very happy!"[14] Consequently, Horowitz closely examined Ralph Kirkpatrick's exhaustive study of Scarlatti, which had been published by the Princeton University Press in 1953. Eventually, he even brought Kirkpatrick to his home for consultation.

Horowitz, recalled Kirkpatrick, "was very much concerned to avoid behaving like a virtuoso. He wanted to be a musician. He knew that I was an authority on Scarlatti and wanted reassurance from me that what he was doing was acceptable."[15] Far from holding Horowitz to a pedantic interpretation, Kirkpatrick, deciding the pianist was being overly cautious, actually found himself "encouraging rather than inhibiting. He had a wonderful sense of balancing notes in a chord, of using silences between notes; and he commanded all grades of *détaché*. His pedaling was impeccable and he played with absolute clarity. Nothing got lost or fudged. He was, however, a little timid about using a wide range of colors and attacks. I kept saying, 'Go ahead, go ahead. Don't be afraid to play more freely.' We played back and forth showing each other what we meant and there was always a conspicuous difference in sound. Horowitz simply had a feel for variety of sound that completely eclipsed anything I had ever heard on the instrument."

Kirkpatrick lent Horowitz microfilms of Scarlatti's manuscripts so that he could correct the many mistakes in the Longo edition. Surrounded by the sonata volumes stacked on the piano, Horowitz and Kirkpatrick listened to the trial recordings of Scarlatti he had made for Columbia. Although Kirkpatrick heard things he did not consider stylistically correct, he kept his reservations to himself, not wanting to risk having Horowitz delete a selection from the record. "He was an infinitely sensitive person who had to be handled very carefully. His playing was beautiful in its own way, so it was better to leave it as it was. For instance, he was way off the mark in L. four eighty; here there are imitations of wind instruments and drums and a kind of underlying brutality that Horowitz prettified. In another sonata, I suggested, in a section imitating trumpets and drums, that he might double the bass and play it even an octave lower, which he proceeded to do with absolutely gorgeous sound. But he evidently thought it was too impure because he didn't record it that way."

Ever since Horowitz had canceled his first recording session in 1962, he had been punctual in appearing at the Thirtieth Street studio when he had promised. As one of the producers working on the Scarlatti album recalled: "He arrived punctually and always knew exactly what he wanted to do. His playing was sometimes indescribably beautiful with a shimmering, luscious tone, technically perfect, so that no more than an average number of splices were necessary. Yet other times there were clunkers by the square inch, which was surprising."[16] Everyone including Ralph Kirkpatrick agreed that the final product melded brilliant piano playing with intelligence and imagination to the Scarlatti style.

After taping some twenty sonatas, Horowitz finally settled on twelve largely unfamiliar ones from Scarlatti's middle and late periods, cannily spacing them in the album as an escalating series of dramatic contrasts and surprises. When the recording was released, Horowitz was generally applauded for successfully adapting such works to the piano, "by making his piano a harpsipiano," as one writer put it. Columbia had spared no hyperbole, advertising the Scarlatti album as "one of the most important musical events of our time." Once again, Horowitz's effort was a financial and critical success. Wrote *Hi-Fi/Stereo Review:* "Nobody else has presented a Scarlatti panorama that so convincingly captures the breadth of the composer's spirit, one which, along with all the sensitivity and formal elegance, combines a certain aristocratic gregariousness with a robust taste for worldly splendor and spectacle."[17]

Although Horowitz had recorded his first two Columbia discs in 1962 in only nine months, the following two took considerably more time, and he was now behind the six-record quota stipulated in his three-year contract. It had become clear that his working habits and exacting standards did not respond to an imposed timetable. At any rate, the great success of his four albums was sufficient to stifle any dissatisfaction among executives at CBS. The producers and engineers assigned to Horowitz, however, had more than their fair share of complaints, as they became all too familiar with the customized treatment Horowitz demanded. During the taping of the Scarlatti album, Tom Frost was unable to attend all the sessions and two other men, Thomas Shepard and Andrew Kazdin, were brought in to assist. Initially thrilled to be involved with Horowitz, Shepard soon cooled, for the work was extremely time-consuming and more than faintly perplexing. Three days after their first session, Goddard Lieberson received a phone call from a petulant Horowitz, who complained, "Mr. Shepard doesn't like me. He doesn't telephone me." Shepard then had to explain to Lieberson that he had seen Horowitz only a few days earlier and had felt he should not bother him. Thereafter, he phoned Horowitz every day for the next week, asking him how he was feeling and discussing repertory for future recordings. At the end of the week, Lieberson received another call from Horowitz: "Why is Mr. Shepard persecuting me with his telephone calls? Please tell him to stop calling me so much!"[18]

Shepard and his colleagues were amused when it came time for Horowitz to choose a photograph for the album cover. One Columbia recording artist recalled, "Tom told me about the impossible photographs Horowitz wanted for the covers. He kept choosing pictures of himself leaning against a piano, with a very, very long cigarette holder, looking out at the camera like sort of a drag version of Marlene Dietrich. They would then have to persuade him that that was not a very good likeness."[19]

Far from amusing, however, were the changes Horowitz demanded, usually concerning volume level or repositioning previously recorded sequences. Kazdin recalled that "after a recording session was over and roughly spliced, Frost and I would go over to Horowitz's house, and Horowitz would say, 'that's pretty good but I did the coda better in another take.' So we would find the coda he was talking about and put it in. Then a week later, he says, 'I think I played a more exciting section on another take.' We finally get this right and send him an acetate test pressing and he says, 'You know, the slow movement, it could be one decibel lower'—and both Frost and I look at each other in disbelief. We knew then that Horowitz was getting outside advice, probably from Jack Pfeiffer. The decibel is the smallest unit of sound, barely detectable by the human ear. The technical term for this sort of thing is bullshit. Nonetheless, we went back and remixed an entire slow movement and made it one decibel lower. Finally, he was happy. Then came the test pressing—something rarely made for other artists—where we had the factory press six or twelve records at the plant. So we would bring the test records to Horowitz before pressing all the rest, and he would say, 'You know, it is noisy on the second side.' So the plant would make another one. Then after the new test pressing was ready, he would say, 'You know, I don't think I like the way I play the second movement.' So then we had to go back to the beginning and start the whole thing over again. I don't know of any other artist who has behaved in this way."[20]

Another Columbia producer, Paul Myers, agreed that the amount of time involved in producing a Horowitz album was often excessive. "Nobody else, to my knowledge, got this kind of treatment," he said. "Normally an artist has three, four, or five sessions to make a record. But Horowitz's records were handcrafted products, and he could take as many days as he liked in the studio. The repeated sessions made the record more expensive and time-consuming to produce, but he would not be pressured by such considerations."[21] Horowitz himself admitted, "I have the time. I take the time with my records. I don't record just like this [making a rapid motion with his fingers] and then good-bye, good-bye. But I think the records I have made have a good standing."[22]

Horowitz had indeed proven that he was at the height of his artistic powers, and that the meticulous attention paid to every technical aspect of his records was reflected in near-unanimous positive reviews and impressive sales. Moreover, he was moving, albeit slowly and cautiously, toward the idea of a return to the concert stage. "I would like to play for students," he told the *New York Herald Tribune,* "because they are the best audience in the country. And I'd like to give my concert in the late afternoon. I don't like to play in the evening. Life in a big city is very tense and difficult for everybody. People are tired in the evening. On Saturday or Sunday in the late afternoon they are more relaxed. The artist is more relaxed, too. But the date, I cannot tell you. When I do it, you'll know it."[23]

The year 1962 had clearly marked the beginning of a renaissance for

Horowitz, not only in terms of his successful recordings, but because his growing self-confidence now made it possible for him to socialize and entertain. In the early 1960's, society columnist Elsa Maxwell reported that when the Horowitzes gave a party in honor of tenor Franco Corelli "the rooms of their apartment were swelling with every great celebrity in music imaginable." Maxwell had said to Horowitz, "Take one giant step, Volodya. You must play again for the millions who are waiting to hear you." But Horowitz shook his head. "No, I have not made up my mind yet."[24]

Nevertheless, he was in a remarkably receptive mood and increasingly eager to have friends over for evenings of canasta and music-making. One frequent guest before 1965 was Arthur Rubinstein. After twenty years of estrangement, the two rivals had reached a reconciliation of sorts in the mid-1950's, largely because of their daughters. "Sonia was a very miserable child, very unhappy," remembered Rubinstein. "My wife and I took pity on her. Except for her aunt Wally, Sonia hated her family and would have little to do with them. Wanda wanted our daughter, Eva, to spend some time with Sonia; she thought it would help. It was at that time that Wanda said to me, 'Look, you must see Volodya.' "[25] At Rubinstein's request, Horowitz had recently sent Rubinstein a formal note of apology for his bad behavior over the broken luncheon date in Paris nearly three decades before. The two men had now established a tentative friendship, but their diametrically opposed personalities and intense competitiveness assured that it would be only a temporary one.

"Instead of amusing me, inviting me and my wife to a nice lunch or dinner," recalled Rubinstein, "he would call at eleven at night and ask us over to talk. He was the same as always—taking, never giving. He started an evening looking gloomy, but ended it looking quite absolutely delighted at two in the morning! But *I* was gloomy and tired by two, and tired to death of trying to persuade him to return to the stage. I told my wife that this whole business of going over to his house was a terrible bore. I couldn't persuade him to play and he would just cackle all night long, running to the piano, saying 'I did something different to the *Carmen* Variations!' He was so impolite, so conceited—a curious combination of arrogance and stupidity. As a person, he was just not interesting, and he was killing me with his childish pranks—staying up all night, coming downstairs in his pajamas. Even Wanda was sometimes in a terrible state from putting up with him. She told me once that she would like to sell the long couch—with him on it! Finally, thank God, he stopped inviting me."[26]

Rubinstein, however, did not entirely stop seeing Horowitz, and despite their underlying rivalry, he did occasionally try to persuade him to resume his public career. He remembered that "Horowitz confessed that if he returned to performing, he believed the public would not accept him without the transcriptions. On that subject, I told him that I hardly even sweated after a concert and asked him why he went to all that trouble. Why did he play those stupid encores—those wedding marches, *Danse Macabres*, *Carmens*? I said it was in bad taste to play such music in serious piano recitals. He just looked at me and replied, 'Ah, they want it, they are used to it, and they wouldn't want me without it.' "[27]

Although Rubinstein may have thought that Horowitz behaved in an intolerably childish manner, Horowitz was in fact quite serious about the possibility of resuming his career. He was arriving at that decision in the same way as always—by exhausting every argument for and against, and by playing devil's advocate. "All my friends, all my colleagues were coming here like I was dead, with condolences," Horowitz said a few years later. "People coming, and sitting here saying 'You have to play, you have to play.' They were very nice, very thoughtful. They were telling me, 'Volodya, you have to start in small towns now, after so many years. Go to Scandinavia, nobody knows you there.' But I was telling Wanda, 'I don't know why they send me away from here. I'm living in New York. I have my own house. If I can play, I can play anywhere. Do I have to go to Scandinavia to try?' But my colleagues were sending me everywhere. I was listening. Listening. Saying, 'Thank you, that is very nice.' I said to my wife, finally, 'I think I can start like that in Carnegie Hall. Not in Copenhagen. Not in Monte Carlo. Just in Carnegie Hall. And this would be the simplest thing. There would be no traveling. This is where I live. Here is my food. Here is my life. I will go from my bed and we will see what happens.' "[28]

PART FIVE
1965 ~ 1982

CHAPTER TWENTY-TWO

REHEARSALS AT CARNEGIE HALL: "IT'S NICE TO BE A VIRTUOSO"

*"The only thing I can say now is that if I announce a recital,
it means I have some message for the public, or I would
not announce it. . . . I wouldn't try if I didn't feel
I had something to say."*[1]

orowitz began seriously to consider a return to the stage in November 1964, just a month after he finished recording the Scarlatti album. He had not given a piano recital in twelve years, and the last time he had been onstage at Carnegie Hall was during a 1959 recording session for RCA Victor. At that time, the sterility of the empty auditorium had depressed him, and for the next three years he refused any further sessions. However, since his switch to Columbia Masterworks, Horowitz had been pleased by both the commercial and artistic successes of his records; he found it satisfying to be appreciated once again by critics and to be popular with the public. The transition from recluse to performer was nearly complete. "My recordings were coming out better," he recalled. "My rehearsals were more satisfactory, and the urge to play again—to communicate directly—was brooding within me."[2]

During this time Horowitz was juggling five or six different recital programs in his mind, trying to decide on a group of works he might privately try out in Carnegie Hall for a few friends. For before committing himself to a public appearance, he wanted to reinvestigate the environment and acoustics of his favorite concert hall. Determined to return to Carnegie Hall, in the city where he had begun his American career in 1928, he continued to regard with disdain any suggestions of warm-up recitals in other halls in smaller cities.

A six-month decision-making period began in early November with a telephone call to Julius Bloom, then executive director of Carnegie Hall. Bloom had not seen Horowitz since the late 1940's, and he knew immediately that an invitation to visit the pianist at his home meant Horowitz "was going to put himself to the test."[3] Nonetheless, at their first afternoon meeting, Horowitz did not tell Bloom he wanted to resume concertizing. Rather, he complained that all his friends were insisting he return to the stage and he found such pressures irritating. Bloom instinctively understood Horowitz would react negatively to blatant pressure of any kind, that the last thing he needed was another push. "What do *you* think is important?" Bloom asked. "If you don't want to play, don't play, because if you do it against your will, you won't be the Horowitz we expect." Horowitz then enumerated the reasons why others believed his return was imperative: he owed it to the concert world; there was a generation of pianists who had never heard him in recital; his recordings didn't capture his unique sonority; he would fulfill himself as an artist; the occasion would be a unique triumph; he could command very high fees. Horowitz countered that he loathed traveling—the wear and tear was "anti-art"; hotels were uncomfortable; he didn't want the pressure of committing himself far in advance to a specific date; he didn't need the money; his recordings continued to keep him in the public eye; he resented the demands of concert managers. The latter point seemed foremost in Horowitz's mind at this initial meeting with Bloom. He did not want to depend on an impresario like Sol Hurok to orchestrate his return, and so he realized the importance of establishing a good working relationship with Bloom. Horowitz told him that he had always liked his "vibrations"; he found Bloom's gentle demeanor and candor appealing, and over the next two months Bloom became a trusted friend. Horowitz continued to meet him in his living room about once a week, while Wanda often met him at an Italian restaurant near Carnegie Hall to "break pasta" and conspire on how to overcome her husband's resistance.

After his twelve-year hiatus, Horowitz quite enjoyed his near-legendary status. However, living up to it was a formidable proposition. Horowitz worried that his physical condition might deteriorate under the strain of a public career, and that his memory might fail him. A few years earlier he had received electroshock therapy, which he described as a wonderful treatment that healed his nerves. But, he complained to Abram Chasins, "my memory started to weaken. When you record, you don't have to play by heart. Memory is a practicing business too."[4] Ralph Kirkpatrick recalled that during the recording of the Scarlatti album, Horowitz was "very sensitive and obviously worried about his musical memory. When playing for his wife, he would say, 'Well, see, I remembered that,' but he seemed in fine form nonetheless."[5] Julius Bloom soon realized that his job would be methodically to discount each of Horowitz's reservations and fears.

A highly cultivated man who had revitalized Carnegie Hall with innovative programming and a forward-looking subscription campaign, the fifty-three-year-old administrator was equal to the challenge. Horowitz found Bloom well versed in languages, philosophy, and musicology, quite unlike managers he had known in the past, and he began to refer to him as "my philosopher." Bloom assured Horowitz that he himself would handle all details related to a Carnegie Hall concert, and that everything—ticket prices, date, time, publicity—would be tailored to Horowitz's specifications. Horowitz feared that his playing one concert would provoke a deluge of offers for engagements he could not possibly fulfill, but Bloom pointed out that such offers did not have to be accepted. If desired, he, Bloom, would take care of the business details so that Horowitz would not have to hire a professional manager. After two months of discussions, Horowitz decided that whether or not he performed publicly again, he wanted to get the feel of playing in a good hall. Would it be possible to do so in Carnegie Hall when it was empty? Realizing that the last thing Horowitz wanted at this point was publicity, Bloom quietly reserved the hall for several afternoons in January 1965.

Early that month, Horowitz went to the Steinway basement and in the course of three visits selected a piano for his tryouts. Since 1940, he had been playing the same instrument, which he now thought sounded too strident, and he chose in its place the concert grand CD 186—"more mellow, more like the human voice."[6] On January 7, Horowitz brought the new piano to Carnegie Hall and began a regimen of afternoon rehearsals once or twice a week, usually at four in the afternoon when he was at his peak energy level. On his first visit, the position of the piano seemed almost as difficult a decision as the selection of the instrument itself. After an hour of trying different areas of the stage, Horowitz finally was satisfied with one, and a small brass stud was hammered into the floor to mark the spot where one leg of the piano was to be put. The

"Horowitz screw," as it came to be known, was left in place, and many pianists have subsequently shown faith in Horowitz's acoustical judgment by positioning their own pianos on it.

Only those in Horowitz's inner circle were permitted into Carnegie Hall during the 4:00 P.M. tryouts: Jack Pfeiffer of RCA Records, Tom Frost of Columbia Records, Wanda's close friend Olga Strumillo, Steinway representative David Rubin, piano tuner Bill Hupfer, and pianists Constance Keene and Ania Dorfman. At Horowitz's suggestion, Columbia Masterworks recorded those sessions, capturing on tape the Buch-Busoni Toccata and Fugue in C Major, the Chopin Ballade in G Minor, the Schumann Fantasy, and several Chopin mazurkas and Debussy etudes. "We all sat there stunned while he played," recalled Bloom. "It was absolutely fantastic. When he finished he turned to us and said, 'Not so bad today.' For a few seconds nobody said anything. Then I blurted out, 'Not so bad! You should have had an audience!' "[7]

The rehearsals dragged on into February and March and Horowitz still refused to commit himself to a public concert. He continued to look to friends for encouragement and constantly solicited advice from them. At a dinner early in 1965, Schuyler Chapin quietly reminded Horowitz of Chapin's offer to "valet" for him. Horowitz's reply was surprising, for he said he had been visiting his tailor and was thinking about having a new morning coat made. What Chapin did not know was that the coat was already finished and that Horowitz was in the final stages of preparation for his historic return. No one was more incredulous about this than his wife. "This was the first time in twelve years that I heard him talk like that. I knew he was getting tired of playing only for a microphone in a studio. There were times when friends would say to him, 'You must play! You must play!' But I never told him that. Not this time either. I felt that the more I would urge him, the less he would play. An artist must want to play, must feel he has to play. It is no use to talk. So this time I said nothing."[8]

Only Bloom continued to prod gently, overcoming the real and imaginary problems that seemed to prevent Horowitz from making a decision. One evening in early March, Bloom successfully rebuffed Horowitz's many complaints about managers, finally convincing him that no manager would be needed, that the enormous amount of business which would inevitably come into Horowitz's life could be entirely taken care of by Bloom, that there would be no great burden. Horowitz was enormously relieved, for during the tryouts Bloom had handled every-thing smoothly and had proved himself equal to the task. Bloom re-membered, "Wanda, Horowitz, and I sat in the downstairs dining room eating lamb and drinking coffee one evening, and I realized that I had finally overcome the last of his objections. Horowitz looked dismayed and then turned to Wanda. 'But Wanda, you're a witness. I didn't say I would definitely play; I said I would consider playing if all my objections were overcome.' "[9]

Bloom considered Horowitz to be a man of his word, so he was not surprised when Horowitz telephoned a few days later to ask him to ar-range a date for that spring. However, it was understood that Horowitz would not have to make a final decision until two or three weeks before. He directed Bloom to schedule the concert for the afternoon. "My mem-ory is better, and it is too tense to wait until evening. Eight o'clock is like the guillotine."[10] The first date selected was April 25, but it was can-celed because a number of other pianists were performing that week and Horowitz didn't want his return to be construed as competitive. Even-tually, a tentative date and time were set: 3:30 P.M., Sunday, May 9—Mother's Day, a relaxed holiday that appealed to Horowitz. Bloom agreed to prepare a publicity campaign for the newspapers and set to work with Wanda on the scaling of tickets and on the drawing up of contractual agreements. "I composed everything according to his wishes," said Bloom, "with no penalty for nonappearance."

Above all, Horowitz did not want to break the news too soon. But de-spite Bloom's efforts at secrecy, word leaked out in the middle of March that he was giving secret recitals. On March 14, the *New York Herald Tribune* ran a story reporting that although Horowitz's afternoons in the hall were ostensibly for recording sessions, he was actually preparing for a return to public life. The article finished by noting that Maria Callas was returning to the Met, Heifetz and Piatigorsky were giving concerts after long absences, and "Vladimir Horowitz is finally returning to Carnegie Hall."[11] "I was a bit shocked," recalled Horowitz. "The next day the *New York Times* called me. 'Why did you tell the *Herald Tribune,* and not us?' I said, 'I haven't. They just printed it. I don't know where they got this information. But all right. I am playing in Carnegie Hall tomorrow and Columbia is taping. Come with a photographer and I will give you an interview. You will see with your own eyes and discover the truth.' "[12]

The next day, March 16, Horowitz stepped out onto the Carnegie Hall stage at 4:36 P.M. and played for a little over an hour for an audience of nine that included *Times* critic Howard Klein. Jauntily dressed in bow tie and sport jacket, Horowitz was in fine spirits, confident and full of good humor. Ever the temperamental perfectionist, he asked his tuner Bill Hupfer to remove a three-foot-long red felt tape, which he called the "fringe," from the back of the piano strings to make the tone more brilliant. But then, when Horowitz played a loud chord, he shook his head and said, "No, it's too bright. I think we have to put the fringe back."[13] When the session ended at 5:40, Horowitz walked to the edge of the stage, perspiring but obviously elated with his performance. *"Wanda, est-ce que tu est là?"*[14] ["Are you there?"] he whispered. Wanda then came to the stage, mysteriously placed a tiny bandage on the tip of his fifth finger, and Horowitz strode off for his interview with Howard Klein.

Arriving at the greenroom, the critic found Horowitz stretched out on the red leather sofa. Having pulled off his bow tie and changed shirts, he was relaxed and in a mood to talk. He said that he would continue rehearsing at the hall until he was completely satisfied but refused to affirm whether or not he would play a public recital. "It went fairly well today. Next time the fringe will be back in the piano and it should be good."[15] Klein explained that although he had reviewed Horowitz's Columbia albums, he had never actually heard a live performance. "Mr. Horowitz, your recordings don't do you justice. You play completely differently. You are like another pianist!" Horowitz was startled. Klein's observation seems to have decided him. "That did it. So that's the younger generation that doesn't know me at all," Horowitz remembered thinking. "This boy must be telling me the truth. He was always very complimentary about my records, but now he tells me I sound totally different. I believed him. I trusted his sincerity, and at that moment I knew I must play again."[16]

VLADIMIR HOROWITZ ON ROAD BACK TO CONCERT STAGE was the *New York Times*'s front-page headline the day after Klein's visit to Carnegie Hall. Later, the pianist admitted, "The front page bath in the newspaper was a big shove. I felt a responsibility. . . . But I also felt artistically and psychologically ready to take the plunge."[17]

The *Times* article set off a veritable chain reaction. Horowitz's business phone began ringing with requests for interviews. Telegrams poured in from concert impresarios in the United States, Italy, France, England, West Germany, and Japan. From Russia, Horowitz's sister, Regina, forwarded a petition signed by a committee of Moscow Conservatory students requesting that he return to his native country for a tour. When a commentator asked him if he would appear in Moscow or Leningrad, Horowitz answered, "Yes, but first I must play Brooklyn."[18]

In response to the great number of requests from reporters, Horowitz called a press conference for Saturday, March 19, at Steinway Hall. On that occasion, he did not reveal the May concert date he had already chosen, but stated that he would play at Carnegie Hall either that spring or in the fall, performing the same recital several times "to let all the people hear the same program." Questioned on repertory, Horowitz proclaimed that he had a new motto: "Simplicity is wisdom." He would avoid the ostentatious transcriptions of the past and extend his repertory in some areas (more Schumann, Scriabin, Chopin, Debussy) while limiting it in others (the modern works he performed during the 1940's and 1950's). "When I hear my recordings now of the Prokofiev Sonatas, Barber or Kabalevsky," he explained, "I think someone else is playing. I don't know where to begin them now. The other music I've cooled on is Liszt. The Sonata I will play, but altogether, less Liszt."[19]

Horowitz explained to reporters that his life-style now was a very quiet one as compared to the frenetic pace of earlier years: two hours of practice every day, a mile walk with his poodle, Pippo, naps before lunch and dinner, evenings with friends. Pressed to explain the reasons for his long retirement, he offered his standard, attenuated rationales—too many trains and hotels, too much exhaustion, the lack of time for reflection—and vowed that he would never again undertake extensive tours. "I would like to play in some big cities again, and, of course, I like the college audiences very much. But I will have no manager. I do not like the pressure from managers or the press."[20] When Horowitz's former colleague at Columbia Artists, F. C. Schang, read that Horowitz had decided to perform without the services of professional management, he was incensed, and wrote sarcastically in *Variety:* "My company managed Horowitz in the early 1930's, but he left for financial reasons. It killed him to pay commissions. . . . We all wish him success even if he wants to lone-wolf it in his old age. For by managing his own affairs, Horowitz will have a manager who pleases him and one that he can afford."[21]

But in truth, Horowitz was depending heavily on Julius Bloom to advise him on his program and supervise the details of the recital. In late March, Bloom, Horowitz, and Wanda worked out a price scale, one of the highest in the history of Carnegie Hall up to that time: first tier, $12.50; parquet, $10; second tier, $9; dress circle, $7 and $5; balcony, $4 and $3. Horowitz wanted to have stage seating, lest it be said that he was afraid of his own audience, but Bloom opposed this, believing that for dramatic impact Horowitz should be absolutely alone on the stage.

During one of Horowitz's rehearsals in late March, Bloom began to feel ill. A week later he suffered a mild heart attack and was hospitalized indefinitely. No firm decision was due on the still tentative May 9 date until the end of April, but during the first week of the month Horowitz called Bloom in the hospital and said that he had definitely decided to play on that date. "I was so happy I started to cry," remembered Bloom. "And Horowitz said, 'Ah, I'm glad you said good; I was hoping this would do good for you.' "[22] Bloom's patience and sensitivity had paid off. On April 22 the official announcement was made: on Sunday, May 9, at 3:30, Horowitz would return to Carnegie Hall to give his first performance in more than a decade. "I don't want to talk about how I will play," Horowitz said to the press. "Let the people decide that for me. I hope I am still a virtuoso; it's nice to be a virtuoso. But I hope they like it because the music is beautiful. It is not easy to play again after twelve years and when you are sixty. Who knows? Maybe I will play like a pig."[23]

CHAPTER TWENTY-THREE

A HISTORIC
RETURN

*"It is difficult to have a legend surround you. To people
I am a legend, but I am still alive. In a way, my future
is in my past and my past in my present. I must now
make the present my future."*[1]

ickets went on sale on Monday, April 26, at ten in the morning.
Horowitz worried that young people might not come to the recital because they had never heard of him, and although Julius Bloom and
Schuyler Chapin assured him he was wrong, and Wanda called him a
Russian pessimist, he remained skeptical, insisting that just in case students were interested there should be plenty of $3 tickets available. On
Sunday, April 25, Horowitz was amazed to learn that many people, most
of them young music students, had begun lining up at the Carnegie Hall
box office at 11:30 that morning. By midnight the line had grown to 278
and by 7:30 the next morning, there were 1,500 waiting four abreast in a
queue that stretched east from Fifty-seventh Street and Seventh Avenue
to the Avenue of the Americas. For this crowd the weather couldn't have
been worse, and in the cold, rainy night, blankets, sleeping bags, um-
brellas, slickers, camp chairs, and even wooden boxes were employed as
shelters. During heavy downpours, people retreated into doorways and
under canopies, numbers being issued so the line could reassemble without anyone's place being jeopardized. Said a thirty-two-year-old accoun-
tant, "This is an opportunity many people never thought they would get.
The price of a ticket—even if it includes waiting in the rain all night—is
worth it."[2]

Twenty policemen were sent to tend this veritable army, a member of
which commented that he had never seen such enthusiasm or endurance
in a crowd. Someone passing wanted to know, "Is this a Beatle
thing?"—to which an exuberant gaggle of students shouted, "No, this is

a Horowitz thing!"[3] Later, Wanda would exclaim proudly, "Mr. Horowitz is like a fifth Beatle!"[4] Many of those assembled had never heard Horowitz play, while others had, but before 1953. "The last time I saw him was in Cleveland in 1950," said Eugene Mancini, a pianist, adding, "I never thought of doing this for anyone else." Anatole Morell, a chemist, exclaimed, "The only other time I ever stood on line was in Russia—for bread!"[5]

When Horowitz heard about the scene at Carnegie Hall, he felt flattered and touched, and especially pleased that so many of the crowd were young people. Feeling responsibility, he asked Wanda to take a taxi to the hall and make sure everything was all right. Taking one look at the sodden fans, she marched into the corner coffee shop to order one hundred cups of coffee, with a second round for the entire crowd later in the evening. Early the next morning, at 4 A.M., Horowitz and Wanda received a telegram: DEAR MAESTRO AND MADAME: THE ONE HUNDRED OF US SPENDING THE NIGHT IN LINE WISH TO THANK YOU FOR THE HEART-WARMING COFFEE AND TO EXPRESS THE JOY AND ANTICIPATION FROM ALL OF US. UNSIGNED.

Inevitably, many of those waiting all night were to be disappointed. Tickets went on sale at 10:00 A.M., with a maximum of four to a person. By noon the management announced that the house was sold out. Of the 1,500 in line, only 300 had been served. But, everyone wanted to know, if 1,200 seats had been sold, where were the rest of the tickets for the 2,760-seat hall? The box office explained that there had been an unusually heavy demand by the press and from abroad, and that quite a few tickets had also been set aside for the Horowitzes, RCA and Columbia Records, and Steinway. More than a thousand people left Fifty-seventh Street that morning disappointed and angry, resenting the fact that they had not been told that more than half of the house was not up for sale. Even those who had managed to purchase tickets were annoyed, because tickets for the first tier and for most of the center and the left, or keyboard side, were unavailable.

With Bloom still recuperating in the hospital, the brunt of the complaints landed on Wanda, forcing her to defend herself to the press. "I could not let Mme. Koussevitzky and Rachmaninoff's daughter stand in line!" she declared. "I got angry letters and so many telephone calls we had to put in an answering service, and I can't even answer the phone when friends call. I am becoming a nervous wreck. All because of those tickets. Now they say the reason there are not tickets is because Mrs. Horowitz has them all. I tell you what Mrs. Horowitz has. Here it is. Mrs. Horowitz took out 296 seats. All except eight are paid for. The seats are for musicians, singers, artists, close friends of ours. Columbia Records got 108 tickets. Carnegie Hall Corporation got 175. Steinway got 36. RCA got 56. The press got 100. I am being blamed for 1,000 tickets I never had!"[6]

During the two weeks before the recital, everyone looked nervous except Horowitz. He felt quite ready, and was amused by the fawning concern of those around him, not only professionals like Chapin and Bloom, but also his neighborhood policemen, postman, barber, and cook. "I have real friends among them," Horowitz later told Abram Chasins. "My barber came here to give me a haircut four days before the concert and said to me, 'Mr. Horowitz, you are in a fine position. Don't worry. You just go out there. They will see you, they will laugh, they will be delirious. Just *you* be quiet. I know you. You will not feel anything.' He started to cut my hair in silence and then said, 'You know, I have a very good idea. Tell Madame Horowitz to pack a little bottle of smelling salts for you.' Then my newsdealer said, 'Mr. Horowitz, I know you're giving a piano recital in a few days, and you have to realize that the public here is merciless, terrible! You have to give them the best plus the super-best or they will tear you to pieces like nobody's business.' After the concert, he said, 'Mr. Horowitz, I have never read such things, such raves. Oh, I'm so happy for you'—at which point, he broke down and sobbed."[7]

Horowitz was genuinely amazed by his prerecital popularity, for he had never received such publicity before a concert. First, there had been the front-page story in the *New York Times,* then the press conference at Steinway Hall, then detailed news reports in several different papers, with pictures, describing the furor over tickets and the loyalty of Horowitz's fans. His high spirits notwithstanding, Horowitz was at times worried about the upcoming recital, knowing he was likely to make many more mistakes than during a rehearsal or recording session. "Everyone told me it wouldn't matter," Horowitz recalled. "They said I could play with one finger and the audience would scream."[8]

The program he had selected was difficult. For his audience's sake, Horowitz was anxious about having placed both the Schumann Fantasy and Scriabin Ninth Sonata on the same recital, as he feared they might prove too great a strain on the public's concentration. He was nonetheless happy overall with his carefully chosen and very personal program. "The Bach-Busoni [Organ Toccata and Fugue in C Major] is comfortable for me," Horowitz explained. "It was the first piece on my debut program after I left Russia forty years ago. As the first piece after twelve years, it presents the pianist quite well. The Schumann *Fantasie* is a fantastic work. It's very beautiful and is Schumann's most important composition for piano. The Scriabin [which had featured on Horowitz's 1953 Silver Jubilee recitals] ... well, he died in 1915 and this is the fiftieth anniversary of his death. As a boy of ten or eleven I played for him. As for the Chopin [Etude, Op. 10, No. 8, Mazurka, Op. 30, No. 4, and Ballade, Op. 23] it is on the program because it is Chopin."[9] For one of the encores, Horowitz had selected Debussy's *Serenade for the Doll,* which represented his revitalized interest in that composer and was a work which had served him well in the past. His continuing predilection for Slavic music was reflected in the next two encores: the Scriabin Etude, Op. 2, No. 1, and the Moszkowski Etude in A-flat Major, Op. 72, No. 11—while the final encore, Schumann's *Träumerei,* was one of Horowitz's longtime favorites. By ending his recital with this quiet, contemplative music, rather than with *The Stars and Stripes Forever* or *Carmen,* he was making a personal statement about himself as a musician.

Bloom was still confined to his home and would be unable to attend the concert, so it was up to Schuyler Chapin to fulfill his promise to be "the best concert-valet in the business." A few days before, Horowitz phoned Chapin to check "just a few things." For instance, the hall's air conditioning: "Is it onstage? I don't want any onstage, but we must be sure the people out front are comfortable. It may be a hot day. And one more thing ... I don't want anyone to talk to me before the concert."[10] Chapin assured Horowitz that the temperature would be regulated to his specifications and that no one except Wanda would be allowed backstage. Horowitz was also worried that he might not remember how to bow correctly, and so he practiced in his bedroom.

Even with his windows blackened and the telephone disconnected, Horowitz could not sleep soundly on the night of May 8. "Usually I sleep well ... but on Saturday night I couldn't sleep much, maybe five hours,"[11] Horowitz later told a reporter. "It was not panic or nervousness—it was anticipation, the anticipation of something very important in my life. I'm not temperamental. I'm high-strung, but not temperamental. I had only to lose—nothing to gain. I was a legend."[12] But for a few panicked moments that Saturday evening, it seemed as if the concert would have to be canceled. Brushing his hair, Horowitz managed to get a bristle stuck in the ball of his right thumb. Gitta Gradova and her husband, Dr. Cottle, were houseguests that night, and Cottle carefully removed the bristle, cleansed the finger, and pronounced Horowitz fit.

Horowitz's need for perfection and for being in absolute control of both himself and his environment had always been a considerable problem. An unpleasant dream, a passing mood, traffic noise outside—anything might jolt his system and upset the perfect balance he believed necessary for a performance. He noted: "Busoni said the tragedy of the artist is that you have to be inspired, wanting to play, and being in good form. It could be that at three-thirty I could have a stomachache. Maybe I will have a cramp. I am a human being. And I have to go onstage anyway."[13]

Chapin, well aware of Horowitz's extreme sensitivity, worried that he might cancel the concert at the last minute. On the restless night before, however, Horowitz was determined to maintain his equilibrium so that he would be able to present his "message to the public." He had often thought of Klein's comment that his playing in person was very different from his recordings, and he was anxious to prove that point. Related to this was his need to play for a generation of listeners who had never heard him in recital and his concern for what he called *le niveau,* or the general level of contemporary pianism. Horowitz felt that present-day performance standards were not up to what they had been in the past, when the competition included figures like Cortot, Hess, Hofmann, Godowsky, Moiseiwitsch, Levitski, Lhévinne and Rachmaninoff. "Most of the young pianists," said Horowitz, "sound the same to me. I can hear a few bars by an older pianist and tell immediately who is playing, but not with the youngsters. They listen to too many recordings. . . . They are picked a little too early, like grapefruit. They are a little sour. They do not sing. They do not meditate on music."[14]

On the morning of the concert, Horowitz demanded complete silence. "Not to be nervous. Not to rush. All the movements quiet. I don't talk. Nobody should interfere and if anyone interferes he gets such a scandal that he never heard!"[15] Wanda recalled that "the others around him suffered in silence, trying to seem as calm as possible on the outside and saying absolutely nothing about anything except trivialities."[16] Horowitz awoke at 10:30 A.M. and had a breakfast of chicken, three slices of bread with honey, and Sanka. He then began to wash, shave, and dress, slowly and systematically preparing himself for the afternoon like an actor making up for a role. "The public pays money and they want to hear and see something aesthetic. I'm the boss of the situation. I have to look like that. I want my suit to fit, my hair to be combed. I want to have a completely clean body and hands, perfume, too. In pajamas, when I play at home, the music is the same but I behave differently. I'm loose. You can have genius ideas at the moment you get out of bed, but when you are explaining them before people you are more concentrated and your ideas are more focused."[17]

Horowitz had chosen an attire for afternoon recitals that he would continue to favor in the future: black pants with faint white stripes, white shirt, gray vest, gray silk tie (the bow tie would come later), and a formal, afternoon cutaway jacket with handkerchief. "I think about small details," he said. "To put on the socks so that they don't press me. To see the shoes are closed. The fly is closed. Then, the moment I feel that cutaway—the moment I am in uniform—it is like a racehorse before the races. I start to perspire. I feel already some electricity. At this moment, I am already an artist. I feel a pressure to be on time. I like to be ten, fifteen minutes early to warm up the fingers. I am a general. My soldiers are the keys and I have to command them."[18]

The only people present in the Horowitz house on May 9 were Jack Pfeiffer, Gitta Gradova, and her husband. At 2 P.M. a rented limousine arrived to pick up Horowitz, Wanda, Pfeiffer, and the butler, James Hunter. As the quartet was leaving for Carnegie Hall, Hunter couldn't face the tension of the afternoon. "I'm just not up to it," he told Wanda. "I can't go." "If that's your decision," Wanda said coolly, "we must accept it."[19]

Of paramount importance to Horowitz was the weather, and, fortuitously, the day was warm and sunny. However, he worried that the temperature would become too warm, and that his refusal to have air conditioning onstage might cause discomfort to those sitting in the front of the orchestra. Schuyler Chapin had been at Carnegie Hall since noon, overseeing every detail—the onstage temperature, the piano placement, the preparation of the greenroom. At one point, Chapin walked through the hall and looked out the entrance. "There, as far as the eye could see, were thousands of people jamming the sidewalks and spilling onto the avenue. Traffic was choked; nothing was moving."[20] Some had come to the hall without tickets, hoping to catch a glimpse of Horowitz arriving. Scalpers were selling $3 tickets for $30, $4 tickets for $40 and $7 tickets for $50. "I went around to the 56th Street entrance," recalled Chapin, "and saw the same thing. I went back into the hall to do a last-minute check on details. By then, it was 3:00 P.M."[21]

Three P.M.—and no sign of Horowitz. The traffic that day was horrendous all over town, and the thirty-seven-block trip from Ninety-fourth Street and Fifth Avenue to Fifty-seventh Street and Seventh Avenue took nearly an hour. Near Carnegie Hall, traffic was at a standstill, blocked by throngs of people. Representatives of the three principal television networks and reporters and photographers from all over the world were crowded in front of the stage entrance on Fifty-sixth Street. The chaos outside, however, was in stark contrast to the serenity backstage, where Chapin and two of the hall's best ushers mounted guard. The only other persons in the area were Tom Frost, several engineers from Columbia Records, and Horowitz's tuner Bill Hupfer.

The dressing room had been meticulously washed and vacuumed, with distilled ice water set alongside the leather couch and the practice piano, in perfect tune, positioned where Horowitz wanted it. The room was cool and inviting, but it was still empty at 3:10, and Chapin began to panic. He peeped into the hall and was startled to see the entire house already filled, including one hundred standees who had been allowed to purchase tickets an hour before the concert time. Chapin had never seen such a punctual audience, and he noted that the tension was tangible as people fanned themselves with their programs in the stuffy auditorium. "Nobody could play to a house like this," muttered a pianist in the audience, reacting to the galaxy of celebrities present: Leopold Stokowski, Igor Stravinsky, George Balanchine, Sir John Gielgud, Leonard Bernstein, Van Cliburn, Rudolf Nureyev, Jennie Tourel, Richard Tucker, and Zero Mostel were only a few of them; and there were others from France, Italy, England, and Germany. "My knees buckled with the sudden thought that if Horowitz did not appear, I would have to go on that stage and tell them,"[22] Chapin recalled. He went to check the Fifty-sixth Street entrance.

Earlier, the crowd had seen Cliburn and Bernstein enter the hall and had hardly paid them any notice. When Stokowski emerged from his car, however, he was enthusiastically applauded. Then impresario Sol Hurok marched through the stage door. "Is he here yet?" he snapped to Chapin.

"No, but he'll arrive," retorted Chapin, with more conviction than he felt. Goddard Lieberson stood by Chapin's side and they looked at each other helplessly. "What are you going to do?" Lieberson inquired. Chapin asked him if he had "any bright suggestions."[23]

Fifteen minutes before concert time, Horowitz, Wanda, and Pfeiffer were still trapped in traffic, while in the hall tension rose. Three-twenty and still no Horowitz. Finally, at 3:25, the black limousine pulled up. Chapin, unsteady on his feet and buffeted by a horde of photographers, opened the car door and Horowitz stepped out, dressed in a topcoat, looking trim, energetic, and calm, smiling and waving to his applauding fans.

"It was traffic, traffic," Horowitz said to Chapin. "We couldn't move. It took us over an hour. How does my suit look?" "Beautiful," replied the harried Chapin, "but I think we ought to move into the hall. There are a lot of people waiting."[24] Horowitz turned and waved as the crowd continued to clap and cheer. Reporters began firing questions, but Chapin kept Horowitz, Wanda, and Pfeiffer moving briskly toward the entrance.

Once inside, Chapin led Horowitz to the dressing room, where Horowitz immediately removed his gray kid gloves and sat down at the piano to warm up. He played odds and ends of scales, not so much to practice as to steady his nerves. He never practiced on the day of a concert because he wanted his muscles relaxed and his responses to the music spontaneous and fresh. Unlike Paderewski, who always spent the last quarter hour backstage in solitude, Horowitz was comforted by the presence of Chapin, Wanda, and Pfeiffer.

"My hands are cold," Horowitz said. He took Chapin's hands to warm his, but Chapin's hands were even colder. "You're like ice," Horowitz complained. Nervously, he reached out to an usher: "Listen, you're young and healthy. Give me your hands to warm my fingers." Horowitz later remembered: "When I felt the boy's hands, I drew mine back quickly. Mine were cold, but his were really icy. He was more nervous than I. Everybody was nervous!"[25]

And that included the audience. It was now 3:35 and the tension in the hall was unbearable. Chapin suggested that they start down to the stage. "What about latecomers?" asked Horowitz. Chapin told him that there had not been an empty place in the hall since 3:00. "Really?" said Horowitz, obviously pleased. Walking toward the stage, Horowitz may

Steinway & Sons

Trying a piano in the basement of
Steinway & Sons in New York, 1952.
Wanda and Sonia look on.

Steinway & Sons

Fishing in the Long Island Sound,
summer of 1952.

Beneath one of the gems of his art collection,
Georges Rouault's *Tête de Jeune Fille*,
Horowitz examines an original first edition
of Clementi sonatas. (1953)

Photograph by the *New York Times*

Wide World Photos

Sonia, age twenty-two, at
Arturo Toscanini's funeral in
New York, January 17, 1957.

On June 30, 1957, Sonia
Horowitz crashed her
motorscooter into a telephone
pole in San Remo, Italy. She
was flown to Milan by U.S.
Army Air Force personnel, for
emergency surgery.

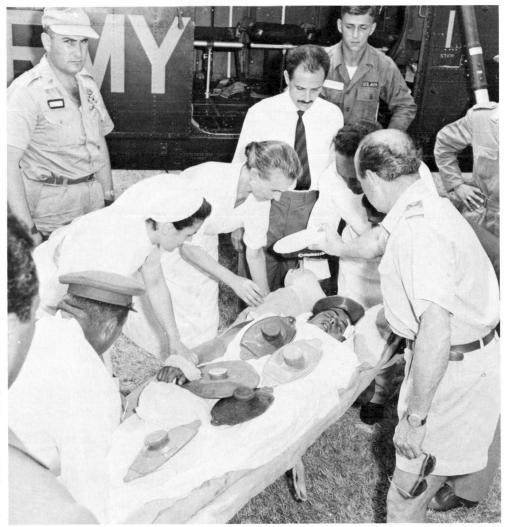

Wide World Photos

Steinway & Sons

Good-bye, Mr. RCA: Horowitz, in 1962, with Goddard Lieberson, president of Columbia Records, signing the exclusive, long-term recording contract that rejuvenated his career in the 1960's.

Photograph by the *New York Times*

Courtesy of Kenneth Glancey

In 1975, flanked by Kenneth Glancy, RCA Records president, and RCA's "Little Nipper," Horowitz signals the end of a five-year hibernation by leaving Columbia Masterworks and returning to RCA.

1965: A HISTORIC RETURN

In 1965, after twelve years away from the concert stage, Horowitz practices at home for his May 9 Carnegie Hall recital. The signed portraits of Arturo Toscanini, Ignace Paderewski, and Sergei Rachmaninoff were permanent fixtures on his piano.

Steinway & Sons

In April 1965, when
Horowitz's return recital was
announced, fifteen hundred
fans waited through a cold,
rainy night to buy tickets.

Photograph by the *New York Times*

Fifteen minutes before the historic recital, Horowitz emerges from his limousine and waves, as Schuyler Chapin escorts him to the stage door of Carnegie Hall.

Horowitz bows during the thunderous standing ovation that greeted him as he came onstage at Carnegie Hall. (May 9, 1965)

Wide World Photos

Photograph by the *New York Times*

Project X: To celebrate the fortieth anniversary of his American debut, Horowitz agreed to film a television concert for CBS, the first classical piano recital in network-television history. It was telecast on February 1, 1968.

Horowitz, Wanda, and their two poodles on Fifth Avenue, near their home. (1966)

During his third retirement from the stage (1969–1974), Horowitz continued to record at Columbia's Thirtieth Street studio in New York. Between takes, he rests on a cot.

Courtesy of Fred Plaut

Photograph by the *New York Times*

Horowitz checks the lighting on the stage of the Metropolitan Opera House during a rehearsal before an invited audience of thirty-five friends. On November 17, 1974, he gave the first piano recital in the Metropolitan's eight years at Lincoln Center.

Steinway & Sons

On the road again in the 1970's, Horowitz had his "beauty" (as he called his favorite Steinway concert grand) hoisted out of a window of his townhouse and shipped to cities in which he was to play.

At age sixty-nine, seven months after a series of electroshock treatments, Horowitz ends a six-year retirement with a recital at Severance Hall in Cleveland on May 12, 1974. "I'm a young man, full of pep!" he exclaimed to reporters at a press conference. "Now I take no more retirements."

United Press International Photo

Wide World Photos

In the 1970's many concert managers found Horowitz and Wanda to be formidable business partners, much concerned with procuring engagements at top dollar. Wanda's temper was legendary, said to rival that of her father, Arturo Toscanini.

Horowitz giving an autograph to actor Tony Randall at Korvettes department store in New York. (1976)

United Press International Photo

"This was his birthday, so I'll do anything," Wanda told a reporter at New York's celebrated discotheque, Studio 54, on October 1, 1978.

Wide World Photos

Decked out in his finest, Horowitz inserts earplugs at Studio 54.

Courtesy of Tedd Joselson

Wearing his favorite black-and-white "keyboard" bow tie, Horowitz gives pianist Tedd Joselson an impromptu lesson at an RCA cocktail party a week before his January 1978 Golden Jubilee appearance with the New York Philharmonic.

United Press International Photo

Horowitz bows with conductor Eugene Ormandy after his January 8, 1978, performance with the New York Philharmonic of the Rachmaninoff Third Concerto, his first appearance with orchestra in twenty-five years.

United Press International Photo

Horowitz and conductor
Zubin Mehta in rehearsal for
(below) and acknowledging
applause at (above) *Horowitz
Live*, a repeat performance of the
Rachmaninoff Third with the
New York Philharmonic,
which was televised live on
the NBC network and
simultaneously transmitted by
satellite to Europe, on
September 24, 1978.

United Press International Photo

Courtesy of Bill Ray

Horowitz, Wanda, and "Fussy" the cat pose in the elegant living room of the Horowitz townhouse for a 1978 *Newsweek* feature article.

The Horowitzes chat with Prince Charles at the Royal Festival Hall, London, after the 1982 charity concert.

Wide World Photos

United Press International Photo

President Carter introducing Horowitz·on the occasion of his February 26, 1978, afternoon recital in the East Room of the White House. "Horowitz," the President declared, "is a national treasure."

Courtesy of the Carter White House Photo Office Collection

Horowitz presenting a copy of his new record of the Rachmaninoff Third Concerto to President and Mrs. Carter in the Oval Office after the 1978 White House recital. Looking on are valet Giovanni Scimonelli (far left), RCA producer John Pfeiffer, and Wanda.

Union-Tribune Publishing Co.

Horowitz and Wanda arriving in San Diego in 1977—their favorite photograph together.

well have felt a familiar pounding of his heart, tightening of the stomach muscles, and shaking in his legs. Half supported by Chapin, he moved like a condemned man, his face pale and gaunt, his brow furrowed. At the doorway leading to the stage area, Horowitz saw his piano tuner. "Hupfer," he asked, "is everything all right?" "Everything's okay, Mr. Horowitz," was the reply.[26]

Chapin and Horowitz were now standing in the wings. Chapin turned to the house electrician, noticed the clock over his head read 3:38 P.M. and said, "House lights down, please." Out front, the audience murmured anxiously. "Stage lights up." The lights were adjusted to exactly the intensity that Horowitz had settled on a few days earlier. There stood the new Steinway piano, looking austere and forbidding, gleaming in the light. Chapin could hear his own breathing as he turned to Horowitz and bowed him forward. But Horowitz did not move. Instead, he stood watching Chapin with a quiet, remote smile. Finally Chapin, gripping Horowitz by one shoulder, turned him 180 degrees, put his hand on his back and gently propelled him out onto the stage.

Horowitz walked slowly, slightly stooped. As the lights caught him the entire audience rose to its feet and erupted into applause and cheers. To those who had seen Horowitz perform years earlier, it seemed that his physical appearance had changed but little. He remained slender and refined, if perhaps less erect than before. With a friendly, self-deprecatory shrug with out-turned hands, as if to say, "I haven't even played yet— sorry to make you come here on this beautiful day," he acknowledged the huge ovation.

Unable to see more than the three front rows of the orchestra because of his nearsightedness, Horowitz stood center stage, his eyes moist, overwhelmed. Fighting for control, he straightened his shoulders, moved downstage, and bowed to each section of the house. "He was elegant, measured, dignified, and welcoming," wrote Chapin. "The audience sensed his pleasure at being there and the roar increased. Finally, he gestured toward the piano and turned his head as if to ask if they would like to hear him play. He sat at the piano bench and the roar increased. There was a slight scuffle as people resumed their seats. Perhaps two seconds of this, and then the most deafening silence I've ever heard in my life."[27]

Horowitz did not fiddle with the bench, or move back and forth on it as he used to. He simply began to play. Extremely nervous, he launched into the Bach-Busoni faster than he had intended and, on the last octaves of the first phrase, he hit a clinker. The audience froze, but Horowitz quickly recovered and settled into the music. Although he played with rhythmic vitality, immaculate articulation, and his incomparable palette of colors, the performance was marred by continued wrong notes. "I was handicapped," Horowitz said the following day. "I am sure I could play it better under different circumstances. It was too emotional for me."[28] Wanda, elegantly dressed in a magenta-and-white silk dress with matching coat, sat with her brother, Walter, and sister, Wally. Midway through the first half of the Bach-Busoni, she left her box to go backstage, as her husband had requested.

In the wings, Chapin suddenly became aware of someone standing next to him. He turned to see Wanda staring out onto the stage, tears streaming down her face, repeating over and over, as if in a trance: "I never thought I'd live to see this day. . . . I never thought I'd live to see this day."[29] (Later she insisted that she did not remember saying any such thing.) Chapin reached out and put his arms around Wanda. Together they listened to the rest of the Bach-Busoni.

When it was finished, the audience let out a collective gasp and then began a thunderous applause. In the *New York Times* the next day, Harold C. Schonberg noted that "in the fugue, every voice was clearly outlined, every note weighted for maximum musical and coloristic effect."[30] When Horowitz walked off the stage and saw Wanda his face relaxed. They looked at each other for a long, awkward moment, and then embraced. Horowitz straightened his coat and walked back onstage to acknowledge the applause. Then, before the next selection, he went back to the dressing room "to wait for latecomers to be seated," as he told Chapin, although there were few if any latecomers.

As Chapin guided Horowitz to the wings once again, they talked about the next work on the program, the Schumann Fantasy in C Major. "What a beautiful piece it is!" Horowitz declared. "So beautiful. You must listen carefully. Now, you promise?" "Yes," Chapin agreed, brushing an imaginary spot of lint from Horowitz's jacket. "I'll listen with all my heart."

The three long movements of the Schumann are difficult to sustain and make coherent, but Horowitz, now considerably more relaxed, played the complex work with breadth and drama. Schumann had once described the Fantasy as the most passionate music he had ever written, and Horowitz's performance was fittingly rhapsodic and driving. "It was a heroic performance," said Schonberg, "that never sounded punched, neurotic or spasmodic."[31] As Horowitz would not allow his conception of the work to be compromised by stage nerves, he was willing to take chances, making no adjustment in tempi and unperturbed by wrong notes. In the treacherous coda of the second movement, the notoriously difficult series of leaps got out of control, just as he had feared. Still, he did not slow the tempo as he had considered doing, and the mistakes must have been of some comfort to the pianists in the audience. "It proved, at least," wrote Schonberg, "that Mr. Horowitz was mortal."

Horowitz later blamed the problems in the Schumann on the uncomfortable temperature. "I perspire when I play," he explained, "and it was humid. You play a piece for thirty minutes and you don't take time to take out your handkerchief. The chords in the second movement are difficult, just like playing billiards. . . . The perspiration was coming down my forehead. I shook my head twice and it would not go away. I closed my eye because water was coming into it . . . and I took two, three wrong notes completely."[32] But as Horowitz left the stage after the Schumann, he was nonetheless grinning broadly at the deafening applause. "Not too bad, I think," he told Chapin. "It will be better the next time."

During intermission, Horowitz stretched out on the greenroom couch and joked with Wanda and the others. "You think they like it?" he asked mischievously. Everyone nodded. "But I've been away from concerts a long time. I should have much more control when I play again."[33] Horowitz wondered whether the recording being made of the recital would have good enough sound to be released and both Chapin and Pfeiffer assured him that the sound would be excellent. In addition, the audience had helped matters by remaining almost completely silent during the first half. One elderly woman, red-faced from attempting to suppress a coughing spasm, had left the hall, at the beginning of the Bach-Busoni. Otherwise, not a cough or a sneeze had been heard. "But all those wrong notes in the Busoni," Horowitz protested. "I was a little nervous, you know. But if the record is released we must keep those notes. It would be unfair to fix them up. What touched my heart was that the audience understood the music. I felt that the message . . . had reached the hearts of the people."[34]

Intermission almost over, Horowitz rose from the couch, put on a new shirt, combed his hair, and carefully inspected the result in the mirror. The second half was to begin with the Scriabin Ninth Sonata. Scriabin had told Horowitz's mother a half century earlier that her son was perhaps destined for greatness as both a pianist and composer. Now, on the fiftieth anniversary of Scriabin's death, his Ninth, or *Black Mass,* Sonata had special meaning for Horowitz. As Harold Schonberg commented: "Nobody plays Scriabin better than Mr. Horowitz. . . . Not only does he have complete affinity with the strange, mysterious world of Scriabin but he also has the technique to make the complicated writing sound as clear as the strands of a Bach invention."[35] Unlike Horowitz's 1953 interpretation, which lasted about six minutes, his 1965 Scriabin Ninth was just short of nine minutes. Although no less exciting than in former years, his performance now had an expansive grandeur and, according to one critic, "an untroubled lyricism that gradually developed into animated breadth."[36]

The program ended with the three Chopin works. As Horowitz finished the final selection, the G Minor Ballade, the enthusiasm of the crowd changed to near-hysteria, and the pandemonium increased as photographers were admitted into the hall and began to set up their cameras near the apron of the stage. Awaiting encores, some of the audience became infuriated by the clicks of cameras and one photographer was actually attacked. Another's tripod was thrown to the red-carpeted floor, while a third was threatened by a man who hissed, "Horowitz is more important than your pictures!" The crowd was not aware that the pianist had granted the press permission to take photographs during the encores.

Horowitz had selected those encores with care. Backstage, as he waited to return to the stage, he asked Chapin coyly, "What do you think I should play?" First was Debussy's *Serenade for the Doll,* which he presented with a childlike wonder and calm simplicity that was in dramatic contrast to the clicking cameras and frenzied audience. Then came Scriabin's Etude in C-sharp Minor, to which he imparted a melancholy lyricism and containment that defied the audience's hunger for more virtuosity. Although there would be no *Stars and Stripes Forever* or *Carmen* this time, Horowitz did finally give the crowd something it wanted, the Moszkowski Etude in A-flat Major, a showcase for the amazing velocity of his fingers. After the final sweep of scales and the four cadential chords that end the piece, Horowitz bounded from his bench with his right hand moving as if still playing. The earlier applause seemed almost tame as compared to the leonine roar that now shook the hall. Returning backstage, Horowitz declared to Chapin, "I had to show them some of the old Horowitz." Wanda, Chapin, the ushers, Hupfer, and even the electrician laughed, and Horowitz marched onstage a last time for his final encore, Schumann's *Träumerei*. ("The whole thing was a dream and that's why I ended with *Träumerei*,"[37] he said later.) The following day, Alan Rich wrote in the *New York Herald Tribune*: "The vision of simple beauty comes late to most men, and often latest of all to performing musicians. This is inevitable, perhaps, in the neurotic world of the performer today. Horowitz knew, and demonstrated in full measure, what a precious thing he has now acquired. He was right to worry about its fragility under public scrutiny. One can only hope that now his worries are at an end."[38]

Harold C. Schonberg was another who perceived a new equanimity in Horowitz's playing: "At this concert one did feel a grander, more spacious line in such works as the Schumann Fantasy and the G Minor Ballade by Chopin. And there were a few other changes. For one thing, Mr. Horowitz uses a little more pedal than he used to. For another, his playing is emotionally more poised, more of a piece, less driving and nervous."[39] Horowitz had also proved that his staggering technique remained intact, that he was one of the last representatives of the grand manner, "one of the knights of the keyboard in the direct Liszt-Anton Rubinstein tradition."[40]

After *Träumerei,* the house lights were turned on. Horowitz took his last bow, but the audience refused to leave and continued its applause. The stage lights were then dimmed, and the piano lid was closed, eliciting loud groans from the audience. Meanwhile, the greenroom was swamped with flowers, photographers, musicians, and friends. Roving reporters were recording celebrities' spontaneous reactions to the concert. Zero Mostel bellowed, "If I could play piano like that, I'd get out of show business!"[41] Sol Hurok quipped, "I'm not as good a pianist as he is. But he had twelve years to practice."[42] Van Cliburn, seeming overwhelmed, declared: "I am thrilled today as are all members of the music world. The sonority is so wonderful. The beauty and excitement are not only in the music but in the hall. It is all about us."[43]

About five forty-five, as the Horowitzes prepared to leave, Jack Pfeiffer entered the dressing room through the crowd and queried Chapin, "How are we going to get him out of here? There is no room to move out there."[44] Chapin broke through the assembled throng, walked out to the limousine, and caught the chauffeur's eye. The milling fans made room for the car to pull up to the stage door. To cries of "Bravo Horowitz!," the pianist put on his gray gloves and overcoat and was escorted from Carnegie Hall by Chapin. "We came out," recalled Wanda, "and there was a big line of people on both sides of us, and somebody said, 'Oh, Mr. Horowitz, we stood in line all night'; and I said, 'You know what? I stood in line for twelve years!' "[45]

Horowitz and Wanda returned home with a group of close friends for a champagne and pastry reception. With Schuyler and Betty Chapin, Jack Pfeiffer, Tom Frost, Abram Chasins, Constance Keene, Ania Dorfman, David Rubin, Gitta Gradova, Maurice Cottle, and Olga Strumillo, Horowitz was in a jocular mood. Lighting a cigarette, he laughed about his mistakes that afternoon: "It happens in the best of families. Pianistically not too bad, although there were far too many wrong notes. This was really too emotional an experience for me. I have to do more homework. And you know the demon inside me. I always have to do better, each time. I should have much more control when I play again."[46]

Not long after, Horowitz retreated upstairs to watch the television news, in case his concert was mentioned. And, indeed, the first item on the *CBS Evening News* was Horowitz's return to the stage. A reporter was shown outside Carnegie Hall interviewing youngsters who were chattering with excitement. One teenaged girl was crying, vowing that her love affair with the Beatles was over, because her "new god" was Horowitz. Chapin nudged Horowitz. "See, I told you there was a young audience for your art. Now you can believe it." "I play because of them,"[47] replied Horowitz.

On the day after the concert, Horowitz gave an interview to the *New York Times*. Dressed in a light-blue robe over blue pajamas, he showed the reporter the fourteen bouquets of flowers that decorated the living room. "Everyone sent me flowers," he boasted. "Sviatoslav Richter sent me flowers and a telegram from Detroit. I have a beautiful telegram from Arthur Rubinstein in Venice: 'I am with you with all my heart. Bravo for your coming back. I wish you the greatest success which you deserve.' " Messages had also arrived from Isaac Stern, Erich Leinsdorf, Eugene Ormandy, Risë Stevens, and fifty others. Horowitz reiterated that the occasion had been too emotional for him and apologized for his wrong notes. "If I play more I will have complete control. All these false notes disappear."[48]

The day's technical lapses continued to bother Horowitz, and he finally decided to correct some of them for the forthcoming Columbia album of the recital. When the record was released on June 7, 1965, it was not generally known that the performances had been "doctored," though the patchwork could be determined easily enough thanks to the many tape pirates who made illegal recordings of the recital. Columbia promoted the album as a live "document" and Horowitz himself told *Life* magazine: "I wouldn't want to change anything at all. You know, this is a document."[49] To Howard Klein at the *New York Times,* he said, "I want to be honest with the public. There were some mistakes but these add to a human quality. And as it goes along, the program gets better."[50] But although Horowitz claimed he didn't mind the mistakes, he positively bristled when one critic wrote that there were more wrong notes in this recital than in all of Horowitz's past recitals combined.

Horowitz especially regretted the faults in the second movement of the Schumann Fantasy and felt justified in returning to Carnegie Hall to rerecord a passage or two. He rationalized that the errors here had not been caused by nerves but rather by perspiration that had gotten into his eyes, and he decided to leave many other wrong notes from the recital intact on the album, including the first mistakes in the Bach-Busoni. But producer Tom Frost was bothered by the idea of releasing the album as a "live" performance when the master tapes had been edited. "I didn't think it was morally right for Columbia to release the album this way," he said later. "It was especially tempting because nearly the entire program had been recorded in a dress rehearsal, so we had both tapes to work with."[51] When Howard Klein discovered he had been duped, he wrote a follow-up piece about the record. "It was since learned that some splicing had been done and that the second movement of the Schumann Fantasy used an ending recorded at another time."[52] Klein went on to raise the ethical questions that had so bothered Frost.

The album nonetheless won three Grammy awards in March 1966 and eventually sold over fifty thousand copies. The plain fact was that no other classical concert of that decade could match the dramatic impact of Horowitz's return to the stage in 1965. "I don't know what to call it. Is it a debut or a resurrection?" Horowitz asked one friend. "If you call it a debut, I am offended. Resurrection, I think, is all right. . . ."[53]

CHAPTER TWENTY-FOUR

"WHAT'S TO BE GAINED?"

"Each time you go out on stage you have to outdo yourself. You have to do better. It's my character. I cannot change myself. You may agree with me, you may disagree with me. You may like me or dislike me. But integrity I think I have."[1]

*I*mmediately after Horowitz's success at Carnegie Hall, he was approached by concert managers from all over the United States—some of them old friends like Harry Zelzer in Chicago and Patrick Hayes in Washington, D.C.—to discuss the possibility of further appearances. Although Horowitz had intimated that he might repeat the same program in other cities, he now was not inclined to do so. He felt let down and depressed after the May 9 concert. "Oh, I don't know if I will ever play again," he said morosely to Abram Chasins. "Maybe the next recital would be anticlimactic. I shouldn't play anymore. No." Chasin's fawning encouragement and unctuous flattery only seemed to deepen Horowitz's reluctance. "My dear Abrasha," he snapped, "after you talk about May so much, you make me sorry I *ever* played!"[2]

For much of the summer of 1965, Horowitz felt tired and generally pessimistic. "My playing isn't satisfactory," he told reporters. "I have to find myself on the stage. Sitting at home I can play wonderfully. Then I go on the stage and I say to myself, 'Oh my God!' It's completely different. There are a thousand more shadings and nuances on the stage. At home, the expression is more subdued."[3] Horowitz did not practice at all and blamed his "laziness" on the weather. "I had a setback this summer. I'm allergic to playing in humid weather," he confided to the *New York Times*. "My instrument doesn't respond and I don't respond. In crisp weather, I have more energy."[4]

To reawaken his dormant enthusiasm, Horowitz decided to do what he had always done when depressed: to "make a challenge to myself."[5]

Toward the end of the summer and in early fall, he set out to learn the Sonata No. 10 of Scriabin, which he asserted was "the most difficult" of that composer's piano sonatas. As he told one friend, "I'm proud of myself, proud that at my age I can do new things."[6]

It turned out that tackling entirely new repertory gave Horowitz the lift he needed, and with the arrival of cool weather, he began practicing regularly, contemplating a Carnegie Hall recital in November or December. Along with the Scriabin, he began to work at other pieces he had not performed or recorded in recent years: the Beethoven Sonata, Op. 10, No. 2, the Mozart Sonata, K. 331, and the Chopin *Polonaise-Fantasie*. On the afternoon of October 27, Horowitz rehearsed his new program alone at Carnegie Hall at 4 P.M., and publicized the session by giving an interview to the *New York Times*. Two weeks later, he felt sufficiently confident to invite a small audience. With Columbia recording engineers taping, he played a program of Scarlatti, Beethoven, and the Scriabin Tenth for two hundred Rutgers University students who had traveled to New York just for the private recital. This occasion turned out to be a memorable one in an unexpected way, for it was November 9, the evening of the first of New York City blackouts. Horowitz had just begun the Chopin *Polonaise-Fantasie* when the lights went off. He continued without missing a note, and after about two minutes a stagehand came onstage with a flashlight and focused it on the keyboard, whispering to Horowitz that the whole block seemed to be black. Horowitz then stopped, listened for a moment, and began the Chopin again, to play it through to the end with the keyboard illuminated by the narrow beam of light.

Whether because of the blackout or, more likely, because Horowitz was neither happy with his performance nor satisfied with his repertory (he was known to have reservations about the Beethoven Sonata, which he later decided was too dull and tame for concert performance), Horowitz aborted his plans for a fall concert. He told the *New York Times*'s Howard Taubman that while it wasn't actually the shock of the sudden blackout that had caused him to cancel the November 28 date that Julius Bloom had put aside for him, he had made up his mind to do so when he read in the newspaper that government and Consolidated Edison officials had admitted that there could be another blackout. "A pianist who had waited twelve years between recitals," wrote Taubman, "could wait a few more months, until he felt comfortable about the city's power situation."[7]

During the early months of 1966, Horowitz continued to resist the idea of giving more concerts. "Some mornings I wake up feeling empty and I think that it makes no sense to give a recital. To prove that I can still play? Didn't I do that last May? Then, I don't need the excitement, the tension again. I've had a long lifetime of it. What's to be gained? Money? I can play in some small town in the middle of America, make a few thousand dollars and not have to face the feverish atmosphere of a New York recital." Although at the time Horowitz was working each day on two different recital programs, his moods were manic, swinging unpredictably between ebullient enthusiasm and depressive lethargy. "Some days I go to that piano and it is nothing," he lamented. Then his voice would lift and the look of despair would twist into a smile. "A few hours later I play and it goes well, very well. My fingers are in good shape; they are even better now than when I was young."[8]

It took nearly a year after the 1965 return concert for Horowitz to push aside his insecurities and ask Julius Bloom to reserve two Sunday afternoons in April for possible recitals. In late March, he decided the date would be April 17. In confidence, Horowitz told Bloom that if the Carnegie Hall performance went well, he would also agree to repeat the program that spring at Rutgers University in New Brunswick, New Jersey. Contrary to Horowitz's fear that another Carnegie Hall recital would be anticlimactic, announcement of the April concert provoked new pandemonium at the box office. Tickets went on sale on April 4, but once again, by midnight of the day before, there was a long line of people—nearly one thousand—waiting patiently in the cold and rain. At midnight, Horowitz headed to the hall in a taxi with his secretary, Kati Melonas, to view the scene, and he shook his head in disbelief at the throng of shivering, dedicated fans. Recognizing him, one shouted, "Don't be nervous, Mr. Horowitz—we're all with you!"—to which he replied, "God bless you!" Miss Melonas was instructed to remain at Carnegie Hall and to buy the crowd coffee and doughnuts, which she did twice during the night. "Moved isn't the word for how he feels," she told the *New York Times*. "I'm too cold to think what the word is, though."[9] The following morning, all tickets were sold within two and a half hours and four hundred people went home frustrated and empty-handed.

On the afternoon of April 17, remembering the mistake-ridden performance of the difficult Bach-Busoni toccata at last year's recital, Horowitz began cautiously, with the short, relatively simple Scarlatti

Sonata, L. 18. This was, he later explained, "to quiet my nerves."[10] Compared to 1965, Horowitz's playing that day was infinitely more controlled, and the carefully chosen, rather chaste program of Scarlatti, Beethoven (Thirty-two Variations), Mozart (Sonata, K. 331), Scriabin (Sonata No. 10) and Chopin (*Polonaise-Fantasie;* Mazurka, Op. 33, No. 4; Nocturne, Op. 72, No. 1; B Minor Scherzo) elicited rave reviews. However, although Horowitz's Mozart was a marvel of rhythmic vitality and romantic lyricism, the usual complaints were uttered about his highly stylized performances of Classical works. "There are too many agogic shifts, too many dynamic fluctuations, too many tempos that sounded un-Mozartean,"[11] wrote Harold C. Schonberg.

Horowitz was in a concentrated, contemplative mood that afternoon, mindful of reducing the number of false notes to a bare minimum. Consequently, his playing during the first half was guarded—at least until he reached full stride in an electric rendition of the Scriabin Sonata that ended the first half of the program. Although the enigmatic harmonies of the mystical Russian composer might ordinarily be beyond the comprehension of many of Horowitz's audience, the concentrated, sumptuously colored performance, replete with jackhammer trills and stunning dynamic contrasts, held his listeners in a trance-like state for the duration.

Horowitz similarly mesmerized his audience at the end of the program with a riveting performance of the Chopin B Minor Scherzo. Although he continued to ignore the temptation of presenting one of his notorious transcriptions, he could not resist rewriting the Scherzo's coda. There he transformed a running scale passage in both hands into a sequence of interlocked octaves, "rolling upward in a blur of two hammering wrists,"[12] as Schonberg put it. Audible gasps were heard when he hit the top B, and "the faces of the many pianists in the audience [turned] positively green,"[13] he wrote. After every piece, Horowitz had been greeted with shouts of bravo and with foot stamping, and as he strode offstage after the Chopin, he was obviously well-pleased with himself. Later, however, he claimed that "these hysterics, they bother me, they make me nervous. The audiences are too hysterical because I play too seldom."[14] Yet Horowitz well understood that the very definition of his legend was his inaccessibility and unpredictability, and throughout the 1960's, 1970's, and 1980's, he would thrive on his mercurial reputation.

After the April 17 recital, Horowitz made good on his promise to play for student audiences at reasonable prices ($2 to $6 per ticket), and on May 8 he went to New Brunswick for the Rutgers concert. The announcement and location of the recital caught the press off guard, for Horowitz would not commit himself to publicizing a concert more than two weeks in advance. (Because Horowitz would not sign with a professional management company, Bloom, now recovered, took charge of his affairs as he had promised.) On the eighth, during a leisurely drive to Rutgers, Horowitz and Wanda noticed a car slowing down beside them on the New Jersey Turnpike. A young woman held up a hastily penned sign reading "Bravo," and flashed two tickets at them. Horowitz, grinning, told the driver to follow the car. "They know where I'm going!"

The festive and relaxed atmosphere in the Rutgers gymnasium delighted Horowitz. Not even a ringing telephone during the Scriabin Sonata perturbed him, and he ended the afternoon by waving energetically to the enthusiastic young crowd in the bleachers. So pleased was he with the Rutgers appearance that he decided to schedule his next concert at another university. Rejecting invitations from managers in Philadelphia, Washington, and Boston, Horowitz chose to play at Yale University's Woolsey Hall on November 13.

The informality of a campus environment permitted him to test the new program that fall without the pressure of a New York audience. Two weeks later, on November 27, he performed the Yale program at Carnegie Hall, and again on December 10, fulfilling his long-standing desire to play an identical program twice there. Having recently signed a five-year contract with Columbia Masterworks, Horowitz had both recitals recorded and a two-record set, "Horowitz in Concert," was later issued, featuring works both from the fall programs and the concert of the previous spring.

In 1965 Horowitz had promised in interviews that he would play more Debussy, and for his 1966 fall recitals he therefore programmed three of the preludes from Book II: *Bruyères, Les fées sont d'exquises danseuses* and *La terrasse des audiences au clair de lune*—and *L'Isle Joyeuse*. Structuring his program in the customary way, he began with a Classical work—in this case Haydn's Sonata No. 23 in F Major—followed it with a short Romantic work, Schumann's *Blumenstück*, Op. 19, and ended the first half with a war-horse, Chopin's B-flat Minor Sonata. The Debussy followed the intermission and the program ended with the seldom-heard Liszt *Vallée d'Obermann* from *Années de Pèlerinage*. Horowitz was especially happy about the Liszt, which he had never played before. Some of its passages, he found, did not lie well in his hand, so he had retouched it, filling in octaves, rewriting some of the cadenzas and adding reinforcements—all of which he considered justifiable within the improvisatory tradition of Liszt as long as the changes were in good taste. "It had to be played with the grand gesture and the big line, with belief and fervency," commented Schonberg. "Mr. Horowitz believes in this music and there was a dignity as well as power in his performance. . . . At the end, he not only resurrected a noble work. He had also brought an age to life."[15]

Although Horowitz rehearsed at Carnegie Hall in March 1967 and seriously considered playing recitals in Chicago, Washington, Boston, and Philadelphia that spring, he did not actually perform again until the following October. The ten-month hiatus was necessary because of special plans. January 1968 would mark the fortieth anniversary of his American debut and he wanted time away from the stage to add drama to the celebration. His only public appearance in that ten-month interval was a tea party held at Steinway Hall, with a guest list drawn from his most loyal fans, the young people who had stood in the rain in 1965 and 1966 in order to hear him play. "I am not running for anything, but I shake all the hands,"[16] Horowitz said wryly at this reception. Seated at a piano beneath a portrait of Handel, he accepted compliments and such gifts as a yellow T-shirt with his portrait painted on it. The sixty-two-year-old pianist greeted a teenager who asked him, "Mr. Horowitz, will you ever play *Danse Macabre* again?" "No," was the tongue-in-cheek reply. "Too macabre." Horowitz gave each of his fans a huge grin and although he was repeatedly begged to play he insisted that the party was "for meeting, not playing. You know," he told the press, "I am not a gregarious person, but I am enjoying this. It's love—mutual love."[17]

Horowitz was, in fact, so taken by his youthful admirers and so energized by the success of his second comeback recording that he considered teaching once again. He asked Peter Mennin, president of the Juilliard School, to recommend potential young pianists, and four Juilliard students—Murray Perahia, Joseph Kalichstein, Jeffrey Siegel, and Albert Lotto—were sent to Ninety-fourth Street to audition for him. However, none of them became Horowitz students; some were scandalized by the high fee Horowitz quoted, while others were hesitant to become involved with Horowitz in view of his peculiar history with his students of the past. "At my audition," recalled Albert Lotto, "he asked me strange questions—did I have money, did I have a girl friend, were my parents still married, etc., etc. I realized that I would not only have to work at the piano but also work at the relationship with Horowitz. Horowitz lived in a fantasy world and I didn't want to become a part of it."[18]

Horowitz eventually discarded the idea of serious work with a student although he did continue his contact with young people by making two more college appearances in the fall of 1967 in New York City, at Queens College on October 22 and Brooklyn College on November 12. Both helped him warm up for his Carnegie Hall recital on November 26 and for a Washington, D.C., recital on December 10, his first visit to the capital in fourteen years. The surprise of Horowitz's Carnegie Hall program and the climax of the afternoon came after he played his first two encores. Stepping onto the stage again, he glanced questioningly at the audience, grinned devilishly, and launched into his famous arrangement of Bizet's *Carmen*. This was the first time he had played one of his own transcriptions since his 1953 retirement, and by doing so he proved himself still capable of outrageous virtuoso fireworks and demonstrated that he no longer feared being pigeonholed as a keyboard acrobat. Horowitz, wrote a critic, "showered the audience with sprays of notes, with volleys of *fortissimos,* with streaking octaves and freakish passagework."[19] It seemed that the old Horowitz was back, possibly for good.

CHAPTER TWENTY-FIVE

PROJECT X

*"At a concert they've got to sit there and hear you but
what happens in the living room when the children want
something to eat and mamma has to go get it?
You become background music!"*[1]

*H*orowitz had not resurrected *Carmen* exclusively for his 1967 fall recitals but rather in preparation for a special celebration planned for the
fortieth anniversary of his American debut: a television special to be
filmed at Carnegie Hall. He had had great difficulty deciding whether he
wanted to do a television program and insisted on absolute secrecy until
he felt positive about it. The show was referred to as "Project X" by everyone involved until its public announcement on January 17, 1968. Ever
since Horowitz had returned to the stage, CBS had tried to persuade him
to make such an appearance, but Horowitz had put endless obstacles in
the way. He had always declined offers from motion pictures and television, wary of anyone's capitalizing on his name and worried that enormous public exposure might interfere with his private life. It took CBS
nearly three years of careful negotiating to change his mind. Horowitz
not only wanted each of his reservations about television refuted to his
satisfaction, but demanded complete control over every aspect of the production.

New York Times critic-at-large Howard Taubman was delegated by CBS
to act as its emissary in the ritual of persuasion. Taubman argued that a
television recital would be by far the most dramatic way to celebrate the
anniversary and make up for the infrequency of Horowitz's public appearances. (Although Horowitz's confidence on the stage had gradually
returned, he still had no intention of making extensive national tours or
of traveling outside the eastern United States.) Taubman reasoned that
with a television concert, Horowitz would in effect be able to perform in
every American city at once, and to reach many persons who had never
bought a record or attended a concert. Such an event, filmed in color and

broadcast during prime time, would also have a special cachet as the first classical piano recital in network-television history. Horowitz himself admitted that he enjoyed watching TV for relaxation, but he shot back that the sound quality of television was poor, inappropriate for serious music, and that elaborate camera tricks would interfere with his concentration and that of his audience. "Everything I've seen on music has been a flop," he said. "There are too many things that distract the eye at the expense of the ear. With a symphony orchestra you jump around the sections. With a singer you see tonsils."[2] But Taubman countered that television had reached a stage of technical and artistic maturity, that the camera would eye him from a few strategic angles in long, uninterrupted shots; that Carnegie Hall would be used instead of a studio; that there would be no script and no set. "Think, if you can," Taubman cooed, "if you had seen a film of Liszt playing the piano, how wonderful that would be."[3]

Horowitz began to show interest in the idea but was full of pragmatic concerns—not just any sponsor, for instance, would be acceptable. "No spaghetti, no macaroni, no deodorants," he admonished. "Let's face it, there are some very cheap things on television."[4] Speaking for CBS, Taubman assured Horowitz that a "high-class sponsor" would be found, and it turned out that the choice suited Horowitz: General Telephone and Electronics agreed to pay $450,000 for the privilege of backing the historic program.

Still the debate continued, with Horowitz insisting upon two full dress rehearsals at Carnegie Hall before committing himself to do the program. He knew his demands were extraordinary, and he felt that CBS "was wonderful" about the whole thing. "They said, 'Why not let us show you how well it would work out? Let us do a dry run. Let us tape hours of you at the piano. Then we'll run it off for you. If you aren't satisfied we'll burn it. If you like it, we'll do the special.' "[5]

Technical concerns were foremost in Horowitz's mind, and it took months for executive producer Taubman, director Roger Englander, and Horowitz's own Columbia Masterworks producer Tom Frost to decide how to film the concert. Frost had been hired by CBS TV to serve as audio consultant and also to edit the tapes for the planned Columbia album, "Horowitz on Television." In view of Horowitz's idiosyncratic recording habits, Frost explained to Englander and Taubman that the pianist was extremely choosy about approving performances for release on record. Frost anticipated problems in editing the program and suggested that film, not videotape, be used, since film was easier to sound-edit. Both Englander and Taubman, however, favored the immediacy of videotape which, they argued, would capture Horowitz's performance with more realism and drama. Conflict quickly arose, not only because of the tape-versus-film argument but also because Taubman felt that, in general, Frost was interfering in a medium he did not understand. One Columbia producer intimately involved with the program recalled that "Frost naturally assumed that he would be in the production staff of the show and he wanted monetary remuneration for his work. He told Taubman that he knew Horowitz well and that his participation would be indispensable."[6] Frost, determined to have a say in the program, became quite stubborn, insisting again and again that his expertise was essential, and generally irritating those involved in the project. Finally, Taubman, sensing that he had the leverage necessary to discard Frost, went to Horowitz and complained that the record producer was jeopardizing the entire production. "Taubman told Horowitz I said it was very difficult working with him," Frost remembered, "that videotape shouldn't be used because Horowitz was impossible to please, and that I was talking behind his back."[7] Horowitz, hypersensitive as always to criticism and resenting the idea of anyone's taking advantage of an association with him, demanded that Frost be removed from the project and that Paul Myers, with whom Horowitz had once worked briefly, replace him.

CBS was spending an estimated $275,000 for the two dress rehearsals on January 2 and 3, and there were worries that Horowitz might withdraw from the project if he found any aspect of the tryouts disagreeable. To protect its investment, the network assigned twenty-eight technicians to the taping of the program. Carpenters were brought in to shore up the stage to prevent creaking when the heavy television cameras were positioned around the piano, and the areas of the floor that were particularly squeaky were carefully marked with masking tape. As a further precaution, a thick layer of talcum powder was spread over the entire stage, for Horowitz had been guaranteed that the cameras would move around him in complete silence.

Leaving nothing to chance, CBS also hired pianist Sheldon Shkolnik to be Horowitz's stand-in, so that Horowitz would not have to endure the hot television lights for prolonged periods of time. While Englander mapped out strategic camera angles and Myers tested volume levels, Shkolnik played through the program. "I had," he said, "always imagined that Horowitz's piano had to be very light-actioned in order for him to achieve his astonishing brilliance and velocity. But I was surprised that this Steinway—the same he used for his 1965 return—was one of the most heavy-actioned instruments I ever encountered. Playing that piano was like running in sand.

"At the first rehearsal on January second, Horowitz warmed up in the most incredible fashion. First, he began to improvise ten- and twelve-note chords with both hands, so softly that there seemed to be no attack; those chords floated like steam rising from the piano. Then came an assertive, trumpet-like melody played with alternate thumbs while the chords continued uninterrupted. To all this he added low bass notes, one at a time, and finally a chromatic counter-melody in the treble register played by the upper fingers of the right hand. He had produced four completely different sonorities simultaneously—as if played by four different pianists on four different pianos, each in perfect control. David Rubin turned to me and gasped: 'Phenomenal. It's like watching Niagara Falls!' "[8]

During the rehearsal, Shkolnik observed CBS executives standing nearby, deferential and nervous, fearful Horowitz might become displeased by some aspect of the production and cancel the program. In contrast, Horowitz, the cameramen, and the technicians quickly established a lively, almost carefree camaraderie. When Horowitz had arrived on stage, he had at first been bothered by the glare of the lights and the movement of the cameras. Then one of the cameramen exclaimed jokingly, "Hey, Vlady baby, it's our job to make you look good, and you're doin' great! Wanna look through the TV monitor?"[9] Horowitz started to banter with the man and soon became so intrigued by the technical aspects of television that he began to suggest his own camera angles. Finally he took a short ride on one of the elevated platforms, peering through the camera and reveling in all the attention he was receiving. "How patient they were," he later declared. "How much they made me feel wanted!"[10]

During those two hectic days, Horowitz spent seven hours at the piano while Paul Myers and Roger Englander, with their respective armies of technicians, continued to experiment with microphone placement and coordinate camera shots for the different repertory. Five cameras were used: two on the stage, one in the pit, and two in the balcony.

Both Horowitz and Wanda became extremely difficult to deal with during the rehearsals. "Horowitz was very naïve," recalled Englander. "He believed that if there were close-ups it would look as if perhaps he himself wasn't actually playing. He and Wanda did not want *any* close-ups, either on his hands or his face."[11]

Horowitz also worried that his unconventional, flat-fingered approach would create a furor with piano pedagogues and their students. "I've never watched my own fingers moving over the keys that way," Horowitz said. "It's fantastic, but sometimes the technique is awful. Things I tell my students not to do, I'm doing!" There was also the question of vanity. "When I play something goes on in me that makes a strange expression come over my face. To show it is almost an invasion of my privacy."[12]

During the taping of the Chopin G Minor Ballade, Wanda watched as three cameras surrounded Horowitz, the first pointing up from the front of the orchestra, the second focused across the top of the piano on his face, and the third, mounted on a dolly, prowling silently around the stage. Englander's zooming camera angles violated Wanda's ground rules, and she marched into the sound booth in a fury. "That first taping session was problematic largely because of Mrs. Horowitz," recalled Paul Myers. "She laid out a series of directions regarding how the cameramen were going to be allowed to film—that every piece had to be static, that there was to be no moving around. We were only to shoot at certain angles and there would be no close-ups of his hands. It was quite a scene when she came storming into the control booth just because one camera was in a position she didn't like. She was giving hell to Roger Englander, who was outside the hall in a mobile trailer unit—shrieking at him—and finally the sound man turned off her sound so that Englander could not hear her. Roger was trying his best to direct the damn thing, but Wanda Horowitz continued to rage."[13]

The one person who seemed able to resolve conflict between Englander and Wanda was Goddard Lieberson—according to Myers, "a giant in his own right who was respected by both Horowitzes."[14] Lieberson attended the screening session and concluded that the results were too static, and he told the Horowitzes that since they knew nothing about television they must stop bullying Englander and his crew. "I think you should let the television people do their job and you do your job and then it will go much better."[15] They agreed, although reluctantly.

Vladimir Horowitz: A Television Concert at Carnegie Hall was taped on

February 1, 1968, before an invited audience of 2,730, including 200 young people who had stood in line overnight in a fruitless attempt to buy tickets for Horowitz's November 26 concert. At 5:59 P.M., a CBS announcer appeared onstage to welcome the crowd and express the hope that the activities of the camera crew would not interfere with their enjoyment of the music. Because Horowitz wanted to capture the excitement of a live performance but without the usual audience noises, CBS had printed special nonrustling programs on paper that had the feel of limp dollar bills. Once again the stage was covered with talcum powder, and the television crew, dressed in dark gray suits, padded about in black-velvet bedroom slippers to ensure absolute silence. Horowitz had been promised there would be no script, so the only introduction was a simple, "Ladies and Gentlemen: Mr. Vladimir Horowitz," as he walked onto the stage in a black morning coat, gray striped trousers, and gray four-in-hand tie.

In choosing the program, Horowitz had complied with CBS's wish that no work last longer than ten minutes. While Horowitz had promised that his repertory would not be too esoteric, he refused to "play down to the public,"[16] as he put it. After months of vacillation, the program he finally decided upon consisted both of trademark works and pieces performed at his recitals the previous fall: the Chopin G Minor Ballade, F Minor Nocturne, and F-sharp Minor Polonaise; two Scarlatti sonatas (L. 23 and L. 335); the Schumann *Arabesque* and *Träumerei;* the Scriabin D-sharp Minor Etude, and the Bizet-Horowitz *Carmen* Fantasy. Horowitz seemed to sail effortlessly through these works, and only one and a quarter hours after it began the concert was over. If the enthusiasm of the invited audience was any gauge, the TV special was going to be a tremendous success.

Over the next four months, Horowitz worked with Myers and Englander, editing both the record and the videotape. "He enjoyed the editing sessions more than anything else," recalled Englander, "and was endlessly astonished at seeing himself play."[17] He was not, however, pleased with some of the audio portions of the live-performance tape and asked Myers to splice in takes from the two rehearsals. During the Chopin *Polonaise,* for instance, CBS inserted a seven-minute section shot in the empty hall on January 1 and then had a graphic artist draw in the tops of people's heads in chalk on a black card so that the insert would match the surrounding shots. Horowitz was also dissatisfied with his February 1 performance of the Schumann *Arabesque* and told Myers to use a version recorded many years before. But Horowitz now played the ending slightly faster, so it was impossible to synchronize the video of his hands with the sound. Finally Myers put the old recording through a machine that sped up the tempo without raising the pitch, and Horowitz was satisfied. Like Tom Frost, Myers found that Horowitz was a demanding taskmaster, and that he had to accustom himself to the Maestro's many foibles. "It was very difficult to edit the *Carmen* Fantasy," he recalled, "because Horowitz wouldn't let me look at the music. He was afraid it might get published and was absolutely obsessed with keeping it to himself."[18]

When the complicated editing was finally completed, Horowitz took to worrying about the ratings of his program. The CBS contract stated that the show could be aired twice, after which the tape became Horowitz's property. But Horowitz bet Taubman that CBS would quietly shelve it after one showing and never rerun it. "Honestly, they'll turn it off by the millions, I know they will," he said. "There's a Russian pessimist for you," Wanda interjected—to which Horowitz retorted: "At a concert they've got to sit there and listen. But what happens in the living room when the children want something to eat and mamma has to go get it? You become background music."[19]

Horowitz lost his bet. CBS aired the special on Sunday, September 22, 1968, and then rebroadcast it on Christmas day. He was, however, quite correct about the general public's reaction to such a program, for it received low ratings as compared to its network competition that September evening, the season premiere of the popular Western series *Bonanza* and a showing of the film *Zorba the Greek*. But, as the *New York Times* put it, "by the ridiculous audience measure of television, Horowitz's concert registered a very low rating, so low that he merely played to more persons in one evening than he could reach in several years' work in the concert halls."[20]

Having been on television, Horowitz was now more recognizable than ever on the streets of New York; in fact, he could hardly walk with his dog on Fifth Avenue near his home without being hounded for autographs. At times, he complained that he should never have played on television, and he donned a beard and moustache given to him by the CBS makeup department as a joke. Aside from his increased visibility, Horowitz found himself attacked by critics for attempting a television recital, one of them pointing out that television sound was little better than a phonograph recording from the 1930's, another that "distortion, flutter, and signal-to-noise ratio are probably a bit worse on television than on a modest mono FM radio."[21] The whole concept of bringing the concert hall into the living room was questioned, and many critics maintained that the television medium intolerably diluted and distorted the concert experience. Horowitz was even taken to task for allowing his program to be aired on the eve of the Jewish holiday Rosh Hashanah, and to this he snapped that "Rosh Hashanah is not Yom Kippur—the service at the temple is rather brief and time is left for going home and watching my program. And don't let anyone tell me that I am violating a holiday by working. The program was taped last February."[22]

Notwithstanding the furor and complaints, *Vladimir Horowitz: A Television Concert at Carnegie Hall* was a highly lucrative venture for Horowitz. For one thing, it enabled him to move out of his rented summer home in Litchfield, Connecticut, and to buy a Colonial-era farmhouse with a large plot of land in New Milford. (Over the next few years, Wanda would stock this house with early American antiques, selling much of the famous art collection in the process.) More important, Horowitz had succeeded in capturing a new audience, including young musicians who might never have had the opportunity to attend one of his Carnegie recitals or sporadic East Coast appearances. Indeed, for pianists across the nation, the television special was an unparalleled opportunity to observe Horowitz's playing at close range. However, despite the fact that the cameras had been allowed more freedom than before in the last taping, the final product was relatively antiseptic, wanting in warmth and excitement. One critic unkindly described Horowitz as looking "like no one so much as Arthur Treacher, the deferential butler of a thousand 1930's movies."[23] The simple truth was that the visceral excitement of Horowitz in concert did not seem to translate well onto television. By refusing to compromise the recital atmosphere at Carnegie Hall—no set, no script, no introductory comments, no elaborate camera work—Horowitz had preserved his integrity but had forfeited an effective television production. "Horowitz's program had one fatal drawback," wrote one newspaper. "He was put on a pedestal."[24]

CHAPTER TWENTY-SIX

THIRD RETIREMENT: RETREAT

*"I'm still alive, still on this planet. They [doctors] say I have
the heart of a forty-five-year-old but I'm tired all the time.
Anything I do I'm tired. I go to the hospital and they put me
to sleep. Shock heals the·nerves. The colitis is from nerves. I'm
going through a difficult time now."*[1]

etween 1965 and 1969, Horowitz's concert appearances increased in
proportion to his growing self-confidence on stage. His television special
had generated more publicity than he had ever previously enjoyed, and it
spurred him to present ten recitals in 1968 as compared to only one in
1965, five in 1966, and four in 1967. Horowitz now ventured outside the
New York City area to appear in Boston on April 7 and Chicago on May
12, his first concerts in those cities since 1953. In Chicago, fans waited in
line all night long as in New York, and Horowitz was lionized in the
press as "the super Big Ben of pianists."[2] On Monday morning, May 13,
Horowitz was so pleased with his performance of the day before and the
reviews that he asked impresario Harry Zelzer to arrange another recital
for the following Sunday. "I have always felt at home here," Horowitz
told the *Chicago Sun Times.* "Chicago is one of the most exciting cities in
the world and its musical standards are among the highest. I realize that
repeating my program May 19 on such extraordinarily short notice has
not ever been done before, but Mr. Zelzer assures me that Chicago is accustomed to breaking with precedent."[3] Tickets for the second performance were sold out in two hours.

The two major works Horowitz featured on his 1968 anniversary programs were the Schumann *Kreisleriana,* which he had never before performed or recorded, and his own version of the Rachmaninoff Sonata
No. 2 in B-flat Minor, realized from the original (1913) and revised
(1931) editions with the composer's consent. The Rachmaninoff, not

performed by Horowitz since the 1940's, was resurrected to mark the twenty-fifth anniversary of the composer's death. By playing scores like the Schumann and Rachmaninoff, Horowitz was not only setting himself a new challenge but was also fulfilling the terms of his five-year contract with Columbia Masterworks.

Since he was now adamant about not recording in the sterile atmosphere of a studio, an entourage of Columbia engineers and producers were present at each of Horowitz's 1968 recitals. But although he wanted all his concerts recorded so as to choose the best performances for his records, he did not want to be distracted by technicians. "Horowitz didn't even want to see them at his concerts," said one producer. "We would try to be as discreet as possible with the placement of microphones so that he would not be more nervous than he already was, and so that the audience would not feel that the concert had turned into a recording session."[4] While the Columbia personnel were remarkably successful in matching the acoustics of different halls, there were other problems involved with Horowitz's insistence on "live" recording, the most important being the variances in Horowitz's performances from concert to concert. A producer who worked with him at this time observed that "Horowitz's playing got better and better as he continued to perform, but his interpretation was constantly changing, making it very difficult to produce one coherent performance. Adding to the problem was the fact that he always practiced a composition in segments and put it all together at the concert. He broke a piece down into display sections which he then seamed together at the last moment. He had always practiced this way and this worked for him in many works, but, for instance, in recording the Beethoven Sonata, Opus one hundred one (which was never released), the results were not effective because such a work is conceived as an organic whole and Horowitz's Beethoven came out sounding compartmentalized."[5]

Some critics noted that despite the obvious growth in Horowitz's playing since his return, he was still subject to pianistic caprices that either obstructed the flow of the music or the intention of the composer, or obscured the style of the composition. After one of Horowitz's Carnegie Hall recitals in the fall of 1968, Harold C. Schonberg lamented that his reading of Haydn's Sonata No. 58 in C Major was stylistically "all wrong," although pianistically wonderful, with "a romantic set of colors, cute little accents and stresses."[6] In his performances of Scarlatti sonatas,

Horowitz did not feel bound to repeat both the A and B sections of the brief works. Rather, as Paul Myers recalled, "he would sometimes repeat the A section, sometimes not. Sometimes the B, sometimes not. Sometimes he would repeat everything, sometimes no repeats at all." In frustration, Myers finally asked Horowitz about his inconsistency, and was told, "I know what the audience wants me to do." Admitted Myers: "He has that instinct. His timing is always perfect—whether it be his entrance into his living room or knowing just when to come out onto the stage—and he employs better than anyone else a superb sense of showmanship."[7]

Horowitz commanded the stage and his audience completely. Even when an A string in the bass of his Steinway snapped, as it once did in 1968 at Carnegie Hall in the middle of the second movement of the Rachmaninoff Sonata, the disaster was viewed as a mere dramatic interlude. On that occasion, Horowitz's piano technician, Franz Mohr, quickly came on stage to remove the broken string, and Horowitz, completely calm, leaned over and whispered, "Take your time, this is very good."[8] Without beginning the movement again, Horowitz continued from where he had left off, finishing what many critics considered his most monumental performance of the Rachmaninoff.

The record that followed the television album, titled "Horowitz Plays Rachmaninoff," and assembled from performances in New York, Philadelphia, and Washington during 1967 and 1968, was hailed as the definitive reading of the B-flat Minor Sonata. It won two Grammy Awards— for best classical album of the year and for best instrumental performance—and Horowitz was lauded as "the *ne plus ultra* in identification with Rachmaninoff's idiom and purposes."[9] Even with this somewhat overblown work, Horowitz could mesmerize his audience and make the music seem profound. According to *Saturday Review,* Horowitz could be convicted of that "heinous crime of making music sound better than it is."[10]

Less successful was Horowitz's interpretation of the Schumann *Kreisleriana.* "What one had not anticipated was a certain kind of unease that extended even to the pianistics," wrote Harold C. Schonberg. "It was a nervous performance in which details were picked over, in which the line often was broken . . . the intimacy and tender beauty of the *Kreisleriana* were missing and the work tended to sound convulsive."[11] Horowitz himself was not pleased enough with his Carnegie Hall performance to approve its release, and decided to venture into Columbia's Thirtieth Street studios in February and December of 1969 to rerecord the work. He paired *Kreisleriana* with the same composer's *Variations on a Theme by Clara Wieck* in an all-Schumann disc released in 1970. For clarity of sound, this album was superior to any of his "live" concert records, and unlike the Rachmaninoff album, this contained no applause, coughs, or sneezes.

Along with Wanda, Julius Bloom was handling all business arrangements related to Horowitz's concert appearances, and he found himself fending off a great number of requests from all over the world, in addition to working overtime to soothe Horowitz's nerves before every recital. "At one performance of *Kreisleriana,* Horowitz was revved up and ready to go, but he seemed overly animated to me," recalled Bloom. "I thought he played the Schumann too fast. When he came backstage, he asked me what I thought, and I told him it was wonderful but perhaps a little too fast, and he seemed hurt and reminded me that no performance was ever the same way twice. Wanda and I sort of sat on him for a few minutes to calm him down, and he was fine for the rest of the program."[12] Bloom often discussed with Horowitz the possibility of an appearance with orchestra, which Columbia Masterworks had been unsuccessfully urging since 1962. Horowitz said that if he did so he would feel obliged to choose the Philadelphia Orchestra under his old friend Eugene Ormandy, but he had no real enthusiasm for the idea. What he really wanted to do was play with Herbert von Karajan and the Chicago Symphony (which he considered the world's best orchestra) at Carnegie Hall. This was no small project, since George Solti, not Karajan, had recently been appointed music director of the Chicago Symphony, but the orchestra's manager, John Edwards, was willing to do what he could to smooth the awkwardness of having Karajan rather than Solti. Unfortunately, Karajan approached Deutsche Grammophon Gesellschaft about recording the concert before Horowitz had made up his mind to say yes. "Wanda telephoned me, blazing mad, and said the concert was off," recalled Bloom. "A friend of hers from another record company had called and wanted to know about the recording. She was angry because Horowitz's appearances were always kept a secret until the last moment, and the date with the Chicago Symphony had not been set. So, although it could have been one of the most sensational concerts of the decade, it never took place."[13]

It seemed to Bloom that Horowitz was not much disappointed. All his appearances in the 1960's were tentative, arranged informally, usually on short notice, and were predicated on Horowitz's day-to-day mood and health. After his December 15, 1968, Carnegie Hall recital, he did not play again until October 26 of the next year. Although he had scheduled a concert for March 30 in New York, he canceled it because he was ill. "Horowitz had few problems with his colitis," recalled Bloom, "but he had frequent little fevers and colds and oftentimes felt lousy. No concerts from December to the following fall was not unusual because he avoided appearances in the winter months when he was most likely to get sick. Also, he didn't want to give frequent or regular concerts but preferred his appearances to be special events. He wanted to be sure that people would come."[14] Horowitz's box-office appeal was greater than ever in the 1960's, and he was paid top dollar for his few appearances. His fee was the highest of any concert pianist. For instance, on February 25, 1968, Arthur Rubinstein played a recital in Boston at Symphony Hall and was paid $8,000, which amounted to 65 percent of the gross with $6 as the top ticket price. Horowitz played at the same hall the following April 7 and got just short of $15,000, taking 75 percent of the gross with a top ticket price of $10.

During the early months of 1969, Horowitz recorded his Schumann album and later that year worked on a transcription of Liszt's Hungarian Rhapsody No. 13, his first new arrangement since the early 1950's. He programmed this in a Boston recital, on October 26, 1969, at Symphony Hall, which proved to be his last public performance for the next five years. "Everything went well until 1969," he recalled. "Then something happened. I played in Boston in October and at intermission I caught a cold because I didn't change my clothes and it was terribly cold in the artist's room. . . . I came home and had a hundred-and-two-degree fever. So, with that I became frightened. I said something disagreed with me. And I stopped again."[15]

Although Horowitz's health was unquestionably the most important reason for his new retirement in 1969, some suggested that a devastating review by the *Boston Globe*'s Michael Steinberg had also contributed. Horowitz had little respect for critics, yet he had always been sensitive to their comments. He later said he had played "quite well" that day, and indeed, Steinberg wrote that he had rarely heard Horowitz perform "with such power, swiftness, color, with such beauty and variety of sound." But

Steinberg also noted that while Horowitz played the audience coughed incessantly, and when he finished they cheered wildly. He conjectured that many in Symphony Hall had purchased a ticket simply to hear a legend, and not to hear the program of Haydn, Chopin, Scriabin, and Liszt. HOROWITZ—BORING, MARVELOUS AND EXCITING read the headline of Steinberg's review, and the critic asserted that Horowitz was "at the deepest level, boring." "Crazily irrelevant," "catastrophic," "fussy," "prissy" and "incoherent"[16] were other epithets attached to his interpretations. These were words that did not usually turn up in Horowitz's reviews, especially now that he seemed to have acquired living-legend status.

Be that as it may, from October 1969 until a recording session in April 1971, Horowitz stopped all professional activity. He told friends that at age sixty-six he was afraid of becoming ill, reiterating that the flu he had caught in Boston had alarmed him. Said Bloom, "He had never wanted to return to giving regular concerts, and he felt he had nothing left to prove. He would say, 'Look, I returned and played; everyone heard me. I proved I could do it and now I've had enough. Do I have to go on? For what?' So he felt he had done his duty and didn't feel compelled to give any more concerts. I have to admit I heaved a sigh of relief."[17]

Contrary to rumor, Horowitz was not, for the most part, physically incapacitated during this time. He was, however, sometimes uninterested in the piano and was often tired and depressed. There were also frequent conflicts at home, especially concerning his daughter. Sonia had never completely recovered from her motorcycle accident and in general she needed someone to look after her, although she frequently attempted to assert her independence. In the early 1960's, perhaps seeking to establish an identity of her own, she had worked on a kibbutz in Israel, where she very much identified with her Jewish heritage; then, in 1964, she had returned to New York, where she attempted once again to settle down and to make a career. Gary Graffman's wife, Naomi, befriended Sonia at this time and recalled that she lived alone at a residential hotel, was reasonably well physically and wanted to find a job. "She was interested in becoming a stenographer and was also excited about the civil-rights movement and wanted to go down to Mississippi. Although she was trying to make her own way, she was a frightened girl, not completely balanced, and very excitable."[18] At times Sonia had lived in Milan, cared for either by her beloved aunt Wally or by Mario Delli Ponti, a concert pianist and family friend. At other times, she lived in Paris, watched over by a friend, pianist Jean Rudolphe Kars. Sonia had become a constant source of friction between Horowitz and Wanda. "What can I do?" Horowitz said to friends during her European sojourn. "She is forty years old. I can't bring her here to live—that wouldn't work—and I don't travel to Europe. What do they want from me?"[19]

Since at this point Horowitz's absence from the stage could hardly be termed a novelty, there was little curiosity in the press. He gave no interviews, made no public appearances. But then, as in the past, he began to get tired of his inactivity, so he decided to resume his career in a small way through recordings. Over the next four years, Columbia released five new albums: "Horowitz Plays Chopin" (1971), "Horowitz Plays Scriabin" (1972), "Vladimir Horowitz: Favorite Beethoven Sonatas" (1973), "Horowitz: Beethoven Moonlight Sonata; Schubert Impromptus" (1973) and "Vladimir Horowitz: New Recordings of Chopin" (1974).

Some of these performances were taken from Horowitz's live concerts from as far back as 1966, but most were made in the studio under the supervision of CBS producer Richard Killough, who had pretty much replaced Tom Frost since Frost's 1967 falling-out with Horowitz. Because the sale of Horowitz records had tapered down from the extraordinary boom of his first few albums, he had agreed to record a more commercial repertory, because, as he put it, "the people know the tunes." He therefore made new recordings of the Beethoven *Moonlight, Appassionata,* and *Waldstein* sonatas and also of many well-known works of Chopin. Newly learned pieces were three of Schubert's impromptus (F Minor, Op. 142, No. 1; A-flat Major, Op. 142, No. 2; E-flat Major, Op. 90, No. 2), Chopin's Introduction and Rondo, Op. 16, and Scriabin's *Vers la Flamme* and *Feuillet d'Album,* Op. 45, No. 1. By principally relying on older live performances and including only a few new works on the albums, Columbia was able to produce a fair number of records without requiring too much of Horowitz's time.

Horowitz continued to record in the late afternoon on Wednesdays, arriving at the studio dressed "like he was going to a cocktail party," said one producer, playing the piano for about an hour and a half and resting on a cot between takes. During this period when his professional life revolved entirely around recording, the Columbia Masterworks staff discovered that Horowitz's notorious idiosyncrasies and demands, his displays of temperament and insecurity had intensified over the years. He now frequently sat in the control room and listened to playbacks. "Pretty good for an old man," he would say to engineer Raymond Moore, cackling maniacally. "Pretty good for a young man!" was the response. Moore recalled that Horowitz "was very sensitive about growing older and was constantly proving to himself that he could still play. He would look to Wanda for encouragement and for her approval on splicing and any other artistic matters."[20]

Moore and the rest of the staff decided that in worrying about his age and his place in history, Horowitz was not mellowing but, rather, was giving in to his eccentricities with even greater fervor than before. In the early 1970's, for instance, he had offered a remarkable rendition of "Tea for Two" during a break in a recording session and this had been taped. A few days later, engineer Paul Gordon and Tom Frost (with whom there had been a reconciliation) were listening to the playback of "Tea for Two" when Gordon's young nephew walked in. The boy later wrote a fan letter to Horowitz, telling him how marvelous it was that an artist of his stature would play a popular work so wonderfully. Horowitz went into a fury, imagining that the engineers were passing around copies of the tape; Fred Plaut, the head engineer, was told that anyone who had a copy would be fired, and Paul Gordon made a formal apology to Horowitz for the innocent mistake of his nephew.[21]

At another session, in December 1972, Horowitz was working on the *Waldstein* Sonata. He had been using the same Steinway (No. 186) since his return to the stage in 1965, and on this day Horowitz was extremely unhappy over its sluggish action, caused by the studio's humidity. Wanda—who listened to playbacks with her eyes closed and feet propped up—and the Columbia staff were all in the soundproof control room when Horowitz abruptly stood up, swung his fist and struck the peg holding up the piano lid, causing the lid to come crashing down. The engineers were nearly deafened by the horrendous sound, and in the studio Horowitz was heard shrieking hysterically. Not even Wanda wanted to go into the studio to try to calm him. Finally, one of the engineers entered the studio and asked quietly, "Mr. Horowitz, is there anything I can do?" The reply was steady and calm: "Yes, I'd like to go home, and go to bed."[22] Subsequently, Horowitz had his own piano shipped from New Milford for each recording session.

Horowitz's five-year contract with Columbia expired in 1973, but even before his last recording session in February of that year, he seems to have decided not to renew his agreement with the company. Each side was dissatisfied with the other, and for precisely the same reasons that caused RCA and Horowitz to terminate their relationship in 1961. With Horowitz guaranteed a minimum of $50,000 per record, Columbia was losing money, but Horowitz was offended by any implication that he was no longer as popular as he had been. "It's very simple," Horowitz told the press. "They don't advertise; they don't give me any publicity. It's very stupid—not for me, but for them. Look, in America you have to advertise everything, even cigarettes."[23]

It was true that Columbia had budgeted less money in the advertising budget for Horowitz's records after his "Historic Return to Carnegie Hall" album in 1965, and that sales both in the United States and Europe had plummeted. Columbia had tried unsuccessfully to persuade Horowitz to make a concerto or even chamber-music recording, and in 1973 Wanda attempted to persuade him to perform publicly again. Horowitz refused everything, and by the time of his fifth post-1969 retirement album, in 1973, a decision had to be made by Columbia. Paul Myers was now director of Artists and Repertoire in the London Division of the company and was charged with the responsibility of trying to make the classical record department a profitable one. "I did very little to keep him on the label," Myers admitted. "His records had not been selling with the same success, and they were, in fact, proving to be something of a loss. By the time we paid him an enormous advance—plus advertising, plus specialized engineering work, plus traveling with him on the road, plus the cost of his limousines—each record was showing quite a deficit. With Horowitz now wanting a raise in his fee and making still greater demands for specialized star treatment, I went to Goddard Lieberson and said, 'Look, this is getting out of hand,' and Lieberson agreed. I told him wouldn't it be lovely to use all that money laid out for Horowitz to develop the career of a young musician—a Murray Perahia, for instance."[24]

Through the spring and summer of 1973, neither Horowitz nor Columbia made a move toward reconciling their differences. Horowitz, increasingly angry, bitter, and moody, groused that he was not interested in making any more records: "Producers make their own dynamics which change my interpretation. I don't like to splice. I don't like recording anymore," he said flatly. "I'm finished with them and very glad."[25] Yet at one point he contemplated recording Nicolai Medtner's Third Violin Sonata with Nathan Milstein and even giving an all-Medtner recital, but nothing came of the ideas. Then Horowitz decided to travel to Washington to test the acoustics of the Kennedy Center but suddenly canceled the trip. Wanda often intimated that she was trying to get her husband to play in concert again, and Horowitz planned a program "every third day" and talked nonstop with friends about Clementi sonatas. To one interviewer he mentioned several works that he was interested in performing with orchestra: the Brahms Second Concerto, the Rachmaninoff First Concerto ("I promised him I would play that") and Third Concerto, the Medtner First Concerto, the Schubert-Liszt *Wanderer Fantasy,* and, possibly, the Prokofiev Second Concerto or the Concerto by the young American composer John Corigliano.[26] But nothing happened. His bursts of enthusiasm were squelched by exasperation, irritation, and obsession with many things: Tom Frost had misquoted him in liner notes on the subject of Scriabin; the editing of his all-Chopin album was being held up by Columbia because a Joel Grey record was in production ("I have nothing against popular music, but Joel Grey cannot sing," Horowitz said indignantly. "He cannot nothing! He's just a zero and they [CBS] will lose their shirts."); Columbia was more interested in pop music than anything else and only in the popular classics; young pianists banged out the Rachmaninoff Third Concerto ("Oh my God! They have their outlet and the public is the victim!"[27]). Once, Harold C. Schonberg wrote an article in the *New York Times* asserting that every one of Rachmaninoff's performances had a certain sameness, and Horowitz launched into a tirade against Schonberg and critics in general: "He doesn't know anything. Nothing! He lives by records. My God, how can he remember? He probably heard Rachmaninoff two or three times in his life. Rachmaninoff was the most emotional pianist I ever knew. But the critics don't know it. They only know old records. It's like children!"[28] There were repeated diatribes against Columbia Masterworks's bad business sense in not more seriously pursuing renewal of his contract, and against recording in general: "You are at the mercy of machines. They can control you."[29]

During the summer of 1973, Horowitz, following a now-familiar pattern, felt physically exhausted, discouraged, and depressed. "I had a kind of letdown this summer," he told a friend. "It's like a nervous breakdown—but physical, completely physical. My brain is completely normal—it's just that the nervous system didn't work. I walk. I do everything. But I'm tired all the time. Anything I do, I'm tired."[30]

Horowitz refused even to touch the piano for a period of eight months—"Nothing. Now I hate music"—and he sank into a depressive lethargy far worse than anything he had experienced in years. During the early 1960's, he had been successfully treated for depression with electro-shock therapy at New York's Columbia Presbyterian Hospital, and he now returned for further treatments at the hospital's Neurological Institute. But his despair remained. "Art is in a messy shape," he would lament. "It is like *Götterdämmerung.*" Of his own abilities, he complained, "My octaves are no good now; they used to be, but not now."[31] Well-meaning friends would try in vain to cheer him up, but he would simply shake his head. "I'm going through a difficult time," he said. "I'm a funny guy, you know. I'm funny now."[32]

CHAPTER TWENTY-SEVEN

REJUVENATION

"After five years in seclusion I am coming out because I don't want to be a legend. I am not a ghost but a real live human being. I really can play. I can deliver the goods, and letters from young people convinced me I should do it. Now I take no more retirements."[1]

*F*inally, the hospital treatments began to work, and Horowitz's depression lifted and his phobia about appearing in public began to fade. He had spent many evenings with New York concert manager Harold Shaw, over a period of a year and a half, discussing the possibility of making concert tours in 1974 or 1975. "Mr. Shaw was coming to me and sitting here and making millions of dollars planning my tours," Horowitz said. "Then I would go to sleep, and I was nowhere. But he had patience. He was wonderful. He knew that I would play because I looked well."[2] Horowitz began practicing again during the winter and spring of 1974, working on the Clementi F-sharp Minor Sonata, Op. 26, No. 2, Schumann's *Kinderscenen,* Scriabin's *Vers la Flamme,* and, as always, works of Chopin. At age sixty-nine, he was obsessed by the inevitability of growing older and the fear of losing his powers, but he boasted often that his doctors found him to be an exceptional physical specimen. One afternoon, fondling one of the two mild Carlton cigarettes he allowed himself each day, he told reporters, "I'm full of pep, like a man in his 40's or 50's. My doctors say I have a heart of a 45-year-old. I walk 30 to 40 blocks a day; I eat only fowl and fish, no meat, and have not had a drink in 20 years. Look, I have no belly, I am everywhere symmetrical: nice green bow tie, matching handkerchief, everything." Wryly, he added, "Only the nose is a little too long."[3]

Shaw had suggested that Horowitz might want to make his return to the stage on May 10, 1974, Mother's Day, the same day he had returned in 1965, but this time Horowitz did not immediately want to face a New York audience. He did, however, seem to like the idea of traveling to a city not far from home, and Shaw telephoned Michael Maxwell, then manager of the Cleveland Orchestra, to inquire about possible dates in May at Cleveland's Severance Hall. Once the idea was planted, Maxwell pursued Horowitz relentlessly by telephone and letter, reminding him that he had not played in Cleveland for twenty-seven years. "Why don't you start in a part of the country where they're longing for you?" Maxwell asked pointedly, adding, "You'll love the acoustics of Severance Hall."[4]

Horowitz considered the Cleveland proposal seriously but, as usual, put off making a decision. There were, after all, so many other offers. One that especially interested him was an invitation to meet with students at Yale University to play for them and discuss music and his career. The unpredictable Horowitz decided to bring the seminar into his own living room, and on Friday, May 3, thirty-eight Yale students and fifteen friends came to the Ninety-fourth Street townhouse for an informal musicale. Horowitz played two works tentatively scheduled for his return recital— the Clementi F-sharp Minor Sonata and Schumann's *Kinderscenen*. That day Horowitz felt, he said, "terrific." Invigorated by his enthusiastic young audience, he impulsively walked over to Harold Shaw when the minirecital ended and said, "Let's go to Cleveland!"[5] Minus the pressure of committing himself to a date far in advance, Horowitz felt enthusiastic about playing again and was certain he would not be deluged with other offers because it was now the end of the concert season. "I'm not an assembly-line pianist," he told Shaw. "I like to decide very fast."[6]

Although Horowitz was skeptical about the acoustics of modern auditoriums, he received general assurance that he would be pleased with Severance Hall. He would not consider any piano in Cleveland, however, and had his "beauty," as he called his favorite Steinway, hoisted out the window of his Connecticut home and transported to Ohio. The recital was to take place on May 12, and arrangements for it were made almost as quickly as Horowitz's snap decision to play: Maxwell was notified on Monday, tickets were printed and newspaper ads taken out on Tuesday, the concert was announced on Wednesday, and Horowitz flew to Cleveland on Thursday. But Horowitz worried: about flying, about how his piano would sound in Severance Hall, about the weather, about ticket sales. In charge of protecting, encouraging, and calming him was an entourage of five: Wanda, her sister, Wally, Harold Shaw, Franz Mohr, and Ralph Hanes, a young employee at Shaw's company assigned to be Horowitz's valet-secretary on the road.

Shaw had pulled off a tremendous coup in getting Horowitz under his management. He was Horowitz's first manager in twenty-one years, and he had succeeded where so many others had failed by guaranteeing that every concert would be completely handcrafted, that Hanes would travel with Horowitz, and that Horowitz would take a whopping 80 percent of the gross proceeds. The pianist had no intention of ever again subjecting himself to uncomfortable hotels, and Maxwell had secured temporary use of an opulent condominium apartment in Cleveland. After 1974, Horowitz traveled with the luxury that Paderewski had once enjoyed, accompanied by a veritable caravan: his wife, valet, manager, piano tuner, cook, truck driver, family friends and relatives, recording engineers and producers. By regulating his daily routine to the minute, and by approximating his home environment wherever he played, Horowitz managed to be considerably more comfortable on the road than ever before.

In Cleveland two days before the recital, on Friday afternoon, May 10, Horowitz called a press conference at the apartment on Bratenahl Place. Before assembled television, radio, and newspaper reporters, he behaved with an unprecedented ease and exuberance. Perched on a blue chair and surrounded by microphones, Horowitz was costumed in a black suit with a gold vest, a peach-colored shirt, and an orange bow tie crosshatched in thin black lines. Laughing frequently, speaking with great animation, sometimes with an unlighted cigarette dangling from his lips, Horowitz quickly dispelled his public image as a reclusive, tortured genius. "I'll admit I'm nervous," he said, "but I'm not neurotic—just high-strung."[7] Horowitz explained away his latest five-year absence from the stage in a characteristically honest if vague manner: "I had good times, bad times, like any human being. Lots of problems, then sometimes no problems. But I just didn't feel like going to the public. To make a break does purify [but] people think that if an artist like me chooses not to play, then I must be locked up somewhere in a mental home. I am not crazy."[8]

At present, he said, he was considering making a tour of the West Coast, where he had not appeared in over twenty years, and he was also interested in playing in his favorite midwestern cities and college towns. "I'm an old trouper," Horowitz said in a hushed voice. "It's not normal not to play for many years. Now I come back. I will play as much as I can. I don't know if I'll be satisfied with only this one concert. I may go to Chicago and do another. I'm a funny artist. I don't like to make dates very far in advance."[9] Wanda, standing behind him, added occasional parenthetical comments ("Ah, Russian pessimist!" "He's in top form and we're all nervous wrecks!" "If I didn't have a sense of humor after forty years, I wouldn't be here at all.")[10] and from time to time tried to silence him if he mentioned things still in the planning stages—for instance, when Horowitz revealed that he was thinking of videotaping a recital at Yale University to air on National Educational Television, a project that never materialized. During the press conference he revealed that another television program was planned, a portrait of Horowitz at home that the German company UNITEL was undertaking, which never came to fruition either. Finally, he revealed that his contract with Columbia Masterworks had expired and he was on the lookout for a new recording company.

As with most of his press conferences over the next few years, there were few questions of substance at this one, and Horowitz rambled on, entertaining reporters with his good humor and his stock of anecdotes about his meeting with Scriabin, his first Josef Hofmann recital, his early desire to be a composer. He touched on only one controversial subject, the price scale for his Cleveland concert, complaining that the tickets had been set too high. To this, Michael Maxwell later retorted: "Shaw and the Horowitzes told me the tickets *should* be priced very high, and they ranged from five dollars to twenty-five dollars per ticket and we didn't quite sell out."[11] The Horowitzes were displeased by the few empty seats, but they had insisted that no tickets at all be given away, not even to critics who came from other cities. "It's legitimate for the local critics who always review the Cleveland Orchestra to have free tickets. After that, nobody,"[12] Horowitz instructed Maxwell.

His performance on May 12 created something of a sensation. HOROWITZ PLAYS AGAIN, FLABBERGASTINGLY read the headline in the *New York Times;* HOROWITZ: AT 69 STILL WITHOUT PEER AT THE PIANO said the *Chicago Tribune.* After three retirements totaling twenty-two years, Horowitz appeared to be completely at home onstage—"as relaxed and patrician as the king who knows his worth,"[13] said the *New York Post.* Horowitz had proved his point: the huge sonority, the endless shifting of colors and dynamics, the clean-edged octaves, arpeggios, and runs were intact. Technically, in his own words, he "played like a young man."[14] Offering an expansive grin after each selection, Horowitz seemed surprised and delighted by the standing ovations the audience gave him. His listeners were more "hysterical" than ever. Because Horowitz was still in contractual limbo with Columbia, the concert was not recorded, but pirate tapes soon became available in the musical underground, and from them it was possible to confirm a *Chicago Tribune* critic's declaration that "Horowitz simply has more of everything—more tension, more control, more mastery of detail, the miraculous ability to take the emotional temperature of each moment of music as he is creating it, to blend, mold, and fuse feelings into compelling unities, to carry us along to the very end of a mood, however fleeting."[15]

Ignoring the multitude of requests for more concerts, Horowitz said to Wanda soon after the performance, "From here, we go home."[16] Three weeks later, however, he repeated the program in Washington, D.C., after which he retreated to his farmhouse in Connecticut for the summer, to begin work on the Scriabin Fifth Sonata. He promised inquiring concert managers that he would reappear in the fall, "if nothing happens to me."[17]

Contrary to Horowitz's assertion that he performed solely on whim, his appearances throughout 1974 were carefully masterminded both by Shaw and by the New York public-relations firm operated by Bernard Gurtman and Jim Murtha, two of Shaw's former colleagues at Sol Hurok management. Shaw's booking and management firm was not equipped with the kind of sophisticated press department Horowitz required, and unlike Horowitz's 1965 comeback, his reappearance in 1974 did not, at first, automatically generate a deluge of news articles. In fact, when the Cleveland recital was first announced, Shaw was rather alarmed by the diminutive piece that appeared in the *New York Times*. "Horowitz was too vain to admit that he—the legend—needed a public-relations firm," explained Peter Gelb, a young man assigned by Gurtman and Murtha to generate publicity for the Horowitz concerts. "But when we saw the tiny article in the *Times* announcing his Cleveland concert, it was obvious that much more could be done. From 1974 to 1978, we handled Horowitz's public relations and were paid directly by Shaw."[18]

Gelb—twenty-four years old at the time, aggressive, charming, and well-connected through his father Arthur Gelb of the *New York Times*—was capable of dealing with the very different temperaments of the mercurial Horowitz and his formidable business partner, Wanda. "Horowitz was childlike, charming, sweet, innocent, and highly egotistical," recalled Gelb, "and Wanda was the foil for his tough dirty work; for instance, on negotiations of contracts."[19] Harold Shaw understood that Horowitz preferred dealing with young people, that being surrounded by contemporaries depressed him and reminded him that he too was getting older. Shaw therefore left many of the day-to-day operations involved with managing Horowitz to Gelb and the amiable young valet, Ralph Hanes.

Gelb's first publicity move had been to arrange a press conference in Horowitz's living room in May 1974, the first such session there. He quickly discovered Horowitz's impeccable business instincts and talent for public relations. "He had the best sense of self-promotion I'd ever come across in any artist. He was very careful not to be overexposed and chose his offers carefully. He played fewer concerts than anyone else, but his fee was two or three times higher. Instead of the fifteen thousand dollars per concert that Rubinstein was paid in the 1970's, Horowitz took eighty percent of the gross, which amounted to anything from thirty-five thousand to sixty thousand dollars per recital, depending on the size of the house. Since the time that his twelve-year retirement ended, his value as a commodity had risen steadily. His third absence had enhanced his mystique even more and, extremely aware of this, Horowitz wanted to be paid what he believed he deserved. The whole image he projected was that you never knew whether his hands would fall off or not."[20]

The first major event after Horowitz's reappearance in 1974 was a New York recital at the Metropolitan Opera on November 17, 1974. For years, Horowitz had attended the Metropolitan whenever possible and had thought of presenting a recital there, but when he suggested this it had always been turned down by Sir Rudolf Bing, the Met's director. "Bing said that if he let me play there, then Mr. Hurok and other managers would try to push their artists into the house," recalled Horowitz. But by the fall of 1974, Bing had retired and Horowitz's friend Schuyler Chapin was executive director of the Met. Chapin knew that if such an event could be organized it would be a public-relations dream—the first instrumental recital in the Met's eight years at Lincoln Center and the first Horowitz concert in New York in six years, presented to celebrate his seventieth birthday. Chapin decided that a benefit concert would be an excellent way of helping to remedy the Met's dire financial condition, and gave his approval at once.

As Horowitz's decision whether or not to play now depended on whether he liked the hall's acoustics, Chapin was willing to gamble $6,000 on two test sessions, and he instructed Cyril Harris, the Met's distinguished acoustician, to design a special shell for placement behind the piano. Then he ordered three Steinways to be positioned on stage, dead center under the proscenium arch. The first tryout was set for June 9, 1974, with a small group of Horowitz's friends invited to offer advice. "As we walked into the auditorium," recalled Chapin, "I realized that there had been a confusion of instructions. The pianos had not been placed under the proscenium but at the very edge of the orchestra pit. I was furious but there was nothing that could be done as Horowitz appeared on stage ready to start. I sat in the back and was convinced that I'd just poured at least $6,000 down the drain in what was bound to be an abortive test."[21] But the mixup turned out to be a blessing, for the sound was entirely satisfactory to Horowitz; in fact, Harris later chided Chapin that "if the pianos had been where you wanted them, this would not have worked."[22]

At the second rehearsal on October 13, Peter Gelb invited Harold Schonberg to come and to bring along a photographer. A larger group of friends and associates than before were in the hall, including Pfeiffer, Shaw, the Chapins, William F. Buckley, Jr., Pierre Boulez, Carlos Moseley, Ania Dorfman, Alice Tully, Constance Keene, and Olga Strumillo. Dressed in a gray business suit with a red polka-dot bow tie, Horowitz sat at the piano and began warming up by improvising sequences of chords and running passages of scales and arpeggios. But then suddenly he stopped. "Much better last time,"[23] he said to Mohr and Harris, insisting that the curved plywood acoustic shell was now in a different position. The stage crew pushed it back three feet and there was a discernible improvement in sound. During the two-hour rehearsal, Wanda wandered about the 3,700-seat hall, listening, reporting and criticizing. Horowitz eventually decided he was pleased with the hall and also with his performances, so he gave Chapin, Shaw, and Gelb the go-ahead for the announcement of the recital. The following day a prominent article by Schonberg appeared in the *New York Times,* along with a dramatic photograph of Horowitz playing on the cavernous stage of the Metropolitan.

The November 17 concert, billed as Horowitz's only New York appearance of the season, was announced at another press conference in Horowitz's living room in early October. The second floor of the house had been entirely redecorated and the French Impressionist paintings were conspicuously gone. "I had to sell them because of the insurance," Horowitz told the gathered reporters. "I couldn't afford it."[24] Over the long sofa, where the Picasso used to hang, there was now a large, opulent

Japanese screen; over the fireplace, a Chinese painting on glass; nearby, a Japanese painting. The furniture had been re-covered with a flowered black fabric, and touches of gold, black, and red were everywhere apparent in the formal, exquisitely elegant living room.

Both Horowitzes had by then become astute connoisseurs of art and wise investors. Some, in fact, thought them obsessed by money, and they were certainly shrewd about arranging the financial aspects of Horowitz's concerts. In the case of the Metropolitan recital, the net profits were to be split fifty-fifty between the Met and Horowitz. Ticket prices were scaled at $200 apiece for members of the Metropolitan Opera Guild, and from $25 to $5 for the general public. When Chapin subtracted the cost of the rental of the Opera House ($15,000) and the additional $6,000 for the two rehearsals, the total box-office gross for the Met amounted to $106,-000—a record anywhere for a solo recital. One expense Chapin did not have to figure into his budget was advertising and public relations, for Gelb and Horowitz himself stage-managed the sale of tickets and the publicity better than any in-house staff at the Met could have. "It was Horowitz's idea that there would be no mail-order or advance sales," remembered Gelb. "He knew that people would stay up all night waiting in line, and he could bring them coffee and doughnuts and generate the same publicity he attracted with his 1965 return."[25]

The plan was that Horowitz, after a recital in Chicago on November 3, would fly back to New York the following day and make a personal visit to those waiting in line. Although people purchasing tickets usually assembled in the basement of the Metropolitan Opera, this time the line would form outside, to intensify the dramatic impact of the vigil. Gelb was to make certain that television and newspaper reporters were waiting to record Horowitz's magnanimous gesture toward his fans. "In New York, it was highly unusual for a classical music figure to attract front-page coverage," said Gelb, "and it was my job to convince the media editors that Horowitz was not just music news but news news."[26]

On the evening of November 4, all the variables fell into place nicely. Five hundred people were lined up outside the Met, and it was another cold and rainy night. Horowitz came to Lincoln Center directly from the airport. When his car pulled up, he coyly announced that he would not walk across the plaza because photographers were present and he did not want his appearance to be construed as a publicity stunt. In the same spirit, he declared, "I'm sometimes frightened of myself! Always, when I play, the people wait on line for a whole night to buy tickets. Why does it happen?"[27] The photographers agreed to come over and take pictures, and many fans followed them to the car. Horowitz and Wanda had ordered coffee and doughnuts, and then the press snapped pictures of the kindly Maestro tossing his fedora to the cheering crowd.

"Horowitz at the Met" would have been a sure-fire best-selling album, but unfortunately Horowitz still had not reached an agreement with Columbia, and because both sides were being tenaciously stubborn, no recording was made. The November 17 concert, however, was only the first of a string of grand occasions that punctuated Horowitz's career during the 1970's. Imelda Marcos, wife of the president of the Philippines, flew to New York especially for it; Vladimir Ashkenazy changed the hour of his own recital on the same day in order to attend; and the Metropolitan Opera House was filled with luminaries such as Jacqueline and Aristotle Onassis, Herbert von Karajan, Leonard Bernstein, Van Cliburn, Isaac Stern, and Daniel Barenboim. Horowitz was immensely proud of himself for having learned the Scriabin Fifth Sonata the previous summer—"Difficult, but I did it. I still have it, you know. I'm like a young man these days"[28]—and this was his first performance of the work. According to Harold C. Schonberg, it was a "sensational" interpretation: "No living pianist, not even Richter, had this kind of insight into Scriabin's music. Strength, color, phenomenal technique, a surging rhythm, an unfaltering line—everything was there."[29] His performances of the Clementi Sonata in F-sharp Minor, the Schumann *Kinderscenen,* and the Chopin Introduction and Rondo, G Minor Ballade, and two of the mazurkas were also well received.

After successful appearances in Cleveland, Chicago, and New York, Horowitz was ready to accept Shaw's challenge of an extended concert tour. "I haven't gone West in twenty-three years," he mused. "There will be pandemonium if I go to California—they will think it is a ghost."[30] He also began to talk more and more frequently about the possibility of traveling to Europe and Japan.

After the Met concert, Horowitz stayed in New York for the Christmas holidays, planning to escape some of the winter by playing in Houston on February 9, and then in Miami. But on January 10, Horowitz and Wanda received terrible news: Sonia was dead in Geneva. "It was a great shock," Wanda said in an interview. "She was just here for the Metropolitan concert in November."[31] Friends of the family who knew how unhappy Sonia had been were not very surprised. For years Sonia had been depressed, directionless, and in and out of sanatoriums. "She had lots of talents," Wanda said with sorrow, "but she never found her own way. She was not married. She was very musical. At one moment, she painted, then she did photography. She was writing quite well . . . but she could never find her way."[32] There were persistent rumors that the forty-year-old woman had committed suicide, but hardly a ripple of this surfaced in the press. In fact, many of Horowitz's fans had never known he had a daughter, and her infrequent visits to New York were never publicized. Although she had evidently been at the Met concert, no one, not even Horowitz's valet, seemed to remember seeing her, so much was she in the background.

Wanda flew immediately to Milan where Sonia was to be buried in the Toscanini family tomb in the Cimitero Monumentale. Although Horowitz reportedly pondered over what music should be played at the funeral, he did not attend. Sonia, he said, was "always a troubled child,"[33] and his manner of dealing with her death was to become detached. The day after the news reached him, he announced matter-of-factly that he would have to postpone the February concert in Houston—"Tell the people in Houston I'm going to play there, but I just can't do it within the next few weeks."[34] He rescheduled his appearance for March 30. As Wanda observed in a 1978 interview: "He draws an iron curtain around himself. He doesn't let unpleasantness touch him."[35]

It was clear that, in contrast, Wanda was deeply grieved by Sonia's death. In an interview later that year, she fended off all questions on the subject. "I'd rather not talk about it," she told one reporter. "For the moment, I have the impression that I will never recover from it. Although you have to go on living. Life is stronger than death. But I don't think the mother can forget such an experience."[36]

Evidently, however, the father could—or at least could try. Intimates felt that Horowitz considered he had lost Sonia long ago, at the time of her 1957 motorcycle accident. They noted that soon after her death Horowitz became noticeably more extroverted, almost as if a great weight had lifted. For the first time, he began to welcome interviews with newspapers, and he started to plan further concert tours with enthusiasm. In early May, a composer friend, Phillip Ramey, gave a Saturday afternoon party for him and Wanda on the terrace of his West Side penthouse. There were about twenty people, most of them, at Horowitz's request, young, and few of them, also at his request, pianists. Remembered Ramey: "A half an hour before, I took a taxi across the park to pick them up. Volodya was smiling and in good spirits, but Wanda was looking grim. It was a beautiful spring day, and I was dressed in a sport jacket and open-necked shirt, while the Horowitzes were more elegantly attired. As we left the house, I noticed Wanda glaring at my tieless neck; suddenly she stopped dead and said, 'I'm sorry, Mr. Ramey, I don't think this is a party for me,' and turned on her heel. In the taxi, Volodya grinned and said, 'Don't worry. Now we'll have more fun! She is depressed and neurotic and very difficult. You know, her daughter died.' I was a little startled by that, and shot back, 'Her daughter?' 'Yeah,' he replied, suddenly looking glum." At the party, Horowitz was charming and convivial, and at one point he took pleasure in posing for photographs with some of the guests. "I remember," said Ramey, "an amusing shot of him with one of my woman friends: she, looking rather like a 1920's flapper with beads and a long cigarette holder, had an arm thrown over his shoulder while he smiled contentedly."[37]

Eventually Wanda, philosophizing that "life was stronger than death," emerged from her depression. She went more frequently to parties and began to travel, eager to sample everything with, as one friend put it, "a rage to live."[38]

Sonia's death made no difference to Horowitz's schedule for the remainder of that season. He traveled to Miami for a recital on March 23, to Houston on the thirtieth, to Ann Arbor on April 20; he played a repeat of the Met recital at Carnegie Hall on April 27 and at Ohio State University on May 18. Once again, he spoke excitedly of Japan: "Oh my God, the offers! Japan offered me fabulous money, but it's too far to travel."[39] He announced a tour to California for the 1975–76 season, dropped new hints about playing with orchestra, and revealed plans for a four-hand recital with Rudolf Serkin to be presented in Vermont that summer on the twenty-fifth anniversary of the Marlboro School. Horowitz intended to perform the Schubert F Minor Fantasy and *Scherzo Brillante* with Serkin, "who I love like a brother,"[40] but he canceled that concert. He was engrossed in learning a new work, Schumann's Sonata No. 3 in F Minor (*Concerto Without Orchestra*), which he described as "one of the most gigantic pieces of Romantic music, which is for some inexplicable reason neglected."[41] Although there were half a dozen recordings of the work available, Horowitz spoke of it as if it were his personal discovery and was clearly proud of being able to master such a big work at his age. "Serkin was the only pianist who played the Sonata twenty-five years ago, and he said it took him eight months to memorize it,"[42] Horowitz told a reporter. "If I don't do research, if I don't look up new things, then I feel older. All the books and all the musicologists put this work down, and I disagree with them. . . . Liszt, who knew something about piano playing, called it one of Schumann's greatest works."[43] In interviews throughout the 1975–76 season, Horowitz continually emphasized the extreme difficulty of the work, especially the moto perpetuo of the last movement.

When Horowitz finally performed the Schumann Sonata in March 1976, he might well have been disappointed by the critical reaction. The *Boston Herald* asserted that "Horowitz himself doesn't really understand what is happening," and that the performance was "disjunct," and "incomprehensible."[44] The *Boston Globe* pointed out that "technical problems didn't seem to faze him; the musical ones did not concern him at all. The result was a pretty dazzling, incoherent jumble of fragments."[45] Indeed, one apparent manifestation of aging was his increased fixation on details to the point of fragmentation: entire movements of a sonata, the exposition, even one phrase, were sometimes broken apart. When Horowitz played the Schumann *Arabesque,* for instance, one critic wrote that the performance was "impossibly sectionalized, lurching, fragmented . . . changes of pace, rhythm and color mark not only formal divisions and individual phrases but also nothing in particular—one had the feeling listening to this grotesque performance that if it were possible to fragment the sound of a single note on the piano once it had been struck and pedaled, Horowitz would want to."[46] Harold Schonberg countered that Horowitz had always concentrated on details—for instance, the weighting of a chord or the color and rubato of a phrase—and while admitting the habit was now more pronounced, he maintained that "Horowitz's playing, as heroic and singing as ever, as boldly romantic and idiosyncratic, has to be taken on its own terms."[47]

During the 1970's, Horowitz not only had little respect for critics, but their comments no longer had much effect on him. He was far more concerned with appearing as frequently as possible and arranging lucrative contracts. In the fall of 1975, the most pressing matter at hand was to become affiliated with a new record company. He had left the lines open at Columbia ("We were close to a contract"[48]), but since no agreement was forthcoming, he began to consider a change. Angel, Capitol, and Deutsche Grammophon were all interested, but in the end Horowitz decided to return to the familiar ground of RCA. Just as he had gone to Columbia in 1962 because he liked and trusted Goddard Lieberson and Schuyler Chapin, he now opted for RCA because its president, Kenneth Glancey, seemed to Horowitz a good businessman and also a good musician. There was also the added benefit of having Jack Pfeiffer producing his records again. As Horowitz explained it, "All the old staff which had been there in the 1950's were gone or retired. Some of them were kicked out and Mr. Glancey is a very great friend of mine."[49] Horowitz felt wanted and needed by RCA. Indeed, since Glancey became president in 1973, one of his main goals had been to bring Horowitz back to the Red Seal label, and after much negotiation, Horowitz agreed to return for the same $50,000 per record he had received from Columbia. Horowitz now spoke happily about the possibility of making his first concerto recording in twenty-six years, of giving a concert in Milan at La Scala, of having all of his upcoming recitals recorded. "It was," remembered Glancey, "like a new life for Horowitz in 1974 and 1975. New concert manager, the PR firm of Gurtman and Murtha, new record company, giving concerts again—a string of cascading successes until 1978, the climax."[50]

CHAPTER TWENTY-EIGHT

ON THE
ROAD AGAIN

*"I think the most important thing in a man's life is
health—mental and physical health. If you have both those
things, then you can do anything. You get older and something
happens to you. Of that I am a little bit frightened. But now
I'm full of pep, like forties or fifties. I can go on and on."*[1]

*D*uring the 1975–76 season, Horowitz scheduled his most extensive
tour since 1953. Harold Shaw booked twenty appearances for him in the
United States and Canada, mostly in the Midwest and on the West
Coast, in cities where Horowitz had not appeared in decades—Seattle,
Portland, Oakland, Pasadena, Los Angeles, Minneapolis, Ann Arbor
(University of Michigan), Ames, Iowa (University of Iowa), Blooming-
ton, Indiana (Indiana University). "Planning tours was fun for
Horowitz and Wanda, rather like mapping out a presidential campaign,"[2] recalled Ralph Hanes of the Shaw office. Wanda prided herself
on her fiscal acumen, and while her husband had the final say, she was
pleased that both Shaw and Horowitz recognized her to be a valuable
business partner. "They say I have a managerial instinct,"[3] Wanda declared proudly. She could also be of practical use. Hanes remembered her
skill at packing a suitcase "so the suit came out better than when it went
in. In every way, she was indispensable to him."[4]

On several occasions Horowitz sat in his living room late into the
night, listening intently as Wanda, Shaw, and Hanes worked out the upcoming tour. He would cackle with delight upon hearing that the local
management in Sarasota was willing to pay his expenses, and rub his
hands with glee thinking of the luxurious manner in which he would
now be traveling. "Until the 1970's, Horowitz had not entirely realized
that he could perform on his own terms," said Peter Gelb, "and that the
concert world would both accommodate his demands and pay him nearly
three times as much as any other artist."[5]

Horowitz's many years away from the stage had cost him considerable income and now he was determined to take advantage of his mystique by charging as much as possible for his concerts. "For years, I sat home and didn't make one cent. . . . It was too long. I'm entitled to make a lot of money now; I'm regaining what I lost."[6] Next to acoustics, money was the most important issue in determining which cities he would play in. "I play now where managers can afford to pay me,"[7] he declared. Even the problem of transportation, which had for years been an obstacle to touring, disappeared in January 1976, when Horowitz took his first long trip by air since 1953, from New York to Seattle, and said that he had enjoyed it. "I went to the pilots immediately to find out the route and to make sure they weren't drinking," he told a reporter in Seattle. "I was frightened of planes, but now I am the Lindbergh of the piano!"[8]

A unique aspect of Horowitz's recital at the Seattle Center Opera House on January 24 was the presence of one hundred Japanese fans, who had traveled from their homeland solely to hear Horowitz. He continued to receive lucrative offers from Japan, but feared that the flight there would be too long and that the time difference would upset his equilibrium. Yet he maintained, "I will do it finally, like I do everything,"[9] and had even sent Wanda to Japan to appraise the acoustics of concert halls in Tokyo, Kyoto, Yokohama, and Osaka. In Seattle, Horowitz, touched by his Japanese fans, invited them to a rehearsal and allowed hundreds of photographs of himself to be taken with them.

Horowitz explained to reporters that a number of factors had gone into his decision to concertize widely again. "First of all," he said, "I like to fly. Second, I play only once a week or every second week so it's not too much. Third, the public enjoys it and they like me. You see, I just discovered that myself, that they love me. And that gives me pleasure since that means they need me. If they need me, I will not be selfish and sit at home."[10] This was a major departure from the past, when Horowitz felt pressured by audience demands and unequal to the brilliance expected from him.

Realizing at last that he would be accepted whatever he chose to do, he no longer worried about playing easily comprehensible repertory. "Before, I was always aware there was a public in the hall, and I played to please them and selected music that I thought would be pleasing to them; today I play music I want and I just try to do my best. Whether the public likes the music I play or not, I don't give a damn."[11]

Horowitz's new, rather cavalier attitude sometimes, even in his own mind, bordered on being "a little bit conceited."[12] "Even when I play not so good, it's good enough," he told one interviewer. "You see, I know it, but the audience doesn't know it, and sometimes even the critics don't know it."[13]

Over the next four seasons, Horowitz would learn one or two new solo works each year, most of them somewhat off the beaten track. During 1975–76, he tackled the Schumann Sonata in F Minor, Op. 14; the following year, the Clementi Sonata Quasi Concerto in C Major, Op. 33. In 1978, aside from resurrecting the Liszt B-Minor Sonata, he added the Fauré Nocturne No. 13 in B Minor, Op. 119, and Impromptu No. 5, Op. 102, to his repertory. "We have special periods in this house," Wanda said, laughingly. "Whole weeks of Medtner or Fauré—who knows?"[14] Horowitz always wanted his repertory to remain secret until the last possible moment, because "the young pianists always copy the older person."[15]

In 1979, after a hard summer of work on a group of Schumann pieces, a Clementi sonata and the seldom-programmed Mendelssohn Scherzo a Capriccio in F-sharp Minor, Horowitz pleaded with a photographer: "Try not to show too much the bags under my eyes—that is because I'm working very hard right now. My nose I don't care; it is big but my wife says it is a Roman nose and she likes it. Most important, don't make me too old," said the seventy-five-year-old pianist. "I'm just fifty-eight. I made my debut at age eight. I feel very young."[16] Nonetheless, mistakes became more frequent in these years, and he was forced to admit, "I am bad for memorizing. Mozart or Beethoven sonatas I can learn in three days, but when it comes to a Fauré nocturne, that takes time. I have no photographic memory."[17]

Horowitz no longer cared what inconvenience his demands for personal attention might cause any local management. "He fed on special treatment and loved to be pampered," observed Gelb. "He knew that the more eccentric, elusive, and demanding he was, the more the public would respond to him."[18] At times, Horowitz quite reveled in his elusive mystique, as when he told the *Toronto Star,* "I am like a ghost now. People come to put flowers on my grave."[19]

Horowitz had told Shaw many times that playing the piano was "the easiest thing in the world. It's all the things around playing the piano that drive me crazy."[20] It was Shaw's responsibility to assure that

Horowitz did not have to concern himself with any of the little and not-so-little curses of touring—poor pianos, eating in restaurants, unfamiliar beds, noisy accommodations. Before each concert, Shaw sent out a detailed list of instructions to local managers on how the Horowitzes expected to be treated. This included some odd items, such as "Is there a fish store that stocks fresh grey sole in your city?" and "Please list the name, address, and telephone number for the meat market with the best chicken."[21] The fussy Horowitz made no exceptions as far as being served either grey sole or red snapper for dinner and chicken for breakfast and lunch, and in 1977 he refused an offer to play in Miami unless the local manager arranged to have eleven fillets of grey sole flown down from New Bedford, Massachusetts.

Further, the Horowitzes were to be met at airports with a large limousine, unless the concert was in one of the smaller college towns, in which case a large station wagon would do. Their accommodations had to be within easy driving distance of both the fish and meat markets and the concert hall, and located in an area of the city suitable for Horowitz's daily constitutionals. Wanda, Shaw, or Hanes would sometimes fly ahead weeks in advance to make sure the living arrangements were acceptable. Occasionally Horowitz took advantage of the hospitality of wealthy music lovers who were willing to move out of their homes or apartments for the duration of Horowitz's visit so that he could have absolute quiet and privacy. His specifications for his home-away-from-home were detailed: the living room had to be large enough to comfortably fit a nine-foot Steinway, the kitchen must be fully equipped with cooking utensils, china and glassware, and serving trays for four. Aside from bringing his own piano, which was trucked ahead, Horowitz also had his own water purifier, as he feared that local water might upset his hypersensitive digestive tract.

On the truck along with the piano were specially fitted suitcases containing Horowitz's personal omelette pans and thick black-velvet draperies for his bedroom. Shaw's questionnaire always required careful measurement of windows because "spring-type curtain rods will be inserted in the sills for black-out thick draperies."[22] Local managers found themselves on their hands and knees helping tape the windows with three preparatory layers of brown paper that Horowitz insisted be in place before the special curtains were hung. His bedroom also had to be equipped with twelve wooden hangers, a firm double bed, a nightstand for his pajamas, a straight-backed chair, and an adjoining bathroom with a stool for washing—this because he would not take a bath or a shower in a strange environment for fear he might slip and fall. If there was a telephone in the room, it had to be removed. When members of the press or local managers called attention to Horowitz's eccentricities, Wanda became incensed, maintaining "he's no more difficult than any other husband. Some woman might prefer an IBM businessman, but my father, Toscanini, was also a famous name in music. I watched my mother manage him and I have emulated her."[23]

The Horowitz traveling party included Jack Pfeiffer and several RCA engineers, who usually arrived a day or two before a performance with Franz Mohr, the piano tuner. When special problems arose, Shaw often would fly in and stand backstage during a recital, ready to calm Horowitz's nerves and collect the check from the local manager. Otherwise, the regulars in the entourage were Wanda, valet Ralph Hanes, driver-bodyguards Toby McCallum or Duane Lewin, and Wanda's close friend Sally Horwich, who kept her company, provided a fourth for canasta, and helped with the cooking. "I dislike cooking; it makes me nervous," Wanda once confided. "But I like to eat well. I do some cooking while on tour with a friend—we take turns."[24] Whether in Los Angeles, Seattle, or Ann Arbor, Horowitz maintained his daily routine of walking, rehearsing, napping, eating, and staying up until one or two o'clock in the morning to play cards and talk. Often, he arrived in a city a few days before a recital and remained there as much as a week later—sometimes even two weeks if the climate was warm.

Around the country, local managers were given to understand that Horowitz played only on Sunday afternoons at four, and that the hall had to be equipped with an orchestra shell; it also must be available for rehearsal the day before the concert, so that Horowitz could test the acoustics, verify the lighting, and position his piano. Clearly, a Horowitz visit was a demanding occasion for a manager. It also was not a very lucrative one since Horowitz took 80 percent of the gross and required many unusual expenditures. In one concert hall seating 3,070, with 150 onstage, for instance, the total of box-office receipts in the late 1970's amounted to $48,965, and $39,152 of this went to the pianist. As the local manager had to spend approximately $7,000 on advertising, tickets, programs, and mailings, his net profit was practically nil.

Nonetheless, many managers felt that the prestige of having Horowitz in their series compensated for their meager profits, and they became angry only when Horowitz suddenly canceled performances. He was highly susceptible to the weather, and with him a cold easily turned into bronchitis. Hanes recalled that "he was physically extremely sensitive, like a barometer, and had continuous problems with his digestion, his colitis, his throat, his fingers—you name it."[25] During the 1970's, Horowitz's cancellations became more and more frequent, and local managers often found themselves caught with sold-out houses and empty pockets. There were any number of reasons given for Horowitz's lapses. "Sometimes he would cancel because of physical illness," said one Shaw employee, "or because of the weather, or fatigue, or because the house was not sold out, or simply because he didn't feel like appearing in a particular city."[26]

When Horowitz canceled a performance in Portland, Oregon, the manager there, his old Russian friend, Ariel Rubstein, had already spent an estimated $8,000 on promoting the concert. "He canceled because he was afraid the house would not be sold out; he said he had a cold but he played in California the following week," recalled Rubstein. He sent the Shaw office a bill for $3,000, but this was neither paid nor acknowledged. "When Shaw's assistant, Paul Gregory, called me to later arrange another date in Portland, I told him what I thought of Horowitz. He is a great artist, yes. But not a great man."[27]

Horowitz, though, insisted that "when I have a cold I don't play, because I don't have the right to play for the public or myself if I am not in top form. I have to be one hundred percent well."[28] Wanda herself admitted that Horowitz "is a little spoiled,"[29] and local newspapers became increasingly impatient with his high-handed behavior. When a Cleveland concert was called off because of a supposed intestinal infection, one critic suggested what that meant was that Horowitz had no stomach for the trip to Cleveland. In April 1977, Horowitz developed a case of water on the knee and canceled a recital in Cincinnati. Danny Deeds, the local manager, believed that Horowitz really canceled "because we did not expect to sell out the house. But the following week he played in Buffalo. Earlier, Shaw had told me that if our ticket sales did not improve, Horowitz would find some way of canceling the concert and indeed he did. I spent seven thousand dollars promoting the concert and wanted to be reimbursed. Shaw refused, citing the paragraph in Horowitz's contract which states the management doesn't have to pay anything if there's a legitimate reason for Horowitz's absence."[30] Deeds finally settled out of court, but went into bankruptcy and had to accept a mere $3,000, which Shaw paid only with reluctance.

One way Horowitz had of avoiding such problems was to refuse to sign a contract with a local manager until *after* he gave the concert. In 1978 one manager, Charles Robb of the Philadelphia Performing Arts Society, decided not to put up with this highly unorthodox practice. In the 1977–78 season, Horowitz had twice canceled appearances at the Philadelphia Academy of Music, first because of a hangnail and then because of snow, and Robb's firm lost $12,000. Horowitz did finally give his Philadelphia recital on Easter Sunday, 1978. But after that experience Robb decided to play it safe, so he demanded a signed contract from Horowitz well in advance of another Philadelphia appearance, scheduled for November 6, 1978. When Robb did not receive a signed contract in a reasonable time, he sent out cancellation notices for the completely sold-out house. "It's the first time in my life any concert manager has done this to me," complained an outraged and incredulous Horowitz. "I was all ready to play. I certainly will not work with that man anymore."[31] To which Robb retorted, "This is a business arrangement and Horowitz is not God!"[32]

Once, the tables were turned. On April 25, 1975, Horowitz gave a recital in Montreal, and the local manager presented him with a check for $35,123.91. But when Horowitz returned to New York and deposited the check it bounced. The promoter of the concert declared bankruptcy, and Horowitz was furious: "I will never go to Canada as long as I live," he told Harold Shaw, but he relented two seasons later when he decided to appear in Toronto.

Usually, Horowitz, coddled by his entourage, was impervious to criticism. He left Harold Shaw to absorb any ire and settle legal disputes. For the glory of being Horowitz's manager, Shaw accepted a reduced commission rate, and he more than earned every penny of it in a job that became enormously time-consuming and frustrating. As one Shaw employee saw it, "That was the most humiliating situation you can imagine. The Horowitzes took eighty percent, made extraordinary demands on Shaw and then treated him like a servant. No one would have stood for that humiliation except for the money and prestige of having Horowitz on the list."[33]

Perhaps worst of all, if tickets to a recital were not sold out, if there was any snag in traveling arrangement or a misprint in the program, if accommodations were not perfect, if an electrician or a piano tuner was not prompt enough at a rehearsal, if a chauffeur was not polite to the right degree, if a partition was not immediately available to be placed in front of those sitting on the stage, if any other major or minor problem arose—then Shaw would have to answer to Wanda. Horowitz once publicly stated that his wife had "an Italian temper," to which Wanda retorted, "No—Italian-Toscanini!"[34] Impresarios everywhere were terrified of her, and in the press she was described (to her delight) as being as stubborn and brilliant as her father: "a formidable woman in her 60s [who] sails into a room with the authority of a ship's figurehead and a voice that can reduce mortals to tears."[35] "I'm a very independent person," she told one interviewer. "I'm straightforward and simply can't lie. I speak right out, and even if I don't say anything my face seems to give me away when I don't like somebody. But I do a very good job for my husband."[36]

Few things angered Wanda as much as empty seats at a Horowitz concert, and despite the astounding profits they were seeing, she would not tolerate any excuses from local managers. In 1979, at a recital at Constitution Hall in Washington, D.C., a few seats were not sold, and Theodore Libbey, then music critic for the *Washington Star,* later recalled that "the top price for a ticket was thirty-five dollars, which I found unprecedented and incredible. There were sixty-four seats unsold when the concert began. Wanda Horowitz came into the box-office in a rage and stood counting those sixty-four tickets at the window, over and over again. She was angry as hell for losing the money and it was embarrassing to see her venal impulse to count those tickets repeatedly until the management was humiliated."[37] As for Horowitz's attitude on the subject, when a Milwaukee concert promoter met him at the airport in 1977 and went into a how-proud-we-are speech, Horowitz gave him an icy glare. "I wouldn't be so proud," he snapped. "I hear you're not sold out."[38]

However, Horowitz almost always played to a full house, and according to his 1978 tour manager, he seemed to be much impressed with his drawing power. "Horowitz was very proud of the fact that he could get people to put out so much money to hear him play. That truly thrilled and amused him. He constantly told the story of the bellhop in Los Angeles who informed Horowitz that he had paid $35 to a scalper for a ticket. I would have given the poor boy $100 just for his enthusiasm, but

Horowitz never thought of getting him a free ticket."[39] Horowitz did, though, give the adoring bellhop a $5 tip. "Now it costs him only thirty dollars,"[40] he told a reporter.

The Horowitzes together often gave amusing performances during press conferences in various cities in the 1970's. Their stock comments were so well rehearsed that once when Horowitz arrived late he told reporters quite sincerely, "She can do a good job without me."[41] At such sessions, Horowitz was chatty and liked to say whatever came to his mind, while Wanda was more restrained, generally standing behind her husband, at all times ready to intervene if she felt he had become too personally revealing. At a press conference in Chicago in 1977, Wanda suddenly decided she wished to give the struggling musicians of America a piece of good advice, and asked reporters to turn off their recorders so she could speak off the record. Some of them did not, so the incident is preserved on tape, and one can hear Horowitz, knowing what she's about to say, groaning, "She's very rude, she's very rude!"[42] Wanda then launches into her diatribe: "No, I'm realistic. I wasn't born with talent to play the piano, so I didn't play. If you want to study music and you are not on top, chamber music is important. But if they are not talented . . . they are struggling because, let's face it, they have small fees, and they come home and they don't eat. So I say, go to a nice school to learn how to be a cook and a butler and you have the most fantastic career—money up to here. They can have five hundred dollars a week." Horowitz, in a disapproving voice, is heard saying, "She is like her papa," to which a reporter rejoins, "She's prettier than papa though!" "She looks like him," sniffs Horowitz, concluding, "I am more diplomatic." Retorts Wanda, "I am not diplomatic, no, but I feel sorry for them."[43]

During the late 1970's, Horowitz became increasingly gregarious. He enjoyed noting that "luckily I am not shy like Rachmaninoff; I am what you call an extrovert." He basked in the public limelight and consented to public-relations gestures unimaginable earlier in his career. When RCA released "The Horowitz Concerts 1975–76," for instance, he was persuaded by Jack Pfeiffer and Peter Gelb to sign autographs in New York at the Korvette department store on Fifth Avenue. At first visibly nervous under the hot television lights, facing one thousand noisy fans, he soon began to enjoy himself, and would boast for weeks after that even a celebrity like Tony Randall had waited in a long line to buy his record.

On December 31, 1977, Peter Gelb persuaded Horowitz, Wanda, and

Sally Horwich to spend an evening at the glittery New York disco, Studio 54. "A gay guy came over and started to kiss Horowitz's feet in adoration," Gelb recalled, "and Wanda poured a bottle of Dom Perignon over the kid's head. I asked her why and she answered 'to cool him off.' "[44] Horowitz told friends that he much preferred an evening at a disco to television or the movies. "I have a tremendous concentration during the day," he said, "and for recreation I like to be a child, a complete child. For three hours, just to go and see how young people dance. I don't drink but if you give me something, just accidentally, then I can dance."[45] Indeed, several months later, on his seventy-fifth birthday, he went back to Studio 54, and this time photographers caught him and Wanda on the dance floor. Although Wanda admitted that Studio 54 wasn't exactly her preference, "this was his birthday, so I'll do anything."[46] With cotton stuffed in his ears, Horowitz stayed at the disco until two in the morning and tipped that night's honorary bartender, Bianca Jagger, $50 for a drink. Increasingly, Horowitz ventured out to gay bars and discos alone, or accompanied by young men from Shaw's office. The older he grew, the freer he seemed to become, anxious to meet men and remain sexually active. "It's very different from the way it used to be," he told a reporter. "You know, because of sexual liberation. In those days it was all *en cachet,* under the table. Now everything is out in the open, which is very healthy: it's *on* the table and I like to see how far it goes."[47]

Although Wanda tolerated Horowitz's antics with a certain resignation and even, occasionally, amusement, there were times when her patience wore thin. One evening, Phillip Ramey arrived at East Ninety-fourth Street dressed in a black-velvet tuxedo and white lace shirt. A few minutes later, Wanda swept into the living room in an elegant designer's gown. "Wanda, Wanda, look how beautiful," Horowitz said of Ramey. "It's as if Chopin visits me!" With a half smile at Ramey, Wanda replied, "Yes, he looks very good. And I look very good. And you? That same old bow tie!"[48] Horowitz grinned at their guest and shrugged. Not long after, Wanda and Ramey began to discuss one of her favorite subjects, the Roman Catholic Church's position on birth control, which they both considered irresponsible. Horowitz, lying full-length on his side on the couch, elegant buckled loafers resting on a pillow, suddenly interjected, with an innocent smile, "The homosexuals will save the world." Pretending not to have heard, Wanda continued her tirade. Again,

Horowitz's voice, this time louder: "The homosexuals will save the world." Not looking at her husband, Wanda paused, her brows beetling, and then started to tell Ramey how enraged Toscanini used to become with the Church over birth control. Suddenly, the voice from the couch, now emphatic: "But I'm *telling* you—the homosexuals will save the world!" Wanda then abruptly turned and snapped, *"Quiet, you!"* at which Horowitz flinched, closed his eyes, and lapsed into silence for the next fifteen minutes.[49]

It was apparent to all who knew the Horowitzes that Wanda was still very much in charge of their domestic life. Horowitz remained hypersensitive to any criticism from her. Once, when publicity pictures were taken in California, Horowitz showed them proudly to Pfeiffer, obviously pleased. Wanda took a quick look and snapped that he was too old to be photographed. The photos were never subsequently approved for release on any of Horowitz's records and he reportedly pouted for weeks afterwards. Although Wanda undeniably protected him from outside intrusions, she herself sometimes greatly upset him; apparently, however, she regarded that as her prerogative. At one rehearsal at Philadelphia's Academy of Music, Wanda sat in the audience with Jack Pfeiffer, talking loudly as onstage Horowitz tried to concentrate. "Quiet, please," he said, but Wanda paid no attention. After repeated pleas for silence, Horowitz finally stopped playing, turned out to the audience and asked, "Wanda, Wanda, how did it sound?" But there was no answer, for Wanda was still noisily conversing with Pfeiffer. Finally, Horowitz shrugged. "I guess today she don't speak to me," he said sadly, and turned his attention back to the piano.[50]

However, on the day of a concert, even Wanda followed Horowitz's strict set of rules. He would awaken at about noon, have his usual breakfast, ignore the piano, and remain utterly silent, expecting the same from everyone around him. He explained, "I don't have stage fright, but nervous anticipation, yes. I want to give the best I can. I'm only nervous to play the conception I have in my head. I am nervous to know if it will come out from me or not. Maybe I will have a cramp. I'm only a human being. The problem is that at exactly four o'clock on Sunday I have to be on top and if at that moment I am not . . . I don't have the right to play. That's what is difficult, the timing of things. The only minute which is unpleasant is the minute when I stand in the wings, just before coming in."[51]

But once his handkerchief had been placed inside the piano and he was comfortably seated on the long bench that he carted everywhere, Horowitz felt that he was sovereign in the auditorium, ready to give his "message to the public." "Without false modesty, I feel that when I am on the stage, I'm the king. Nobody may interfere with me because I have something to do. I have my integrity. I have my duty.[52]

Onstage, Horowitz was able to immerse himself completely in the music he was playing, and his concentration had a like effect on his audience. "Once I sit down I transform myself. I see the composer. I am the composer. The music gives me that sense. It needs a lot of concentration to achieve [that] and a lot of electricity. Then, the current has to reach the public and wrap them. I want them to feel what I feel. I want when I cry on the piano or when I laugh that the public also cries and laughs [but] sometimes I feel they are not with me, and I am unhappy. So I gradually try to seduce them. If I don't succeed with one piece, then I try another with another sound, a more spectacular playing. Pyrotechnics or something like that. Then I go back to something more concentrated, more quiet. That's how I build a program. In the end they will be with me. Unless I don't feel well. Silence is the greatest thing. When you get silence in the audience, it means you are a success."[53]

After a concert, Horowitz's fans would line up outside the greenroom and a few of them, mostly musicians and local dignitaries, would be allowed backstage for a few minutes with the Maestro until Wanda, Sally, or Shaw indicated with a nod that the audience was over. "When I finish I am happy to go home. I go to bed right away. I sleep fifteen minutes, half an hour. I wake up. I dine. I feel like there was no concert."[54]

During the 1976–77 season, Horowitz embarked on a tour of seventeen cities, carefully coordinating his appearances so that he could enjoy the warmth of California during the winter. No New York recital was scheduled that year since Horowitz was saving up for a spectacular series of concerts to celebrate the fiftieth anniversary of his American debut in January 1978. His last appearance in New York before his Golden Jubilee was on May 18, 1976, when he was to appear in a unique chamber-music performance to help celebrate the eighty-fifth birthday of Carnegie Hall. Isaac Stern and Julius Bloom had decided to organize a gala concert, the proceeds of which would help to create a $6.5 million Carnegie Hall National Endowment Fund. Both Bloom and Stern managed to persuade many of the most illustrious musicians of the day to participate in the event, billed as "The Concert of the Century"—among them, Leonard Bernstein, Dietrich Fischer-Dieskau, Yehudi Menuhin, Mstislav Rostropovich, Martina Arroyo, the Oratorio Society of New York, and members of the New York Philharmonic. There were to be no solo roles in this concert, which was conceived, rather, in terms of ensembles, with the various musicians performing together in a sonata, double concerto, a *lieder* cycle, and a trio. All of the artists were to donate their services.

Horowitz, of course, felt a deep affection for Carnegie Hall, where he had enjoyed so many triumphs, and he liked the idea of playing chamber music, especially a song-cycle with Fischer-Dieskau. "Horowitz told me that he was going to return the favor one day after I helped him come back in 1965,"[55] Bloom recalled. Nevertheless, when the idea of the concert was first broached, Horowitz was typically hesitant because he was enthusiastic, indeed firmly opposed, to performing in concert with Isaac Stern. The relationship between Stern and Horowitz had never been a close one and Horowitz said he wouldn't play with him. He could never warm up to Stern as a person and used to say half-jokingly, "Don't call it 'Carnegie Hall,' call it 'Isaac Stern Hall,' " because he felt Stern was imposing too much of his own personal image on the hall. Stern, on the other hand, was eager to play with Horowitz, hungry for the status of such an opportunity, and finally persuaded Horowitz to agree to an informal evening meeting on Ninety-fourth Street. But Horowitz's cold demeanor that night quickly prompted Stern to telephone Bloom for help.

"When I arrived the atmosphere was freezing," said Bloom. "Horowitz was glad to see me and during the entire evening he played the Rachmaninoff Cello Sonata, croaking out the cello part and flatly ignoring the Sterns and the matter at hand, the idea of programming the first movement of the Tchaikovsky A Minor Piano Trio with Stern and Rostropovich." Sitting on the piano bench next to Horowitz and turning pages, Bloom whispered in his ear, "Volodya, look, you've just got to do the Tchaikovsky with Stern; otherwise life is not going to be bearable"; to which Horowitz hissed, "He doesn't practice enough. I just can't play with a man like that."[56]

Eventually breaking away from Wanda, Stern came to the piano to see how things were going. Bloom told him Horowitz never made a decision until one in the morning and that he must be patient. "Please do something," Stern implored Bloom in an aside. "We've got to play the Tchaikovsky." At one in the morning, Horowitz told Bloom he would decide

by noon the following day, which Bloom recognized as Horowitz's be-
grudging way of saying yes. The next day Horowitz did in fact consent
to play with Stern, and also expressed his desire to accompany Fischer-
Dieskau in the entire Schumann *Dichterliebe*. Stern agreed, and Horowitz
was then signed for his first chamber-music appearance since the 1930's.

On the day of the trio rehearsal at Horowitz's house, Stern and Rostropovich got caught in traffic and arrived late. Horowitz came down the
stairs in his pajamas and bathrobe. "I have only half an hour," he said,
"because I have to have lunch."[57] The rehearsal went extremely well and
ended at three o'clock, Rostropovich packing away his cello for a flight
back to Washington, D.C. But then Horowitz began playing a few notes
from the Rachmaninoff Cello Sonata, which he had always wanted to
play with Rostropovich. "The next thing I knew," recalled Stern, "Slava
literally dove under the piano for his cello, opened it up, and began to
play. Volodya yelled for his wife to find the music, and the two of them
read through the slow movement and then the first. Volodya's immov-
able lunch took place at 5 P.M.!"[58]

The next day, Martina Arroyo called Stern to say that she had
wrenched her back during a performance of *Aida* in Dallas and would be
unable to participate in the concert. So, in her place, Stern asked
Horowitz and Rostropovich if it would be possible to prepare the second
movement of the Rachmaninoff with only one afternoon rehearsal on the
day of the performance. Both said yes.

On Tuesday afternoon, May 18, Horowitz arrived at Carnegie Hall for
the rehearsal looking dapper in a brown-and-white-checked jacket, rust-
colored trousers and matching rust bow tie, and gray suede gloves. He
was discernibly tense, for he disliked performing at night and it had been
such a long time since he'd played chamber music. But under the spell of
Rostropovich's expansive personality, Horowitz slowly relaxed and
began to enjoy himself during the rehearsal. "Horowitz found a Russian
brother in Rostropovich," recalled Bloom. "Their Russian heritage and
mutual respect established a rapport that was mirrored in what turned
out to be the most moving and technically polished performance of the
evening."[59] About the Rachmaninoff, *Rolling Stone* later commented that
"here were two sons of Mother Russia carrying on a conversation so
tender, so loving and so Russian that only a Nabokov could describe the
bittersweetness of the memories that must have been passing through
their heads."[60] At the end of their performance, Rostropovich gave
Horowitz a bear hug and the two left the stage ecstatic, almost tearful.

The rapport between Fischer-Dieskau and Horowitz was hardly less intense. At the rehearsal, Horowitz looked up at the baritone and smiled, saying, "We are very much together. I feel when you breathe."[61] Before the performance, Horowitz had difficulty determining the protocol for coming on stage with another great artist—who went first? Horowitz suggested they go together, so out they came, the towering Fischer-Dieskau hand in hand with the much slighter Horowitz, and that was how they took their curtain calls as well. At the end, Horowitz, smiling and gesticulating with his free hand, was heard to say to Fischer-Dieskau, "I followed you all the way!"[62]

Perhaps the most unsettling moment of the evening for Horowitz occurred just before the Tchaikovsky Trio. He had walked onto the stage to a huge ovation, and then a hush had fallen over the house. He straightened his back, brought his fingers to the keys, and struck an experimental C major chord, which provoked laughter from the audience. Unamused, Horowitz gave a regal nod and led Rostropovich and Stern into the music.

Of all the personalities on the stage, Horowitz caused the most excitement. Harold C. Schonberg, for instance, noted that while Leonard Bernstein was "jumping all over the place, wiggling and waggling, and levitating and having a wonderful time bathing his ego in the music," the comparatively immobile Horowitz let off far more electricity: "There is the feeling of unleashed force in that taut body; a feeling that he and the stage and the piano are somewhere along the line going to explode, taking the audience with them."[63]

The memorable evening ended with an exuberant performance of the "Hallelujah Chorus" from Handel's *Messiah*. Horowitz, Fischer-Dieskau, Rostropovich, Stern, Bernstein, Menuhin, and Bloom all assembled on-stage with the chorus of the Oratorio Society. "May the Lord have mercy and forgive us for what we are about to do," exclaimed Stern. "If I sing this, nobody will ever come here anymore,"[64] declared Horowitz, and each time during the subsequent rendition that he reached a note that was too low for him, he marked it with a sharp downward chop of his right hand, much to the delight of the audience.

Among the letters Horowitz received after the "Concert of the Century" was one that amused him greatly. This was from a young singer who wrote: "Dear Mr. Horowitz: My name is Mr. Katz. I live in Brooklyn and I sing only arias in my concerts. I have a good personality and would like to have you play for me."[65] Laughing loudly, Horowitz showed the missive to a reporter from the *New York Post*. He took more seriously another letter from former Metropolitan Opera star Risë Stevens, now president of the Mannes College of Music, for she asked him to join her piano faculty. It was widely known that over the years Juilliard's president, Peter Mennin, had tried unsuccessfully to lure Horowitz into teaching, so Miss Stevens was surprised along with everyone else when Horowitz accepted her offer. "The year 1978 will be the 50th anniversary of my debut here, and I wanted to contribute something to this century,"[66] Horowitz told the press in July 1976 in yet another brilliantly executed publicity blitz orchestrated by Peter Gelb. Horowitz went on to explain that "Mannes is a big family that needs some help, a shot in the arm. I am joining the staff to attract new talent to the school. Nadia Reisenberg and Claude Frank are good friends and are screening the applicants for me."

Horowitz never agreed to any contract without presenting a long list of detailed specifications, and his teaching appointment was no exception. Students chosen were going to have to match Horowitz's expectations. He refused to accept any student already enrolled at Mannes because he did not want to create friction with any of the faculty by absconding with a protégé. Any student of his, Horowitz said, would have to have musicianship and solid technique. He didn't want one with "too much chutzpah,"[67] nor one too shy, yet he insisted that there must be a well-developed personality. "When I teach, I don't inflict my own personality on anybody. It has to exist already."[68] There were other requirements as well, but they were to be kept secret. When Horowitz had considered teaching at Juilliard, he had told Peter Mennin that he was not interested in teaching either Orientals or women. "Women," recalled Mennin, "because he said they got married eventually and then all his work was for naught. Orientals because he thought they didn't feel Western music deeply enough—they just imitated."[69] Horowitz now repeated these reservations at Mannes. The dean of the college recalled that "there was a strict verbal agreement made between Horowitz and Risë Stevens. He simply wasn't interested in teaching women or Orientals. Also, Horowitz was to be paid a whopping fee of $150 per hour, a fact kept confidential because it was about three times what the very top-rank faculty were getting."[70]

Preliminary auditions were held at Mannes, and two pianists emerged as finalists—Dean Kramer, who was then a student of Adele Marcus at

Juilliard, and Boris Bloch, an Israeli. Horowitz chose the attractive and personable Kramer, even though most of the jury thought Bloch the better musician by far. For about eight months, from April to November 1977, Kramer received an average of one lesson per month, but Horowitz soon became distracted with preparations for his Golden Jubilee season. "I tried to contact Horowitz during the time that he was arranging his jubilee tour," remembered Kramer, "but had no success for two months. He had stipulated that I not enter any competitions or play concerts while studying with him and I felt stalemated—I was not getting lessons and I wasn't performing. So I went to the dean and asked him to find out what was going on. Horowitz's secretary, Beatrice Stein, said that Mr. Horowitz would not be available until the fall of 1980 and at that point the whole thing fell apart. I was horribly disappointed, frustrated, and angry. Adele Marcus had warned me against the move. She had, in fact, launched into a two-hour diatribe against both Horowitz and his wife, but I had taken the chance."[71]

Horowitz had been attracted to the Mannes because it was a new challenge and perhaps because of the publicity it generated, but he was apparently not deeply interested in the teaching itself, so considered he had overextended himself. In the spring of 1978, Risë Stevens resigned as head of the Mannes School, and Horowitz immediately withdrew from the faculty. "Mannes doesn't exist anymore," he announced. "I gave up because I have to take children, and with children I have no patience. It took three hours and I was so exhausted I couldn't teach anymore. When you take them when they are over twenty, they think they know more than the teacher and you cannot shape them."[72]

CHAPTER TWENTY-NINE

THE GOLDEN
JUBILEE

*"I'm full of pep, very active now, and I play like a young man.
And I love young people. Usually when an artist gets older
he sees more white hair in the audience, but the older I get,
the younger the people are!"*[1]

"In other words, you have no intention whatsoever of retiring?"
Mike Wallace, 60 Minutes (1978) *"Oh, my God, no!"*[2]

"WHOOOOOOOOOOPEEEEEEEEEE!!!!!!!!!! I am as excited as a child!" wrote Carlos Moseley, president of the New York Philharmonic, to Eugene Ormandy. "I cannot exaggerate to you how pleased I am that you will be conducting the Philharmonic, and to know that you and Horowitz will be playing such a program for us is a glorious thought."[3]

Moseley's high exuberance was commensurate with the difficulty he had had in persuading Horowitz to appear again with orchestra. For nearly three years he had persistently reminded the pianist that "an extraordinarily important anniversary date is looming"—namely January 12, 1978, the fiftieth anniversary of Horowitz's New York debut with Sir Thomas Beecham and the New York Philharmonic—and had suggested he consider playing again with the Philharmonic. Giants such as Rachmaninoff and Hofmann had celebrated their golden jubilees in regal fashion and Horowitz, also, wanted "to do something special." Nonetheless, he had remained ambivalent about playing with orchestra.

His last concerto appearance had been exactly twenty-five years earlier, when he marked his Silver Jubilee with a performance of the Tchaikovsky Concerto with the New York Philharmonic under George Szell. An entire generation of concertgoers had never heard Horowitz in a concerto and, as Harold Shaw once remarked to Moseley, they probably never would. After two letters to Horowitz in 1975 and 1976 went unanswered, Moseley was more than a little surprised to receive a call from Shaw in the early winter of 1977 saying that Horowitz was seriously considering his invitation. With no definite commitment, Moseley reserved all of the Sunday afternoons in Carnegie Hall in January 1978, and since the New York Philharmonic was prohibited by contract from performing on Sunday afternoons, Moseley and the orchestra's manager, Albert K. Webster, negotiated into a new labor contract a special clause allowing such performances on special occasions for special artists. Still, Horowitz kept vacillating, and it was not until March 1977 that he finally said yes.

The principal reason for Horowitz's hesitation was that he was not certain he could find the right conductor, one who would yield to his interpretation and not in any way take the spotlight from him. Horowitz never seriously considered the flamboyant Leonard Bernstein. "You can't accompany," he told Bernstein. "The more important the player, the more you steal the show. Lenny, don't play the stud with me, don't dominate me, please"; and although Bernstein vowed to be his "musical slave,"[4] Horowitz was not convinced. Georg Solti, Daniel Barenboim, Zubin Mehta, Seiji Ozawa, and James Levine were all considered, but in an interview with the *New York Post,* Horowitz lambasted each of them. Actually, there were no conductors that were ideal for him, he said. Ormandy was "too old," and the younger men were all "too fast." Only Herbert von Karajan (with, perhaps, the Brahms B-flat Major Concerto) and Carlo Maria Giulini passed muster—"but with neither one would I work in Russian music. There is no one I know who is good there."[5]

Although Horowitz had dismissed his contemporary Ormandy as too elderly, it turned out that Ormandy was the only conductor Horowitz could reconcile himself to without enormous difficulty. Horowitz remembered that Ormandy had wielded the baton for Rachmaninoff himself in his own concertos during the Philadelphia Orchestra's 1939 Rachmaninoff Cycle, and Horowitz knew Ormandy well, admired and trusted him, and believed he would do everything possible to accommodate his interpretation. Moseley wrote Ormandy that "of all the conductors, his heart is set upon having you conduct if you will be willing. He feels that you truly understand him and his kind of approach."[6] Horowitz sweetened the bid by offering to play a benefit concert with Ormandy and the Philadelphia Orchestra later in the season if Ormandy conducted his Philharmonic concert in New York.

There had been a long-standing rift between Eugene Ormandy and the

New York Philharmonic which complicated the negotiations. Ormandy had never appeared in New York with the Philharmonic during his long, distinguished career, and had not conducted it anywhere since 1947. However, he finally agreed to the Horowitz program, and the pianist told one reporter, "I was pleased that this concert brought peace between Ormandy and the Philharmonic."[7]

Horowitz now pushed ahead and stage-managed arrangements for the concert with characteristic zeal. Thanks to the new labor contract, the Philharmonic was able to perform at Horowitz's favorite hour, 4 P.M. Although the orchestra's home was Avery Fisher Hall at Lincoln Center, Horowitz had vowed he would never play there because of what he considered inferior acoustics. He had managed to persuade Moseley and Webster to hold the concert in Carnegie Hall. Another obstacle to be surmounted was that both the Philharmonic and Ormandy were under contract to Columbia Masterworks, but a special arrangement was made with CBS whereby Horowitz's performance would be recorded and released by his own company, RCA.

The actual date of Horowitz's anniversary was January 12, but as he was insistent upon performing only on a Sunday, the jubilee concert would have to be on the eighth. Besides, he rationalized, he had always thought of his real debut as having occurred on the eighth of January rather than the twelfth, because that was when he had first played for Rachmaninoff in the Steinway basement.

Rather than the Tchaikovsky First Concerto, his 1928 debut piece, Horowitz opted for the Rachmaninoff Third Concerto. "Without false modesty," he said. "I brought this Concerto to light. I brought it to life, and everywhere! Rachmaninoff had not won the recognition with the Concerto that he thought he deserved."[8] Nineteen seventy-eight marked the thirty-fifth anniversary of Rachmaninoff's death and the golden anniversary of the beginning of their friendship, and he was playing the Third Concerto in his memory. As far as the Tchaikovsky, Horowitz felt that "some pianists have made it a little *démodé*. I would play it again but I have much more to show off in the [Rachmaninoff] D Minor. It's much more idiomatic."[9] At seventy-four, Horowitz wanted not only to prove that he could play again with orchestra but also that he could still perform one of the most difficult works in the repertory with the vigor of youth. "Time is marching, but I prove to myself that I can do it, at this age which I am now—fifty-three!"[10] he joked.

Horowitz's appearance with the New York Philharmonic was announced to the music world in April 1977, with a warning from Horowitz that he was not ready to consider any other concerto dates. The remainder of his jubilee celebration would be a series of solo recitals—Ann Arbor, Toronto, Philadelphia, Chicago, Cleveland, Boston, New York, Washington, D.C., San Francisco, and Los Angeles. Hundreds of requests for interviews poured in even before the new season began, and Wanda, Horowitz's secretary Beatrice Stein, Harold Shaw, and Peter Gelb were deluged with an unprecedented amount of paper work. Ralph Hanes, Horowitz's traveling companion since 1974, decided at this time that he had had enough of the concert business and left Shaw's employ at the end of the summer. Needing an immediate replacement for the busy season ahead, Shaw hired Giovanni Scimonelli, an adventurous Italian travel agent—young, diplomatic, and charming. Immediately after Scimonelli accepted the position, Shaw gave him prudent advice. Remembered Scimonelli: "He warned me not to mention the names of other pianists to Horowitz, especially the younger ones, because the Maestro was unhappy about getting older. The fact that he was a member of the older generation bothered him immensely."[11]

Scimonelli turned out to be an ideal and near-constant companion. He moved into the Horowitz house, where he occupied Sonia's old room, and he was the perfect foil for Horowitz, good at protecting him from the public and bolstering his moods. He would chat amiably in French with the pianist and in Italian with Wanda, who approved of his suave and solicitous manners. In the afternoons Scimonelli listened to Horowitz practice, and in the evenings he played canasta with Wanda and her friends. At the latter occasions, everyone was amused when Horowitz sometimes provided "music to play cards by," in Wanda's words. "Sometimes he's very nice and plays background music, but if he starts to play Beethoven, Haydn, or Chopin, we ask him to stop. But when he plays operetta music, then we like that."[12] Occasionally, late at night, Horowitz would launch into one of his famous opera transcriptions and, remembered Scimonelli, eventually "Wanda would say 'Enough! Get to bed!' and Horowitz *jumped* up, and up the stairs and into his room. I discovered that Wanda and Horowitz were very different personalitywise. Horowitz, for instance, would say 'I hate the country,' and he much preferred living in New York; he adored his townhouse and bedroom, where he spent a lot of time. Wanda, however, loved best the house in New Milford, loved the country and animals—

she had a brood of four cats and one dog—loved traveling, shopping, movies, and meeting people. But, most of all, she was devoted to taking care of Horowitz, and she did that exquisitely."[13]

Scimonelli became immersed in the endless details of planning Horowitz's travels and accommodations for the 1977–78 season. "This was the most exciting period of his career, and the world was literally at his feet. Horowitz was treated like a movie star." The pianist now enjoyed hobnobbing with politicians, entertainers, and media personalities—dinner with Henry Kissinger, a visit to Danny Kaye's house, frequent evenings with Mike Wallace. Among the many interviews and appearances lined up for the jubilee season were a television interview with Mike Wallace on CBS's 60 Minutes show and extensive articles in the New York Times Sunday Magazine and in Newsweek. (Horowitz was, in fact, scheduled for the cover of the January 23, 1978, issue of Newsweek, but was bumped at the last moment when Hubert Humphrey died.) Although the newspaper and magazine coverage was immense in 1978, nothing thrilled Horowitz more than the 60 Minutes program, which was aired on December 26, 1977, and viewed by approximately 45 million people. This, along with a televised appearance with the New York Philharmonic in September 1978 and a recital broadcast live from the White House in February 1978, would be the final step in Horowitz's ascent to media celebrity.

The producer of the 60 Minutes show, David Lowe, recalled that "six or seven meetings of persuasion were necessary before Horowitz agreed to film the program, though Mrs. Horowitz wanted the program very badly and was anxious to be on camera herself. Mike and I would talk about Horowitz's cats, the living room decor, the weather—anything to warm him up to the idea. He loved flattery, complained that he didn't want to be recognized, but in fact he really did. That the Horowitzes finally agreed to do the program was in large part due to Mike Wallace. The Horowitzes were very celebrity conscious and wanted Mike in their social circle. Horowitz was in awe of Mike and vice versa, so they became fast friends."[14] Lowe remembered Wanda as being extremely nervous during the taping, ever ready to direct the conversation, either to censure her husband or to encourage him and protect him from Wallace's penetrating questions. What, asked Wallace, were the real reasons for Horowitz's twelve years of retirement? Was he really as temperamental and impossible as some newspaper stories suggested? Horowitz gave charmingly nuanced but evasive answers to such questions, revealing no more of himself than usual. "I believe in astrology and am born Libra," he told Wallace. "It is said that the Libra is a little bit narcissistic. So they like compliments. But I think every artist likes compliments. I will not tell you I am an angel. I have some weaknesses, I suppose. I don't know where they are. My weaknesses, I cannot talk about them."[15] "He was," said Lowe, "a wonderful showman, but completely in his own world. On one omitted portion of the videotape, Horowitz said, 'Oh, I didn't have a daughter. We don't have children,' and Wanda corrected him—'We had a child.' Horowitz was like a little boy during the filming."[16]

CBS shot seven and a half hours in the Horowitz living room, which was edited into a sixteen-minute interview. Horowitz had insisted that he would not perform during the program, but the determined Wallace coaxed him into playing a portion of his now-legendary transcription of *The Stars and Stripes Forever*. Horowitz claimed he had forgotten the work, couldn't possibly play it, but then suddenly got up and went to the piano, with the cameras rolling. He played a brilliant excerpt and finished with riotous laughter. Throughout the interview, Horowitz revealed an almost puerile charm, mischievously playing the child to Wanda's stern tongue-in-cheek parent. For those members of the public accustomed to thinking of Horowitz as elusive, shy, and serious, here instead was a Horowitz who revealed his love of pranks—for instance, putting hairbrushes and ashtrays in the beds of his wife and his valet to entertain himself on the road during boring stays in hotels.

In November 1977, Horowitz gave a different kind of interview, unusual in that it concentrated for the most part on music itself, that of Rachmaninoff. Phillip Ramey, who had interviewed Horowitz six years previously for the liner notes of a Columbia Chopin album, had since become friendly with the pianist. In 1972 Ramey had written a virtuoso piano work titled *Leningrad Rag* which was published two years later bearing a dedication to Horowitz, with his permission. Horowitz had played *Leningrad Rag* at home and told the Metropolitan Opera's Francis Robinson, "It's very effective. Perhaps I'll do it as an encore." Horowitz and Ramey saw each other every so often and frequently talked on the telephone.

At the beginning of the 1977–78 season, Ramey was appointed the New York Philharmonic's program editor, and he immediately approached Horowitz with the idea of doing an interview for the Golden Jubilee program book. Knowing Ramey to be a musician rather than a journalist, Horowitz agreed, and on the evening of November 29 Ramey arrived at East Ninety-fourth Street with his tape recorder and a list of carefully considered questions. Horowitz had always seemed relaxed with the young man, so that night Wanda eschewed her usual dragon-at-the-gate posture with interviewers and absented herself from the living room for the better part of two hours. The result was one of the most intelligent and candid interviews of Horowitz's career.

Ramey spent much of the following two weeks transcribing the conversation, structuring an articulate, coherent whole. He did not mind the long hours because he felt that including the interview in the Philharmonic's program book could only enhance the occasion. "I was," he said, "tired of reading bizarre things in the press about Horowitz—his disco flings and so on. I was also impatient with silly quotes from press conferences, quotes that made him sound rather idiotic, and also of hearing about what a dope he was from musicians who had spent only short periods of time with him. A serious interview would, I hoped, help counter such impressions."[17]

Not long before the concert, RCA suddenly decided to print a special booklet to be passed out at Carnegie Hall with the programs and also included in the forthcoming album. They asked Ramey if his interview might be used there instead of the program book, and after consulting with the Philharmonic, Ramey agreed, but asked RCA for a small fee. "After all," he said, "I had put a great deal of effort into that project, which was no part of my duties. I was willing to do this gratis for our own program, but certainly not for a commercial enterprise like RCA Records."[18] When RCA balked at the figure he named, Ramey good-naturedly halved it. The interview was then sent to Horowitz with the invitation to make any changes or deletions he wished, and it came back a few days later approved by both Horowitz and Wanda. Only minor alterations were requested, such as the omission of a paragraph in which Horowitz had criticized Rachmaninoff's own recordings of his concertos and *Rhapsody on a Theme of Paganini,* and of an observation that Egon Petri had been a "dry and academic" pianist.

The next day, RCA informed Ramey that the interview was not to be published because Wanda had changed her mind. It seemed that she considered him not sufficiently distinguished to question her husband and that she was offended that Ramey's name came before his in the question-answer format. Ramey remembered: "I remarked to Jack Pfeiffer that perhaps Mrs. Horowitz would prefer that Horowitz question *me* about his career and opinions of Rachmaninoff's music. Jack looked harried and didn't smile. He told me Wanda was in one of her famous tempers, was being impossible about every aspect of the record, and had just that day shot down a second cover. There was, he said, nothing he could do." Concerning Wanda's behavior, Ramey mused, "Doubtless, she's had a difficult life with Horowitz. Still, Samuel Barber, who knew them both for nearly half a century, once told me Wanda had always been badly behaved, that even as a young woman she delighted in making scenes. So perhaps it's in her genes."[19]

The Golden Jubilee season demanded that Wanda be in the public eye far more than in past years and she gave a number of interviews on her own, but only to publications she considered properly prestigious. "We are not like Lenny Bernstein," she sniffed to a reporter. "We do not want to be in *People* magazine."[20] Business was transacted at 9:30 P.M. in the living room, and Wanda expected any reporter or guest to be properly dressed for an audience with either Horowitz or herself. Wanda had glared at Horowitz's short-lived student, Dean Kramer, when he arrived one day for a lesson without a tie. In Horowitz's presence, male visitors were to wear ties and jackets, Wanda had decided; she would tolerate no exceptions when it came to the respect she expected for her husband. In the course of interviews, Wanda was afforded the opportunity of surveying and appraising her role as wife and the arduous ordeal of her marriage. "You know how people are," she said on one occasion. "They predicted the marriage wouldn't last three weeks, but we've been together almost forty-five years. . . . He's no more difficult than any other husband."[21]

Although often portrayed as a stern taskmaster, Wanda revealed in a 1978 interview her softer and more private side. She told a reporter, "We have a farmhouse. I love it. I take care of the flowers and the garden. We have four cats and a dog. Unfortunately, I can't have cows and horses, but sometimes I think I should have married a farmer. I love nature very much."[22] Wanda had always been an animal lover and she occasionally worked as a volunteer at the New York ASPCA; she had also set aside some of their New Milford property to be used as a bird sanctuary and park. Three of Wanda's cats were, she said, "Connecticut girls," foundlings from the woods. They were, however, subordinate to the favored cat of the household, Horowitz's. Wanda would explain that Horowitz had never been particularly fond of cats until one night when a light-colored animal wandered onto the balcony outside his bedroom. "Since it was so late, I suggested that we leave him on the terrace," recalled Wanda, "and the next morning I found the cat at the foot of my husband's bed! He became the most important person in the house."[23] Horowitz loved the animal, took care of it himself, bought cans of food and litter and named it Foosi. When an interviewer unused to his Russian accent asked Horowitz, "Foosi? Why Foosi?," Horowitz exclaimed in exasperation, "Because she's *foosy* [fussy]!"[24]

So strong was Wanda's love of animals, especially cats (she was featured in a book called *Cat People* by Bill Hayward), that she scheduled an animal-watching safari in Africa in the spring of 1978. Scimonelli remembered that she was highly excited about this trip but ultimately canceled it rather than miss the last concert of her husband's jubilee season. Scimonelli tried to convince her that Horowitz would be fine, that Scimonelli, Pfeiffer, Sally Horwich, and a maid could attend to Horowitz, but Wanda retorted, "No, no, what if something goes wrong?," and sacrificed her plans. "She simply would not leave him alone," says Scimonelli, "despite the fact that she was dying to do so. What if there was a wrinkle in his shirt and he canceled the concert?"[25]

As Horowitz began his jubilee season, he was forced to cancel three of seven recitals between October and December 1977—the first because of a hangnail, the second because of an intestinal flu, and the third due to a cold. He was being extremely cautious because he wanted to be in absolute top form for his January 8 concerto appearance, an event that weighed heavily on his mind. Three other such appearances were to follow—with Zubin Mehta and the Los Angeles Philharmonic on February 5, Ormandy and the Philadelphia Orchestra on April 16, and another performance with Ormandy and the Philadelphia Orchestra in Ann Arbor on April 30. Horowitz was so worried about playing with orchestra again that Harold Shaw arranged a dry run with Ormandy and the Philadelphia Orchestra at Carnegie Hall in the fall of 1977. This rehearsal was such a closely guarded secret that even the orchestra members weren't told about it until the last moment. When the players sat down for what they believed was a rehearsal of the Verdi *Requiem,* they saw on their music stands the parts for the Rachmaninoff Third Concerto, and a minute later Vladimir Horowitz strode onto the stage with a huge grin.

The run-through was an unqualified success. Horowitz had prepared himself for his performance as thoroughly as an athlete might train for the Olympics. "First," he told a reporter, "I played through all the great Romantic Russian operas on the piano, *Sadko, Mazeppa, Snow Maiden, Iolanta, Pique Dame*. I had to feel the right spirit again. I had to sing."[26] Then Horowitz began to work on the Rachmaninoff Concerto, using an old score that contained occasional penciled notations in the composer's own hand. After long evenings of discussion with Pfeiffer, Horowitz decided to play the Concerto without the standard cuts, omitting only two bars in the first-movement cadenza which he considered "absolutely impossible"[27] musically. Of the two cadenzas Rachmaninoff wrote for the opening movement, Horowitz chose the less complicated one, and for a legitimate musical reason: "The alternate cadenza," he said, "is like an ending in itself. It's not good to end the Concerto before it's over! Rachmaninoff was a tremendous virtuoso and what he wrote was wonderful. But later, when he looked at [the alternate cadenza] in relation to his whole Concerto, he knew it wasn't right. He didn't play it, so I don't."[28] Horowitz also decided not to omit the third of the four variations in the central section of the last movement, although he had done so in past performances.

At the first rehearsal with Ormandy and the Philharmonic at Carnegie Hall, Horowitz prided himself on having studied not only the piano part but every instrumental line in the Concerto. "I couldn't do it any other way," he explained. "The Philharmonic was surprised that I knew their parts, not just mine. I had to feel the composer, the whole work, not just the solo part."[29] Singing along with the orchestra, stopping Ormandy from time to time to discuss a change in dynamics or tempo, encouraging the strings with discreet bowing motions of his hand, playing the flute or oboe parts on the piano at will, Horowitz took complete charge of the Concerto. Ormandy proved a perfect accompanist, yielding in every way to Horowitz's interpretation, even though Horowitz sometimes took enormous liberties with the score. One observer wrote that he made a habit of "inverting dynamics [and] stretching time to extreme limits. At times he slowed the breakneck pace almost to a halt to create movements of quivering tension in which the musical line threatened to break."[30] Asked to describe his behavior at the rehearsal, Horowitz replied, "I play freely in the grand manner. And the Philharmonic is not really accustomed to this style. I am a nineteenth-century romantic. I am the last. I take terrible risks. Because my playing is very clear, when I make a mistake you hear it [but] the score is not a bible and I am never afraid to dare. The music is behind those dots. You search for it, and that is what I mean by the grand manner. I play, so to speak, from the other side of the printed score, looking back."[31]

However, Horowitz's psychological attitude toward the performance did not necessarily work to his own best advantage. He was hell-bent on proving to the audience, and perhaps to himself, that he could still play like a young man, that he could top his own legendary 1930 and 1951 recordings of the Rachmaninoff Third. This process of, in effect, competing with his younger self and defying his present physical limitations created enormous pressure, and he worried that he might have a memory slip. When, during a tape-recorded interview, Phillip Ramey asked him about the possibility of that happening in the Rachmaninoff, Horowitz positively shrieked in dread: "No! I never did [but] now I'm older. Oh my God, you make me crazy now! Maybe I will forget, it can happen. I don't know. There are so many notes, some of them unnecessary. Rachmaninoff conceded that."[32]

Horowitz was increasingly superstitious during the 1970's, and he once asserted that if the gods were with him at 4 P.M. on a Sunday afternoon, if his emotion, intellect, and mechanical ability were in perfect harmony, and if the audience was quiet and the conductor responsive—then he would play well. "I will hope that physically I will feel well, that everything will be balanced and all my spiritual control will be there in place,"[33] he told a friend. But right up to the last moment Horowitz was not entirely sure that the Philharmonic performance would actually take place. In a conversation with pianist Ted Joselson not long before the concert, Horowitz held up his fifth finger and asked, "Do you see the little cut?" Joselson did not see anything wrong, but Horowitz insisted, "Yes, there is a cut, and I need a strong pinky for the Rachmaninoff. You want to hear the Rachmaninoff, don't you? Well, it won't be. 'Horowitz has cut, and cancels jubilee!'—you will read it in the newspapers."[34]

Until a week before, the Public Broadcasting Service was slated to televise the concert, but Horowitz feared that the combined pressure of a live audience, the RCA microphones, and the TV cameras would be too much, and he scrapped the idea. Already, there was pressure enough at home, where ticket requests had turned the Horowitz house into a battleground. Nine thousand such requests had to be turned down, and

Horowitz proudly predicted that the New York Philharmonic was going to make "lots of money." He was right: ticket prices for the benefit ran from $10 to $250, and a record $168,000 was grossed for the Philharmonic's pension fund. On January 8, half an hour before the concert, scalpers were in the lobby offering single tickets for $1,000 each.

Horowitz was tremendously nervous that afternoon, but he felt physically well and thought himself up to the task. Franklin Delano Roosevelt had sent a letter of congratulation to Josef Hofmann on the occasion of his Golden Jubilee, and a similar message to Horowitz from his admirer Jimmy Carter was read to the audience before the historic performance. Coming onstage after intermission, Horowitz received a tumultuous greeting. But his rendition of the Rachmaninoff Concerto aroused mixed feelings. The orchestra had some difficulty following Horowitz, and the performance seemed to one critic "less than a paragon of refinement." Yet the work's passion and drama were intact, because of Horowitz's unique sonority and a drive that even nerves and slips of the fingers could not compromise. "Only Rachmaninoff himself had that crashing, yet articulated, left-hand passage work, that rhythmic thrust and steel-like projection of every individual note,"[35] declared Harold C. Schonberg.*

Horowitz's two previous recordings of the work had been clean-edged, with coherent phrasing and tautly held rhythm. The controversial 1978 performance was much freer in its metrical patterns, richer in harmonic textures, with inner voices much emphasized and far more varied dynamics. Still, in many places Horowitz's grand manner seemed simply over-mannered, a somewhat grotesque parody of well-known Horowitzisms. Wrote one critic: "Horowitz accelerates and snaps off the ends of phrases, retards the middles, transposes accents, rushes, and generally storms along his own course while the orchestra plays its notes and tries both to keep up and stay out of his way. . . . The piece itself becomes fragmented and the lack of coordination between keyboard and orchestra makes it sound at times rather startlingly modern. . . . Terrific excitement is purchased at the cost of just about everything else. In short, then, this is one

---

* Horowitz himself might not have agreed with that appraisal of Rachmaninoff's performance. Concerning the composer's own record of the Third Concerto, he told Phillip Ramey in 1977 in a taped interview: "It is a little placid—awful, one of the worst [recordings] he ever did. [On records] he played the First Concerto beautifully, the Second fair (he played that much better in concert), and the Third terrible! This was because he was absolutely frustrated with the Concerto, that he couldn't have success with it. He gave it to me. 'That's Gorovitz's,' he would say."

of the great ego trips of our time."[36] Even Horowitz's old friend Nathan Milstein expressed disappointment. "The performance was bad," he said bluntly. "A little of the fire is gone, the phrasing is bad and there is an ostentatious quality to his physical gestures. His economy of motion is somewhat tarnished. He is always trying to do something to the music instead of letting the music come out simply."[37]

His shoulders somewhat constricted, Horowitz had clearly been struggling in some parts of the Concerto, especially in the two *più mosso* sections of the last movement—in the toccata-like, rhythmic coda, during much of which the piano and the orchestra were not synchronized and produced some striking dissonances, and in the dramatic cadenza-flourish just before the grandiose finale. At the end of the performance, Horowitz was dripping wet. A sustained ovation followed, and Horowitz bowed hand in hand with Ormandy, beaming, looking happy and triumphant.

At the concert, the stage had been festooned with sixteen microphones, which, chief engineer Edwin Begley later admitted, had been carelessly placed. On tape, the piano was too prominent, overpowering and diluting the sound of the orchestra even in accompaniment passages, and the orchestra mix was not good. "We did not have enough time to set up the equipment and to make tests for the best placement of the microphones," Begley complained, also noting that Horowitz's piano was so juiced up, so brilliantly voiced, that it sounded like "a rock piano."[38] Horowitz's tone seemed to have become more brittle—"atrophic with time," wrote one critic. "The young Horowitz was a painter, dazzling us with a bright display of color and technique, while today's Horowitz has exchanged his brush for a mallet."[39] Nonetheless, RCA was eager to rush the new record to dealers in order to capitalize on the immense publicity of the event. Advance sales for the first Horowitz concerto recording in twenty-seven years were "just phenomenal," according to Irwin Katz, RCA's director of Red Seal merchandising, and it was hoped that the album would outdo the sales of Van Cliburn's Tchaikovsky First Piano Concerto, which had been possibly the largest selling classical record of all time. Horowitz did his part in promoting the album by agreeing to an autograph session at Sam Goody's record store in Manhattan, where he signed two hundred copies. But the enthusiasm of adoring fans could not offset the general disappointment the record caused in the music world. Many thought it puzzling that RCA had released a technically inferior, mistake-ridden version when it could have waited until Horowitz played the Concerto again later that season. Pfeiffer privately admitted that the more relaxed performance with Zubin Mehta in Los Angeles a few months later was better, but said that RCA felt obliged to release the "live, historic performance" that marked the fiftieth anniversary.

Immediately after the concert, RCA had scheduled a session with Horowitz and the Philharmonic to redo sonically unacceptable portions of the Concerto. Such, at least, was the rationale, and it may have been partially true, but the fact is that, as with the 1965 Carnegie Hall recital album, much of the patchwork was necessitated by the unacceptable quality of areas of the performance. Phillip Ramey, who wrote the Philharmonic's program note for the Concerto and knew the music well, was present at the concert and later had access to a pirated tape recording of it. He felt that the statement RCA had appended in tiny print on the back of the record jacket reading "for technical recording reasons, some portions of this album were rerecorded following the concert" was intentionally misleading. "I said as much to Jack Pfeiffer and he told me the Horowitzes had insisted on it," noted Ramey. "Much of what you hear on the record is not what we heard at the concert. Most if not all of the patches were done, I think, for the purpose of correcting performance mistakes—for instance, the coda of the last movement. There is one spot that was rerecorded—the marchlike episode at the beginning of the finale—where Horowitz does something unusual which he had not done either in his previous recordings, at the January 1978 concert, or when he played it for me in his living room a couple of months before that concert: he articulates the left-hand accompaniment over the right-hand melody-chords, and the result is unique and quite marvelous."[40]

There was another large-scale work that Horowitz programmed for his jubilee season, the Liszt B Minor Sonata. "I can play it," he told a reporter. "I might take the octaves a little slower, but this is not a piece to show off octaves."[41] His performance was severely criticized as being fragmented, eccentric, overmannered and exaggerated. Similarly, RCA's album of it was, in general, poorly received. "I am surprised," wrote one critic, "that Horowitz consented to the release of a performance so immobile and bogged down in detail, further beset by an alarmingly high incidence of dropped and missed notes."[42] To make matters worse, RCA's engineering falsified Horowitz's tone: *"fortissimos* put forth with a bleak, nasty sound; delicate filigree, which in live performance had such caressing nuance, here emerges note by note with glockenspiel-like construction,"[43] concluded one magazine. After the release of the Rachmaninoff and Liszt albums, a critic wrote: "RCA should do some rethinking. It would be a shame indeed if these late years of Horowitz's illustrious career were to be represented to posterity only by such dubious examples as these two discs."[44] Pfeiffer's task was formidable; he had to prod Horowitz to keep recording throughout the 1970's, and because Horowitz refused to step into a studio, Pfeiffer had to patch performances together from live concerts. The finished sheen of Horowitz's pre-1965 Columbia albums was conspicuously missing.

After solo recitals in San Francisco and Los Angeles in February 1978, Horowitz headed back east for another highlight of his jubilee year, his first appearance at the White House since he had played for President Hoover in 1931. He had been invited to the White House by Presidents Eisenhower, Kennedy, Johnson, Nixon, and Ford, but had always refused. But when the invitation came from President Carter, "I told Mr. Shaw to tell them it should be a concert just like when Casals came and played for Kennedy. The President should invite three or four hundred people who love music but who are not specialists. But not politicians, not people who just look at their watches to see when I will finish because they are bored to death."[45]

Horowitz had been assured by the President, a classical-music fan who often listened to Horowitz's recordings in the Oval Office, that his appearance would be a traditional recital, not connected to any visit of any head of state and not after-dinner entertainment, so he had agreed to come. Horowitz settled into the Watergate apartments on February 25, and then headed up Pennsylvania Avenue for the rehearsal, accompanied by Pfeiffer, Mohr, Wanda, and Scimonelli. Arriving at the White House, they were taken to the Winston Churchill Room to wait for the President. Not long after, Jimmy Carter entered dressed in suede shoes and a cardigan sweater. This titillated Scimonelli but clearly did not amuse Wanda, who insisted that every man wear a tie in *her* home. The President asked Horowitz if he would like to see the family living quarters, and Horowitz replied, "No, I'd like to see the piano."[46] The East Room, where he was to play, proved too full of echo, and Horowitz told the President that it needed carpets to absorb the sound. Mrs. Carter remembered that there were a number of Oriental rugs in storage upstairs, and the White House ushers along with the President and Mrs. Carter went upstairs to find them, returning fifteen minutes later, much to Horowitz's delight, with the rugs in tow. While the President and his attendants pulled and tugged, Horowitz directed the placement of the carpets. "As a person, Mr. Carter could not have been more gracious or human," Scimonelli recalled. "He stayed for the first half of the rehearsal before apologizing that he had to go back to work."[47] Later Wanda positively gushed about President Carter: "After my husband finished playing the Chopin Sonata [at the actual concert], the President got up from his chair, came over and kissed me. As I remember, he kissed me four times while we were there!"[48]

The White House recital, given Sunday afternoon, February 26, 1978, was a great success. The audience in the East Room included a smattering of politicians but was mostly made up of musicians and celebrities from the art world, including Eugene Ormandy, Isaac Stern, Mstislav Rostropovich, Samuel Barber, Byron Janis, Kitty Carlisle Hart, Avery Fisher, and Alice Tully. Before it began, President Carter introduced Horowitz by reminiscing about how, as a midshipman at the U.S. Naval Academy, he had spent whatever extra money he had on recordings of classical music and had thus discovered Vladimir Horowitz. "At that time," Carter said, "I learned of the brilliance of his playing [and] his fearless expression of emotion."[49] Carter ended his introduction by calling Horowitz "a national treasure." Horowitz gave a bemused shrug and a sardonic smile and then stepped onto a platform elegantly surrounded by flowers.

His program consisted of Chopin (B-flat Minor Sonata, two waltzes, and the A-flat Major Polonaise), Schumann (*Träumerei*), Rachmaninoff (*Polka de W.R.*) and his newly revised *Carmen* Fantasy. Horowitz had not performed this last since 1968 but was now featuring it on each of his anniversary recital programs. "It was a special idea of mine to put on the *Carmen*," he told the press. "I never listen to my own recordings, so I don't remember how the music sounded when I played it fifty years ago. But I know that *Carmen* always changes. It's never the same from performance to performance."[50]

Horowitz was not especially anxious about appearing at the White House, but he was concerned about the television program of his recital which Public Broadcasting was to air at 6 P.M. that evening, nationwide and around the globe. The director, Kirk Browning, was instructed to keep his cameras a respectful distance from Horowitz's hands and face. "He did not want his face photographed too much when he was playing," said Browning. "From certain angles, he felt it didn't express what he was thinking. It was always a fascinating face, but not one that registered in performance the way some do."[51] Immediately after the concert, the Horowitzes, Pfeiffer, RCA engineer Begley, Scimonelli, Browning, and a few close friends hurried back to the Watergate Hotel to watch the program. "The sound on the first delayed broadcast in the United States was very poor," recalled Begley. "The television technicians had taken the RCA sound and pushed it through a compressor or something. Horowitz was very upset, but by the time of the broadcast in Europe the sound was fixed."[52] Horowitz's televised appearance in Europe marked the first time he had been seen there in many years, and it had the effect of bolstering international sales of his records.

For the foreign distribution rights to the program, Horowitz received a fee of $193,964, which proved embarrassing for the White House, the sponsoring Washington station, WETA, and the PBS television network. This was because the public had been led to believe that the recital had been donated, and it was a long-standing rule of the government that such performances were not to be televised or recorded for commercial purposes. It turned out that Horowitz had also hoped to make an RCA record of his performance, but the White House would not allow that. When the President's staff learned that Horowitz had cashed in on the program in a manner that was not actually illegal but could hardly be called ethical, the next four artists to appear at the White House were told in no uncertain terms that they were not to sell foreign television rights. The administration stated it did not want any further publicity "about people making money from White House functions."[53]

Horowitz gave no apologies. Although his jubilee-year performances may have had their artistic flaws, they were an unprecedented financial triumph. After the publicity generated by 60 Minutes and Newsweek, Wanda in particular felt that ticket prices should be raised, and in some cases for performances that had already been sold out. In Philadelphia, impresario James Robb refused to do such a thing, and as a result received a phone call from Wanda. "She was just enraged, but finally we struck a compromise," he remembered. "The orchestra and the boxes were already sold out, so we raised prices in the family circle and amphitheater, which was only half sold out. The changes she insisted upon were from seven dollars to seven fifty in the amphitheater and from ten dollars to twelve fifty in the family circle."[54] Averaging $40,000 per recital (a grand total of nearly $440,000 that season) and with an additional $350,000 from a televised concert appearance with Zubin Mehta and the New York Philharmonic in the fall of 1978, Horowitz earned upwards of $1 million that year—and this did not include profits from the White House performance which eventually topped $200,000. Nonetheless, he sometimes seemed ambivalent about his phenomenal earning power. At one moment he would declare, "They can pay!" but then, perhaps more conscious of his public image, he would modify his tone, as when he told Mike Wallace during the *60 Minutes* interview: "I am not proud of this, but it is so. Well, I didn't do it my whole life. After fifty years I got this."

Procuring a ticket for a Horowitz concert had for some time been a real feat for his fans, and now a ticket scandal ensued which eventually caused Horowitz to pledge that he would never again appear in Carnegie Hall. His two Golden Jubilee recitals there, on March 12 and 19, 1978, attracted huge crowds which, as usual, camped outside overnight hoping for tickets. On the morning of January 17, when the box office opened, 3,444 tickets were purchased by 861 people, a maximum of 4 tickets per person. That left 1,000 tickets unaccounted for, and following hundreds of telephone calls and letters from angry fans who had been denied tickets, the New York Deputy Attorney General decided to investigate. After the tickets held for Horowitz's friends, business associates, and the press were counted, 300 were found to be missing. Eventually, it was discovered that these tickets had been funneled to a scalper in New Jersey to be sold for nearly $3,000 above their face value. It was also learned that Isaac Stern's wife, Vera, had held back a number of tickets for wealthy Carnegie Hall donors who had been unwilling to stand in line. The head box-office treasurer resigned and Isaac Stern, as president of the Carnegie Hall Corporation, was severely embarrassed by the matter. One Carnegie Hall executive recalled that "when Mrs. Horowitz heard that even Vera Stern had held tickets and had given them to her friends instead of having them set aside for those who waited in line, she was wild with rage. She detested Mrs. Stern, Horowitz disliked Isaac, and Horowitz vowed that he would never play there again as long as Stern was president. Subsequently, Horowitz was begged to return, but he would not budge."[55]

It turned out that Horowitz's last appearance at Carnegie Hall was on

May 7, 1978, before the ticket scandal had been completely uncovered. He had long been besieged by invitations to play in both Europe and Asia, but as always, he feared the long flights and the time changes. However, the idea of an "international" concert, held in the United States for foreign admirers willing to travel there to hear Horowitz, had been germinating in Harold Shaw's mind ever since the incident of the one hundred Japanese in Seattle. Horowitz agreed to Shaw's plan and Shaw duly announced the special Carnegie Hall date, explaining that tickets would be sold as part of a package tour which would also include hotels, round-trip air fare and a potpourri of cultural activities ranging "from ballet to Bloomingdale's," in Horowitz's words. Horowitz decided to play only Chopin, explaining, "I thought a festival of one composer would attract the most people, and globally speaking, I thought people would like Chopin the most. I'm against doing this in general. But I'm doing it because you have to tell people who come so many thousands of miles what they will hear. I cannot give them a mixed program. That would be very difficult to advertise."[56] Applications were received from 1,200 people from 14 different countries, including 140 Japanese who agreed to spend $1,740 per person.

Horowitz's last major performance during his jubilee season was a television special of the Rachmaninoff Third Concerto with Zubin Mehta and the New York Philharmonic. The NBC network, an RCA affiliate, broadcast the program live on Sunday afternoon, September 24, sponsored by the American Telephone and Telegraph Corporation, and it was rebroadcast on public television on March 11, 1979. This was Horowitz's first appearance in Avery Fisher Hall, which would be the site of his future concerts in New York. Although he seemed nervous during the performance, his hands visibly shaking, this was a far more relaxed and polished reading than the earlier one with Eugene Ormandy. The *New York Times* noted that Mehta, "with the instinct that a fine collaborator must have, consistently pushed the soloist to the brink of the impossible. . . . There was an element of competition, such as one can hear in the pianist's famously incendiary recordings with Toscanini, but also an underlying agreement as to the music's emotional core that subjugated visceral excitement to musical meaning." The critique continued: "When he was younger, Horowitz played the Concerto in a straightforward manner, though with extraordinary drive and power. These days his performance is infinitely more mannered and self-indulgent. He takes all

439

kinds of liberties with the rhythms, he inserts many more punctuation points, he breaks the line at will for expressive purposes [and] some of this is actually vulgar. But it still remains Vladimir Horowitz at the piano—the Horowitz of massive sonorities, tremendous (though no longer infallible) technique, penetrating tone and musical electricity."[57]

The Golden Jubilee year had spotlighted Horowitz as, in President Carter's words, "a national treasure," and so he was. But a half century is, after all, a great span, and despite Horowitz's assertions that he now played like a young man, time had inevitably taken its toll on his playing. Yet whatever Horowitz had lost in accuracy or endurance was more than compensated for by his uncanny ability to stage-manage music for optimum effect. He still reveled in his own playing and bridled at the notion that what he did best at the keyboard was in any way diminished by age: "I do not have the greatest mechanics in the world," he admitted, "but I never did. There are pianists who have more than me, but they don't make an impression because the sound, the colors are not there. That's how I'm different. The *sound* of my piano—*staccato, legato, portamento, pianissimo, piano, mezzo-forte, fortissimo*—twenty-five or thirty colors in the same line. That's what I have, and that's technique!"[58]

In 1978, buoyed by his jubilee celebrations, Horowitz was adamant about continuing to perform. In an unusually candid moment, he declared, "Yes, I am young too," and then lapsed into a quiet reflection. "But I'm very sorry for myself. Yes, sorry for myself because I know I will have to get older. I know I will have to stop playing someday. People tell me these things. I don't want to hear them because I still feel young. . . . When I feel that I can no longer give pleasure, aesthetic pleasure, then I will not play. It could be tomorrow, next year, I don't know. But I will know when it happens. And I will stop."[59]

Perhaps this determination about his career had a connection with the overall disappointment of his personal life. He had never invested much of his energies in continuing friendships, never nurtured such relationships nearly as carefully as he had groomed his celebrity, his reputation as the grand eccentric of the keyboard. Horowitz had, in fact, grown to believe in his own legend, and in some ways he was a victim of it. Having rejected and separated from many of his contemporaries, he found his social life somewhat barren. More and more, he was to be seen in gay bars and nightspots with Shaw employee Paul Gregory—observing, disco-dancing, bantering with startled patrons (for whom he sometimes consented to write an autograph), and, on occasion, even arm wrestling. "I am young too!" he would insist to all and sundry, from waiters to interviewers. (Increasingly, Wanda led a social life of her own, allowing Horowitz the freedom to spend time with his male friends. On weekends, she sometimes relaxed at the house in Connecticut while Horowitz maintained his daily routine on Ninety-fourth Street, taken care of by a maid, cook, and male companion, usually Paul Gregory.)

Horowitz may have felt young in spirit, but beyond all of his cavortings he seemed a lonely man. One intimate noted that the pianist had practically no close friends aside from his inner circle of Jack Pfeiffer, Gitta Gradova, Wanda's traveling companion, Sally Horwich, and the loyal secretary, Beatrice Stein. "It was sad," he remarked, "that people passed in and out of Horowitz's life so quickly. No one stayed for long."[60]

Now, after years of canceling concerts, alienating concert managers, driving record companies to distraction, and treating friends and associates cavalierly, Horowitz experienced a backlash. Practically no one in the music world seemed to speak well of him as a person. Many who had associated with Horowitz would no longer tolerate his fits of temperament and his boundless ego.

Even Jack Pfeiffer, who continued to patch together lackluster albums for RCA from live performances, distanced himself somewhat from him, finding that he could not persuade Horowitz to do anything he didn't want to and that Wanda, as always, was obstructive. Of course, Wanda was Horowitz's main support—a woman whom he must have resented at times, but upon whom he depended greatly. "Wanda was a wonderful friend to him," said one family friend. "Their life together had been very mixed up and she went through hell with him, but her loyalty was amazing. By 1978, there was a gallantry and gratitude on his part that was rather charming. He was grateful that she had stuck to him and protected him."[61]

During these later years, there was frequent tension between them over Horowitz's insistence that he could continue to perform indefinitely. Wanda would scoff at the idea and, to prepare him for the inevitable, would sometimes fantasize jokingly about how she envisioned their future together. "Five years from now, maybe ten," she told Mike Wallace, "I'm going to open a little restaurant and serve cakes and coffee and he will play the piano. We'll have a hamburger supreme, for twenty-five dollars with coffee included. And a little piano ... playing light music."[62]

That scenario aside, Horowitz was frequently offended by Wanda's intimations that he neither looked young anymore nor played as well as before. "I'm an old trouper,"[63] he insisted proudly. His obsession with youth and his fascination with the extraordinary sums he could command, propelled him into concocting showcases to attract new audiences. He unashamedly let it be known that, aside from his physical state, his sporadic appearances hinged in large part on the size of the check—this as Wanda carefully marshaled the receipts from each dwindling season of concerts.

One method of injecting new life into a career that had already been rewarded with every imaginable success and accolade was to make some kind of change in *modus operandi*. So it was that in 1981 he decided to rock the boat by leaving Shaw Concerts, Inc. Since 1974 the relationship between manager and client had deteriorated, perhaps because Shaw felt exploited by the fact that the minimal commission he was paid was out of all proportion to the time expended. During the 1980–81 season, Horowitz's last with Shaw, the pianist had canceled the majority of his engagements and was "in a slump," according to Jack Pfeiffer. Horowitz's contract with RCA was up for renewal, he was depressed by negative reviews from the previous season, and he was otherwise plagued by a recurrent bronchial infection. Pfeiffer confided to friends that he wasn't certain Horowitz would ever play or record again.

But then, in the fall of 1981, the situation changed when Horowitz announced he was leaving Shaw. A new manager, he reasoned, was just the thing to rejuvenate his post-Jubilee letdown, and he chose the young man who had managed the publicity for his 1974 return, Peter Gelb. The ambitious Gelb, after leaving Gurtman and Murtha, had worked for the Boston Symphony and now was engaged by Columbia Artists as a vice-president to be exclusively in charge of Horowitz. Horowitz's return to Columbia Artists, after a thirty-eight-year absence, prompted a terse statement by Shaw to the press: "As you know, caring for Mr. Horowitz has requirements that exceed those of other artists, and I think that after ten years, I have done my share for the public. It seems only fair to me now that some other agency take up that responsibility." Horowitz's retort was: "We had no grudge, no quarrel. He worked very hard for me. I was satisfied ... but I felt I had to change. That's all. It is sometimes good to have a change."[64]

Horowitz followed the Shaw announcement with a recital at the Metropolitan Opera House on November 1, 1981. Then he called a press conference and revealed that he would make a spring 1982 tour of Europe, his first overseas trip in thirty-one years—since the short 1951 tour of England and France. "In the end, I do everything!"[65] he exclaimed.

Initially, Horowitz contemplated appearances in London, Paris, Amsterdam, and Milan, but he eventually decided to perform only in London, with two recitals (on May 22 and 29) in the Royal Festival Hall, one to benefit the Royal Opera, Covent Garden—"at the invitation of Prince Charles,"[66] he said proudly. With a highly lucrative contract for a worldwide television broadcast of the first of these events, Horowitz had once again succeeded in providing himself with a challenge and another showcase for his mercurial genius.

Now, it seemed that nothing could hold him back. Gitta Gradova observed: "He can put aside all the unhappiness and conflict in his life and still play the piano. This is remarkable, and a sign of his tremendous will and ability to concentrate."[67] In news conferences, Horowitz, at age seventy-nine, exclaimed over and over: "I have tremendous will power! Tremendous!"[68]—and with his eye on the future, he proclaimed that he was years away from retirement. He would keep playing, he said, as long as he felt "the devil and the angel" from within.

SOURCE NOTES

* telephone interview
° Horowitz tape-recorded

PART ONE

CHAPTER ONE

1. °Vladimir Horowitz interviewed by Abram Chasins on National Public Radio, New York, February 27, 1976.

2. Press Book for Josef Hofmann, Wolfsohn Musical Bureau, New York, 1913.

3. Harold C. Schonberg, *The Great Pianists* (New York: Simon & Schuster, 1963).

4. Natasha Saitzoff interviewed by Glenn Plaskin, Washington, D.C., October 8, 1979.

5. The exact place and year of Horowitz's birth are in question. After leaving Russia in 1925, Horowitz and his subsequent managers supplied Western sources with the following information: "Vladimir Horowitz was born in Kiev, Russia, on October 1, 1904" (Concert Management Arthur Judson, 1928).

This information is contradicted, however, by Paul Kogan, Horowitz's first concert manager in Russia. In his book of recollections, *Together with Musicians,* Kogan states: "Vladimir Horowitz was born in Berdichev. Not being able to thrive (in Horowitz's own words) in this little town, he and his family moved to Kiev where Horowitz spent his childhood and adolescence."

Moreover, despite Horowitz's continued insistence that he was born in Kiev, both Nicolas Slonimsky (*Baker's Biographical Dictionary of Musicians*) and Izrail Yampolsky (*Great Soviet Encyclopedia of Music*) confirm Berdichev as Horowitz's correct place of birth—"a fact as well documented as anything in my experience," asserted Slonimsky. In an August 16, 1981, letter to the author, Slonimsky elaborated: "[Horowitz's] place of birth, Berdichev, was testified to by a rabbi in a sworn document in the Hebrew language [and] such an oath by a Jewish cleric is absolutely binding. The document was discovered by Michael Goldstein who now lives in Hamburg, and he gave it to Yampolsky, editor of the Russian Musical Encyclopedia [i.e., *Great Soviet Enclycope-dia of Music*]." Then why the contradiction?

Russian history and psychology play a factor here. The traditionally precarious position of Jews in Russia is symbolized by the town of Berdichev. Czarist governments were notorious for a long tradition of anti-Semitism which manifested itself in periodic purges of Jews, who were forced to leave large cities and settle in smaller, less attractive places like Berdichev. Because of this strong, pre-Revolutionary anti-Semitism, Horowitz may have been sensitive, when setting out to establish his career in Europe and in America, about having been born in Berdichev. As Slonimsky put it to the author: "Anyone born in Berdichev would have been considered by some to be 'the lowest of the low.' It was not uncommon for Jews to deny their place of birth in the Ukraine, for instance, adopting as a more desirable birthplace the cultural and commercial capital, Kiev."

Also in question is the year of Horowitz's birth, listed as 1904 in most sources. The 1937 *Who's Who in Music* lists it as 1900. But Horowitz's first cousin Natasha Saitzoff, who has kept meticulous family records, insists that Horowitz was born in 1903. Mme. Saitzoff explained (interview with author, 10/8/79) that Horowitz's father changed his son's birth date to make him seem a year younger, so that the Bolsheviks could not detain him in Russia for military service. Only a birth certificate could now resolve this dilemma, but various correspondence over the years indicate 1903 as the likely date of birth. In a 1976 radio interview (see Chapter Two, source note 1), Horowitz himself explained: "I had permission to study in Europe and I, a little bit, forged my age."

6. Natasha Saitzoff interviewed by Glenn Plaskin, Washington, D.C., October 8, 1979.

7. Florence Leonard, "Technique the Outgrowth of Musical Thought, An Education Conference with Vladimir Horowitz," *The Etude,* March 1932.

CHAPTER TWO

1. °Vladimir Horowitz interviewed by Digby Peers and Don Newlands for the Canadian Broadcasting Corporation, New York, February 17, 1976.

2. Natasha Saitzoff interviewed by Glenn Plaskin, Washington, D.C., October 8, 1979.

3. Ariel Rubstein interviewed by Glenn Plaskin. *Portland, Ore., November 28, 1979; January 14, 1980.

"A Talk with Vladimir Horowitz," *Neue Freie Presse* (Vienna), February 21, 1929.

SOURCE NOTES

4. Rubstein-Plaskin interview.

5. ibid.

6. Press Book for Vladimir Horowitz, Concert Management Arthur Judson, Inc., 1940.

7. ibid.
°Vladimir Horowitz interviewed by Evans Mirageas on Michigan radio station WUOM, Ann Arbor, April 19, 1975; October 8, 1977.

8. Chotzinoff, op. cit.

9. Sergei Tarnowsky interviewed by Caine Alder, Los Angeles, November 1, 1969.

10. °Vladimir Horowitz interviewed by Abram Chasins on National Public Radio, New York, February 27, 1976.

11. °Vladimir Horowitz interviewed by Tom Willis for *Profiles of Greatness* radio series, New York, September 1974.

12. ibid.

13. Anatole Kitain interviewed by Glenn Plaskin, Orange, N.J., May 27, 1980.

14. Tarnowsky-Alder interview.

15. Rubstein-Plaskin interview.

16. ibid.

CHAPTER THREE

1. °Vladimir Horowitz interviewed by David Dubal on WNCN radio station, New York, February, 1980.
°Vladimir Horowitz interviewed by Helen Epstein for "The Grand Eccentric of the Concert Hall," *New York Times Sunday Magazine,* January 8, 1978.

2. Sergei Tarnowsky interviewed by Caine Alder, Los Angeles, November 1, 1969.

3. Ariel Rubstein interviewed by Glenn Plaskin. *Portland, Ore., November 28, 1979; January 14, 1980.

4. Orrin Howard, "Vladimir Horowitz and His Neglected Mentor," *Los Angeles Times,* September 22, 1968.

5. Arthur Judson Concert Bureau, written statement by Vladimir Horowitz, New York, March 12, 1930.

6. °Horowitz-Dubal interview.

°Vladimir Horowitz interviewed by Evans Mirageas on Michigan radio station WUOM, Ann Arbor, April 19, 1975; October 8, 1977.

7. Howard Taubman, "The Horowitz Story, Or What Makes a Pianist," *New York Times Sunday Magazine,* October 17, 1948.

8. Florence Leonard, "Technique the Outgrowth of Musical Thought, An Education Conference with Vladimir Horowitz," *The Etude,* March 1932.

9. ibid.

10. °Vladimir Horowitz interviewed by Phillip Ramey, New Milford, Conn., July 21, 1971.

11. °Vladimir Horowitz interviewed by Tom Willis for *Profiles of Greatness* radio series, New York, September 1974.

12. Heinrich Neuhaus, *The Art of Piano Playing* (New York: Praeger Publishers, 1973), p. 222.

13. °Horowitz-Ramey interview.

14. °Vladimir Horowitz interviewed by Helen Epstein for "The Grand Eccentric of the Concert Hall," *New York Times Sunday Magazine,* January 8, 1978.

Hubert Saal, "Lord of the Piano," *Newsweek,* January 23, 1978.

15. Vernon Duke (Vladimir Dukelsky), *Passport to Paris* (Boston: Little, Brown & Company, 1955), p. 37.

16. Sergei Bertensson and Jay Leyda, *Sergei Rachmaninoff: A Lifetime in Music* (New York: New York University Press, 1956), p. 229: letter from Felix Blumenfeld to Sergei Rachmaninoff, January 1, 1922.

17. °Horowitz-Epstein interview.

18. °Horowitz-Willis interview.

19. °Horowitz-Epstein interview.

CHAPTER FOUR

1. °Vladimir Horowitz interviewed by Helen Epstein for "The Grand Eccentric of the Concert Hall," *New York Times Sunday Magazine,* January 8, 1978.

2. Vera Resnikov interviewed by Caine Alder, New York, October 17, 1969.

3. Elyse Mach, *Great Pianists Speak for Themselves* (New York: Dodd, Mead & Company, 1980).

4. ibid.

5. *Musical America,* July 1974.

6. ibid.

7. Hubert Saal, "Lord of the Piano," *Newsweek,* January 23, 1978.

8. Samuel Chotzinoff, *A Little Nightmusic* (London: Hamish Hamilton, 1964).

9. Saal, loc. cit.

10. Heinrich Neuhaus, *The Art of Piano Playing* (New York: Praeger Publishers, 1973), p. 91.

11. *Musical America,* July 1974.

12. Chotzinoff, op. cit.

13. *The Gramophone,* April 1975.

14. Raya Garbousova interviewed by Glenn Plaskin, *Hartford, December 5, 1979.

15. Gregor Piatigorsky, *Cellist* (New York: Da Capo Press, 1976).

16. Paul Kogan, "First Steps," *Together with Musicians* (Moscow: Muzgiz, 1964).

17. ibid.

18. ibid.

19. ibid.

20. Natasha Saitzoff interviewed by Glenn Plaskin, Washington, D.C., October 8, 1979.

21. David Rabinovich, "Vladimir Horowitz and the Russian Piano Tradition," *Soviet Music Magazine* (Moscow), January 1965.

22. °Vladimir Horowitz interviewed by David Dubal on WNCN radio station, New York, February 1980.

23. Rabinovich, loc. cit.

24. Artur Schnabel, *My Life & Music* (London: Longmans, 1961), p. 189.

25. Kogan, op. cit.

26. °Vladimir Horowitz interviewed by Tom Willis for *Profiles of Greatness* radio series, New York, September 1974.

27. °Horowitz-Epstein interview.

28. °Vladimir Horowitz interviewed by Digby Peers and Don Newlands for the Canadian Broadcasting Corporation, New York, February 17, 1976.

29. Lydia Zhukova interviewed by Glenn Plaskin, New York, November 9, 1980; December 10, 1980.

30. ibid.

31. ibid.

32. Rabinovich, loc. cit.

33. Alexander Eydelman interviewed by Glenn Plaskin, New York, June 24, 1979.

34. Ariel Rubstein interviewed by Glenn Plaskin, *Portland, Ore., November 28, 1979; January 14, 1980.

35. Saal, loc. cit.

36. Rabinovich, op. cit.

37. Anatole Kitain interviewed by Glenn Plaskin, Orange, N.J., May 27, 1980.

38. Kogan, op. cit.

39. Chotzinoff, op. cit.

40. °Vladimir Horowitz interviewed by Phillip Ramey, New York, November 29, 1977.

41. Kogan, op. cit.

42. David Thorstad and John Lauritsen, *The Early Homosexual Rights Movement* (*1864–1935*) (New York: Times Change Press, 1974).

43. Victor Chapin, *Giants of the Keyboard* (Philadelphia: J.B. Lippincott Co., 1967).

44. Alexander Merovitch, unpublished diaries, c. 1948.

45. ibid.

46. ibid.

47. *Musical America,* July 1974.

48. Kogan, op. cit.

49. Alexander Steinert interviewed by Glenn Plaskin, New York, June 6, 1980.

50. Saitzoff-Plaskin interview.

51. Berthe Malko interviewed by Glenn Plaskin, New York, January 23, 1980.

52. Steinert-Plaskin interview.
Maria Merovitch interviewed by Glenn Plaskin, *Ft. Lauderdale, Fla., November 8, 1980.
Michel Michelet (real name Levin) interviewed by Glenn Plaskin, Los Angeles, January 24, 1980. ["I was a young professor at the Kiev Conservatory," recalled composer Michelet, "and will never forget that Horowitz's brother, George, committed suicide in 1925 at age twenty-three. My colleagues and friends of the Horowitz family were shocked to read this in the local newspapers."]

53. Nathan Milstein interviewed by Glenn Plaskin, London, February 16, 1980.

54. Saitzoff-Plaskin interview.

55. Kitain-Plaskin interview.

56. Press Book for Vladimir Horowitz, Arthur Judson Concert Bureau, c. 1928.

57. °Horowitz-Dubal interview.

58. Chotzinoff, op. cit.

PART TWO

CHAPTER FIVE

1. Press Book for Vladimir Horowitz, Concert Management Arthur Judson, Inc., New York, 1940.

2. Abram Chasins, *Speaking of Pianists* (New York: Alfred A. Knopf, 1958), p. 139.

°Vladimir Horowitz interviewed by Helen Epstein for "The Grand Eccentric of the Concert Hall," *New York Times Sunday Magazine,* January 8, 1978.

°Vladimir Horowitz interviewed by David Dubal on WNCN radio station, New York, February 1980.

3. Peter Gay, *Weimar Culture* (New York: Harper & Row, 1970), p. 130.

4. ibid., p. 132.

5. Harold C. Schonberg, *The Great Pianists* (New York: Simon & Schuster, 1963), p. 419.

6. Gay, op. cit., p. 129.

7. °Horowitz-Epstein interview.

8. *Chicago Tribune,* November 24, 1928.

9. Nicolas Slonimsky, *Baker's Biographical Dictionary of Musicians,* 6th Ed. (New York: Schirmer Books, 1978), p. 1455.

10. Jan Holcman, "Horowitz at Home," *Stereo Review,* April 30, 1960 (unedited transcript of interview with Vladimir Horowitz).

11. ibid.

12. °Horowitz-Epstein interview.

13. Schonberg, op. cit., p. 420.

14. °Vladimir Horowitz interviewed by Winthrop Sargeant, New York, 1978.

15. Schonberg, op. cit., p. 401.

16. °Horowitz-Sargeant interview.

17. ibid.

18. °Horowitz-Epstein interview.

19. ibid.

20. Alexander Merovitch, unpublished diaries, c. 1948.

21. ibid.

22. ibid.

23. ibid.

24. °Horowitz-Dubal interview.

25. ibid.

26. Chasins, op. cit., p. 137.

27. Merovitch diaries.

28. °Horowitz-Dubal interview.

29. *Allgemeine Musikzeitung* (Berlin), January 15, 1926.

30. *Allgemeine Musikzeitung* (Berlin), January 8, 1926.

31. °Horowitz-Epstein interview.

32. *Deutsche Zeitung* (Berlin), January 28, 1926.

33. °Horowitz-Epstein interview.

34. Gregor Piatigorsky, *Cellist* (New York: Doubleday & Company, 1965), p. 51.

35. ibid., p. 161.

36. ibid., p. 162.

37. ibid., p. 162.

38. ibid., p. 163.

39. ibid., p. 163.

40. Chasins, op. cit., p. 138.

41. *Hamburger Fremdenblatt,* January 20, 1926.

42. Chasins, op. cit., p. 138.

43. ibid.

44. ibid.

45. ibid.

46. ibid.

47. Merovitch diaries.

48. Caine Alder, "The Recordings of Vladimir Horowitz," *High Fidelity,* July 1973.

49. Nathan Milstein interviewed by Glenn Plaskin, London, February 18, 1980.

50. Piatigorsky, op. cit., p. 164.

51. ibid.

52. Merovitch diaries.

CHAPTER SIX

1. Abram Chasins, *Speaking of Pianists* (New York: Alfred A. Knopf, 1958), p. 140.

2. Hubert Saal, "Lord of the Piano," *Newsweek,* January 23, 1978.

3. Henry Prunières, *La Revue Musicale* (Paris), April 1926.

4. Prunières, op. cit., April 1927.

5. Alexander Merovitch, unpublished diaries, c. 1948.

6. Chasins, op. cit., p. 140.

7. Maria Merovitch interviewed by Glenn Plaskin, *Ft. Lauderdale, Fla., July 14, 1980.

8. Arthur Judson, "The Making of a Name," *The Etude,* June 1940. Biography of Arthur Judson supplied by Ralph Kolin.

9. ibid.

10. *Seattle Star,* November 10, 1945.

11. *Gramophone,* April 1975.

12. Piatigorsky, op. cit., p. 130.

13. Charles Cooke, "Maestro's Son-in-Law," *Esquire,* April 1935.

14. *Jewish Tribune,* June 29, 1928.

15. Gitta Gradova interviewed by Glenn Plaskin, *Chicago, November 11, 1979.

16. Anatole Kitain interviewed by Glenn Plaskin, Orange, N.J., May 27, 1980.

17. Saal, loc. cit.

18. Peter Gay, *Weimar Culture* (New York: Harper & Row, 1970), pp. 129–130.

19. °Vladimir Horowitz interviewed by Evans Mirageas on Michigan radio station WUOM, Ann Arbor, April 19, 1975; October 8, 1977.

20. Nathan Milstein interviewed by Glenn Plaskin, London, February 18, 1980.

21. *Hamburger Fremdenblatt,* November 13, 1926.

22. °Vladimir Horowitz interviewed by Helen Epstein for "The Grand Eccentric of the Concert Hall," *New York Times Sunday Magazine,* January 8, 1978.

23. ibid.

24. *Berliner Tageblatt,* February 5, 1927.

25. *Schlesische Zeitung Breslau,* November 28, 1926.

26. Gay, op. cit., p. 129.

27. *Berliner Tageblatt,* November 12, 1927.

28. *Breslauer Zeitung,* November 10, 1926.

29. *Rheinischer Merkur Dortmund,* February 1, 1927.

30. *Berliner Tageblatt,* February 5, 1927.

31. *Breslauer Zeitung Wroclaw,* February 19, 1927.

32. *Breslauer Zeitung,* February 19, 1927.

33. °Horowitz-Mirageas interview.

34. °Horowitz-Epstein interview.

35. Rudolf Serkin interviewed by Glenn Plaskin, *Brattleboro, Vt., January 24, 1980.

36. Merovitch diaries.

37. Chasins, op. cit., p. 141.

38. *De Telegraaf* (Amsterdam), November 20, 1927.

39. London *Times,* April 18, 1927.

40. °Vladimir Horowitz interviewed by Phillip Ramey, New York, November 29, 1977.

41. *Hamburger Nachrichten,* October 10, 1927.

42. ibid.

43. *Vossische Zeitung* (Berlin), November 27, 1927.

44. °Horowitz-Ramey interview.

45. *Vossische Zeitung* (Berlin), April 13, 1927.

46. *Allgemeine Musikzeitung* (Berlin), December 2, 1927.

CHAPTER SEVEN

1. °Vladimir Horowitz interviewed by Phillip Ramey, New York, November 29, 1977.

2. *The Gramophone,* June 1931, pp. 11, 12.

3. Linton Martin, *Philadelphia Inquirer,* February 11, 1928. Arthur Judson Press Book, New York City, 1940.

4. Alexander Merovitch, unpublished diaries, c. 1948.

5. *Boston Globe,* March 25, 1928.

6. *New York Herald Tribune,* January 11, 1953.

7. °Horowitz-Ramey interview.

8. ibid.

9. ibid.

10. Abram Chasins, *Speaking of Pianists* (New York: Alfred A. Knopf, 1958), p. 137.

11. °Horowitz-Ramey interview.

12. Pitts Sanborn, *New York Telegram,* January 13, 1928.

13. Harold Schonberg, *The Great Conductors* (New York: Simon & Schuster (Paperback Printing), 1970), p. 293.

14. °Vladimir Horowitz interviewed by Mary Rousculp on Ohio radio station WOSU, Columbus, May 17, 1975.

15. ibid.

16. Barbara Amiel, "Horowitz on the Road," *The Canadian,* July 10, 1976.

17. Olin Downes, *New York Times,* January 13, 1928.

18. Sanborn, loc. cit.

19. Downes, loc. cit.

20. °Horowitz-Rousculp interview.

21. Olin Downes, *New York Times,* January 15, 1928.

22. Henrietta Straus, *The Nation,* March 7, 1928.

23. W.J. Henderson, *New York Evening Sun,* January 13, 1928.

24. Pitts Sanborn, *New York Telegram,* January 13, 1928.

25. *New York Evening World,* January 13, 1928.

26. Olin Downes, *New York Times,* February 21, 1928.

27. *The Nation,* March 7, 1928.

28. Olin Downes, *New York Times,* January 15, 1928.

29. Olin Downes, *New York Times,* January 13, 1928.

30. Hubert Saal, "Lord of the Piano," *Newsweek,* January 23, 1978.

31. °Horowitz-Rousculp interview.

32. Chasins, op. cit.

33. °Vladimir Horowitz interviewed by David Dubal on WNCN radio station, New York, February 1980.

34. °Horowitz-Ramey interview.

35. °Horowitz-Dubal interview.

36. Olin Downes, *New York Times,* February 21, 1928.

37. ibid.

38. *Musical America,* March 3, 1928.

39. Olin Downes, *New York Times,* February 21, 1928.

40. ibid.

41. Pitts Sanborn, *New York Telegram,* February 21, 1928.

42. Olin Downes, *New York Times,* February 21, 1928.

43. ibid.

44. Pitts Sanborn, *New York Telegram,* February 21, 1928.

45. ibid.

46. *Musical America,* March 3, 1928.

47. *Boston Herald American,* March 19, 1928.

48. *Boston Globe,* March 19, 1928.

49. *Boston Globe,* March 25, 1928.

50. ibid.

51. *Boston Globe,* March 19, 1928.

52. ibid.

53. ibid.

54. ibid.

55. *Boston Globe,* March 25, 1928.

56. Helen L. Kaufmann, and Eva E. Hansl, *Artists in Music of Today* (New York: Grosset & Dunlap, 1933), p. 53.

CHAPTER EIGHT

1. Alexander Steinert interviewed by Glenn Plaskin, New York, June 9, 1980.

2. Arthur Rubinstein interviewed by Glenn Plaskin, New York, June 30, 1980.

3. Thomas Manshardt interviewed by Glenn Plaskin, *Montreal, January 28, 1981.

4. *La Semaine à Paris,* June 5, 1928.

5. Letter from Vladimir Horowitz to Alexander Greiner, Vichy, France, September 8, 1928. Steinway & Sons Archive.

6. Alexander Steinert interviewed by Glenn Plaskin, New York, June 9, 1980.

7. ibid.

8. °Vladimir Horowitz interviewed by Tom Willis for *Profiles of Greatness* radio series, New York, September 1974.

9. Steinert-Plaskin interview, June 30, 1980.

10. Harold Schonberg, *The Great Pianists* (New York: Simon & Schuster, 1963), p. 416.

11. ibid., p. 413.

12. ibid., p. 414.

13. Arthur Rubinstein, *My Many Years* (New York: Alfred A. Knopf, 1980), p. 251.
   Rubinstein-Plaskir. interview, June 30, 1980.

14. Alyesa Forsee, *Artur Rubinstein, King of the Keyboard* (New York: Thomas Y. Crowell Company, 1969).

15. Rubinstein, op. cit., p. 255.

16. ibid., p. 256.

17. Arthur Rubinstein interviewed by Glenn Plaskin, New York, June 30, 1980.

18. Rubinstein, op. cit., p. 256.

19. ibid., p. 258.

20. Rubinstein-Plaskin interview.

21. Rubinstein, op. cit., p. 256.

22. ibid., pp. 289–290.

23. Manshardt-Plaskin interview.

24. ibid

25. ibid.

26. *Hamburger Fremdenblatt,* September 27, 1928.

27. *Breslauer Nachrichten,* February 23, 1929.

28. Axcl Sandal, *Musikkens Store Navne* cited in *Great Names in Music from the Concert Hall, Opera, Radio and Gramophone* (*32 Biographies of Contemporary and Deceased Artists* by Sverre Forchhammer), Denmark: C.A. Reitzels Forlag, 1946.

29. °Unedited transcript of Vladimir Horowitz at Chicago press conference, October 25, 1974.

CHAPTER NINE

1. Neville Cardus, *Manchester Guardian,* May 8, 1933.

2. Samuel Chotzinoff, *A Little Nightmusic* (London: Hamish Hamilton, 1964), p. 47.

3. Pitts Sanborn, *New York Telegram,* November 3, 1928.

4. ibid.

5. ibid.

6. Olin Downes, *New York Times,* November 3, 1928.

7. ibid.

8. *New York American,* November 3, 1928.

9. Kurt Weinhold interviewed by Glenn Plaskin, *New York, April 20, 1981.

10. Alexander Merovitch, unpublished diaries, c. 1948.

11. *Chicago Tribune,* November 24, 1928

12. ibid.

13. Charles Cooke, "Maestro's Son-in-Law," *Esquire,* April 1935.

14. *Musical Courier,* December 20, 1928.

15. ibid.

16. ibid.

17. *Neue Freie Presse* (Vienna), February 21, 1929.

18. Gregor Piatigorsky, *Cellist* (New York: Doubleday & Company, 1965), p. 167.

19. Arthur Rubinstein, *My Many Years* (New York: Alfred A. Knopf, 1980), p. 303.

20. *Lyrica Paris,* June 1929.

21. *Neue Freie Presse* (Vienna), October 23, 1929.

22. Piatigorsky, op. cit., p. 167.

23. ibid., p. 175.

24. ibid., p. 206.

25. Press Book for Vladimir Horowitz, Concert Management Arthur Judson, Inc., New York, 1940.

26. Cooke, loc. cit.

27. ibid.

28. ibid.

29. Anatole Kitain interviewed by Glenn Plaskin, Orange, N.J., May 27, 1980.

30. *Rocky Mountain News,* November 29, 1929.

31. *New York Times,* December 27, 1929.

32. *Rocky Mountain News,* November 29, 1929.

33. *Oregon Journal,* February 9, 1931.

34. °Vladimir Horowitz interviewed by Abram Chasins, New York, June 1965.

35. Eugene Stinson, *Chicago Daily News,* January 29, 1931.

36. Rom Landau, *Ignace Paderewski* (New York: Thomas Y. Crowell Co., 1934), p. 283.

37. Glenn Dillard Gunn, *Chicago Herald and Examiner,* April 11, 1931.

38. Cooke, loc. cit.

39. ibid.
Hubert Saal, "Lord of the Piano," *Newsweek,* January 23, 1978.
Chicago Tribune, February 25, 1931.

40. Piatigorsky, op. cit., p. 198.

41. ibid., p. 168.

42. Alexander Steinert interviewed by Glenn Plaskin, New York, June 9, 1980.

43. Letter from Alexander Merovitch to Alexander Greiner, Crans Sur Sierre, September 9, 1931. Steinway & Sons Archive.

44. Piatigorsky, op. cit., p. 168.

45. °Vladimir Horowitz interviewed by Phillip Ramey, New York, November 29, 1977.

46. Piatigorsky, op. cit., p. 171.

47. *Neue Freie Presse* (Vienna), November 11, 1933.

48. Piatigorsky, op. cit., p. 171.

49. ibid., p. 171.

50. ibid., p. 170.

51. ibid., p. 170.

52. ibid., p. 170.

53. ibid., p. 171.

54. *Musical Courier,* May 23, 1931.

55. *New York Times,* March 31, 1932.

56. ibid.

57. Piatigorsky, op. cit., p. 229.

58. ibid., pp. 198–199.

59. Letter from Harold Holt to Alexander Merovitch, May 19, 1932.

60. London *Times,* April 13, 1932.

61. °Vladimir Horowitz interviewed by Edward Greenfield, New York, May 10, 1978.

62. London *Times,* November 11, 1932.

63. L.M.G. Arntzenius, "Vladimir Horowitz Talks," *De Telegraaf.* An interview in Amsterdam, November 20, 1932.

64. *Musical America,* February 10, 1933.

65. Ronald Gelatt, *Music Makers* (New York: Alfred A. Knopf, 1953), pp. 236–237.

66. Arntzenius, loc. cit.

67. *Chicago Daily News,* April 12, 1933.

68. *Milwaukee Journal,* April 18, 1933.

CHAPTER TEN

1. Samuel Chotzinoff, *A Little Nightmusic* (London: Hamish Hamilton, 1964), p. 48.
°Vladimir Horowitz interviewed by John Gruen, November 9, 1975.
°Vladimir Horowitz interviewed by Digby Peers and Don Newlands for the Canadian Broadcasting Corporation, New York, February 17, 1976.

2. °Vladimir Horowitz and Wanda Toscanini Horowitz interviewed by Mike Wallace for CBS's *60 Minutes,* December 26, 1977.

3. Charles Cooke, "Maestro's Son-in-Law," *Esquire,* April 1935.

4. °Vladimir Horowitz interviewed by David Dubal on WNCN radio station, New York, February 1980.

5. *Allegri,* April 8, 1972, p. 56.

6. Cooke, loc. cit.

7. *Allegri,* April 8, 1972, p. 56.

8. °Vladimir Horowitz interviewed by Winthrop Sargeant, New York, 1978.

9. *New York Times,* April 24, 1933.

10. ibid.

11. Helen L. Kaufmann, and Eva E. Hansl, *Artists in Music of Today* (New York: Grosset & Dunlap, 1933), p. 53.

12. *New York Times,* April 24, 1933.

13. °Vladimir Horowitz and Wanda Toscanini Horowitz interviewed by Edward Greenfield, New York, May 10, 1978.

14. Tex McCrary and Jinx Falkenburg, "New York Close-Up," January 24, 1951.

15. °Wanda Toscanini Horowitz interviewed by Mary Rousculp on Ohio radio station WOSU, Columbus, May 17, 1975.
   °Wanda Horowitz-Wallace interview.

16. Harvey Sachs, *Toscanini* (New York: J.B. Lippincott Co., 1978), p. 92.

17. ibid., p. 74.

18. °Wanda Horowitz-Greenfield interview.

19. °Wanda Horowitz-Rousculp interview.

20. ibid.

21. °Wanda Horowitz-Greenfield interview.

22. ibid.

23. °Wanda Horowitz-Rousculp interview.

24. °Wanda Horowitz-Wallace interview.

25. Neville Cardus, *Manchester Guardian,* May 8, 1933.

26. °Wanda Horowitz-Greenfield interview.

27. Yehudi Menuhin, *Unfinished Journey* (London: MacDonald & Jane's, 1976), p. 108.

28. °Wanda Horowitz-Greenfield interview.

29. Sachs, op. cit., p. 170.

30. °Wanda Horowitz-Rousculp interview.

31. Sachs, op. cit., p. 229.

32. *New York Herald Tribune,* January 11, 1928.

33. Interview with anonymous source, citing diaries, c. 1933.

34. ibid.

35. ibid.

36. ibid.

37. ibid.

38. ibid.

39. L.M.G. Arntzenius, *De Telegraaf* (Amsterdam), October 10, 1933.

40. Berthe Malko interviewed by Glenn Plaskin, New York, January 28, 1980.

41. Interview with anonymous source.

42. Malko-Plaskin interview.

43. *Chicago Tribune Press Service* (Paris), October 6, 1933.

44. Interview with anonymous source.

45. ibid.

46. ibid.

47. Alexander Steinert interviewed by Glenn Plaskin, New York, June 9, 1980.

48. London *Times,* November 6, 1933.

49. Vera Resnikoff interviewed by Caine Alder, New York, October 17, 1969.

50. *New York Post,* March 28, 1978.

51. Mary Jane Matz interviewed by Glenn Plaskin, *New York, January 20, 1981.

52. Hubert Saal, "Lord of the Piano," *Newsweek,* January 23, 1978.

53. Arthur Rubinstein interviewed by Glenn Plaskin, New York, June 30, 1980.

54. *New York Post,* March 28, 1978.

55. Sachs, op. cit., p. 55.

56. John Selby, *New York American,* January 12, 1934.

57. *Chicago Tribune,* January 6, 1934.

58. Cooke, loc. cit.

59. *Rocky Mountain News,* March 6, 1934.

60. Pitts Sanborn, *New York Telegram,* January 31, 1934.

61. ibid.

62. Cooke, loc. cit.

CHAPTER ELEVEN

1. °Vladimir Horowitz interviewed by Abram Chasins, New York, June 1965.

2. Charles Cooke, "Maestro's Son-in-Law," *Esquire,* April 1935.

3. Gitta Gradova interviewed by Glenn Plaskin, *Chicago, March 10, 1980.

4. Nathan Milstein interviewed by Glenn Plaskin, *New York, October 8, 1980.

5. Maria Merovitch interviewed by Glenn Plaskin, *Ft. Lauderdale, Fla., July 14, 1980.

6. Ella Brailowsky interviewed by Glenn Plaskin, *New York, November 27, 1980.

7. Merovitch-Plaskin interview.

8. Arthur Rubinstein interviewed by Glenn Plaskin, New York, June 30, 1980.

9. Rubinstein-Plaskin interview.
Arthur Rubinstein, *My Many Years* (New York: Alfred A. Knopf, 1980), pp. 334–335.

10. Natasha Saitzoff interviewed by Glenn Plaskin, Washington, D.C., October 8, 1979.

11. Alexander Steinert interviewed by Glenn Plaskin, New York, June 6, 1980.

12. Saitzoff-Plaskin interview. (The date of Simeon Horowitz's death is unknown.)

13. Unpublished journal of Nicolai Malko, entry of October 17, 1934. (Permission: Berthe Malko.)

14. ibid., October 20, 1934.

15. Berthe Malko interviewed by Glenn Plaskin, New York, January 23, 1980.

16. ibid.

17. Unpublished journal of Nicolai Malko, entry of October 17, 1934.

18. Malko-Plaskin interview.

19. °Vladimir Horowitz and Wanda Toscanini Horowitz at Chicago press conference, November 8, 1977.

20. Gregor Piatigorsky, *Cellist* (New York: Doubleday & Company, 1965), p. 109.

21. Ted Joselson interviewed by Glenn Plaskin, New York, March 11, 1980.

22. °Vladimir Horowitz interviewed by Mike Wallace for CBS's *60 Minutes,* December 26, 1977.

23. Interview with anonymous source.

24. John Frieman interviewed by Glenn Plaskin, *New York, January 23, 1981.

25. Samuel Chotzinoff, *A Little Nightmusic* (London: Hamish Hamilton, 1964), p. 48.

26. °Vladimir Horowitz interviewed by John Gruen, November 9, 1975.

27. °Vladimir Horowitz interviewed by Digby Peers and Don Newlands for the Canadian Broadcasting Corporation, New York, February 17, 1976.

28. *Le Soir* (Brussels), December 1, 1934.

29. London *Times,* January 18, 1935.

30. Leonard Liebling, *New York American,* April 14, 1935.

31. *New York Sun,* April 14, 1935.

32. Edwin Bachmann interviewed by Glenn Plaskin, New York, March 9, 1980.

33. Olin Downes, *New York Times,* March 15, 1935.

34. *Musical America,* March 25, 1935.

35. *New York Sun,* April 14, 1935.

36. *Chicago Tribune,* March 29, 1935.

37. Stockholm Theatre Column, October 23, 1935.

38. Vladimir Horowitz news clipping file, Lincoln Center Library of the Performing Arts (Rotterdam, November 8, 1935).

39. ibid. (Milan, January 8, 1936).

40. °Horowitz-Chasins interview.

41. ibid.

42. Vladimir Horowitz news clipping file, Lincoln Center Library of the Performing Arts (Martin Cookes, London, April 1936).

43. London *Times,* February 26, 1936.

44. Gradova-Plaskin interview.

45. Saitzoff-Plaskin interview.

46. Oscar Levant, *The Memoirs of an Amnesiac* (New York: G.P. Putnam's Sons, 1965), p. 219.

47. Saitzoff-Plaskin interview.

48. Gradova-Plaskin interview.

49. *New York Times,* January 25, 1938.

50. *New York Times,* December 24, 1939.

51. Kurt Blaukopf, *Les Grands Virtuoses* (Paris: Éditions Correa, 1955).

52. Abram Chasins, *Speaking of Pianists* (New York: Alfred A. Knopf, 1958), p. 141.

53. Steinert-Plaskin interview.

54. Interview with anonymous source.

55. Letter from Wanda Toscanini Horowitz to Sergei Rachmaninoff, July 3, 1937. Steinway & Sons Archive.

56. Steinert-Plaskin interview.

57. Letter from Sergei Rachmaninoff to Vladimir Robertovitch Wilshau, August 3, 1935. Courtesy of Francis Joseph Crociata.

58. Francis Joseph Crociata, interviewed by Glenn Plaskin, New York, July 5, 1979.

59. °Vladimir Horowitz interviewed by David Dubal on WNCN radio station. New York, February, 1980.

60. °Vladimir Horowitz interviewed at Chicago press conference, January 10, 1979.

61. Milton Cross, and David Ewen, *The Milton Cross New Encyclopedia of the Great Composers and Their Music* (New York: Doubleday & Company, 1969), p. 742.

62. Letter from Dr. Nicolai Dahl to Sergei Rachmaninoff, Bayreuth, May 21, 1938. Courtesy of Francis Joseph Crociata.

63. °Horowitz-Peers interview.

64. Rudolf Serkin interviewed by Glenn Plaskin, *Brattleboro, Vt., January 24, 1980.

65. °Horowitz-Chasins interview.

66. Chotzinoff, op. cit., p. 51.

67. °Horowitz-Gruen interview.

68. °Vladimir Horowitz interviewed by Phillip Ramey, New York, November 29, 1977.

69. °Horowitz-Gruen interview.

70. °Horowitz-Ramey interview.

71. ibid.

72. *Le Figaro,* July 17, 1938.

73. *New York Sun,* January 25, 1938.

74. *Le Figaro,* July 19, 1938.

75. *Neue Zuericher Zeitung,* September 29, 1938.

76. *De Telegraaf* (Amsterdam), February 29, 1938.

77. Letter from Vladimir Horowitz to Alexander Greiner, November 18, 1938. Steinway & Sons Archive.

78. ibid.

79. Undated letter from Vladimir Horowitz to Sergei Rachmaninoff, Gstaad, Switzerland, 1939. Steinway & Sons Archive.

80. Undated letter from Vladimir Horowitz to Alexander Greiner. Steinway & Sons Archive.

81. *New York Times,* December 24, 1939.

82. *New York Sun,* January 13, 1940.

83. Blaukopf, op. cit., p. 125.

84. *De Telegraaf* (Amsterdam), November 30, 1938.

85. *Niewe Rotterdamse Courant,* March 12, 1939.

86. London *Times,* March 22, 1939.

87. London *Times,* March 1, 1939

88. *New York Times,* March 5, 1939.

89. *Le Figaro,* February 12, 1939.

90. ibid.

91. *De Telegraaf* (Amsterdam), February 29, 1938.

92. Letter from Vladimir Horowitz to Alexander Greiner, The Hague, November 18, 1938. Steinway & Sons Archive.

93. ibid.

94. Harvey Sachs, *Toscanini* (New York: J.B. Lippincott Co., 1978), p. 154.

95. ibid., p. 211.

96. ibid., p. 267.

97. °Vladimir Horowitz interviewed by Winthrop Sargeant, New York, 1978.

98. *Atlanta Journal,* October 8, 1939.

PART THREE

CHAPTER TWELVE

1. °Vladimir Horowitz interviewed by Helen Epstein for "The Grand Eccentric of the Concert Hall," *New York Times Sunday Magazine,* January 8, 1978.

2. *Boston Globe,* February 12, 1940.

3. *New York Sun,* January 13, 1940.

4. Press Book for Vladimir Horowitz, Concert Management Arthur Judson, Inc., New York, 1940.

5. Milton Katims interviewed by Glenn Plaskin, *Houston, March 23, 1980.

6. *New York Sun,* January 13, 1940.

7. *Milwaukee Journal,* March 2, 1949.

8. *Boston Post,* February 12, 1940.
New York Sun, January 13, 1940.

9. Press Book for Vladimir Horowitz, op. cit.

10. ibid.

11. *New York Times,* January 13, 1940.

12. *Boston Herald,* February 12, 1940.

13. *New York Times,* December 24, 1939.

14. ibid.

15. B.H. Haggin, *A Decade of Music* (New York: Horizon Press, 1973). Originally written for *The Nation,* January 13, 1940.

16. *New York Herald Tribune,* February 1, 1940.

17. *New York Times,* February 16, 1940.

18. Jerome D. Bohm, February 16, 1940.

19. *New York Times,* April 13, 1940.

20. ibid.

21. *New York Times,* May 7, 1940.

22. ibid.

23. °Vladimir Horowitz interviewed by Digby Peers and Don Newlands for the Canadian Broadcasting Corporation, New York, February 17, 1976.

24. Edwin Bachmann interviewed by Glenn Plaskin, New York, March 9, 1980.

25. *New York Times,* May 7, 1940.

26. *New York Tribune,* October 14, 1940.

27. *New York Sun,* October 16, 1940.

28. Draft of letter sent by Alexander Merovitch to Ernesto De Quesada, undated. University of Oregon Library.

29. Letter sent by Alexander Merovitch to Ernesto De Quesada, April 5, 1948. University of Oregon Library.

30. Lowell Benedict interviewed by Glenn Plaskin, Lambertville, N.J., July 15, 1981. Telephone interviews on May 27, June 9, June 26, 1980; July 14, 1981.

31. ibid.

32. Letter from Vladimir Horowitz to Arthur Judson, January 27, 1941. University of Oregon Library.

33. Telegram from Vladimir Horowitz to Alexander Merovitch, January 31, 1941. University of Oregon Library.

34. Benedict-Plaskin interview.

35. ibid.

36. *Kansas City Times,* March 1, 1941.

37. *New York Herald Tribune,* March 20, 1941.

38. *New York Times,* March 20, 1941.

39. Benedict-Plaskin interview.

40. Joachim Kaiser, *Great Pianists of Our Time* (New York: Herder & Herder, 1971), p. 75.

41. *New York Times,* April 20, 1941.

42. Charles O'Connell, *The Other Side of the Record* (New York: Alfred A. Knopf, 1947), p. 242.

43. ibid., p. 243.

44. Arthur Rubinstein, *My Many Years* (New York: Alfred A. Knopf, 1980), p. 468.

45. Lehman Engel interviewed by Glenn Plaskin, New York, April 10, 1980.

46. Letter from Wanda Toscanini Horowitz to Sergei Rachmaninoff, November 20, 1941. Library of Congress Archive.

47. Benedict-Plaskin interview.

48. ibid.

49. Engel-Plaskin interview.

50. Benedict-Plaskin interview.

CHAPTER THIRTEEN

1. Vladimir Horowitz, "Why I Transcribed *The Stars and Stripes Forever*," Press Book for Vladimir Horowitz, Concert Management Arthur Judson, Inc., New York, 1940.

2. Natasha Saitzoff interviewed by Glenn Plaskin, Washington, D.C., October 8, 1979.

3. °Vladimir Horowitz interviewed by David Dubal on WNCN radio station, New York, February 1980.

4. Saitzoff-Plaskin interview.

5. Lowell Benedict interviewed by Glenn Plaskin, Lambertville, N.J., July 15, 1981.

6. °Wanda Toscanini Horowitz interviewed by Edward Greenfield, New York, May 10, 1978.

7. Henry Simon, March 7, 1942.

8. Kurt Weinhold interviewed by Glenn Plaskin, *New York, April 15, 1981.

9. Marilyn Meyer Holzer interviewed by Glenn Plaskin, New York, December 13, 1981.

10. Ted Joselson interviewed by Glenn Plaskin, New York, March 11, 1980.

11. William Judd interviewed by Glenn Plaskin, *New York, May 7, 1980.

12. Letter from Vladimir Horowitz to Arthur Judson, March 7, 1942. Courtesy of Lowell Benedict.

13. Letter from Calvin Franklin to Vladimir Horowitz, March 13, 1942. University of Oregon Library.

14. Letter from Vladimir Horowitz to V. Bezikin, 1942. Courtesy of Lowell Benedict.

15. Lowell Benedict interviewed by Glenn Plaskin, New York, April 10, 1980.

16. Virgil Thomson, *New York Herald Tribune,* March 7, 1942.

17. *Los Angeles Times,* February 12, 1978.

18. Sergei Bertensson, and Jay Leyda, *Sergei Rachmaninoff* (New York: New York University Press, 1956), p. 376.

19. ibid., pp. 371–372.

20. Samuel Chotzinoff, *A Little Nightmusic* (London: Hamish Hamilton, 1964), p. 47.

21. *Milwaukee Journal,* April 13, 1943.

22. Chotzinoff, op. cit., p. 48.

23. °Vladimir Horowitz interviewed by Phillip Ramey, New York, November 29, 1977.

24. *New York Daily News,* February 23, 1943.

25. Phillip Ramey interviewed by Glenn Plaskin, May 15, 1982.

26. *New York Herald Tribune,* April 26, 1943.

27. Lehman Engel, *This Bright Day* (New York: Macmillan Co., 1974), pp. 133–136.

28. *Milwaukee Journal,* April 30, 1943.

29. Lehman Engel interviewed by Glenn Plaskin, New York, April 10, 1980.

30. Natasha Saitzoff interviewed by Glenn Plaskin, Washington, D.C., October 8, 1979.

31. °Horowitz-Dubal interview.

32. RCA Liner Note from *"The Horowitz Collection,"* ARMI-2952.
°Vladimir Horowitz interviewed by Abram Chasins on National Public Radio, February 27, 1976.

33. *New York Herald Tribune,* March 15, 1944.

34. ibid.

35. *Chicago Tribune,* April 30, 1943.

36. Jerome D. Bohm, May 18, 1943.

37. Guy Maier, "The Pianist's Page," *Etude,* June 1948.

38. *Los Angeles Times,* November 26, 1950.

39. *New York Times,* January 24, 1950.

40. *Atlanta Constitution,* February 28, 1950.
Cleveland Plain Dealer, January 7, 1950.

41. Olin Downes, *New York Times,* January 24, 1950.

42. Horowitz, "Why I Transcribed *The Stars and Stripes Forever.*"

43. *Chicago Tribune,* February 13, 1945.

44. *Denver Post,* January 27, 1949.

CHAPTER FOURTEEN

1. °Vladimir Horowitz interviewed by Helen Epstein for "The Grand Eccentric of the Concert Hall," *New York Times Sunday Magazine,* January 8, 1978.

2. Adele Marcus interviewed by Glenn Plaskin, *New York, December 11, 1979.

3. Byron Janis interviewed by Glenn Plaskin, New York, *March 11, 1980; April 12, 1980.

4. *New York Post Home News,* December 23, 1948.

5. Marcus-Plaskin interview.

6. ibid.

7. Janis-Plaskin interviews.

8. ibid.

9. ibid.

10. Vladimir Horowitz, "Students Must Help Themselves," *Etude,* September 1951.

11. ibid.

12. *Los Angeles Times,* November 26, 1950.

13. Janis-Plaskin interviews.

14. ibid.

15. Letter from Wanda Toscanini Horowitz to Alexander Merovitch, August 8, 1944. University of Oregon Library.

16. *Los Angeles Times,* November 26, 1950.

17. Janis-Plaskin interviews.

18. ibid.

19. ibid.

20. ibid.

21. *Los Angeles Times,* November 26, 1950.

22. Janis-Plaskin interviews.

23. *New York Times,* October 31, 1948.

24. Janis-Plaskin interview.

25. Byron Janis interviewed by Gregor Benko, New York, March 23, 1980.

26. ibid.

27. Byron Janis interviewed by Glenn Plaskin, New York, September 26, 1982.

28. Nelly Walter interviewed by Glenn Plaskin, *New York, March 11, 1980.

29. Marcus-Plaskin interview.

30. *New York Times,* November 2, 1960.

31. Byron Janis interviewed by Gregor Benko, New York, March 23, 1980.

32. ibid.

33. ibid.

CHAPTER FIFTEEN

1. °Vladimir Horowitz interviewed by Abram Chasins, New York, June 1965.

2. ibid.

3. Ronald Gelatt, *Music Makers* (New York: Alfred A. Knopf, 1953), pp. 236–237.

4. Hubert Saal, "Lord of the Piano," *Newsweek,* January 23, 1978.

5. °Vladimir Horowitz interviewed by Digby Peers and Don Newlands for the Canadian Broadcasting Corporation, New York, February 17, 1976.

6. Horowitz-Chasins interview.

7. Irving Kolodin, *New York Sun,* February 4, 1947.

8. B.H. Haggin, *The Nation,* April 3, 1948.

9. *The Nation,* July 7, 1945.

10. *New York Sun,* January 18, 1949.

11. *New York Herald Tribune,* April 9, 1946.

12. °Horowitz-Chasins interview.

13. ibid.

14. Arthur McKenzie interviewed by Glenn Plaskin, Boston, June 11, 1980.

15. Irving Kolodin, "The Music Box," *New York Sun,* February 10, 1952.

16. °Vladimir Horowitz interviewed by Evans Mirageas on Michigan radio station WUOM, Ann Arbor, April 19, 1975; October 8, 1977.

17. °Vladimir Horowitz interviewed by David Dubal on WNCN radio station, New York, February 1980.

18. *New York Sun,* March 29, 1947.

19. Olin Downes, Carnegie Hall Program Notes, March 28, 1947.

20. °Horowitz-Dubal interview.

21. *New York Times,* November 28, 1948.

22. Arthur Berger, January 18, 1949.

23. *Musical America,* Volume 73, 1953.

24. *New York Times,* September 22, 1968.

CHAPTER SIXTEEN

1. °Vladimir Horowitz interviewed by Evans Mirageas on Michigan radio station WUOM, Ann Arbor, April 19, 1975; October 8, 1977.

2. Samuel Chotzinoff, *A Little Nightmusic* (London: Hamish Hamilton, 1964), p. 45.

3. Press Book for Vladimir Horowitz, Concert Management Arthur Judson, Inc., New York, 1940.

4. Arthur Rubinstein interviewed by Glenn Plaskin, New York City, June 30, 1980.

5. Leonard Lyons, June 15, 1952. Unidentified newspaper column, Vladimir Horowitz news clipping file, Lincoln Center Library of the Performing Arts.

6. Lowell Benedict interviewed by Glenn Plaskin, Lambertville, N.J., July 15, 1981.

7. °Vladimir Horowitz interviewed by Tom Willis for *Profiles of Greatness* radio series, New York, September 1974.

8. Oscar Levant, *The Unimportance of Being Oscar* (New York: G.P. Putnam's Sons, 1968), p. 144.

9. °Horowitz-Mirageas interview.

10. Oscar Levant, *The Memoirs of an Amnesiac* (New York: G.P. Putnam's Sons, 1965), p. 217.

11. ibid.

12. Letter from Wanda Toscanini Horowitz to Alexander Merovitch, July 22, 1947. University of Oregon Library.

13. Alexander Steinert interviewed by Glenn Plaskin, New York, June 6, 1980.

14. Benedict-Plaskin interview.

15. Royal Marks interviewed by Glenn Plaskin, New York, March 27, 1980.

16. Lowell Benedict interviewed by Glenn Plaskin, New York, June 6, 1980.

17. ibid.

18. Edwin Bachmann interviewed by Glenn Plaskin, New York, March 9, 1980.

19. *Chicago Times Herald,* August 10, 1947.

20. *Milwaukee Journal,* March 2, 1949.

21. John Frieman interviewed by Glenn Plaskin, *New York, January 23, 1981.

22. Alexander Steinert interviewed by Glenn Plaskin, New York, June 6, 1980.

23. *Upstate,* May 30, 1982.

24. Gitta Gradova interviewed by Glenn Plaskin, *Chicago, March 10, 1980.

25. Natasha Saitzoff interviewed by Glenn Plaskin, Washington, D.C., October 8, 1979.

26. Harvey Sachs, *Virtuoso* (London: Thames & Hudson, 1982).

27. Steinert-Plaskin interview.

28. ibid.

29. Interview with anonymous source.

30. Letter from Vladimir Horowitz to Alexander Greiner, September 10, 1949. Steinway & Sons Archive.

31. Carl Erpf, Jr., interviewed by Glenn Plaskin, New York, June 6, 1980.

32. ibid.

33. Kenneth Leedom interviewed by Glenn Plaskin, *New York, November 12, 1981.

34. *Salt Lake City Tribune,* November 2, 1951.

35. ibid.

36. *Milwaukee Journal,* March 2, 1949.

37. °Vladimir Horowitz interviewed by Abram Chasins on National Public Radio, February 29, 1976.

38. *Salt Lake City Tribune,* December 8, 1950.

39. Howard Taubman, "The Transformation of Vladimir Horowitz," *New York Times Sunday Magazine,* January 11, 1953.

40. Vladimir Horowitz news clipping file, Lincoln Center Library of the Performing Arts.

41. °Horowitz-Chasins interview.

42. *Musical Opinion,* December 1951.

43. London *Times,* October 9, 1951.

44. Letter from Wanda Toscanini Horowitz to Alexander Greiner, October 9, 1951. Steinway & Sons Archive.

45. *Musical Times,* December 1951.

46. Letter from Wanda Toscanini Horowitz to Alexander Greiner, October 9, 1951. Steinway & Sons Archive.

47. Vladimir Horowitz news clipping file, Lincoln Center Library of the Performing Arts, June 15, 1952.

48. *New York Herald Tribune,* January 11, 1953.

49. °Horowitz-Mirageas interview.

50. *New Orleans Times Picayune,* November 30, 1949.

51. *New York Times,* January 13, 1953.

52. Ronald Gelatt, *Music Makers* (New York: Alfred A. Knopf, 1953), pp. 232–240.

53. Chotzinoff, op. cit., p. 49.

54. Albert Goldberg, *Los Angeles Times,* December 11, 1952.

55. *New York Herald Tribune,* February 26, 1953.

56. *Saturday Review,* December 26, 1953.

57. B.H. Haggin interviewed by Glenn Plaskin, New York, March 15, 1980.

58. Taubman, loc. cit.

PART FOUR

CHAPTER SEVENTEEN

1. °Vladimir Horowitz interviewed by Abram Chasins on National Public Radio, New York, February 27, 1976.
Hubert Saal, "Lord of the Piano," *Newsweek,* January 23, 1978.

2. Wanda Toscanini Horowitz interviewed by Mike Wallace for CBS's *60 Minutes,* December 26, 1977.

3. °Vladimir Horowitz interviewed by Abram Chasins, New York, June 1965.

4. Harold Schonberg, *The Great Pianists* (New York: Simon & Schuster, 1963), p. 412.

5. Saal, loc. cit.
Arthur McKenzie interviewed by Glenn Plaskin, Boston, June 25, 1980.
Arthur Rubinstein interviewed by Glenn Plaskin, New York, June 30, 1980.

6. °Vladimir Horowitz interviewed by John Gruen, New York, November 9, 1975.

7. Lowell Benedict interviewed by Glenn Plaskin, Lambertville, N.J., May 27, 1980.

8. Fritz Steinway interviewed by Glenn Plaskin, *Amherst, Mass., November 28, 1979.

9. George Marek interviewed by Glenn Plaskin, New York, October 28, 1979.

10. Rubinstein-Plaskin interview.

11. Interview with anonymous source.

12. °Horowitz-Chasins interview, February 27, 1976.
°Vladimir Horowitz interviewed by Digby Peers and Don Newlands for the Canadian Broadcasting Corporation, New York, February 17, 1976.

13. Kenneth Leedom interviewed by Glenn Plaskin, *New York, November 12, 1981.

14. °*60 Minutes* interview.

15. °Horowitz-Gruen interview.

16. McKenzie-Plaskin interview.

17. °Horowitz-Peers interview.

18. John Pfeiffer, "Manhattan Holiday," *High Fidelity,* October 1957.

19. °Horowitz-Peers interview.

20. Quotations regarding Clementi taken from the following recorded interviews:
°Horowitz-Peers interview.

°Vladimir Horowitz interviewed by Evans Mirageas on Michigan radio station WUOM, Ann Arbor, April 19, 1975; October 8, 1977.

°Vladimir Horowitz interviewed by David DuBal on WNCN radio station, New York, February 1980.

°Vladimir Horowitz interviewed by Phillip Ramey, New Milford, Conn., July 21, 1971.

21. Pfeiffer, loc. cit.

22. See footnote 20.

23. Pfeiffer, loc cit.

24. ibid.

25. Gary Graffman, *I Really Should Be Practicing* (New York: Doubleday & Co., 1981), p. 141.

26. °Horowitz-Chasins interview, June 1965.
    °Horowitz-Gruen interview.

CHAPTER EIGHTEEN

1. °Vladimir Horowitz interviewed by John Gruen, New York, November 9, 1975.

2. John Pfeiffer, "Manhattan Holiday," *High Fidelity,* October 1957.

3. ibid.

4. ibid.

5. ibid.

6. ibid.

7. Irving Kolodin, *Saturday Review,* November 26, 1955.

8. °Wanda Toscanini Horowitz interviewed by Edward Greenfield, New York, May 10, 1978.

9. °Vladimir Horowitz interviewed by David Dubal on WNCN radio station, New York City, February 1980.

10. Pfeiffer, loc. cit.

11. ibid.

12. ibid.

13. ibid.

14. ibid.

15. ibid.

16. °Vladimir Horowitz interviewed by Abram Chasins, New York, June 1965.

17. *Saturday Review,* April 1956.
RCA Victor Showcase series, unedited tape.

18. °Horowitz-Chasins interview.

19. Pfeiffer, loc. cit.

20. Charles Rosen interviewed by Glenn Plaskin, *New York, December 7, 1979.

21. Arthur McKenzie interviewed by Glenn Plaskin, Boston, June 25, 1980.

22. Abram Chasins, *Speaking of Pianists* (New York: Alfred A. Knopf, 1958), p. 142.

23. Pfeiffer, loc. cit.

24. ibid.

25. Robert Marsh, *Record Reviews,* April 28, 1957.

26. *Saturday Review,* April 1956. Letter from Alan Kayes to the editor, April 28, 1956.

27. °Horowitz-Chasins interview.

28. Pfeiffer, loc. cit.

29. ibid.

30. Harvey Sachs, *Toscanini* (New York: J.B. Lippincott, 1978).

31. ibid.

32. Harvey Sachs, *Virtuoso* (London: Thames & Hudson, 1982).

33. Camilla Cederna, *La voce dei padroni Milano* (Milan: Longanesi & Company, 1962), pp. 259–260.
AP (Associated Press), Wide World Photos, July 8, 1957.

34. George Marek interviewed by Glenn Plaskin, New York, October 28, 1979.

SOURCE NOTES

CHAPTER NINETEEN

Unless otherwise noted, all quotations in this chapter are derived from the following interviews:

Coleman Blumfield interviewed by Glenn Plaskin, New York, October 7, 1979.

Alexander Fiorillo interviewed by Glenn Plaskin, Philadelphia, December 7, 1979.

Ivan Davis interviewed by Glenn Plaskin, New York, September 15, 1979.

Ronald Turini interviewed by Glenn Plaskin, *London, Ontario, January 9, 1980.

Byron Janis interviewed by Glenn Plaskin, New York, April 14, 1980.

Gary Graffman interviewed by Glenn Plaskin, New York, December 12, 1979.

1. °Vladimir Horowitz interviewed by Abram Chasins, New York, June 1965.

2. °Vladimir Horowitz interviewed by Evans Mirageas on Michigan radio station WUOM, Ann Arbor, April 19, 1975; October 8, 1977.

3. Gary Graffman, *I Really Should Be Practicing* (New York: Doubleday & Co., 1981), p. 139.

4. ibid.

5. °Unedited transcript of Vladimir Horowitz at Chicago press conference, October 25, 1974.

6. °Wanda Toscanini Horowitz interviewed by Edward Greenfield, New York, May 10, 1978.

7. Graffman, op. cit.

8. Arthur McKenzie interviewed by Glenn Plaskin, Boston, June 25, 1980.

9. °Horowitz-Chasins interview.

10. Gitta Gradova interviewed by Glenn Plaskin, *Chicago, March 10, 1980.

11. Nelly Walter interviewed by Glenn Plaskin, *New York, March 11, 1980.

12. °Vladimir Horowitz interviewed by Digby Peers and Don Newlands for the Canadian Broadcasting Corporation, New York, February 17, 1976.

13. ibid.

CHAPTER TWENTY

1. °Vladimir Horowitz interviewed by John Gruen, New York, November 9, 1975.

2. Robert C. Marsh, *High Fidelity,* April 1960.

3. *Stereo Review,* February 1961.

4. °Vladimir Horowitz interviewed by Abram Chasins, New York, June 1965.

5. George Marek interviewed by Glenn Plaskin, New York, October 28, 1979.

6. ibid.

7. °Horowitz-Gruen interview.

8. Alan Kayes interviewed by Glenn Plaskin, *New York, October 27, 1981.

9. ibid.

10. Marek-Plaskin interview.

11. Schuyler Chapin, *Musical Chairs* (New York: G.P. Putnam's Sons, 1977), p. 152.

12. Schuyler Chapin interviewed by Glenn Plaskin, New York, October 5, 1979.

13. Chapin, op. cit., p. 154.

14. ibid., p. 155.

15. °Horowitz-Gruen interview.

16. Chapin, op. cit., p. 154.

17. Marek-Plaskin interview.

18. °Horowitz-Gruen interview.

19. Chapin-Plaskin interview.

20. Raymond Ericson, "Horowitz Records May Herald the Pianist's Return to Stage," *New York Times,* March 11, 1962.

21. ibid.

22. Chapin, op. cit., p. 156.

23. °Horowitz-Chasins interview.

24. Thomas Frost, "Horowitz on Music: His Reflections and Impressions," Columbia Record VH Stereo KS 6371, program booklet.

25. Thomas Frost interviewed by Glenn Plaskin, New York, October 5, 1979.

26. *New York Times,* March 11, 1962.

27. Chapin, op. cit., p. 157.

28. Frost, loc. cit.

29. ibid.

30. ibid.

31. Chapin, op. cit., p. 157.

32. ibid., p. 158.

33. Fred Plaut interviewed by Glenn Plaskin, New York, November 19, 1979.

34. Frost-Plaskin interview.

35. Chapin, op. cit., p. 159.

36. *High Fidelity,* October 1962.

37. Chapin, op. cit., p. 159.

38. °Wanda Toscanini Horowitz interviewed by Winthrop Sargeant, New York, 1978.

39. °Horowitz-Gruen interview.

CHAPTER TWENTY-ONE

1. Roland Gelatt, "Music Makers," *High Fidelity,* October 1962.

2. *Musical America,* October 1962.

3. Schuyler Chapin, *Musical Chairs* (New York: G.P. Putnam's Sons, 1977), p. 159.

4. Thomas Frost interviewed by Glenn Plaskin, New York, October 5, 1979.

5. Chapin, op. cit., p. 160.

6. Andrew Kazdin interviewed by Glenn Plaskin, *New York, December 2, 1979.

7. Chapin, op. cit., p. 160.

8. *New York Herald Tribune,* March 1, 1964.

9. *Time,* November 10, 1961.
   °Vladimir Horowitz interviewed by Mike Wallace for CBS's 60 *Minutes,* December 26, 1977.
   Jan Holcman, "Dialogue With Horowitz." *Milwaukee Journal,* June 8, 1962. (unedited transcript of interview)

10. *New York Herald Tribune,* March 1, 1964.

11. ibid.

12. *Hi-Fi Stereo Review,* May 1964.

13. ibid.

14. °Vladimir Horowitz interviewed by David Dubal on WNCN radio station, New York, February 1980.

15. Ralph Kirkpatrick interviewed by Glenn Plaskin, *Princeton, N.J., November 19, 1979.

16. Kazdin-Plaskin interview.

17. *Hi-Fi Stereo Review,* May 1964.

18. Paul Myers interviewed by Glenn Plaskin, New York, November 2, 1979.

19. Charles Rosen interviewed by Glenn Plaskin, *New York, December 7, 1979.

20. Kazdin-Plaskin interview.

21. Myers-Plaskin interview.

22. °Vladimir Horowitz interviewed by Digby Peers and Don Newlands for the Canadian Broadcasting Corporation, New York, February 17, 1976.

23. *New York Herald Tribune,* March 1, 1964.

24. Elsa Maxwell, *New York Journal American,* February 22, 1961.

25. Arthur Rubinstein interviewed by Glenn Plaskin, New York, June 30, 1980.

26. ibid.

27. ibid.

28. °Vladimir Horowitz interviewed by John Gruen, New York, November 9, 1975.
°Vladimir Horowitz interviewed by Abram Chasins on National Public Radio, New York, February 27, 1976.

PART FIVE

CHAPTER TWENTY-TWO

1. °Vladimir Horowitz interviewed by Mike Wallace for CBS's 60 *Minutes*, December 26, 1977.

2. °Vladimir Horowitz interviewed by Abram Chasins on National Public Radio, New York, February 27, 1976.

3. Julius Bloom interviewed by Glenn Plaskin, New York, September 26, 1979.

4. °Vladimir Horowitz interviewed by Abram Chasins, New York, June 1965.

5. Ralph Kirkpatrick interviewed by Glenn Plaskin, *Princeton, N.J., November 19, 1979.

6. *New York Post,* May 2, 1965.

7. Bloom-Plaskin interview.

8. *New York Times,* May 9, 1965.

9. Bloom-Plaskin interview.

10. *Time,* May 17, 1965.
°Vladimir Horowitz interviewed by Helen Epstein for "The Grand Eccentric of the Concert Hall," *New York Times Sunday Magazine,* January 8, 1978.

11. *New York Herald Tribune,* March 14, 1965.

12. °Horowitz-Chasins interview, June 1965.

13. *New York Times,* March 17, 1965.

14. ibid.

15. ibid.

16. *High Fidelity,* October 1965.

17. °Horowitz-Chasins interview, June 1965.

18. ibid.

19. *New York Times,* April 22, 1965.

20. ibid., March 17, 1965.

21. *Variety,* March 24, 1965.

22. Bloom-Plaskin interview.

23. *New York Times Sunday Magazine,* May 9, 1965.

CHAPTER TWENTY-THREE

1. *New York Times,* March 17, 1965.

2. *New York Post,* April 26, 1965.

3. ibid.

4. *New York Times,* May 9, 1965.

5. ibid., April 26, 1965.

6. *New York Post,* May 2, 1965.

7. °Vladimir Horowitz interviewed by Abram Chasins, New York, June 1965.

8. ibid.

9. *New York Times,* April 22, 1965.

10. Schuyler Chapin, *Musical Chairs* (New York: G.P. Putnam's Sons, 1977), p. 162.

11. *New York Times,* May 11, 1965.

12. ibid.
    °Horowitz-Chasins interview.

13. °Vladimir Horowitz interviewed by Helen Epstein for "The Grand Eccentric of the Concert Hall," *New York Times Sunday Magazine,* January 8, 1978.

14. *Look,* February 8, 1966.

15. °Horowitz-Chasins interview.

16. *New York Post,* May 23, 1965.

17. °Horowitz-Epstein interview.

18. ibid.

19. *New York Post,* May 23, 1965.

20. Chapin, op. cit., p. 163.

21. ibid.

22. ibid., p. 164.

23. ibid.

24. ibid.

25. Schuyler Chapin interviewed by Glenn Plaskin, New York, October 5, 1979.

26. Chapin, op. cit., p. 164.

27. ibid., pp. 165–169.

28. *New York Times,* May 11, 1965.

29. Chapin, op. cit., p. 165.

30. *New York Times,* May 10, 1965.

31. ibid.

32. ibid., May 11, 1965.
    °Vladimir Horowitz interviewed by Digby Peers and Don Newlands for the Canadian Broadcasting Corporation, New York, February 17, 1976.

33. Chapin, op. cit., p. 166.

34. °Horowitz-Chasins interview.

35. *New York Times,* May 10, 1965.

36. *High Fidelity,* August, 1965.

37. *Look,* February 8, 1966.

38. *New York Herald Tribune,* May 10, 1965.

39. *New York Times,* May 10, 1965.

40. ibid., May 16, 1965.

41. *Boston American Globe,* May 10, 1965.

42. ibid.

43. ibid.

44. Chapin, op. cit., p. 168.

45. °Wanda Toscanini Horowitz interviewed by Mike Wallace for CBS's *60 Minutes,* December 26, 1977.

46. °Horowitz-Chasins interview.

47. Chapin, op. cit., p. 169.

48. *New York Times,* May 10, 1965.
°Horowitz-Chasins interview.

49. *Life,* May 21, 1965.

50. *New York Times,* June 6, 1965.

51. Thomas Frost interviewed by Glenn Plaskin, New York, March 14, 1980.

52. *New York Times,* April 23, 1967.

53. *Look,* February 8, 1966.

CHAPTER TWENTY-FOUR

1. *New York Times,* October 28, 1965.

2. °Vladimir Horowitz interviewed by Abram Chasins, New York, June 1965.

3. *New York Times,* October 28, 1965.

4. ibid.

5. Phillip Ramey interviewed by Glenn Plaskin, New York, May 15, 1982.

6. ibid.

7. *New York Times,* March 22, 1966.

8. ibid.
Look, February 8, 1966.

9. *New York Post,* April 5, 1966.
New York Times, April 5, 1966.

10. *New York Journal American,* April 18, 1966.

11. Harold C. Schonberg, *New York Times,* April 18, 1966.

12. ibid.

13. ibid.

14. *Time,* April 29, 1966.

15. *New York Times,* November 28, 1966.

16. ibid., January 10, 1967.

17. ibid.

18. Albert Lotto interviewed by Glenn Plaskin, New York, April 21, 1980.

19. *New York Times,* November 27, 1967.

CHAPTER TWENTY-FIVE

1. *Detroit News,* September 22, 1968.

2. *Time,* September 20, 1968.

3. Roger Englander interviewed by Glenn Plaskin, New York, December 17, 1979.

4. *New York Times,* February 2, 1968.

5. *Detroit News,* September 22, 1968.

6. Andrew Kazdin interviewed by Glenn Plaskin, New York, December 2, 1979.
Paul Myers interviewed by Glenn Plaskin, New York, November 29, 1979.
Thomas Frost interviewed by Glenn Plaskin, New York, March 14, 1980.

7. ibid.

8. Sheldon Shkolnik interviewed by Glenn Plaskin, *Chicago, May 10, 1982.

9. ibid.

10. *Detroit News,* September 22, 1968.

11. Englander-Plaskin interview.

12. *Time,* September 20, 1968.

13. Myers-Plaskin interview.

14. ibid.

15. ibid.

16. *New York Times,* September 20, 1968.

17. Englander-Plaskin interview.

18. Myers-Plaskin interview.

19. *Detroit News,* September 22, 1968.

20. *New York Times,* October 6, 1968.

21. *Washington Star,* September 23, 1968.

22. *Los Angeles Times-Washington Post News Service,* September 22, 1968.

23. *New York Times,* October 6, 1968.

24. ibid.

CHAPTER TWENTY-SIX

1. Phillip Ramey interviewed by Glenn Plaskin, New York, May 15, 1982.

2. *Chicago Tribune,* May 12, 1968.

3. *Chicago Sun Times,* May 14, 1968.

4. Paul Myers interviewed by Glenn Plaskin, New York, November 29, 1979.

5. Thomas Frost interviewed by Glenn Plaskin, New York, March 14, 1980.

6. *New York Times,* November 25, 1968.

7. Myers-Plaskin interview.

8. Arthur McKenzie interviewed by Glenn Plaskin, Boston, June 25, 1980.

9. *Saturday Review,* July 31, 1971.

10. ibid.

11. *New York Times,* November 25, 1968.

12. Julius Bloom interviewed by Glenn Plaskin, *New York, December 2, 1981.

13. ibid.

14. ibid.

15. °Vladimir Horowitz interviewed by John Gruen, New York, November 9, 1975.

15. Michael Steinberg, *Boston Globe,* October 28, 1969.

17. Bloom-Plaskin interview.

18. Naomi Graffman interviewed by Glenn Plaskin, New York, December 12, 1979.

19. Bloom-Plaskin interview.

20. Raymond Moore interviewed by Glenn Plaskin, *New York, January 14, 1980.

21. Frost-Plaskin interview.
Myers-Plaskin interview.

22. Moore-Plaskin interview.

23. *New York Post,* October 15, 1974.

24. Myers-Plaskin interview.

25. °Ramey-Plaskin interview.
Billboard, October 26, 1974.

26. ibid.

27. Vladimir Horowitz interviewed by Phillip Ramey, New York, November 29, 1977.

28. ibid.

29. *Chicago Tribune,* October 20, 1974.

30. Ramey-Plaskin interview.

31. ibid.

32. ibid.

CHAPTER TWENTY-SEVEN

1. *Houston Chronicle,* March 29, 1975.

2. °Vladimir Horowitz interviewed by John Gruen, New York, November 9, 1975.

3. *New York Times,* May 10, 1974.

4. Michael Maxwell interviewed by Glenn Plaskin, New York, March 27, 1980.

5. *Cleveland Press,* May 11, 1974.

6. ibid.

7. *Washington Star,* June 1, 1974.

8. *New York Post,* May 10, 1974.

9. ibid.

10. *People,* May 27, 1974.

11. Maxwell-Plaskin interview.

12. ibid.

13. *New York Post,* May 13, 1974.

14. *New York Times,* May 10, 1974.

15. *Chicago Tribune,* October 28, 1974.

16. *New York Post,* May 10, 1974.

17. *Minneapolis Star,* June 8, 1974.

18. Peter Gelb interviewed by Glenn Plaskin, New York, December 13, 1979.

19. ibid.

20. ibid.

21. Schuyler Chapin, *Musical Chairs* (New York: G.P. Putnam's Sons, 1977), p. 384.

22. ibid.

23. *New York Times,* October 14, 1974.

24. ibid.

25. Gelb-Plaskin interview.

26. ibid.

27. *Cleveland Plain Dealer,* November 23, 1975.

28. °Vladimir Horowitz interviewed at Chicago press conference, October 25, 1974.

29. *New York Times,* November 18, 1974.

30. *Newsweek,* December 22, 1974.

31. *New York Times,* January 11, 1975.

32. °Wanda Toscanini Horowitz interviewed by Mary Rousculp at University of Ohio radio station WOSU, Columbus, May 17, 1975.

33. *Newsweek,* January 23, 1978.

34. *Houston Post,* January 11, 1975.

35. *Newsweek,* January 23, 1978.

36. °Wanda Horowitz-Rousculp interview.

37. Phillip Ramey interviewed by Glenn Plaskin, New York, May 15, 1982.

38. Lanfranco Rasponi interviewed by Glenn Plaskin, *New York, October 20, 1981.

39. °Vladimir Horowitz interviewed by Helen Epstein for "The Grand Eccentric of the Concert Hall," *New York Times Sunday Magazine,* January 8, 1978.

40. *Los Angeles Times,* February 12, 1978.

41. *Chicago Sun Times,* November 9, 1975.

42. °Horowitz-Gruen interview.
Louisville Courier, October 27, 1975.

43. *Chicago Sun Times,* November 9, 1975.

44. *Boston Herald,* March 15, 1976.

45. *Boston Globe,* March 15, 1976.

46. ibid.

47. *New York Times,* November 17, 1975.

48. *New York Post,* October 15, 1974.

49. °Horowitz-Gruen interview.

50. Kenneth Glancey interviewed by Glenn Plaskin, New York, March 3, 1980.

CHAPTER TWENTY-EIGHT

1. °Vladimir Horowitz interviewed by Helen Epstein for "The Grand Eccentric of the Concert Hall," *New York Times Sunday Magazine,* January 8, 1978.

2. Ralph Hanes interviewed by Glenn Plaskin, New York, June 20, 1979.

3. *New York Post,* March 28, 1978.

4. Hanes-Plaskin interview.

5. Peter Gelb interviewed by Glenn Plaskin, New York, December 13, 1979.

6. *Sunday Oregonian,* January 8, 1978.

7. °Horowitz-Epstein interview.

8. °Vladimir Horowitz interviewed by Mary Rousculp at University of Ohio radio station WOSU, Columbus, May 17, 1975.
   Seattle Times, January 22, 1976.

9. °Horowitz-Epstein interview.

10. °Vladimir Horowitz interviewed by Mike Wallace for CBS's *60 Minutes,* December 26, 1977.

11. *Piano Quarterly,* Volume 23, 1975.

12. °Horowitz-Epstein interview.

13. ibid.

14. *Music and Musicians,* August 23, 1975.

15. ibid.

16. *Sunday Oregonian,* January 8, 1978.

17. °Vladimir Horowitz interviewed by Evans Mirageas on Michigan radio station WUOM, Ann Arbor, April 9, 1975; October 8, 1977.

18. Gelb-Plaskin interview.

19. *Toronto Star,* May 7, 1976.

20. *Cleveland Plain Dealer,* November 23, 1975.

21. Harold Shaw Concerts, Inc., Advance Instructions for Vladimir Horowitz.

22. ibid.

23. *New York Post,* March 28, 1978.

24. °Wanda Toscanini Horowitz interviewed by Edward Greenfield, New York, May 10, 1978.

25. Hanes-Plaskin interview.

26. Edward Klein interviewed by Glenn Plaskin, New York, February 15, 1980.

27. Ariel Rubinstein interviewed by Glenn Plaskin, *Portland, Ore., November 28, 1979; January 14, 1980.

28. °Horowitz-Wallace interview.

29. ibid.

30. Danny Deeds interviewed by Glenn Plaskin, *Cincinnati, April 17, 1977. *Cincinnati Post,* April 17, 1977.

31. *New York Times,* November 7, 1978.

32. ibid.

33. Klein-Plaskin interview.

34. °Vladimir Horowitz and Wanda Toscanini Horowitz interviewed at Chicago press conference, November 8, 1977.

35. "Horowitz on the Road," *Canadian Magazine,* July 10, 1976.

36. °Wanda Toscanini Horowitz interviewed by Mike Wallace for CBS's *60 Minutes,* December 26, 1976.

37. Theodore W. Libbey interviewed by Glenn Plaskin, Washington, D.C., October 9, 1979.

38. Hubert Saal, "Lord of the Piano," *Newsweek,* January 23, 1978.

39. Giovanni Scimonelli interviewed by Glenn Plaskin, Hudson, N.Y., August 20, 1980.

40. *Los Angeles Times,* February 12, 1978.

41. °Vladimir Horowitz interviewed at Chicago press conference, November 8, 1979.

42. °Vladimir Horowitz and Wanda Toscanini Horowitz interviewed at Chicago press conference, November 8, 1977.

43. ibid.

44. Gelb-Plaskin interview.

45. °Horowitz-Mirageas interview.

46. Wanda Horowitz, October 2, 1978.

47. *Chicago Tribune,* April 15, 1979.

48. Phillip Ramey interviewed by Glenn Plaskin, New York, May 15, 1982.

49. ibid.

50. Paul Myers interviewed by Glenn Plaskin, New York, November 29, 1979.

51. °Horowitz-Epstein interview.

52. ibid.

53. ibid.

54. ibid.

55. Julius Bloom interviewed by Glenn Plaskin, New York, December 2, 1981.

56. ibid.

57. *New Yorker,* June 7, 1976.

58. ibid.

59. Bloom-Plaskin interview.

60. *Rolling Stone,* July 15, 1976.

61. *New Yorker,* June 7, 1976.

62. ibid.

63. *New York Times,* May 30, 1976.

64. *New Yorker,* June 7, 1976.

65. *New York Post,* October 20, 1976.

66. *New York Times,* July 26, 1976.

67. *New York Post,* October 20, 1976.

68. *New York Times,* July 26, 1976.

69. Peter Mennin interviewed by Glenn Plaskin, *New York, December 11, 1979.

70. David Tcimpidis interviewed by Glenn Plaskin, *New York, December 15, 1979.

71. Dean Kramer interviewed by Glenn Plaskin, *New York, December 5, 1979.

72. °Vladimir Horowitz interviewed at Chicago press conference, January 10, 1979.

CHAPTER TWENTY-NINE

1. °Vladimir Horowitz interviewed by Evans Mirageas on Michigan radio station WUOM, Ann Arbor, April 19, 1975; October 8, 1977.

2. °Vladimir Horowitz interviewed by Mike Wallace for CBS's 60 *Minutes,* New York, December 26, 1977.

3. Letter from Carlos Moseley to Eugene Ormandy, March 15, 1977. New York Philharmonic Archive.

4. *New York Post,* October 20, 1976.
   Leonard Bernstein interviewed by Glenn Plaskin, New York, February 16, 1981.

5. Speight Jenkins interviewed by Glenn Plaskin, *New York, January 25, 1980.

6. Letter from Carlos Moseley to Eugene Ormandy, March 10, 1977. New York Philharmonic Archive.

7. *Philadelphia Inquirer,* January 20, 1978.

8. *Chicago Sun Times,* January 15, 1978.
   °Vladimir Horowitz interviewed by Phillip Ramey, New York, November 29, 1977.

9. °Horowitz-Wallace interview.

10. ibid.

11. Giovanni Scimonelli interviewed by Glenn Plaskin, Hudson, N.Y., August 20, 1980.

12. °Wanda Toscanini Horowitz interviewed by Mike Wallace for CBS's 60 *Minutes,* New York, December 26, 1977.

13. Scimonelli-Plaskin interview.

14. David Lowe interviewed by Glenn Plaskin, New York, November 20, 1979.

15. °Horowitz-Wallace interview.

16. Lowe-Plaskin interview.

17. Phillip Ramey interviewed by Glenn Plaskin, New York, May 15, 1982.

18. ibid.

19. ibid.

20. °Wanda Toscanini Horowitz interviewed by Helen Epstein for "The Grand Eccentric of the Concert Hall," *New York Times Sunday Magazine,* January 8, 1978.

21. *New York Post,* March 28, 1978.

22. °Wanda Toscanini Horowitz interviewed by Mary Rousculp at University of Ohio radio station WOSU, Columbus, May 17, 1975.

23. Bill Hayward, *Cat People* (New York: Doubleday & Co., 1978).

24. Ramey-Plaskin interview.

25. Scimonelli-Plaskin interview.

26. *Los Angeles Times,* February 12, 1978.

27. °Horowitz-Ramey interview.

28. ibid.
    RCA Victor program booklet: Vladimir Horowitz Golden Jubilee: CRL 1 2633.

29. *Los Angeles Times,* February 12, 1978.

30. Hubert Saal, "Lord of the Piano," *Newsweek,* January 23, 1978.

31. ibid.
    New Yorker, January 23, 1978.

32. °Horowitz-Ramey interview.

33. *Montreal Gazette,* September 23, 1978.

34. Ted Joselson interviewed by Glenn Plaskin, New York, March 11, 1980.

35. Harold Schonberg, *New York Times,* January 9, 1978.

36. *Stereo Review,* May 1978.

37. Nathan Milstein interviewed by Glenn Plaskin, London, February 16, 1980.

38. Edwin Begley interviewed by Glenn Plaskin, New York, March 3, 1980.

39. *Dallas Morning News,* February 17, 1978.

40. Ramey-Plaskin interview.

41. °Horowitz-Ramey interview.

42. *High Fidelity,* June 1978.

43. ibid.

44. ibid.

45. °Vladimir Horowitz interviewed at Dallas press conference, January 8, 1977.

46. Scimonelli-Plaskin interview.

47. ibid.

48. *New York Post,* March 28, 1978.

49. *New York Times,* February 27, 1978.

50. ibid., November 9, 1977.

51. Kirk Browning interviewed by Glenn Plaskin, *New York, February 16, 1980.

52. Begley-Plaskin interview.

53. *Washington Journalism Review,* April/May 1979.

54. James Robb interviewed by Glenn Plaskin, New York, October 16, 1979.

55. Interview with anonymous source.

56. *Phoenix Gazette,* April 18, 1978.

57. *New York Times,* September 26, 1978.

58. °Horowitz-Ramey interview.

59. *Chicago Tribune,* April 15, 1979.

60. Scimonelli-Plaskin interview.

61. Alexander Steinert interviewed by Glenn Plaskin, New York, June 9, 1980.

62. °Wanda Horowitz-Wallace interview.

63. °Ramey-Plaskin interview.

64. *New York Times,* August 13, 1981.

65. ibid.

66. °Horowitz-Epstein interview.

67. Gitta Gradova interviewed by Glenn Plaskin, *Chicago, November 16, 1979.

68. *New York Times,* May 14, 1982.

DISCOGRAPHY

COMPILED BY ROBERT MCALEAR

INTRODUCTION

This discography lists all known commercial recordings and all subsequent American and British releases by Vladimir Horowitz. Limitation of space has necessitated the omission of recordings by Horowitz issued in countries other than the United States and the United Kingdom, although two of the most important of these international releases are cited in the footnotes.

From 1945 to 1951 Horowitz had his Carnegie Hall recitals privately recorded for his own use. None of the twenty-two 78-rpm shellac transcription discs made for him by the Carnegie Hall Recording Company are listed here.

Selections are arranged in alphabetical order by composer, and the date a work was recorded and the matrix or job number of the selection are given. From 1928 through 1959, Horowitz's recordings were designated by individual matrix numbers by record companies; beginning in 1962, job numbers (which designate a specific recording session rather than a particular composition) were used.

Magnetic tape, which was introduced in the early 1950's, facilitated the splicing together of segments from different "takes" or sessions. In the case of Horowitz, the exact placement of such splices is not documented in the files of either RCA Red Seal (formerly RCA Victor Records) or Columbia Masterworks. Nor has this information been forthcoming from any of Horowitz's producers.

ACKNOWLEDGMENTS

To Don German of Columbia Masterworks and John F. Pfeiffer of RCA Red Seal, both of whom made available certain logs and files from their respective companies pertaining to Horowitz's recordings.

To John Watson of EMI Limited who was most attentive to all appeals for information concerning Horowitz's British recordings and releases.

To a host of private record collectors and Horowitz enthusiasts in both the United States and the United Kingdom who supplied a surprisingly large amount of information concerning Horowitz's recordings which was not available through any of the record companies with which Horowitz has been associated.

KEY TO ABBREVIATIONS

ANG	Angel (United Kingdom)
FMR	Franklin Mint Recordings (United States)
HMV	His Master's Voice (United Kingdom)
RCA	RCA Victor/Red Seal (United States)
SER	Seraphim (United States)
SUP	Sony Superscope (United States)
TLR	Time-Life Records (United States)
UK COL	Columbia Masterworks (United Kingdom)
US COL	Columbia Masterworks (United States)
WLR	Welte Legacy Recordings (United States)

An asterisk (*) following the recording date indicates that the recording session in question was also the occasion of a live concert performance.

The serial numbers of stereophonic (and simulated stereophonic) records are underscored.

The abbreviation s. denotes the side number of a disc.

COMPOSER AND SELECTION:	DATE RECORDED:	MATRIX-TAKE OR JOB NUMBER:	U.S. AND U.K. RELEASES:
BACH-BUSONI			
"Ich ruf' zu dir, Herr Jesu Christ," BWV 639	6/-2/69	ZSM-152670-1A	COL 33rpm: No Serial No.[1]
"Nun freut, euch lieben Christen," BWV 734	5/6/34	OB-6196-1	HMV 78 rpm: DA-1388 RCA 78rpm: 1690 ANG 33rpm: COLH-300
"Nun komm' der Heiden Heiland," BWV 599	9/€/47	D7-RC-6932-1	RCA 78rpm: DM-1284 M-1284 RCA 45rpm: WDM-1284 WDM-1605 RCA 33rpm: ARM1-2717 LM-1171
Toccata, Adagio, and Fugue in C Major, BWV 564	5/9/65*	77219	UK COL 33rpm: MET-2110 SET-2110 US COL 33rpm: M2L-328 M2S-728
BARBER:			
Sonata in E-flat Minor, Opus 26—s. 1 s. 2 s. 3 s. 4	5/15/50	EO-RC-965-2 EO-RC-966-1 EO-RC-967-1A EO-RC-968-1	RCA 78rpm: DM-1466 RCA 45rpm: WDM-1466 HMV 33rpm: RB-6554/5 RCA 33rpm: ARM1-2952 LD-7021 LM-1113

BEETHOVEN:

COMPOSER AND SELECTION:	DATE RECORDED:	MATRIX-TAKE OR JOB NUMBER:	U.S. AND U.K. RELEASES:
Concerto No. 5 in E-flat Major, Opus 73 ("Emperor") (With the RCA Victor Symphony Orchestra, conducted by Fritz Reiner)—s. 1	4/26/52	E2-RC-0792-1	RCA 45rpm: WDM-1718
s. 2	)	E2-RC-0793-1	HMV 33rpm: ALP-1280
s. 3	)	E2-RC-0794-1	RB-16114
s. 4	)	E2-RC-0795-1	RCA 33rpm: ARM1-3690
s. 5	)	E2-RC-0796-1	CRM4-0914
s. 6	)	E2-RC-0797-1	LM-1718
s. 7	)	E2-RC-0798-1	VICS-1636(e)[2]
s. 8	)	E2-RC-0799-1	
Sonata No. 7 in D Major, Opus 10 #3—I	5/29 and 6/10/59)[3]	K2-RB-3386	HMV 33rpm: RB-16230
—II	)	K2-RB-3387	SB-2102
—III	)	K2-RB-3388	RCA 33rpm: LM-2366
—IV	)	K2-RB-3389	LSC-2366
Sonata No. 8 in C Minor, Opus 13 ("Pathétique")	11/4/63	85254	COL 33rpm: ML-5941
			MS-6541
			M-34509
Sonata No. 14 in C-sharp Minor, Opus 27 #2 ("Moonlight")—1st recording—s. 1	11/21/46	D6-RC-6419-1A	RCA 78rpm: DM-1115
s. 2	)	D6-RC-6420-1A	M-1115

	Date	Matrix	Issue
s. 3 s. 4	11/26/46	D6-RC-6421-1A D6-RC-6422-3	RCA 45rpm: ERA-144 WDM-1115 HMV 33 rpm: BLP-1014 RCA 33rpm: LM-1027
—2nd recording—I —II —III	6/5/56)	G2-RB-1295-1 G2-RB-1296-1 G2-RB-1297-1	RCA 33rpm: LM-2009 LM-2574[4]
—3rd recording	April and May/72[5]	Various[6]	UK COL 33rpm: 73175 US COL 33rpm: M-32342 M-34509
Sonata No. 21 in C Major, Opus 53 ("Waldstein")			
—1st recording—I —II and III	5/10/56 5/11 and 6/5/56[7]	G2-RB-1298-1 G2-RB-1299	RCA 33rpm: LM-2009
—2nd recording	12/6 and 12/20/72	95511 and 95555	US COL 33rpm: M-31371
Sonata No. 23 in F. Minor, Opus 57 ("Appassionata")			

—1st recording—I
—II
—III
	May/59[8]	K2-RB-2754
		K2-RB-2755
		K2-RB-2756
			HMV 33rpm: RB-16230
			    SB-2102
			RCA 33rpm: LM-2366
			    LSC-2366

—2nd recording	October and December/72[9]	Various[10]	US COL 33rpm: M-31371 M-34509
Thirty-two Variations in C Minor, WoO 80—s. 1 s. 2 s. 3	5/6/34	OB-6193-2 OB-6194-2 OB-6195-3	HMV 78rpm: DA-1387/8 RCA 78rpm: 1689/90 ANG 33rpm: COLH-300

COMPOSER AND SELECTION:	DATE RECORDED:	MATRIX-TAKE OR JOB NUMBER:	U.S. AND U.K. RELEASES:
BRAHMS:			
Concerto No. 2 in B-flat Major, Opus 83 (With the NBC Symphony Orchestra, conducted by Arturo Toscanini)—s. 1	5/9/40	CS-048837-2A[11]	HMV 78rpm: DB-5861/6
s. 2	)	CS-048838-2	DB-8884/9
s. 3	)	CS-048839-2	RCA 78rpm: AM-740
s. 4	)	CS-048840-2	DM-740
s. 5	)	CS-048841-2	M-740
s. 6	)	CS-048842-2A	RCA 45rpm: WCT-38
s. 7	)	CS-048843-2	HMV 33rpm: AT-103
s. 8	)	CS-048844-2A	RCA 33rpm: ARM1-2874
s. 9	)	CS-048845-2	CRM4-0914
s. 10	)	CS-048846-2	LCT-1025
s. 11	)	CS-048847-2	
s. 12.	)	CS-048848-3	
Intermezzo in B-flat Minor, Opus 117 #3	4/23/51*	Unknown	HMV 33rpm: RB-16019
			RCA 33rpm: ARM1-2873
			LM-1957
			VICS-1649(e)[2]
Violin Sonata No. 3 in D Minor, Opus 108 (With Nathan Milstein, violinist)—s. 1	6/22/50	EO-RC-1200-1	RCA 45rpm: WDM-1551
s. 2	)	EO-RC-1201-1A	RCA 33rpm: ARM1-2718
s. 3	)	EO-RC-1202-1	LM-106
s. 4	)	EO-?-1203-1	

s. 5   EO-RC-1204-1

s. 6   6/29/50)   EO-RC-1205-2

Waltz No. 15 in A-flat Major, Opus 39 #15   10/10/50   EO-RC-1854-1

RCA 78rpm: 10-3424
RCA 45rpm: 49-3424
RCA 33rpm: ARM1-2873
            VICS-1649(e)[2]

CHOPIN:

Andante Spianato and Grande Polonaise
Brillante in E-flat Major, Opus 22—s. 1   10/6/45   D5-RC-1221-3A

s. 2   9/22/45   D5-RC-1222-1

s. 3   )   D5-RC-1223-1

RCA 78rpm: DM-1034
            M-1034
RCA 45rpm: ERB-7051
            WDM-1034
HMV 33rpm: BLP-1079
            RB-6554/5
            7ER-5071
RCA 33rpm: ARM1-2953
            LD-7021
            LM-1137
            LRM-7051
            VIC-1605

Ballade No. 1 in G Minor, Opus 23
—1st recording—s. 1   5/19/47   D7-RC-7534-1C

s. 2   )   D7-RC-7535-3B

HMV 78rpm: DB-6688
RCA 78rpm: DM-1165
            DV-29
            M-1165
            V-29
RCA 45rpm: ERB-7018
            WDM-1165
HMV 33rpm: ALP-1087

COMPOSER AND SELECTION:	DATE RECORDED:	MATRIX-TAKE OR JOB NUMBER:	U.S. AND U.K. RELEASES:
—2nd recording	5/9/65*	77219	RCA 33rpm: ARM1-3268 LM-1235 LRM-7018 VIC-1605 XRL1-4329 UK COL 33rpm: MET-2110 SET-2110 US COL 33rpm: M2L-328 M2S-728
—3rd recording	2/1/68*[12]	14093	UK COL 33rpm: 72720 79340[55] US COL 33rpm: MS-7106 M3-36935[55]
Ballade No. 4 in F Minor, Opus 52			
—1st recording[13]—s. 1 s. 2	12/28/49)	D9-RC-2143-1 D9-RC-2144-1	HMV 78rpm: DB-21503
—2nd recording—s. 1 s. 2	5/8/52)	E2-RC-0805-1 E2-RC-0806-1	RCA 45rpm: ERB-7018 WDM-1707[14] HMV 33rpm: ALP-1111 RCA 33rpm: ARM1-2953 LM-1707[14] LRM-7018

—3rd recording | 11/1/81* | Unknown | RCA 33rpm: <u>ATC1-4260</u>[15]

Barcarolle in F-sharp Major, Opus 60

—1st recording	2/23/57	H2-RB-807-1	HMV 33rpm: RB-16064 RCA 33rpm: ARM1-2953 LM-2137
—2nd recording	April and May/80*[38]	Unknown	HMV 33rpm: RL-14322 RCA 33rpm: <u>ARL1-4322</u>

Etude No. 3 in E Major, Opus 10 #3

—1st recording	4/29/51	E1-RC-3435-1	RCA 45rpm: ERA-241 WDM-1707 HMV 33rpm: ALP-1111 RCA 33rpm: ARM1-2716 LM-1707
—2nd recording	7/6/72	79906	UK COL 33rpm: <u>76307</u> <u>79340</u>[55] US COL 33rpm: <u>M-32932</u> <u>M3-36935</u>[55]

Etude No. 4 in C-sharp Minor, Opus 10 #4

—1st recording	6/2/35	2EA-2075-2	HMV 78rpm: DB-2788 RCA 78rpm: 14140 ANG 33rpm: COLH-300 TLR 33rpm: STL-P06[16]
—2nd recording[17]	1/5/52	E2-RC-0021-1	RCA 33rpm: ARM1-2716 VIC-1605
—3rd recording	2/8/73	95725	UK COL 33rpm: <u>76307</u> <u>79340</u>[55] US COL 33rpm: <u>M-32932</u> <u>M3-36935</u>[55]

COMPOSER AND SELECTION:	DATE RECORDED:	MATRIX-TAKE OR JOB NUMBER:	U.S. AND U.K. RELEASES:
Etude No. 5 in G-flat Major, Opus 10 #5 ("Black Key")—1st recording	5/12/34	2B-7209-2	HMV 78rpm: DB-2238[18]
—2nd recording	6/2/35	2EA-2075-2	HMV 78rpm: DB-2788 RCA 78rpm: 14140 ANG 33rpm: COLH-300 TLR 33rpm: STL-P06[16]
—3rd recording	4/7 and 4/14/71	76124 and 76157	UK COL 33rpm: 72969 79340[55] US COL 33rpm: M-30643 M3-36935[55]
—4th recording	April and May/80*[38]	Unknown	HMV 33rpm: RL-14322 RCA 33rpm: ARL1-4322
Etude No. 8 in F Major, Opus 10 #8 —1st recording	11/15/32	OB-4507-1	HMV 78rpm: DA-1305 ANG 33rpm: COLH-300
—2nd recording	5/9/65*	77219	UK COL 33rpm: MET-2110 SET-2110 US COL 33rpm: M2L-328 M2S-728
Etude No. 12 in C Minor, Opus 10 #12 ("Revolutionary")—1st recording	11/4/63	85254	US COL 33rpm: ML-5941 MS-6541

—2nd recording	7/5/72	79906	UK COL 33rpm: 76307 / 79340[55] US COL 33rpm: M-32932 / M3-36935[55]
Etude No. 15 in F Major, Opus 25 #3[19]	5/12/34	2B-7209-2	HMV 78rpm: DB-2238[18]
Etude No. 19 in C-sharp Minor, Opus 25 #7 —1st recording	11/14/63	85311	US COL 33rpm: ML-5941 / MS-6541
—2nd recording	April and May/80*[38]	Unknown	HMV 33rpm: RL-14322 / RCA 33rpm: ARL1-4322
Impromptu No. 1 in A-flat Major, Opus 29	10/21/51	2EA-15978-3	HMV 78rpm: DB-21425 / RCA 45rpm: ERA-241, WDM-1707 / HMV 33rpm: ALP-1111 / RCA 33rpm: ARM1-2716, LM-1707, VIC-1605
Introduction and Rondo in E-flat Major, Opus 16	4/7 and 4/14/71	76124 and 76157	UK COL 33rpm: 72969 / 79340[55] US COL 33rpm: M-30643 / M3-36935[55]
Mazurka No. 7 in F Minor, Opus 7 #3 —1st recording	11/15/32	OB-4506-1	HMV 78rpm: DA-1305 / RCA 78rpm: 1654 / ANG 33rpm: COLH-300
—2nd recording	12/22/47	D7-RC-8281-1	HMV 78rpm: DB-6953 / RCA 78rpm: 12-0427

COMPOSER AND SELECTION:	DATE RECORDED:	MATRIX-TAKE OR JOB NUMBER:	U.S. AND U.K. RELEASES:
—3rd recording	5/12/68*	14108	RCA 45rpm: ERA-241 / 49-0458 RCA 33rpm: LM-1137 / VICS-1649(e)[2]
Mazurka No. 13 in A Minor, Opus 17 #4	4/7 and	76124 and	UK COL 33rpm: 76307 / 79340[55] US COL 33rpm: M-32932 / M3-36935[55]
	7/14/71	76157	UK COL 33rpm: 72969 / 79340[55] US COL 33rpm: M-30643 / M3-36935[55]
Mazurka No. 17 in B-flat Minor, Opus 24 #4	3/5/51*	Unknown	HMV 33rpm: RB-16019 RCA 33rpm: LM-1957
Mazurka No. 20 in D-flat Major, Opus 30 #3 —1st recording	12/28/49	D9-RC-2145-1	HMV 78rpm: DB-21561 RCA 78rpm: DM-1446 RCA 45rpm: ERA-31[20] / WDM-1446 HMV 33rpm: ALP-1069 / 7ER-5006 RCA 33rpm: LM-1109 / LVT-1032

—2nd recording	2/8/73	95725	UK COL 33rpm: 76307, 79340[55] US COL 33rpm: M-32932, M3-36935[55]

Mazurka No. 21 in C-sharp Minor, Opus 30 #4

—1st recording	3/26/28	BVE-43412-1	HMV 78rpm: DA-982 RCA 78rpm: 1327 RCA 45rpm: E2LW-1007[21] RCA 33rpm: LM-2993
—2nd recording	12/28/49	D9-RC-2146-1A	HMV 78rpm: DB-21561 RCA 78rpm: DM-1446 RCA 45rpm: ERA-31[20], WDM-1446 HMV 33rpm: ALP-1069, 7ER-5006 RCA 33rpm: LM-1109, LVT-1032
—3rd recording	5/9/65*	77219	UK COL 33rpm: MET-2110, SET-2110 US COL 33rpm: M2L-328, M2S-728

Mazurka No. 23 in D Major, Opus 33 #2

	2/8/73	95725	UK COL 33rpm: 76307, 79340[55] US COL 33rpm: M-32932, M3-36935[55]

Mazurka No. 25 in B Minor, Opus 33 #4

	4/17/66*	77310	UK COL 33rpm: 72794 US COL 33rpm: M2L-357, M2S-757

COMPOSER AND SELECTION:	DATE RECORDED:	MATRIX-TAKE OR JOB NUMBER:	U.S. AND U.K. RELEASES:
Mazurka No. 26 in C-sharp Minor, Opus 41 #1	5/11/49	D9-RC-1747-2A	RCA 78rpm: DM-1446 RCA 45rpm: ERA-31[20] ERB-7018 WDM-1446 HMV 33rpm: ALP-1069 RCA 33rpm: LM-1109 LRM-7018 LVT-1032
Mazurka No. 27 in E Minor, Opus 41 #2			
—1st recording	5/29/33	OB-6724-1	HMV 78rpm: DA-1353 ANG 33rpm: COLH-300
—2nd recording	2/15/73	95754	UK COL 33rpm: 76307[55] 79340[55] US COL 33rpm: M-32932[55] M3-36935[55]
Mazurka No. 32 in C-sharp Minor, Opus 50 #3			
—1st recording	6/2/35	2EA-2074-2	HMV 78rpm: DB-2788 RCA 78rpm: 14140 ANG 33rpm: COLH-300 SER 33rpm: 60207
—2nd recording	12/30/49	D9-RC-2149-1	RCA 78rpm: DM-1446 RCA 45rpm: ERA-31[20] WDM-1446

—3rd recording 2/15/73 95754

HMV 33rpm: ALP-1069
RCA 33rpm: ARM1-3268
LM-1109
LVT-1032
VIC-1605
UK COL 33rpm: 76307
79340[55]
US COL 33rpm: M-32932
M3-36935[55]

Mazurka No. 38 in F-sharp Minor, Opus 59 #3
—1st recording 5/10/50 EO-RC-948-1

HMV 78rpm: DB-21590
RCA 78rpm: DM-1446
RCA 45rpm: ERA-31[20]
WDM-1446
HMV 33rpm: ALP-1069
7ER-5006
RCA 33rpm: LM-1109
LVT-1032

—2nd recording 2/15/73 95754

UK COL 33rpm: 76307
79340[55]
US COL 33rpm: M-32932
M3-36935[55]

Mazurka No. 40 in F Minor, Opus 63 #2
12/30/49 D9-RC-2148-1

HMV 78rpm: DB-21590
RCA 78rpm: DM-1446
RCA 45rpm: ERA-31[20]
WDM-1446
HMV 33rpm: ALP-1069
7ER-5006
RCA 33rpm: LM-1109
LVT-1032

COMPOSER AND SELECTION:	DATE RECORDED:	MATRIX-TAKE OR JOB NUMBER:	U.S. AND U.K. RELEASES:
Mazurka No. 41 in C-sharp Minor, Opus 63 #3	12/30/49	D9-RC-2148-1	HMV 78rpm: DB-21590 RCA 78rpm: DM-1446 RCA 45rpm: ERA-31[20] WDM-1446 HMV 33rpm: ALP-1069 7ER-5006 RCA 33rpm: LM-1109 LVT-1032
Nocturne No. 2 in E-flat Major, Opus 9 #2	5/14/57	H2-RB-803-4	HMV 33rpm: RB-16064 RCA 33rpm: ARM1-2716 LM-2137 VIC-1605
Nocturne No. 3 in B Major, Opus 9 #3	2/23/57	H2-RB-804-5	HMV 33rpm: RB-16064 RCA 33rpm: LM-2137
Nocturne No. 4 in F Major, Opus 15 #1	2/23/57	H2-RB-805-5	HMV 33rpm: RB-16064 RCA 33rpm: LM-2137
Nocturne No. 5 in F-sharp Major, Opus 15 #2	5/19/47	D7-RC-7536-1A	HMV 78rpm: DB-6627 RCA 78rpm: DM-1165 DV-29 M-1165 V-29 RCA 45rpm: ERB-7018 WDM-1165

Nocturne No. 7 in C-sharp Minor, Opus 27 #1

2/23/57 — H2-RB-805-2

HMV 33rpm: ALP-1087
RCA 33rpm: ARM1-3268
LM-1235
LRM-7018
VICS-1649(e)[2]

Nocturne No. 15 in F Minor, Opus 55 #1
—1st recording

4/28/51 — EO-RC-1986-3

HMV 33rpm: RB-16064
RCA 33rpm: ARM1-3268
LM-2137

RCA 45rpm: ERB-7051
WDM-1707
HMV 33rpm: ALP-1111
BLP-1079
RCA 33rpm: ARM1-2716
LM-1707
LRM-7051

—2nd recording

2/-/68*[12] — 14093

UK COL 33rpm: 72720
79340[55]
US COL 33rpm: MS-7106
M3-36935[55]

Nocturne No. 19 in E Minor, Opus 72 #1
—1st recording[22]

1/5/52 — E2-RC-0020-1

RCA 45rpm: ERA-241

—2nd recording

2/25/53* — E3-RP-5251

RCA 45rpm: ERG-6014
HMV 33rpm: ALP-1430/1
RCA 33rpm: LM-6014
VICS-1649(e)[2]

—3rd recording

4/17/66* — 77310

UK COL 33rpm: 72794
US COL 33rpm: M2L-357
M2S-757

COMPOSER AND SELECTION:	DATE RECORDED:	MATRIX-TAKE OR JOB NUMBER:	U.S. AND U.K. RELEASES:
Polonaise No. 3 in A Major, Opus 40 #1 ("Military")	7/6/72	79906	UK COL 33rpm: 76307 / 79340[55] US COL 33rpm: M-32932 / M3-36935[55]
Polonaise No. 5 in F-sharp Minor, Opus 44	2/1/68*[12]	14093	UK COL 33rpm: 72720 / 79340[55] US COL 33rpm: MS-7106 / M3-36935[55]
Polonaise No. 6 in A-flat Major, Opus 53 —1st recording—s. 1 s. 2	10/6/45)	D5-RC-1224-2 D5-RC-1225-2	HMV 78rpm: DB-10131 RCA 78rpm: DM-1034 M-1034 11-9065 18-0013 RCA 45rpm: WDM-1034 RCA 33rpm: ARM1-3268 LM-1137
—2nd recording	5/4/71	76233	UK COL 33rpm: 72969 / 79340[55] US COL 33rpm: M-30643 / M-35118 / M3-36935[55]

Work / Recording	Date	Matrix	Releases
Polonaise-Fantasie in A-flat Major, Opus 61			
—1st recording	4/23/51*	Unknown	HMV 33rpm: RB-16019 / RCA 33rpm: ARM1-2953 / LM-1957
—2nd recording	4/17/66*	77310	UK COL 33rpm: 72969 / 79340[55] / US COL 33rpm: M-30643 / M3-36935[55]
Prelude No. 6 in B Minor, Opus 28 #6	7/6/72	79906	UK COL 33rpm: 76307 / 79340[55] / US COL 33rpm: M-32932 / M3-36935[55]
Scherzo No. 1 in B Minor, Opus 20			
—1st recording—s. 1	4/29/51)	E1-RC-3433-1	RCA 45rpm: ERB-7051 / WDM-1707 / HMV 33rpm: ALP-1111 / BLP-1079 / RCA 33rpm: ARM1-3268 / LM-1707 / LRM-7051
s. 2	)	E1-RC-3434-1	
—2nd recording	2/25/53*	E3-RP-5251	RCA 45rpm: ERG-6014 / HMV 33rpm: ALP-1430/1 / RCA 33rpm: ARM1-2873 / LM-6014 / VIC-1605
—3rd recording	11/14/63	85311	US COL 33rpm: ML-5941 / MS-6541

COMPOSER AND SELECTION:	DATE RECORDED:	MATRIX-TAKE OR JOB NUMBER:	U.S. AND U.K. RELEASES:
Scherzo No. 2 in B-flat Minor, Opus 31	2/23/57	H2-RB-801-3	HMV 33rpm: RB-16064 RCA 33rpm: LM-2137
Scherzo No. 3 in C-sharp Minor, Opus 39	1/15/57	H2-RB-802-1	HMV 33rpm: RB-16064 RCA 33rpm: LM-2137
Scherzo No. 4 in E Major, Opus 54—s. 1 s. 2	3/9/36)	2EA-3136-1 2EA-3137-1	HMV 78rpm: DB-3205 RCA 78rpm: 14634 ANG 33rpm: COLH-300
Sonata No. 2 in B-flat Minor, Opus 35 —1st recording—s. 1 s. 2 s. 3 s. 4 s. 5 s. 6	5/13/50)))))	EO-RC-950-1A EO-RC-951-2A EO-RC-952-2 EO-RC-953-2B EO-RC-954-1A EO-RC-955-1A	HMV 78rpm: DB-9658/60 DB-21312/4 RCA 78rpm: DM-1472 RCA 45rpm: WDM-1472 HMV 33rpm: ALP-1087 RCA 33rpm: ARM1-2716 LM-1113 LM-1235
—2nd recording	April and May/62[23]	Various[24]	UK COL 33rpm: 79340[55] US COL 33rpm: KL-5771 KS-6371 M3-36935[55] FMR 33rpm: 12[25] TLR 33rpm: STL-P06[16]

Waltz No. 3 in A Minor, Opus 34 #2

—1st recording 9/23/45 D5-RC-1226-1
RCA 78rpm: DM-1034
M-1034
RCA 45rpm: ERA-59
WDM-1034
HMV 33rpm: 7ER-5071
RCA 33rpm: LM-1137

—2nd recording 2/25/53* E3-RP-5253
RCA 45rpm: ERG-6014
HMV 33rpm: ALP-1430/1
RCA 33rpm: ARM1-3268
LM-6014

—3rd recording 5/4/71 76233
UK COL 33rpm: 72969
79340[55]
US COL 33rpm: M-30643
M3-36935[55]

Waltz No. 7 in C-sharp Minor, Opus 64 #2

—1st recording 11/29/46 D6-RC-6463-1
HMV 78rpm: DB-21425
RCA 78rpm: 11-9519
RCA 45rpm: ERA-59
49-0133
RCA 33rpm: ARM1-3268
LM-1137
LM-2993
VIC-1605

—2nd recording 4/7/58* 14099
UK COL 33rpm: 76307
79340[55]
US COL 33rpm: M-32932
M-35118
M3-36935[55]

COMPOSER AND SELECTION:	DATE RECORDED:	MATRIX-TAKE OR JOB NUMBER:	U.S. AND U.K. RELEASES:
Waltz No. 9 in A-flat Major, Opus 69 #1	11/1/81*[56]	Unknown	HMV 33rpm: RL-14260[15] RCA 33rpm: ATC1-4260[15]
CLEMENTI:[26]			
Sonata in F Minor, Opus 13 #6[27]	October/54[28]	Unknown	HMV 33rpm: ALP-1340 RCA 33rpm: ARM1-3689 LM-1902
Sonata in B-flat Major, Opus 24 #2 —Third Movement: Rondo[29]	5/17/50	EO-RC-970-2	RCA 45rpm: 49-3303 HMV 33rpm: RB-6554/5 RCA 33rpm: ARM1-2719 LD-7021 TLR 33rpm: STL-P06[16]
Sonata in F-sharp Minor, Opus 25 #5[30]	October/54[28]	Unknown	HMV 33rpm: ALP-1340 RCA 33rpm: ARM1-3689 LM-1902
Sonata in C Major, Opus 33 #3[57]	April/79*[34]	Unknown	HMV 33rpm: RL-14322 RCA 33rpm: ARL1-4322
Sonata in G Minor, Opus 34 #2	October/54[28]	Unknown	HMV 33rpm: ALP-1340 RCA 33rpm: ARM1-3689 LM-1902

CZERNY:

Variations on a Theme by Rode, Opus 33

—"La Ricordanza"—s. 1	12/23/44)	D4-RC-688-2	HMV 78rpm: DB-6274
s. 2	)	D4-RC-689-2	RCA 78rpm: DM-1001
			M-1001
			HMV 33rpm: RB-6554/5
			RCA 33rpm: ARM1-2719
			LD-7021

DEBUSSY:

Children's Corner Suite:

No. 3 Serenade for the Doll—1st recording	3/26/28	BVE-43414-1	HMV 78rpm: DA-1032
			DA-1160
			RCA 78rpm: 1353
			RCA 45rpm: E2LW-1007[21]
			RCA 33rpm: LM-2993
—2nd recording	5/16/47	D7-RC-7529-3A	HMV 78rpm: DB-6971
			RCA 78rpm: 12-0428
			RCA 45rpm: WDM-1605[31]
			49-1042
			RCA 33rpm: ARM1-2717
			LM-1171
—3rd recording	2/25/53*	E3-RP-5253	RCA 45rpm: ERG-6014
			HMV 33rpm: ALP-1430/1
			RCA 33rpm: LM-6014
—4th recording	5/9/65*	77219	UK COL 33rpm: MET-2110
			SET-2110
			US COL 33rpm: M2L-328
			M2S-728
			M-35118

COMPOSER AND SELECTION:	DATE RECORDED:	MATRIX-TAKE OR JOB NUMBER:	U.S. AND U.K. RELEASES:
Etude, Book II, No. 11: Pour les arpèges composés	5/6/34	OB-6197-1	HMV 78rpm: DB-2247 RCA 78rpm: 8996 ANG 33rpm: COLH-300
L'Isle Joyeuse	11/27/66*	77328	UK COL 33rpm: 72974 US COL 33rpm: M2L-328 M2S-728
Preludes, Book II:			
No. 4 "Les fées sont d'exquises danseuses"	11/4/63	85254	US COL 33rpm: ML-5941 MS-6541
No. 5 Bruyères	11/4/63	85254	US COL 33rpm: ML-5941 MS-6541
No. 6 "General Lavine"—eccentric	11/4/63	85254	US COL 33rpm: ML-5941 MS-6541
DOHNÁNYI:			
Concert Etude in F Minor, Opus 28 #6 ("Capriccio")	12/4/28	BVE-49156-3	HMV 78rpm: DA-1140 RCA 78rpm: 1455 RCA 45rpm: E2LW-1007[21] RCA 33rpm: LM-2993
FAURÉ:			
Impromptu No. 5 in F-sharp Minor, Opus 102	6/22/76	Unknown	HMV 33rpm: RL-12548 RCA 33rpm: ARL1-2548

Title	Date	Matrix	Issues
Nocturne No. 13 in B Minor, Opus 119	6/22/76	Unknown	HMV 33rpm: RL-12548 RCA 33rpm: <u>ARL1-2548</u>

HAYDN:

Title	Date	Matrix	Issues
Sonata in F Major, Hob. XVI: 23	11/27/66*	77328	US COL 33rpm: M2L-357 <u>M2S-757</u>
Sonata in E-flat Major, Hob. XVI: 52			
—1st recording—s. 1	11/11/32)	2B-4487-2	HMV 78rpm: DB-1837/8
s. 2	)	2B-4488-2	RCA 78rpm: 8489/90
s. 3	)	2B-4485-1	SER 33rpm: 60063
s. 4	)	2B-4486-1	
—2nd recording	4/23/51*	Unknown	HMV 33rpm: RB-16019 RCA 33rpm: ARM1-3263 LM-1957

HOROWITZ:

Title	Date	Matrix	Issues
Danse Excentrique[32]	3/4/30	BVE-58687-1	HMV 78rpm: DA-1146 RCA 78rpm: 1468 RCA 33rpm: LM-2993
Variations on a Theme from Bizet's "Carmen"			
—1st recording	4/2/28	BVE-43411-5	HMV 78rpm: DA-982 RCA 78rpm: 1327 RCA 33rpm: LM-6074[33]
—2nd recording	12/22/47	D7-RC-8280-1	HMV 78rpm: DB-6953 RCA 78rpm: 12-0427

COMPOSER AND SELECTION:	DATE RECORDED:	MATRIX-TAKE OR JOB NUMBER:	U.S. AND U.K. RELEASES:
—3rd recording	2/1/68*[12]	14093	RCA 45rpm: ERA-74 / WDM-1605 / 49-0458 RCA 33rpm: ARM1-2717 / LM-1171 TLR 33rpm: STL-P06[16] UK COL 33rpm: 72720 US COL 33rpm: MS-7106 / M-35118

KABALEVSKY:

Sonata No. 3 in F Major, Opus 46—s. 1	12/22/47	D7-RC-8269-1	RCA 78rpm: DM-1282 / M-1282
s. 2		D7-RC-8270-1	RCA 45rpm: WDM-1282
s. 3		D7-RC-8271-1	RCA 33rpm: LM-1016 / LM-2993
s. 4		D7-RC-8272-1	

LISZT:

Années de Pèlerinage, Première Année, Suisse: No. 4 Au bord d'une source	5/19/47	D7-RC-7537-1C	HMV 78rpm: DB-6627 RCA 78rpm: DM-1165 / DV-29 / M-1165 / V-29 RCA 45rpm: ERB-7019 / WDM-1165

Title	Date	Matrix/Number	Issue
			HMV 33rpm: ALP-1087 / BLP-1048 RCA 33rpm: LM-1235 / LM-2584 / LRM-7019
No. 6 Vallée d'Obermann	11/27/66*	77328	UK COL 33rpm: 72794 US COL 33rpm: M2L-357 / M2S-757
Années de Pèlerinage, Deuxième Année, Italie: No. 6 Sonetto 104 del Petrarca—s. 1 s. 2	4/28/51	EO-RC-1992-3 EO-RC-1993-2	RCA 45rpm: ERB-7019 / WDM-1534 HMV 33rpm: BLP-1048 RCA 33rpm: LM-100 / LM-2584 / LM-9021 / LRM-7019 / LVT-1043
Ballade No. 2 in B Minor	11/1/81*[56]	Unknown	HMV 33rpm: RL-14260[15] RCA 33rpm: ATC1-4260[15]
Consolation No. 3 in D-flat Major	April/79*[34]	Unknown	HMV 33rpm: RL-13433 RCA 33rpm: ARL1-3433
Études d'exécution transcendante d'après Paganini: No. 2 in E-flat Major	3/4/30	BVE-58689-1	HMV 78rpm: DA-1146 / DA-1160 RCA 78rpm: 1468 RCA 45rpm: E2LW-1007[21] RCA 33rpm: LM-2993

COMPOSER AND SELECTION:	DATE RECORDED:	MATRIX-TAKE OR JOB NUMBER:	U.S. AND U.K. RELEASES:
Harmonies poétiques et religieuses:			
No. 7 Funérailles —1st recording—s. 1	11/15/32)	OB-4504-1	HMV 78rpm: DB-1848
s. 2	)	OB-4505-1	RCA 78rpm: 14515
			ANG 33rpm: COLH-72
			SER 33rpm: 60114
—2nd recording—s. 1	12/29/50)	EO-RC-1990-1A	RCA 45 rpm: ERB-7019
s. 2	)	EO-RC-1991-1A	WDM-1534
			HMV 33rpm: BLP-1048
			RCA 33rpm: LM-100
			LM-2584
			LM-9021
			LRM-7019
			LVT-1043
			VICS-1649(e)[2]
Hungarian Rhapsody No. 6 in D-flat Major—s. 1	5/16/47	D7-RC-7530-1B	HMV 78rpm: DB-6659
s. 2	5/19/47	D7-RC-7531-2B	RCA 78rpm: DM-1165
			DV-29
			M-1165
			V-29
			HMV 45rpm: 7R-142
			RCA 45rpm: ERA-10[20]
			WDM-1165

Sonata in B Minor

—1st recording—s. 1 11/12/32 2B-4490-2 HMV 33rpm: ALP-1087
    s. 2   2B-4491-2 RCA 33rpm: LM-1235
    s. 3   2B-4492-2   LM-2584
    s. 4   2B-4493-2 HMV 78rpm: DB-1855/7
    s. 5   2B-4494-2   DB-2455[35]
    s. 6   2B-4495-1   DB-7334/6

RCA 78rpm: AM-380
               DM-380
               M-380
ANG 33rpm: COLH-72
SER 33rpm: 60114

—2nd recording 11/21/76* Unknown HMV 33rpm: RL-12548
                                              RCA 33rpm: ARL1-2548

Valse Oubliée No. 1 in F-sharp Major

—1st recording 2/25/30 BVE-49155-8 HMV 78rpm: DA-1140
                                             RCA 78rpm: 1455

—2nd recording 4/28/51 EO-RC-1993-2 RCA 45rpm: ERB-7019
                                             WDM-1534
HMV 33rpm: BLP-1048
RCA 33rpm: LM-100
               LM-2584
               LM-9021
               LRM-7019
               LVT-1043
               VICS-1649(e)[2]

COMPOSER AND SELECTION:	DATE RECORDED:	MATRIX-TAKE OR JOB NUMBER:	U.S. AND U.K. RELEASES:
LISZT-BUSONI:			
Mephisto Waltz No. 1	April/79*[34]	Unknown	HMV 33rpm: RL-13433 RCA 33rpm: ARL1-3433
LISZT-HOROWITZ:			
Hungarian Rhapsody No. 2 in C-sharp Minor	2/25/53*	E3-RP-5252	RCA 45rpm: ERG-6014 HMV 33rpm: ALP-1430/1 RCA 33rpm: LM-2584 LM-6014
Hungarian Rhapsody No. 15 in A Minor ("Rakóczy March")—s. 1	5/9/49	D9-RC-1738-1	RCA 78rpm: 12-3154 RCA 45rpm: WDM-1534 49-3154 RCA 33rpm: LM-100 LM-2584 LM-9021 LVT-1043
s. 2	5/17/50	EO-RC-969-2	
Hungarian Rhapsody No. 19 in D Minor	April and May/62[23]	Various[24]	US COL 33rpm: KL-5771 KS-6371 M-35118 FMR 33rpm: 12[25] TLR 33rpm: STL-P06[16]

MEDTNER:

Fairy Tale in A Major, Opus 51 #3[36]	6/12/69	ZSW-152671-1A	COL 33rpm: <u>CSS-1033</u>[37] <u>No Serial No.</u>[1]

MENDELSSOHN:

Scherzo a Capriccio in F-sharp Minor	April and May/80*[38]	Unknown	HMV 33rpm: <u>RL-13775</u> RCA 33rpm: <u>ARL1-3775</u>

Songs Without Words:

No. 25: "May Breezes," Opus 62 #1	10/29/46	D6-RC-6415-1	HMV 78rpm: DB-6613 RCA 78rpm: DM-1121 DV-28 M-1121 V-28 RCA 45rpm: ERA-59 WDM-1121
No. 30: "Spring Song," Opus 62 #6	10/29/46	D6-RC-6416-1A	HMV 78rpm: DB-6613 RCA 78rpm: 11-9519 RCA 45rpm: WDM-1605[31] 49-0133 HMV 33rpm: RB-6554/5 RCA 33rpm: ARM1-2717 LD-7021 LM-1171 <u>VICS-1649(e)</u>[2]

COMPOSER AND SELECTION:	DATE RECORDED:	MATRIX-TAKE OR JOB NUMBER:	U.S. AND U.K. RELEASES:
No. 35: "Shepherd's Complaint," Opus 67 #5	10/29/46	D6-RC-6415-1	HMV 78rpm: DB-6613 RCA 78rpm: DM-1121 DV-28 M-1121 V-28 RCA 45rpm: ERA-59 WDM-1121 HMV 33rpm: RB-6554/5 RCA 33rpm: ARM1-2717 LD-7021 <u>VICS-1649(e)</u>[2]
No. 40: "Elegy," Opus 85 #4	10/29/46	D6-RC-6416-1A	HMV 78rpm: DB-6613 RCA 78rpm: 11-9519 RCA 45rpm: WDM-1605 49-0133 HMV 33rpm: RB-6554/5 RCA 33rpm: ARM1-2717 LM-1171 LD-7021 <u>VICS-1649(e)</u>[2]
Variations Sérieuses in D Minor, Opus 54 — s. 1 s. 2 s. 3	10/25/46 11/22/46))	D6-RC-6412-1 D6-RC-6413-4A D6-RC-6414-4	RCA 78rpm: DM-1121 DV-28 M-1121 V-28 RCA 45rpm: ERA-103

MENDELSSOHN-LISZT-HOROWITZ:

RCA 33rpm: ARM1-2719
LM-21
LM-9021
LVT-1043

Wedding March and Variations—s. 1   11/22/46   D6-RC-6417-1A
s. 2   )   D6-RC-6418-2A

RCA 78rpm: DM-1121
DV-28
M-1121
V-28
11-9693
RCA 45rpm: ERA-10[20]
WDM-1121
RCA 33rpm: ARM1-2717
LM-21
LM-9021
LVT-1043

MOSZKOWSKI:

Étincelles, Opus 36 #6   4/23/51*   Unknown

HMV 33rpm: RB-16019
RCA 33rpm: ARM1-2717
LM-1957

Etude in F Major, Opus 72 #6   10/10/50   EO-RC-1862-1

RCA 78rpm: 10-3424
RCA 45rpm: ERA-59
49-3424

Etude in A-flat Major, Opus 72 #11
—1st recording   10/10/50   EO-RC-1855-3

HMV 33rpm: RB-6554/5
RCA 33rpm: ARM1-2717
LD-7021

COMPOSER AND SELECTION:	DATE RECORDED:	MATRIX-TAKE OR JOB NUMBER:	U.S. AND U.K. RELEASES:
—2nd recording	5/9/65*	77219	UK COL 33rpm: MET-2110 / SET-2110 US COL 33rpm: M2L-328 / M2S-728 / M-35118

MOZART:

COMPOSER AND SELECTION:	DATE RECORDED:	MATRIX-TAKE OR JOB NUMBER:	U.S. AND U.K. RELEASES:
Sonata No. 11 in A Major, K. 331 —Third Movement: Rondo alla Turca	10/25/46	D6-RC-6409-2	RCA 78rpm: 12-0429 RCA 45rpm: WDM-1605[31] / 49-0597 RCA 33rpm: ARM1-2717 / LM-1171
Sonata No. 11 in A Major, K. 331	4/17/66*	77328	US COL 33rpm: M2L-357 / M2S-757
Sonata No. 12 in F Major, K. 322—s. 1 s. 2 s. 3	11/6/47)))	D7-RC-7693-2A D7-RC-7694-3C D7-RC-7695-1	RCA 78rpm: DM-1284 / M-1284 RCA 45rpm: WDM-1284 HMV 33rpm: BLP-1014 / RB-6554/5 RCA 33rpm: ARM1-2719 / LD-7021 / LM-1027

MUSSORGSKY-HOROWITZ:

By the Water (From the Song Cycle "Without Sun")	11/21/47	D7-RC-8004-1A	RCA 78rpm: DM-1249 / DV-30 / M-1249 / V-30 RCA 45rpm: ERA-103 / WDM-1249 / WDM-1605 RCA 33rpm: ARM1-2717 / LM-1171
Pictures at an Exhibition —1st recording—s. 1	11/7/47	D7-RC-7968-1	RCA 78rpm: DM-1249 / DV-30 / M-1249 / V-30 RCA 45rpm: WDM-1249 RCA 33rpm: ARM1-3263 / LM-1014 / LVT-1023
s. 2)		D7-RC-7969-1A	
s. 3	11/21/47	D7-RC-7970-4	
s. 4	11/7/47	D7-RC-7971-1	
s. 5)		D7-RC-7972-1	
s. 6)		D7-RC-7973-1	
s. 7)		D7-RC-7974-1	
—2nd recording	4/23/51*	Unknown	FMR 33rpm: 46[25] HMV 33rpm: RB-16194 RCA 33rpm: LM-2357 / LSC-3278(e)[2]

POULENC:

Pastourelle in B-flat Major	11/11/32	2B-4484-1	HMV 78rpm: DB-1869[39] / DB-2247 RCA 78rpm: 8996 ANG 33rpm: COLH-300 TLR 33rpm: STL-P06[16]

COMPOSER AND SELECTION:	DATE RECORDED:	MATRIX-TAKE OR JOB NUMBER:	U.S. AND U.K. RELEASES:
Presto in B-flat Major	5/16/47	D7-RC-7529-3A	HMV 78rpm: DB-6971 RCA 78rpm: 12-0428 RCA 45rpm: 49-1042
Toccata	11/11/32	2B-4484-1	HMV 78rpm: DB-1869[39] DB-2247 RCA 78rpm: 8996 ANG 33rpm: COLH-300 TLR 33rpm: STL-P06[16]
PROKOFIEV:			
Sonata No. 7 in B-flat Major, Opus 83—s. 1	9/22/45)	D5-RC-1217-1A	RCA 78rpm: DM-1042
s. 2	)	D5-RC-1218-1	M-1042
s. 3	10/6/45	D5-RC-1219-3A	RCA 45rpm: WDM-1042
s. 4	9/22/45	D5-RC-1220-1	HMV 33rpm: RB-6554/5 RCA 33rpm: ARM1-2952 LD-7021 LM-1016
Sonata No. 7 in B-flat Major, Opus 83 —Fourth Movement: Precipitato	2/25/53*	E3-RP-5253	RCA 45rpm: ERG-6014 HMV 33rpm: ALP-1430/1 RCA 33rpm: LM-6014
Toccata in C Major, Opus 11	11/21/47	D7-RC-8007-1	HMV 78rpm: DB-6971 RCA 78rpm: 12-0428

RACHMANINOFF:

Barcarolle in G Minor, Opus 10 #3   April/79[*34]   RCA 45rpm: ERA-103
                 WDM-1605[31]
                 49-1042
            RCA 33rpm: ARM1-2717
                 LM-1171
            TLR 33rpm: STL-P06[16]

                     Unknown   HMV 33rpm: RL-13433
            RCA 33rpm: ARLl-3433

Concerto No. 3 in D Minor, Opus 30
(With the London Symphony Orchestra,
conducted by Albert Coates)

  —1st recording—s. 1   12/30/30   CC-20723-3   HMV 78rpm: DA-1486/90
               s. 2   CC-20724-3   DB-7468/72
               s. 3   CC-20725-3   RCA 78rpm: AM-117
               s. 4   CC-20731-2   DM-117
               s. 5   CC-20726-2   M-117
               s. 6   CC-20727-2   SER 33rpm: 60063
               s. 7   CC-20728-2
               s. 8   CC-20729-1
               s. 9   CC-20730-2

(With the RCA Symphony Orchestra,
conducted by Fritz Reiner)

  —2nd recording—s. 1   5/8/51   E1-RC-3437-1   RCA 45rpm: WDM-1575
               s. 2   E1-RC-3438-1   HMV 33rpm: ALP-1017

COMPOSER AND SELECTION:	DATE RECORDED:	MATRIX-TAKE OR JOB NUMBER:	U.S. AND U.K. RELEASES:
s. 3)		E1-RC-3439-2	RCA 33rpm: CRM4-0914
s. 4)		E1-RC-3440-1	LM-1178
s. 5)		E1-RC-3441-1A	
s. 6	5/10/51	E1-RC-3442-1	
s. 7)		E1-RC-3443-1	
s. 8)		E1-RC-3444-1	
s. 9)		E1-RC-3445-1	
s. 10)		E1-RC-3446-1	
(With the New York Philharmonic, conducted by Eugene Ormandy)			
—3rd recording	1/8/78*[40]	Unknown	HMV 33rpm: RL-12633 RCA 33rpm: CRL1-2633
Étude-Tableau in C Major, Opus 33 #2			
—1st recording	April and May/62[23]	Various[24]	US COL 33rpm: KL-5771 KS-6371 TLR 33rpm: STL-P06[16]
—2nd recording	12/10/67*	14080	UK COL 33rpm: 72940 US COL 33rpm: M-30464
Étude-Tableau in E-flat Minor, Opus 33 #6	12/10/67*	14080	UK COL 33rpm: 72940 US COL 33rpm: M-30464
Étude-Tableau in E-flat Minor, Opus 39 #5	April and May/62[23]	Various[24]	US COL 33rpm: KL-5771 KS-6371

Title	Date	Number	Recording
Étude-Tableau in D Major, Opus 39 #9	12/10/67*	14030	FMR 33rpm: 12[25] TLR 33rpm: STL-P06[16] UK COL 33rpm: 72940 US COL 33rpm: M-30464
Humoresque in G Major, Opus 10 #5	April/79*[34]	Unknown	HMV 33rpm: RL-13433 RCA 33rpm: ARL1-3433
Moment Musical No. 2 in E-flat Minor, Opus 16 #2	November/77 and March/78*[58]	Unknown	HMV 33rpm: RL-14322 RCA 33rpm: ARL1-4322
Moment Musical No. 3 in B Minor, Opus 16 #3	12/15/68*	14146	UK COL 33rpm: 72940 US COL 33rpm: M-30464 FMR 33rpm: 12[25]
Polka de W.R. in A-flat Major	April and May/80*[59]	Unknown	HMV 33rpm: RL-14322 RCA 33rpm: ARL1-4322
Prelude No. 6 in G Minor, Opus 23 #5 —1st recording[41]	6/12/31	2D-473-2	HMV 78rpm: DA-1490 DB-7468 RCA 78rpm: AM-117 DM-117 M-117
—2nd recording	11/1/81*[56]	Unknown	HMV 33rpm: RL-14260[15] RCA 33rpm: ATC1-4260[15]
Prelude No. 16 in G major, Opus 32 #5	November/75*[60]	Unknown	HMV 33rpm: RL-14322 RCA 33rpm: ARL1-4322

COMPOSER AND SELECTION:	DATE RECORDED:	MATRIX-TAKE OR JOB NUMBER:	U.S. AND U.K. RELEASES:
Prelude No. 23 in G-sharp Minor, Opus 32 #12	12/15/68*	14146	UK COL 33rpm: 72940 US COL 33rpm: M-30464 M-35118 FMR 33rpm: 12[25]
Sonata No. 2 in B-flat Minor, Opus 36 —1st recording	12/15/68*	14146	UK COL 33rpm: 72940 US COL 33rpm: M-30464
—2nd recording	April and May/80*[38]	Unknown	HMV 33rpm: RL-13775 RCA 33rpm: ARL1-3775 XRL1-4329
RIMSKY-KORSAKOV–RACHMANINOFF:			
The Flight of the Bumble-Bee[19]	11/11/32	2B-4489-1	HMV 78rpm: DB-1869[39]
SAINT-SAËNS–LISZT–HOROWITZ:			
Danse Macabre—s. 1 s. 2	9/10/42))	PCS-072583-1 PCS-072584-1	HMV 78rpm: DB-6275 RCA 78rpm: DM-1001 M-1001 HMV 33rpm: RB-6554/5 RCA 33rpm: ARM1-2717 LD-7021

SCARLATTI:

	Date	Matrix	Issue(s)
Sonata in E Major, L. 21 [K. 162]	May/June September/64[42]	Various[43]	UK COL 33rpm: 72274 US COL 33rpm: ML-6058 MS-6658
Sonata in E Minor, L. 22 [K. 198]	May/June September/64[42]	Various[43]	UK COL 33rpm: 72274 US COL 33rpm: ML-6058 MS-6658
Sonata in E Major, L. 23 [K. 380]			
—1st recording	10/24/46	D6-RC-6410-1	RCA 78rpm: MO-1262
—2nd recording	4/23/51*	Unknown	HMV 33rpm: RB-16019 RCA 33rpm: ARM1-2719 LM-1957
—3rd recording	2/1/68*[12]	14093	UK COL 33rpm: 72720 US COL 33rpm: MS-7106
Sonata in E Major, L. 25 [K. 46]	11/27/46	D6-RC-6411-3	RCA 78rpm: MO-1262
Sonata in B Minor, L. 33 [K. 87]			
—1st recording	6/4/25	2EA-2076-2	HMV 78rpm: DB-2847 ANG 33rpm: COLH-300 TLR 33rpm: STL-P06[16]
—2nd recording	11/21/47	D7-RC-7966-2	HMV 78rpm: DB-6882 RCA 78rpm: MO-1262
—3rd recording	11/1/81*[56]	Unknown	HMV 33rpm: RL-14260[15] RCA 33rpm: ATC1-4260[15]
Sonata in F Minor, L. 118 [K. 466]			
—1st recording	May/June September/64[42]	Various[43]	UK COL 33rpm: 72274 US COL 33rpm: ML-6058 MS-6658

COMPOSER AND SELECTION:	DATE RECORDED:	MATRIX-TAKE OR JOB NUMBER:	U.S. AND U.K. RELEASES:
—2nd recording	11/1/81*[56]	Unknown	HMV 33rpm: RL-14260[15] RCA 33rpm: ATC1-4260[15]
Sonata in D Major, L. 164 [K. 491]	May/June/September/64[42]	Various[43]	UK COL 33rpm: 72274 US COL 33rpm: ML-6058 MS-6658
Sonata in A-flat Major, L. 186 [K. 127]	11/1/81*[56]	Unknown	HMV 33rpm: RL-14260[15] RCA 33rpm: ATC1-4260[15]
Sonata in F Minor, L. 187 [K. 481]	May/June/September/64[42]	Various[43]	UK COL 33rpm: 72274 US COL 33rpm: ML-6058 MS-6658
Sonata in F Major, L. 188 [K. 525]	4/23/64	90659	UK COL 33rpm: 72274 US COL 33rpm: ML-6058 MS-6658
Sonata in F Minor, L. 189 [K. 184]	11/1/81*[56]	Unknown	HMV 33rpm: RL-14260[15] RCA 33rpm: ATC1-4260[15]
Sonata in E-flat Major, L. 203 [K. 474]	May/June/September/64[42]	Various[43]	UK COL 33rpm: 72274 US COL 33rpm: ML-6058 MS-6658
Sonata in G Major, L. 209 [K. 455] —1st recording	10/24/4(	D6-RC-6410-1	RCA 78rpm: MO-1262

Work	Date	Matrix	Issues
—2nd recording	November and December/62[44]	Various[45]	UK COL 33rpm: 72117 US COL 33rpm: ML-5811 MS-6411
Sonata in E Major, L. 224 [K. 135]	11/1/81*[56]	Unknown	HMV 33rpm: RL-14260[15] RCA 33rpm: ATC1-4260[15]
Sonata in A Minor, L. 239 [K. 188]	10/11/51	2EA-15979-1	HMV 78rpm: DB-21359 HMV 45rpm: 7R-155
Sonata in A Minor, L. 241 [K. 54]	May/June/September/64[42]	Various[43]	UK COL 33rpm: 72274 US COL 33rpm: ML-6058 MS-6658
Sonata in G Major, L. 335 [K. 55]	2/1/68*[12]	14093	UK COL 33rpm: 72720 US COL 33rpm: MS-7106
Sonata in A Major, L. 391 [K. 39]	4/23/64	90659	UK COL 33rpm: 72274 US COL 33rpm: ML-6058 MS-6658 M-35118
Sonata in D Major, L. 424 [K. 33]	May/June/September/64[42]	Various[43]	UK COL 33rpm: 72274 US COL 33rpm: ML-6058 MS-6658
Sonata in E Major, L. 430 [K. 531] —1st recording	11/7/47	D7-RC-7967-2	HMV 78rpm: DB-6882 RCA 78rpm: MO-1262
—2nd recording	November and December/64[44]	Various[45]	UK COL 33rpm: 72117 US COL 33rpm: ML-5811 MS-6411

COMPOSER AND SELECTION:	DATE RECORDED:	MATRIX-TAKE OR JOB NUMBER:	U.S. AND U.K. RELEASES:
Sonata in D Major, L. 465 [K. 96]	May/June/September/64[42]	Various[43]	UK COL 33rpm: 72274 US COL 33rpm: ML-6058 MS-6658
Sonata in A Major, L. 483 [K. 322] —1st recording	11/27/46	D6-RC-6411-3	RCA 78rpm: MO-1262
—2nd recording	10/11/51	2EA-15981-1A	HMV 78rpm: DB-21359 HMV 45rpm: 7R-155
—3rd recording	November and December/64[44]	Various[45]	UK COL 33rpm: 72117 US COL 33rpm: ML-5811 MS-6411
Sonata in G Major, L. 487 [K. 125]	6/2/35	2EA-2077-1	HMV 78rpm: DB-2847 ANG 33rpm: COLH-300 TLR 33rpm: STL-P06[16] HMV 33rpm: RL-14260[15]
Sonata in A Major, L. 494 [K. 101]	11/1/81*[56]	Unknown	HMV 33rpm: RL-14260[15] RCA 33rpm: ATC1-4260[15]
SCARLATTI-TAUSIG:			
Capriccio in E Major [L. 375/K. 20]	4/2/28	BVE-43413-3	HMV 78rpm: DA-1032 RCA 78rpm: 1353 RCA 45rpm: E2LW-1007[21] RCA 33rpm: LM-2993

SCHUBERT:

Impromptu in E-flat Major, Opus 90 #2 [D 899]	1/10 and 1/24/73	95602 and Unknown	UK COL 33rpm: 73175 US COL 33rpm: M-32432
Impromptu in G-flat Major, Opus 90 #3 [D 899] —1st recording[46]	1/4/53	E3-RC-2104-1	RCA 33rpm: VICS—1649(e)[2]
—2nd recording	November and December/62[44]	Various[45]	UK COL 33rpm: 72117 US COL 33rpm: ML-5811 MS-6411
Impromptu in A-flat Major, Opus 90 #4 [D 899]	1/10 and 1/24/73	95602 and Unknown	UK COL 33rpm: 73175 US COL 33rpm: M-32432
Impromptu in F Minor, Opus 142 #1 [D 935]	1/10 and 1/24/73	95602 and Unknown	UK COL 33rpm: 73175 US COL 33rpm: M-32432
Impromptu in A-flat Major, Opus 142 #2 [D 935]	1/10 and 1/24/73	95602 and Unknown	UK COL 33rpm: 73175 US COL 33rpm: M-32432
Sonata in B-flat Major, Opus Posthumous [D 960] —s. 1 s. 2	2/25/53)*)*	E3-RP-5250 E3-RP-5251	RCA 45rpm: ERG-6014 HMV 33rpm: ALP-1430/1 RCA 33rpm: ARM1-2873 LM-6014

COMPOSER AND SELECTION:	DATE RECORDED:	MATRIX-TAKE OR JOB NUMBER:	U.S. AND U.K. RELEASES:
SCHUMANN:			
Arabeske in C Major, Opus 18[47]			
—1st recording—s. 1	5/6/34)	OB-6722-3	HMV 78rpm: DA-1381
s. 2	)	OB-6723-4	RCA 78rpm: 1713
			ANG 33rpm: COLH-72
			SER 33rpm: 60114
—2nd recording	April and May/62[23]	Various[24]	US COL 33rpm: KL-5771
			KS-6371
			TLR 33rpm: STL-P06[16]
—3rd recording	2/1/68*[21]	77329	UK COL 33rpm: 72720
			US COL 33rpm: MS-7106
Blumenstück in D-flat Major, Opus 19	12/10/66*	77329	UK COL 33rpm: 72794
			US COL 33rpm: M2L-357
			M2S-757
Concerto Without Orchestra in F Minor, Opus 14 ("Grand Sonata No. 3")	February and May/76*[48]	Unknown	HMV 33rpm: ARL1-1766
			RCA 33rpm: ARL1-1766
Concerto Without Orchestra in F Minor, Opus 14 ("Grand Sonata No. 3") —Third Movement: Variations on a Theme by Clara Wieck —1st recording	3/5/51*	Unknown	HMV 33rpm: RB-6554/5
			RB-16019

	Recording date	Matrix	Label/catalog numbers
—2nd recording	2/5 and 2/14/69	40009 and 40072	RCA 33rpm: ARM1-2719 / LD-7021 / LM-1957 UK COL 33rpm: 72841 / US COL 33rpm: MS-7264
Dichterliebe, Opus 48 (With Dietrich Fischer-Dieskau, baritone)	6/18/76*	78291	UK COL 33rpm: 79200 / US COL 33rpm: M2-34256
Fantasie in C Major, Opus 17	5/9/65*[49]	77219	UK COL 33rpm: MET-2110 / SET-2110 US COL 33rpm: M2L-328 / M2S-728
Fantasiestücke, Opus 12: No. 7 Träumeswirren	11/15/32	OB-4508-1	HMV 78rpm: DA-1353 RCA 78rpm: 1654 ANG 33rpm: COLH-72 SER 33rpm: 60114
Fantasiestücke, Opus 111	April and May/80*[38]	Unknown	HMV 33rpm: RL-13775 RCA 33rpm: ARL1-3775
Humoreske in B-flat Major, Opus 20	April/79*[34]	Unknown	HMV 33rpm: RL-13433 RCA 33rpm: ARL1-3433

COMPOSER AND SELECTION:	DATE RECORDED:	MATRIX-TAKE OR JOB NUMBER:	U.S. AND U.K. RELEASES:
Kinderscenen, Opus 15 —1st recording—s. 1 s. 2 s. 3 s. 4	5/10/50 5/17/50 5/10/50)	EO-RC-944-2A EO-RC-945-4A EO-RC-946-2 EO-RC-947-2C	RCA 78rpm: DM-1447 RCA 45rpm: WDM-1447 HMV 33rpm: ALP-1069 RCA 33rpm: ARM1-2718 LM-1109 LVT-1032 XRL1-4329
—2nd recording	November and December/62[44]	Various[45]	UK COL 33rpm: 72117 US COL 33rpm: ML-5811 MS-6411 FMR 33rpm: 11[25] TLR 33rpm: STL-P06[16]
Kinderscenen, Opus 15: No. 7 Träumerei —1st recording	11/21/47	D7-RC-8006-2	RCA 78rpm: 12-0429 RCA 45rpm: WDM-1605[31] 49-0597 RCA 33rpm: LM-1171
—2nd recording[30]	5/17/50	EO-RC-945-4A	HMV 33rpm: RB-6554/5 RCA 33rpm: LD-7021 VICS-1649(e)
—3rd recording	5/9/65*	77219	UK COL 33rpm: MET-2110 SET-2110 US COL 33rpm: M2L-328 M2S-728

—4th recording	2/1/68*[12]	14093	UK COL 33rpm: 72720 US COL 33rpm: MS-7106 M-35118
Kreisleriana, Opus 16	12/1/69	06592	UK COL 33rpm: 72841 US COL 33rpm: MS-7264 FMR 33rpm: 11 [25]
Nachtstück in D-flat Major, Opus 23 #3	April and May/80*[38]	Unknown	HMV 33rpm: RL-13775 RCA 33rpm: ARL1-3775
Nachtstück in F Major, Opus 23 #4	April and May/80*[38]	Unknown	HMV 33rpm: RL-13775 RCA 33rpm: ARL1-3775
Presto Passionato in G Minor—s. 1 s. 2	11/15/32)	OB-4502-1 OB-4503-2	HMV 78rpm: DA-1301 RCA 78rpm: 1638 ANG 33rpm: COLH-72 SER 33rpm: 60114
Toccata in C Major, Opus 7 —1st recording	5/12/34	2B-6725-3	HMV 78rpm: DB-2238[18] ANG 33rpm: COLH-72 SER 33rpm: 60114
—2nd recording	November and December/62[44]	Various[45]	UK COL 33rpm: 72117 US COL 33rpm: ML-5811 MS-6411 TLR 33rpm: STL-P06[16]

SCRIABIN:

Etude in C-sharp Minor, Opus 2 #1 —1st recording	5/17/50	EO-RC-971-2	RCA 45rpm: 49-3303

COMPOSER AND SELECTION:	DATE RECORDED:	MATRIX-TAKE OR JOB NUMBER:	U.S. AND U.K. RELEASES:
—2nd recording	November and December/62[44]	Various[45]	UK COL 33rpm: 72117 US COL 33rpm: ML-5811 MS-6411 M-35118 TLR 33rpm: STL-P06[16]
—3rd recording	5/9/65*	77219	UK COL 33rpm: MET-2110 SET-2110 US COL 33rpm: M2L-328 M2S-728
Etude in F-sharp Minor, Opus 8 #2	April and May/72[5]	Various[6]	UK COL 33rpm: 73072 US COL 33rpm: M-31620
Etude in B-flat Minor, Opus 8 #7	2/25/53*	E3-RP-5252	RCA 45rpm: ERG-6014 HMV 33rpm: ALP-1430/1 RCA 33rpm: ARM1-2952 LM-6014
Etude in A-flat Major, Opus 8 #8	April and May/72[5]	Various[6]	UK COL 33rpm: 73072 US COL 33rpm: M-31620
Etude in D-flat Major, Opus 8 #10	April and May/72[5]	Various[6]	UK COL 33rpm: 73072 US COL 33rpm: M-31620
Etude in B-flat Minor, Opus 8 #11	April and May/72[5]	Various[6]	UK COL 33rpm: 73072 US COL 33rpm: M-31620

Work	Recording	Date	Matrix	Labels
Etude in D-sharp Minor, Opus 8 #12	—1st recording	November and December/62[44]	Various[45]	UK COL 33rpm: 72117 US COL 33rpm: ML-5811 MS-6411 TLR 33rpm: STL-P06[16]
	—2nd recording	2/1/68*[12]	14093	UK COL 33rpm: 72720 US COL 33rpm: MS-7106
Etude in F-sharp Major, Opus 42 #3		April and May/72[5]	Various[6]	UK COL 33rpm: 73072 US COL 33rpm: M-31620
Etude in F-sharp Major, Opus 42 #4		April and May/72[5]	Various[6]	UK COL 33rpm: 73072 US COL 33rpm: M-31620
Etude in C-sharp Minor, Opus 42 #5	—1st recording	2/25/53*	E3-RP-5252	RCA 45rpm: ERG-6014 HMV 33rpm: ALP-1430/1 RCA 33rpm: ARM1-2952 LM-6014
	—2nd recording	April and May/72[5]	Various[6]	UK COL 33rpm: 73072 US COL 33rpm: M-31620
Feuillet d'Album in E-flat Major, Opus 45 #1		April and May/72[5]	Various[6]	UK COL 33rpm: 73072 US COL 33rpm: M-31620
Poème in F-sharp Major, Opus 32 #1	—1st recording	November and December/62[44]	Various[45]	UK COL 33rpm: 72117 US COL 33rpm: ML-5811 MS-6411
	—2nd recording	5/9/65*	77219	UK COL 33rpm: MET-2110 SET-2110 US COL 33rpm: M2L-328 M2S-728

COMPOSER AND SELECTION:	DATE RECORDED:	MATRIX-TAKE OR JOB NUMBER:	U.S. AND U.K. RELEASES:
Poème, Opus 69 #1	April and May/72[5]	Various[6]	UK COL 33rpm: 73072 US COL 33rpm: M-31620
Poème, Opus 69 #2	April and May/72[5]	Various[6]	UK COL 33rpm: 73072 US COL 33rpm: M-31620
Prelude in C Major, Opus 11 #1	1954/55[51]	Unknown	HMV 33rpm: ALP-1429 RCA 33rpm: LM-2005
Prelude in G Major, Opus 11 #3	1954/55[51]	Unknown	HMV 33rpm: ALP-1429 RCA 33rpm: LM-2005
Prelude in D Major, Opus 11 #5	1954/55[51]	Unknown	HMV 33rpm: RB-16019 RCA 33rpm: ARM1-2952 LM-1957
Prelude in E Major, Opus 11 #9	1954/55[51]	Unknown	HMV 33rpm: ALP-1429 RCA 33rpm: LM-2005
Prelude in C-sharp Minor, Opus 11 #10	1954/55[51]	Unknown	HMV 33rpm: ALP-1429 RCA 33rpm: LM-2005
Prelude in G-flat Major, Opus 11 #13	1954/55[51]	Unknown	HMV 33rpm: ALP-1429 RCA 33rpm: LM-2005
Prelude in E-flat Minor, Opus 11 #14	1954/55[51]	Unknown	HMV 33rpm: ALP-1429 RCA 33rpm: LM-2005
Prelude in B-flat Minor, Opus 11 #16	1954/55[51]	Unknown	HMV 33rpm: ALP-1429 RCA 33rpm: LM-2005

Title	Date		Recordings
Prelude in B Minor, Opus 13 #6	1954/55[51]	Unknown	HMV 33rpm: ALP-1429 RCA 33rpm: LM-2005
Prelude in F-sharp Minor, Opus 15 #2	1954/55[51]	Unknown	HMV 33rpm: ALP-1429 RCA 33rpm: LM-2005
Prelude in B Major, Opus 16 #1	1954/55[51]	Unknown	HMV 33rpm: ALP-1429 RCA 33rpm: LM-2005
Prelude in E-flat Minor, Opus 16 #4	1954/55[51]	Unknown	HMV 33rpm: ALP-1429 RCA 33rpm: LM-2005
Prelude in G-sharp Minor, Opus 22 #1	1954/55[51]	Unknown	HMV 33rpm: RB-16019 RCA 33rpm: ARM1-2952 LM-1957
Prelude in G Minor, Opus 27 #1	1954/55[51]	Unknown	HMV 33rpm: ALP-1429 RCA 33rpm: LM-2005
Prelude in D-flat Major, Opus 48 #3	1954/55[51]	Unknown	HMV 33rpm: ALP-1429 RCA 33rpm: LM-2005
Prelude in A Minor, Opus 51 #2	1954/55[51]	Unknown	HMV 33rpm: ALP-1429 RCA 33rpm: LM-2005
Prelude, Opus 59 #2	1954/55[51]	Unknown	HMV 33rpm: ALP-1429 RCA 33rpm: LM-2005
Prelude, Opus 67 #1	1954/55[51]	Unknown	HMV 33rpm: ALP-1429 RCA 33rpm: LM-2005
Sonata No. 3 in F-sharp Minor, Opus 23	1954/55[51]	Unknown	HMV 33rpm: ALP-1429 RCA 33rpm: LM-2005

COMPOSER AND SELECTION:	DATE RECORDED:	MATRIX-TAKE OR JOB NUMBER:	U.S. AND U.K. RELEASES:
Sonata No. 5, Opus 53	2/29/76*	Unknown	HMV 33rpm: ARL1-1766 RCA 33rpm: ARL1-1766
Sonata No. 9, Opus 68 ("Black Mass") —1st recording	2/25/53*	E3-RP-5252	RCA 45rpm: ERG-6014 HMV 33rpm: ALP-1430/1 RB-6554/5 RCA 33rpm: LD-7021 LM-6014
—2nd recording	5/9/65*	77219	UK COL 33rpm: MET-2110 SET-2110 US COL 33rpm: M2L-328 M2S-728
Sonata No. 10, Opus 70	4/17/66*	77310	UK COL 33rpm: 72794 73072 US COL 33rpm: M2L-357 M2S-757 M-31620
Vers la Flamme, Opus 72	April and May/72[5]	Various[6]	UK COL 33rpm: 73072 US COL 33rpm: M-31620
SOUSA-HOROWITZ:			
The Stars and Stripes Forever —1st recording	12/29/50	EO-RC-1850-1	RCA 78rpm: 10-3424 RCA 45rpm: ERA-74 49-3424

—2nd recording	4/23/51*	Unknown	HMV 33rpm: RB-16019 RCA 33rpm: ARM1-2717 LM-1957

STRAVINSKY:

Danse Russe from "Petrushka"[19]	11/11/32	2B-4489-1	HMV 78rpm: DB-1869[39]

TCHAIKOVSKY:

Concerto No. 1 in B-flat Minor, Opus 23 (With the NBC Symphony Orchestra, conducted by Arturo Toscanini)

—1st recording—s. 1	5/6/41	CS-065300-1	HMV 78rpm: DB-5988/91 DB-8922/5
s. 2	)	CS-065301-1A	RCA 78rpm: DM-800 M-800
s. 3	)	CS-065302-2A	
s. 4	)	CS-065303-1A	
s. 5	5/14/41	CS-065304-3	RCA 45rpm: ERBT-3 WCT-16
s. 6	)	CS-065305-2A -3 -3A[52]	HMV 33rpm: AT-103 CSLP-505
s. 7	)	CS-065306-3	RCA 33rpm: LCT-1012 VIC-1554
s. 8	5/6/41	CS-065307-2A	
—2nd recording	4/25/43*	Unknown	HMV 33rpm: RB-16190 RCA 33rpm: CRM4-0914 LM-2319

COMPOSER AND SELECTION:	DATE RECORDED:	MATRIX-TAKE OR JOB NUMBER:	U.S. AND U.K. RELEASES:
Dumka in C Minor, Opus 59—s. 1 s. 2	10/29/42 9/27/42	PCS-072579-3 PCS-072580-1	HMV 78rpm: DB-6273 RCA 78rpm: DM-1001 M-1001 RCA 33rpm: LM-2993
Piano Trio in A Minor, Opus 50 —First Movement: Pezzo elegiaco (With Mstislav Rostropovich, cellist, and Isaac Stern, violinist)	5/18/76*	78291	UK COL 33rpm: 79200 US COL 33rpm: M2-34256

PIANO ROLLS

COMPOSER AND SELECTION:		DATE RECORDED:[53]	DUO-ART NUMBER:	WELTE-MIGNON NUMBER:	LP DISC TRANSFERS:
BACH-BUSONI:					
Prelude and Fugue in D Major, BWV 532		ca. 1927		4127	SUP 33 rpm: <u>KBI 4-A068</u>
CHOPIN:					
Etude No. 6 in E-flat Minor, Opus 10 # 6		ca. 1928	7287-4		
Etude No. 24 in C Minor, Opus 25 # 12		ca. 1928	7287-4		
Mazurka No. 21 in C-sharp Minor, Opus 30 # 4		ca. 1927		4126	SUP 33rpm: <u>KBI 4-A068</u>
Mazurka (Key and Opus number undetermined)		ca. 1927		4126	
HOROWITZ:					
Moment Exotique (Danse Excentrique)		ca. 1927		4119	WLR 33rpm: <u>GCP-771B-14</u>[54]
Variations on a Theme from Bizet's "Carmen"	(1st Roll)	ca. 1927		4120	
	(2nd Roll)	ca. 1928	7250-4		
Waltz in F Minor		ca. 1928	7360-3		

COMPOSER AND SELECTION:	DATE RECORDED:[53]	DUO-ART NUMBER:	WELTE-MIGNON NUMBER:	LP DISC TRANSFERS:
LISZT-BUSONI:				
Fantasia on Two Motives from Mozart's "Marriage of Figaro"	ca. 1927		4128	
RACHMANINOFF:				
Prelude No. 6 in G Minor, Opus 23 # 5	ca. 1927		4118	
Prelude No. 16 in G Major, Opus 32 # 5	ca. 1927		4123	SUP 33rpm: KBI 4-A068
Prelude No. 19 in A Minor, Opus 32 # 8	ca. 1928	7450-8		
Prelude No. 21 in B Minor, Opus 32 # 10	ca. 1928	7450-8		
Prelude No. 23 in G-sharp Minor, Opus 32 # 12	ca. 1927		4123	SUP 33rpm: KBI-4-A068
SAINT-SAËNS–LISZT:				
Danse Macabre	ca. 1928	A-108		
SCHUBERT-LISZT:				
Liebesbotschaft (No. 1 from the Song Cycle "Schwangesang," D 957)	ca. 1928	7282-3		
TCHAIKOVSKY:				
Dumka in C Minor, Opus 59	ca. 1928	7281-4		

NOTES

1. Columbia Masterworks produced a small quantity of this 7-inch 33⅓-rpm disc in late 1969. Its label bears the inscription "Merry Christmas '69," and it was given to certain Columbia executives as a Christmas present. This record was never commercially released to the public.

2. This record was issued in simulated stereo sound. All of the selections on the record were originally recorded in monophonic sound.

3. Horowitz recorded several takes of each movement of this Sonata on both May 29 and June 10, 1959. RCA files, however, are inconclusive in determining which particular takes were eventually issued to the public.

4. RCA Victor record number LM-2574 was an anthology entitled "60 Years of Music America Loves Best," and included recordings by various artists, both "popular" and "classical." Only the first movement of this, Horowitz's second recording of the *Moonlight* Sonata was included on the record.

5. It is impossible to determine the exact date(s) on which this item was recorded. Columbia files indicate that it was recorded at one or more of the recording sessions that occurred on: April 20, 1972, April 27, 1972, May 4, 1972, and May 31, 1972.

6. The job number(s) for this selection cannot be determined exactly. The job numbers for the recording sessions during which it was recorded are 79642, 79667, 79692, and 79787 respectively.

7. Horowitz recorded two takes of the second and third movements of this Sonata: one on May 11, 1956, and one on June 5, 1956. RCA files, however, are inconclusive in determining which take was eventually issued to the public.

8. Horowitz recorded several takes of each movement of this Sonata on May 14, 1959, and May 18, 1959. Two additional takes of the first movement were also made on May 25, 1959. RCA files, however, are inconclusive in determining which particular takes were eventually issued to the public.

9. Horowitz recorded either the entire Sonata or portions of it on October 25, 1972, October 30, 1972, and December 6, 1972. Columbia files, however, are inconclusive in determining which portions of which recordings were eventually issued to the public.

10. The job number(s) for this selection cannot be determined exactly. The job numbers for the recording sessions during which it was recorded are 95383, 95394, and 95511 respectively.

11. Although no first takes of this selection were issued, it is important to note that RCA Victor recorded a live concert performance of this Concerto with the same principals on May 6, 1940, and assigned it the same matrix numbers that would be used for the recording session of May 9, 1940. The live concert performance, therefore, was considered "take 1," so that all the second takes of the May 9, 1940, recording session are really first attempts at recording the work under studio conditions.

12. This particular recording session was also the occasion of the taping of a television recital which was broadcast on the CBS television network throughout the United States on September 22, 1968.

13. Horowitz never approved the release of this, his first recording of the Ballade, to the public. It was issued by HMV erroneously and has not been subsequently reissued in any form.

14. The original versions of both LM-1707 and WDM-1707 were produced with a recording of the Ballade No. 4 in F Minor, Opus 52 by Chopin that Horowitz recorded on January 5, 1952. These original versions were subsequently withdrawn from production and modified slightly at Horowitz's request. The revised versions of LM-1707 and WDM-1707, which were eventually issued to the public, differed from the original versions in that they lacked recordings of the Etude No. 4 in C-sharp Minor, Opus 10 #4 and the Nocturne No. 19 in E Minor, Opus 72 #1, both by Chopin. In addition, the recording of the Ballade No. 4 in F Minor, Opus 52 which appeared on the original versions of LM-1707 and WDM-1707 was replaced by a new recording of the same work made on May 8, 1952. It is unlikely that any of the original versions of either LM-1707 or WDM-1707 were ever issued to the public since production was halted before its scheduled release date. RCA Victor, however, confused matters by neglecting to adjust either the liner notes of LM-1707 and WDM-1707 or their own record catalogues, which list both the above mentioned Etude and Nocturne among the

contents of LM-1707 and WDM-1707, notwithstanding the fact that these two selections were finally omitted from the issued records.

15. This record was pressed in Germany, but produced and mastered in New York City using the "digital" process of recording.

16. Time-Life Records issued a three-record set (STL-P06) of recordings by Horowitz in 1981 as part of their "Great Performers" series. These records are, consequently, available only through Time-Life Records as part of a subscription.

17. This recording of the Etude was originally intended to be released on RCA 45-rpm set WDM-1707 and 33⅓-rpm disc LM-1707 in October 1952. The contents of these records were modified at Horowitz's request, however, and this item was omitted.

18. The release of this disc was halted at Horowitz's request. It is possible, however, that a small number of records were inadvertently released to the public for a short time. Of the items contained on the disc (Chopin's Etude No. 5 in G-flat Major, Opus 10 #5 (Black Key), Etude No. 15 in F Major, Opus 25 #3, and Schumann's Toccata in C Major, Opus 7), only the recording of the Black Key Etude has not been subsequently reissued in any form.

19. This selection has been reissued on only one 33⅓-rpm long-playing disc to date: EMI-Pathé C 061-01902, which was produced and released in France.

20. RCA originally intended their classical series of "extended play" 45-rpm records to be designated with the letters "WERP." These letters were later changed to "ERA." Thus, some of the earlier pressings of both ERA-10 and ERA-31 are labeled WERP-10 and WERP-31.

21. RCA record number E2LW-1007 was a 7-inch extended-play 45-rpm disc that was distributed to American radio stations in December 1952 as a "Christmas Receiver Record." It was never issued for commercial sale.

22. This recording of the Nocturne was originally intended to be released on the 45-rpm set WDM-1707 and the 33⅓-rpm disc LM-1707 in October 1952. The contents of these records were modified at Horowitz's request, however, and this item was omitted.

23. It is impossible to determine the exact date(s) on which this item was recorded. Columbia files indicate that it was recorded at one or more of the recording sessions that occurred on: April 5, 1962, April 18, 1962, April 24, 1962, May 9, 1962, and May 14, 1962.

24. The job number(s) for this selection cannot be determined exactly. The job numbers for the recording sessions during which it was recorded are 77437, 77456, unknown, 77536, and 77562 respectively.

25. This record was produced by The Franklin Mint as part of their series of records entitled "The 100 Greatest Recordings of All Time," and is only available through a subscription to the Franklin Mint.

26. The opus numbers used to designate the works of Clementi in this section are those listed in Alan Tyson's *Muzio Clementi: Thematic Catalogue* (Tutzing: Hans Schneider, 1967). Very often the opus numbers listed on the labels and record sleeves of Horowitz's recordings of works by Clementi are inaccurate. These errors are clarified in the footnotes.

27. This Sonata is erroneously labeled "Opus 14 #3" on the labels and record sleeves of many of Horowitz's recordings of it.

28. According to the liner notes of RCA 33⅓-rpm disc ARM1-3689, this selection was recorded in October 1954. The RCA recording logs for these sessions have been lost, and it is impossible to ascertain any exact recording dates.

29. This Sonata is erroneously labeled "Opus 47 #2" on the labels and record sleeves of many of Horowitz's recordings of it.

30. This Sonata is erroneously labeled "Opus 26" on the labels and record sleeves of many of Horowitz's recordings of it.

31. Some versions of WDM-1605 were issued as four-record sets and some versions as two-record sets. This particular selection was issued only in the four-record format of WDM-1605.

32. The original 78-rpm disc labels of this selection list the composer as "Demeny-Horowitz" and "Demeny, arr. Horowitz."

33. RCA Victor LM-6074 was a two-record anthology entitled "60 Years of Music America Loves Best," and included recordings by various artists, both "classical" and "popular."

34. This selection was recorded at one (or more) of the live concert performances that were recorded by RCA on April 8, 1979, April 15, 1979 (both in Orchestra Hall, Chicago), and April 22, 1979 (in Constitution Hall, Washington D.C.). The unavailability of RCA Red Seal recording logs has made it impossible to ascertain which portions of which performances comprise the final product.

35. HMV 78-rpm DB-2455 was part of a two-record set (along with DB-2454) entitled "Cavalcade of Famous Artists," a promotional gift given to purchasers of HMV gramophones in the 1930's. Only two sides of the Liszt Sonata were issued on DB-2455; however, the EMI Archives do not possess the files which would ascertain which two sides.

36. Horowitz's recording of this *Fairy Tale* was wrongly described as being "incomplete" in Eric Hughes's Medtner discography ("Music by Medtner," *Recorded Sound*, LXX–LXXI, April–July 1978, p. 795). In fact, Horowitz recorded the entire *Fairy Tale*.

37. Columbia Special Products produced CSS-1033 which was entitled "Great Songs of Christmas–Album Nine" and was an anthology of Christmas songs and melodies performed by various artists, both "classical" and "popular." The Medtner *Fairy Tale* performed by Horowitz is listed as "A Christmas Tale for Children." The record was distributed by Goodyear outlets throughout the United States.

38. This selection was recorded at one (or more) of the live concert performances that were recorded by RCA on April 13, 1980 (in Symphony Hall, Boston), May 4, 1980, and May 11, 1980 (both in Avery Fisher Hall, New York).

39. The release of this disc was halted at Horowitz's request. A small number of copies were released to the public, however, and are of extreme rarity today. All of the items on this disc have been subsequently reissued.

40. Horowitz, Ormandy, and the New York Philharmonic returned to Carnegie Hall on January 11, 1978, and re-recorded portions of the Concerto, most notably in the second movement.

41. This selection has been reissued on only one 33⅓-rpm long-playing disc to date: EMI-Electrola C 053-03038, which was produced and released in Germany.

42. It is impossible to determine the exact date(s) on which this item was recorded. Columbia files indicate that it was recorded at one or more of the recording sessions that occurred on: May 4, 1964, May 18, 1964, June 4, 1964, September 24, 1964, and September 28, 1964.

43. The job number(s) for this selection cannot be determined exactly. The job numbers for the recording sessions during which it was recorded are 90701, 90772, 90839, 92051, and 92062 respectively.

44. It is impossible to determine the exact date(s) on which this item was recorded. Columbia files indicate that it was recorded on one or more of the recording sessions that occurred on: November 6, 1962, November 13, 1962, November 29, 1962, and December 18, 1962.

45. The job number(s) for this selection cannot be determined exactly. The job numbers for the recording sessions during which it was recorded are 78329, 78357, 78388, and 84011 respectively.

46. In this recording of the *Impromptu*, Horowitz used the edition prepared by Hans von Bülow, in which the entire work is transposed up a semitone into G Major, and in which a few minor alterations are made to the text. In his second recording of the work, Horowitz plays the piece in its original tonality, and without any changes in the text. (In concert performances of this work during the 1980/81 season, however, Horowitz returned to the von Bülow version.)

47. Horowitz also made a recording of the *Arabesque* on December 27, 1950, which was to have been released on the RCA 45-rpm disc 49-3304. This disc was withdrawn from production at Horowitz's request, and although it is possible that a small number of copies might have been made available to the public, this is unlikely.

48. This work was recorded at one or both of the live concert performances recorded by RCA on February 15, 1976 (in Paramount Auditorium, Oakland), and on February 22, 1976 (in the Ambassador Hall Auditorium, Pasadena). Portions of it were rerecorded in May 1976 in New York City.

49. Horowitz returned to Carnegie Hall on May 10, 1965, and rerecorded sections of this work, most notably in the second movement.

50. This recording of *Träumerei* is taken from Horowitz's complete recording of *Kinderscenen* recorded on May 10, 1950, and May 17, 1950.

51. The RCA recording logs for these sessions have been lost, and it is therefore impossible to ascertain the exact date on which this item was recorded. All reports indicate, however, that it was recorded between the fall of 1954 and the spring of 1955.

52. Two different versions of this 1941 recording of the Tchaikovsky Concerto No. 1 in B-flat Minor, Opus 23 were issued to the public in the early 1940's. Horowitz was displeased with only a small portion of a particular take, and requested that RCA recording engineers combine different portions of two different takes to manufacture a completely "new" take. This was done on June 6, 1941, when take -2A and take -3 of matrix number CS-065305 (the second half of the second movement of the Concerto) were combined to produce CS-065305-2R, which was issued to the public as part of the complete recording of the Concerto. Horowitz, however, was still not satisfied with the results and requested further changes. RCA withdrew the records from retail outlets (not before some had been sold), and on August 29, 1941, take -2A and take -3A of matrix number CS-065305 were combined to produce CS-065305-12R, which met with Horowitz's approval, and which was released to the public.

53. It has to date been impossible to determine the exact dates on which Horowitz cut his piano rolls. All reports indicate that the rolls made by Horowitz for Welte-Mignon were cut shortly after his Berlin debut in January 1926, and those made for the Duo-Art company were cut sometime after May 1928.

54. This record was part of a fourteen-record set which was available exclusively to colleges and universities.

55. This set of records was pressed in Germany, but released by Columbia Masterworks in both the United States and in the United Kingdom.

56. Certain portions of this selection might have been recorded at a rehearsal that took place at the Metropolitan Opera House on October 25, 1981.

57. This Sonata is erroneously called "Opus 36, #3" on the labels and record sleeves of many of Horowitz's recordings of it.

58. This selection was recorded at one or more of the live concert performances that were recorded by RCA on November 6, 1977, November 13, 1977 (both in Orchestra Hall, Chicago), March 12, 1978, and March 19, 1978 (both in Carnegie Hall, New York). The unavailability of RCA Red Seal recording logs has made it impossible to ascertain which portions of which performances comprise the final product.

59. This selection was recorded at one or both of the live concert performances that were recorded by RCA on April 13, 1980 (in Symphony Hall, Boston), and May 4, 1980 (in Avery Fisher Hall, New York). The unavailability of RCA Red Seal recording logs has made it impossible to ascertain which portions of which performances comprise the final product.

60. This selection was recorded at one or more of the live concert performances that were recorded by RCA on November 2, 1975 (in Orchestra Hall, Chicago), November 16, 1975, and November 23, 1975 (both in Carnegie Hall, New York). The unavailability of RCA Red Seal recording logs has made it impossible to ascertain which portions of which performances comprise the final product. (Horowitz also recorded this work under studio conditions on June 22, 1976, and it is possible that a portion or portions of this studio performance also comprise a part of the final product.)

REPERTORY LISTING

This repertory listing contains all of the compositions recorded by Vladimir Horowitz (including those never released), as well as many works he has performed in concert but never recorded. This listing is not all-inclusive, but rather representative, and includes most of the works that Horowitz has programmed since his American debut in 1928. Undoubtedly, Horowitz's private repertory extends beyond this listing.

BACH:

Das Wohltemperierte Klavier, Book II:
  Prelude and Fugue No. 12 in F Minor, BWV 881
Toccata in C Minor, BWV 911

BACH-BUSONI:

"Chaconne," from the violin Partita No. 2 in D Minor, BWV 1004
Chorale Preludes:
  No. 3: "Nun komm' der Heiden Heiland," BWV 599
  No. 4: "Nun freut, euch lieben Christen," BWV 734
  No. 5: "Ich ruf' zu dir, Herr Jesu Christ," BWV 639
Prelude and Fugue in D Major, BWV 532
Toccata, Adagio, and Fugue in C Major, BWV 564

BALAKIREV:

Islamey

BARBER:

Four Excursions, Opus 20:
  No. 1 in C Minor
  No. 2 in C Major
  No. 3 in G-flat Major
  No. 4 in F Major
Sonata in E-flat Minor, Opus 26

BEETHOVEN:

Concerto No. 5 in E-flat Major, Opus 73 ("Emperor")
Sonata No. 7 in D Major, Opus 10 #3
Sonata No. 8 in C Minor, Opus 13 ("Pathétique")
Sonata No. 14 in C-sharp minor, Opus 27 #2 ("Moonlight")
Sonata No. 18 in E-flat Major, Opus 31 #3
Sonata No. 21 in C Major, Opus 53 ("Waldstein")
Sonata No. 23 in F Minor, Opus 57 ("Appassionata")
Sonata No. 28 in A Major, Opus 101
Thirty-two Variations in C Minor, WoO 80

BIZET:

(See Horowitz listing)

BRAHMS:

Concerto No. 1 in D Minor, Opus 15
Concerto No. 2 in B-flat Major, Opus 83
Intermezzo in B-flat Minor, Opus 117 #2
Klavierstücke, Opus 119:
   No. 3: Intermezzo in C Major
   No. 4: Rhapsody in E-flat Major
Sonata for Violin and Piano No. 3 in D Minor, Opus 108
Variations on a Theme of Paganini, Opus 35
Waltz No. 15 in A-flat Major, Opus 39 #15

BUSONI:

(See Bach-Busoni and Liszt-Busoni listings)

CHOPIN:

Andante Spianato and Grande Polonaise Brillante in E-flat Major, Opus 22
Ballade No. 1 in G Minor, Opus 23
Ballade No. 2 in F Major, Opus 38
Ballade No. 3 in A-flat Major, Opus 47
Ballade No. 4 in F Minor, Opus 52

Barcarolle in F-sharp Major, Opus 60
Etude No. 3 in E Major, Opus 10 #3
Etude No. 4 in C-sharp Minor, Opus 10 #4
Etude No. 5 in G-flat Major, Opus 10 #5 ("Black Key")
Etude No. 6 in E-flat Minor, Opus 10 # 6
Etude No. 8 in F Major, Opus 10 #8
Etude No. 12 in C Minor, Opus 10 #12 ("Revolutionary")
Etude No. 14 in F Minor, Opus 25 #2
Etude No. 15 in F Major, Opus 25 #3
Etude No. 18 in G-sharp Minor, Opus 25 #6
Etude No. 19 in C-sharp Minor, Opus 25 #7
Etude No. 21 in G-flat Major, Opus 25 #9 ("Butterfly")
Etude No. 22 in B Minor, Opus 25 #10 ("Octave")
Etude No. 23 in A Minor, Opus 25 #11 ("Winter Wind")
Etude No. 24 in C Minor, Opus 25 #12
Fantasie in F Minor, Opus 49
Impromptu No. 1 in A-flat Major, Opus 29
Introduction and Rondo in E-flat Major, Opus 16
Mazurka No. 7 in F Minor, Opus 7 #3
Mazurka No. 13 in A Minor, Opus 17 #4
Mazurka No. 17 in B-flat Minor, Opus 24 #4
Mazurka No. 19 in B Minor, Opus 30 #2
Mazurka No. 20 in D-flat Major, Opus 30 #3
Mazurka No. 21 in C-sharp Minor, Opus 30 #4
Mazurka No. 23 in D Major, Opus 33 #2
Mazurka No. 25 in B Minor, Opus 33 #4
Mazurka No. 26 in C-sharp Minor, Opus 41 #1
Mazurka No. 27 in E Minor, Opus 41 #2
Mazurka No. 32 in C-sharp Minor, Opus 50 #3
Mazurka No. 38 in F-sharp Minor, Opus 59 #3
Mazurka No. 40 in F Minor, Opus 63 #2
Mazurka No. 41 in C-sharp Minor, Opus 63 #3
Nocturne No. 2 in E-flat Major, Opus 9 #2
Nocturne No. 3 in B Major, Opus 9 #3
Nocturne No. 4 in F Major, Opus 15 #1
Nocturne No. 5 in F-sharp Major, Opus 15 #2
Nocturne No. 7 in C-sharp Minor, Opus 27 #1
Nocturne No. 8 in D-flat Major, Opus 27 #2
Nocturne No. 15 in F Minor, Opus 55 #1
Nocturne No. 19 in E Minor, Opus 72 #1

CHOPIN:

Nouvelle Etude (Key and Number Unknown)
Polonaise No. 1 in C-sharp Minor, Opus 26 #1
Polonaise No. 3 in A Major, Opus 40 #1 ("Military")
Polonaise No. 5 in F-sharp Minor, Opus 44
Polonaise No. 6 in A-flat Major, Opus 53
Polonaise Fantasie in A-flat Major, Opus 61
Prelude No. 6 in B Minor, Opus 28 #6
Prelude No. 16 in B-flat Minor, Opus 28 #16
Prelude No. 20 in C Minor, Opus 28 #20
Scherzo No. 1 in B Minor, Opus 20
Scherzo No. 2 in B-flat Minor, Opus 31
Scherzo No. 3 in C-sharp Minor, Opus 39
Scherzo No. 4 in E Major, Opus 54
Sonata No. 2 in B-flat Minor, Opus 35
Sonata No. 3 in B Minor, Opus 58
Waltz No. 3 in A Minor, Opus 34 #2
Waltz No. 6 in D-flat Major, Opus 64 #1 ("Minute")
Waltz No. 7 in C-sharp Minor, Opus 64 #2
Waltz No. 9 in A-flat Major, Opus 69 #1
(See also Rachmaninoff listing)

CLEMENTI:

Adagio (Key and Opus Number Unknown)
Rondo (Key and Opus Number Unknown)
Sonata in E-flat Major, Opus 12 #2:
   Third Movement: Rondo
Sonata in F Minor, Opus 13 #6
Sonata in B-flat Major, Opus 24 #2:
   First Movement: Allegro con brio
   Third Movement: Rondo
Sonata in F-sharp Minor, Opus 25 #5
Sonata in A Major, Opus 33 #1
Sonata in C Major, Opus 33 #3
Sonata in C Major, Opus 34 #1:
   Second Movement: Un poco Andante, quasi Allegretto
Sonata in G Minor, Opus 34 #2

CLEMENTI-HOROWITZ:

Duet in C Major, Opus 14 #1:
  Second Movement: Adagio

CZERNY:

Variations on a Theme by Rode, Opus 33—"La Ricordanza"

DEBUSSY:

Children's Corner Suite:
  No. 1: Doctor Gradus ad Parnassum
  No. 3: Serenade for the Doll
  No. 5: The Little Shepherd
Etudes, Book I:
  No. 1: Pour les "cinq doigts"—d'après Monsieur Czerny
  No. 3: Pour les quarts
  No. 4: Pour les sixtes
  No. 6: Pour les huit doigts
Etudes, Book II:
  No. 8: Pour les agréments
  No. 11: Pour les arpèges composés
L'Isle Joyeuse
Preludes, Book II:
  No. 4: "Les fées sont d'exquises danseuses"
  No. 5: Bruyères
  No. 6: "General Lavine"—eccentric
  No. 7: La terrasse des audiences au clair de lune

DOHNÁNYI:

Concert Etude in F Minor, Opus 28 #6 ("Capriccio")

FAURÉ:

Impromptu No. 5 in F-sharp Minor, Opus 102
Nocturne No. 13 in B Minor, Opus 119

HAYDN:

Sonata in F Major (Hoboken XVI: 23)
Sonata in C Major (Hoboken XVI: 48)
Sonata in E-flat Major (Hoboken XVI: 52)

HOROWITZ:

Danse Excentrique (Moment Exotique)
Variations on a Theme from Bizet's "Carmen"
Waltz in F Minor
(See also Clementi-Horowitz, Liszt-Horowitz, Mendelssohn-Liszt-Horowitz, Mussorgsky-Horowitz, Saint-Saëns–Liszt–Horowitz, and Sousa-Horowitz listings)

KABALEVSKY:

24 Preludes, Opus 38:
  Selections (At least ten)
Sonata No. 2 in E-flat Major, Opus 45
Sonata No. 3 in F Major, Opus 46

KREISLER-RACHMANINOFF:

Liebesleid

LIADOV:

Musical Snuff Box, Opus 32

LISZT:

Années de Pèlerinage, Première Année, Suisse:
  No. 4: Au bord d'une source
  No. 6: Vallée d'Obermann
Années de Pèlerinage, Deuxième Année, Italie:
  No. 5: Sonetto 104 del Petrarca
  No. 6: Sonetto 123 del Petrarca
Ballade No. 2 in B Minor

Concerto No. 1 in E-flat Major
Concerto No. 2 in A Major
Consolation No. 3 in D-flat Major
Consolation No. 5 in E Major
Harmonies poétiques et religieuses:
    No. 7: Funérailles
Hungarian Rhapsody No. 6 in D-flat Major
Hungarian Rhapsody No. 13 in A Minor
Réminiscences de "Don Juan" d'après Mozart
"Rigoletto": Paraphrase de Concert d'après Verdi
Sonata in B Minor
Transcendental Etudes:
    No. 4: Mazeppa
    No. 5: Feux-follets
Transcendental Etudes after Paganini:
    No. 2 in E-flat Major
    No. 5 in E Major ("La Chasse")
Valse Oubliée No. 1 in F-sharp Major
(See also Mendelssohn-Liszt-Horowitz, Saint-Saëns–Liszt, Saint-Saëns–Liszt–
Horowitz, and Schubert-Liszt listings)

LISZT-BUSONI:

Fantasie on Two Motives from Mozart's "The Marriage of Figaro"
Mephisto Waltz No. 1

LISZT-HOROWITZ:

Hungarian Rhapsody No. 2 in C-sharp Minor
Hungarian Rhapsody No. 15 in A Minor ("Rakóczy March")
Hungarian Rhapsody No. 19 in D Minor
Légende No. 2: "Saint François de Paule marchant sur les flots"
Scherzo and March

MEDTNER:

Fairy Tale in A Major, Opus 51 #3
Forgotten Melodies, Opus 38: Volume I:
    No. 1: Sonata Reminiscenza in A Minor
Sonata in G Minor, Opus 22

MENDELSSOHN:

Three Etudes, Opus 104, Book II:
  No. 3 in A Minor
Prelude and Fugue in F Minor, Opus 35 #5
Scherzo a Capriccio in F-sharp Minor
Songs Without Words:
  No. 25: "May Breezes," Opus 62 #2
  No. 30: "Spring Song," Opus 62 #6
  No. 33: "Song of the Pilgrim," Opus 67 #3
  No. 35: "The Shepherd's Complaint," Opus 67 #5
  No. 36: "Lullabye," Opus 67 #6
  No. 40: "Elegy," Opus 85 #4
Variations Sérieuses in D Minor, Opus 54

MENDELSSOHN-LISZT-HOROWITZ:

Wedding March and Variations

MOSZKOWSKI:

Étincelles, Opus 36 #6
Etude in A Minor
Etude in F Major, Opus 72 #6
Etude in A-flat Major, Opus 72 #11

MOZART:

Adagio (Key and Köchel Number Unknown)
Sonata No. 10 in C Major, K. 330
Sonata No. 11 in A Major, K. 331
Sonata No. 12 in F Major, K. 332
Sonata No. 13 in B-flat Major, K. 333
(See also Liszt and Liszt-Busoni listings)

MUSSORGSKY-HOROWITZ:

By the Water (No. 6 of the Song Cycle "Without Sun")
Pictures at an Exhibition

PAGANINI:

(See Brahms and Liszt listings)

POULENC:

Intermezzo (Unknown Number and Key)
Novelette No. 1 in C Major
Pastourelle in B-flat Major (from the ballet "L'Eventaille de Jeanne")
Presto in B-flat Major
Toccata in A Minor

PROKOFIEV:

Three Pieces from "Cinderella," Opus 95:
  No. 1: Intermezzo in B-flat Major
  No. 3: Valse Triste in D-flat Major
Sonata No. 6 in A Major, Opus 82
Sonata No. 7 in B-flat Major, Opus 83
Sonata No. 8 in B flat Major, Opus 84
Toccata in C Major, Opus 11
Twenty Visions Fugitives, Opus 22:
  Selections

RACHMANINOFF:

Barcarolle in G Minor, Opus 10 #3
Concerto No. 3 in D Minor, Opus 30
Étude-Tableau in C Major, Opus 33 #2
Étude-Tableau in E-flat Minor, Opus 33 #6
Étude-Tableau in E-flat Minor, Opus 39 #5
Étude-Tableau in D Major, Opus 39 #9
Étude-Tableau in C Minor, Opus 39 (#1 or #7)
Humoresque in G Major, Opus 10 #5
Moment Musical No. 2 in E-flat Minor, Opus 16 #2
Moment Musical No. 3 in B Minor, Opus 16 #3
Polka de W.R. in A-flat Major
Prelude No. 6 in G Minor, Opus 23 #5
Prelude No. 7 in E-flat Major, Opus 23 #6
Prelude No. 8 in C Minor, Opus 23 #7

Prelude No. 15 in E Minor, Opus 32 #4
Prelude No. 16 in G Major, Opus 32 #5
Prelude No. 19 in A Minor, Opus 32 #8
Prelude No. 21 in B Minor, Opus 32 #10
Prelude No. 23 in G-sharp Minor, Opus 32 #12
Sonata for Cello and Piano in G Minor, Opus 19:
    Third Movement: Andante
Sonata No. 2 in B-flat Minor, Opus 36
Variations on a Theme by Chopin, Opus 22
(See also Kreisler-Rachmaninoff and Rimsky-Korsakov–Rachmaninoff listings)

RAVEL:

Gaspard de la Nuit
Jeux d'eau
Oiseaux tristes

RIMSKY-KORSAKOV–RACHMANINOFF:

The Flight of the Bumble-Bee

SAINT-SAËNS–LISZT:

Danse Macabre

SAINT-SAËNS–LISZT–HOROWITZ:

Danse Macabre

SCARLATTI:

Sonata in C Major, L. 1 [K. 514]
Sonata in C Minor, L. 9 [K. 303]
Sonata in E Major, L. 21 [K. 162]
Sonata in E Minor, L. 22 [K. 198]
Sonata in E Major, L. 23 [K. 380]
Sonata in E Major, L. 25 [K. 46]

Sonata in B Minor, L. 33 [K. 87]
Sonata in F-sharp Major, L. 35 [K. 319]
Sonata in F Minor, L. 118 [K. 466]
Sonata in G Major, L. 124 [K. 260]
Sonata in G Major, L. 129 [K. 201]
Sonata in B Minor, L. 147 [K. 197]
Sonata in D Major, L. 164 [K. 491]
Sonata in A-flat Major, L. 186 [K. 127]
Sonata in F Minor, L. 187 [K. 481]
Sonata in F Major, L. 188 [K. 525]
Sonata in F Minor, L. 189 [K. 184]
Sonata in E-flat Major, L. 203 [K. 474]
Sonata in G Major, L. 209 [K. 455]
Sonata in E Major, L. 224 [K. 135]
Sonata in A Minor, L. 239 [K. 188]
Sonata in A Minor, L. 241 [K. 54]
Sonata in G Major, L. 335 [K. 55]
Sonata in G Major, L. 349 [K. 146]
Sonata in A Major, L. 391 [K. 39]
Sonata in D Major, L. 417 [K. 161]
Sonata in D Major, L. 424 [K. 33]
Sonata in E Major, L. 430 [K. 531]
Sonata in F Major, L. 433 [K. 446]
Sonata in D Major, L. 465 [K. 96]
Sonata in A Major, L. 483 [K. 322]
Sonata in G Major, L. 487 [K. 125]
Sonata in A Major, L. 494 [K. 101]

SCARLATTI-TAUSIG:

Capriccio in E Major [L. 375/K. 20]

SCHUBERT:

Impromptu in E-flat Major, Opus 90 #2 [D 899]
Impromptu in G-flat Major, Opus 90 #3 [D 899]
Impromptu in A-flat Major, Opus 90 #4 [D 899]
Impromptu in F Minor, Opus 142 #1 [D 935]
Impromptu in A-flat Major, Opus 142 #2 [D 935]
Sonata in B-flat Major, Opus Posthumous [D 960]

SCHUBERT-LISZT:

Liebesbotschaft (No. 1 of the Song Cycle "Schwangesang") [D 957]

SCHUBERT-TAUSIG:

Marche Militaire in D-flat Major, Opus 51 #1

SCHUMANN:

Arabeske in C Major, Opus 18
Blumenstück in D-flat Major, Opus 19
Concerto Without Orchestra in F Minor, Opus 14 ("Grand Sonata No. 3")
Dichterliebe, Opus 48
Fantasie in C Major, Opus 17
Fantasiestücke, Opus 12:
  No. 1: Des Abends
  No. 7: Träumeswirren
Fantasiestücke, Opus 111:
  No. 1 in C Minor
  No. 2 in A-flat Major
  No. 3 in C Minor
Humoreske in B-flat Major, Opus 20
Kinderscenen, Opus 15
Kreisleriana, Opus 16
Nachtstücke, Opus 23:
  No. 3 in D-flat Major
  No. 4 in F Major
Presto Passionato in G Minor
Toccata in C Major, Opus 7

SCRIABIN:

Etude in C-sharp Minor, Opus 2 #1
Etude in C-sharp Minor, Opus 8 #1
Etude in F-sharp Minor, Opus 8 #2
Etude in B Major, Opus 8 #4
Etude in B-flat Minor, Opus 8 #7
Etude in A-flat Major, Opus 8 #8
Etude in D-flat Major, Opus 8 #10

Etude in B-flat Minor, Opus 8 #11
Etude in D-sharp Minor, Opus 8 #12
Etude in F-sharp Major, Opus 42 #3
Etude in F-sharp Major, Opus 42 #4
Etude in C-sharp Minor, Opus 42 #5
Etude, Opus 65 #3
Fantasie, Opus 28
Feuillet d'Album, Opus 58
Three Pieces, Opus 45:
   No. 1: Feuillet d'Album in E-flat Major
Poème in F-sharp Major, Opus 32 #1
Poème Opus 69 #1
Poème Opus 69 #2

SCRIABIN:

Prelude in C-sharp Minor for the Left Hand Alone, Opus 9 #1
Prelude in C Major, Opus 11 #1
Prelude in G Major, Opus 11 #3
Prelude in D Major, Opus 11 #5
Prelude in E Major, Opus 11 #9
Prelude in C-sharp Minor, Opus 11 #10
Prelude in G flat Major, Opus 11 #13
Prelude in E-flat Minor, Opus 11 #14
Prelude in B-flat Minor, Opus 11 #16
Prelude in B Minor, Opus 13 #6
Prelude in F-sharp Minor, Opus 15 #2
Prelude in B Major, Opus 16 #1
Prelude in E-flat Minor, Opus 16 #4
Prelude in G-sharp Minor, Opus 22 #1
Prelude in G Minor, Opus 27 #1
Prelude in D-flat Major, Opus 48 #3
Prelude in A Minor, Opus 51 #2
Prelude, Opus 59 #2
Prelude, Opus 67 #1
Sonata No. 3 in F-sharp Minor, Opus 23
Sonata No. 5, Opus 53
Sonata No. 6, Opus 62
Sonata No. 9, Opus 68 ("Black Mass")
Sonata No. 10, Opus 70
Vers la flamme, Opus 72

SOUSA-HOROWITZ:

The Stars and Stripes Forever

STRAVINSKY:

Three Movements from "Petrushka":
  No. 3: Danse Russe

TAUSIG:

(See Scarlatti-Tausig and Schubert-Tausig listings)

TCHAIKOVSKY:

Concerto No. 1 in B-flat Minor, Opus 23
Dumka in C Minor, Opus 59
Trio for Cello, Violin and Piano in A Minor, Opus 50:
  First Movement: Pezzo elegiaco

VERDI:

(See Liszt listing)

ZHELOBINSKY:

Six Short Etudes, Opus 19

INDEX

INDEX

INDEX